For Reference

Not to be taken from this room

NOVELS
for Students

Advisors

Erik France: Adjunct Instructor of English, Macomb Community College, Warren, Michigan. B.A. and M.S.L.S. from University of North Carolina, Chapel Hill; Ph.D. from Temple University.

Kate Hamill: Grade 12 English Teacher, Catonsville High School, Catonsville, Maryland.

Joseph McGeary: English Teacher, Germantown Friends School, Philadelphia, Pennsylvania. Ph.D. in English from Duke University.

Timothy Showalter: English Department Chair, Franklin High School, Reisterstown, Maryland. Certified teacher by the Maryland State Department of Education. Member of the National Council of Teachers of English.

Amy Spade Silverman: English Department Chair, Kehillah Jewish High School, Palo Alto, California. Member of National Council of Teachers of English (NCTE), Teachers and Writers, and NCTE Opinion Panel. Exam Reader, Advanced Placement Literature and Composition. Poet, published in *North American Review, Nimrod,* and *Michigan Quarterly Review,* among other publications.

Jody Stefansson: Director of Boswell Library and Study Center and Upper School Learning Specialist, Polytechnic School, Pasadena, California. Board member, Children's Literature Council of Southern California. Member of American Library Association, Association of Independent School Librarians, and Association of Educational Therapists.

Laura Jean Waters: Certified School Library Media Specialist, Wilton High School, Wilton, Connecticut. B.A. from Fordham University; M.A. from Fairfield University.

NOVELS
for Students

Presenting Analysis, Context, and Criticism on Commonly Studied Novels

VOLUME 33

Sara Constantakis, Project Editor

Foreword by Anne Devereaux Jordan

GALE
CENGAGE Learning

Detroit • New York • San Francisco • New Haven, Conn • Waterville, Maine • London

Novels for Students, Volume 33

Project Editor: Sara Constantakis

Rights Acquisition and Management: Leitha Etheridge-Sims, Kelly Quin, Tracie Richardson, Mardell Glinski Schultz

Composition: Evi Abou-El-Seoud

Manufacturing: Drew Kalasky

Imaging: John Watkins

Product Design: Pamela A. E. Galbreath, Jennifer Wahi

Content Conversion: Katrina Coach

Product Manager: Meggin Condino

For product information and technology assistance, contact us at
Gale Customer Support, 1-800-877-4253.
For permission to use material from this text or product,
submit all requests online at **www.cengage.com/permissions.**
Further permissions questions can be emailed to
permissionrequest@cengage.com

Gale
27500 Drake Rd.
Farmington Hills, MI, 48331-3535

ISBN-13: 978-1-4144-4171-9
ISBN-10: 1-4144-4171-1

ISSN 1094-3552

This title is also available as an e-book.
ISBN-13: 978-1-4144-4949-4
ISBN-10: 1-4144-4949-6
Contact your Gale, a part of Cengage Learning sales representative for ordering information.

Printed in the United States of America
1 2 3 4 5 6 7 14 13 12 11 10

Table of Contents

The Informed Dialogue: Interacting with Literature

When we pick up a book, we usually do so with the anticipation of pleasure. We hope that by entering the time and place of the novel and sharing the thoughts and actions of the characters, we will find enjoyment. Unfortunately, this is often not the case; we are disappointed. But we should ask, has the author failed us, or have we failed the author?

We establish a dialogue with the author, the book, and with ourselves when we read. Consciously and unconsciously, we ask questions: "Why did the author write this book?" "Why did the author choose that time, place, or character?" "How did the author achieve that effect?" "Why did the character act that way?" "Would I act in the same way?" The answers we receive depend upon how much information about literature in general and about that book specifically we ourselves bring to our reading.

Young children have limited life and literary experiences. Being young, children frequently do not know how to go about exploring a book, nor sometimes, even know the questions to ask of a book. The books they read help them answer questions, the author often coming right out and *telling* young readers the things they are learning or are expected to learn. The perennial classic, *The Little Engine That Could, tells* its readers that, among other things, it is good to help others and brings happiness:

> "Hurray, hurray," cried the funny little clown and all the dolls and toys. "The good little boys and girls in the city will be happy because you helped us, kind, Little Blue Engine."

In picture books, messages are often blatant and simple, the dialogue between the author and reader one-sided. Young children are concerned with the end result of a book—the enjoyment gained, the lesson learned—rather than with how that result was obtained. As we grow older and read further, however, we question more. We come to expect that the world within the book will closely mirror the concerns of our world, and that the author will *show* these through the events, descriptions, and conversations within the story, rather than *telling* of them. We are now expected to do the interpreting, carry on our share of the dialogue with the book and author, and glean not only the author's message, but comprehend how that message and the over-all affect of the book were achieved. Sometimes, however, we need help to do these things. *Novels for Students* provides that help.

A novel is made up of many parts interacting to create a coherent whole. In reading a novel, the more obvious features can be easily spotted—theme, characters, plot—but we may overlook the more subtle elements that greatly influence how the novel is perceived by the reader: viewpoint, mood and tone, symbolism, or the use of humor. By focusing on both the obvious and more subtle literary elements within a novel, *Novels for Students* aids readers in both analyzing for message and in determining how and why that message is communicated. In the discussion on Harper Lee's *To Kill a Mockingbird* (Vol. 2), for example, the mockingbird as a symbol of innocence is dealt with, among other things, as is the importance of Lee's use of humor which "enlivens a serious plot, adds depth to the characterization, and creates a sense of familiarity and universality." The reader comes to understand the internal elements of each novel discussed—as well as the external influences that help shape it.

"The desire to write greatly," Harold Bloom of Yale University says, "is the desire to be elsewhere, in a time and place of one's own, in an originality that must compound with inheritance, with an anxiety of influence." A writer seeks to create a unique world within a story, but although it is unique, it is not disconnected from our own world. It speaks to us *because* of what the writer brings to the writing from our world: how he or she was raised and educated; his or her likes and dislikes; the events occurring in the real world at the time of the writing, and while the author was growing up. When we know what an author has brought to his or her work, we gain a greater insight into both the "originality" (the world of the book), and the things that "compound" it. This insight enables us to question that created world and find answers more readily. By informing ourselves, we are able to establish a more effective dialogue with both book and author.

Novels for Students, in addition to providing a plot summary and descriptive list of characters—to remind readers of what they have read—also explores the external influences that shaped each book. Each entry includes a discussion of the author's background, and the historical context in which the novel was written. It is vital to know, for instance, that when Ray Bradbury was writing *Fahrenheit 451* (Vol. 1), the threat of Nazi domination had recently ended in Europe, and the McCarthy hearings were taking place in Washington, D.C. This information goes far in answering the question, "Why did he write a story of oppressive government control and book burning?" Similarly, it is important to know that Harper Lee, author of *To Kill a Mockingbird,* was born and raised in Monroeville, Alabama, and

that her father was a lawyer. Readers can now see why she chose the south as a setting for her novel—it is the place with which she was most familiar—and start to comprehend her characters and their actions.

Novels for Students helps readers find the answers they seek when they establish a dialogue with a particular novel. It also aids in the posing of questions by providing the opinions and interpretations of various critics and reviewers, broadening that dialogue. Some reviewers of *To Kill A Mockingbird,* for example, "faulted the novel's climax as melodramatic." This statement leads readers to ask, "Is it, indeed, melodramatic?" "If not, why did some reviewers see it as such?" "If it is, why did Lee choose to make it melodramatic?" "Is melodrama ever justified?" By being spurred to ask these questions, readers not only learn more about the book and its writer, but about the nature of writing itself.

The literature included for discussion in *Novels for Students* has been chosen because it has something vital to say to us. *Of Mice and Men, Catch-22, The Joy Luck Club, My Antonia, A Separate Peace* and the other novels here speak of life and modern sensibility. In addition to their individual, specific messages of prejudice, power, love or hate, living and dying, however, they and all great literature also share a common intent. They force us to *think*—about life, literature, and about others, not just about ourselves. They pry us from the narrow confines of our minds and thrust us outward to confront the world of books and the larger, real world we all share. *Novels for Students* helps us in this confrontation by providing the means of enriching our conversation with literature and the world, by creating an *informed* dialogue, one that brings true pleasure to the personal act of reading.

Sources

Harold Bloom, *The Western Canon, The Books and School of the Ages,* Riverhead Books, 1994.

Watty Piper, *The Little Engine That Could,* Platt & Munk, 1930.

Anne Devereaux Jordan
Senior Editor, TALL (Teaching and Learning Literature)

Introduction

Purpose of the Book

The purpose of *Novels for Students* (*NfS*) is to provide readers with a guide to understanding, enjoying, and studying novels by giving them easy access to information about the work. Part of Gale's "For Students" Literature line, *NfS* is specifically designed to meet the curricular needs of high school and undergraduate college students and their teachers, as well as the interests of general readers and researchers considering specific novels. While each volume contains entries on "classic" novels frequently studied in classrooms, there are also entries containing hard-to-find information on contemporary novels, including works by multicultural, international, and women novelists. Entries profiling film versions of novels not only diversify the study of novels but support alternate learning styles, media literacy, and film studies curricula as well.

The information covered in each entry includes an introduction to the novel and the novel's author; a plot summary, to help readers unravel and understand the events in a novel; descriptions of important characters, including explanation of a given character's role in the novel as well as discussion about that character's relationship to other characters in the novel; analysis of important themes in the novel; and an explanation of important literary techniques and movements as they are demonstrated in the novel.

In addition to this material, which helps the readers analyze the novel itself, students are also provided with important information on the literary and historical background informing each work. This includes a historical context essay, a box comparing the time or place the novel was written to modern Western culture, a critical essay, and excerpts from critical essays on the novel. A unique feature of *NfS* is a specially commissioned critical essay on each novel, targeted toward the student reader.

The "literature to film" entries on novels vary slightly in form, providing background on film technique and comparison to the original, literary version of the work. These entries open with an introduction to the film, which leads directly into the plot summary. The summary highlights plot changes from the novel, key cinematic moments, and/or examples of key film techniques. As in standard entries, there are character profiles (noting omissions or additions, and identifying the actors), analysis of themes and how they are illustrated in the film, and an explanation of the cinematic style and structure of the film. A cultural context section notes any time period or setting differences from that of the original work, as well as cultural differences between the time in which the original work was written and the time in which the film adaptation was made. A film entry concludes with a critical overview and critical essays on the film.

To further help today's student in studying and enjoying each novel or film, information on media adaptations is provided (if available), as well as suggestions for works of fiction, nonfiction, or film on similar themes and topics. Classroom aids include ideas for research papers and lists of critical and reference sources that provide additional material on the novel. Film entries also highlight signature film techniques demonstrated, and suggest media literacy activities and prompts to use during or after viewing a film.

Selection Criteria

The titles for each volume of *NfS* are selected by surveying numerous sources on notable literary works and analyzing course curricula for various schools, school districts, and states. Some of the sources surveyed include: high school and undergraduate literature anthologies and textbooks; lists of award-winners, and recommended titles, including the Young Adult Library Services Association (YALSA) list of best books for young adults. Films are selected both for the literary importance of the original work and the merits of the adaptation (including official awards and widespread public recognition).

Input solicited from our expert advisory board—consisting of educators and librarians—guides us to maintain a mix of "classic" and contemporary literary works, a mix of challenging and engaging works (including genre titles that are commonly studied) appropriate for different age levels, and a mix of international, multicultural and women authors. These advisors also consult on each volume's entry list, advising on which titles are most studied, most appropriate, and meet the broadest interests across secondary (grades 7–12) curricula and undergraduate literature studies.

How Each Entry Is Organized

Each entry, or chapter, in *NfS* focuses on one novel. Each entry heading lists the full name of the novel, the author's name, and the date of the novel's publication. The following elements are contained in each entry:

Introduction: a brief overview of the novel which provides information about its first appearance, its literary standing, any controversies surrounding the work, and major conflicts or themes within the work. Film entries identify the original novel and provide understanding of the film's reception and reputation, along with that of the director.

Author Biography: in novel entries, this section includes basic facts about the author's life, and focuses on events and times in the author's life that inspired the novel in question.

Plot Summary: a factual description of the major events in the novel. Lengthy summaries are broken down with subheads. Plot summaries of films are used to uncover plot differences from the original novel, and to note the use of certain film angles or other techniques.

Characters: an alphabetical listing of major characters in the novel. Each character name is followed by a brief to an extensive description of the character's role in the novel, as well as discussion of the character's actions, relationships, and possible motivation. In film entries, omissions or changes to the cast of characters of the film adaptation are mentioned here, and the actors' names—and any awards they may have received—are also included.

Characters are listed alphabetically by last name. If a character is unnamed—for instance, the narrator in *Invisible Man*—the character is listed as "The Narrator" and alphabetized as "Narrator." If a character's first name is the only one given, the name will appear alphabetically by that name.

Variant names are also included for each character. Thus, the full name "Jean Louise Finch" would head the listing for the narrator of *To Kill a Mockingbird*, but listed in a separate cross-reference would be the nickname "Scout Finch."

Themes: a thorough overview of how the major topics, themes, and issues are addressed within the novel. Each theme discussed appears in a separate subhead and is easily accessed through the boldface entries in the Subject/Theme Index. While the key themes often remain the same or similar when a novel is adapted into a film, film entries demonstrate how the themes are conveyed cinematically, along with any changes in the portrayal of the themes.

Style: this section addresses important style elements of the novel, such as setting, point of view, and narration; important literary devices used, such as imagery, foreshadowing, symbolism; and, if applicable, genres to which the work might have belonged, such as Gothicism or Romanticism. Literary terms are explained within the entry but can also be found in the Glossary. Film entries cover how the director conveyed the meaning, message, and mood of the work using film in comparison to the author's use of language, literary device, etc., in the original work.

Historical Context: in novel entries, this section outlines the social, political, and cultural climate in which the author lived and the novel was created. This section may include descriptions of related historical events, pertinent aspects of daily life in the culture, and the artistic and literary sensibilities of the time in which the work was written. If the novel is a historical work, information regarding the time in which the novel is set is also included. Each section is broken down with helpful subheads. Film entries contain a similar Cultural Context section because the film adaptation might explore an entirely different time period or culture than the original work, and may also be influenced by the traditions and views of a time period much different than that of the original author.

Critical Overview: this section provides background on the critical reputation of the novel or film, including bannings or any other public controversies surrounding the work. For older works, this section includes a history of how the novel or film was first received and how perceptions of it may have changed over the years; for more recent novels, direct quotes from early reviews may also be included.

Criticism: an essay commissioned by *NfS* which specifically deals with the novel or film and is written specifically for the student audience, as well as excerpts from previously published criticism on the work (if available).

Sources: an alphabetical list of critical material used in compiling the entry, with full bibliographical information.

Further Reading: an alphabetical list of other critical sources which may prove useful for the student. It includes full bibliographical information and a brief annotation.

In addition, each entry contains the following highlighted sections, set apart from the main text as sidebars:

Media Adaptations: if available, a list of audiobooks and important film and television adaptations of the novel, including source information. The list also includes stage adaptations, musical adaptations, etc.

Topics for Further Study: a list of potential study questions or research topics dealing with the novel. This section includes questions related to other disciplines the student may be studying, such as American history, world history, science, math, government, business, geography, economics, psychology, etc.

Compare and Contrast: an "at-a-glance" comparison of the cultural and historical differences between the author's time and culture and late twentieth century or early twenty-first century Western culture. This box includes pertinent parallels between the major scientific, political, and cultural movements of the time or place the novel was written, the time or place the novel was set (if a historical work), and modern Western culture. Works written after the mid-1970s may not have this box.

What Do I Read Next?: a list of works that might give a reader points of entry into a classic work (e.g., YA or multicultural titles) and/or complement the featured novel or serve as a contrast to it. This includes works by the same author and others, works from various genres, YA works, and works from various cultures and eras.

The film entries provide sidebars more targeted to the study of film, including:

Film Technique: a listing and explanation of four to six key techniques used in the film, including shot styles, use of transitions, lighting, sound or music, etc.

Read, Watch, Write: media literacy prompts and/or suggestions for viewing log prompts.

What Do I See Next?: a list of films based on the same or similar works or of films similar in directing style, technique, etc.

Other Features

NfS includes "The Informed Dialogue: Interacting with Literature," a foreword by Anne Devereaux Jordan, Senior Editor for *Teaching and Learning Literature* (*TALL*), and a founder of the Children's Literature Association. This essay provides an enlightening look at how readers interact with literature and how *Novels for Students* can help teachers show students how to enrich their own reading experiences.

A Cumulative Author/Title Index lists the authors and titles covered in each volume of the *NfS* series.

A Cumulative Nationality/Ethnicity Index breaks down the authors and titles covered in each volume of the *NfS* series by nationality and ethnicity.

A Subject/Theme Index, specific to each volume, provides easy reference for users who may be studying a particular subject or theme rather than a single work. Significant subjects, from events to broad themes, are included.

Each entry may include illustrations, including photo of the author, stills from film adaptations, maps, and/or photos of key historical events, if available.

Citing Novels for Students

When writing papers, students who quote directly from any volume of *Novels for Students* may use the following general forms. These examples are based on MLA style; teachers may request that students adhere to a different style, so the following examples may be adapted as needed.

When citing text from *NfS* that is not attributed to a particular author (i.e., the Themes, Style, Historical Context sections, etc.), the following format should be used in the bibliography section:

> "*Night*." *Novels for Students*. Ed. Marie Rose Napierkowski. Vol. 4. Detroit: Gale, 1998. 234–35.

When quoting the specially commissioned essay from *NfS* (usually the first piece under the "Criticism" subhead), the following format should be used:

> Miller, Tyrus. Critical Essay on "*Winesburg, Ohio*." *Novels for Students*. Ed. Marie Rose Napierkowski. Vol. 4. Detroit: Gale, 1998. 335–39.

When quoting a journal or newspaper essay that is reprinted in a volume of *NfS*, the following form may be used:

> Malak, Amin. "Margaret Atwood's *The Handmaid's Tale* and the Dystopian Tradition." *Canadian Literature* 112 (Spring 1987): 9–16. Excerpted and reprinted in *Novels for Students*. Vol. 4. Ed. Marie Rose Napierkowski. Detroit: Gale, 1998. 133–36.

When quoting material reprinted from a book that appears in a volume of *NfS*, the following form may be used:

> Adams, Timothy Dow. "Richard Wright: 'Wearing the Mask.'" In *Telling Lies in Modern American Autobiography*. University of North Carolina Press, 1990. 69–83. Excerpted and reprinted in *Novels for Students*. Vol. 1. Ed. Diane Telgen. Detroit: Gale, 1997. 59–61.

We Welcome Your Suggestions

The editorial staff of *Novels for Students* welcomes your comments and ideas. Readers who wish to suggest novels to appear in future volumes, or who have other suggestions, are cordially invited to contact the editor. You may contact the editor via e-mail at: **ForStudentsEditors@cengage.com**. Or write to the editor at:

Editor, *Novels for Students*
Gale
27500 Drake Road
Farmington Hills, MI 48331-3535

Literary Chronology

1775: Jane Austen is born on December 16 in Steventon, Hampshire, England.

1799: Honoré de Balzac is born on May 20 in Tours, France.

1811: Jane Austen's *Sense and Sensibility* is published.

1812: Charles Dickens is born on February 7 in Portsmouth, England.

1817: Jane Austen dies on July 18 in Winchester, Hampshire, England.

1834–1835: Honoré de Balzac's *Le Pére Goriot* is published.

1837–1839: Charles Dickens' *Nicholas Nickleby* is published.

1850: Honoré de Balzac dies on August 19 in Paris, France.

1850: Robert Louis Stevenson is born on November 30 in Edinburgh, Scotland.

1870: Charles Dickens dies of a paralytic stroke on June 18 in Gad's Hill, Kent, England.

1873: Willa Cather is born on December 7 in Back Creek Valley, Virginia.

1886: Robert Louis Stevenson's *Kidnapped* is published.

1890: Agatha Christie is born on September 15 in Torquay, Devon, England.

1894: Robert Louis Stevenson dies on December 3 in Apia, Samoa.

1897: William Faulkner is born on September 25 in New Albany, Mississippi.

1908: Ann Petry is born on October 18 in Old Saybrook, Connecticut.

1915: Saul Bellow is born on June 10 in Lachine, Quebec, Canada.

1923: Willa Cather's *A Lost Lady* is published.

1930: Chinua Achebe is born on November 16 in Ogidi, Nigeria.

1934: Agatha Christie's *Murder on the Orient Express* is published.

1936: Judith Guest is born on March 29 in Detroit, Michigan.

1937: Walter Dean Myers is born on August 12 in Martinsburg, West Virginia.

1946: Ann Petry's *The Street* is published.

1947: Willa Cather dies of a cerebral hemorrhage on April 24 in New York, New York.

1948: William Faulkner's *Intruder in the Dust* is published.

1950: Edward Bloor is born on October 12 in Trenton, New Jersey.

1952: Robin McKinley is born on November 16, in Warren, Ohio.

1953: Saul Bellow's *The Adventures of Augie March* is published.

1954: Saul Bellow's *The Adventures of Augie March* wins the National Book Award.

1960: Chinua Achebe's *No Longer at Ease* is published.

1961: Chinua Achebe's *No Longer at Ease* wins the Nigerian National Trophy.

1962: William Faulkner dies of a heart attack on July 6 in Byhalia, Mississippi.

1976: Agatha Christie dies of natural causes on January 12 in Wallingford, England.

1976: Judith Guest's *Ordinary People* is published.

1978: Robin McKinley's *Beauty: A Retelling of the Story of Beauty and the Beast* is published.

1980: The film *Ordinary People* is released.

1981: The film *Ordinary People* wins Academy Awards for Best Director, Best Picture, Best Adapted Screenplay, and Best Supporting Actor.

1994: Walter Dean Myers' *The Glory Field* is published.

1997: Ann Petry dies of respiratory complications on April 28 in Old Saybrook, Connecticut.

1995: The film *Sense and Sensibility* is released.

1996: The film *Sense and Sensibility* wins an Academy Award for Best Adapted Screenplay.

1997: Edward Bloor's *Tangerine* is published.

2005: Saul Bellow dies on April 5 in Brookline, Massachusetts.

Acknowledgments

The editors wish to thank the copyright holders of the excerpted criticism included in this volume and the permissions managers of many book and magazine publishing companies for assisting us in securing reproduction rights. We are also grateful to the staffs of the Detroit Public Library, the Library of Congress, the University of Detroit Mercy Library, Wayne State University Purdy/Kresge Library Complex, and the University of Michigan Libraries for making their resources available to us. Following is a list of the copyright holders who have granted us permission to reproduce material in this volume of *NfS*. Every effort has been made to trace copyright, but if omissions have been made, please let us know.

COPYRIGHTED EXCERPTS IN *NfS*, VOLUME 33, WERE REPRODUCED FROM THE FOLLOWING PERIODICALS:

The ALAN Review, v. 24, fall, 1996. Reproduced by permission.—*The Atlantic Monthly*, v. 192, October, 1953 for "A Rolling Stone" by Charles J. Rolo. Copyright 1953, renewed © 1981 by The Atlantic Monthly Company. Reproduced by permission of the Literary Estate of Charles J. Rolo.—*Chicago Sun Times*, January, 1980. Reprinted with permission of *The Chicago Sun Times*.—*Commonweal*, v. 58, October 2, 1953; v. 123, March 8, 1996. Copyright © 1953, 1996 Commonweal Publishing Co., Inc. Both reproduced by permission of Commonweal Foundation.—*The*

English Journal, v. 70, September, 1981. Copyright © 1981 by the National Council of Teachers of English. Reproduced by permission of the publisher.—*The Faulkner Journal*, v. 22, fall 2006/spring, 2007. Reproduced by permission.—*The French Review*, v. 69, February, 1996. Copyright © 1996 by the American Association of Teachers of French. Reproduced by permission.—*The Globe and Mail*, September 27, 1980. Copyright © 1980 Globe Interactive, a division of Bell Globemedia Publishing, Inc. Reproduced by permission.—*The Horn Book*, v. 71, March, 1995; v. 73, July-August, 1997. Copyright © 1995, 1997 by The Horn Book, Inc., Boston, MA, www.hbook.com. All rights reserved. Both reproduced by permission.—*The Lion and the Unicorn*, v. 12, December, 1988. Copyright © 1988 The Johns Hopkins University Press. Reproduced by permission.—*Literature/Film Quarterly*, v. 15, 1987. Copyright © 1987 Salisbury State College. Reproduced by permission.—*MELUS*, v. 27, winter, 2002. Copyright *MELUS: The Society for the Study of Multi-Ethnic Literature of the United States*, 2002. Reproduced by permission.—*Midstream*, v. 49, September-October, 2003 for "Inside the Hornet's Head" by Jerome Charyn. Copyright © 2003 Theodor Herzl Foundation. Reprinted by permission of Georges Borchardt, Inc. on behalf of the author.—*The New Criterion*, v. 17, February, 1999 for "The Magic of Contradictions: Willa Cather's 'Lost Lady'" by Morris Dickstein. Copyright © 1999 by Morris Dickstein. Reprinted by permission of Georges

Borchardt, Inc. on behalf of the author.—*The Southern Literary Journal*, v. 38, spring, 2006. Copyright © 2006 by the University of North Carolina Press. Used by permission.—*St. Petersburg Times*, February 18, 2002. Copyright © 2002 *St. Petersburg Times*. Reproduced by permission.—*Twentieth Century Literature*, v. 53, June 22, 2007. Copyright © 2007 Hofstra University Press. Reproduced by permission.—*The Women's Review of Books*, v. 9, July, 1992. Copyright © 1992 Old City Publishing, Inc. Reproduced by permission.—*Writing!*, v. 26, February 1, 2004. Copyright © 2004 Weekly Reader Corporation. Reproduced by permission.

COPYRIGHTED EXCERPTS IN *NfS*, VOLUME 33, WERE REPRODUCED FROM THE FOLLOWING BOOKS:

Amossy, Ruth. From "Fathers and Sons in Old Goriot: The Symbolic Dimension of Balzac's Realism," in *Approaches to Teaching Balzac's Old Goriot*. Edited by Michael Peled Ginsburg. The Modern Language Association of America, 2000. Copyright © 2000 by the Modern Language Association of America. All rights reserved. Reproduced by permission of the Modern Language Association of America.—Birns, Nicholas and Margaret Boe Birns. From "Agatha Christie: Modern and Modernist," in *The Cunning Craft: Original Essays on Detective Fiction and Contemporary Literary Theory*. Edited by Ronald G. Walker and June M. Frazer. Western Illinois University, 1990. Copyright © 1990 by Western Illinois University. Reproduced by permission.—Monod, Sylvere. From *Dickens the Novelist*. University of Oklahoma Press, 1968. Copyright © 1968 University of Oklahoma Press. Reproduced by permission.—Muoneke, Romanus Okey. From *Art, Rebellion and Redemption: A Reading of the Novels of Chinua Achebe*. Peter Lang, 1994. Copyright © 1994 Peter Lang Publishing, Inc., New York. All rights reserved. Reproduced by permission.—Ojinmah, Umelo. From *Chinua Achebe: New Perspectives*. Spectrum Books Limited, 1991. © Umelo Ojinmah 1991. All rights reserved. Reproduced by permission of author.—Riddy, Felicity. From "Language as a Theme in 'No Longer at Ease,'" in *Critical Perspectives on Chinua Achebe*. Edited by C. L. Innes & Bernth Lindfors. Three Continents Press, 1978. Copyright © 1978 by Three Continents Press. All rights reserved. Used by permission of Lynne Rienner Publishers.—Sackelman, Ellen R. From "More Than Skin Deep: Robin McKinley's 'Beauty': A Retelling of the Story of Beauty and the Beast," in *Women in Literature: Reading through the Lens of Gender*. Edited by Jerilyn Fisher and Ellen S. Silber. Greenwood Press, 2003. Copyright © 2003 by Jerilyn Fisher and Ellen S. Silber. All rights reserved. Reproduced by permission of Greenwood Publishing Group, Inc., Westport, CT.

Contributors

Ira Allen: Allen holds a Master's degree in English from Indiana University. He has published scholarly articles on topics ranging from nineteenth-century literature to censorship of the arts in contemporary Singapore. Entry on *Le Père Goriot*. Original essay on *Le Père Goriot*.

Melanie Bush: Bush holds a Master's degree in English. She is a teacher and writer in upstate New York. Entry on *Nicholas Nickleby*. Original essay on *Nicholas Nickleby*.

Michelle Lee: Lee is an assistant professor of literature and composition at Daytona State College with a Ph.D. in English from the University of Texas at Austin. She has published poetry, fiction, and nonfiction, along with her academic work. Entries on *Ordinary People* and *Sense and Sensibility*. Original essays on *Ordinary People* and *Sense and Sensibility*.

Laura Noll: Noll is a freelance editor and writer. Entry on *The Street*. Original essay on *The Street*.

A. Petruso: Petruso holds degrees from the University of Michigan and the University of Texas. Entries on *The Glory Field*, *A Lost Lady*, and *Tangerine*. Original essays on *The Glory Field*, *A Lost Lady*, and *Tangerine*.

Roger K. Smith: Smith, a freelance writer based in Ithaca, New York, pens articles on politics and government, literature, history, and media. Entry on *No Longer at Ease*. Original essay on *No Longer at Ease*.

Patrick Walsh: Walsh holds a Ph.D. in history from the University of Texas and has served as a professor of English, American Studies, and Multidisciplinary Studies. Walsh has published many articles on topics and figures in twentieth century literature and history. Entry on *The Adventures of Augie March*. Original essay on *The Adventures of Augie March*.

Greg Wilson: Wilson is a freelance writer who has contributed material to dozens of books ranging in subject matter from statistics to mythology. Entries on *Beauty*, *Kidnapped*, and *Murder on the Orient Express*. Original essays on *Beauty*, *Kidnapped*, and *Murder on the Orient Express*.

The Adventures of Augie March

SAUL BELLOW

1953

Published in 1953, Saul Bellow's sweeping, comedic novel *The Adventures of Augie March*, was heralded by many reviewers as an instant classic, and it established its author as a major voice in American fiction. It is a bold, ambitious novel that claims that the story of a young, poor, fatherless, Jewish man belongs at the center of American literature as well as at the center of the American experience itself. In the course of the novel, Augie seeks to find his place in the world, and his desire for what he calls his "better fate" leads him on dozens of adventures, some tedious, some exhilarating, from selling coal to training an eagle to stealing college textbooks. Intertwined with these many occupations are numerous romantic escapades with chambermaids, heiresses, actresses, and others, through which Augie strives to find both true love and amorous excitement.

Centered in Chicago, the story is told from Augie's point of view in a seemingly endless torrent of words. The novel teems with American idiom, slang, and the music of urban immigrant speech. Through Augie, Bellow paints intensely rich, and often hilarious, portraits of Chicagoans of all stripes from the years before the stock market crash of 1929, through the Great Depression and World War II, finally coming to rest in postwar Paris. The joy with which Bellow presents this world, combined with Augie's liberal use of references from classical mythology and European literature as he describes his

Saul Bellow (The Library of Congress)

(1964), and *Humboldt's Gift*, which won a Pulitzer Prize in 1975. In 1976, Bellow was awarded the Nobel Prize in Literature.

Although he had worked for left-wing magazines in earlier years, Bellow became disenchanted with liberal views as the years passed. After 1966, Bellow taught at the University of Chicago and increasingly became identified with conservative thinkers at that school. He traveled the college lecture circuit and often clashed with the liberal counterculture that was sweeping the country. In 1970, students at San Francisco State University booed Bellow off stage following a speech he gave there.

In the 1980s Bellow married for a fifth time and took a position at Boston University. Perhaps because his work reflected his growing cynicism about American society, critics were less enthusiastic about the novels he continued to write. In 2000, however, Bellow published a final novel, *Ravelstein*, which met with highly positive reviews. Bellow died in 2005.

experiences, elevates the story to the level of a truly American coming-of-age epic.

AUTHOR BIOGRAPHY

Saul Bellow was born in 1915 in Lachine, Quebec, Canada, and was the fourth child of parents who had emigrated from Russia just two years before. When he was nine, his family moved again, settling in Chicago. After finishing high school, Bellow attended the University of Chicago for a year before transferring to Northwestern University, where he graduated with honors in sociology in 1937. His first two novels, *Dangling Man* and *The Victim*, appeared in 1944 and 1947, respectively, to mostly positive reviews but did not sell widely. In the late 1940s, Bellow traveled Europe, part of the time as a Guggenheim Fellow. With the publication of *The Adventures of Augie March* in 1953, Bellow moved into the top tier of American writers both in terms of popularity and critical reputation. *Augie March* won the National Book Award for Fiction in 1953, the first of three times Bellow would win the award. Over the next half century, Bellow produced a number of successful and important novels, including *Seize the Day* (1956), *Henderson the Rain King* (1959), *Herzog*

PLOT SUMMARY

Chapters 1–4

The first four chapters of *The Adventures of Augie March* introduce us to Augie and his family and the immigrant, Jewish world of his section of Chicago. Augie, the narrator and main character, declares in the opening sentence that "I am an American, Chicago born ... and go at things as I have taught myself, freestyle, and will make the record in my own way." Augie introduces his "simple-minded" mother, who has very few teeth and poor eyesight; his "idiot" brother, Georgie; and his older brother, Simon. His father is apparently dead, and Augie knows next to nothing about him. Ruling over the household is Grandma Lausch, who is not really a relative but instead a willful boarder who hopes to make something of the March boys. When Augie is beaten up by neighborhood boys, who appear to pick on him because he is Jewish, Grandma begins his worldly education, telling Augie that the beating is his own fault and he should not try to fit in with whomever is around him.

Grandma arranges for Augie to pass out handbills for a theater. Then, when he is twelve, she sends him to Chicago's North Side to work for his successful cousins, the Coblins. Simon, meanwhile, is sent to work at a resort hotel. At the Coblin's, Augie is treated kindly by Anna Coblin, who buys him new shoes and a jackknife. He helps deliver newspapers for Coblin and also helps Anna's brother, known as Five Properties, on his route as a milk truck driver. Although Anna hopes Augie will marry into the family, he already has his eye on a different future.

With Grandma's help, the teenaged Augie takes on a series of jobs. In fact, he declares that understanding the term "various jobs" unlocks the meaning to his "entire life." Meanwhile, Simon is transformed by waiting on the rich at the resort, and although he is valedictorian of his graduating class, he is no longer interested in following Grandma's advice. He tells Augie, "She's really nothing to us." With Simon's help, Augie gets a job selling newspapers; he loses the job. He then works along with a friend, Jimmy Klein, as one of Santa's elves at Deever's, a neighborhood department store. Realizing that the cash they take from customers is not followed closely, the boys begin pocketing some of it. This scheme is discovered and Augie is severely scolded by Grandma and Simon. Jimmy's cousin, Clem Tambow, joins the boys in fantasizing about burning down Deever's, and Jimmy's older sister, Eleanor, flirts with Augie. For his part, Augie falls for Hilda Novinson, his first crush. These teenage dreams are pushed aside when Grandma demands that Georgie be put into a mental institution before he does something harmful. Augie resents this, but shows his younger brother how to open and close his suitcase before tearfully taking him to an institution.

Chapters 5–7

In the fall of 1929, just before the stock market crash, Augie goes to work for a local businessman named William Einhorn. Augie calls Einhorn "the first superior man I knew" and becomes the "arms and legs" of his severely handicapped mentor. The Einhorn fortune was made by Einhorn's father, the Commissioner. Augie is essentially adopted by the Einhorn family, which includes Einhorn's younger half brother, known by all as Dingbat, as well as Einhorn's wife, Tillie, and his college-student son, Arthur. Augie does everything for Einhorn, serving as his "secretary, deputy, agent, companion." In return, Einhorn replaces Grandma as Augie's mentor, though his advice and actions are not always honorable. Augie learns that Einhorn carries on "with one woman after another," including his employee Lollie Fewter, with whom Augie also has a romantic liaison. Later, Augie observes Einhorn burning his own living room

for the insurance money when Tillie demands they redecorate. Consequently, Augie receives a fire-damaged set of *Harvard Classics*, books that will also shape the way he looks at the world.

As he begins his senior year in high school, Augie's world is shaken by the rapid deterioration of both Grandma Lausch's health and Mama's eyesight. When Simon appeals to Grandma's sons for help, they respond by placing her in the Nelson Home for the Aged and Infirm. Soon after, it becomes clear that the Commissioner is dying. Following the funeral, Augie sits with Einhorn as he writes his father's obituary and burns some of his personal papers. Soon after, the stock market crashes and the Einhorns lose much of their wealth and sense of power. The March family also loses its savings when their bank closes. Simon toys with radical politics and Augie falls in with a petty gangster named Joe Gorman. Gorman convinces Augie to help him rob a handbag store. When Einhorn hears of the robbery he counsels Augie to steer clear of criminals like Gorman. He observes that Augie has a strong desire to oppose the world around him, but notes that the prisons are full of just such men. Augie is stunned by Einhorn's insight and realizes that Einhorn's advice is not to follow his example but to chart a different course. Even so, Einhorn enlists Augie's help to swindle a gangster, and he takes Augie to a prostitute on the night of his graduation from high school.

Chapters 8–11

"From here a new course was set," declares Augie. He attends a city college at night and finds work at a clothing store during the day. Simon works in the same store, and the family is doing well enough to hire a mulatto (a person of both black and white ancestry), Molly Simms, to help the increasingly blind Mama with the housework. But Simon soon spends the night with her and then fires her. Augie drops out of school and begins selling high-end sporting goods for a man named Mr. Renling. At first, Augie feels like a "house slave," but soon Renling and his wife become mentors for Augie, teaching him how to act in high society. When Augie begins dating a waitress, Mrs. Renling demands that he stop. She has Augie drive her to Benton Harbor, a Michigan resort where, at her side, he learns still more about the rich. He then meets a wealthy heiress, Thea Fenchel, and her younger sister, Esther. Augie decides he has fallen in love with Esther while Thea seems very interested in him. Esther completely rebuffs Augie's advances, causing him to faint. As Augie broods about Esther, Thea appears and declares that she is in love with him. The Fenchels leave soon after. Simon arrives with his girlfriend, Cissy Flexner, whom Augie finds "a sly girl, soft though she seems." Simon tells Augie he hopes to marry her soon.

Returning from the resort, the Renlings suggest that they adopt Augie. Though drawn by their wealth, Augie declines the offer. He confesses that he likes his own flawed family, and besides, "the unvarnished truth is that it wasn't a fate good enough for me." Breaking with the Renlings, Augie returns to the South Side of Chicago and takes a job trying to sell paint on commission to hotels and hospitals. Augie runs into Joe Gorman coming out of a train station, and the dapper criminal suggests they work together to bring in illegal immigrants from Canada. Humiliated by his failure as a paint salesman, Augie joins Gorman and they speed toward the border in what turns out to be a stolen car. When they stop to eat, they realize a state trooper is looking at the car, so Augie and Gorman split up and run. Augie later sees a beaten Gorman in the back of a police car. Augie makes his way to Buffalo, New York, where he wires Simon for money so that he can return home by bus. When none arrives, Augie makes his way west by hopping freight trains. Along the way he befriends a man named Stoney, is beaten by police, and spends a night in jail. Finally, he arrives in Chicago to find that Grandma Lausch has died, Simon has sold the family furniture, and Mama is living in a tiny rented room. He also learns that Five Properties is going to marry Cissy Flexner, Simon's old girlfriend. Frustrated at how Mama is being treated, Augie helps arrange to put her in a home for the blind.

Einhorn helps Augie find a job working with an elite dog groomer. Augie is struck by how often the groomer, Guillaume, uses a hypodermic needle to sedate the dogs. Augie moves into a house near the University of Chicago and befriends Manny Padilla, a brilliant math student who supplements his scholarship by stealing and then selling textbooks. Padilla convinces Augie to do the same, though Augie is often distracted by reading the books he steals. Simon finally makes amends with Augie about not wiring him money and proudly announces he plans to marry a rich girl named Charlotte Magnus. Clem Tambow also visits, in part because he is enamored with Mimi Villars, a young woman who lives in Augie's student house. Mimi is in love with a young graduate

student in political science named Frazer. Augie learns that his old friend Sylvester, now a Communist organizer who wants to recruit Frazer, was once married to Mimi's sister.

Simon prepares to marry Charlotte, and her coarse Uncle Charlie helps set up Simon as the owner of a coal yard. When Augie meets the Magnuses it is clear that they adore Simon. Augie goes to work for Simon at the coal yard, where he meets Happy Kellerman, the yardmaster. At first Simon struggles with the coal yard. But soon, in part thanks to Charlotte's excellent business sense, he is making money and enjoying his new style of life. Even so, Augie is concerned that there is a new desperation about Simon.

Chapters 12–15

Simon and Charlotte marry, and Simon hatches a plan for Augie to marry Lucy Magnus, Charlotte's cousin. The Magnuses, however, are not enthusiastic about Augie, largely because of his seeming lack of ambition and direction. He continues to work hard as Simon's assistant at the coal yard, and business for the ruthless Simon rapidly improves. Mimi Villars tells Augie she is pregnant by Frazer, and Augie drives her to get an illegal and dangerous abortion. She bleeds badly afterward and Augie fears for her health. At the abortionist's, Augie runs into Kelly Weintraub, a cousin of the Magnuses who had lived in Augie's old neighborhood. Kelly spreads the rumor that Mimi is Augie's girlfriend, and the Magnuses break off his relationship with Lucy. Augie returns to reading his books and takes a job with the Works Progress Administration, one of the New Deal programs. He walks through the slums of Chicago, working on a housing survey. Through Mimi he meets a man named Grammick who makes him a union organizer for the Congress of Industrial Organizations, or CIO. He is struck by how many people want to sign up. One new member is a Greek chambermaid named Sophie Geratis with whom Augie begins a love affair. Although Augie feels tenderly toward Sophie, he is drawn away from her by the dramatic return of Thea Fenchel.

In typical fashion Augie throws himself headfirst into his relationship with Thea, and he is prepared to do whatever she asks. She tells him she is on her way to Mexico to get a divorce from her husband, and she urges Augie to accompany her. Thea also has an idea to make money on their trip; namely, to train an eagle to catch lizards.

Augie takes this odd news in stride, deciding, "I could not find myself in love without it should have some peculiarity." Although Thea's behavior seems somewhat erratic, and despite the advice of such friends as Mimi, he decides to accompany her to Mexico. Together they drive south, stopping near the Texas border to buy an eagle from a man Augie believes to be a crook. Still, he is impressed with how natural Thea is with the eagle. In Nuevo Laredo, Mexico, Augie names the bird Caligula, after the sound of the Spanish world for "eagle." In Mexico, Thea begins training Caligula to fly after a piece of meat on a fishing lure. Augie is afraid of the bird but impressed by Thea's command of it. Augie assumes he and Thea will marry when her divorce is finalized.

Chapters 16–20

Augie and Thea settle in the town of Acatla, in a house owned by her family. Augie begins to wonder just why he is in Mexico. Thea has said earning money was the goal, but training an eagle to catch lizards seems to be a strange way of doing it. He also finds himself feeling sympathy for the lizards brought in by Jacinto, the young son of the housekeeper. Thea is somewhat annoyed at this display of compassion and becomes enraged when Caligula is bitten by a lizard and seems to lose all interest in hunting. Augie is struck that, "while she was unpleasantly stirred against Caligula I felt a little condemned with him." Thea declares Caligula to be "chicken" and abandons the eagle for a new pastime: developing photographs.

Eventually, Thea agrees to give Caligula another chance. She and Augie ride into the mountains where iguanas live, but Augie's burro loses its footing and falls down the mountain, kicking Augie in the head. Thea shoots the injured burro dead. As Augie recuperates, Thea sends Caligula to a zoo in Indiana. Weeks pass and Thea becomes bored. Augie begins to gamble with the little colony of Americans, and Thea hunts for poisonous snakes. Augie realizes that he has "no more stretch" for Thea; he can't get excited about her snake-catching. Augie suggests they marry and Thea simply shakes her head.

Augie increasingly spends his time in the company of the town's bohemian colony of writers, artists, and other characters, including a woman named Stella, whom Augie feels immediately drawn to. One day, he catches sight of the exiled Russian Communist leader Leon Trotsky

outside the village church. Augie is stunned to realize that one of the bodyguards is his old friend Sylvester. Their conversation is superficial, but the encounter reminds Augie of the world he'd left behind. Soon after, Stella's jealous boyfriend, Oliver, discovers American lawmen are looking for him, and Stella, who is frightened of Oliver, turns to Augie for help. Meanwhile, Thea asks Augie to drive farther south with her, her only reason being that there are "interesting animals" in the area. Augie agrees but is clearly distracted by Stella's precarious situation. At a party thrown by Oliver, Stella takes Augie aside, telling him she fears for her safety and begging him to help her flee to Mexico City. She tells Augie that "you and I are the kind of people other people are always trying to fit into their schemes." Augie realizes she is right and agrees to help her. When Augie tells Thea of his plan she is furious and jealous, even when he invites her to come as well. He leaves with Stella, and on their way through the mountains they spend the night together. When he returns to Thea she accuses him of betraying her and tells him, "You're not special. You're like everybody else."

Thea leaves and Augie remains, brooding and filled with guilt. He hears that one of his acquaintances in Mexico is actually an ex-lover of Thea's and that he, too, has left for the south. Augie follows and confronts Thea. He asks again for them to continue on together. Thea refuses, and Augie returns to Acatla. Sylvester and Frazer convince him to take a job as a companion to Trotsky; Augie agrees, but he fears that he will be "sucked into another one of those great currents where I can't be myself," Fortunately, the plan falls through. Augie moves in with an old friend of Trotsky's, a Yugoslavian named Paslavitch who loves French culture, and the two of them become good friends.

Chapters 21–26

Augie returns to Chicago, stopping to see his brother Georgie along the way. He is impressed that Georgie has learned the craft of shoemaking. He then drops in on Mama, finding her in a nicer apartment at her institution. She tells him to go see Simon, and Augie is thrilled to hear that Simon often talks to Mama about him. When Augie meets Simon he realizes that no matter what Simon does or becomes, "I loved him again. I couldn't help it." Simon is rich but unhappy and treats people around him with thinly disguised contempt. Augie then visits Einhorn, Mimi, Padilla, and Clem Tambow, all of whom offer advice as to what he should do next with his life. Clem tells Augie he needs to pick up an exciting specialty like Egyptology, but Augie feels it's exactly the need for specialization that he doesn't like about the modern world. Augie then lands a job as a research assistant to an eccentric millionaire named Robey. Robey claims to be writing a book on human happiness, but Augie perceives that he just wants to hear himself talk.

Augie begins teaching at a public school where his old neighbor, Kayo Obermark, is also teaching. Augie has dinner with Kayo and his family and ends up selling his run-down car to Kayo's brother without telling him quite how bad it is. Augie tries to make amends, but in the end his friendship with Kayo is damaged. Sophie Geratis reappears, now married, but still interested in Augie. Augie has a profound philosophical conversation with Clem. Augie declares that life is only good when it conforms to what he calls its "axial lines" of "Truth, love, peace, bounty, usefulness, harmony!" Augie's goal is to keep seeking these lines. His new plan is to get married and start a boarding school and bring Mama and Georgie to live at it. Clem is impressed but skeptical. However, before Augie can act on this new dream, World War II breaks out and he volunteers for military service. But in the process of signing up, Augie learns he has a hernia, undergoes surgery, and must wait to recuperate. During this time he sees Simon again and meets Simon's longtime mistress, Renee. Augie finds her a "suspicious girl," but Simon is devoted to her, seeing her before and after work every day. Augie is struck by the lack of trust in their relationship and is distressed by the rage he sees in Simon. One day, Simon tells Augie that Renee has attempted suicide, though he is not sure if she was serious about killing herself. Simon explains that Renee demands all the luxuries that Charlotte gets, and that Charlotte has found out about Renee. There was a confrontation between Charlotte and Renee, and now Renee claims to be pregnant. Augie notes that Simon "went to defy his wife, and soon found himself twice-married."

Augie travels to New York and prepares to ship out as a purser aboard a warship. He hears that Stella is in that city and goes to visit her, thinking, "What use was war without love?" Again he is irresistibly drawn to her and she to him. Before he

ships out they share their hopes for the future, declare their love for each other, and decide to get married as soon as Augie completes his training.

Through Stella, Augie meets a man named Mintouchian, who is an experienced divorce lawyer. He is also having an affair with Stella's friend Agnes Kuttner. Mintouchian, like so many before him, gives Augie advice, in this case about marriage and adultery. At first Augie is suspicious of his tales of lies and secrets, but he is delighted when Mintouchian concludes that "pureheartedness" and simplicity are the keys to happiness. Mintouchian then takes Augie to meet his wife, who tells a stunned Augie that she knows all her husband's secrets, but, like Augie, thinks Mintouchian is "great, even if he is all too human."

Augie prepares for marriage and war feeling bolstered and ennobled by the purity of his love. Augie and Stella wed, with Frazer, Sylvester, Robey, Mintouchian, and Agnes in attendance. After a short honeymoon he ships out. Because of his duties and his character, Augie swiftly becomes the "ship's confidant," hearing the secrets of many of his shipmates. Augie counsels prudence: "Nobody is perfect. I advocated love especially." But this job comes swiftly to an end when the ship is torpedoed, leaving Augie clinging desperately to a lifeboat. He helps another man into the boat but the favor isn't returned. Augie manages to get into the boat and furiously beats his new companion. This man, the only other survivor, is named Basteshaw. Also from Chicago, his father did business with Einhorn. But Augie does not like him, the way he speaks of his father, or his pretensions of being a genius. Basteshaw claims to have created life and wants Augie to join him as his assistant. Basteshaw tells Augie they are headed straight toward the Canary Islands, where they will be able to set up a laboratory. Augie is impressed by Basteshaw's intellect but finds him less than sane. When Augie tries to signal for help, Basteshaw attacks him and ties him up. Eventually Augie gains control of the boat and the two of them are rescued. They are taken to Naples, Italy, nowhere near where Basteshaw claimed they had been. Six months later, Augie is back in New York with Stella.

The novel concludes with Augie and Stella in France. His plan for his "academy and foster-home" is gone, sacrificed to his love for Stella and her goal of being a film actress. He hopes to have children and to return to America, but Stella is uninterested. Augie works for Mintouchian, moving goods on the black market, and Mintouchian tells him that Stella long ago had an important romance that Augie has never heard about. He then learns that she is threatening to sue her former lover. Augie realizes that Stella lies "more than is average," and that Stella's desire to make it as an actress is in large part driven by her desire to show her old lover that she can be successful without him.

Simon and Charlotte come to Paris. Augie innocently asks Simon what has become of Renee, and Charlotte flies into a rage. Augie learns that she was never pregnant, has "disappeared," and has married another wealthy man. Augie is once again overwhelmed with love for his brother as well as with pity as he realizes how much Simon wants to have the child he thought Renee was going to have.

In the final scene, Augie travels with his maid, Jacqueline, to northern France, where she is going to visit her uncle's farm. Walking the final few kilometers, they begin singing. Augie sings a Mexican song, and she tells him it has always been her dream to travel to Mexico. Augie laughs hard at this, in part delighted that a woman who has had such a hard life "will still refuse to lead a disappointed life." Or perhaps, he thinks, the joke is on nature for thinking that it can keep us from hoping and dreaming. Reflecting on his life's experiences, Augie muses, "Look at me, going everywhere! Why, I am a sort of Columbus.... I may well be a flop at this sort of endeavor. Columbus too thought he was a flop, probably, when they sent him back in chains. Which didn't prove there was no America." In the end, Augie is full of hope, despite his half-success at finding his "axial lines."

CHARACTERS

Caligula

Caligula is the young eagle trained to hunt lizards by Augie and Thea Fenchel. When he turns out to be "chicken," Augie's sympathy for him contributes to the tension between Augie and Thea.

Uncle Charlie

Charlotte Magnus's uncle, Uncle Charlie helps set up Simon in the coal business. However, he takes less of a liking to Augie, who is more interested in romance and adventure than making money and obtaining power.

Anna Coblin

Anna Coblin serves as a surrogate mother to Augie in his youth. He lives briefly with the Coblins and works for Anna's brother, Five Properties. A kindly and emotional woman, Anna is devastated when her son runs away to enlist in the Marine Corps.

The Commissioner

The patriarch of the Einhorn family. He passes away before the stock market crash wipes away much of the family's wealth. Like his son, he is a womanizer.

Dingbat

Einhorn's younger, less intelligent half brother. Augie and Dingbat briefly work together managing an unsuccessful prizefighter.

Einhorn

Augie goes to work for William Einhorn while still in high school. Einhorn loses much of his family's wealth during the Great Depression. Augie does everything for the crippled Einhorn, including carrying him when necessary. In Augie's mind, his words have the weight of wise figures like Julius Caesar or the hero of Homer's *Odyssey*, Ulysses.

Arthur Einhorn

The only son of the Einhorn family, Arthur is a student at the University of Illinois. He falls in love with Mimi Villars and, much to his father's disgust, becomes her lover.

Tillie Einhorn

Einhorn's wife. She acts as a surrogate mother to Augie.

Esther Fenchel

Augie meets Esther when he is living with the Renlings. She is wealthy and unobtainable, rebuffing Augie's advances because she believes he is Mrs. Renling's lover.

Thea Fenchel

Esther's older sister, Thea falls for Augie as he falls for Esther. Thea is determined and emotional. She proclaims her love for Augie before he leaves the Renlings, telling him they will meet again. She reappears when he has taken up with Sophie Geratis. Augie leaves Sophie for Thea, believing the latter is the love of his life. The couple travels to Mexico, where she demands he assist her in training an eagle to fight iguanas. The project fails, and Augie's doubts about it drive them apart. After Augie spends a night with Stella, Thea rejects him and leaves him in Acatla.

Lollie Fewter

An employee of Einhorn's, Lollie begins but then halts a romantic relationship with Augie. Augie then learns she is also involved with Einhorn. She is later murdered by another lover.

Five Properties

Anna Coblin's brother, with whom Augie works when Grandma Lausch sends him to live with the Coblins. Five Properties marries Cissy Flexner, an attractive girl whom Simon March had planned to wed.

Cissy Flexner

Cissy Flexner is Simon March's attractive girlfriend, whom he hopes to marry. Cissy refuses to marry him, however, instead marrying his cousin, Five Properties, because Simon is essentially penniless.

Frazer

Frazer is Mimi Villars's lover when Augie meets him as one of Padilla's stolen-book customers. He is a graduate student in political science at the University of Chicago. He gets Mimi pregnant but responds by going to an academic convention in Louisiana. When Augie is in Mexico, Frazer appears and tries to convince Augie to help protect the exiled Communist Leon Trotsky by traveling with him posing as his nephew.

Sophie Geratis

A Greek chambermaid whom Augie meets when he works as a union organizer. They become and remain lovers until Thea Fenchel tracks him down. After his return from Mexico, Augie briefly returns to the kind and now-married Sophie.

Joe Gorman

A small-time Chicago gangster who twice convinces Augie to join him in crime. When Augie is still in high school, Gorman enlists him to rob a store. When Einhorn hears of the robbery, he lectures Augie about staying away from violent crime, using Gorman as an example. Years later, when Augie is down on his luck, he meets Gorman and they drive to Canada in a stolen car to bring illegal aliens into the country. The plan goes awry and Augie last sees Gorman bloodied and in the back seat of a police car.

Grammick

Grammick is the genteel law student and union organizer who recruits Augie to become an organizer for the Congress of Industrial Organizations (CIO).

Jacinto

The son of Thea and Augie's maid in Acatla. He helps them find lizards for Caligula.

Happy Kellerman

Simon's experienced yardmaster at the coal yard.

Jimmy Klein

A neighborhood boy and friend of Augie's. Together they steal quarters while working as Santa's elves in a department store at Christmas time. Augie runs into Jimmy again when the latter, now a policeman, catches Augie stealing textbooks.

Agnes Kuttner

Stella's best friend and the lover of Augie's friend and employer, Mintouchian.

Grandma Lausch

A Russian immigrant of apparently important background, Grandma Lausch lives with the March family during Augie's boyhood. While she is no relation to the rest of the family, she strives to mold the March boys into successes. When she becomes senile and increasingly hard on Augie's mother, Grandma is placed in a mental institution.

Charlotte Magnus

The heavyset daughter of a well-to-do family, Charlotte is targeted for marriage by Simon March after he is dumped by Cissy Flexner. Charlotte turns out to be a help to Simon in business, though their marriage is not a happy one.

Lucy Magnus

Charlotte's cousin, whom Simon hopes Augie will marry. She is keen on Augie, calling him "husband," but her family cuts off the affair.

Mama

Augie's mother, whose name is Rebecca, is a kindly but somewhat weak-willed woman of failing eyesight. At the beginning of the novel she is dominated by Grandma Lausch. Later, when she has gone blind, she lives comfortably in an institution for the blind and is supported by Simon.

Augie March

The central figure of the novel, Augie begins the story as a Jewish teenager in a mostly non-Jewish, poor section of Chicago. Looking for his place in the world, he tries all sorts of occupations—some legal, some not. Eventually he graduates from high school and leaves college to pursue his adventures. He attracts a number of mentors who try to bend him to their way of seeing the world. But Augie is "oppositional" and wants to find his way on his own terms. His journeys take him to Mexico and Europe, where he settles into married life while working in the postwar black market.

Georgie March

Augie's mentally challenged brother, Georgie is eventually institutionalized. When Augie visits him years later, he is impressed and somewhat jealous that Georgie has become a shoemaker.

Simon March

Simon is Augie's older brother, and his desire for wealth, power, and prestige serves as a counterpoint to Augie's adventures. Simon is valedictorian at his high school, but a summer waiting tables at a wealthy resort creates a burning desire to achieve status at any cost. This is reinforced when his beautiful girlfriend, Cissy Flexner, refuses to marry Simon and instead weds his cousin, Five Properties, because Simon could not raise enough money for the marriage. Simon in turn marries Charlotte Magnus for her money and uses her family connections to become rich in the coal business and other concerns. He also takes up with a young lover, Renee. Despite his success, by the story's end his affair has collapsed into a threatened lawsuit and public humiliation.

Mintouchian

An older Armenian lawyer whose specialty appears to be messy divorces. He befriends Augie because his lover, Agnes Kuttner, is Stella's best friend. After World War II, Augie works for Mintouchian on the European black market. Mintouchian tells Augie about important secrets about her past that Stella has been keeping from him.

Hilda Novinson

Hilda, the daughter of a neighborhood tailor, is Augie's first crush, though he never speaks a word to her.

Kayo Obermark

Kayo Obermark lives in the room between Augie and Mimi Villars and overhears much of their conversation. Near the end of the novel, Kayo and Augie teach at the same school. Their friendship is temporarily damaged when Augie sells his car to Kayo's brother.

Oliver

Oliver is a member of the American colony in Acatla and, when Augie meets him, Stella's lover. It turns out he is on the run from the police. Stella tells Augie that Oliver has a violent temper and convinces Augie to help her escape from him.

Manny Padilla

A brilliant student of math and science who steals textbooks to finance his education. Padilla helps Augie become a book thief as well.

Paslavitch

An emotional Russian Communist who meets Augie in Mexico through Frazer and Sylvester.

Mr. Renling

Owner of a successful sporting goods business, Mr. Renling hires Augie as a salesman.

Mrs. Renling

Mrs. Renling, an immigrant from Luxembourg, takes Augie under her wing with the intention of teaching him the ways of the wealthy. She takes Augie to the resort town of Benton Harbor, Michigan, where he serves as her companion. Mrs. Renling becomes fond of Augie and offers to adopt him.

Robey

The eccentric millionaire whom Augie serves as a research assistant.

Molly Simms

The African American housekeeper hired by Simon to take care of the Marchs' house because of Mama's failing eyesight. On New Year's Eve, Simon sleeps with Molly and then fires her.

Stella

Stella is a beautiful film actress whom Augie meets in Acatla, Mexico. She asks Augie for help escaping from her lover, Oliver, and when he agrees, his car breaks down. They make love, essentially ending Augie's relationship with Thea. They meet again as Augie readies to ship out to World War II. They fall in love and marry. After the war, they settle in France, and Stella pursues her interest in acting. Because he loves her, Augie seems to give up his dream of having children and opening an "academy and foster-home." He also accepts the fact that she "lies more than is average."

Stoney

Stoney is a sympathetic African American hobo with whom Augie travels on his way back to Chicago from Buffalo.

Sylvester

Sylvester turns up many times in Augie's life. As a boy, Augie passes out handbills for Sylvester's father's theater. Later, Augie discovers that Sylvester was married to the sister of Mimi Villars. In Mexico, Augie again runs into Sylvester, who is now a bodyguard for the exiled Russian Communist leader Leon Trotsky.

Clem Tambow

Jimmy Klein's cousin, Clem talks with the boys about burning down Deever's Department Store. Later, as a student at the University of Chicago, he falls for Mimi Villars, Augie's neighbor. Clem and Augie have an important conversation in which Clem urges Augie to find an exciting specialty in life. Clem suggests they go into business together, but Augie tells him of his desire to follow life's "axial lines."

Mimi Villars

Augie has a more meaningful relationship with Mimi than with any other woman in the novel except perhaps for Stella, though Mimi and Augie are not romantically involved. Mimi lives in the student housing where Augie and Kayo Obermark also have rooms. She is a waitress and is clearly intelligent. Mimi dates Frazer until she becomes pregnant by him. After Augie helps Mimi get through her experience of having an abortion, she begins to date Arthur Einhorn.

Kelly Weintraub

Weintraub is from Augie's neighborhood and is a cousin to the Magnus family. Augie runs into him while helping Mimi get an abortion, and he spreads the rumor that Mimi is pregnant by Augie. This leads the Magnuses to break off Augie's relationship with Lucy Magnus.

THEMES

Self-Realization

Perhaps the central theme of *The Adventures of Augie March* is its protagonist's lifelong struggle

TOPICS FOR FURTHER STUDY

- Research the ways in which Saul Bellow used his own experience and the people he knew growing up as inspiration for *The Adventures of Augie March*. What did he change? How did he elaborate on his experiences or on neighborhood characters? Write a paper looking at the choices Bellow made as an author to flesh out his personal history into the plot of *Augie March*, speculating on the reasons for the literary license he took at certain points.

- When he wrote *Augie March*, Bellow was trying to write "The Great American Novel." What do writers and critics mean by this phrase? List the kinds of qualities such a novel is supposed to have. What does a novel that encompasses the American experience need to have in it? Discuss with classmates the ways in which the term "American" can be limited in terms of race, class, and gender when it comes to this list. What would a woman's "Great American Novel" look like?

- Although it has been very popular for fifty years, there has never been a film made of this novel. Write a scene-by-scene screenplay. What elements of the film would work well on film? Which would not? Lead a discussion in which you talk about novels that have become successful films. What is it about these books that lend themselves to film?

- Some critics argue that male writers cannot possibly create fully developed female characters. Similarly, some argue writers cannot truly understand the experience of someone of another race or ethnicity. Research this controversy and write a paper framing the debate and detailing your position on this question.

to discover who he truly is and what his place in the world should be. This epic search for a path through life is what launches Augie into his "various jobs," including smuggler, thief, teacher, and shoe salesman. But his quest for realization is not as simple as finding his preferred occupation. Instead, Augie must deal with a string of would-be mentors whose advice is only sometimes geared to actually helping him. Grandma Lausch, Einhorn, Simon, Mrs. Renling, Basteshaw, and Mintouchian all dish out pages of wisdom to Augie, but he learns to perceive which words are meant for him and which are intended to advance their own interests. On the other hand, Augie believes that he will be fully realized when he is able to discern and follow what he calls "the axial lines of life." He can feel these lines only when "striving stops"; then he becomes vaguely aware of "Truth, love, peace, bounty, usefulness, [and] harmony." Thus, from childhood, he can turn away from "all my persuaders, just on the obstinacy of these lines, never entirely clear." This explanation is a bit vague, but it seems that Augie believes in his inner voice and its connection to larger, indefinable currents. When he can step away from the whirl of his life, when he listens to his own mind, he believes in what he hears. It is not clear whether or not Augie has succeeded in his quest for self-realization by the end of the novel. In the final paragraph, he looks back on his adventures and reflects, "I may well be a flop in this endeavor." But failing to follow his axial lines does not mean he was wrong to seek them.

The Primacy of Love

The Adventures of Augie March centers on Augie's "various jobs" and his many romances. But underlying these two important themes is Augie's guiding belief in love. If what Einhorn describes as the "opposition" in Augie drives him to experiment with many occupations and relationships, his desire to feel and give love is a complementary force. This includes more than romantic love, but brotherly and filial love as well. Though his mother is weak-willed and blind, his brother Georgie is mentally challenged, and his brother Simon is hollowed out by his drive for wealth, Augie deeply loves them all. Each time he encounters Simon, Augie reflects on how much he loves him and how the sight of Simon eclipses whatever other emotion Augie had been feeling toward him. Augie's desire for familial love keeps him from being hurt by Einhorn's refusal to see him as a son despite their close relationship. It also drives Augie to refuse the Renlings's offer of adoption and accompanying wealth. Furthermore, it helps maintain emotional distance from Basteshaw, who hates

his own father, something the fatherless Augie cannot abide. With women, Augie is sensual but never unloving. He may not plan to marry Sophie but he is gentle with her because he recognizes that she deserves love. In his relationship with Thea, his response to her behavior in Mexico was to ask, "What was wrong with the enjoyment of love, and what did there have to be an eagle for?" Augie is disappointed that, for Thea, simple love is not enough. But he accepts that "I could not find myself in love without it should have some peculiarity." He needs this flexibility with Stella as well as it becomes clear she has no intention of giving up her career for his dream of a "private green place" where unloved children could be loved, but, as Augie reflects, "I understood that I would mostly do as she wanted because it was I who loved her most." Augie's love is perhaps passive, but it is also forgiving. When he becomes the counselor for the men aboard a ship headed into war, he reminds his comrades that "nobody is perfect," and he "advocated love, especially."

The American Dream

Several versions of the American Dream coexist within *The Adventures of Augie March*. It is arguably the Great American Novel of immigrant America and offers numerous tales of new Americans (or their children) seeking their success in their new country. There is Einhorn, with his pretense to dynasty and his curious collection of pamphlets and other kinds of self-help information. Einhorn is interested in creating a kind of old-world fiefdom and ultimately appears to be a symbol of a pre-modern kind of power, in this case over a neighborhood. There is Simon and his ruthless and ultimately empty pursuit of spiteful power and wealth. For Simon, achieving the American Dream means climbing socially into the wealthy classes. His intellect is directed only at the acquisition of money and power, especially power over the wealthy, as Augie observes when they visit Simon's club. Other immigrants also dream of American success: Padilla, with his studies and his book-stealing business; Grandma, with her plans for the March boys; Sophie Geratis, with her demand for honest pay. And of course, there is Augie's final pastoral dream of a school for unwanted children. It is worth noting that a book that seems to celebrate the energy and amorality of urban life climaxes with a vision of a little country school at which orphans and foster children can find shelter. And Augie's own

The eagle is a symbol in the novel. *(Image copyright FloridaStock, 2009. Used under license from Shutterstock.com)*

American Dream also contrasts with the fierce individualism exhibited by so many of the book's characters, including Augie himself. But this dream is not realized, and Augie concludes that it is "only one of those bubble-headed dreams of people who haven't yet realized what they're like nor what they're intended for." In fact, none of the main characters seem to have realized their version of the American Dream, but the stronger among them still have hope.

STYLE

The Coming-of-Age Novel
The Coming-of-Age Novel, also known as a *Bildungsroman*, tells the story of a young person discovering their true self and the nature of the world as they come into adulthood. Other examples include *Catcher in the Rye* by J. D. Salinger and *Great Expectations* by Charles Dickens. *The Adventures of Augie March* is arguably a good example of this genre, because it begins with Augie as a young adolescent and

follows him for some twenty years, well into adulthood. In the course of the novel, Augie learns about the nature of work, love, and identity, and comes to his own conclusions on each of these themes.

The Picaresque Novel
The Adventures of Augie March is also arguably a *picaresque* novel. Picaresque novels usually consist of the adventures of a rambling trickster from a low social class. They are comic novels, in which the hero often has many romances and narrow escapes from situations of his or her own making. In such stories, the author uses the wandering rascal's interactions with people from all walks of life in order to comment on society. Augie certainly fits the description of a picaresque hero well, except for his sincerity and kindheartedness, which is often the cause of his trouble. Bellow's title, with its reflection of the title of Mark Twain's picaresque, *The Adventures of Huckleberry Finn*, suggests his intention to write such a novel.

Point of View

Perhaps what is most striking stylistically about *The Adventures of Augie March* is the utterly distinct voice of the narrator, Augie March. The story is told in the first person, from Augie's point of view. What is so conspicuous about Augie as a narrator is his constant use of working-class, Jewish, Chicago vernacular—in other words, the local dialect of Augie's world. But Bellow makes Augie even more compelling as a narrator by designing him as a self-taught student of classical literature and then sprinkling his speech with often obscure references to history and mythology. Armed with this voice, the novel tumbles out of Augie in a torrent of words. Riding an elevator in Chicago's City Hall, for example, Augie notices "bigshots and operators, commissioners, grabbers, heelers, tipsters, hoodlums, wolves, fixers, plaintiffs, flatfeet, men in Western hats and women in lizard shoes and fur coats." With Augie as the narrator, the novel becomes an epic lexicon of American English.

HISTORICAL CONTEXT

The Great Depression

Much of the action of the novel takes place during the Great Depression, widely considered the most serious economic downturn in United States history. The Great Depression began in the autumn of 1929, when the largely unregulated stock market plunged and American industry came almost to a standstill. By the early 1930s, between a quarter and a third of Americans were unemployed. During the Depression, which affected people throughout the world, radical political movements enjoyed rising success. In Germany, for example, millions sought relief in the programs and nationalistic rhetoric of the National Socialist, or Nazi, Party. Significantly, Germany's second most popular party in the early 1930s was the Communist Party, as many lost faith in capitalism's ability to deliver prosperity. In the same way, in the United States socialist and Communist beliefs enjoyed new popularity, although they were never embraced as widely as in Europe and parts of Asia. Nevertheless, the Socialist Party candidate for president in 1932, Norman Thomas, earned almost a million votes, over two percent of the overall tally. Most Americans turned to liberal politicians during the Great Depression. The most important of

these was President Franklin Delano Roosevelt. Elected four times beginning with the 1932 election, Roosevelt changed the relationship between the United States government and its citizens. His "New Deal" programs, such as the Works Progress Administration (1935–1943), responded to the economic crisis by employing millions of Americans to build roads, schools, and bridges. In order to stabilize the economy after the crash of the stock market, Roosevelt created numerous government programs and offices, including such regulatory institutions as the Federal Deposit Insurance Corporation (FDIC). The economy rebounded in the mid-1930s but fell back into recession in 1937. The onset of World War II returned American industry to full capacity and brought the Depression to an end by about 1940.

The Cold War

The Adventures of Augie March was written and published in the early 1950s, in an era known to historians as the Early Cold War. The name "Cold War" signifies that although the United States and the Soviet Union (and the People's Republic of China) were not engaged in a conventional war, they battled for global supremacy in the years after the end of World War II in 1945. American political and social life was dominated by the adversarial relationship between the United States and the Soviet Union. In the early 1950s, the United States fought a war in Korea in order to repel an invasion of South Korea by Communist North Korean forces supported by both the Soviet Union and the People's Republic of China. Domestic politics were also dominated by the Cold War, as Republicans and Democrats vied to lead the fight against communism abroad and communist "infiltration" at home. The Congress held hearings on communism in the film industry and in the Department of State. President Harry S. Truman instituted loyalty oaths for federal employees, and the Supreme Court ruled that the Communist Party was essentially a criminal organization. American culture was also marked by a fear of communism. Because of so-called "blacklists" in Hollywood and elsewhere, writers and artists feared standing out as "different" for fear of being labeled as communists. This was especially true for those who, like Saul Bellow, had a background in left-wing or radical organizations. Because of the Cold War, a sense of conformity descended over society, from the architecture of the new suburban housing developments to the conservative clothing styles of the day. The

COMPARE
&
CONTRAST

- **1930s:** After a decade of economic growth, much of it based on rising debt and unregulated speculation, the stock market crashes and the Great Depression begins. Unemployment in the early 1930s is between 25 and 33 percent, and American industry is operating at a fraction of capacity.

  1950s: Because the United States is the only superpower left undamaged by World War II, the U.S. economy grows swiftly in the early 1950s. Unemployment is low and per capita income increases rapidly for all sectors of the population.

  Today: The economy of the United States is weakened by a stock market that has fallen due to unscrupulous lending practices and unregulated markets in complex commodities such as derivatives. Unemployment is as high as it has been any time in the past generation, but still less than half of what it was at the beginning of the Great Depression.

- **1930s:** Anti-Semitism is widespread in America. Many country clubs and universities are restricted to non-Jews. Popular media figures, such as radio commentator Father Edward Coughlin, are openly hostile to Jewish people and Judaism.

  1950s: The attempted extermination of the European Jews by the Nazis during World War II makes anti-Semitism unacceptable in much of America.

  Today: Anti-Semitism is no longer publicly accepted in mainstream American society.

  Jewish Americans serve in every position in private and public society. In 2000, Joseph Lieberman became the first Jewish American to be the candidate for vice president of a major political party.

- **1930s:** After the crash of the stock market, Republican president Herbert Hoover—the third consecutive Republican president in the 1920s—becomes increasingly identified by most Americans as having done little or nothing to alleviate their suffering. In 1932, Americans elect Franklin Delano Roosevelt of New York, beginning a twenty-year period of liberal, Democratic rule in Washington. Roosevelt will be reelected three times.

  1950s: Dwight D. Eisenhower assumes the presidency, the first Republican to do so since 1933. Cold War tensions run high in the United States and anti-Communist sentiment runs strong in all three branches of the federal government as well as with the people themselves. Many Americans who expressed radical ideas in the 1930s are fired from government jobs or blacklisted from working in the media or entertainment industries.

  Today: Because of the breakup of the Soviet Union in the 1990s and the opening of China to foreign investment more recently, few Americans see communism as a threat to their way of life. After an era of retreat from liberal government in the 1980s and 1990s, more Americans support liberal, Democratic policies.

Cold War does not really play any role in the action of the novel; the scenes that take place after World War II are primarily in Europe, and Augie is not concerned about either communism or fervent anti-communism. However, the book is full of radical characters, from Frazer to Leon Trotsky.

CRITICAL OVERVIEW

Most contemporary reviewers found *The Adventures of Augie March* refreshing and inspiring. It was seemingly a complete departure from Bellow's first two novels, astonishing in its scope and energy, and wholly new in voice and language. In

Depression-era Chicago

his 1953 review, "Adventure in America" for *Partisan Review*, Delmore Schwartz called *The Adventures of Augie March* "a new kind of book," because Bellow had transcended "the blindness of affirmation and the poverty of rejection," in his take on America. Instead, he had risen to see America as a place where "anything might happen, wonderful or awful, but a guy has a fighting chance to be himself, find out things for himself, and find out what's what." Other critics were not so upbeat as Schwartz about the long section in which Augie and Thea become eagle trainers in Mexico, but all the early reviews echo Schwartz's excitement about the energy of Augie's American language and Bellow's mature but optimistic take on life in America.

As Bellow's career lengthened, critics began identifying clearer connections between *The Adventures of Augie March* and his other, more subdued novels. In her study, *Saul Bellow's Enigmatic Laughter*, for example, Sarah Blacher Cohen notes that like the protagonists of *Dangling Man* and *The Victim*, Augie "yearns to discover his purpose" while being "wary that his contribution to others might involve too

great a sacrifice to himself." Other critics argue about whether the novel represented an example of picaresque literature, a style in which a rascal of the lower classes makes his way in the world by using his wits. As Bellow's career as a writer came to a close after the publication of *Ravelstein* in 2000, numerous writers hailed *Augie March* as one of his key achievements in a lifetime of important work. Writing in *The New Yorker*, Joan Acocella notes that although Augie was truly a creation of the 1950s, "one must love the book on artistic grounds," though what really lasts is Bellow's "hopefulness" about the promise of America. Novelist Martin Amis suggests that it could be "the Great American Novel."

CRITICISM

Patrick J. Walsh

Walsh is a former Fulbright Lecturer at the University of Passau in Germany and is currently a teacher of history at the Catlin Gabel School in Portland, Oregon. In this essay, he searches for

WHAT DO I READ NEXT?

- Mark Twain's 1884 novel, *Adventures of Huckleberry Finn*, is a great American novel of adventure and freedom. Twain uses the picaresque style to attack racism and celebrate the American desire for liberty and equality.

- Theodore Dreiser's 1900 novel, *Sister Carrie*, is a classic of American naturalistic literature, portraying Chicago as a swiftly growing metropolis where people are subject to social and environmental forces beyond their control.

- F. Scott Fitzgerald's 1925 novel, *The Great Gatsby*, considers the meaning, and cost, of success in America, through the eyes of a young man and his interactions with the newly wealthy.

- *Bread Givers: A Novel*, by Anzia Yezierska, dramatizes the life of a young Jewish immigrant, the daughter of a rabbi, in 1920s New York. The protagonist, who is torn between family duty and independence, runs away to become a teacher. It was published in 1925.

- Richard Wright's 1940 novel, *Native Son*, tells the story of an African American boy coming of age in Chicago in the 1930s. Thus, Wright offers a story set in the same time and place, but with an outlook colored by the experience of being black in 1930s America.

- J. D. Salinger's classic novel of disgruntled youth, *Catcher in the Rye*, appeared in 1951, just two years before *Augie March*. Holden Caulfield, the cynical teenage narrator, became an unlikely hero to generations of young Americans.

- Chaim Potok's classic coming-of-age novel, *The Chosen* (1967), tells the story of two Jewish boys in New York. It powerfully shows the complexities within Jewish society and the difficulties of religious immigrants in coming to terms with life in America.

- *Making of the New Deal: Industrial Workers in Chicago, 1919–1939* (1990), by Lizbeth Cohen, is an important work of social history. It recounts the history of ethnic workers in Chicago in the 1920s and 1930s, including the rise of labor unions.

- *Ravelstein*, published in 2000, is Bellow's final novel and covers similar themes to *Augie March*, although at a completely different historical moment. Abe Ravelstein, a professor of philosophy at the University of Chicago, is dying of AIDS and asks a friend and fellow professor to write a memoir about him.

- *The American Dream: A Short History of an Idea That Shaped a Nation*, by Jim Cullen (2004), looks at the particularly American ideas of success from a historical standpoint, from the Puritans to the dream of suburban home ownership centuries later.

---

the philosophical messages implicit in *Augie March's* many adventures as well as Saul Bellow's goals in offering such a complex and, at times, rambling novel.

Why do so many literary critics prize *The Adventures of Augie March* so highly? It is a novel in which a young man comes of age in Chicago yet cannot settle down to one career or commit to one relationship. It is a novel in which, after several hundred pages, the hero, Augie March, suddenly goes to Mexico to train an eagle to hunt lizards. Eagles in Mexico? Such a plot twist is a rather odd way to show that Augie is susceptible to the desires of others, and perhaps Saul Bellow could have made his point without such an abrupt change of setting and action. Yet perhaps a story that at its heart is a celebration of the energy and diversity of America should be a little wild itself. It is not a perfect novel: it rambles and at times bogs down in philosophical dialogue; most of the female characters are not fully realized. And then there is that trip to Mexico. Yet Augie, the

"
HIS LIFE TOUCHES SO MANY OTHER WORLDS,
BUT HE DOES NOT TRULY BECOME A PART OF ANY
OF THEM."

"man of no commitments," as Robert Penn Warren calls him, still speaks to us. He is unmistakably American in his ambition, individualism, and self-interest. His restlessness is the restlessness of Americans throughout their history. Bellow clearly thought deeply about the United States as a land of immigrants and radicals, of innovators and hobos, and into Augie he poured all these types and produced an epic novel of America between the world wars.

Augie's simultaneous claim of American identity and his clear Jewishness was startling to many readers when the novel appeared in 1953. Bellow's goal was to write both a novel of immigrants as well as the "Great American Novel," a bold act for a young writer's third book. So he has Augie proclaim at the story's opening: "I am an American, Chicago born... and go at things as I have taught myself." This reads almost like a claim by the poet Walt Whitman. But in the following paragraphs we learn that hearing Yiddish in Augie's house is common while he finds his brother's "English schoolboy notions of honor" foreign and strange. Augie's Chicago is a city of immigrants, of Jews, of gangsters and schemers. "The fact that its citizens... express themselves in four or five different languages," writes Joan Acocella in *The New Yorker*, "does not mean that they are marginal. It means that they are central—the inheritors." Bellow's novel is unapologetically cosmopolitan, seemingly casual about the diversity of its cast. And the fact that Jews in the novel run the entire range of human qualities, whatever Bellow's intentions, is his way of laying claim to American citizenship for all immigrants and native-born Americans willing to take part. As Bellow's biographer, James Atlas, notes, Bellow insisted that his book was "a novel by an American writer who happened to be a Jew. To claim otherwise would have diminished its universality." In this way, *The Adventures of Augie March* is a work of national pride, showing off the diversity, warts and all, of

the new world power coming into its own after World War II and the Holocaust.

If Augie and his author were assimilating into a larger, expansive Americanness, what was it they were conforming to? Throughout the novel, numerous characters attempt to influence Augie's development and purpose. He clearly recognizes this himself: "All the influences were lined up waiting for me. I was born, and there they were to form me," the Machiavellian characters hoping to free Augie from whatever trap they feel life has set for him. Grandma Lausch, the March's domineering boarder, wants to teach the ten-year-old Augie to work the social welfare system, but also to stay away from a life of petty crime. "I'm trying to make something of you," she tells him. "I want you to be a *mensch*." Einhorn tries to shepherd Augie into manhood, suggesting a life of the mind even if he seems helpless before his physical handicaps and the destruction of the Great Depression. Mrs. Renling promises to make Augie "perfect" by stripping him of his ethnic and religious markers and thrusting him into a world of manners and surfaces. Next, Simon recruits Augie to follow him into the wealth and power of the Magnus family even as Augie is drawn into the labor movement. It is no surprise, then, that when Thea lovingly beckons him south into an unknown world, he is ready to follow. Thea is on a quest for power, however, over Augie and life itself, demanding he accompany her on a dangerous and truly ludicrous journey.

Augie's "opposition," a characteristic pointed out by Einhorn and accepted by Augie at face value, is his way of resisting the influence of those who wish to mentor or control him. His life touches so many other worlds, but he does not truly become a part of any of them. In this sense, he is, at least at first, a rather empty character, always running away from any kind of commitment, until he falls in love with Thea. Critic Keith Michael Opdahl argues that Augie's failure with Thea causes him to see the hollowness in his search for adventure: "This insight and struggle give Augie an inner life and a substantial identity." It is after he betrays her with Stella and is left to find his way home from Mexico that Augie becomes more than a happy-go-lucky adolescent. He is wounded and confused. Yet he is not alienated or enfeebled because of his belief in a transcendent level of truth. He tells Clem Tambow of how, ever since childhood, he has been aware of "axial lines of life," supporting external existence with their unalterable truth. They are,

Augie claims, what has made him turn away from all his potential teachers. They call him away from the bewildering specialization the modern world demands, and to which Clem calls him. Instead, in his vision, in his own scheme, Augie wants to create a school in the country for children like himself, a place where he might teach languages or learn to fix his car. In short, he has a pastoral vision of family and simplicity, one which he believes will take him ever closer to the transcendental experience he now seeks.

At the climax of the novel, then, Bellow appears to suggest that Augie's appropriate response to his many mentors (and there will be more before the novel draws to a close) is to turn to the simple, interior life. This solution is emotionally appealing and would have an American pedigree—Emerson and Thoreau come quickly to mind. But what would a retreat to the country do to Bellow's portrait of a nation of schemers and doers? He can't really have both idylls. So Bellow begins World War II immediately after Augie's "axial lines" speech, and the introspection and philosophizing give way to action once again. Augie volunteers, undergoes an operation to meet the physical requirements of the military, and prepares to ship out. While doing so he meets Stella again, and falls for her without really bothering to know who she is or what has happened to her. Despite warning signs, Augie rushes into marriage and casts away his dream, despite having told Clem that "I'd never loan myself again to any other guy's scheme." The novel concludes with Augie in Paris, living in Europe to support Stella's desire to be an actress, and working in the black market. Augie doesn't want to be in Europe and finds communicating with Stella about anything important extremely difficult. He tells himself he is doing it for love. "I am a person of hope," he tells himself, and he continues to long for children of his own and a simpler life.

The final vignette of the novel leaves the reader with a laughing Augie, thinking about all his travels and having a truly hopeful vision of his life. He declares that "I am a sort of Columbus of those near-at-hand and believe you can come to them in this immediate terra incognita that spreads out in every gaze." Augie still believes he can escape the interior world and find communion with people around him, though he admits, "I may well be a flop at this line of endeavor." On a broader level, *The Adventures*

of Augie March uses Bellow's beloved American spirit to say something about human happiness. If the unresolved ending seems unsatisfying, any other option would undo the main arguments of the novel. The reader is invited to watch Augie find his way in the world, not to come to a tidy conclusion to his adventures. If in the final chapter Augie was to be found in the classroom of his school, doling out wisdom to his foster children, then the pleasure a reader takes in the grit of Chicago life would have to be sacrificed. His victory over his wanderings would be a repudiation of them. As it is, Augie is fine. Because a "man's character is his fate," as he proclaims in the first paragraph, Augie's character requires he continue searching the "terra incognita" around him, even if it is the hidden spaces between him and his wife.

So what is Bellow trying to tell us about America by leaving Augie singing Mexican songs with a French maid? Clearly, both Augie and his creator unambiguously love America in all its earthy promise. Augie is happy to be the Renlings's "house slave" if it means he out-earns his brother. He will sell his junker of a car to a sucker, though he may feel regret later. And he will be a smuggler if the price is right. His energy and "opposition" make him an innovator of his own being. He is constantly experimenting, constantly reinventing himself yet always with an eye on his axial lines. Thus, he is of the world if not part of it. Augie puts his shoulder to the wheel when it suits him, but when he senses a "better fate" over the horizon, he strikes out like a Huckleberry Finn of Chicago. As Robert R. Dutton has noted, "In this role as wanderer, Augie is intended by Bellow to be what we may call the backbone of American literature, or, as . . . the spirit of that literature." His Americanness is his restless need for liberty and experience. He is not alienated. He reminds Americans that "one is only ostensibly born to remain in specified limits. That's what you'll be told in the ranks." But for those like Augie, "nothing that others did [was] so inconceivable for me." He believes he can do whatever moves him. In this sense, Augie is a precursor to the dreamers of the following decade, the 1960s, who follow the beat of their own drummers in search of a meaningful life. Bellow himself would turn against what he saw to be the hedonistic excesses of the counterculture, but in the conformist atmosphere of the early 1950s, his message was one of personal liberation, even if that liberation never came.

BUT BELLOW'S BOOK WOULD GIVE A PARTICULAR NUDGE TO JEWISH-AMERICAN WRITERS, MAKE THEM VISIBLE FOR THE FIRST TIME, NOT AS VENTRILOQUISTS, BUT AS HUMAN BEINGS WITH A SINGULAR VISION AND VOICE THAT COULD REACH ACROSS AMERICA."

Source: Patrick J. Walsh, Critical Essay on *The Adventures of Augie March* in *Novels for Students*, Gale, Cengage Learning, 2010.

Jerome Charyn

In the following essay, Charyn states that the lasting legacy of The Adventures of Augie March *is the novel's profound influence on generations of Jewish American writers and readers.*

I did not stumble upon [The Adventures of Augie March] lightly. I gave it as a gift to the most beautiful girl in my high school class, Valerie K. Hadn't it won awards? And wasn't it about a Jewish bumpkin like myself? (So I'd heard secondhand.) I meant the book to bring me closer to Valerie, but it never did. And then, a year or two later, I actually read it and was overwhelmed by its bounty. It was a book that never stopped to breathe, and I was breathless in its wake. Leslie Fiedler calls it "unlike anything else in English except *Moby Dick*." It had the same largeness of imagination . . . and a wondrous eagle called Caligula instead of a white whale.

But it was much more than that. It was a model and a manifest for a boy from the Bronx, a kind of open-sesame into the art of writing. I'd been nowhere, had seen nothing outside my own little ghetto: all I had was a crazy babble of tongues, an exalted gangster talk, a mingling of Yiddish, Russian, and all the books I'd ever read—whole scenes ripped from *Anna Karenina,* whose heroine would have been much better served in the Bronx, where we loved tall, aristocratic women with husbands that were beneath their dignity—all the dialogue from every film I'd ever seen, which included the entire repertoire of MGM and the other majors, and the rough but chivalrous language of the street,

where we were all knights in pegged pants. And when Augie says that "we are meant to be carried away by the complex and hear the simple like the far horn of Roland when he and Oliver are being wiped out by the Saracens," I knew what the hell he was talking about.

Augie's adventures have little to do with the magical places he visits—the mountains of Mexico or the plains of Paris. They are only desiderata, icons, throwaways, bits and pieces of decér in a landscape that shifts right under our feet and sends us scrambling onto the next page and the next. Augie, says Leslie Fiedler, is "a footloose Jewish boy [who] becomes Huck Finn," with his own Mississippi—a river of words. If the Mississippi gives Huck a godlike strength, nurtures him, soothes him, allows him to shove beyond the perimeter of his own lies, then it is language that soothes Saul Bellow and carries Augie March from adventure to adventure, so that he is never used up, no matter how much narrative is crammed into a single sentence. The book is a constant rush of dialogue and detail, of shenanigans and magic tricks, or as Bellow himself writes in "Where Do We Go from Here: The Future of Fiction," the modern hero is "an oddly dispersed, ragged, mingled, broken, amorphous creature whose outlines are everywhere, whose being is bathed in mind as the tissues are bathed in blood, and who is impossible to circumscribe in any scheme of time." He's a "cubistic" character, an "uncertain, eternal, mortal, someone who shuts and opens like a concertina and makes a strange music."

To read The Adventures of Augie March is to live inside a hornet's head—to hear and feel an endless clatter . . . whose sting is a source of terror and delight. We cannot recover from Augie March. Its sting remains with us for life. And we have to ask why. Part of the answer is in Bellow's bona fides. Born in Quebec in 1915, he grew up in Chicago's South Side ghetto during the reign of America's most notorious beer baron, Al Capone—and almost all of Bellow's male characters in Augie March have some kind of gangster mentality. They strut, they wear swell clothes, and they bully us with their words, which Fiedler reminds us, land "like kisses or blows." And they capture the *tumult* of the city. Like George Gershwin, who had his share of little wars on Manhattan's Lower East Side, another cradle of gangsters [and Capone's original turf], he was raised "in the heart of noise." As one of Gershwin's own colleagues said: "He hears the noise and finds music in it." And Augie March might be considered Bellow's own "Rhapsody in Blue," but with a much more hysterical and alarming beat.

"I am American, Chicago born," Bellow insists at the very beginning of the novel, "and go at things as I have taught myself, free–style and will make the record in my own way." We're not caught within some ghetto tale, a lightning rise from rags to riches, a celebration of America's ability to spit out righteous little citizens— noble, healthy, and clean. Augie is a monster of the New World, more American than America itself. And we have to examine this within the context of the Jewish-American writer. It's not the success of Augie March that's startling—a Book of the Month selection and winner of the National Book Award for fiction [it was published in 1953]. But suddenly, with one blow, like a fist coming out of nowhere, Saul Bellow made "[h]is appearance as the first Jewish-American novelist to stand at the center of American literature," as Fiedler says. It's hard to grasp this fifty years after the fact. But Jewish-American writers had always lived in a terrible kind of ghetto, as if they were quaint little children, talented ventriloquists who were miming the American idiom for their Yankee readers, and if they were good, they might be rewarded with a few leftovers and shown off as the most current Jewish clown . . . until another clown was discovered and took this clown's place. They were entertainers, dimwits, who couldn't really enter the canon of American literature, like Hemingway, Faulkner, Fitzgerald, or Edith Wharton and Eudora Welty, when women began to be noticed as writers, rather than quaint knitters of patch-quilt prose. Henry James, America's first "experimental" writer, who understood the music and the hieroglyphics of modern fiction, couldn't even fathom the idea of a Jewish-American writer. When he visited the Lower East Side in 1907, he was repelled by what he saw and heard in "the flaring streets . . . There is no swarming like that of Israel when once Israel has got its start," he writes in *The American Scene*. He discovered "a Jewry that had burst all bounds." He worried over "the Hebrew conquest of New York." And East Side cafés were nothing but "torture-rooms of the living idiom."

James's words were echoed in every English Department of every prominent university in the United States, where Jews couldn't possibly teach English literature, because they couldn't enter into the spirit of Milton, or Chaucer, or Shakespeare, no matter how hard they mimed. Lionel Trilling, the son of a Bronx tailor, and America's most eloquent literary critic, was the first American Jew to receive tenure in the English Department of an Ivy League school [Columbia], and it didn't happen until 1945! The tailor's boy had already published books on Matthew Arnold and E. M. Forster, essays on Sherwood Anderson, Kipling, and F. Scott Fitzgerald, and would soon publish essays on Henry James and *Huckleberry Finn*. And he might never have taught at Columbia if he hadn't had such a melodious name—Lionel Trilling. Also, by 1945, America—and much of the world—had begun to change. The first images of GIs liberating the ghostly remains of Hitler's concentration camps had brought attention to the Jews, and a kind of niggling sympathy that *almost* humanized them. It was the Jewish freedom fighters and terrorists of the Haganah and the Irgun that finally altered the psychological and symbolic landscape, as Jews were seen as warriors rather than victims, and as "winners" once the State of Israel was voted into existence in 1948. America was now ready for Bellow's "atomic bomb." The country seemed to need an urban myth, as "relentless urbanization [had made] rural myths and images no longer central to our experience," according to Fiedler.

Bellow had literally concocted a new America in Augie March, with language as American as the Mississippi, and with rhythms that seemed to incorporate Faulkner, Dreiser, and Sherwood Anderson, as if Bellow were a country boy and a city boy at the same time, rural *and* urban, and as if his concertina could include every strand of music out of America's past . . . except for one, that of Ernest Hemingway. In his best stories, Hemingway was a minimalist who believed, with Flaubert, that each particular sentence was an island unto itself, that the white space between sentences could contain an entire planet, and that the real thunder of a text derived from the reader's own imagination. The reader connected these islands inside his head. He (or she) was as much the creator as "Hem." But Bellow's own daring was to narrow that space between sentences, almost eliminate it, as if he returned to the picaresque of Fielding and Cervantes, but with a modern twist—the hero is as schizoid and haunted as the 20th century. And Augie is always around, exhausting the reader with his parodies and puns, his constant riffs, thrusting the reader right inside the hornet's head, where he experienced Augie March like an abundance of battlefields ...

And so America had a king, at least that part of America that could read a book. Just as Dostoevsky had said that all Russian writers of fiction had come out from under Gogol's overcoat (Gogol had written a bizarre, surreal story about a stolen overcoat that assumes a life of its own), so American writers at mid-century, Jews and gentiles, had come out from under the wings of Caligula, Bellow's eagle who "crackled his feathers or hissed as if snow was sliding." Suddenly the novel had burst out of its narrative skin and had become an assault on language itself, a great whooping war cry. And other warriors and adventurers, demonic jokesters, including Nabokov, Pynchon, John Hawkes, and John Barth, would soon gain acceptance and recognition in good part because of Bellow. I doubt that Gunther Grass's *The Tin Drum* and Gabriel Garcia Marquez's *One Hundred Years of Solitude* would have found many followers in the U.S. if there had been no Augie March to initiate readers into the notion that a novel could be a jungle of words ... or a much wilder thing. Even Faulkner, the wildest of American novelists after Melville, was grounded in his imagined South, his "postage stamp" of Yoknapatawpha County, and Bellow was grounded in nothing at all. Like Caligula, his language could soar and then rocket down into some abyss. No one was safe, neither Augie March nor the reader.

But Bellow's book would give a particular nudge to Jewish-American writers, make them visible for the first time, not as ventriloquists, but as human beings with a singular vision and voice that could reach across America. Bellow himself would help Isaac Bashevis Singer (an immigrant who'd arrived in America as an adult and wrote exclusively in Yiddish) with a superb and stunning translation of "Gimpel the Fool." And the fire that Bellow breathed into the story, his own magical rhythm, came from Bellow's largeness of spirit, the almost Talmudic need of one master to recognize another. Singer's concerns are less elliptical than Bellow's, but in "Gimpel," at least, we can find a prototype of Augie March—the dreamer who weaves stories out of the air—yet Augie's world is comic, and Singer's comedy spills into nightmare.

Bellow would also solidify the reputation of a younger writer, Philip Roth, in *Commentary*, a magazine that was one of the first to value this new, farcical American voice that could often be so mocking of Jews themselves. In the late forties (*Commentary* was founded in 1945), the fifties and early sixties, the magazine didn't follow any pattern of "political correctness." Under Elliot Cohen, Theodore Solotaroff, and Norman Podhoretz (at first), the magazine seemed eager to experiment and to discover and sustain new writers. Singer, Roth, and Bernard Malamud were all published with a certain regularity and rhythm within its pages.

Malamud and Roth would both win the National Book Award in the 1950s, after Augie March, and with books of stories rather than novels, a difficult feat, since publishers *hated* books of stories—stories weren't supposed to sell. The three of them—Bellow, Malamud, and Roth— were soon called the Hart Schaffner & Marx of American fiction (Hart Schaffner & Marx being an upscale Jewish clothier that dressed successful Jewish gangsters, singers, actors—the whole hoi polloi). Bellow would remain the spiritual father of this little club, with Singer as a kind of kissing cousin from an older world.

But there were more immediate cousins, like Stanley Elkin, Herbert Gold, Grace Paley, Cynthia Ozick, Tillie Olsen, Leonard Michaels, and Leonard Cohen, who had the same sense of danger in their prose, a crazy concertina with its own variety of registers that could play on and on without the need to end. Elkin seems the closest to Bellow in his insistence upon the mingling of high and low styles, rhetoric and tough–guy talk, and his first novel, *Boswell* (1964), is like a mirror word of Augie March, homage in the form of parody. Elkin, Paley, Ozick, and Roth all have a particular thing in common with Bellow—the invention of an idiolect that has exploded traditional English, flooded it with rhythms that had never been there before, given it an elasticity and an electrical pull. It's hardly an accident. Elkin's language, like Bellow's, is a lethal weapon, a dive bomber readying to attack the American heartland, to take revenge on a white Protestant culture that had excluded all minorities for so long (not just Afro–Americans and Jews), but the attack is always masked; it comes with a kiss, with a jibe and a bit of buffoonery. One can find the same sabotage in the films of Woody Allen, like *Annie Hall* (1977), where Allen's alter ego, Albie Singer, attacks *all* of America outside of

New York City, and still managed to win an Academy Award as best picture of the year . . .

But Bellow's attack is buried in the nucleus of his book; Augie's an orphan of sorts who never knew his dad. It's as if that monster, Augie March, gave birth to himself. "Look at me, going everywhere! Why, I am a sort of Columbus of those near–at–hand . . . I may well be a flop at this line of endeavor. Columbus too thought he was a flop, probably, when they sent him back in chains. Which didn't prove there was no America."

And that's how the novel ends, with Augie the self-creator bumping along on his little life-boat of words.

Source: Jerome Charyn, "Inside the Hornet's Head," in *Midstream*, Vol. 49, No. 6, September–October 2003, pp. 17–22.

T. E. Cassidy

In the following review, Cassidy characterizes The Adventures of Augie March *as a series of narrative vignettes and contends that "there is no real power here and no tremendous insight that Bellow certainly was striving to achieve."*

Augie March lives quite a life [in *The Adventures of Augie March*]. Up from the depths of poverty to the heights of success, back down, back up, and all in most peculiar fashion. Jobs, journeys, jolts—and women, women, women. Crime and college, labor unions and athletic clubs, Chicago and Mexico, slums and society, thievery and high honor: these form the panorama for Augie. And that's the book. It's a chronicle of an age and a case history of assorted human beings, most of whom are engaged, in one way or another, in using their fellow–men and helping or hurting their families and friends. A good many of these people are psychopathic; at best they have interesting eccentricities, and at worst they are criminals. And they are colorful, sometimes, and boring at other times. Augie himself never quite arrives anywhere and unless he is tormenting himself, he never is quite happy.

Saul Bellow has some fine things in this book. The characterization is complete to the point of exhaustion. The dialogue, when it's on–the–spot exchange, is sharp. When his people wander and meander in the realm of philosophy, garden variety or formal, they are windy and repetitious, and sound like cheap imitations of Proustians. The liberal–radical overtones of some sections are overdone and do not ring with authenticity. For

Augie to break off his organizing activity for a quick but grand passion with one of the organizees, and then to flee to the arms of a wealthy nymphomaniac, is almost comic opera, twentieth century style.

But the best and the weirdest episode is the sojourn in Mexico with the latter lady. The two train an eagle to catch lizards, and the eagle is a flop. The society that surrounds them is full of nuts and cranks, and the eagle will catch anything and everything in the animal kingdom, except a mongoose. The Mexican stay is full of riot and rot, and at times is supremely funny.

The portraits of old families and their ties and splits are in great style. Indeed, several of them could be simply extracted and presented as very thorough national and racial profiles. These are the portraits that make the book, because as a novel there is no depth and no great theme. All the events are loosely tied, and people run in and out of the various stages of Augie's strange progress through life and the world. The one constant thread is the great but bumpy love between Augie and his money–worshipping brother, Simon. But there is no real power here and no tremendous insight that Bellow certainly was striving to achieve. I suppose the scene with Augie in a lifeboat with a maniac, off the Canary Islands, is as typical of the work as any. It's that kind of a book.

Source: T. E. Cassidy, "From Chicago," in *Commonweal*, Vol. 58, No. 26, October 2, 1953, p. 636.

Charles J. Rolo

In the following review, Rolo argues that The Adventures of Augie March *presents the "archetypal" story of "the American as a rolling stone" but notes that the novel's protagonist lacks emotional depth.*

Saul Bellow, who is now publishing his third novel, *The Adventures of Augie March*, has taken a fruitful hint from Cervantes's great parody of a classic Spanish type. His hero–narrator—in whom there is a "laughing creature" forever rising up—unfolds to us a slightly kidding but essentially serious version of an archetypal American saga: the saga of the American as a rolling stone, an irrepressible explorer who doesn't quite know who he is and is always trying "to become what I am"; who keeps seeking the fullest experience of life. The self-educated Augie tells his story in a freshly personal style which intermixes slang and literary English, and which has a quality rare in contemporary American fiction—a great variety of tone: grimness and exuberance, touches of clowning and touches of the fantastic; a current of comedy and intimations of the tragic.

Augie March comes of a poor Jewish family in Chicago. His father has vanished, and the ruling influence of his childhood is Grandma Lausch, who has known plushier days in Odessa. This picturesque old matriarch is one of a dozen or more sharply individual characterizations in Mr. Bellow's spacious novel, whose settings range from the slums to the abodes and playgrounds of the rich.

By the time he is a high–school junior and the Depression has set in, Augie has sampled half a dozen jobs; has once been fired for stealing; and has dabbled in more serious crime. A lucky break turns him into a salesman of expensive sporting goods on the millionaire circuit in Evanston. His wealthy employers take him into their home; polish him up generally; and acquaint him with the life of luxury. But when they want to adopt him and arrange his future, Augie moves on. And when his hardheaded, successful brother has found a rich wife for him and staked him to a job, Augie moves on again.

He moves from job to job, from girl to girl. He has a consuming and bizarre love affair with a glamorous millionairess who takes him to Mexico to help her train eagles, and who eventually leaves him down and out. When we see the last of him— though he is now married to a lovely and erratic siren—he is still the adventurer, chasing after big deals in Europe on behalf of an Armenian tycoon.

With its variousness, its vitality, its strong sense that life is worth living, Mr. Bellow's novel is a notable achievement, and it should be one of the year's outstanding successes. I cannot suppress a slight regret that a novelist with as large a talent as Mr. Bellow's has not tried to take us more deeply inside his hero. His story, at times, comes perilously close to being a catalogue of actions. It certainly tells us all *about* Augie March; but I do not even begin to know and understand him in the way the reader knows and understands, say, Stendhal's Julien Sorel.

Source: Charles J. Rolo, "A Rolling Stone," in *Atlantic Monthy*, Vol. 192, No. 4, October 1953, pp. 86–87.

SOURCES

Acocella, Joan, "Finding Augie March: Saul Bellow's First Novels," in *New Yorker*, October 6, 2003, pp. 112–117.

Amis, Martin, "A Chicago of a Novel," in *Atlantic Monthly*, October 1995, pp. 114–127.

Atlas, James, *Bellow: A Biography*, Random House, 2000, pp. 185–196.

Bellow, Saul, *The Adventures of Augie March*, Viking, 2003, 1953.

Cohen, Sarah Blacher, "The Animal Ridens," in *Saul Bellow's Enigmatic Laughter*, University of Chicago Press, 1974, pp. 64–89.

Doidge, Norman, "Bellow, Restive Soul," in *Maclean's*, Vol. 118, No. 16, 18 April 2005, p. 52.

Dutton, Robert R., "The Adventures of Augie March," in *Saul Bellow*, rev. ed., Twayne Publishers, 1982, pp. 42–74.

Opdahl, Keith Michael, "Life Among the Machiavellians," in *The Novels of Saul Bellow: An Introduction*, Pennsylvania State University Press, 1967, pp. 70–95.

Schwartz, Delmore, "Adventure in America," in *Critical Essays on Saul Bellow*, edited by Stanley Trachtenberg, G.K. Hall & Co., 1979, pp. 8–10; originally published in *Partisan Review*, Vol. 21, No. 1, 1954, pp. 112–115.

Warren, Robert Penn, "The Man of No Commitments," in *New Republic*, Vol. 129, No. 14, 2 November 1953, pp. 22–23.

FURTHER READING

Cronin, Gloria L., *A Room of His Own: In Search of the Feminine in the Novels of Saul Bellow*, Syracuse University Press, 2000.

> Bellow is often criticized for looking at the world only through male eyes and not developing his female characters. In this recent study, Cronin employs a French feminist reading of Bellow's novels.

Cronin, William, *Nature's Metropolis*, Norton, 1992.

> This epic work of history tells the story of Chicago from an environmental point of view.

Lambert, Josh, *American Jewish Fiction*, Jewish Publication Society of America, 2009.

> A guide to over 100 works by American Jewish authors, including Philip Roth and Norman Mailer. The guide offers author biographies and historical context to each work.

Miller, Ruth, *Saul Bellow: A Biography of the Imagination*, St. Martins, 1991.

> This biography of Bellow is unique because it draws on the biographer's own correspondence and friendship with Bellow.

Beauty: A Retelling of the Story of Beauty and the Beast

ROBIN MCKINLEY

1978

Robin McKinley's *Beauty: A Retelling of the Story of Beauty and the Beast* (1978) is a novel-length expansion of the classic fairy tale that was first written in France in the eighteenth century. The story concerns Beauty, a young woman who must go to live with a monstrous creature in his castle to keep the creature from killing her father. As Beauty spends time with the Beast, she realizes that he is not as monstrous as she first believed, and begins to develop feelings for him.

Beauty was McKinley's first novel, though it contains certain characteristics that are trademarks of much of her later work. First, it is a retelling of a classic fairy tale; McKinley has returned to fairy tales several times over the years, creating new visions of familiar stories such as Robin Hood and Sleeping Beauty. Second, the novel contains a heroine who is smart, honorable, and takes charge of her own fate—something seldom seen in the traditional tales or in other retellings, but common in nearly every McKinley story since.

AUTHOR BIOGRAPHY

McKinley was born Jennifer Carolyn Robin Turrell McKinley on November 16, 1952, in Warren, Ohio. An only child with a father in the navy and a mother who was a teacher, McKinley moved often while young, but showed a tremendous interest in books. Eventually McKinley attended preparatory school and college in Maine, and

graduated summa cum laude in 1975. Following her college years, McKinley began working on a story set in a world called Damar. However, the world continued to expand in her imagination until she realized it could only resolve itself in more than one tale. At around the same time, McKinley watched a made-for-television adaptation of the tale of Beauty and the Beast starring George C. Scott. She was so displeased with the version that she set about writing her own novel-length retelling of the tale. *Beauty* became McKinley's first published novel in 1978, when the author was twenty-six years old.

After her success with *Beauty* and a collection of additional retold fairy tales titled *The Door in the Hedge* (1981), McKinley returned to the world of Damar and produced her second novel, *The Blue Sword* (1982), which was selected as a Newbery Honor book. *The Hero and the Crown* (1985), another Damar novel and the prequel to *The Blue Sword*, won the Newbery Medal. She has also written several short stories set in the world of Damar, some of which were collected in *A Knot in the Grain and Other Stories* (1996).

McKinley has also returned to the world of fairy tales, with novel-length retellings of several popular tales and legends. *The Outlaws of Sherwood* (1988) offers a different view of Robin Hood and his band of merry men and women. *Deerskin* (1993) is a dark fantasy aimed at adults, based on a tale written by Charles Perrault at the end of the seventeenth century. *Spindle's End* (2000) is an adaptation of the tale of Sleeping Beauty. McKinley even wrote another retelling of Beauty and the Beast, *Rose Daughter*, in 1997.

In recent years, McKinley has concentrated on writing fantasy novels not involving fairy tales or Damar, such as *Dragonhaven* (2007) and *Chalice* (2008). In 2003, she wrote a novel dealing with vampires, werewolves, demons, and other creatures of legend titled *Sunshine*. The book received the Mythopoeic Fantasy Award for Adult Literature the following year.

As of 2009, McKinley was living and working in Hampshire, England, with her husband, author Peter Dickinson, whom she married in 1992.

PLOT SUMMARY

Part One

Beauty tells the story of a young girl whose given name is Honour, the youngest daughter of a wealthy shipping merchant named Roderick Huston, who lives in a large city by the sea. Her sisters are named Grace and Hope. Honour, upon hearing her father explain the meaning of her name at five years of age, decides that she would rather be called "Beauty." The nickname sticks, though Beauty describes herself as uglier and more awkward-looking than her stunning—though totally different—sisters.

Beauty was only two when her mother died during the birth of a fourth daughter, Mercy, who also died shortly after. As Beauty grows up, she becomes attracted to books and intellectual pursuits, and her father's wealth allows her access to a huge library. She secretly dreams of attending a university when she gets older, though such a thing is unheard of for a woman.

When Beauty is twelve, her oldest sister Grace becomes engaged to one of their father's ship captains, Robert Tucker. After the engagement is set, Tucker departs on a sea voyage meant to last for three years, hoping that he will return wealthy and respectable before the marriage. Two years pass, and Beauty's other sister, Hope, confides that she has also fallen in love. The man she loves, however, is a lowly ironworker in their father's shipyard—not at all the kind of wealthy gentleman she would be expected to marry. On top of that, the man, named Gervain Woodhouse, wants to move back to his home region in the rural north and work as a blacksmith. This would require that Grace leave her family and live modestly, instead of living in a mansion with many servants. Beauty also cannot shake the idea that "the north was a land rather overpopulated by goblins and magicians, who went striding about the countryside muttering wild charms."

Before the girls can speak of Gervain to their father, however, the family receives news that destroys their fortunes. Roderick's entire fleet of four ships is reported to be missing or destroyed, with all cargo and many crew members lost; Tucker's boat, the *White Raven*, is one of the ships unaccounted for, though it is believed to have been lost during a storm. Roderick is financially devastated by the loss, and the family must sell all their possessions, including their estate, to cover the business debts. Gervain approaches Roderick and proposes that the family move with him to a small town up north, where he has secured a position as a blacksmith. They would share a modest house, and ultimately Gervain would like to take Hope's hand in marriage. Roderick agrees.

Before the family departs, a local horse trainer named Tom Black visits Beauty and gives her Greatheart, one of his largest and most prized stallions. Beauty had originally named the horse and did much of his training, but stopped visiting when the family fortunes took a bad turn. Beauty tries to refuse the gift, but Black claims that without Beauty around to care for him, the horse will not eat.

The family sets off on their journey north, and after two months of traveling they arrive in Blue Hill, where Gervain's aunt—Melinda Honeybourne—runs a tavern called the Red Griffin. She takes them to the blacksmith's house where they will live, just outside of town and on the border of a great, dark forest. Gervain makes every member of the family promise not to go into the forest unsupervised; he later reveals to Beauty that the forest is believed by locals to be cursed, and that a monster lives in a castle in the center of the woods.

The family adjusts to their new way of life, and even prospers. Gervain becomes a renowned blacksmith sought after by those in nearby towns, Beauty's father, Roderick, starts his own woodworking business, and Beauty trains Greatheart to pull heavy loads. A year after their arrival in Blue Hill, Gervain and Hope marry. On the wedding day, Gervain's occasional assistant in his forge, an awkward boy named Ferdy, kisses Beauty. She does not return his affection, and he later apologizes; Beauty accepts his apology, but avoids him thereafter. Hope gives birth to twins the following spring.

In September, Roderick receives a message from a friend in the city: one of his missing ships has returned to port. Grace holds out hope that the ship belongs to her long-missing fiancé, Robert Tucker. Roderick decides that he must make the two-month journey back to the city, where he can dispose of the boat and its cargo and possibly bring home some money for his family. Before leaving he asks his daughters if they would like any gifts from the city. Hope jokes about him bringing back fancy jewels for them to wear the next time they visit the king and queen, but Beauty simply asks for a few rose seeds to plant in the garden.

Roderick returns home in March, just after a terrible blizzard. He enters the house holding a rose, which he hands to Beauty. His saddlebags are full, but he appears distraught. Grace places the rose in a vase, and it later loses a petal; as the petal falls to the ground, it inexplicably turns to gold. Although Roderick reveals that the returned ship was not Robert Tucker's, he refuses to tell the rest of his story until the next day, after he has had a chance to rest.

Part Two

When Roderick finally wakes at around noon the next day, Beauty notices that he looks years younger than he had before he left on his trip. After supper, Roderick finally tells the family his strange story.

After arriving back in the city, Roderick sold the cargo from the returned ship and paid off the crew, leaving himself with a small profit. No longer wishing to continue his life as a merchant, he also sold the ship. Realizing that he no longer felt comfortable in the city, especially because he would have to rely on the hospitality of his friends, Roderick decided to return north before the end of winter—a risky proposition, though the winter had so far been mild. He bought a horse from Tom Black and headed home. When he reached the town just south of Blue Hill, a blizzard struck and left him lost in the forest.

Eventually, he happened upon a trail in the forest and followed it. The trail led to a hedge fence and a gate, which opened at his touch. Roderick continued along the trail, and arrived at a great stone castle. As he approached the castle, the snow-covered ground gave way to green vegetation, and he found himself in a beautiful garden in full bloom despite the winter cold. Roderick entered the castle and found a sumptuous feast laid out as if someone were expecting him. However, he could find no one inhabiting the place. He indulged in the delicious meal, and then fell asleep on a couch prepared for him by unseen servants.

The next morning, he thanked his invisible hosts for their hospitality, left the castle, and began riding away through the garden. Upon seeing a bush of unusually beautiful roses in the garden, he remembered his promise to bring back rose seeds for Beauty; he had been unable to get them in the city. Roderick snapped off a single rose to bring back to his daughter, and was immediately confronted by a monstrous figure who accused him of stealing his most prized roses.

The Beast vowed to take Roderick's life for his thievery, but after hearing of Roderick's family, decided to spare the man on one condition: one of Roderick's daughters must come to live with him at his castle, and she must do it willingly. The monster swore that the daughter would not be harmed in any way. Roderick objected, but the Beast would not hear it. It gave Roderick one month to bring the daughter to his castle, or else it would come and find him. Roderick was then sent off, and arrived home still reeling from all that had happened, and still holding the stolen rose.

After hearing this story, Beauty insists on being the one who goes to live with the Beast. The entire family objects, but Beauty insists, and no one can come up with a better solution. When Roderick finally opens his saddlebags from his journey, he finds that the Beast has somehow filled them with money, fancy housewares, and exquisite jewelry for his daughters. For Beauty, there is a small wooden box containing rose seeds. Beauty finds humor in this, and wonders how bad the Beast can be. Also in the box Beauty finds a ring decorated like a griffin. She keeps the ring in her pocket with her wherever she goes.

Beauty plants the rose seeds along the side of the house and barn, even though the winter snow has not even melted. Just before the end of her final month of freedom, the enchanted roses sprout and bloom almost overnight. On her final morning with her family, Beauty gathers her few belongings, along with her horse Greatheart—whom everyone in the family insists she take with her—and sets off after an emotional farewell. Her father travels with her into the forest, and they soon reach the road that leads to the Beast's castle.

Part Three

CHAPTERS 1–2

Beauty and her father follow the road to the hedge surrounding the Beast's grounds. Beauty insists that her father return home, and rides through the gate alone. She passes through lush gardens—curiously devoid of living creatures—and finally reaches the enormous castle, which "rose up before us like sunrise, its towers and battlements reaching hundreds of feet into the sky." She approaches the stable, which automatically opens to welcome Greatheart. After stalling as long as possible, she enters the castle.

She feels herself guided through the halls by an invisible force like a breeze, which leads her to an enormous dining hall where a great feast awaits. She dines alone, and then begins a search of the castle, ready to confront her captor. She quickly

gets lost amid the maze of halls and rooms, none of which contain any mirrors. When she finally happens upon a door with a plaque that reads, "Beauty's Room," she enters to find a hot bath waiting for her. After her bath, she once again resumes her search for the Beast. She finally finds him in a dim study; he is seven feet tall and finely dressed, with a massive frame, fur-covered body, clawed paws, and unsettlingly human eyes set in the face of an animal.

The Beast confirms that he will not harm her, and her fear subsides. He tells her that he seeks companionship, and asks her if she will marry him. She answers no, and he bids her good night. Back in her room, she tries to sleep but finds herself restless. She decides to go visit Greatheart in his stable, but discovers that the door to her room is locked, and she cannot escape. She pounds until her hands are bloody, then falls asleep, exhausted.

The next morning, she finds her hands bandaged and breakfast prepared for her. The door to her room is no longer locked. She visits Greatheart, and later, after complaining about the lack of birds in the sky surrounding the castle and its lands, finds a box of bird seed provided by unseen servants. She spreads it across her windowsill, hoping to attract sparrows.

She goes for a long ride with Greatheart, and when she returns to the garden at sunset, finds the Beast there. The two walk together and have a pleasant conversation; the Beast tells her that she was locked in her room the previous night so that she might not witness his own beastly behavior, which happens after dark. The two then retire to the dining hall for dinner. Although the Beast cannot eat with utensils, he sits and watches as Beauty dines, savoring the companionship. The Beast reveals to Beauty that the invisible forces she feels around her are two invisible handmaids he has assigned to care for her. Other invisible servants light the halls as she passes, serve food and drink at her command, and perform any other task she needs. The Beast also tells Beauty that he is around two hundred years old, though he does not know for certain. After dinner, he once again asks Beauty if she will marry him, and she again refuses.

After several weeks, Beauty falls into a comfortable pattern in her new life at the castle: a morning walk in the garden with Greatheart, followed by reading and studying some of the books from the small library in her room; lunch, followed by additional studies; a late afternoon ride across the Beast's immense grounds; and finally, a sunset walk through the garden with the Beast, followed by dinner. Every night, after dinner and before Beauty retires to her room, the Beast asks her if she will marry him. Every night, Beauty refuses. Beauty's attempt to draw birds to her windowsill proves successful, and it brings not only sparrows but also several other small birds.

One rainy morning, the Beast offers to give Beauty a tour of the castle, and she accepts. One of the most memorable rooms is the portrait gallery, which contains a series of paintings of what appear to be family members. The most recent one, still evidently quite old, depicts a handsome, intense young man standing beside a horse. The most impressive room, however, is the massive library. In it, Beauty has access not only to every book ever written, but every book yet to be written. The Beast recommends a poetry collection by Robert Browning.

After the rain stops, Beauty strikes upon the idea of introducing Greatheart to the Beast. The Beast had previously avoided the horse, knowing that animals react to him with terror. However, with Beauty's encouragement, Greatheart eventually approaches him, much to the Beast's surprise. That night, before going off to sleep, Beauty hears the voices of the invisible servants in her room, though the servants are unaware that she can hear. One of them sounds hopeful that Beauty will soon understand what she must do, though Beauty has no idea what this means.

CHAPTERS 3–5

By summer, Beauty begins to look forward to the time she spends each day in the company of the Beast. One night, she even feeds him some of her cake at dinner, since he cannot handle utensils himself. However, she still refuses his proposal each night when he asks her. She implores him to stop asking, but he insists that he cannot.

One day, Beauty tells the Beast that she misses her family dearly. He tells her that he is sorry, but he cannot let her go to see them. Upset, Beauty tries to flee, and as she pounds on the door, she faints. When she wakes, she finds herself in the Beast's arms; he had caught her as she fell, and carried her to a couch. She recoils and flees to her room.

Beauty begins to hear the invisible servants' voices more clearly, and even discovers that she can sense when the Beast is near. The Beast explains that she is growing accustomed to the enchantments of the castle. By autumn, Beauty begins having vivid dreams about her family— dreams that appear real, and in which her family talks about their own dreams, in which they seem to be able to see Beauty at the castle. She tells the Beast about this, and he acknowledges that he sends the dreams to her family to comfort them. He also reveals that he has a magical way of observing events from afar, which is how he watches over Beauty's family. She asks him to show her, and he agrees.

The Beast takes her to his study, where he has a table whose surface allows her to see and hear her sisters talking in their parlor. By listening to the conversation, Beauty discovers that Pat Lawrey, the clergyman from Hope and Gervain's wedding, would like to marry Grace. Even though he is a decent man, Grace refuses to entertain the notion because she holds out hope that her long-lost fiancé, Robert Tucker, might still return. However, Hope manages to convince Grace that marrying Lawrey is the best decision. After seeing this, Beauty wonders aloud about Robert Tucker's fate. The magic table suddenly shows Tucker stepping off a ship in the port from which her father once ran his fleet. Although he appears haggard, he is alive and once again home.

Beauty begs the Beast for a chance to go home and tell Grace of Tucker's return so that she will not marry Lawrey, whom she does not love. The Beast consents, and hands her a rose to keep with her. When one week has passed, Beauty must return, or she will find the Beast— like the rose—dying. Beauty assures him that she will return, and will never again ask to leave. She quickly departs, and finds herself back at her family's cottage by nightfall.

When Beauty is reunited with her family, she realizes that she has grown several inches during her time away, and is now the tallest of the three sisters. She tells her family about the enchanted castle and her life with the Beast, though they have a difficult time understanding her affection for the monstrous creature that terrorized Roderick and stole Beauty away from her home. As she sits with them, even though she enjoys being around her family once again, she realizes that she no longer feels as if she belongs there. Her home is now with the Beast, and the thought even occurs to her that she loves him.

A few days pass before Beauty tells Grace of Robert Tucker's return. Roderick and Grace both write letters to be delivered as soon as possible to

Tucker, asking him to join the family up north. With the exciting news about Tucker, the next few days pass quickly. On her last night, Beauty's family begs her to stay just one extra day. Not wanting to disappoint them, and feeling she will probably never be able to see them again, she agrees. However, she does not enjoy her extra day, and cannot help but feel that she should be back at the castle. Late that night, she dreams that the Beast is dead. When she wakes, she sees that the rose he gave her is dying. She immediately leaves the cottage while everyone else is still asleep and heads back through the forest toward the castle.

She spends the entire day trying to locate the path to the castle—which can only be found by getting lost in the forest—and manages to locate it just as the sun goes down. By the time she reaches the castle, it is late at night; the invisible servants who once tended to her every need appear to be gone. She searches all night long throughout the massive castle, trying to locate the Beast. Finally, she sees a faint light coming from a room. She finds the Beast in the same room she left him, sitting next to the magic table. He appears to be near death, but improves once he hears her voice. As the first light of dawn appears through the window, Beauty tells the Beast that she loves him, and that she will marry him.

Suddenly Beauty finds herself engulfed in light and noise, and when it stops, the Beast is gone. He has been replaced by a handsome man. She does not understand at first, so the man explains that he is indeed the Beast. Beauty then recognizes him as the handsome young man from the final family portrait. He explains that a local magician placed a curse on his family, and he—as the first family member to exhibit moral weakness—was the one who fell victim to the curse. He was transformed into a hideous beast, and would remain so until he could find someone to love him despite his appearance. As soon as Beauty agreed to marry him, the curse was lifted.

However, Beauty insists that she cannot marry him. He is, after all, noble and handsome, and she is not fit to be his wife. He walks her to a mirror so she can see herself, and she is stunned: not only is she taller than she thought, but her features have developed from awkwardness into true beauty. He asks her for the final time if she will marry him, and she agrees. The two look out upon the courtyard, and as if by magic, Beauty's

family arrives, Robert Tucker included, followed by a large crowd. The Beast suggests that the wedding will be a triple ceremony: Beauty and the Beast, Grace and Robert Tucker, and Roderick and Melinda Honeybourne, who have also fallen in love. Beauty mentions that she does not know the Beast's name; he admits that he has forgotten it after so many years, and gives her the task of coming up with a new one. Beauty then takes the Beast to meet her family as the celebration begins.

CHARACTERS

The Beast

The Beast is a cursed prince who lives in an enchanted castle in the middle of a forest near Blue Hill. His monstrous form is seven feet tall and fur-covered, with the teeth and paws of a beast yet the eyes of a human. Despite his beastly appearance, he dresses impeccably in velvet outfits with lace cuffs. Though he threatens to kill Roderick Huston after the man plucks a rose from his enchanted garden, the Beast later tells Beauty that he would never have hurt the man. His goal was simply to compel one of his daughters to live with him, so that she might fall in love with him and break the curse under which he lives. According to the Beast, a magician placed the curse on his family over two hundred years before; the Beast was the first member of the family to show moral weakness, and therefore succumb to the curse. It can only be broken when he finds a woman who truly loves him and agrees to marry him.

After Beauty agrees to marry him, the Beast is transformed back into a handsome prince, roughly forty years old in appearance (even though about two hundred years have passed since he was transformed). The Beast does not remember his human name, and after his transformation back to human form, he tells Beauty that she must choose a name for him.

Bessie

Bessie is one of the two invisible handmaids assigned to take care of Beauty while she is in the Beast's castle. Although she is not seen, Beauty is able to hear her conversations with Lydia, another handmaid. During these conversations, Bessie remains optimistic that Beauty will figure out what she must do to break the Beast's curse.

Tom Black

Tom Black is a stable owner in the city who breeds horses of both common stock and of the finest stock fit for royalty. One of these finely bred horses, Greatheart, becomes so attached to Beauty that when her family decides to leave the city, Tom Black gives Beauty the horse, claiming Greatheart will not eat if she does not spend time with him.

Tom Bradley

Tom Bradley is a man who escorts groups of travelers from the city to the rural lands of the north. He takes a liking to the Huston family during their journey to Blue Hill, taking care of their needs on the road and teaching them how to care for themselves.

Ferdy

Ferdy is a young man who helps Gervain with his blacksmith business from time to time, becomes friends with Beauty, and develops a crush on her. She describes him as "very tall and thin, with bony hands and a big nose and a wild thatch of red hair." At Hope's wedding, Ferdy kisses Beauty, but she does not reciprocate the sentiment. He later apologizes, though Beauty still no longer feels comfortable around him.

Frewen

Frewen is a wealthy merchant who lives in the city, and who remains a friend to Roderick Huston after the family leaves the city. It is Frewen who sends a letter to Roderick informing him that one of his missing ships has made it back to port, prompting Roderick to travel back to the city so that he can finalize his business affairs regarding the ship and its crew and cargo.

Greatheart

A massive, strong horse bred to carry royalty and knights, Greatheart is given to Beauty by stable owner Tom Black before they leave the city. He contends that Greatheart will not eat without Beauty present; indeed, Beauty helped raise and train Greatheart from a young age, and even gave him his name. When Beauty goes to live with the Beast in his castle, Greatheart accompanies her. Although the horse is at first terrified of the Beast, he learns to tolerate the monster's company for the sake of Beauty.

Melinda Honeybourne

Melinda Honeybourne is Gervain's aunt who lives in Blue Hill. It is Melinda who tells Gervain about the available blacksmith position there, which prompts him and the entire Huston family to move there. Melinda is a widow with six children who runs a tavern called the Red Griffin. As time passes and the Hustons settle into their new life, Beauty notices a connection between her father Roderick and Melinda. At the end of the story, it is suggested that Roderick and Melinda get married during the same ceremony as Beauty and the Beast.

Beauty Huston

Beauty is the youngest surviving daughter of merchant Roderick Huston, whose wealth has brought the family a large estate in the city with many servants. Beauty's given name is Honour; however, when she is five years old, she tells her father that she would rather be called Beauty, though she later regrets it. She does not consider herself beautiful at all, particularly compared to her older sisters. She describes herself as "thin, awkward and undersized, with big long-fingered hands and huge feet." She spends her time engaged in intellectual pursuits such as reading, or working with the horses in Tom Black's stable.

When her father plucks a rose from the Beast's garden and is told he must give up one of his daughters, Beauty volunteers immediately. She knows her father picked the flower for her, and also assumes that she will be missed the least of any family member. Her family, knowing her stubbornness, can do nothing but consent. As she grows to know the Beast, she also grows in physical beauty and in her own ability to recognize that beauty. When shown herself in a mirror near the end of the book, she at first does not believe that the reflection is accurate; soon, however, she is able to see that the mirror's image is true, and that her name fits.

Grace Huston

Grace is the oldest of Roderick Huston's three daughters. Beauty describes Grace as tall and slender, with wavy yellow hair, rosy skin, and blue eyes. At the age of nineteen, Grace becomes engaged to Robert Tucker, a captain for one of her father's merchant ships. When Tucker's ship disappears and is believed to be lost, Grace remains true to him, waiting six years for him to return. She is finally convinced by her sister Hope that she should marry the clergyman Pat

Lawrey, whom she does not love, and forget about Tucker. However, when Beauty visits her family, she tells Grace that Tucker is indeed alive. In the end, it is suggested that Grace and Tucker will marry in the same wedding ceremony as Beauty and the Beast.

Honour Huston
See Beauty Huston

Hope Huston

Hope is the middle sister in the Huston family. Hope is described by Beauty as having ivory skin, dark brown hair, and large green eyes, along with a slim build, small waist, and petite hands and feet. Hope falls in love with Gervain Woodhouse, an ironworker at her father's shipyard, even though she knows she is expected to marry a man from a prominent and wealthy family. Because Grace's fiancé is lost at sea, Hope becomes the first to marry, a year after the family moves to Blue Hill. Hope and Gervain have twin children soon after, a boy named Richard and a girl named Mercy. Hope is the one who convinces Grace that she should marry Pat Lawrey, since she believes—incorrectly—that Robert Tucker is long dead.

Roderick Huston

Roderick Huston is a wealthy merchant who owns a shipyard in the city. He has three daughters, Grace, Hope, and Beauty, though his wife died years before while delivering a fourth, who also died. Roderick's fortunes change drastically when his entire fleet of merchant ships becomes lost or wrecked; he is forced to sell off all his assets to pay creditors, and he and his family move north to the small town of Blue Hill to live with one of his former employees, Gervain Woodhouse. It is Roderick's plucking of a rose from the Beast's garden—found after Roderick gets lost in the forest during a snowstorm—that sets off the events that lead to Beauty staying with the Beast in his castle.

Pat Lawrey

Pat Lawrey is a local clergyman in Blue Hill who performs the ceremony at Hope and Gervain's wedding. Lawrey then becomes interested in Hope's older sister, Grace, who is still engaged to the missing sea captain Robert Tucker. Eventually, Hope convinces Grace that Lawrey is a good man, and that she should marry him. However, before that happens, Beauty returns to visit

the family and brings news that Robert Tucker is still alive.

Lydia

Along with Bessie, Lydia is one of the invisible handmaids assigned to care for Beauty during her stay in the Beast's castle. Although she is never seen, Beauty is able to hear her conversations with Bessie. During these conversations, Lydia appears doubtful that Beauty will be able to figure out what she must do to break the Beast's curse.

Robert Tucker

Robert Tucker is one of Roderick Huston's best captains, and he falls in love with Roderick's oldest daughter, Grace. The two become engaged before Tucker sets off on a three-year voyage aboard one of Roderick's merchant ships. However, the ship goes missing, and Tucker does not turn up again until six years later—long after the Hustons have left for Blue Hill. It is Beauty's vision of Tucker returning to port that prompts her to beg the Beast for a chance to visit her family, so that she may tell Grace of Tucker's return.

Gervain Woodhouse

Gervain Woodhouse is an ironworker in Roderick Huston's shipyard. He meets and falls in love with Roderick's daughter Hope. After the Huston family becomes destitute, Gervain approaches Roderick with a plan. He suggests that Roderick's family move with him to Blue Hill in the north, where he has secured a job as a blacksmith, and where, he plans, he will marry Hope once his career is established. It is Gervain who tells Beauty of the mysterious and magical north lands, and of the curse that keeps villagers from entering the forest of the Beast's castle.

THEMES

The True Nature of Love and Beauty

A recurring theme in the novel is the nature of beauty. In the beginning, Beauty describes her nickname as entirely unbefitting, since she views herself as ugly when compared to her sisters. It is also worth noting that, unlike previous versions of the fairy tale, the author designates "Beauty" as a nickname and not the main character's given name, which is Honour. This suggests that there is more to Beauty than simply superficial appearances. And

TOPICS FOR FURTHER STUDY

- *Beauty* is often credited as presenting in its main character a positive and realistic role model for young girls, something seldom seen in fantasy literature at the time of its publication. Compare *Beauty* to an older version of the tale of Beauty and the Beast, such as the one written by Madame Le Prince de Beaumont in the 1700s. How does McKinley's version attempt to provide a more positive model for female readers than the older tale? In your opinion, do these changes successfully shape Beauty as a positive role model, or is there still room for improvement? Write a short essay explaining these changes.

- It has been suggested by some scholars that the tale of Beauty and the Beast was once intended to quell the fears of girls who were placed into arranged marriages, in which the bride had no choice over her husband and often did not meet him until their wedding day. Do you think this is a valid reading of

the tale? Why or why not? Write an essay to support your view, providing examples from the story to support your points.

- Almost twenty years after writing *Beauty*, McKinley returned to the tale of Beauty and the Beast as inspiration for her novel *Rose Daughter* (1997). Read *Rose Daughter*, and write an essay comparing the two books. What elements of the original tale do they share? What elements are changed? Why do you think the author chose to revisit the same story decades later, and which do you consider the more successful version?

- At the end of *Beauty*, the Beast tells Beauty that he no longer remembers his given name, and that she must provide one for him. Write a proposal in which you provide your suggestion of what the Beast's name should be, along with supporting reasons why Beauty should choose this name.

---

although Beauty later discovers that she has grown into a physically beautiful woman, it is suggested that this is largely an issue of her own perception of herself, and that she was always physically beautiful even though she did not acknowledge it. Likewise, by looking past the physical appearance of the monstrous Beast, Beauty is able to see his inner beauty, which ultimately becomes manifest in his outer appearance when the curse is lifted.

Loves lost and found are also a recurring theme in the work. Beauty's oldest sister, Grace, is the first to fall in love, but her fiancé disappears for six years and is believed by many to be dead. He is finally found just in time to prevent Grace from marrying a man she does not love, simply because her family wants her to move on with her life. Beauty's father, Roderick, loses the love of his life, Beauty's mother, many years before the story begins. However, he finds love again in the end with Melinda Honeybourne, a widow who has also lost her first love. And Beauty, who in a sense loses

the love of her family when she is compelled to leave it, finds love in the most unlikely place of all: with the Beast, a monstrous creature who threatens to kill her father and essentially holds her as a prisoner in his enchanted castle.

The Gap between the Social Classes
The novel depicts quite starkly the gap between the different social classes in the story world. At the beginning, the Huston family lives in the city in an eighteen-room mansion complete with a two-story ballroom, and they are cared for by a veritable army of servants, from maids to governesses. The daughters's calendars are filled with social events intended to bring about marriage to a wealthy young man from a prestigious family. From this, they end up heading north with a small wagon full of their last possessions, and find themselves living in a tiny blacksmith's cottage at the edge of a tiny town.

The difference appears again when Beauty leaves the humble existence she has grown

Illustration depicting the "Beauty and the Beast" story (© *Leonard de Selva / Corbis*)

accustomed to in Blue Hill, and stays with the Beast in his extravagant castle in the forest. Once again, she is given the finest accommodations, food, and clothing; however, she would much rather be back with her family in their small cottage. When Beauty returns to visit her family and finds her saddlebags filled with opulent gifts, the family reacts somewhat negatively to them, finding the valuable items crude and not at all practical (with the exception of a new bellows, which Gervain puts to immediate use in his forge).

Strong and Independent Women

Beauty is notably different from earlier versions of the fairy tale in its depiction of female characters. Traditionally, Beauty's sisters in the tale are vain and malicious; when Beauty returns from the Beast's castle to visit, they are jealous at all the riches she enjoys, so they conspire to keep her from returning to the castle on time. Also in these earlier versions, Beauty herself is primarily just a pretty girl who must accept her fate. In McKinley's retelling, Beauty's sisters, Hope and Grace, are sympathetic and worthy of admiration. They handle the impoverishment of the family with good spirit and a lack of complaining, even though their way of life changes dramatically. They both find love and remain true to the men they care about, and are not at all jealous when Beauty returns to visit.

Beauty herself takes charge of her fate throughout the book, most notably when she insists on going to the Beast's castle to save her father. She also indelibly changes whatever environment she inhabits—another example of her strength and independent nature. For example, she plants rose seeds at the cottage before she leaves, and the beautiful flowers flourish there as a reminder to her family of her vitality and spirit. At the castle, she decides that it is too quiet outside, and she decides to somehow attract birds to this place where wild animals seem to be forbidden to tread. Much to the surprise of her invisible handmaids, she is successful.

A prime example of a strong and independent woman is Gervain's aunt, Melinda Honeybourne. A widow, she raises a family on her own and at the same time runs a tavern in Blue Hill. She is well respected throughout the town. She also shows herself to be quite clever, questioning the family's story of Beauty staying with a mysterious aunt when she is actually at the Beast's castle.

STYLE

The Fairy Tale and Gothic Fiction

Beauty is modeled on a traditional fairy tale, but as a novel, it also reveals stylistic elements common in Gothic fiction. Fairy tales often take

COMPARE & CONTRAST

- **1970s:** Fantasy fiction is dominated by heroic male characters who battle gruesome creatures to win the hearts of beautiful princesses.

  Today: Fantasy fiction has flourished into a genre containing many strong female lead characters and covering a wide variety of themes.

- **1970s:** Women's rights groups support a proposed amendment to the Constitution granting women equal legal rights to women; the amendment fails to be ratified by enough states before its deadline.

  Today: Equality amendments continue to be presented in Congress, though none has been approved for ratification.

place in an indistinct setting—typically rural—and contain at least one supernatural element such as a magical creature or curse. They are often concerned with the main character achieving happiness by finding wealth or true love.

Gothic fiction, which became popular in the mid-eighteenth century thanks to the Horace Walpole novel *The Castle of Otranto* (1764), exhibits some of the same characteristics as the fairy tale, including the inclusion of supernatural elements. Gothic fiction is also described by its atmosphere of foreboding or horror, and by other specific literary traits: the use of a castle as the setting; the existence of a terrible family curse; the presence of a "damsel in distress" and unseen beings such as ghosts; and the use of darkness to signify mystery, danger, or evil. McKinley makes use of each of these characteristics in *Beauty*, sometimes taking traditional notions about Gothic fiction and giving them a modern twist; for example, instead of ghosts, the Beast's castle is inhabited by invisible servants.

HISTORICAL CONTEXT

Beauty is not set in a specified time or place. This creates a certain sense of timelessness regarding the events of the novel, a feature common to many fairy tales and folk tales, passed down and re-told over the course of centuries. However, McKinley also uses elements from the real world to indicate a setting in the past that generally fits with modern readers' assumptions when reading fairy tales: a time before the Industrial Revolution, in a place ruled by royalty and featuring castles and taverns and blacksmiths. Another important characteristic of the setting is that women are viewed largely as pretty, delicate creatures who should not be troubled by things like knowledge and hard labor.

The Second Wave of Feminism

Feminism, the movement dedicated to achieving equal recognition and rights for women, is generally divided into distinct waves. The first wave of feminism took place mostly in the United States and United Kingdom during the nineteenth century, culminating in 1920 when American women were granted the right to vote; similar rights were granted in the United Kingdom in 1918 and then expanded in 1928. The second wave of feminism began in earnest in the 1960s, with two books often credited with igniting the cause: Simone de Beauvoir's *The Second Sex*, first published in English in 1953, and Betty Friedan's *The Feminine Mystique* (1963). While the first wave of feminism was largely focused on achieving a specific goal—the right to vote—the second wave dealt more with expanding overall equality in social and corporate realms, while maintaining a woman's right to be feminine. Along with the second wave of feminism came an impulse to reevaluate works of art and literature from this new perspective. Traditional

Scene from the Disney film version of the story
(The Kobal Collection. Used by permission.)

stories, such as that of Beauty and the Beast, were evaluated in terms of how they depicted women and their place in society. It was during this second wave, in the 1970s, that McKinley wrote *Beauty*, which has been praised for offering a feminist interpretation of the traditional fairy tale.

CRITICAL OVERVIEW

Beauty was first published in 1978 as McKinley's first novel, and it earned the author decent if not glowing reviews. A reviewer for *Choice* calls the novel "gentle" and "pretty," and compliments "the writer's deft handling of the enchantments." The reviewer concludes, "the book is sure to attract young adult readers—and some old ones too." Betsy Hearne, in a review for *Booklist*, calls it a "captivating first-person fantasy novel that explores and expands some of the compelling elements of the original tale while leaving others untouched." While Hearne acknowledges that the author leaves a few unanswered questions,

she concludes that "the book has a style and holding power all its own, however, and offers enjoyment to casual readers on the one hand and fields for thought and comparison to those who delve further." In a 1983 review for *Growing Point*, Margery Fisher states of the book, "it is a strange, absorbing narrative, squarely concrete and domestic in one way, haunting and oblique in another." Fisher concludes, "the reinterpretation of fairy-tale could hardly go further."

Even reviewers who found fault with the novel still offered a fair amount of praise. Algis Budrys, in a review for *The Magazine of Fantasy and Science Fiction*, criticizes the melodrama of the book's early events and the hasty ending. "But as gentle fantasies go," Budrys states, "*Beauty* is a warm and essentially innocent spell of quiet reading; a book whose author clearly had a defined idea of what beauty is, and set out to evoke it." Patty Campbell of *Wilson Library Bulletin* argues that the author takes the traditional fairy tale and "turns it into an adolescent identity novel," making changes that weaken the original message of the tale. "Nevertheless," Campbell concedes, "it's hard to keep a good story down, and the magic shines through." A reviewer for *Kirkus Reviews* contends that McKinley offers very little original perspective to the classic tale, and calls the book "simply a filling out of the story, with a few alterations." However, the reviewer notes that the author "does accomplish all of this with some success."

In 1998, *Beauty* was chosen as an Honor Book for that year's Phoenix Award, given to a work of children's literature published twenty years before and not sufficiently honored at the time of its original publication. In a 2003 review by Adele Geras in *The Guardian*, concurrent with the book's release in the United Kingdom twenty-five years after its first publication in the United States, Geras praises the work as a "lovely retelling" that can be enjoyed by "anyone who appreciates prose that's poetic without being cloying."

CRITICISM

Greg Wilson

Wilson is an author, literary critic, and mythologist. In this essay, he plays detective as he attempts to pinpoint a real-world setting, both in time and place, for McKinley's fantasy novel.

WHAT DO I READ NEXT?

- *Rose Daughter* (1997) is McKinley's second retelling of the tale of Beauty and the Beast. In it, roses are magical creations, and Beauty has a special touch with them. Unlike previous versions of the tale, Beauty gets to choose the Beast's final physical form: as the beastly creature she has fallen in love with, or as the human that he existed as before the curse.

- *Spindle's End* (2000) is another retelling of a classic fairy tale by McKinley, the inspiration this time being the tale of Sleeping Beauty. As in the original tale, a cursed princess is taken into hiding by a fairy so that she might escape a fate of eternal sleep. However, McKinley continues her tradition of updating classic tales by offering strong female characters who are well equipped to solve their own problems, and do not rely upon a prince to save them.

- *The Hero and the Crown* (1985) is McKinley's Newbery Award–winning novel set in the fictional country of Damar. Aerin, daughter of the king but unsure of her place in the world, decides to slay a dragon to prove her worth. She succeeds, but that is only the beginning of her quest to discover her true purpose and potential.

- In *The Outlaws of Sherwood* (1988), McKinley offers a decidedly different telling of the legend of Robin Hood and his merry band of thieves. In this version, Robin's reputation as an archer is entirely undeserved, and Maid Marian is entirely capable of holding her own with the men.

- *Beastly* (2007) by Alex Flinn is a different take on the tale of Beauty and the Beast, setting the tale in modern-day New York City. The main character is Kyle Kingsbury, a cocky teenage boy who is cursed after playing a practical joke on a girl in his English class. Kyle is transformed into a beast, and is given two years to find love with a girl who can see past his monstrous exterior.

- *Beast* (2000) by Donna Jo Napoli also recasts the tale of Beauty and the Beast from the perspective of the beast. However, the main character of Napoli's tale is an Islamic prince, and he is transformed into a lion. The novel focuses as much on the prince's existence as a lion as it does on the relationship he forges with Beauty.

Robin McKinley's *Beauty: A Retelling of the Story of Beauty and the Beast* is notable for both its fidelity to the original fairy tale and for its subtle tweaking of the story line for modern readers. McKinley is especially clever in her use of real-world elements to ground the more fantastical parts of her tale; in fact, although the author never specifies, the story feels as if it happens during an actual historical time and in a real place. Specific details, such as the books Beauty reads, firmly place the story somewhere and sometime in the "real" world. In the course of examining these details, is it possible to piece together the clues offered by the author and pinpoint an actual time and place setting for the novel?

McKinley offers numerous clues as to the location of the tale. First, there is a strong suggestion that Beauty and others in the tale speak English. This is expressed in several ways. When she talks of studying languages while in the Beast's castle, she remarks that she has studied Latin, Greek, and French—which indicates that none of these are her native language. Assuming a European setting for just a moment, this still does not rule out other likely countries such as Spain or Germany, but it narrows the field. In addition to these clues, Beauty and her sisters refer to a king being in charge of their home country. In fact, Hope makes a joking reference to visiting the king *and* queen—an important

THE NEED FOR A "VILLAGE BLACKSMITH," AS GER BECOMES IN THE STORY, SUGGESTS THAT THE NOVEL TAKES PLACE PRIOR TO THE INDUSTRIAL REVOLUTION. BEAUTY SPECIFICALLY MENTIONS THAT GER TEACHES HER HOW TO MAKE CHARCOAL, WHICH WAS USED IN THE FORGING OF IRON BECAUSE OF ITS PURITY AS IT BURNED."

detail, the significance of which will come into play later. For now, it is simply worth noting that England has been ruled by a monarchy for much of the past thousand years, which is consistent with the author's depiction of the book's setting.

Furthermore, Beauty's given name is spelled "Honour," even in American editions of the novel; this is a particularly British convention, and the fact that an American author chooses to use it is rather telling. The author chooses the same British spelling of "harbour." Similarly, early in the book Beauty shares that she dreams of "going to University," a phrase that in modern usage is more common in British parlance than American. To make special effort to Anglicize certain elements of the text suggests that the author wants the reader to envision England as the setting.

Another clue regarding the setting of the novel is the fact that Beauty's family hails from a large port city. If one assumes the city is in England, then some possibilities might include London, Bristol, Liverpool, and Portsmouth. Tom Black, the stable-owner who gives Beauty the massive horse Greatheart to take with her, breeds and trains "Great Horses" intended for royalty. It would make sense that Tom Black's stable, then, is in or near the same city as the king and queen, which would make London the obvious choice as Beauty's hometown. The evidence is purely circumstantial, but tantalizing.

Beauty also notes that the lands to the north of the city are rural, and viewed by those in the city with a sort of superstitious caution as places where magic might well exist. This also fits well with an English setting, since the most developed and

urban areas tend to be along the southern portion of the country, with the northern areas being more rural and the extreme north—Scotland—being culturally distinct enough to cultivate supernatural suspicions about its residents.

The climate in their city is mild, which is true for most port cities in England. Beauty mentions that although snow falls there, it rarely stays on the ground for very long; this is consistent with London, where snow usually falls a few times each year but tends to melt rather quickly. The region to which they move, far in the north, is much colder and serves up bitter winters complete with blizzards. This detail is not entirely consistent with any part of England, which generally remains mild throughout the year. However, the Pennines, a low mountain range that runs up the center of the country, qualify as one of the harsher climatic regions to be found in England—and they are located north by northwest of London (or nearly straight north from Portsmouth).

The family spends two months traveling to reach their new home. At a conservative pace of five miles per day, this makes their journey about three hundred miles long. This number happens to align nicely with earlier versions of the fairy tale, which describe the family's new home as being about one hundred leagues (equivalent to three hundred miles) from the city. From London, this could easily put the family in the northern Pennines, and could even place them as far north as Scotland; from Portsmouth, the family would probably end up somewhere around the Yorkshire Dales. While this is not a perfect match to the climate described in the book, it is about as close as one is likely to find in England.

As one might expect, northern England does not contain a town called Blue Hill, the name of the village where Beauty's family takes up residence. However, it is worth noting that there is a Blue Hill in Maine, and that author McKinley lived in Maine, not far from this town, during the years immediately prior to writing the novel. While her description of winter conditions might fit this region, her geographic descriptions in the book do not otherwise match.

If one accepts the argument that the book is suggested to be set in England, then all that remains is to determine *when* the story is set. There are many general clues that point toward a general time frame, but there are also some hints that provide specific date boundaries in which the tale must be contained.

To begin with the more general clues, Beauty's father makes a living as an importer and exporter who owns several ships. The description of trade by ship suggests that the book takes place no earlier than the 1600s, when such trade became an important part of the European economy. The ship brought back by John Tucker is specifically identified as two-masted, which makes it likely the ship—intended for long ocean trips—was a brig or brigantine. This would suggest that the story takes place in the 1700s or early 1800s, during the height of popularity for such ships. One of the ships, the *Fortune's Chance*, was even taken by pirates after a storm; the most active period for pirates in the Caribbean and Atlantic was from the early 1600s through the early 1700s. Looking solely at this evidence, then, would suggest that the time period of the novel is around the early 1700s.

Another important detail is revealed by Beauty when she speaks of her desire to attend University. The oldest university in England is the University of Oxford; while it has existed since the twelfth century, it did not abandon medieval-style instruction for more modern methods until the 1600s. It is this more modern style of learning, with an emphasis on classical studies and sciences, that fits with the given description of Beauty in the book. Beauty also notes that it is unheard of for a woman to attend University at this time. Indeed, Oxford and Cambridge did not integrate women into their institutions until the twentieth century, though women's colleges affiliated with the universities were formed in the mid-nineteenth century. This suggests a time frame of anywhere from around 1650 until about 1850, which coincides well with the estimate obtained from the details of the ship trade.

The need for a "village blacksmith," as Ger becomes in the story, suggests that the novel takes place prior to the Industrial Revolution. Beauty specifically mentions that Ger teaches her how to make charcoal, which was used in the forging of iron because of its purity as it burned. In the late 1700s, advances in metalworking technology—coupled with a loss of available wood to make charcoal—meant that the forging of iron was usually performed using fuels other than charcoal. This led to the rapid development of the iron industry, and local blacksmiths ultimately became a thing of the past. Based upon this, then, the

setting of the book is probably not any later than the late 1700s, but could be earlier.

Finally, more definitive clues are offered by the books that Beauty reads. She notes that *Le Morte d'Arthur*, Thomas Malory's account of the tales of King Arthur, has already been written at the time the novel takes place. *Le Morte d'Arthur* was first published in 1485, with several reprintings taking place until the 1630s, when the book again became unavailable for almost two hundred years. This only confirms that the story takes place sometime after 1485—not the most helpful clue. However, Beauty also mentions that she is already familiar with at least the first two cantos of *The Faerie Queene* by Edmund Spenser, which means the story must take place after 1590, when the first half of Spenser's epic was published.

Equally important are references to books that have *not* been written yet, which Beauty finds in the magical library within the Beast's castle. Several modern books appear, including *The Once and Future King* by T. H. White and *The Screwtape Letters* by C. S. Lewis. Much attention is paid to the poems of Robert Browning, whose works, having been published throughout the mid-1800s, did not yet exist in the world of the novel. Most important, however, is the fact that Beauty discovers the work of an author who does not yet exist—or at least has not yet published anything—by the name of Sir Walter Scott. Since the well-read Beauty is not familiar with Scott's work, the story must take place prior to 1814, when Scott's first novel, *Waverley*, was published.

Taking into account all the clues, this provides a time frame that encompasses most of the eighteenth century. However, there is one last clue, already mentioned earlier: Beauty's sister Hope and her reference to both a king and a queen, which happens about two years after the family leaves the city. It is not likely that she would refer to both a king and a queen unless both were alive and actively ruling at the time. Interestingly, during the 1700s, England was ruled by both a king and a queen only about half the time. The first period lasted from 1727 until 1737, and the second from 1761 through the beginning of the nineteenth century. This suggests that the story takes place during one of these two time periods.

It is worth noting that the first published version of the tale of Beauty and the Beast was written by Madame Gabrielle de Villeneuve and published in 1740. However, a shorter and somewhat altered

Scene from a 1997 production of Beauty and the Beast *in Stuttgart, Germany* (AP Iimages)

version of the tale, more recognizable to modern readers, was written in 1756 by Madame Le Prince de Beaumont. Is it possible that McKinley simply set her story around the time of the first published versions of the fairy tale, and transported the location of the French-originated tale to England? It seems likely, even though the comments referring to the monarchy are not an exact match with this date range. One could argue that the story officially begins when Beauty is twelve and her sister Grace becomes engaged. If one aligns this with the first published English translation of Madame Le Prince de Beaumont's version of the tale in 1757, the dates come dangerously close to fitting quite well.

It might seem an exercise in literal mindedness to take a novel of fantasy, in which rose petals turn to gold and a cursed prince is trapped in the body of a monster, and analyze its details for glimmers of realism. However, it is precisely because of McKinley's care at injecting realism into the novel that the fantasy elements resonate

all the more deeply. And as this analysis shows, her use of real-world elements does not at all appear to be haphazard or fanciful, but quite deliberate and meaningful.

Source: Greg Wilson, Critical Essay on Robin McKinley's *Beauty, Novels for Students*, Gale, Cengage Learning, 2010.

Ellen R. Sackelman

In the following essay, Sackelman delineates the ways in which McKinley's title character upends traditional gender roles.

Robin McKinley's *Beauty: A Retelling of the Story of Beauty and the Beast* examines the life and education of the title character as she resolves issues of self-image and self-worth. Set somewhere "once upon a time," McKinley's text redefines the role of the fairy-tale heroine and allows the protagonist, the youngest of three motherless sisters, to narrate her story in a matter-of-fact manner and explore her identity within the structure of her family, alone in captivity, and in the company of her lover. Beauty's numerous self-defining gestures help her recognize the difference between physical attractiveness and integrity, and resolve the discrepancy between the way she sees herself and the manner in which others do.

After her father is unable to provide 5-year-old Honour with a satisfactory explanation of what it means to be honorable, she renames herself Beauty and thus sets up the first of many contrasts to her gorgeous siblings. When she suffers from ache and oversized hands and feet during adolescence, Beauty admits that her self-chosen appellation had evolved into something of a gentle family joke. These and other wry observations engage even the most reluctant male readers, who may approach this novel with their own bias against the genre of fairy tales. Indeed, Beauty's subsequent refusal to allow her father to escort her past the gates to the Beast's castle and her nightly rejections of the Beast's marriage proposals distinguish her as a heroine not often encountered by young readers: a female voice negating male desires.

Prior to these instances when Beauty negotiates with male authority, McKinley reverses other familiar aspects of characterization within the genre. Instead of passively awaiting marriage, sequestering herself indoors, or perceiving herself as "a weak woman," as one sister does, the intrepid protagonist dreams of attending the university and reads voraciously. In addition, unlike her sisters, Beauty communicates with her father, and her affectionate exchanges with her brother-in-law foreshadow her own healthy, romantic relationship. Despite her obvious rejection of the roles her sisters occupy, Beauty does not reject or demean them, a welcome development to the way females interact with one another in fairy tales. Encouraged to closely contrast McKinley's depiction of familial relationships and gender roles to those in other well-known fairy tales, students begin to recognize their own conditioned, sexist expectations. Such realizations elicit reactions of surprise and heighten students' awareness of how deeply entrenched and frequently reinforced in everyday life gender stereotypes truly are.

McKinley's Beauty embodies a delightfully rebellious spirit as well as some traditional aspects of the female role. Functioning as nurturer, for example, Beauty has raised her own horse, even bottle-feeding it after the death of its mother. Her labor in the garden establishes her as an integral member of the family. However,

like others who perform domestic duties in their own homes, Beauty is unable to recognize her value to her family. After her father attempts to fulfill her request for rose seeds, another symbol of the vitality that Beauty brings to her surroundings, she easily exchanges her life for his as a result of his bargain with the Beast.

She attributes her decision to leave her family and live with the Beast to what she believes is her worthlessness, namely, her looks. Of her sisters, she says she is the "ugliest." More than once in the course of the text, she refers to herself as having masculine—or unfeminine—attributes. For example, she claims that her household responsibilities can be maintained by "any lad in the village." At the Beast's castle, she sees herself as a "poor plain girl," not worthy of dressing like a princess. Interestingly, Beauty refuses repeatedly to succumb to the elaborate wardrobe her invisible handmaidens make available to her, an assertive act not only emphasizing Beauty's determination to do as she pleases, but also serving as a reminder to the reader how paralyzing an obsession with looks can be. Yet, even after her declaration of unconditional love for the Beast releases him from his enchantment, Beauty questions whether she is attractive enough to be the wife of such a handsome man. Only in his company does she gain a sense of her comely appearance, and because of this, Beauty's moment of actualization may be perceived as a troubling one. In a text lacking an obvious villain, Beauty's poor self-image makes her her own worst enemy.

Strikingly, the relationship between Beauty and her Beast offers an alternative to love affairs in other pieces of fiction usually assigned to the teenage reader. Theirs is not as impulsive or as tragic a union as Romeo and Juliet's, nor is it as torturous as Pip's devotion to Estella. Rarely is Beauty described as powerless or passive. More than once, she is reminded that "she's stronger than she knows." In fact, she determines the pace and nature of her interaction with her Beast, inviting him to share a sunset or a walk in the garden when she wants company. Additionally, with the Beast, Beauty is able to renew her education. Her thirst for knowledge, a trait her sisters disparaged, brings Beauty closer to him. They read together and often. McKinley's unconventional use of a flower to serve as a metaphor for the male protagonist's health and his misgivings about his appearance can propel discussion relevant to both sexes regarding literary characterizations and symbols typically associated with gender.

By the novel's close, Beauty is reunited with her family and set to marry a prince. In the final paragraphs of the text, she must name her husband, a task that recalls her earlier decision to name herself. The privilege in giving a human name to the Beast makes final and more significant Beauty's sense of control over her world.

Using *Beauty* in the classroom allows students to detect the pervasive gender bias in literature and/or video for young "readers" on which they have been raised. Asking them to analyze whether McKinley's text fulfills the criteria of the traditional fairy tale, or complies with parameters set forth by male-dominated quest legends, serves as an introduction to feminist literary theory. Thus, *Beauty* occupies an important place in the gender-balanced curriculum.

Source: Ellen R. Sackelman, "More Than Skin Deep: Robin McKinley's *Beauty*: A Retelling of the Story of Beauty and the Beast," in *Women in Literature: Reading through the Lens of Gender*, edited by Jerilyn Fisher and Ellen S. Silber, Greenwood Press, 2003, pp. 32–34.

Lynn Moss Sanders

In the following excerpt, Sanders argues that McKinley's heroines fulfill an important role by providing physically and mentally independent models for young female readers.

Fantasy fiction is especially popular among young adolescents, both male and female, perhaps because it allows some escape from the problems of modern adolescence. If the escapist nature of fantasy fiction is appealing to young people, that quality of fantasy fiction also makes it a good vehicle for exploring contemporary social issues, including stereotypical gender roles, a subject skillfully explored by fantasy writer Robin McKinley. Although certainly it is important for young adults to read realistic fiction that shows a balanced view of gender roles, fantasy fiction can serve a useful function in allowing young readers, particularly young female readers, to imagine themselves performing feats of physical strength, something that is not required of most young people in our society, unless they are talented athletes. In fantasy fiction, physical strength and bravery are often equated, and these books allow readers to imaginatively conquer their own more realistic dragons.

McKinley's first novel, *Beauty*, does not describe a heroine who fights battles and rules kingdoms, but the main character has important traits that the author develops further in the Damarian novels. The premise of McKinley's retelling of the "Beauty and the Beast" fairy tale is that this Beauty, whose given name is Honour, is not really beautiful: she is a gawky adolescent. Beauty deals with her insecurity about her looks in the time-honored manner of many adolescent girls: she concentrates on books and horses. She tells us, "My intellectual abilities gave me a release"; and she dreams of becoming a true scholar and reads the Greek poets to her horse, Greatheart.

Beauty agrees to live with the Beast in order to save her father's life, but it is her love for books that first helps her achieve the sympathy for the Beast that is necessary to break the spell. She and the Beast read to each other and discover a common bond in the intellect, the first step towards their eventual love. It is interesting to note that in the recent Walt Disney animated film version of "Beauty and the Beast," Belle is also known for her fondness for books, a trait which puzzles her provincial neighbors. Again, the Beast begins to win Belle's heart when he gives her his library. In this case, Robin McKinley may have helped to influence a generation of young girls into believing that one can be both beautiful, good-hearted, and intellectual.

McKinley also portrays Beauty as a fairy tale heroine with a sense of humor. Much of the humor is self-deprecating, focusing on her lack of physical beauty, but humor is also her weapon in helping her to face her destiny. This quality of McKinley's writing separates her from many fantasy writers whose tone is often too serious to be palatable to mature readers. Adolescents frequently take themselves too seriously; it is refreshing to read books for young people where a sense of humor is just as important as sword-wielding skills.

In *Beauty*, *The Blue Sword*, *The Hero and the Crown*, *Deerskin*, and *The Outlaws of Sherwood* Robin McKinley not only avoids the fantasy stereotype of the damsel in distress, she creates a new role for women in fantasy fiction. McKinley's heroes, Beauty, Harry, Aerin, Lissar, Marion, and Cecily provide different positive role models for young women and men. Her characters are winners in the eternal fantasy battle between good and evil, partially through magical help, but largely through their own physical skills as riders and swordfighters, their extraordinary courage and insight, their willingness to defy convention to do what is right, all traditionally the hallmarks of the male fantasy hero.

McKinley herself has commented that it bothers her that she receives many letters from people "saying something on the order of, 'At last! Girls who do things!'" She continues that it is her hope that "young readers who identify with Harry and Aerin and the others and wish to be like them will also realize that they are. And this should be true . . . of boy readers as well as the girls; both sides of our gender-specific event horizon need to be extended" (*Horn Book*, p. 405). And of course this should be true, because what *Beauty*, *The Blue Sword*, *The Hero and the Crown*, *Deerskin*, and *The Outlaws of Sherwood* are about is the freedom to choose to be oneself, and to occupy one's life with honorable endeavors.

Source: Lynn Moss Sanders, "Girls Who Do Things: The Protagonists of Robin McKinley's Fantasy Fiction," in *ALAN Review*, Vol. 24, No. 1, Fall 1996, pp. 38–42.

Betsy Hearne

In the following excerpt, Hearne compares McKinley's version of the fairy tale to more traditional tellings.

Since 1978, adolescents have been captivated by Robin McKinley's novel *Beauty*. The creation of a contemporary, first-person. young adult novel from a fairy tale could raise a host of technical problems for the novelist and objections from devotees of traditional lore. *Beauty, A Retelling of the Story of Beauty and the Beast* was included by American Library Association committees in both the Notable Children's Books and the Best Books for Young Adults lists for 1978. It was Robin McKinley's first novel, written in the throes of a negative reaction to the television adaptation starring George C. Scott, in which McKinley felt that the point had been missed and the aesthetic thinned. The story, she maintains, is about honor. Honour is her heroine's real name, given to match her two older sisters', Grace and Hope, by a mother who does not survive the birth of baby Mercy, who also dies. In the tradition of the story from its origins, Beauty is a nickname, but one bestowed here ironically on a five-year-old who cannot comprehend the concept of Honour and requests Beauty instead, an appellation retained into a gawky adolescence.

For a 247-page novel, the cast is compact, with secondary characters introduced and developed naturally within the context of the traditional plot. Grace, Hope, and Honour (nicknamed Beauty) Huston are the sisters. Their father, Roderick Huston, is a shipwright/merchant and carpenter. Robert Tucker is a sailor and fiancé of Grace; Gervain Woodhouse is an iron-worker/blacksmith who marries Hope. Great-heart, a horse given to Beauty by a family friend, leads her to the palace of the Beast and keeps her company there. Lydia and Bessie are two breezes who attend Beauty in the palace.

A few minor characters make brief appearances essential to McKinley's revisions: Ferdy, whose first kiss repels Beauty in a reaction that presages her resistance to admitting love for the Beast: Pat Lawry, who courts Grace in Robbie's absence; Mercy and Richard, twins born to Hope and Gervaine; Melinda Honeybourne, Gervaine's widowed aunt, manager of the Red Griffin and Roderick Huston's eventual wife; and Orpheus the canary, who cheers the company throughout their resettlement in the country. All but Orpheus further the theme of male/female relationships, and the canary serves as a link with the birds Beauty later coaxes to her palace window—a sign that her involvement is weakening the Beast's enchantment.

There are no villains here. And where fairy-tale brevity benefits from the Beast's initial and terrible impression to lend tension to Beauty's dilemma, it is McKinley's task to maintain that tension through a longer work in which the Beast's essential nobility quickly becomes apparent. The conflict, of course, is shifted to an internal level with Beauty's rite of passage. It seems ultimately fitting that modern teenage fiction should emerge from an old tale of the journey into maturation.

To sharpen this focus, McKinley has altered the father's weakness and the sisters' villainy (those faults shifted the onus of responsibility from Beauty's self-determined choices), in much the same way that Villeneuve either omitted or explained away the family flaws. All three are paragons of integrity, as are the girls' suitors, their virtue fortunately relieved by practical, down-to-earth humor and genuine affection. Beauty herself is strong-willed to obstinate, plain and thin, a tomboy passionate only about animals and books. She is a smart, adolescent ugly duckling, with everyone else's assurance that she will eventually turn into a swan. True to life, Beauty believes only her own critical assessment. She is as deprecatory of her physical appearance and as apprehensive of mirrors as the Beast (there are none in her room or home nor in the palace of the Beast).

The narrative, covering Beauty's fifteenth to eighteenth years, is structured into three parts. The first established the family background and situation, the courtship of the older girls, the loss of the ships (and with them, Grace's fiancé), the auction of goods, the removal to Gervaine's childhood home in the north country, his marriage to Hope and prohibition not to enter the reputedly enchanted forest behind their home, the birth of their twins, and the father's trip to the city to recover one ship, from which he returns with a rose.

In section two, the father tells his story of finding the Beast's castle and picking the fateful flower, after which his saddle-bags are opened to reveal rich gifts. Beauty determines to go back in his stead after a month's reprieve and dreams twice of the castle as she prepares to depart. The third and last part comprises more than half of the book, beginning with the farewell of father and daughter at the castle gate and ending with her declaration of love for the Beast and the celebration. With unexpected holding power, McKinley amplifies descriptions of Beauty's settlement into life at the palace, the development of her relationship with the Beast, her homesickness and desperation to tell Grace of Robbie's return (seen through a magic glass, or nephrite plate, belonging to the Beast) before another suitor proposes, and the visit home, which convinces Beauty of her love for the Beast and delays her return till almost too late. The reader knows that Beauty must finally accept her own physicality and release the Beast, but the questions of how and when raise anticipation and even anxiety during Beauty's last ride, when the Beast's magic weakens and she must find him on the strength of her own love.

Sustaining the plot are the book's compatibly blended point of view, pace, style, tone, and theme. The first-person narrative lends immediacy, fosters a reader's identification with the protagonist, and allows a candid look at Beauty's internal journey. The Beast shows mature perceptions, developed during his 200 years of brooding alone in the palace, on their first meeting, when he tells her he would only have sent her father home unharmed had she decided not to come to the palace herself.

"You would?" I said; it was half a shriek. "You mean that I came here for nothing?"

A shadowy movement like the shaking of a great shaggy head. "No. Not what you would

count as nothing. He would have returned to you, and you would have been glad, but you also would have been ashamed, because you had sent him, as you thought, to his death. Your shame would have grown until you came to hate the sight of your father, because he reminded you of a deed you hated, and hated yourself for. In time it would have ruined your peace and happiness, and at last your mind and heart."

But Beauty's knowledge, limited to an honest if impetuous intuition at the book's beginning, develops through her solitude at the palace and her experiences with the Beast, as evidenced in self-examinations that slowly raise her to the Beast's level of awareness.

I had avoided touching him, or letting him touch me. At first I had eluded him from fear; but when fear departed, elusiveness remained, and developed into habit. Habit bulwarked by something else; I could not say what. The obvious answer, because he was a Beast, didn't seem to be the right one. I considered this.

Without becoming too confessional, these insights bond the reader to Beauty as she progresses through nightly more difficult denials of the Beast's proposal to taking his arm and finally realizing her feelings in the face of the family's animosity toward the Beast.

I knew now what it was that had happened. I couldn't tell them that here, at home with them again, I had learned what I had successfully ignored these last weeks at the castle; that I had come to love him. They were no less dear to me, but he was dearer yet.

The frequency of vivid scenes keeps Beauty's development from dwindling into a diary. A confrontation she forces between her horse Greatheart and the Beast, whom all creatures fear, is gripping. Beauty's discovery, in the library, of books that have never been written and her attempts to understand Robert Browning or to envision modern inventions referred to in other works is quite funny, as are the struggles of the two attendant breezes to outfit her like a lady. Her encounters with the Beast are natural, as often light as moving.

"It's raining," I said, but he understood the question, because he answered:

"Yes, even here it rains sometimes . . . I've found that it doesn't do to tinker with weather too much . . . Usually it rains after nightfall," he added apologetically.

The occasion on which she feeds him her favorite dessert, however, proceeds from a touching note to a powerful confrontation—the last barrier she throws up against him before her vision (literally, in this case) begins to clear for a new sensual awareness.

A deceptively simple style blends drama with detail. Part of the book's appeal is certainly its descriptions of a life anyone might long for—leisure spiced with high cuisine and horseback riding, with learning for learning's sake thrown in at will. These descriptions are by turn specific and suggestive, allowing readers to luxuriate in a wish-fulfilling existence but leaving room for them to grow their own fantasies. The marvels of palace life are quite explicit.

> I returned my gaze to the table. I saw now that it was crowded with covered dishes, silver and gold. Bottles of wine stood in buckets full of gleaming crushed ice; a bowl big enough to be a hip bath stood on a pedestal two feet tall, in the shape of Atlas bearing the world on his shoulders; and the hollow globe was full of shining fresh fruit. A hundred delightful odours assailed me. At the head of the table, near the door I had entered by, stood a huge wooden chair, carved and gilded and lined with chestnut-brown brocade over straw-coloured satin. The garnet-set peak was as tall as a schooner's mast. It could have been a throne. As I looked, it slid away slightly from the table and turned itself towards me, as another chair had beckoned my father. I noticed for the first time that it was the only chair at that great table, and there was only one place laid, although the table gleamed to its farther end with the curved backs of plate covers, and with goblets and tureens and tall jeweled pitchers.

Other passages leave a strategic amount of information to the reader's imagination. During Beauty's first conversation with the Beast, she sees only his "massive shadow", heightening a dread peak when he finally stands to reveal himself. Even then, only his body is delineated: the specifics of his face are implied by Beauty's reaction.

> 'Oh no,' I cried, and covered my own face with my hands. But when I heard him take a step towards me, I leaped back in alarm like a deer at the crack of a branch nearby, turning my eyes away from him... What made his gaze so awful was that his eyes were human.

Bit by bit, through references to long white teeth and mangy fur, readers can construct an image of the Beast, but it is largely their own.

There are twists of humor throughout dialogue and description that balance the darkest hours of both Beauty and the Beast for a tone

alternately sweet and bitter, ingenuous and sophisticated. Underlying all the various shades of emotion, however, is a sense of inevitable destiny, the fairy-tale security that all will be well in spite of threats and confusions. The roses Beauty plants in winter bloom to comfort her before she leaves home. A griffin on the ring (and later necklace) given her by the Beast looks powerful but not predatory. In spite of Beauty's association of the Beast with the Minotaur when Gervaine first tells her of the rumored enchantment, the mazes she encounters at the castle simply mirror her own internal loss of direction.

> I dreamed of the castle that Father had told us about. I seemed to walk quickly down halls with high ceilings. I was looking for something, anxious that I could not find it. I seemed to know the castle very well; I did not hesitate as I turned corners, went up stairs, down stairs, opened doors...
>
> ...
>
> ... I found myself in the castle again, walking through dozens of handsome, magnificently furnished rooms, looking for something. I had a stronger sense of sorrow and of urgency this time; and also a sense of some other—presence; I could describe it no more clearly. I round myself crying as I walked, flinging doors open and looking inside eagerly, then hurrying on as they were each empty of what I sought.
>
> ...
>
> I walked across more corridors, up and down more stairs, and in and out of more rooms than I cared to count... I soon lost my sense of direction, and then most of my sense of purpose, but I kept walking... After a while, perhaps hours, I came to a door at the end of a corridor. just around a corner...
>
> ...
>
> Nearly every day we found ourselves traveling over unfamiliar ground, even when I thought I was deliberately choosing a route we had previously traced; even when I thought I recognized a particular group of trees or flower-strewn meadow, I could not be sure of it. I didn't know whether this was caused by the fact that my sense of direction was worse than I'd realized, which was certainly possible, or whether the paths and fields really changed from day to day—which I thought was also possible.
>
> ...
>
> 'I can't seem to keep the corridors straight in my head somehow, and as soon as I'm hopelessly lost, I turn a corner and there's my room again. So I never learn anything. I don't mean

to complain,' I added hastily. 'It's just that I get lost so very quickly that I don't have the chance to see very much before they—or—send me home again.'

It is Beauty's inner pressure and the Beast's need that tell time; there are no clocks in the palace. Like Cocteau, McKinley is intrigued with different dimensions of reality. The space, time, and logic of the Primary World are suspended in the Secondary World. Beauty's bridging of both requires some adjustment.

> You look at this world—my world, here, as you looked at your old world, your family's world. This is to be expected; it was the only world, the only way of seeing, that you knew. Well; it's different here. Some things go by different rules.
>
> . . .
>
> . . . it was slowly being borne in on me that my stories about the castle and my life there had little reality for my family. They listened with interest to what I told—or tried to tell—them, but it was for my sake, not for the sake of the tale. I could not say if this was my fault or theirs, or the fault of the worlds we lived in.

And as Cocteau admonishes, only true believers can know a world other than the mundane. Beauty's sisters are too pragmatic even to receive a message from the Beast. Her father accepts the dreams sent to comfort him by the Beast, and Gervaine believes in the rumored enchantment of the forest and in Beauty's fate after she has drunk from the forest stream. Beauty herself develops her already strong instincts into a sixth sense so sharpened that she can not only see, hear, and smell the ordinary more keenly but also divine the invisible: envision the Beast in his palace from her country house without a magic glass; understand her attendant breezes' gossip.

As the mysterious becomes familiar, it is less awesome. One reviewer accused McKinley of fettering archetypes with concrete realization, of reducing the larger-than-life to normal. Another critic countered this charge with a defense of the book's fairytale facets, quoting Tolkien on the creation of a Secondary World.

> Fantasy is a natural human activity. It certainly does not destroy or even insult Reason; and it does not either blunt the appetite for, nor obscure the perception of, scientific verity. On the contrary. The keener and the clearer is the reason, the better fantasy will it make.
>
> (In Tolkien, "Tree and Leaf" 74–75)

Fairy tales assume belief, on either a literal or symbolic plane. Fantasies assume only a suspension of disbelief; the rest is a matter of persuasion. As McKinley told me when I interviewed her in 1983, it was her determination to make the story immediate to contemporary readers, to keep the fantastical effect to a minimum and thus obey the rules of convincing fantasy.

Source: Betsy Hearne, "Beauty and the Beast: Visions and Revisions of an Old Tale," in *Lion and the Unicorn*, Vol. 12, No. 2, December 1988, pp. 74–111.

SOURCES

Budrys, Algis, Review of *Beauty. The Magazine of Fantasy and Science Fiction*, Vol. 62, No. 5, May 1982, p. 36.

Campbell, Patty, Review of *Beauty: A Retelling of the Story of Beauty and the Beast. Wilson Library Bulletin*, vol. 53, no. 3 (November 1978): 273.

Fisher, Margery, Review of *Beauty. Growing Point*, Vol. 22, No. 4, November 1983, p. 4160.

Geras, Adele, "Saturday Review: Children's Books: Fresh telling of a tale as old as time: Adele Geras applauds an elegant version of Beauty and the Beast: *Beauty* by Robin McKinley, 259 pp, David Fickling, pounds 10.99." *The Guardian*, May 3, 2003, p. 33.

Hearne, Betsy, Review of *Beauty: A Retelling of the Story of Beauty and the Beast*, *Booklist*, Vol. 75, No. 2, September 15, 1978, p. 222.

McKinley, Robin, *Beauty: A Retelling of the Story of Beauty and the Beast*. Eos, 2005.

Review of *Beauty: A Retelling of the Story of Beauty and the Beast*, *Choice*, Vol. 16, Nos. 5 & 6, July–August 1979, p. 668.

Review of *Beauty*, *Kirkus Reviews*, Vol. XLVI, No. 23, December 1, 1978, p. 1307.

FURTHER READING

Bettelheim, Bruno, *The Uses of Enchantment: The Meaning and Importance of Fairy Tales*, Penguin Books Ltd, 1991.

> Bettelheim, a well-known child psychologist, explores the ways in which fairy tales can help shape the way children interpret and interact with the world around them. The work won both a National Book Award and the U.S. Critic's Choice Prize.

Perrault, Charles, *The Complete Fairy Tales of Charles Perrault*, translated by Nicoletta Simborowski and Neil Philip, Clarion Books, 1993.

This collection of tales by the acclaimed French author includes such well-known works as "Little Red Riding Hood" and "Cinderella," as well as lesser-known tales such as "The Fairies" and "Tufty Ricky."

Tatar, Maria, ed., *The Classic Fairy Tales*, W. W. Norton & Co., 1999.

Despite the name, this Norton Critical Edition is far from just a collection of fairy tales. It focuses on six specific tales and analyzes the different variations that exist in different times and cultures; the book also contains critical essays by scholars such as Jack Zipes and Vladimir Propp.

Von Franz, Marie-Louise, *The Feminine in Fairy Tales*, Shambhala (revised edition), 2001.

In this work, psychologist Von Franz examines fairy tales from different cultures in an attempt to determine how each culture's feelings toward women are reflected in the tales. Von Franz was a student of analytical psychologist Carl Jung.

The Glory Field

WALTER DEAN MYERS

1994

The sweeping saga *The Glory Field*, published in 1994, is one of many popular young adult novels written by the prolific Walter Dean Myers. Like a number of Myers's books, *The Glory Field* focuses on the African American experience and explores the development of youth. The protagonists in each segment of the novel are young people who face significant challenges.

In *The Glory Field*, Myers tells the story of multiple generations of the African American Lewis family in five separate but interconnected stories. Muhammad Bilal is the dynasty's founder, who was brought to the United States as a young slave from Africa. Through subsequent segments, Muhammad's descendants emerge from slavery to own a piece of land they once worked in servitude in South Carolina. Named Glory Field, it serves as a representation of their sacrifice and standing in the local community. Later, the land is a link to the past as the Lewises live in such far-flung locales as Chicago and New York City and deal with twentieth-century problems.

Throughout the novel, Myers emphasizes such themes as the importance of family and the value of kinship. While exploring ideas of the tension between freedom and captivity, he also shows the effects of racism and racist behavior on members of the Lewis clan in such important historical moments as the post–Civil War era and the civil rights movement. Given the period covered in the novel, there are descriptions of violence against

Walter Dean Myers *(Photo by Constance Myers, courtesy of Walter Dean Myers.)*

members of the Lewis clan, including whippings and threats of physical harm. Myers also uses authentic language, including derogatory terms for African Americans. In the final segment of *The Glory Field*, Shep Lewis struggles crack cocaine addiction (discussed, but not depicted, in the text).

Critics generally responded positively to the depth and breadth of *The Glory Field*. Writing about the novel in the *Christian Science Monitor*, Karen Williams notes, "This riveting work brings alive the times each character represents. Although Myers depicts many triumphs of this African-American family, he also vividly shows the high cost of every victory."

AUTHOR BIOGRAPHY

Born Walter Milton Myers in Martinsburg, West Virginia, on August 12, 1937, the author is the son of George and Mary Myers. When he was two, his mother died giving birth to his younger sister, Imogene. Because his father was impoverished and could not care for all of his children, Myers was raised in Harlem by Herbert and Florence Dean. The working-class Deans were friends of Myers's mother and they served as his lifelong foster parents. Myers took their last name and made it his middle name in honor of their loving care.

As a child, Myers had a speech impediment that hindered his spoken communication even though he was a good student. A teacher encouraged him to write down his thoughts in poems and short stories, and he won the first of what would be many awards for his writing. Myers also became an avid reader and spent many hours at the public library. Bitter because of the limited opportunities due to his race and socioeconomic status, he left Stuyvesant High School at sixteen and joined the U.S. Army the following year. Myers remained in the service until 1957. He held various jobs, including postal clerk and messenger, and he wrote at night after work. Myers later studied at the State College of the City of New York and earned his BA from Empire State College.

After a stint working as an employment supervisor for the New York State Department of Labor in the late 1960s, Myers joined the publishing industry. He was frustrated by the lack of books by African American authors that accurately reflected the black experience. His picture book *Where Does the Day Go?* (1969), won a contest sponsored by the Council on Interracial Books for Children in 1968. Myers then found employment as a senior trade-book editor at Bobbs-Merrill Company while continuing to write primarily picture books.

After learning the business side of publishing for seven years, Myers became a full-time writer in 1977. He was highly productive, and by the late 1970s often published several books each year. Myers primarily wrote fiction for children and young adults, but he also penned nonfiction and poetry works for the same age groups. To find the voice he needed to write many of his books, he got away from the familiar in his life and stayed in hotels and other settings related to what he wanted to write. While writing *The Glory Field* (1994), for example, Myers resided in Charleston, South Carolina, for a time.

In the late 1990s and early 2000s, as Myers reached the age at which many people retire, he continued to produce several new works each year. They included *Monster* (1999), which was illustrated by his son Christopher and won the first Michael L. Printz Award. As of 2009, Myers lives in New Jersey where he continues to primarily write young adult fiction, nonfiction, and poetry.

PLOT SUMMARY

July 1753. Off the Coast of Sierra Leone, West Africa

Muhammad Bilal is traveling on a slave ship from Africa, where he was captured by slave traders. He is trapped with other slaves in close quarters for a voyage of at least a month. Like the others, he suffers from pain and thirst, and longs for the end of the journey.

March 1864. Live Oaks Plantation. Curry Island, South Carolina

Muhammad becomes a slave at Live Oaks, and is one of the first slaves bought by the Lewis family to work their plantation. All the slaves are made to work on a Sunday, harvesting sweet potatoes under the watchful eye of overseer Joey Haynes. This Sunday labor is required in part because Joshua (the brother of elder slave Moses) and Moses' son Lem have run away, and white patrollers are after them. Lem is found and brought back, then taken off by whites who tie him to a tree overnight so he will reveal where Joshua is. Miss Julia, the Lewis's daughter, uses an excuse to get Lizzy, a young slave, to the main house. There, Julia fawns over her while trying to get information from her. When Lizzy returns to slave quarters, she does not believe the words of Grandma Dolly (Moses' mother), who tells her that Julia is using her. Saran, Moses' wife, believes that Joshua is "chasing his freedom dream north."

Like the other slaves, Lizzy hopes that Lem is not seriously hurt, and in the middle of the night she goes to the tree where he is tied. Grandma Dolly sees her leave and tries to warn her of the dangers of her actions, but Lizzy still goes, taking water with her. As Lizzy walks in the night, she remembers seeing another slave named Bill whipped and does not want to suffer the same fate. At the tree, Lizzy finds Lem beaten and uses the water to clean him up. As she helps him, she feels the pain of the whip wielded by Joe Haynes. Lizzy gets whipped until her clothing is shredded. The whipping only stops when Joshua tackles Joe. While holding Joe down, Joshua tells Lizzy to pick up the rifle. Joshua tells Lizzy that she

must leave with him and Lem or they will have to kill Joe. Lizzy is allowed to go back to the quarters and say good-bye.

At the slave cabins, Miss Julia is looking for her. Lizzy gets a change of clothing, and Saran tells her to go with Joshua and Lem. Following Saran's advice, Lizzy gets rid of Julia. Leaving with Joshua and Lem, Lizzy is excited and fearful about what is ahead. During the first day of their journey, they hide in trees, but they find Joshua is gone when they wake up at night to resume walking. Lem and Lizzy keep going, but they hear patrollers and their hounds looking for them. They finally reach an enclave of Union soldiers (in 1864, the United States Civil War was under way, pitting the Union against the Confederate States of America), both white and black, who feed them and let them sleep. In the morning, Lizzy is given work cleaning the boots of white officers and packing wagons while Lem becomes a soldier. They learn that Joshua is a soldier there, too. Lem and Joshua leave with their unit, and Lizzy is given the option of going North with them. Lizzy accepts.

April 1900. Curry Island, South Carolina

After the Civil War ends, Moses and Saran take the last name Lewis and are given eight acres of land next to Live Oaks. They name their land Glory Field. Lizzy marries Lem's brother Richard, and they have a son named Elijah who works the land with other members of the family. The African American Lewis family works hard to keep their land. Like many African Americans, they struggle to pay the taxes on their land. To help with expenses, Richard moves to Georgia with Lizzy to work in pulp factories.

On Sunday, Moses consecrates the burial ground behind the church the Lewises and others have built. At the gathering afterward, Elijah flirts with Goldie, a girl he thinks he wants to marry. Saran tells Elijah to tend to the cemetery once a week. Lem, who died in the Civil War, has a grave there, although his body is really buried under Glory Field. Saran has a job watching a little white blind boy named David Turner during the week. David's mother is dead and his father, Hamlin Turner, has entrusted Mr. Foster, an alcoholic, to watch his son over this weekend. Mr. Turner stops by the gathering and tells Saran that he does not know where his son is. Saran worries because the weather is about to turn bad. She sends Elijah and his male cousin Abby to look for David on the water, as it is believed Mr. Foster took him fishing on a nearby island.

When Elijah and Abby reach the riverbank, a group has gathered. There is a $25 reward for any white person finding David; the reward is only $10 for blacks. Nevertheless, Elijah negotiates a $35 reward with Mr. Turner, but must deal with the resentful attitude from the whites present. As the storm picks up, Elijah and Abby use their boat to search, and Sheriff Glover comes with them. When they encounter difficulties, the sheriff pulls a gun on them and tells them to go back. There is a stare-down, and the search party continues.

They make it to Key Island despite the worsening weather. After dropping anchor offshore, Abby stays with the boat while Elijah and Sheriff Glover go ashore. They split up, and in the driving rain Elijah finds David and the injured Mr. Foster. Elijah carries David to the boat, then comes back to help the sheriff with Foster. Everyone is happy when they return, but the sheriff takes credit for finding David and Mr. Foster. The sheriff tells Elijah and Abby they will only get half of the reward money. They are upset but leave the issue alone.

When Elijah is in town a few days later, he visits Mr. Turner, who gives him the $35 he promised. Later, two white men—Frank Petty and his uncle J. D. Petty—want to borrow the boat that Elijah and Abby own. Elijah turns them down, and the tense situation ends only when others on the beach, both black and white, come over. Elijah returns home, gives the reward money to Moses and Saran for taxes, and happily works the fields. As he labors, Sheriff Glover warns Elijah's family that some men, including Petty, are coming that night to whip Elijah. Elijah does not want to be whipped, so Saran suggests that he should leave. They give Elijah $17 of the reward money and he gets on a train headed to Chicago, where Joshua and his wife, Neela, live. Before he leaves, Goldie promises not to marry anyone else.

May 1930. Chicago, Illinois

Elijah marries Goldie in Chicago, where they have two children, Richard and Luvenia. The sixteen-year-old Luvenia does not want to move back to Curry Island and work Glory Field the way her father did. Elijah has gone back to South Carolina with Goldie and Richard while Luvenia stays in the city. Elijah spent the past three decades in Chicago working and sending money to help keep Glory Field, but he grew nostalgic for the land when he went back to South Carolina for Moses' funeral. Luvenia likes the city and wants to go to the University of Chicago using the money from her job as a live-in servant for the Deets family and from hairdressing. She also tries to get a bank loan so she can cover college expenses. Luvenia dreams of being a teacher and knows she is intelligent enough to go to college. Luvenia enlists the help of her best friend and godmother, Miss Etta, who promises to help write a letter to her father so she can stay and achieve her goals.

On Sunday, Luvenia and Miss Etta go to church together at Bethel Tabernacle. Luvenia sings in the choir and performs an impressive solo. After going home and stopping at Miss Etta's, Luvenia returns to the Deets's home that night. While cleaning, she suggests to Mrs. Deets that perhaps the Deets could help her obtain her loan for school. The bank has told Luvenia that if she has guaranteed employment, she will be approved. Mrs. Deets dismisses her desire to go to school.

The next day, Luvenia plans on asking for the help of Florenz Deets, a seventeen-year-old who attends the University of Chicago. Instead, Florenz and her friend Katie catch Luvenia up in a scheme so that Florenz can begin to drive her father's second car. Florenz promises to talk to her father about the loan for Luvenia in return. With Luvenia's help, Florenz lies to her father about Luvenia being sick and pregnant. Because of Luvenia's alleged illness, Florenz is given permission to drive Luvenia to a hospital. Instead, Florenz, Katie, and Luvenia take a joy ride around town. Luvenia is unhappy and upset about the deceit, especially about the lie added by Florenz about Luvenia being pregnant and what it implies about her. Florenz and Katie let Luvenia out when they see a boy from school, and Luvenia walks home, uncomfortable with her role in the scheme.

At home, Luvenia gets a telegram from Mr. Deets telling her that she is fired. Distraught, she goes to Miss Etta's place. Miss Etta tells her losing a job is not a bad thing and distracts Luvenia by sending her to a funeral. Thinking over her situation while helping to deal with a broken coffin, Luvenia comes to believe Florenz will tell the truth and she will get her job back. Calling Mr. Deets from Miss Etta's boyfriend's phone later that night, Luvenia learns Florenz did tell the truth, but Mr. Deets will only give Luvenia a reference, not her job back. Luvenia decides to make her living as a hairdresser, and understands that her destiny is different from, but still a part of, her family's tradition. Even her father understands, and he admits in a letter that he might have to again live in Chicago part-time to pay for the support of Glory Field. Miss Etta throws a rent party (house party in which guests give money to help pay the host's rent, or pay some other expense) for her, and Luvenia plans to use the proceeds to start her business venture.

January 1964. Johnson City, South Carolina

Although Abby is dead, his grandson Tommy Lewis is alive and living on Curry Island. A basketball star with good grades at Curry High School, Tommy impresses all those present at the All-City Tournament. Curry wins the tournament because of Tommy's play at the end of the game. After the game, Coach Smith introduces Tommy to Leonard Chase, a white man who once played at Johnson City State. Tommy and his love interest, Mandy, go to the Chase home. There, Chase asks if Tommy would like to skip his last year of high school to attend State as one of the first African Americans at the university. Tommy would have a scholarship and have a chance to make the basketball team. Chase warns him that it will be hard. At home, Tommy's mother, Virginia, is unsure about his skipping his senior year of high school for college, while his father, Robert, trusts Chase more.

The next morning, Tommy's mother wakes him and tells him that Skeeter Jackson was bitten by a snake and Tommy's father is driving him to the hospital. Skeeter is a fifteen-year-old white friend whose parents are at a revival in North Carolina. Skeeter was bitten by a rattlesnake while shooting hoops after the game. Because Robert takes him to a "white" hospital, he and Tommy must wait outside while Skeeter receives treatment. While waiting, Tommy tells his father that he thinks he can handle college, and his father sees his attendance there as progress for blacks in the community. The doctor eventually comes out and tells them that Skeeter will recover, but must stay in the hospital overnight.

At the Lewis home, Jennie Epps, a schoolmate of Tommy's, is looking at the Lewis family Bible while she, Tommy, and Mrs. Lewis talk about a racist teacher at Curry High School. Reverend McKinnon comes over with his daughter Mandy. The reverend is concerned that the Ku Klux Klan, also known as the White Citizens' Council, has announced they are having a demonstration in Johnson City on the same day as the previously announced march planned by local black citizens. Sheriff Moser wants the black march called off, but organizers refuse because they believe things will not change if they do not march. McKinnon wants Robert to be a leader of the march and the whole Lewis family in attendance because they are landowners.

That night, Tommy goes to work at the Clark's Five-and-Dime. He works on fixing a burst water pipe while listening to his manager, Miss Robbins, and fellow employee Jed Sasser lament the march, the attendance of Martin Luther King Jr., and people like him who "stir up the coloreds." Tommy points out that blacks cannot eat at the store, but Miss Robbins argues that they just cannot eat at the counter. Jed and Miss Robbins emphasize that the races should stay separate, not mix, and remain in their own place. As Tommy sweeps, he thinks about how he does not like to have to look for a water fountain labeled "colored." Later, Chase calls Tommy and tells him that the school's trustees have agreed to look at the applications of four black students, including his. Chase tells him that if he does not demonstrate or get into any trouble, the governor should approve his application.

Later that night, Jennie comes into Tommy's room and tells him that she has been offered a scholarship to attend Meharry Medical College and she will become a doctor. She also informs him that King cannot come to the march, so there will be little press coverage. Tommy realizes that he does not want to attend State but would rather march to show he does not like the way blacks are treated. He also believes that Miss Robbins is right in that people should stick with their own.

Early the next morning, Tommy rides his bike to Johnson City and watches the White Citizens' Council set up their demonstration. The sheriff gets them to tone it down, but they still make their statement in front of television crews. Tommy then watches the African Americans march from a distance, and observes other people throwing things at them. Jennie finds him after the march and yells at him for not taking part. He allows her to ride on the back of his bike back to his house where there is a social gathering. There, Skeeter has been brought after being beaten badly by some whites for participating in the black march. Later, Tommy wonders what he would have done in Skeeter's place.

The next morning, Tommy attends Sheriff Moser's news conference instead of going to school. There, the sheriff announces a meeting between blacks, business leaders, and White Citizens' Council leaders. Tommy brings the shackles and chains that his ancestor, Muhammad, wore when brought from Africa. When the sheriff says that there were no injuries as a result of yesterday's march, Tommy shackles himself to the sheriff with the chains. He is sent to jail for the day. Tommy is later released and his family and friends praise his actions.

August 1994. Harlem, New York

Malcolm Lewis, the fifteen-year-old grandson of Richard Lewis and great-grandson of Elijah and Goldie Lewis, is a young, talented musician living in New York City with his parents. His dream about playing with his band, String Theory, is interrupted by a call from his great-aunt Luvenia, who has become a successful businesswoman selling cosmetics and beauty supplies for African Americans and Hispanics. His great-aunt is coming over shortly, as is Jenn Che Po, who is trying out for the band. Malcolm's parents and sister have already gone to Curry Island for a family reunion, but Malcolm has stayed behind for now to work for Luvenia's cosmetics factory loading trucks.

Jenn shows up first, then Luvenia, who is patient while Malcolm plays a String Theory song for Jenn. When Malcolm plays it a second time, Jenn starts playing along with her cello. After Jenn leaves, Luvenia gives Malcolm money for two plane tickets to South Carolina—one for Malcolm, and one for his cousin Shep—so that they can attend the family reunion. Luvenia wants Malcolm to find Shep, who she believes has a drinking problem. However, Malcolm knows that he is using crack cocaine. Luvenia says they must show up by Monday night for the reunion.

Malcolm first looks in the last place he saw Shep, a park in Harlem. Not finding Shep there, Malcolm reflects on the reunion, which will be the last that focuses on Glory Field as a farm, since the land will soon be turned into a resort. A child nicknamed Mr. Brooks gives Malcolm a tip on where he can find Shep: he is selling tapes in front of the Apollo Theater. Malcolm finds Shep there, but Shep is not interested in going to the reunion. Shep finally agrees, but wants his half of the money and says he will meet Malcolm

at the airport. Malcolm believes he will use the cash for drugs, but after Shep shows him where he is staying—the East Harlem Restoration Center, a homeless shelter—and agrees to go with him the next day, Malcolm gives him the money.

The next morning, Jenn calls to tell him that she wants to be in the band and Malcolm agrees. As he packs for the trip, he reflects on how his aunt's company and some Johnson City Lewises are putting up money to turn the Lewis land on Curry Island into a resort. Later, Malcolm learns that his great-aunt made reservations for them to take a plane at 2:30 PM out of LaGuardia Airport. When he goes to pick up Shep at the shelter, Shep says his part of the money has been stolen and he cannot go. Malcolm convinces him that they can take a bus.

Shep gets sick on the bus, and the driver leaves them behind after a stop in Virginia. A waitress at the diner helps them get a ride with a trucker. Malcolm and Shep both find the journey difficult and hate the feeling of being trapped. During the ride, Shep admits to using the ticket money for crack. The trucker drops them outside Johnson City and the pair feel better in fresh air. They make it to the city, then ride another bus to Curry Island. At the main house, Jennie—who married Tommy and had a daughter with him before he died fighting in Vietnam—gets them settled.

In the morning, Malcolm learns that everyone will be helping to harvest the last sweet potato crop on the Lewis land. He is working with Tommy's father, who now calls himself Planter. They harvest sweet potatoes in Glory Field for several back-breaking days. Planter tells Tommy stories, including how he bought back the slave chains Tommy used at the press conference from a sheriff's department auction for $209. On the third day, Shep gets sick and Jennie, who is a doctor, helps take care of him. The day after they finish the harvest, Luvenia and a representative of the bank tell the family that the resort will be organized into shares that the family will hold.

Epilogue

Malcolm and String Theory are playing their first major concert at Brown University. Jenn adds a new dimension to the group, although the group members are unsure of their future because they are going to different colleges. During the gig, Malcolm remembers Planter, who recently died. Malcolm attended his funeral in Curry. After his death, the shackles were sent to

Malcolm as Planter arranged. Malcolm plays his music with Planter in his heart.

CHARACTERS

Aiken
In the 1964 segment, Aiken is a player for Delaney High School, against whom Tommy Lewis plays hard.

Annie
Annie is Lizzy's cousin in the 1864 segment of the novel. She does not understand why Joshua and Lem ran away.

Bob Archer
At the end of the 1964 segment, Bob Archer drives Tommy home after he spends the night in jail, and then helps guard the Lewis home with a shotgun.

Virginia Bates
The wife of Robert Smalls Lewis and the mother of Tommy Lewis, Virginia appears in the 1964 segment. Initially she does not appreciate the offer Tommy receives to help integrate Johnson City State, but ultimately she supports her son in all that he does.

Muhammad Bilal
When Muhammad Bilal is eleven years old and living in Africa, he is captured by slave traders, put on a slave ship, and sent to America. He does not know if his parents, Odebe and Saran, have knowledge about what happened to him. Although the trip is difficult, he survives and becomes a slave on the Live Oaks plantation in South Carolina. The property of the Lewis family, he helps to build the plantation. Muhammad becomes the founder of his own dynasty of African American Lewises. Dolly is his granddaughter. He lives to the age of 110.

Bill
Bill is a slave on the Live Oaks plantation in the 1864 segment.

Bobby Joe
In the 1964 segment, Tommy shares a jail cell with Bobby Joe. The latter is given a gun by a deputy and implies that he might use it on Tommy.

Mother Bradley
Mother Bradley is the wife of Reverend Bradley in the 1930 segment.

Reverend Bradley
In the 1930 segment, Reverend Bradley is the minister of Bethel Tabernacle, the church Luvenia attends.

Mr. Brooks
In the 1994 segment, Mr. Brooks is the child who tells Malcolm where he can find Shep.

Deacon Brown
In the 1930 segment, Deacon Brown serves at Free Will Baptist Church and helps with Sister Stovall's funeral.

Dr. Calloway
In the 1964 segment, Dr. Calloway is an African American doctor who treats Skeeter Jackson after he is beaten up.

James Caro
James Caro is the head of the White Citizens' Council in the 1964 segment.

Leonard Chase
In the 1964 segment, Leonard Chase is a white man and former basketball star at Johnson City State. He is now married to Sally and is successful in the business operated by his wife's family. Leonard understands that integration is coming, and he believes Tommy would be an ideal candidate to integrate his alma mater. Leonard offers Tommy a full scholarship and a chance to play for the basketball team, as long as Tommy stays out of trouble and away from civil rights marches. When Tommy shackles himself to the sheriff, Leonard withdraws his offer.

Sally Chase
Sally Chase is the gossip-loving wife of Leonard Chase in the 1964 segment.

Norman Chesterfield
In the 1930 segment, Norman Chesterfield is known for collecting numbers (a form of lottery gambling). When he shows up at Bethel Tabernacle he sticks out from the rest of the congregation.

Sister Clinton
The light-skinned, plump Sister Clinton appears in the 1900 segment at the gathering following the consecration of the burial ground. She annoys Saran, but tells her that she saw David Turner with Mr. Foster.

Daoud

In the 1994 segment, Daoud is a member of Malcolm's band, String Theory.

Florenz Deets

Florenz Deets is the seventeen-year-old daughter of Mr. and Mrs. Deets in the 1930 segment. She attends the University of Chicago and has what Luvenia describes as "a real vitality, a kind of bubbly air" about her. Florenz contributes to Luvenia's losing her job with the Deets family by having her lie about being ill and pregnant, so that Florenz can drive her father's old car.

Mr. John Deets

Mr. Deets is Luvenia's employer in the 1930 segment. Luvenia works as a live-in servant for his family. Mr. Deets owns several delicatessens in the Chicago area. Because he values honesty in his employees, he fires Luvenia when she participates in Florenz's scheme to gain regular access to her father's second car. Mr. Deets refuses to give Luvenia her job back—a decision that compels Luvenia to start her own business.

Mrs. Deets

Mrs. Deets is Luvenia's employer in the 1930 segment. Luvenia works as a live-in servant for the family. Luvenia asks Mrs. Deets to help her obtain a loan to attend the University of Chicago by guaranteeing her employment, but Mrs. Deets dismisses her ambitions by asking, "And why ever would you be interested in college?"

Reverend Dexter

Also known as Elder Dexter, he is the minister at the church the Lewis family attends in the 1900 segment.

Grandma Dolly

The granddaughter of Muhammad Bilal, the mother of Joshua and Moses, and grandmother of Lem, Richard, and Yero, she is a slave on the Live Oaks plantation in 1864. She offers guidance and advice—not always wanted—to those around her.

Jennie Epps

In the 1964 segment, teenager Jennie Epps is a friend of the Lewis family. She is ambitious and already has a scholarship offer to attend Meharry Medical College, where she can become a doctor. Jennie is interested in Tommy, but he finds her too aggressive. Nevertheless, Jennie ends up marrying

Tommy and having their daughter, Linda, as well as becoming a doctor. Jennie also briefly appears in the 1994 segment at the Lewis family reunion at Curry Island.

Miss Etta

In the 1930 segment, Miss Etta is a friend and godmother of Luvenia Lewis, Elijah, and Goldie. Miss Etta has a romantic interest in Mr. Harrison. She first befriended Elijah and Goldie when they moved to Chicago. When Elijah, Goldie, and Richard return to Curry Island and Glory Field, Miss Etta keeps an eye on Luvenia. Miss Etta hires Luvenia to do her hair, goes to church with her, supports her through the job-loss crisis, and throws a rent party for her, which allows Luvenia to start her own business.

Mr. Foster

Mr. Foster runs the telegraph office in Johnson City and is a known alcoholic. Over the weekend depicted in the 1900 segment, he takes care of David Turner, a blind white boy. When he takes him fishing on his boat, he gets caught on Key Island with a broken leg. Foster is rescued by Sheriff Glover and Elijah Lewis, but dies shortly thereafter.

Neela Foster

Neela is the wife of Joshua, whom she married on the sly because she was a slave on the Foster plantation. After Joshua runs away and the war ends, he and Neela live in Chicago.

George

In the 1994 segment, George is a member of Malcolm's band, String Theory. He plays drums.

Sheriff Glover

In the 1900 segment, Sheriff Glover is the law-enforcement official in Johnson City and Curry Island. He accompanies Elijah and Abby Lewis when they rescue David Turner and Mr. Foster. Glover takes credit for finding David, although Elijah really made the discovery, and says that Elijah will only get half of the $35 reward Hamlin Turner promised.

Sister Graham

Sister Graham attends Bethel Tabernacle in the 1930 segment.

Dr. Grier

In the 1964 segment, Dr. Grier is a white doctor who helps treat Skeeter Jackson after he is beaten.

Mary Hardin

In the 1900 segment, Mary is Abby's girlfriend. They later marry and have a son, Robert Smalls Lewis. Her grandson is Tommy Lewis, the focal character of the 1964 segment. Mary briefly appears in the 1964 segment eating a meal with her son's family.

Mr. Harrison

In the 1930 segment, Mr. Harrison is Miss Etta's love interest.

Bernie Hatfield

In the 1994 segment, Bernie is the truck driver who gives Malcolm and Shep a ride from Virginia to the outskirts of Johnson City.

Mister Joe Haynes

In the 1864 segment, Mister Joe Haynes is the overseer at Live Oaks plantation, and he is not afraid to use force when needed to keep slaves in line. When he finds Lizzy cleaning up Lem at the tree, for example, he whips Lizzy until her clothes are shredded.

Henry

Henry is a participant in the gathering after the burial ground is consecrated in the 1900 segment.

Hepplewhite

In the 1964 segment, Hepplewhite is a big player on the Delaney High basketball team.

Katie Hornung

In the 1930 segment, Katie Hornung is Florenz Deets's friend from the University of Chicago. While she helps with Florenz's car scheme, she feels bad when Luvenia loses her job with the Deets because of it. Katie finds another job for Luvenia with a family in Oak Park, but Luvenia turns it down to found her own business.

Grady Lee Jackson

In the 1964 segment, Grady is an oysterman and the father of Skeeter. He is a quiet man but does not like African Americans.

Mrs. Jackson

In the 1964 segment, Mrs. Jackson is the mother of Skeeter Jackson.

Skeeter Jackson

A fifteen-year-old white friend of Tommy Lewis, Skeeter gets bitten by a rattlesnake early in the 1964 segment. Skeeter also participates in the march by blacks in Johnson City later in the segment. For his participation, Skeeter is beaten up by whites. It is implied that he might lose an eye, but he has no regrets.

Miss Julia

Miss Julia is the seventeen-year-old daughter of Old Master Lewis. She has Lizzy come to the main house during the 1864 segment and tries to get information on Joshua and Lem's whereabouts and on what is being said in the slave quarters.

Laurel

In the 1930 segment, Laurel attends Bethel Tabernacle and sings in the church choir.

Abby Lewis

Abby Lewis is the son of Yero Lewis and Lois Quincy, and the cousin of Elijah Lewis. In the 1900 segment, he and Elijah own a boat (the *Pele Queen*), and he believes they should be fishermen. Abby helps man their boat when Elijah and the sheriff find and save David Turner and Mr. Foster. Abby later marries Mary Hardin and has a son, Robert Smalls Lewis, also known as Planter. Abby's grandson Tommy Lewis is the primary character in the 1964 segment.

Charles Lewis

In the 1994 segment, Charles Lewis is the son of Richard Lewis (featured in the 1930 segment) and his wife Harriet Sheppard. He is also the brother of Fletcher Lewis. He is married to Celia Owens and the father of Malcolm Lewis. Charles attends the Lewis family reunion with his wife. He is happy when his son arrives.

Elijah Lewis

Elijah Lewis is the son of Richard Lewis and Lizzy; in addition he is the cousin of Abby Lewis. As a fifteen-year-old in the 1900 segment, he helps work the land of Glory Field and owns a boat with his cousin. His grandmother, Saran, relies on him to tend to the consecrated burial ground behind the church on a weekly basis and to find David Turner when he is lost. Elijah is very responsible, reliable, and resourceful. When he learns the family needs to raise money to pay taxes on their land, he convinces Hamlin Turner to pay a $35 reward to locate David, then risks his life in a storm and saves him. Unfortunately, Elijah is forced to leave Curry when two white men, the Pettys, threaten him with violence after he refuses to lend them his boat. Elijah moves to Chicago, where he brings Goldie and marries her. They have two children, Richard and Luvenia. Although he spends much of his adult life in Chicago, he returns to Glory Field and tries to work the land again in 1930.

Fletcher Lewis

In the 1994 segment, Fletcher Lewis is the son of Richard Lewis (from the 1930 segment) and his wife Harriet Sheppard. He is also the brother of Charles Lewis and the father of Sheppard G. Lewis.

Joshua Lewis

The son of Dolly and brother of Moses, Joshua Lewis runs away from Live Oaks in the 1864 segment of *Glory Field* because he believes that the Foster family is going to sell his wife, Neela. Joshua runs away with his nephew Lem and, later, with Lizzy. Joshua joins the Union Army and later makes his home in Chicago with Neela.

Lem Lewis

Lem is son of Moses and Saran and the brother of Richard and Yero. In the 1864 segment, he runs away from the plantation with his uncle Joshua. He is captured by Mister Joe Haynes and tied to a tree for hours so that he will give up information on Joshua's location. After escaping Haynes, Lem joins the Union Army and he dies in combat.

Luvenia Lewis

Introduced in the 1930 segment, Luvenia Lewis is the daughter of Elijah Lewis and Goldie Paige. In 1930, she is sixteen years old and living in Chicago. She has a job working as a live-in servant for the Deets family and also is a hairdresser on the side for Miss Etta and other women. Ambitious, Luvenia wants to attend the University of Chicago but cannot raise the funds or get a loan. A scheme of Florenz Deets results in Luvenia losing her job with the Deets. Luvenia seizes the opportunity to become an entrepreneur, first with a hair salon and later as the owner of a large cosmetics company targeting African Americans and Hispanics. By the 1994 segment, Luvenia is the matriarch of the Lewis family and helps organize turning the family land into a resort.

Malcolm Lewis

Malcolm Lewis is the primary character in the 1994 segment, the son of Charles Lewis and Celia Owens. He is a good student and musician who plays saxophone and flute in his band, String Theory, to which he adds Jenn Che Po. His great-aunt Luvenia Lewis entrusts him to get himself and his cousin Shep to the Lewis family reunion. After finding Shep and convincing him to go, Malcolm goes through a difficult yet character-building journey to reach Curry Island. Once there, he helps bring in the last harvest on Glory Field, mentored by Planter (Robert Smalls Lewis). While doing the back-breaking work, Malcolm learns much about his family and grows close to Planter. After the reunion, Malcolm's band becomes successful, which makes him question his college plans. When Planter dies, he sends Malcolm the slave chains that were placed on Muhammad when he was brought to America.

Moses Lewis

The leader of the slaves in the 1864 segment of *Glory Field*, he is the brother of Joshua, husband of Saran, and father of Lem, Richard, and Yero. When Lem is caught as a runaway, he asks Mister Joe Haynes to not hurt him much. By the 1900 segment, Moses is the patriarch of the African American Lewis family of former slaves. He is the moral compass of the family and community, and takes the lead on such acts as consecrating the burial ground behind the church.

Old Master Lewis

Old Master Lewis, also known as Manigault Lewis, is the owner of the Live Oaks plantation in the 1864 section.

Richard Lewis

In the 1864 and 1900 segments, Richard Lewis is the son of Moses Lewis and Saran, the brother of Lem and Yero Lewis, and the father of Elijah Lewis. He is married to Lizzy and helps support the family in South Carolina by working in pulp factories in Georgia. In the 1930 segment, Richard Lewis is the son of Elijah Lewis and Goldie Paige, as well as the elder brother of Luvenia Lewis. Unlike his sister, he is passive and goes along with the idea of returning to Curry Island with his parents.

Robert Smalls Lewis

The son of Abby Lewis and Mary Hardin, Robert Smalls Lewis is also known as Planter (which was the name of a boat stolen by a slave, Robert

Smalls, from the Confederate Army and given to the Union Army during the American Civil War). He marries Virginia Bates and has a son, Tommy, who is the main character of the 1964 segment. Robert is a leader in the black community and is aware of the institutionalized racism in the area. Still, he helps out others as needed. He drives Skeeter Jackson to the white hospital after he is bitten by a snake, for example. Unlike his wife, Robert believes that Tommy should take Chase's scholarship offer and integrate Johnson City State. Later, in the 1994 segment, Robert mentors Malcolm during the last Lewis family harvest on Curry Island. He arranges for Malcolm to receive, after his own death, the slave chains that had shackled Muhammad and which Tommy used in his act of civil disobedience.

Sheppard G. Lewis

In the 1994 segment, Sheppard G. Lewis, commonly known as Shep, is a sixteen-year-old who is living in a Harlem homeless shelter and has an addiction to crack cocaine. He tries to get out of going to the Lewis family reunion, despite Malcolm's best efforts. After Malcolm gives him money for his plane ticket, Shep spends it on drugs and then tells Malcolm the cash has been stolen. Despite his problems, he agrees to take a bus with Malcolm to Curry Island. Because he gets sick on the bus, the driver leaves the cousins behind and they are forced to take a ride in the back of a truck driver's rig. Shep makes it through the journey with the help of Malcolm. Shep gets sick again—this time taking in the last harvest. But Jennie Lewis helps him with his problems.

Thomas Lewis

Known as Tommy, Thomas Lewis is the son of Robert Smalls Lewis and Virginia Bates and the grandson of Abby Lewis and Mary Hardin. In the 1964 segment, Tommy is the primary character, a star basketball player and a good student at Curry High School in Curry Island. Because of his success, Leonard Chase believes Tommy will be an ideal candidate to help integrate Johnson City State. Tommy is unsure if he wants to be among the first black students at the college and miss his senior year of high school, but he knows that he does not like Jim Crow laws that force him to use only "colored" drinking fountains. Tommy decides to take the scholarship and go to Johnson City State, and follows Chase's

admonishment to stay out of the march or any other trouble. But ultimately he believes he must stand up for what he comes to believe about civil rights and uses Muhammad's slave chains to shackle himself to Sheriff Moser. Tommy spends the night in jail and loses his chance to attend Johnson City State. Although Tommy is interested in Mandy McKinnon in the 1964 segment, he eventually marries Jennie Epps, with whom he has a daughter, Linda. Tommy dies before his daughter is born, while serving in Vietnam.

Yero Lewis

The son of Moses and Saran and brother of Lem and Richard, Yero is a slave on the Live Oaks plantation in the 1864 segment. Called "fun," Yero "was also a little touched in the head."

Young Master Lewis

Young Master Lewis, also known as Manigault Lewis, is the son of Old Master Lewis, the owner of the Live Oaks plantation, and his wife, Miss Ruth. He is also the brother of Miss Julia. Appearing in the 1864 segment, he is a soldier in the Confederate Army and dies in the American Civil War.

Aunt Lillian

In the 1964 segment, Aunt Lillian visits her nephew Skeeter Jackson in the hospital after he is bitten by a snake.

Lizzy

In the 1864 segment, thirteen-year-old Lizzy is the primary protagonist. She and her mother had been sold to Old Master Lewis when she was young, and her mother died six years ago. She is the informally adopted daughter of Moses and Saran. Because she is a favorite of Miss Julia, Miss Julia tries to use that relationship to find out where Joshua and Lem have run away by promising her a fun life in Johnson City. Instead, Lizzy follows her feelings for Lem and visits him at the tree, then runs away with Joshua and Lem. Like them, she goes North with Union troops. Lizzy eventually marries Lem's brother Richard, gives birth to Elijah, and later lives in Georgia where her husband has found work.

Sister Lois

Sister Lois is a participant in the gathering after the burial ground is consecrated in the 1900 segment.

Jimmy Manigault

In the 1964 segment, Jimmy plays on the Curry High basketball team.

Miss Mary

See Mary Hardin

Sister Maslan

In the 1930 segment, Sister Maslan attends Bethel Tabernacle and, at fifty-seven, is the oldest singer in the choir.

Mandy McKinnon

In the 1964 segment, Mandy is the daughter of Reverend McKinnon and is the love interest of the teenaged Tommy Lewis.

Reverend McKinnon

In the 1964 segment, Reverend McKinnon is the father of Mandy, a community leader, and the organizer of an African American march in Johnson City.

Sheriff Moser

In the 1964 segment, Sheriff Moser is the primary law enforcement official in Johnson City. At a press conference following demonstrations by both the White Citizens' Council and African Americans, the sheriff tries to diffuse racial tensions, hoping to limit such activities in the future. Instead, Tommy uses Muhammad's slave chains to shackle himself to Sheriff Moser.

Virgil Moser

In the 1964 segment, Virgil works as a fruit seller and gives Tommy a peach on credit.

Mister Oakes

Mister Oakes is the slave trader mentioned as a possible candidate to buy Lem in the 1864 segment.

Celia Owens

In the 1994 segment, Celia is married to Charles Lewis and is the mother of Malcolm. She is very supportive of her son and his musical efforts.

Goldie Paige

In the 1900 segment, Goldie Paige is the love interest of Elijah. She is younger than Elijah, and she promises not to marry anyone else when he is forced to leave Curry Island at the end of the segment. Later, Goldie goes to Chicago to marry him. There she gives birth to Richard and Luvenia.

Tom Pawley

In the 1930 segment, Tom Pawley is a student at the University of Chicago. Florenz and Katie drop off Luvenia when they see Tom and offer him a ride.

Mr. Parrish

Mr. Parrish lives in Luvenia's building in the 1930 segment. He gives her the telegram in which she learns that she has been fired from her job with the Deets.

Frank Petty

A white man in the 1900 segment. Frank does not like Elijah and Abby's attitude about wanting more reward money for finding David Turner. He later demands to borrow their boat and when refused by Elijah, threatens during a drinking binge to physically harm him. Because of the threats made by Frank and his uncle J. D. Petty, Elijah leaves town and moves to Chicago.

J. D. Petty

The uncle of Frank Petty in the 1900 segment. He is as racist as his nephew and is condescending when Elijah refuses to lend him his boat.

Planter

See Robert Smalls Lewis

Jenn Che Po

In the 1994 segment, Jenn Che Po tries out for Malcolm's band, String Theory. She plays amplified cello and adds a new dimension to the band. Malcolm has a romantic interest in Jenn.

Precious

Precious is the brown-and-white Pekingese lapdog owned by the Deets in the 1930 segment.

Miss Robbins

In the 1964 segment, Miss Robbins is the manager of Clark's Five-and-Dime, where Tommy works. Miss Robbins believes that races should be socially separate and decries any move toward integration.

Saran

The wife of Moses Lewis and mother of Lem, Richard, and Yero, Saran is a slave on the Live Oaks plantation. Although white people call her Sara before the slaves are freed, she prefers her real name. She is greatly troubled by Lem and Joshua running away, but gives Lizzy advice on how to survive. After she gains her freedom, she helps maintain the land she and her husband inherited, which they call Glory Field. Although she struggles to find enough money to pay taxes, she cares more about finding David Turner, the young, blind white boy she cares for in the 1900 segment. (Saran had been the nanny of David's father, Hamlin.) Her grandson Elijah finds the boy with the help of another grandson, Abby. Elijah gives Saran the money for taxes from the reward he earns, but she returns him half to leave when he is threatened with violence by white men in town. Such incidents trouble her, but she relies on her faith.

Jed Sasser

In the 1964 segment, Jed Sasser is an employee at Clark's Five-and-Dime, where Tommy works. Jed believes that races should be socially separate and that black civil rights leaders are not what they seem. He does not believe in blacks marching or moving toward integration.

Deepak Singh

In the 1994 segment, Deepak is a member of Malcolm's band, String Theory. He plays sitar.

Coach Smith

Coach Smith coaches the Curry High School basketball team in the 1964 segment.

Macon Smith

A black fisherman in the area around Curry Island, Smith declines to use his boat in the storm for the $10 reward to find David Turner.

Johnnie Mae Stokes

In the 1930 segment, Johnnie Mae Stokes is a member of the Bethel Tabernacle and sings in the church choir.

Sister Stovall

A deceased acquaintance of Miss Etta. Luvenia goes to her funeral in the 1930 segment. Sister Stovall's casket is broken.

Sukey

Sukey is the mule Elijah uses to work the land in the 1900 segment.

David Turner

David Turner is the young blind son of Hamlin Turner and his deceased wife. In the 1900 segment, Saran has a job taking care of him. One

weekend that she has off, David is cared for by Mr. Foster, who gets stranded with him on a small island during a major storm. He is rescued by Elijah Lewis and others.

Hamlin Turner

Hamlin Turner is the father of David Turner. Prosperous because he inherited a hotel in Wraggstown, he employs Saran, who had once been his nanny, to take care of his son. Hamlin is distraught when Mr. Foster, the weekend care-giver he hired, goes missing with his son. Hamlin agrees to pay Elijah and Abby Lewis $35 to find his son. Although Sheriff Glover tries to undermine them, Hamlin pays Elijah the full amount.

Mary Turner

In the 1930 segment, Mary Turner attends Bethel Tabernacle and sings in the church choir.

Wilson

In the 1964 segment, Wilson plays center on the Curry High School basketball team.

THEMES

The Importance of Family and Land

One overriding theme of the saga that is *The Glory Field* is the value of kinship and relations. Myers expresses this idea by emphasizing the importance of the relationships between the generations of the Lewis family and their holding onto the land they own in Curry Island, South Carolina. Before each section of the novel, Myers presents a genealogical tree of where the characters in this segment fit in the Lewis family. These trees both provide a guide to the readers about the characters in this part of the story and emphasize a link between the generations of the Lewis family.

The African American Lewis family began with Muhammad Bilal, who was brought from Africa as a slave as a young child. He was one of the first slaves bought by the white Lewis family to work Live Oaks, which became a viable plantation. Most of Muhammad's descendants remained in slavery working the land on Live Oaks until they were freed after the American Civil War ended. Then, Moses Lewis and his children gained part of the plantation for their own, and named it Glory Field. In the 1900 segment, Myers emphasizes the lengths to which

TOPICS FOR FURTHER STUDY

- Read both *The Glory Field* and another book by Myers, *Harlem Summer* (2007). The latter focuses on a young boy, Mark Purvis, who is in a jazz band during the Harlem Renaissance of the 1920s. In an essay, compare and contrast Mark with Malcolm in the 1994 segment of *The Glory Field*. How do their experiences as musicians and residents of Harlem differ? How much do they have in common? Do you think that Mark is more like Malcolm or Luvenia from the 1930 segment of *The Glory Field*?

- Research the history of Jim Crow laws in the United States, using both books and the Internet. Focus on finding out what Jim Crow laws were, how and where they regulated the lives of African Americans, and how the civil rights movement brought them to an end. For your class, create a presentation that includes your findings. Use examples from *The Glory Field* to illustrate your findings as well.

- In a small group, watch part or all of the 1977 television miniseries adaptation of Alex Haley's nonfiction novel, *Roots: The Saga of an American Family* (1976), then discuss how *Roots* compares with *The Glory Field*. How are the characters and their struggles alike or different? Have each member of the group summarize a part of your conclusions on an aspect of both *Roots* and *The Glory Field* for the class.

- In *The Glory Field*, Myers includes a genealogical tree of the Lewis family that stretches from Muhammad Bilal to Malcolm Lewis. Create a genealogical tree of your family as far back as you can find, perhaps using genealogical resources on the Internet to help. Then, pick an ancestor and research the time and place in which he or she lived. Write a short story based on your findings and what knowledge you can gain about this person.

---

members of the Lewis family went to keep that land. Over the years, they bought more of the land around Glory Field and kept growing sweet potatoes until 1994, when the Lewis clan, led by Luvenia Lewis, turned the property into a resort owned by the family. Although the segments in 1930, 1964, and 1994 are removed from Glory Field itself, the Lewis' connection to that piece of land is continually emphasized. The field is the physical reminder of the family and how these various connected family members share a common, loving kinship.

Slavery and Racism

Much of *The Glory Field* explores ideas about race relations, beginning with slavery. Myers also looks at racial conflicts in various post-slavery generations, and at acts of racism, subjugation, oppression, and repression. The first manifestation of racism is young Muhammad's journey in shackles

after he is forcibly removed from Africa and taken on a ship to America, where he is sold to the Lewis family. He is treated without dignity in the overcrowded quarters; there is little food or water.

In the 1864 segment, the slaves on the Lewis plantation are forced to labor even on Sunday, are prohibited from marrying whomever they want, as in the case of Joshua and Neela, and face whippings or worse for running away. Lem is beaten because he ran away, and so is Lizzy, just for bringing water to Lem after he is tied to a tree so that he will reveal Joshua's whereabouts. Most of the whites in that segment of *The Glory Field* do not see blacks as people like themselves, but treat them as property.

This situation does not improve much in the 1900 and 1964 segments, which are also set in Curry. In 1900, the Lewis family may own Glory Field, but the bank in Johnson City will not give them a loan because of their race. When the search party is formed to find blind David Turner and Mr. Foster, his alcoholic caregiver for the weekend, Mr. Turner initially offers $25 to whites but only $10 to blacks to find his son. Elijah negotiates a better deal and eventually gets his money, Sheriff Glover takes credit for finding David although it was Elijah who made the discovery. Elijah is forced to leave town at the end of the 1900 segment because he refuses to lend the boat that he and Abby own to two white men, the Pettys. Elijah goes to Chicago rather than be whipped by the Pettys.

While the 1964 segment features a civil rights march, Tommy and others must deal with the lingering effects of such Jim Crow restrictions as separate drinking fountains, hospitals, and doctors for blacks and whites. Although Leonard Chase wants Tommy, a model student, athlete, and citizen, to integrate Johnson City State, Chase says, "I'm not sure if integration is good on a grade school level. Nothing to do with race, either." Tommy's manager and coworker at Clark's Five-and-Dime are more virulent in their belief that the races should be separated and blacks kept in their place. Tommy is unsure if he wants to go to Johnson City State because he does believe that blacks and whites should sometimes stick with their own, but he is inspired to create his own act of civil disobedience after observing the Ku Klux Klan demonstration, the African American march, and his white friend Skeeter's beating after showing his support for the cause.

Although the 1930 and 1994 segments are set in big cities—Chicago and New York City, respectively—the members of the Lewis family experience racism and issues related to race relations there. In 1930, Luvenia finds her employer, Mrs. Deets, unwilling to help her go to college. Luvenia becomes more distressed when Florenz Deets goes beyond telling her father that Luvenia is sick so she can drive her father's second car around; Florenz adds that Luvenia is pregnant, a lie that appalls and hurts the honorable Luvenia. In 1994, race relations are less overtly tense, but Malcolm and Shep do get left behind by the bus driver in Virginia in part because of their race. As Myers writes, "They were young and black, and Shep had thrown up on the bus." When they make it to outside Johnson City, no one will stop to give them a ride to the nearest phone or into town. No matter what the era or intensity of the

racism, however, the Lewis family perseveres and keeps moving forward.

Captivity vs. Freedom

Another theme central to *The Glory Field* are the ideas of captivity versus freedom. In the first few segments of the novel, this tension can be seen in race and social-related situations of the characters. Muhammad is literally a captive stuck in a small space with many other Africans shackled on a slave ship. When he arrives in America, he is a slave, as are several generations of his descendants. Joshua, Lem, and Lizzy in the 1864 segment escape slavery and the restrictions that go along with it by serving the Union Army. In 1900, Elijah is a free man and part of a land-owning family, but racial restrictions limit his freedom. To escape a whipping by white men—an act of control in itself—he goes to Chicago where he can be more free.

Elijah's daughter Luvenia demonstrates that even in the North African Americans can be trapped because of their race. Whites do not believe she can become educated or be more than a servant, but she finds freedom by starting her own business. Back in South Carolina in 1964, Tommy experiences a type of captivity because of his race. He must act in an uncontroversial way to get his scholarship; he is not allowed to eat at the lunch counter of the store in which he works. Tommy uses the idea of being held captive in his act of civil disobedience when he uses Muhammad's shackles on himself and the white sheriff. For that action, Tommy is put in jail and the sheriff tries to intimidate him by having a fellow prisoner hold a gun on him.

By 1994, Malcolm does not experience being trapped until he and his cousin have no choice but to ride in the back of a truck driver's trailer to Johnson City. Both Malcolm and Shep are challenged by the heat and lack of fresh air, but both feel free they can breathe more easily when they are dropped off outside the city. Shep is the final example of what the struggle between captivity and freedom has come to mean. As a drug addict with a crack cocaine problem, he is trapped by his drug use and its effect on his life, but finds freedom with Malcolm's help on the trip and with his family's help in South Carolina. While Shep's captivity is his own choice, it is also his choice to get up and choose freedom.

Slaves being transported on a slave ship (*Rischgitz | Hulton Archive | Getty Images*)

STYLE

Saga

As a novel, *The Glory Field* can be considered a saga. While the term *saga* originally referred to twelfth- to fourteenth-century stories about the families who originally populated Iceland as well as their descendants, the term has come to include other multigenerational narratives. *The Glory Field* is a saga because the novel tells the story of the Lewis family from its founding member, a slave from Africa named Muhammad Bilal, who arrives in what would become the United States in 1753, through multiple generations into the late twentieth century. *The Glory Field* uses the sweeping nature of the saga to emphasize the connectedness between the generations and their effect on the world around them.

Episodic Structure

Myers uses an episodic structure to tell the story of the saga that is *The Glory Field*. An episode is

an incident that forms part of the story. In the case of this novel, the episodes are each of the dated segments. Each of these segments is a self-contained narrative, which is one kind of episode. The other kind of episode contains events that depend on a larger context for their sense and importance. Myers uses this kind of episode as well, as each segment adds to the story of the Lewis family from generation to generation.

Motif

A motif is a theme, character type, image, metaphor, or other element that recurs throughout a literary work. In *The Glory Field*, chain, or shackles, are a motif that run through the novel. These are literal chains—the chains that bind Muhammad on his terrible journey in the slave ship. Each time the reader encounters the chains, the context is different and the chains have a differing meaning. In the prologue, the chains that bind Muhammad are both a painful reality and a potent symbol of the state of bondage in which Muhammad lives.

In the 1900 section, Moses shows Elijah the chains just as Elijah is preparing to leave town. In this case, Moses shows Elijah the chains to remind him "where we come from," and to give him the strength to find a new life for himself. In the 1964 section of the book, the very same chains become a symbol of protest and a demand for equal rights when Tommy uses them to chain himself to the sheriff in an act of civil disobedience. In the 1994 section, the same chains appear again, reclaimed by Planter at an auction held by the sheriff. When Planter dies, Malcolm inherits the chains that had been passed down for generations through his family. This time, the chains are a symbol of everything his family has gone through, suffered, and overcome in the past, something for him to respect and be proud of. He thinks about putting on the chains, but does not, because the experience of being chained "was't his to experience, only his to know about, to imagine how hard it had been."

Prologue

The prologue is the introductory section of a literary work. In *The Glory Field*, the segment "July 1753. Off the Coast of Sierra Leone, West Africa" acts as a prologue. Prologues usually contain information that establishes the situation of the characters. They also can present information about the setting, time period, or action. The prologue of *The Glory Field* shows how the Lewis family was founded by Muhammad Bilal. The prologue also hints at some of the major themes of the novel, including racism, captivity versus freedom, and the importance of family.

HISTORICAL CONTEXT

African Americans in Southern Society

While Africans had been brought to South Carolina by the early sixteenth century, it was not until the mid-eighteenth century that most American Colonies voted to allow slavery. Southern states, including South Carolina, continued to import thousands of men, women, and children taken from Africa each year throughout the eighteenth century. The import of slaves was banned in the United States in 1808, but the slave population continued to grow through natural increase.

In the South, a plantation economy dominated from the time the colonies were settled until the American Civil War and led to the reliance on slaves. Many landowners controlled large tracts of land, often between two thousand and ten thousand acres, and grew such crops as tobacco, cotton, rice, and sweet potatoes. To make a profit off their farming activities, plantation owners needed many workers who did not cost much.

Slaves fit the bill—often even for smaller farmers in the South—and plantations used slaves to work the land, take care of farm animals, clean and maintain the home, and perform everyday household and upkeep duties. Slaves received no compensation for their work except food, clothing, and shelter. Their ability to marry was limited, and children could be sold away from their parents by their owners. Some slaves tried to escape to the North and freedom, but many failed to make it, and were pursued by their owners and other white men who worked as patrollers to return such runaways.

In 1863, slaves were technically made free when President Abraham Lincoln issued the Emancipation Proclamation. The Civil War was still under way, however, and the proclamation had little practical effect on the lives of many slaves in the South. After the Civil War ended in 1865, slaves were truly freed, and in many Southern states they were compensated by receiving land during the period known as Reconstruction. There were several ways in which former slaves received land. In some cases, plantation lands were split among the slaves who had worked it. In other cases, the U.S. government helped former slaves buy land at reduced cost. Still other former slaves received no land at all but worked land as renters or sharecroppers. As Myers explained in *The Glory Field*, some African Americans lost land they owned because they could not pay taxes or afford to bear the costs of farming themselves. Sharecropping continued into the twentieth century and remained the most impoverishing type of tenant farming.

While slavery had legally ended in the South in 1863, many African Americans faced economic, social, and political subjugation through Jim Crow laws, which severely limited African Americans' civil rights. Most Southern states passed laws in the 1880s and 1890s. The U.S. Supreme Court case *Plessy v. Ferguson* had stated that establishing "separate but equal" public facilities for black and whites was legal, paving the way for segregation in virtually all aspects of daily life in the South. In practice, separate schools, hospitals, restrooms,

COMPARE
&
CONTRAST

- **1864:** African Americans are often free in the North, but are enslaved in the South. As slaves, they are considered the property of their owners.

  1994: While African Americans have been free from slavery for well over a century, they do not benefit as much as whites from the booming "New Economy."

  Today: African Americans continue to live in freedom, but on average earn 40 percent less than whites.

- **1964:** While the Civil Rights Act of 1964 ends many forms of discrimination in the United States, very few African Americans serve in the highest levels of the federal government. Augustus F. Hawkins, a Democrat from California, is the only African American in the House of Representatives.

  1994: Colin Powell is the first African American Chairman of the Joint Chiefs of Staff, the highest post in the U.S. military.

  Today: Barack Obama is the first African American president of the United States.

- **Early 1900s:** Madam C. J. Walker (born Sarah Breedlove) became a millionaire by developing and selling hair products for African American women. African American women must buy such specialty products because most major cosmetics companies do not market products for them.

  1994: Most major cosmetics and personal-care companies still market their products primarily to white consumers.

  Today: In the early 2000s, major cosmetics and personal care companies such as Procter & Gamble and L'Oréal began developing and selling products for African Americans.

---

drinking fountains, entrances to public buildings, and the like, but were rarely equal. Many African Americans also saw their voting rights compromised by poll taxes, literacy and property taxes, and discrimination against those blacks who could pay the taxes or pass the tests. The civil rights movement of the 1950s and 1960s sought to redress such legal inequalities. It achieved major legal victories, such as the U.S. Supreme Court's decision in *Brown v. the Topeka Board of Education* (1954), which struck down *Plessy v. Ferguson*. It also saw major legislative victories, including the 1964 Civil Rights Act and the 1965 Voting Rights Act. By the 1990s, African Americans in the South had achieved legal equality but still dealt with racial tensions and faced discrimination, especially in rural areas.

African American Life in Northern Cities

In contrast to life in the South, African Americans living in the North, especially in its cities, faced less discrimination in the late nineteenth and twentieth centuries. While blacks had lived in the North's urban areas in freedom since the post–Revolutionary War period, it was not until the post–American Civil War period that their numbers greatly increased. After the Civil War ended, many African Americans living in the South had to deal with racism and poor living conditions as well as few job opportunities. The failure of the U.S. government to fulfill the goals of Reconstruction in the 1880s and 1890s worsened the situation.

To find greater freedom and opportunity, a significant number of African Americans migrated to the North and West in the late nineteenth and early twentieth centuries. Between 1910 and 1930, more than one million blacks moved from the rural South to urban areas in the North and West as well as in the South in what became known as the Great Migration. Industrial cities such as Detroit, Chicago, Pittsburgh, and New York were primary destinations for African Americans who could find jobs and greater educational, social, and

Some African Americans served in the Union Army during the Civil War. *(MPI | Hulton Archive | Getty Images)*

political opportunities. In the Northern cities, many blacks relied on kinship and community networks to receive guidance as they made the transition to city life and establish themselves.

While life in the North was generally better than in the South, African Americans still faced discrimination. Most African Americans could only find jobs that required few or no skills and had little chance of upward mobility. Like Luvenia in the 1930 segment, many African American women worked as domestics or cleaners.

Many blacks were segregated into black neighborhoods and found rents there to be quite high. However, such black enclaves as the South Side of Chicago and Harlem in New York City became vital African American communities, particularly in the 1920s with the Harlem Renaissance. Myers himself was raised in Harlem in the 1940s and 1950s as the civil rights movement started in earnest. Although discrimination was

not as overt in the North, many African Americans fought to ensure that they and their Southern brethren received their full civil rights.

By the 1990s, life for African Americans in Harlem and other Northern cities could be difficult. In the post–World War II period, Harlem began to struggle with issues of unemployment, poverty, and crime that continue through today. While the economic prosperity of the 1990s led to the rebuilding of certain sections of the neighborhood and a second renaissance began in the early 2000s, Harlem's core remains impoverished.

CRITICAL OVERVIEW

Critical response to *The Glory Field* has been mostly positive from the time it was published in 1994. Reviewers generally praise the novel and its far-reaching narrative. In *Book Report*, Brenda B. Little calls it a "glorious work of African-American family heritage and pride." Carol Jones Collins in *School Library Journal* believes "This moving, effective novel is a sort of *Roots* for young adults."

Reviewing the novel in the *Pittsburgh Post-Gazette*, Andrea L. Jones summarizes the appeal of *The Glory Field* by noting, "Masterly writing ties each generation to the next in a fluent and intense style." Similarly, Katy Kelly in *USA Today* writes, "This is a lovely book about a strong family that overcomes incredible hardship."

A few critics believed the scope of *The Glory Field* was too ambitious because of the many years covered by Myers. Writing in *Booklist*, Hazel Rochman notes that "The slavery episode is powerful, but afterwards, this becomes a long, sprawling docu-novel, with little of the taut intensity of *Somewhere in the Darkness* (1992)." Rochman concludes, "This books works better as essay than as fiction."

CRITICISM

A. Petruso

Petruso has a B.A. in history from the University of Michigan and an M.A. in screenwriting from the University of Texas at Austin. In this essay, she looks at the concepts of risk-taking and perseverance as experienced by each of the primary protagonists in The Glory Field.

In an interview with *Reading Today*, author Walter Dean Myers states, "One of the things that brings young people to books is seeing something they recognize in their own lives. If there is nothing in the books they read that reflects their lives, they see reading only as an opportunity to fail." Throughout *The Glory Field*, Myers tries to connect with young readers by showing them that, although many young people before them have stumbled and even failed in some way, taking risks and persevering in the darkest hour of life is a worthy way to live.

While this essay looks at each of the primary protagonists in the six sections of *The Glory Field*, Myers summarizes this theme in the 1930 segment in Chicago in the words and thoughts of Luvenia. She tells Miss Etta that she loves the Lewis family land on Curry Island just like her father, but does not want to live there and

> BY HELPING TO BRING IN THE LAST HARVEST ON GLORY FIELD AND OTHER PLOTS, MALCOLM AND SHEP CONNECT WITH THE PAST AND ALL THE SACRIFICES THEIR FAMILY MEMBERS HAVE MADE ALONG THE WAY."

work it directly. Luvenia then defines Myers's thoughts on risk-taking and perseverance when Luvenia explains, "I want to be part of what Negroes are doing today. I want to be building something, making something, I don't know. I feel like I could even discover something."

After her father gives her permission to stay in Chicago, the newly unemployed Luvenia thinks about the family tradition of living one's dream. Myers writes, "And for her what was it all about? Perhaps stretching the tradition, perhaps building on it, perhaps just finding her place in it. As so many Negroes moved from the south, that was what they would have to do for themselves, find their places in new traditions." In these words, Myers defines an important aspect of the book and its young protagonists. Each of them struggles to find their place in the Lewis family and the world at large, but this struggle is a family tradition as are the qualities of perseverance and taking risks in the face of what often seems like insurmountable odds. Each of them triumphs in unexpected ways.

The origins of the Lewis family values are found in the 1753 segment that opens *The Glory Field*. While this section is brief, it defines these qualities in stark terms. Muhammad Bilal is a child when he is ripped from his home in Africa and put in shackles on a slave ship going to America. Although Muhammad does not have a choice about the situation he finds himself in and suffers greatly in his captivity, he does not give up and give into death like others around him. Muhammad fights against death for months, "from breath to breath . . . trying to think of being free again." For Muhammad, simply staying alive is an amazing act of perseverance.

In the next section, set in 1864 on the Live Oaks plantation in South Carolina, Lizzy is a

WHAT DO I READ NEXT?

- *Now Is Your Time!: The African-American Struggle for Freedom*, published in 1991, is a nonfiction book by Myers. In the book, he chronicles the black experience in the United States through the stories of significant African Americans such as Abd al Rahman Ibrahima and George Latimer.

- *Letters from a Slave Girl: The Story of Harriet Jacobs*, published in 2007, is a young adult novel by Mary E. Lyons. Based on the autobiography of the real Jacobs, the book chronicles her life as a slave in the mid-nineteenth century.

- *Somewhere in the Darkness*, published in 1992, is a young adult novel by Myers. The novel focuses on fourteen-year-old Jimmy Little who has been raised by a family friend after the death of his mother. He goes on a quest to understand his family after his convict father, Crab, shows up in his life.

- *The Captive*, published in 1994, is a young adult novel by Joyce Hansen. In the book, Hansen tells the story of Kofi, an eighteenth-century African boy who is sold into slavery in America but escapes with the help of the captain of a ship.

- *A Hero Ain't Nothin' but a Sandwich*, published in 1973, is a young adult novel by Alice Childress. The award-winning novel focuses on the troubled life of Benjie Johnson, a thirteen-year-old drug addict living in Harlem in the early 1970s.

- *Witness to Freedom*, published in 1994, is a young adult nonfiction work by Belinda Rochelle. In the book, Rochelle chronicles the contributions of a number of young African Americans to key events in the civil rights movement.

- *On the Bus with Rosa Parks: Poems*, published in 2000, is a collection of poems by Rita Dove. Dove's poems, especially "Lady Freedom Among Us," reflect different aspects of the African American experience.

- *Madam C. J. Walker*, published in 1992, is a young adult biography by A'Lelia Perry Bundles. This biography of the well-known African American woman cosmetics and hair products entrepreneur includes numerous pictures of Walker.

---

young teenage slave and the primary protagonist. She has been informally adopted by Moses Lewis and his wife Saran, and later marries their son Richard. Young Lizzy takes several risks, even in the face of physical punishment and personal danger. She has feelings for Lem, the runaway son of Moses and Saran, and brings him water when he is tied to a tree. For this, Lizzy is viciously whipped by Mister Joe Haynes, the plantation overseer. After Joshua tackles the overseer and Lizzy disarms him, she runs away with Lem and Joshua. Although fearful, Lizzy runs with Lem and Joshua, not giving up even when she and Lem lose track of Joshua and are nearly caught by white patrollers out looking for runaway slaves. Lizzy and Lem make their way to a Union Army camp where they are protected. Lizzie is given the chance of trying to go North with a group of people or staying with the soldiers (whom Lem has joined). She follows the soldiers, as Myers writes, "never looking back." Lizzy's willingness to take risks and to stick with her course of action allow her to gain her freedom.

Lizzy and Richard's son Elijah has a similar experience in the 1900 segment. Forced to deal with the lingering racism, segregation, and Jim Crow laws in place in Curry and Johnson City in this time period, Elijah takes risks to ensure his grandparents have enough money to cover the taxes on Glory Field while saving a beloved young, white, blind boy. When David Turner goes missing with the drunken Mr. Foster one Sunday, Elijah negotiates a $35 reward with David's father, Hamlin, for finding his son in the dangerous stormy weather. Only Elijah and his cousin Abby are willing to risk taking their boat out to Key Island to find the boy. During the journey they must deal with Sheriff Glover pulling a gun on them as well as hazardous weather conditions. Although Elijah is the one to find David, Sheriff Glover takes credit for the rescue and denies that the Lewises will get their full reward.

Elijah does not give up in the face of Glover's deceit. Elijah goes to Hamlin Turner's home and is given the full amount because Hamlin knows who really rescued his son. Elijah gives the money to his grateful grandparents. Unfortunately, Elijah faces more challenges and is forced to persevere in the face of the kind of racism similar to what Lizzy experienced. Two white men, Frank Petty and his uncle J. D., demand to borrow his boat the morning after the rescue, and Elijah turns them down, telling them that he does not lend it out. Elijah is forced to leave Curry Island because the Pettys threaten to whip him, if not commit other acts of violence against him. Elijah takes the first train out of town with $17 of the reward money. Before he leaves, Moses shows him the shackles and reminds him of the past. Moses says, "This is where we come from, and what we overcome. It's up to you where you go from here."

Where Elijah goes is Chicago, where his great-uncle Joshua lives. Years later, Elijah's sixteen-year-old daughter, Luvenia, shares his independent spirit, ability to take risks, and persevere in the face of much adversity. Living in the city, Luvenia works as a live-in servant for the white Deets family and styles hair on the side for women like Miss Etta. But Luvenia has greater ambitions. She wants to go to the University of Chicago like Florenz Deets. Luvenia has enough credits to graduate from high school and knows she can keep up with the demands of college because she has read Florenz's textbooks. Luvenia even goes to a bank to get a loan to go to college, but needs a letter from her employers guaranteeing her job to get it. Luvenia's hopes are dashed when she loses her job suddenly. Luvenia struggles with losing her job and her college goal for several days, but comes to see it as an opportunity. Though she was denied one goal, she perseveres, changes course, and pursues

another. Miss Etta throws a party for Luvenia to help her raise money to start her own hair care business. As Myers writes, "She knew that if she could make as much doing hair and selling as she thought she could, things would be all right." There were few successful African American businesswomen in the 1930s, so Luvenia takes an enormous risk in pursuing this plan. Later in *The Glory Field*, readers learn that Luvenia becomes extremely successful and owns a major business producing and selling cosmetics for African Americans and Hispanics.

In the 1964 segment, Luvenia's relative Tommy Lewis shows similar bravery. Living in Curry during the early days of the civil rights movement, Tommy comes to question the institutionalized racism, segregation, and position of the Ku Klux Klan still prevalent in the area. While his manager and a fellow employee at Clark's Five-and-Dime at least somewhat respect his work, they express racist, if not ignorant, views about segregation and black civil rights leaders. Tommy is given a chance to influence civil rights because of his skills as a basketball player, but ends up ruining it for the greater good. A white alumnus of Johnson City State, a local college, gives Tommy the chance to perhaps be one of the first African Americans to integrate the school. The alum, Leonard Chase, believes that integration is coming and wants ideal candidates to take the first steps.

Tommy chooses to do what he thinks is right and takes a risk, even though he will lose his college scholarship and potential to change the local community through his attending Johnson City State. He ponders the humiliation and injustice of having to search for a drinking fountain labeled "colored". He watches as his white friend Skeeter suffers severe injuries by marching with African Americans. Tommy does not march with his friends and family, in part because Chase told him to stay clear of trouble as a condition of the offer. But Tommy abides by his conscience and makes a bold statement at Sheriff Moser's press conference. Tommy puts Muhammad's shackles on himself and the sheriff as an act of civil disobedience and to bring attention to the problems in the area. This incident earns him the respect of his community. Tommy emerges stronger and more sure of himself for his risk and perseverance.

The last section of *The Glory Field* is set in Harlem in 1994. It focuses on Malcolm, the grandnephew of Luvenia. Compared to the stories of his relatives told to this point, teenaged Malcolm lives a relatively easy life. He has a band (String Theory), a job, and is being educated at a good school. Malcolm knows he is going to college and simply must choose which one. It is the connection to the Lewis family land that tests Malcolm and gives him a chance to show his ability to persevere in difficult circumstances. Luvenia charges him with the seemingly impossible task of getting his homeless, drug-addicted cousin Shep to the family reunion on Curry Island.

Over the course of the next few days, Malcolm draws on all his skills and strength to find Shep and come up with an alternate way to get to South Carolina after Shep spends his airplane ticket money on drugs. Their journey is fraught with peril after their bus driver deliberately leaves them behind after a rest stop. Malcolm makes Shep take a ride with a trucker who will drop them outside Johnson City. This ride is challenging for both of them, as Malcolm—like Muhammad centuries ago—is trapped in a small space, unable to breathe freely, and he must take care of Shep, who is struggling with his withdrawal from crack cocaine. Before the truck ride even ends, Malcolm recognizes that these experiences are making him stronger and building his character. Myers writes, "He had already survived Shep's rage, his wild fighting, his tortured frenzy. He, Malcolm, was exploring what it meant to be black."

Continuing to persevere and take risks as they make their way to Curry Island, Malcolm and Shep find something more at the Lewis family land. By helping to bring in the last harvest on Glory Field and other plots, Malcolm and Shep connect with the past and all the sacrifices their family members have made along the way. Although Malcolm is the primary character in this segment of *The Glory Field*, Shep, too, steps up to the challenge and makes it to Curry Island just as his great-aunt wanted. When Shep collapses in the fields, he stands up by himself, a symbolic victory.

After the harvest is completed, Myers writes, "They were proud of themselves, the Lewis family. Malcolm could see it. He was proud of himself, too. Every ache in his body said that he had done something, that he had helped to move them all to a different place." Malcolm eventually inherits Muhammad's chains from Planter, whom Malcolm first sees at the reunion. Before Malcolm receives them, he has already had experiences that define the Lewis family, if not all of humanity,

including readers looking for a connection in literature. He has taken risks in the face of adversity, and he has persevered.

Source: A. Petruso, Critical Essay on *The Glory Field*, in *Novels for Students*, Gale, Cengage Learning, 2010.

Don Gallo

In the interview that follows, Myers discusses his background as an author.

What does this award-winning writer have to say about his past, his books, and his writing techniques? In this interview, which appeared in a longer form at Authors4Teens.com, Don Gallo finds out.

Don Gallo: You have written about being a foster child, especially in your vivid memoir Bad Boy. Can you tell readers more about your early years?

Walter Dean Myers: I was born in Martinsburg, West Virginia about ten miles from the plantation that my people had been held on during slavery. Some of my family still live in Martinsburg, and others live in Harpers Ferry, the site of the John Brown raid in 1859. A great-great-great uncle claimed to have seen John Brown on his way to trial in Charlestown.

My mother died when I was less than two, leaving my father, George Myers with a large family. The Depression was in full swing, and jobs in West Virginia were virtually nonexistent. Informal adoptions were fairly common among poor people of all races, and I was given, informally, to the Dean family, who lived in Harlem.

What kinds of books do you remember reading as a teenager?

Myers: My first "good" books were things like Huckleberry Finn, Little Men, Robin Hood, etc. A ninth grade teacher, Mrs. Finley, gave me four tragedies and four comedies of Shakespeare that I loved. I also read tons of comic books.

Your early works were mainly children's picture books. What led you to start writing novels for and about teenagers?

Myers: My agent thought that I could write a novel for teenagers because much of my short fiction was about young, inner city males. She gave one of my short stories to an editor, touting it as a potential novel. The editor said that she had read the "first chapter" and asked me how the rest of it went. The book turned out to be *Fast Sam, Cool Clyde & Stuff*, which is really a book of related short stories.

What's your usual writing schedule? What's a typical writing day for you?

Myers: I work five days a week. I write seven pages a day; the writing ends when I've done my seven pages.

There's no warm-up, no sharpening of pencils, etc. I'm always eager to start. On the previous day I have stopped work at the end of seven pages, often in the middle of an idea, or a scene. The idea/scene has been on my mind since my last session and needs to be released onto the paper.

How do you organize your thoughts for writing?

Myers: I have notebooks full of preliminary outlines. Then I'll do a regular outline, on lined paper. I sometimes expand this outline even more, doing a scene-by-scene breakdown. I allow myself the luxury of learning more about my characters as I go along. But with all this prewriting, the structure will invariably be strong enough to allow me to finish the piece.

In your prewriting, do you usually begin with characters, an idea, a conflict . . . how?

Myers: I begin with an idea and try to develop that idea into a conflict that can be resolved by the central character. How do I turn it into a clear conflict? If I find a way of doing this, I can structure the book in the traditional way: develop the character, impose the conflict at a point of crisis, allow the character to attempt to resolve the conflict, then allow insights through personal growth, which leads to some sort of resolution.

When you've finished a book, how do you decide what your next project is going to be? Do you make an effort to choose an interesting subject, or do the ideas seem to choose you?

Myers: The ideas come from every source. A series of prison interviews led to *Monster*, and also to *Handbook for Boys*. In London a few years ago, I found a group of letters by and about a little African girl who was brought to England in 1849. These letters, plus a lot of research, became *At Her Majesty's Request*. This year I bought a group of photographs of black American aviators who fought in the war between Italy and Ethiopia. This could easily become a book. I have a huge list of topics in which I'm interested.

Of what value to your writing are the many school visits you make each year?

Myers: I firmly believe that good writing skills can be learned. When I talk about writing in schools, it's like a review of what I've learned, and it invariably affirms my own skills. It improves my writing.

Discovering a Painful Truth

One of the most emotional things **Walter Dean Myers** wrote about in Bad Boy was discovering that his father had never learned to read. As he tells it to Don Gallo, he never knew about his father's illiteracy when his father was alive—but he put the clues together after his father's death.

"Sometimes my father would have me read something to him, telling me it was because of his weak eyes. During the last months of his life, when he was dying of cancer in a Veterans' Administration hospital. I left him a book I had written about Little League baseball which was based on my son Christopher's experiences. He made no comment on the book which really hurt me. I think I was looking for a final blessing from him.

After his death, I went through his papers and saw the childlike scrawl that he used to fill out forms, and the misunderstandings he had of those forms . . . Other correspondence indicated that his business affairs were being supervised by a friend at his job. It was then I realized that he had never commented on any of my books because he couldn't read them."

Source: Don Gallo, "A Man of Many Ideas," in *Writing!*, Vol. 26, No. 5, February 1, 2004, pp. 10–13.

Peter D. Sieruta

In the following essay, Sieruta finds The Glory Field *to be an ambitious novel.*

Though the intergenerational saga is a staple of adult literature, few have been written for younger readers—perhaps due to the assumption that the lifespan experiences of a fictional character are not of interest once the character reaches adulthood. In one of his most ambitious novels to date, Walter Dean Myers avoids this concern by focusing only on turning points in the lives of adolescent characters, as he traces the history of an African-American family over two hundred and forty years. Beginning with the harrowing stories of Muhammad, traveling from West Africa on a slave ship, and his descendant Lizzy, who breaks the bonds of slavery, the novel follows six generations of the Lewis family. At the turn of the twentieth century. Elijah helps save his family's South Carolina land—known as the *Glory*

Field—but is forced to leave the home he loves. In Depression–era Chicago, Luvenia resolves to achieve success when her dream of a college education is shattered. Tommy has the opportunity to integrate a white university if he'll avoid joining the 1964 civil rights demonstrations but, in one of the novel's strongest scenes, chooses to chain himself to a racist sheriff with the shackles that once enslaved his ancestors. The final section of the book concerns contemporary teenager Malcolm, who accompanies his crack-addicted cousin from Harlem to a Lewis family reunion at the *Glory Field*. Each time period is accurately depicted, although the extraneous subplots and characters that provide historical flavor sometimes cause the lengthy book to ramble. And despite the helpful genealogical charts, it is occasionally difficult to sort out family relationships because the characters don't follow a direct line of descent. Yet all together, the mothers and fathers, children, grandparents, and cousins of this extended family celebrate the freedom, pride, and unity that has endured for many generations.

Source: Peter D. Sieruta, "*The Glory Field*," in *Horn Book Magazine*, Vol. 71, No. 2, March 1, 1995, pp. 200–201.

SOURCES

Collins, Carol Jones, Review of *The Glory Field*, in the *School Library Journal*, November 1994, pp. 121–122.

Jones, Andrea L., "Past and Present, Heroes for Our Children," in the *Pittsburgh Post-Gazette*, February 19, 1995, p. J12.

Kelly, Katy, "Courage and Calculations/A Family's Brave Saga; Fun with Arithmetic," in *USA Today*, December 13, 1994, p. 2D.

Little, Brenda B., Review of *The Glory Field*, in *Book Report*, Vol., 13, No. 3, November/December 1994, p. 47.

Myers, Walter Dean, *The Glory Field*, Scholastic, 1994.

Rochman, Hazel, Review of *The Glory Field*, in *Booklist*, Vol., 91, No. 3, October 1, 1994, p. 319.

"Scoring with Reading: To Engage Adolescent African American Males in Reading, Books Must Reflect Their Lives," in *Reading Today*, October–November 2007, p. 40.

Williams, Karen, "Celebrate America!," in the *Christian Science Monitor*, November 4, 1994, p. 10.

FURTHER READING

Burshtein, Karen, *Walter Dean Myers*, Rosen Publishing Company, 2004.
>
> This biography of the author is targeted at a young adult audience. It covers the whole of his life and looks at several of his better-known books, including *Hoops*, in depth.

Jordan, Denise M., *Walter Dean Myers—Writer for Real Teens*, Enslow Publishers, 1999.
>
> This young adult biography covers Myers's life from his birth in Virginia until the turn of the twentieth century. The volume includes photographs of the author and his life.

Lane, R. D., "'Keepin' It Real': Walter Dean Myers and the Promise of African-American Children's Literature," in *African American Review*, Spring 1998, p. 125.
>
> This critical article looks at Myers's place and active role in promoting children's literature featuring and targeting African Americans.

Levine, Ellen S., *Freedom's Children: Young Civil Rights Activists Tell Their Own Stories*, Putnam Juvenile, 2000.
>
> This nonfiction book offers the stories of children and young adults who participated in the civil rights movement in the 1960s as well as those who lived out its ramifications.

Myers, Walter Dean, *Bad Boy: A Memoir*, Amistad, 2002.
>
> This young adult memoir covers Myers's childhood growing up in Harlem in the 1940s and 1950s. He touches on the difficulties in his life as well as the beginnings of his writing career.

Intruder in the Dust

WILLIAM FAULKNER

1948

Intruder in the Dust, first published by Random House in 1948, is a novel by William Faulkner that defies easy description. On the surface, it is a classic "whodunit," a murder mystery after the manner of the Sherlock Holmes stories written by British author Arthur Conan Doyle (1859–1930). In *Intruder in the Dust*, a man is falsely accused of murder; much of the plot of the novel involves unraveling what actually happened, finding the real murderer, and setting the innocent man free. What complicates this basic, simple situation is the time, the place, and the race of the characters: the man accused of murder is black, the victim is white, and the story is set in Mississippi long before the civil rights movement. This is the era of what is still called "Jim Crow," a collective term for all the rules that kept blacks and whites separate in the southern United States, the states that had formed the rebellious Confederacy during the American Civil War (1861–1865). Further complicating the situation is the personality of Lucas Beauchamp, the accused black man. He is a man who, throughout his life, has refused to obey all the subservient rules of Jim Crow, and for being so "uppity," to use the old Southern slang term, he is in particular danger of being lynched—of being hauled out by an angry crowd and summarily hanged.

These are familiar themes in Faulkner's work. Much of his writing, including *Intruder in the Dust*, is set in a fictional county in Mississippi he called Yoknapatawpha, and in that writing, race relations play a central role. The reader first approaching

William Faulkner *(Getty Images)*

Faulkner should be aware that he tries always to represent the speech of his place and time realistically, so racial slurs are present throughout, sometimes on every page. These slurs were a part of everyday speech in that era, in constant use by most people. The novel was a financial success, was made into a film, and did much to repair both Faulkner's finances and his reputation as an author at a point in his life when both were in danger of failing.

AUTHOR BIOGRAPHY

William Cuthbert Falkner—Faulkner himself later changed the spelling of his name—was born on September 25, 1897, in New Albany, Mississippi, and was the eldest son of Murry and Maud Butler Falkner. He was named "William" after his great-grandfather, a dashing figure who had fought as a colonel in the Civil War, been a successful businessman, published a best-selling novel, and been killed in a duel. His was a hard act to follow, and

Faulkner's own father did not live so spectacularly. In 1902, Murry Falkner moved the family to Oxford, Mississippi, where he worked in family businesses and later for the University of Mississippi, the famous "Ole Miss," located in Oxford. Young William spent much of his life in and around Oxford, which became the model for his fictional Yoknapatawpha County; Oxford itself was the model for the Yoknapatawpha County seat, Jefferson. An important early figure in his life was his childhood sweetheart, Estelle Oldham. Although the two enjoyed a romance as youngsters, Oldham was popular and dated others. When one of her boyfriends proposed, she accepted, thinking the proposal was not entirely serious. Her family thought it a good match, however, and finding no way out of the situation, Estelle was married.

The First World War provided some distraction for the heartbroken William. He was rejected by the U.S. Army Air Corps because of his height (he stood just under five feet six inches tall), and so entered the Canadian Royal Air Force, pretending to be British on his application. He even put on a British accent for the recruiters, and while there are many stories about how he added the "u" to the family name, one version has him adopting it when he applied to become an air cadet, because he thought "Faulkner" looked more British. He was accepted for training, but the war was over before he saw any action. Still, he returned to Oxford filled with stories about his wartime exploits, which were largely or entirely fictional. Even though he had not finished high school, he entered the University of Mississippi under a special provision that allowed veterans to attend. While at the university, he began writing poems and short stories, and he helped found a drama club. He left the university after only three semesters, however, and entered a period during which he held a series of odd jobs. Later, when he became famous, his stint as university postmaster became a comic legend. He somehow held the job for three years, even though he refused to serve customers, spent his time playing cards with friends, and would even throw mail in the garbage rather than deliver it.

In 1925, he moved to New Orleans, and his writing career picked up speed. He became part of a crowd of writers that included Sherwood Anderson, the author of the classic collection of short stories, *Winesburg, Ohio* (1919). Faulkner published a book of poetry, spent several months living in Paris, and then began writing novels. Everything changed for him when he followed a piece of advice Sherwood Anderson had given him. Told to write about his native region, Faulkner published, in 1929, the novel *Sartoris*, and began to weave his elaborate mythology of Yoknapatawpha County, Mississippi. While he tried to sell *Sartoris*, he also worked on a manuscript that he thought at first unpublishable, a thing he wrote entirely for his own pleasure. That novel turned out to be *The Sound and the Fury*, published in 1929. *The Sound and the Fury* is a revolutionary work often regarded as Faulkner's first masterpiece. It is his most difficult book to read. For instance, the first section of the novel is told from the point of view of a severely mentally disabled adult who has no sense of time, and whose story jumps back and forth between present and past seemingly at random, and without warning. Faulkner may not have known it, but he had turned a corner.

Money would become more of a worry now, because he suddenly found himself a family man. His childhood sweetheart Estelle had divorced her first husband, and she married Faulkner soon after, in June 1929. She brought to the marriage two children, so money was indeed an issue; he wrote his next novel, *As I Lay Dying*, while working nights in a power plant. He was further in debt after he bought a house built before the Civil War. The house, which he named Rowan Oak and lived in periodically for the rest of his life, is today maintained as a museum by the University of Mississippi. Faulkner discovered that, while his novels did not sell as well as he would have liked, he could make money writing short stories for national magazines. Perhaps the most famous of these, "A Rose for Emily," appeared during this period (1930). In 1932, Faulkner began what became a long-term, part-time profession as a screenwriter in Hollywood. He divided his time between Oxford, Hollywood, and elsewhere, accumulating more dependents all along: Estelle gave birth to a daughter, Jill, and after his father died, Faulkner also took care of his mother.

In 1936, he made the first of many stays at Wright's Sanitarium, a nursing home in Byhalia, Mississippi. He went there to recover from a drinking binge, and he later made the same trip for the same purpose repeatedly. Among the legends that have grown up around Faulkner, those about his drinking may be the most persistent: many believe he drank for inspiration, and

would write while drunk. Biographers now believe that alcohol was a release he turned to under the weight of a stressful life, and common sense dictates that no human could have produced novels as complex as his while drunk.

His life followed a familiar pattern for some time to come: novels that were a labor of love but did not sell well, short stories that did better on the market, and forgettable hackwork in Hollywood. By the mid-1940s, Faulkner had been largely forgotten in the United States, although his reputation was favorable in Europe. The success of *Intruder in the Dust*, as well as its film version, helped improve this situation somewhat. Of greater importance was the decision to award him the 1950 Nobel Prize in Literature. Of even greater significance was the acceptance speech he wrote. He delivered it rapidly and in such a low voice that the Swedish audience understood nothing, but when the speech was reprinted in the newspapers the next day, it was hailed for its striking eloquence in grim circumstances. Writing of the just-begun Cold War between the United States and the Soviet Union, and the possible extinction of humanity in a nuclear holocaust, he wrote:

> I decline to accept the end of man.... I believe that man will not merely endure: he will prevail. He is immortal, not because he alone among creatures has an inexhaustible voice, but because he has a soul, a spirit capable of compassion and sacrifice and endurance. The poet's, the writer's duty is to write about these things.... The poet's voice need not merely be the record of man, it can be one of the props, the pillars to help him endure and prevail.

He was now very much a public figure—CBS-TV, for instance, ran a documentary showing his life at home in Oxford—and he found his privacy hard to protect. But he was also growing more comfortable in his role as a public figure. He accepted more readily requests by the U.S. State Department to speak abroad, and no longer turned down, as he often had, invitations to speak at events in the United States. His position on racial relations in the South, however, confused nearly everyone. As his Confederate great-grandfather had been, he was a believer in "states' rights," that is, in the constitutional liberty of the Southern states to deal with racial problems on their own, without interference from the North. At the same time, he regarded slavery as a kind of Southern original sin, and thought that segregation was an abuse that had to be addressed. His was a moderate position that left few satisfied. In the meantime, he continued his new life as a public figure. He became writer-in-residence at the University of Virginia, and later willed all his manuscripts to the William Faulkner Foundation there. In 1961, he published a final novel, *The Reivers*, which earned him a second Pulitzer Prize, awarded posthumously. (He received his first Pulitzer in 1954 for his novel *A Fable* in 1954.) On June 17, 1961, Faulkner suffered a fall from a horse. It was hardly his first fall, but this one led to a fatal heart attack on July 6, 1962. The day happened to be his great-grandfather William's birthday.

PLOT SUMMARY

Chapters 1–2

The novel opens with the news that Lucas Beauchamp, a black man living in the countryside of Yoknapatawpha County, has been accused of murdering a white man, Vinson Gowrie. The novel is told from the point of view of sixteen-year-old Charles "Chick" Mallison, and the news reminds him of the first time he met Beauchamp, four years earlier.

As a twelve-year-old boy, he had gone rabbit hunting on the Edmonds plantation, where Beauchamp lives, and accidentally fell into a frigid creek. After the accident, Lucas Beauchamp takes him to his cabin, where his wife, Molly, feeds Chick while his clothes are drying. Chick is impressed by Beauchamp's manner, which is self-confident to the point of being contemptuous—odd behavior for a black man in Mississippi in the late 1940s. Chick tries to pay for the meal, but Beauchamp refuses the seventy cents he offers; insulted, Chick throws the money on the floor. He leaves feeling that he must reestablish the proper relations between the races (from his point of view, Beauchamp, as a racial inferior, should have accepted the money the way a waiter accepts a tip). Chick only feels free of the burden when, after some years, Beauchamp seems no longer to recognize him during his rare trips to Jefferson, the county seat, where Chick lives.

Chick hears frequent stories about what the people of Yoknapatawpha regard as Beachamp's arrogant behavior. Then, Gowrie is murdered. Next to a country store, Beauchamp is caught with a pistol in his hip pocket, standing over Gowrie's corpse. The murder happens in a

MEDIA ADAPTATIONS

- A film version of the novel appeared in 1949, starring David Brian as Gavin Stevens, Claude Jarman Jr. as Chick Mallison, and Juano Hernandez as Lucas Beauchamp. The film was shot in Faulkner's hometown of Oxford, Mississippi. It is available in VHS format but not in DVD, and can be hard to find. It was admired by Ralph Ellison, one of the most prominent black authors of the twentieth century. The film appears in his essay "The Shadow and the Act."

district of the county called Beat Four, a kind of rural slum inhabited by "white trash," to use the old Southern slang term. The locals want to lynch Beauchamp right away, but it is Saturday night, only three hours before Sunday, and they do not want to have to rush; etiquette dictates that lynchings do not happen on Sundays. Beauchamp spends the night chained to the local constable's bed, and Sheriff Hampton escorts him to jail in Jefferson the next day. As he arrives at the jail, Beauchamp sees Chick in the crowd and tells him he wants to speak to Chick's uncle, the attorney Gavin Stevens.

Chapters 3–4

Chick and Stevens visit Beauchamp at the jail. Beauchamp reveals that he has summoned Stevens to hire him to do a job that he is vague about, but he assures Stevens he can pay for it. Stevens refuses at first, in anger. He is quite convinced that Beauchamp is guilty of the murder. When he calms himself, he asks Beauchamp to explain what happened, and Beauchamp begins to unfold the story: The murdered Vinson Gowrie and another man were partners in a sawmill operation. The other man, however, was stealing the lumber at night, selling it in another town, and pocketing the money; Lucas had seen him doing it. Stevens is still angry, but offers to attempt a legal maneuver that will at least save Beauchamp's life: he will request a change of venue for the trial to

Mottstown, which is far enough away that no one there knows Beauchamp. He will then, in the trial, point out Beauchamp's advanced age and previous good record, and hope he will not be executed, but rather sent to the penitentiary.

After they leave the jail, Chick and Stevens part ways, and Chick considers turning his back on the situation. Instead, he returns to the jail and offers to take the job Beauchamp had wanted his uncle to do. Beauchamp wants Chick to dig up Vinson Gowrie's body, saying that Gowrie had not been shot with Beauchamp's gun. Chick is aghast. However, it is four hours until midnight, at which point Sunday will be over and Beauchamp can expect to be lynched. Chick realizes that there is not enough time left to open the grave by official, legal channels. Passing his uncle Stevens's office, he enters to find Stevens talking to Miss Habersham, an elderly woman who lives at the edge of town. Chick does try to get his uncle to consider exhuming the body, but the uncle rejects the idea flatly. Chick asks his friend Aleck Sander to help him; he, too, is aghast, but agrees to help. When Miss Habersham discovers what Chick plans to do with Aleck Sander, she offers to join them, to Chick's surprise. She owns a truck. They set out, taking Chick's horse to help with the task. Racing the clock, they find the grave in a country churchyard, dig it up, and discover that Vinson Gowrie is not in his own coffin. Instead, the body is that of a lumber buyer named Montgomery.

Chapters 5–6
After they fill in the grave, Chick, Miss Habersham, and Aleck Sander go first to Gavin Stevens, who then goes to the sheriff; it is now time to seek legal authority to open the grave officially. The sheriff, interrupted during his breakfast and a little irritated, calls the district attorney and arranges for the exhumation. The group begins to formulate a plan. Miss Habersham will replace Will Legate, the crack shot who has been guarding the entry to the jail; Will needs to rest and tend to his farm, and Miss Habersham plans on guarding the jail door herself. Her sheer moral authority as an elderly white woman will keep any lynch mob from physically moving her out of the way to get at Beauchamp. There is some debate about whether Chick should go to school, or perhaps just home to bed, but Chick enlists his uncle to convince his parents to let him go along on the trip back to the churchyard for the official exhumation. Chick, woozy with exhaustion, drinks the first coffee he has ever had. Even the coffee

precipitates an argument with his parents, who seem to want to keep him a child as long as possible.

As his mother leaves to help Miss Habersham guard the jail, the jolt from the caffeine causes Chick to remember a detail from the previous night: Aleck Sander had heard a man on a mule, and had seen him carrying a burden in front of him as he rode. Chick remembers the whole episode in detail; the group had decided that the man had something to do with the crime, and feared ambush as they left the area of the churchyard. Chick returns to town and finds what he feared he would—the lynch mob is there. He catches sight of his mother and Miss Habersham, calmly sewing in the doorway of the jail, and effectively blocking it. Chick, who had been determined to return to the churchyard, now wants to stay and protect his mother, but his uncle reveals a secret: Beauchamp is no longer in the jail. The sheriff has snuck him into his own house, just before dawn. So Stevens and Chick set out for the churchyard.

Chapters 7–8
Chick and his uncle drive back to the graveyard. In an expansive mood, Gavin Stevens comments on race relations in general. Attempts by the federal government to force desegregation and civil rights failed after the Civil War; there is no reason to believe, Stevens thinks, that they will work now, in the middle of the twentieth century. Change will have to come from within the South, and slowly. The sheriff has arrived with two black convicts for laborers, and the convicts begin reopening the grave. Suddenly, Vinson's father, Nub Gowrie, and other members of the clan appear, insisting that the grave be left alone. To back up his point, Gowrie pulls a gun. The sheriff convinces Gowrie to open the grave, but Gowrie only agrees if his sons do the digging rather than the convicts. The sons open the grave, and find that the coffin is now empty.

The sheriff begins to try to figure out what happened. Aleck Sander had seen a man with a mule carrying, presumably, a body. What had that man done with it? Stevens speculates that the murderer had buried Jake Montgomery in the Gowrie grave the previous night, but then heard Miss Habersham, Aleck Sander, and Chick digging it up again. This unknown person would have had to get rid of the body he was carrying quickly, so the group searches the sand next to a nearby creek, which would be an easy place to dig. They find a shallow grave containing Montgomery, and guess that his was the second body the murderer disposed of that night. The shallow grave suggests it had been dug in a hurry, with dawn approaching. The group then finds Vinson Gowrie's body in quicksand nearby.

Given all this evidence, it appears that the murderer had dug up Vinson, put Montgomery in his grave, dumped Vinson in the quicksand, then had been forced to move Montgomery when he realized that Miss Habersham, Aleck Sander, and Chick had discovered the substitution. Lucas Beauchamp, therefore, is innocent. Montgomery had been present, alive, at Vinson's funeral, at which time Lucas had been in jail. The sheriff can also tell that Vinson was not shot by Beauchamp's gun. The murder weapon belongs to another member of the Gowrie clan, Crawford.

Chapters 9–11

The sheriff, Stevens, and Chick haul Montgomery's body back to Jefferson to be examined by a coroner. The sheriff, certain that Vinson was killed by his brother, returns his body to his father to bury yet again. The group arrives back in Jefferson, and the lynch mob, realizing that there will be no lynching, breaks up. Sheriff Hampton and Stevens now begin to unravel the plot, based partly on what Beauchamp is willing to tell them.

Vinson and Crawford Gowrie, they learn, had a business selling timber, but Crawford had been cheating his brother, selling part of the timber on the sly to Jake Montgomery. Beauchamp stumbled onto the plot himself. When Vinson learned of it, Crawford hatched a plan to murder Vinson and make it look like Beauchamp did it. Crawford invited Beauchamp to bring his gun to the country store (Beauchamp usually wore the gun on Saturdays as a kind of ornament). Crawford challenged Beauchamp to a feat of difficult shooting; Crawford then lured Vinson to the spot and shot him. The crowd, streaming from the store and finding Beauchamp with a freshly fired weapon, assumed he was the murderer.

Jake Montgomery discovered the truth, he and blackmailed Crawford. But Jake, it seems, was going to have Crawford arrested anyway, and was digging up Vinson's body as evidence when Crawford caught him, killed him, buried Montgomery in Vinson's grave, and dumped Vinson in the quicksand. Later that same night, Crawford saw Miss Habersham, Aleck Sander,

and Chick digging up the grave, and knew he would have to get rid of Montgomery's body, too. Sheriff Hampton arrests Crawford, who quickly commits suicide in jail. In the final scene, a free Beauchamp visits Chick and his uncle. His uncle charges Beauchamp two dollars for his expenses in the case, and Beauchamp, troublesome to the last, pays a fourth of the bill in pennies and demands a receipt.

CHARACTERS

Lucas Beauchamp

Lucas Beauchamp is one of the central characters in the novel, the man accused of murdering Vinson Gowrie. Although still vigorous, he is in his seventies as the story takes place. The black owner of a small cabin and farm on the Edmonds estate, Beauchamp is in fact a direct descendent of Carothers McCaslin, who founded the estate long ago. Beauchamp is self-assured to the point that he seems contemptuous of all who meet him. This is a dangerous trait for a black man in the South of the 1940s. Faulkner describes his face as "not arrogant, not even scornful: just intractable and composed." For years, the county, it seems, has been waiting to teach him a lesson and put him in his place as a subordinate within this segregated culture. This may be one reason the white residents of Beat Four are so eager to lynch him, and even seem intent on burning him alive (hence, the frequent references Faulkner makes to the lynch mobs carrying gasoline).

Molly Beauchamp

Molly is Lucas Beauchamp's wife, who feeds Chick after he falls in the creek at the beginning of the story. Faulkner describes her as a "tiny, doll-like woman." She dies not long afterward, and when Chick next sees Lucas Beauchamp, he realizes Lucas is grieving. Chick had not, until then, understood that a black person was capable of such emotion.

Carothers Edmonds

Edmonds is the landowner on whose property Lucas Beauchamp lives; he is a friend of Gavin Stevens, Chick's uncle, and now owns the two-thousand-acre plantation founded by the patriarch Carothers McCaslin before the Civil War.

Ephraim

Ephraim is Paralee's father, and has died by the time the central action of the novel takes place. He gives the young Chick a crucial piece of advice about how women and children are better than men at doing uncommon things.

Doyle Fraser

Fraser is the son of the proprietor of the country store where the murder takes place. He had saved Lucas Beauchamp during an earlier fight with the locals. After the murder, he saves Beauchamp yet again, keeping the crowd at bay until the constable arrives to take Beauchamp into custody. He seems, therefore, an unusual person—secretly opposed to lynching and other racial violence.

Crawford Gowrie

Crawford Gowrie is the murderer of both his brother Vinson and Jake Montgomery. He enters the plot late in the novel, and not much is revealed about his personality—except that he would have to be vicious in the extreme to behave as he does.

Nub Gowrie

Nub Gowrie is the father of the Gowrie boys, Vinson and Crawford. He is missing an arm, but nevertheless pulls a gun on the sheriff during the official exhumation. He is a classic denizen of Beat Four, living with his children alone on a piece of land from which they together pursue professions that are either marginal or outright illegal.

Vinson Gowrie

Vinson Gowrie is the man Lucas Beauchamp is supposed to have murdered. His family, the Gowrie clan, is considered the worst and most criminal group in Beat Four. Vinson himself is the only member of the family to have any business sense, and actually has both money in the bank and some property at the time of his death.

Miss Eunice Habersham

Miss Habersham is an elderly lady, a member of the oldest family in Yoknapatawpha County. Although she dresses elegantly, she lives in a decayed house at the edge of town with a pair of black servants. She grew up with Molly, Lucas Beauchamp's wife; the two had been as close as sisters, even though Molly was black and Miss Habersham was white. The relationship partly explains why Miss Habersham is eager to help Beauchamp, the widower of her closest friend.

Hope Hampton

Hampton is the county sheriff. Faulkner describes him as "a big, tremendous man with no fat and little hard pale eyes in a cold almost bland pleasant face." He is a farmer in addition to being sheriff, and is in fact brave and skilled at his job. He takes on Crawford Gowrie alone, even though he knows Gowrie will be armed, and thinks nothing of it.

Joe

Joe is the black son of one of Carothers Edmonds's tenants. With Aleck Sander, he goes on the rabbit hunting trip at the start of the novel. After Lucas Beauchamp refuses the money Chick offers and Chick throws it on the floor, Joe helps Aleck Sander pick up the coins.

Will Legate

Legate is a farmer known as the best shot with a deer rifle in the county. When Lucas Beauchamp is in the Jefferson jail, Legate is stationed at the entrance of the jail with a shotgun, in an effort to warn off any lynch mob that might develop.

Mr. Lilley

Lilley is the owner of a small store in Jefferson with whom Gavin Stevens speaks briefly at the start of chapter three. Although Lilley's customers are black, and he even lets them get away with a little shoplifting now and then, he is eager to be present and help with the lynching.

Charles "Chick" Mallison

Chick is the sixteen-year-old from whose point of view the story is told; although much of the novel is focused on Lucas Beauchamp and Gavin Stevens, *Intruder in the Dust* is usually regarded as Chick's story. Raised in a racist society, he is thoroughly bigoted at the beginning of the novel. When Beauchamp refuses the money Chick offers him at the start of the story, after Beauchamp has fed and cared for him, Chick is outraged; he feels that his race has been insulted by Beauchamp's refusal to accept his subordinate status as a servant.

Yet when Beauchamp asks for his help after the murder, Chick does help him, summoning his uncle, Gavin Stevens, then going even further, exhuming what is supposed to be the body of the man Beauchamp has murdered. In the process, he discovers the beginning of the trail of evidence that will set Beauchamp free. He goes well out of his way to help a man his society has told him is both lowly and dangerously arrogant. In the process, he establishes much of the independence from his parents that he has been longing for.

Maggie Mallison

Maggie Mallison is Chick's mother. She is highly protective of Chick, and is not quite ready to let go and allow him to become an adult. Her husband, Charles Sr., Chick's father, plays only a minor role in the novel, but he, too, is highly protective. One of Chick's major challenges in life is getting his parents to allow him more independence.

Jake Montgomery

It is Jake Montgomery's body that turns up in what is supposed to be Vinson Gowrie's grave when Chick, Aleck Sander, and Miss Habersham open it. Montgomery had run a saloon in Tennessee before being chased out of the state by the police after a man was killed in his place. He is working as a lumber buyer with Vinson Gowrie when last seen alive.

Paralee

Paralee is the mother of Aleck Sander, Chick's childhood playmate. Chick recalls playing around their cabin in bad weather, and also remembers the meals Paralee often cooked for Aleck Sander and him, which he ate without thinking the situation at all unusual, even though Paralee was black. She still lives in the cabin with Aleck Sander when Vinson Gowrie is murdered.

Aleck Sander

Sander is Chick's black childhood playmate. He goes along on the rabbit hunting trip at the start of the novel, and is present when Lucas Beauchamp refuses to take the seventy cents Chick offers him, helping pick up the coins when Chick throws them on the floor. He is almost exactly Chick's age, and the two are in fact as close as brothers. Chick assumes Aleck Sander will help him dig up Vinson Gowrie's body, even though it is a dreadful and dangerous task, and in fact Aleck does help.

Skipworth

Skipworth is the constable in Beat Four. He takes Beauchamp under custody and keeps him chained to his bed until the sheriff arrives. Faulkner portrays him as ineffectual, describing him as a "little driedup wizened stonedeaf old man not much larger than a half-grown boy," but Skipworth does have the wherewithal to keep the lynch mob at bay.

Gavin Stevens

Stevens is Chick Mallison's uncle, and is an attorney in the town of Jefferson, the county seat of Yoknapatawpha. He is a highly educated man, having been to Harvard and the University of Heidelberg before he went to law school long enough to become county attorney. He is a small-town philosopher, loves to talk, and can be emotional. He is convinced from the start that Beauchamp is guilty, but is willing to consider the evidence and wants to prevent a lynching. He also becomes something of an ally of Chick against his parents; they want him to stay out of the Beauchamp affair, but Stevens lets Chick become ever more deeply involved. Where segregation is concerned, he is a moderate. He does not believe the federal government can force the South to treat its black neighbors better. Change will have to come from within the South.

Tubbs

Tubbs is the jailer guarding Beauchamp. Faulkner describes him as "a snuffy untidy potbellied man with a harried concerned outraged face." He is torn to the point of being frantic as he guards Beauchamp; he wants to do his duty and keep the jail secure, but is unwilling to die merely to protect a black prisoner.

THEMES

Debt and Payment

The incident at the start of the novel, when Beauchamp refuses the seventy-cent tip from Chick, is in fact complex. On one level, the young and thoughtless Chick regards it as an insult to his race. More is happening here, however. The incident swells in his mind in part because he feels he owes an unpaid debt to Beauchamp, and he continually tries to repay it. In the end, he succeeds. He goes against the common sense of his time and place, opens the Gowrie grave, and finds the first piece of evidence that will save Beauchamp's life and set him free. The debt, however, operates at a symbolic level, too. Chick owes Beauchamp seventy cents, but he owes him much more, because his society had enslaved Beauchamp's ancestors, and presently keeps them in a new bondage that takes the form of strict segregation and poverty.

TOPICS FOR FURTHER STUDY

- An obvious comparison with *Intruder in the Dust* is the 1960 novel *To Kill a Mockingbird* by Harper Lee. The plots are strikingly similar: a black man is falsely accused of a heinous crime in the Jim Crow South, and a white lawyer comes to his defense. Read *To Kill a Mockingbird* and write an essay comparing Lucas Beauchamp and Tom Robinson, the accused man in *To Kill a Mockingbird*. In what specific ways do the two differ?

- film version of *Intruder in the Dust* and the film of *To Kill a Mockingbird*, which was made into a classic piece of cinema in 1962, with Gregory Peck in the central role. Break into small groups and argue this simple question: Which is the better film? Make a list of examining the strengths and weaknesses of each film.

- Does Chick Mallison change in his attitude toward race relations? How does he develop? Write a paper in which you explain how Chick changes—or fails to change—during the course of the novel.

- While Faulkner was writing *Intruder in the Dust*, the 1948 presidential campaign was under way. Democrat candidate President Harry Truman was running for reelection. While Faulkner was still working on the novel, Truman sent to Congress a legislative package dealing exclusively with civil rights. Southern Democrats reacted with anger, in some cases fury. Faulkner comments in the novel on these contemporary events (a rare occurrence, in his work). Do some research on the Internet about the 1948 campaign and the impact civil rights had on the race. Write a paper in which you explain how the novel is commenting on presidential politics.

Chick's debt symbolizes something much bigger: all of the South owes a debt to Beauchamp and his race, and Beauchamp knows it.

Race

It is quite rare for Faulkner to comment on political issues or events that are exactly contemporary with his own time, but *Intruder in the Dust* is an exception. As noted, President Truman introduced civil rights legislation while Faulkner was writing the novel. When, in his speech in chapter seven, Gavin Stevens refers to "the necessity of passing legislation to set Lucas Beauchamp free," that is surely a reference to Truman's bill. In certain ways, the characters in the novel are constructed so that each embodies one among the varying reactions Southerners had to the new pressure for civil rights coming from Washington, D.C. Lucas Beauchamp is of the radical black faction, demanding equality now. Various other black characters might be considered to be "accomodationists," just trying to survive in a world they did not make. Characters like the Gowrie clan represent the most violent of the traditional segregationists. Gavin Stevens is a moderate. And so on; each of the other characters' attitude toward segregation can be similarly identified within the novel.

Social Innovation

Near the end of chapter three, old Ephraim gives Chick a crucial piece of advice: "If you ever needs to get anything done outside the common run, dont waste yo time on the men-folks; get the womens and children to working on it." Ephraim's basic idea returns over and over in the novel; so it is that, when no one else in the county is interested, young Aleck Sander and Chick, and the elderly Miss Habersham, open the grave and find the first crucial piece of evidence that ends with the discovery of the truth behind the murder. Faulkner is making a wider point with incidents like this. He suggests that change, in the South, will have to come from outside the

Claude Jarman, Jr. as Chick Mallison and Juano Hernandez as Lucas Beauchamp in the 1949 film version of the novel (Hulton Archive | Getty Images)

present ruling class of elderly men—and, as a matter of historical fact, it was youths of Aleck Sander and Chick's generation who experienced the civil rights revolution.

STYLE

Stream of Consciousness

"Stream of consciousness" is the term literary critics use to describe a technique of telling a story from inside a character's mind. The technique was brought to a high level of development during the 1920s by authors like James Joyce, Virginia Woolf, Ernest Hemingway, and Faulkner himself. All of these novelists had come to understand that the human mind is not, in fact, very orderly; thoughts jump backward and forward in time, leap from topic to topic, are easily interrupted, and are further tangled up by such distractions as

snatches of music. These authors set out to try to capture this chaos on the page. Faulkner's sentence style seems a part of his own effort to do so. He has noted that, in the mind, language is not divided into neat grammatical packages, and so he frequently constructs sentences a page or more in length (first-time readers of Faulkner often find this the most difficult aspect of his style). He does occasionally use italics to indicate such important shifts as jumps in time or perspective.

Plot

When literary critics speak of "plot," they are referring to the order in which events are arranged in a story. A plot can be quite orderly and straightforward, or it can be disconnected and episodic. The plot of *Intruder in the Dust* is actually deceptive, in a modest way. It appears to be a conventional crime novel or murder mystery. In such a novel, a crime is committed, and the central character has to figure out who the guilty party is. The reader knows as much as the central character, who puts together the clues until, at the end, the identity of the criminal is revealed. But this aspect of *Intruder in the Dust* actually seems less important as one studies the book. The real plot is the history of Yoknapatawpha since the Civil War, and the nature of race relations there. In a way, Faulkner does not hide the identity of the villain so much as he hides his actual topic behind the veneer of a conventional crime story.

Southern Gothic

The term "Gothic" fiction refers to stories that include elements of the supernatural or grotesque; famous Gothic novels include Mary Shelley's *Frankenstein* (1818) or Bram Stoker's *Dracula* (1897). The term "Southern Gothic" was invented to describe a kind of story by a Southern author, usually set in the South, which relies on similarly grotesque elements and characters. In practice, Southern Gothic writers have normally been thought of as critics of the South, of its religiosity, its conservatism, or its problems with race relations. These writers did not work together to form a conscious "school" of literature, and many who are identified with Southern Gothic (Tennessee Williams, Erskine Caldwell, Carson McCullers, Flannery O'Connor, Eudora Welty, and many others) would resist the idea that they fit the definition. Only part of Faulkner's work could be considered Southern Gothic, although *Intruder in the Dust* could be regarded as a good candidate for inclusion in the group. Note how much of the plot involves opening fresh graves, as in the classic Frankenstein movies.

HISTORICAL CONTEXT

The Antebellum, or Pre– Civil War, South

Events in the South during Faulkner's life cannot be understood without knowing something of the American Civil War (1861–1865). The essence of the situation is that the northern and southern sections of the United States had, over the course of the last two centuries before the Civil War, followed different paths. The North had become, by 1860, an industrial powerhouse, a full participant in the Industrial Revolution that was then sweeping across the advanced nations of the world. The South had remained agrarian, growing cotton, sugar, and rice. After

the invention of the cotton gin, a device that separated cotton from its seeds with high efficiency, the South became the Cotton Kingdom, exporting vast quantities to Great Britain, where the cotton was spun into cloth. The entire system, unfortunately, rested on the backs of millions of slaves, who grew the cotton and kept the gins running.

Because they followed different paths, the two regions, North and South, began to look like different countries, with their own separate languages and cultures. When Northern activists began to make some progress toward their long-cherished goal of banning slavery, it looked, to Southerners, like an attack on their entire economic system. When the war began, it seemed an invasion of a sovereign nation by another nation bent on conquest. The average Confederate infantryman was not wealthy enough to own slaves; he was fighting the invasion of his native country. And, in spite of the Confederacy's impressive military qualities, he lost. The South was devastated, and the slaves were freed, at the end of the Civil War in 1865.

Segregation and Integration

To deal with the former slaves, in what remained a thoroughly racist society, the South soon developed a system of segregation. All public facilities would be, as the phrase went, "separate but equal." So blacks and whites lived almost entirely separate lives, interacting only as white employers and black employees. In practice, the separate facilities for blacks were never equal to white facilities; a black school, for instance, never got as much money as a white school of comparable size. Blacks tolerated the situation because they were usually outnumbered, and violence could break out if, like Lucas Beauchamp, they insisted on their dignity. In practice, many simply left the South in what historians call the "great migration," leaving for Northern cities, just as Beauchamp's married daughter left for Detroit.

But as of 1948, the year of *Intruder in the Dust*, change was coming fast. In 1947, Jackie Robinson had broken the color barrier in major league baseball. In 1948, Harry Truman introduced the first civil rights legislation. That summer, Truman took matters into his own hands, signing an executive order that desegregated the United States armed forces, which had previously been separated into black and white units. What is now called "the Civil Rights Movement" gathered speed throughout

COMPARE
&
CONTRAST

- **1940s:** Russia was still part of the "Soviet Union" and was ruled by the Communist dictator Josef Stalin. The Soviets and the Americans were finding themselves locked in an increasingly dangerous standoff called the Cold War.

  Today: While relations with Russia are frequently tense, the sense of impending doom is gone, because the former Soviet Union has disintegrated.

- **1940s:** Faulkner's South was segregated: blacks and whites lived in separate neighborhoods, went to separate schools, stayed

in separate hotels, used separate drinking fountains, and so on.

  Today: While blacks and whites frequently lead separate lives, and equality of opportunity is imperfect at best, segregation is illegal everywhere.

- **1940s:** In many places, black people were kept from running for public office or even voting.

  Today: The United States has elected a black man, Barack Hussein Obama, as president of the United States.

---

the 1950s, especially under the leadership of the charismatic Martin Luther King Jr. The movement culminated in the federal Civil Rights Act of 1964, which substantially outlawed racial segregation.

CRITICAL OVERVIEW

Intruder in the Dust was an immediate monetary success for Faulkner. It was his first full-length book since *Go Down, Moses*, six years before, and it made clear to the public that he still had some creative life in him. The MGM movie studio paid his publisher $50,000 for the film rights, of which Faulkner received $40,000; such sums are large still today, but were enormous in the 1940s. It provided Faulkner the financial comfort he needed. And the book sold well, moving about 18,000 copies during its first year, more than any of his previous books. The novel has, however, usually been considered a second-rank book, compared to his major classics like *The Sound and the Fury*. Any search of the scholarly databases that collect literary criticism reveals a vast gap between the mountain of commentary on *The Sound and the Fury* and the relatively minimal discussion of *Intruder in the Dust*. The

book nevertheless remains popular among readers, and has attracted its share of commentary by critics, as is inevitable: William Faulkner is one of the most important authors in U.S. literary history.

When the book was new, some dismissed it as a mere crime novel, and one early critic to come to its defense was Donna Gerstenberger, who analyzed the novel at length in a 1961 article. The novel, she writes, "is too often dismissed as a propaganda-bearing tract, thinly disguised as a not very clear murder mystery. Yet *Intruder in the Dust* has a clear design and a significant form." One question some have considered is the title itself, which Faulkner had trouble with. He went through various versions, and seems to have become genuinely irritated by the problem; some believe the title he ended with, "Intruder in the Dust," was merely a last-minute improvisation. Lorie Watkins Fulton looks at this question and discovers that the title actually communicates some crucial information and works on many different levels. For instance,

> Faulker's emphasis on the process of substitution puts forward two characters as possible intruders: Jake Montgomery, the 'shoestring' timber buyer whose dead body Chick Mallison,

A man reads the funeral announcements for four African Americans murdered by a lynch mob in 1946, two years before Faulkner published Intruder in the Dust. *Below, a notice from the Federal government threatens prosecution for anyone attempting to prevent an African American from voting.* (FPG / Hulton Archive / Getty Images)

Miss Habersham, and Aleck Sander find literally intruding upon the ground of Vinson Gowrie's grave, and Lucas Beauchamp, the black man who stands accused of Gowrie's murder after essentially intruding into the scam which led to that death.

Ticien Marie Sassoubre analyzes *Intruder in the Dust* in the context of Southern history, both the general history of the region and the legal history of race relations there. She notes that the young Faulkner had an experience that surely had a lasting impression on him, where racial justice is concerned. A black man accused of slitting the throat of a white woman was arrested, and hauled out of jail by a huge mob and lynched the very same night. Local authorities had tried to stop the lynching, but they were urged on by a respected Oxford lawyer. As Sassoubre notes, "The young Faulkner may well have heard, if he did not in fact see, the lynching—his childhood home was only a few blocks from the Oxford jail."

CRITICISM

Scott Herring

Scott Herring teaches both twentieth-century American literature and writing at the University of California, Davis. In this essay, he considers how inheritance and disinheritance works in the world Faulkner creates in Intruder in the Dust, *as well as in the actual Mississippi in which he lived.*

William Faulkner was a legendary drinker in two senses: He could consume truly enormous amounts of alcohol, and some contended that he needed alcohol as a kind of potion that gave him creativity and inspiration as an artist. However, common sense states that no one could have produced novels as complex as he did while under the influence of alcohol. This becomes especially clear when considering the almost unbelievably complex family trees that Faulkner constructed for his imaginary families in Yoknapatawpha County. A number of prominent families in the county appear in novel after novel, and Faulkner would follow the history of each clan backward and forward in time, keeping the relationships, birth dates, and death dates of each member in mind as he constructed their stories (and further mixing the families together in any given story or novel; again, no one could have accomplished this feat while as inebriated as the legends say he was).

Of the prominent Yoknapatawpha clans, the one most important in understanding *Intruder in the Dust* is the McCaslin family; without an understanding of its twists and turns, a crucial level of meaning is missed in the novel.

One source of confusion for a reader of *Intruder in the Dust* is that the McCaslin family history does not appear primarily in this book. The main source for much of this information is Faulkner's *Go Down, Moses* (1942), a collection of long short stories that are closely related to one another—so closely that the book is often considered a novel.

The details of what happens to the McCaslin clan are a key to understanding Lucas Beauchamp's personality and actions. The Yoknapatawpha McCaslin clan is founded by a man with the resounding name of Lucius Quintus Carothers McCaslin, who lives from 1772 to 1837, and is normally known simply as Carothers McCaslin. By the era of *Go Down, Moses*, his grandchildren have entered the picture, cousins Ike McCaslin and Cass Edmonds. Ike is due to inherit the huge plantation established back in the 1800s by

WHAT DO I READ NEXT?

- Any serious student of Faulkner, and any-one who wants to fully understand *Intruder in the Dust*, should also read Faulkner's 1942 collection *Go Down, Moses*. The earlier book gives a great deal of valuable back-ground on the characters in the later novel.

- Although it is about another time and place, a student of *Intruder in the Dust* can benefit by reading "Shooting an Elephant," an essay written by the English novelist George Orwell in 1936. It is in many anthologies, and is even available free on the Internet. In it, Orwell tells the story of how he had to confront a dangerous elephant while work-ing as a police officer in a British colony in the 1920s. It provides some key insight into the psychology of people who set themselves up as masters over what they regard as an inferior race of people.

- *The Civil War* is a 1990 PBS film by Ken Burn. It is impossible to fully understand Faulkner without some knowledge of the American Civil War. An easy way to approach this complex conflict is to watch Burns's famous documen-tary. Also read the companion book to the series (*The Civil War*) which is a good way to review the material at a slower pace. The book was issued as a paperback in 1994.

- *The Souls of Black Folk* (1903) by W. E. B. DuBois provides an African American view on race relations in the South. DuBois was a Harvard-educated professor, but was closely familiar with black life in the South, and gives a thorough view of that life when the Jim Crow system was at its height. It, and the next three items, are all widely available in libraries and paperback editions.

- Another view from the black author's perspec-tive is the 1912 novel *The Autobiography of an Ex-Coloured Man*, by James Weldon John-son. It tells the story of a light-skinned black man who, in a time of segregation, lives some parts of his life in the white world, and some in the black. The novel ends with a horrific description of a lynching, which suggests what would be in store for Lucas Beauchamp if the lynch mob were to get hold of him.

- For a very different view, again by a black author, see the collection of essays by Zora Neale Hurston, published in 1979 under the title *I Love Myself When I Am Laughing*. Hurston was from Florida, and she brought an absolutely unique perspective to the debate. A conservative who regularly voted for Republicans, Hurston liked to point out some of the *positive* qualities of the relation-ship between blacks and whites in the South—the sense of community and mutual aid, for instance.

- For another novel written from a black wom-an's viewpoint, see Nella Larsen's *Quicksand*. As in *The Autobiography of an Ex-Coloured Man*, the central character moves through various situations, in both the white and black worlds, and finally marries a black preacher in the South. The reader then learns just how exhausting work and childbearing was for women under such circumstances.

Carothers McCaslin. Ike is, however, an idealist. Because he feels a kind of collective guilt for how the South has treated black people, he does not want to have anything to do with the system. He therefore transfers ownership of the plantation to Edmonds. So it is to the "Edmonds place" that Chick goes to hunt rabbits at the start of *Intruder in the Dust*.

Carothers McCaslin, however, has had many children, not all of them with his wife. As was common among slaveholders before the Civil War, he has at least two children by two of his slaves. One of them, Tomasina, is Lucas Beau-champ's grandmother; her son is Lucas's father. Lucas is thus a direct descendant of the patriarch Carothers McCaslin, which explains his otherwise

> **[LUCAS BEAUCHAMP] IS ACTUALLY THE RIGHTFUL OWNER OF THE VAST ESTATE WHERE HE HAS HIS TINY CABIN. HE HAS BEEN DISINHERITED BY THE RACIAL TRADITIONS OF THE SOUTH, AN INJUSTICE THAT EXPLAINS MUCH OF THE ANGER THAT SEEMS TO SIMMER JUST BENEATH THE SURFACE OF HIS PERSONALITY."**

potentially confusing comment when he is attacked at the crossroads store near the start of Chapter Two. The man who attacks him calls Lucas a "biggity stiff-necked stinking burrheaded Edmonds sonofabitch." Lucas calmly replies, "I aint a Edmonds. I dont belong to these new folks. I belongs to the old lot. I'm a McCaslin". He regards the Edmonds family, which has only recently taken charge of the land, as interlopers, intruders into the old dynasty.

Among the aristocracy in Europe, the system for dividing huge estates was one called "primogeniture." It is a term from common law, and while the system can take multiple forms, it usually refers to the practice of having the first-born son of a family inherit the land and, in a country with nobility, the title. The Old South modeled itself on Europe and followed this practice. The McCaslin and Edmonds families have, however, violated the system. They specifically did so when Ike McCaslin transferred the land to Cass Edmonds.

Cass descends from a daughter of old Carothers McCaslin, and under the system of primogeniture, he should not be in charge. That position should go to the male heir. The male line, however, is made up of slaves and the descendants of slaves, ending in Lucas Beauchamp. Lucas should possess the whole two-thousand-acre plantation, but does not because of his race and his parents' condition as slaves. The family is aware of the problem and has tried to make amends, after a fashion. As Chick approaches Lucas's house after the fall in the creek, he remembers the rest of the story of Lucas's land: "How Edmonds' father had deeded to his Negro first cousin and his heirs in perpetuity the house and the ten acres of land it sat

in—an oblong of earth set forever in the middle of the two-thousand-acre plantation like a postage stamp in the center of an envelope."

Lucas obviously regards this gesture as inadequate, and it colors his behavior toward everyone. He is actually the rightful owner of the vast estate where he has his tiny cabin. He has been disinherited by the racial traditions of the South, an injustice that explains much of the anger that seems to simmer just beneath the surface of his personality. He veers constantly between something like dignity and something like arrogance—just as a wealthy planter would. The description of Lucas, as seen from Chick's point of view just after he has fallen in the river, sums up his personality and situation. The appearance and attitude of Lucas Beauchamp's face is something new to Chick:

> [W]hat looked out of it had no pigment at all, not even the white man's lack of it, not arrogant, not even scornful: just intractable and composed. Then Edmonds' boy said something to the man, speaking a name: something Mister Lucas: and then he knew who the man was, remembering the rest of the story which was a piece, a fragment of the country's chronicle which few if any knew better than his uncle: how the man was son of one of old Carothers McCaslin's, Edmonds' great grandfather's, slaves who had been not just old Carothers' slave but his son too: standing and shaking steadily now for what seemed to him another whole minute while the man stood looking at him with nothing whatever in his face. Then the man turned, speaking not even back over his shoulder, already walking, not even waiting to see if they heard, let alone were going to obey: 'Come on to my home.'

When Lucas refuses the coins in payment for the meal he has given Chick, it is a crucial moment in Chick's life, because it is the first time he has been bested by a black man. The coins so humiliate Chick that he disposes of them quickly:

> [He] drew the four coins from his pocket and threw them out into the water: and sleepless in bed that night he knew that the food had been not just the best Lucas had to offer but all he had to offer; he had gone out there this morning as the guest not of Edmonds but of old Carothers McCaslin's plantation and Lucas knew it when he didn't and so Lucas had beat him, stood straddled in front of the hearth and without even moving his clasped hands from behind his back had taken his own seventy cents and beat him with them, and writhing with impotent fury he was already thinking of the man whom he had never seen but once and

that only twelve hours ago, as within the next year he was to learn every white man in that whole section of the country had been thinking about him for years: *We got to make him be a nigger first. He's got to admit he's a nigger. Then maybe we will accept him as he seems to intend to be accepted.*

What is happening here is that Lucas is insisting on his rightful position as the owner of old Carothers McCaslin's property. As a host, he delivers food to the wayfarer free of charge, according to the rules of hospitality. Refusing the money is a way of making it clear that he is neither an innkeeper nor a black servant; the money would make him servile, while the free gift of food makes him an equal, and truly master of this domain. The twelve-year-old Chick is a product of the white society in which he has been raised, so this declaration of social equality is intolerable. It is normal behavior for Lucas, who believes himself to have been cheated out of his rightful inheritance by his race.

Source: Scott Herring, Critical Essay on *Intruder in the Dust*, in *Novels for Students 33*, Gale, Cengage Learning, 2010.

Lorie Watkins Fulton

In the following excerpted essay, Fulton pays careful attention to the significance of the title of Faulkner's Intruder in the Dust.

Whom, exactly, William Faulkner intends readers to envision as the intruder in *Intruder in the Dust* seems a question almost as complex as the mystery contained within the pages of the novel itself. The lack of any definite candidate for the position, combined with Faulkner's difficulty in selecting a title, tempts one to treat his choice as a throwaway, unimportant because likely chosen in a moment of desperation. The beginnings of his frustration appear in a letter Robert K. Haas, his literary agent, received from him on March 15, 1948, in which he complains, "By the way, first time in my experience, I cant find a title." Actually, he already knew that he wanted to use the phrase "in the dust," and searched only for the perfect word to combine with it. He wrote to Haas, "I want a word, a dignified (or more dignified) synonym for 'shenanigan,' 'skulduggery'; maybe" (*Selected Letters* 264–265). Faulkner's correspondence shows that his mild irritation at his inability to choose a title soon escalated, and he followed his first letter with another to Haas approximately a week later proposing *Intruder in the Dust* as a title, along with

> IN THE PROCESS OF HELPING LUCAS, CHICK INADVERTENTLY DESTROYS HIS WORLD AS HE KNOWS IT BY PUTTING THE EVENTS INTO MOTION THAT SEVER THE PHILOSOPHICAL AND EMOTIONAL TIES BINDING HIM TO IT."

several other possible (though perhaps not completely serious) combinations including the likes of "Imposter," "Sleeper," "Malfeasance," and even "Malaprop" (265). After initially composing the letter, Faulkner returned to it six hours later and typed, "I believe Intruder In The Dust is best yet," and even added in ink on the following Tuesday, "Still like Intruder In The Dust" (265). Clearly, the matter continued to prey upon his mind, and he hardly settled it so easily. On April twentieth, Faulkner, still in search of a title, again wrote to Haas that he sought a word synonymous with "substitution by sharp practice." Although "Jugglery" came closest to expressing the meaning he searched for, he rejected it because he thought it a "harsh ugly word" (266). He finally settled firmly upon the title, though not without reservations, by the time he wrote to Bennett Cerf in early May, that "lacking any short word for substitution, swap, exchange, sleight-of-hand, I think Intruder In The Dust is best" (268).

Faulker's emphasis on the process of substitution puts forward two characters as possible intruders: Jake Montgomery, the "shoestring" timber buyer whose dead body Chick Mallison, Miss Habersham, and Aleck Sander find literally intruding upon the ground of Vinson Gowrie's grave, and Lucas Beauchamp, the black man who stands accused of Gowrie's murder after essentially intruding into the scam which led to that death. The meaning of the title, though, perhaps should depend more upon the phrase "in the dust" than the initial word that Faulkner never quite found adequate. From the beginning, he seemed sure of the final part of his title, and Patrick Samway implies that the latter phrase might occupy a more central position than the word which precedes it when he notes in his introduction to the novel's concordance that Faulkner uses the word "intruder" only in the title, but the phrase "in the dust" is "used 3 times and in each case there is an association with blacks" (ix). Samway's observation, though astute, limits the importance of the central image, dust, with its focus on the entire phrase. Reducing the phrase to its essential image infinitely expands the implications of the title. Various forms of "dust" float throughout the pages of *Intruder in the Dust,* and an examination of that dust, in all its various guises, narrows the possibilities for who the intruder might actually be, and, perhaps more importantly, clarifies what, exactly, that character intrudes upon.

Faulkner refers to many types of soil in *Intruder in the Dust,* and they all serve specific functions. His deliberate usage emphasizes the importance of such subtle differences; for example, as Chick and his uncle, Gavin Stevens, drive through the streets of Jefferson after Chick's all-night adventure in the graveyard, Chick notices the "string of cars and trucks stained with country mud and dust". Faulkner carefully differentiates "mud" from "dust," and such specificity undercuts the otherwise likely possibility that the dust of his title simply refers to the dust of Vinson Gowrie's or, for that matter, any other grave. Faulkner never associates any of the novel's various graves with the word "dust": Aleck Sander and Chick shovel "dirt" from Vinson Gowrie's grave, "dirt" trickles back into it after Hope Hampton later finds it empty, Jake Montgomery's body resides in a "mound of fresh shaled earth" and the Gowrie family pulls Vinson's body from "quicksand".

Whatever elements compose the dust in this novel, they seem to come from a source other than the cemetery. Faulkner's most intriguing reference to dust suggests a connection with a passing of another sort and has more to do with Jefferson's mythic history than with any one specific person. As Chick first enters the jail with Stevens, whose legal services Lucas wishes to retain, he remembers:

> his uncle had said once that not courthouses nor even churches but jails were the true records of a county's, a community's history, since not only the cryptic forgotten initials and words and even phrases cries of defiance and indictment scratched into the walls but the very bricks and stones themselves held, not in solution but in suspension, intact and biding and potent and indestructible, the agonies and shames and griefs with which hearts long since unmarked and unremembered *dust* had strained and perhaps burst.

For Chick, and, of course, Stevens, the jail evokes the very essence of Jefferson's strife-filled past. As the various individuals become absorbed into this shared communal history, the "dust," all that remains of the particular hearts, stays, for the most part "unmarked and unremembered" in that collective past. Thus Faulkner's complex construction loosely equates "dust" with some sort of past communal strife, and employs the jail as a symbol of it. Accordingly, Faulkner's language reinforces this connection in that the jail gives off a decidedly "dusty" aura as the "dim dusty flyspecked bulb" which lights the jail generates, at best, a "dusty glare". Lucas, while held in the very heart of that dusty jail, the lone cell, convinces Chick to violate Vinson Gowrie's grave and obtain the evidence that will prove his innocence. In doing so, Chick unearths something far more disturbing than a dead body; he discovers the depth of Jefferson's ingrained racial prejudices and realizes the lengths to which its citizens will go to maintain their self-serving ideology of white supremacy.

This realization, though, happens gradually, and Chick's relationship to the history represented by the jail is complicated. The building occupies such a representative position, Chick theorizes, "because it and one of the churches were the oldest buildings in the town, the courthouse and everything else on or in the Square having been burned to rubble by Federal occupation forces after a battle in 1864." More importantly, Chick goes on to establish that the jail stands as such a monument because "scratched into one of the panes of the fanlight beside the door was a young girl's single name, written by her own hand into the glass with a diamond in that same year". Though he does not refer to her by name, Chick most likely speaks of the town legend concerning Cecilia Farmer that Faulkner later recounts more fully in *Requiem for a Nun* . . .

Cecilia's story, then, for Chick both represents the sort of conflict that his uncle's complicated reference concerning dust highlights and gives him a context for his own musings about the past and how history might remember him in a similar fashion. Appropriately enough, this Civil War story grounds that strife at the crux of the South's racially troubled past, and Chick's identification with Cecilia intensifies as the novel progresses. Chick admits that with his efforts on Lucas's behalf, he wants "to leave his mark too on his time in man, but only that, no more than that, some mark on his part in earth". In attempting to leave this mark, though, Chick, gets far more than he bargained for:

> certainly he hadn't expected this:—not a life saved from death nor even a death saved from shame and indignity nor even the suspension of a sentence but merely the grudging pretermission of a date; not indignity shamed with its own shameful cancellation, not sublimation and humility with humility and pride remembered nor the pride of courage and passion nor of pity nor the pride and austerity and grief, but austerity itself debased by what it had gained, courage and passion befouled by what they had had to cope with.

Indeed, self-interest motivates Chick when he agrees to help Lucas; he initially wants only to eradicate the childhood debt that he incurs as the novel begins, and he secretly hopes that he might become a significant part of Jefferson's history in the process. Although he only wants to leave his mark on that collective history, as he thinks Cecilia did, he instead comes to see the crowd that almost lynches Lucas, "his people his blood his own" as "a Face monstrous unravening omniverous and not even uninsatiate". In the process of helping Lucas, Chick inadvertently destroys his world as he knows it by putting the events into motion that sever the philosophical and emotional ties binding him to it. Thus he intrudes into this conflict at what, for him, becomes quite a high price.

As Chick watches the mob gather and realizes that, for the white citizens of Jefferson, Lucas remains largely incidental to his own impending trial for murder, Faulkner writes, "something like a skim or a veil like that which crosses a chicken's eye and which he [Chick] had not even known was there went flick! from his own [eye] and he saw them [the townspeople] for the first time."

Some of Faulkner's more minor references to dust point to Chick as the novel's intruder as well. In the initial flashback scene, Chick enters Lucas's yard and describes it as "completely bare, no weed no sprig of anything, the dust each morning swept by some of Lucas' womenfolks". In some ways, dust seems to epitomize the general condition of Jefferson's African American population. Faulkner again makes reference to the "grassless treeless yards" of similar residences as Chick and his uncle drive to the exhumation, and Chick earlier noticed that he "had not seen one Negro" walking the "dusty roads" leading into town. Chick's observation implies, of course, that only the poorest of whites would have walked through the road's dust in a similar fashion, without even a mule to lift them above it. And, most obviously, the jail's inmate population consists of "five Negroes" incarcerated separately from Lucas in the "dusty glare" of Jefferson's jail.

As Chick intrudes into this world filled with the metaphorical dust, indeed the fallout, generated by the intersection of race and history, Faulkner necessarily goes with him. From a modern standpoint, this incursion seems somewhat less than revolutionary. As Richard C. Moreland observes, Faulkner's attempt to deal with racial issues in a contemporary fictional setting "includes more than its share of clumsiness and embarrassment". Faulkner's delineation of Lucas likely presents the novel's most problematic element; after all, he hardly comes across as a radical figure. He epitomizes, as Erik Dussere points out, "a version of the perfect Negro Faulkner invokes in his public writings, the one who is required to be *superior* to white people in order to be deserving of equality". Such criticism, of course, seems obvious enough in the twenty-first century, but we cannot forget that, as a product of the 1940s, *Intruder in the Dust* bears these and many other marks of the era of its composition. Therefore it seems even more remarkable that Faulkner intrudes, however problematically, into the social and political situation of his own day by putting his theories about how the South might solve its racial dilemma through individual action into play in the unlikely persons of two young boys and a spunky old lady. Sure, the fictional effort stands as a single occurrence, an isolated action, but as Chick—and perhaps even his uncle—comes to learn, change has to begin somewhere. Stevens predicts that "in time he [the black man] will vote anywhen and anywhere a white man can and send his children to the same school anywhere the white man's children go and travel anywhere the white man travels as the white man does it. But it wont be next Tuesday". For once Stevens is right, and in many ways we continue to wait for next Tuesday. By depicting the possibilities inherent in Chick's experience, though, Faulkner takes us a bit closer to that day his fiction envisions, one when the dust might finally settle.

Source: Lorie Watkins Fulton, "Intruder in the Past," in *Southern Literary Journal*, Vol. 38, No. 2, Spring 2006, pp. 64–73.

> THROUGH HIS DESCRIPTION OF WHITE SOUTHERNERS' IDEOLOGICALLY RITUALIZED RESPONSE TO AN ALLEGED RACE MURDER, FAULKNER MAKES THE POINT THAT, IN REDUCING THE CHAOTIC COMPLEXITY OF REALITIES TO SIMPLE NOTIONS, THE RACIALLY CLICHÉD LANGUAGE OF THE SOUTH DENIES PEOPLE A DISCOURSE IN WHICH TO THINK OR ACT OUTSIDE THE SCOPE OF IDEOLOGY."

Masami Sugimori

In the following excerpted essay, Sugimori analyzes Faulkner's careful, almost tortuous negotiation of whiteness and racism in Intruder in the Dust.

Coming out of Faulkner's "dark years," after his period of "authentic originality and greatness" (Minter 192–93), *Intruder in the Dust* has attracted relatively little critical attention since its publication. When critics do discuss the novel at length, their approach has often drawn upon the general conception that "Faulkner failed to give it the intensity and resonance we associate with his finest work" such as *The Sound and the Fury, Light in August*, and *Absalom, Absalom!* (Minter 212). Accordingly, most of this scholarship has treated *Intruder in the Dust* as a kind of political novel and thus focused on Faulkner's personal attitude toward contemporary Southern race relations and how this attitude manifests in his narrative. Unlike the "work of authentic originality and greatness" from his prolific years, the novel's philosophical investigation of race itself has suffered critical disregard.

With its major attention to the author's explicit or implicit self-expression, the prevailing political approach to the novel predicates itself upon a rather simplistic question of whether, and to what degree, the character of Gavin Stevens represents Faulkner. Observing that "Stevens clearly echoes many of the author's recorded sentiments," Carl Dimitri identifies one with the other and attributes Stevens's inconsistency on racial equality to Faulkner's own inconsistency: "It is a testimony to the confused nature of Faulkner's stance on civil rights, as well as to the confused nature of *Intruder in the Dust* itself, that Stevens contradicts [himself on] these sentiments" (21). In contrast, while admitting their shared moderate conservatism, Noel Polk emphasizes there is "plenty of distance between Gavin Stevens and William Faulkner" (143), between the hypocritical character "so completely wedded, even if he does not know it, to the status quo" and the author whose "concern was consistently with the *individual* Negro" (141). Pointing to a middle ground, John E. Bassett describes Faulkner's attitude toward Stevens as "identification mixed with self-irony" (212). However, resorting to the same framework which reduces their relationship to identification, opposition, or in-between and, in so doing, presupposes a "politicizably" unproblematical, monolithic notion of race, Bassett misses Faulkner's socioepistemological inquiry into race itself—an inquiry made *through* his characters' ideologically charged practices. Thus, for Bassett, *Intruder in the Dust* conveys the novelist's message more explicitly than his preceding "great works": "In one sense the message had been implicit ever since Faulkner first considered the modes of knowing and communicating [racial blackness] in *Light in August*. Now in the last novel in which he confronts the issue directly, it is more explicit" (216).

Keith Clark's study of Lucas Beauchamp overcomes the reductive critical model of placing the character on the same level as the author: "In my treatment of Lucas . . . I approach Faulkner's protagonist not so much as an extension of the author's own views on race and racism, but instead as a character in the matrix of Faulkner's art" (67) . . .

Indeed, through his characterization of Lucas in *Intruder in the Dust*, Faulkner points to the problematical nature of Southern whiteness as a construct predicated upon the reductive operation of language in ordering (by signification) the essentially chaotic world. With no intrinsic signified in material reality, whiteness as a signifier defines itself only as opposed to blackness which, as the "liminal" Lucas plainly shows, also lacks a substantial foothold. The novel dramatizes the situation where, as dominant ideology penetrates people's mental activity through a particular language it endorses, Southern whites, with their monolithic subjectivity authorized by the Southern racial ideology, cannot conceive of blacks except as an abstract and homogeneous otherness nor question their own ritualized social practices such as lynching, thus further reinforcing the same ideology that determines their behavior. Therefore, I shall argue, Lucas's silence indicates not only his "marginalization" but also a liberation from the ideologized language that reductively defines him as a "nigger" and in turn helps "whites" to become such. Chick Mallison's attempt to save Lucas from impending lynching corresponds with his struggle with ideo-linguistically charged whiteness which, as exemplified by Gavin Stevens's talkative acquiescence to mob violence, limits one's thinking to that of racism.

In the postbellum Southern setting of the novel, the "one-drop rule" serves to binarize a chaotic variety of individuals into "whites" and "blacks," with the former on the top of the hierarchy. To reinforce the racial hierarchy on which it founds itself, the white-supremacist society further describes/ inscribes "blacks" with another trope, "niggers," which not only suppresses their diversity, individuality, and personhood but also attaches to them stereotypically inferior—and somewhat mutually contradicting—attributes such as "ignorance," "cowardice," "childishness," "subservience," "savageness" and "brutality." Thus, white men in the novel insist on imposing the "nigger" label upon Lucas all the more for his essentially unclassifiable (and so potentially disruptive) in-betweenness in terms of race, appearance (e.g., his eyes belong to "not black nor white either", and behavior ("not arrogant at all and not even scornful: just intolerant inflexible and composed"): "*We got to make him be a nigger first. He's got to admit he's a nigger. Then maybe we will accept him as he seems to intend to be accepted*". Faulkner also utilizes Chick's interior monologue to demonstrate how the white youth, influenced by his discursive environment, unwittingly thinks in a fashion already built into the highly racialized language. Looking at Lucas sleep silently in jail on the night following his alleged crime, Chick conceives of the suspect as a "nigger":

> *He's just a nigger after all for all his high nose and his stiff neck and his gold watch-chain and refusing to mean mister to anybody even when he says it. Only a nigger could kill a man, let alone shoot him in the back, and then sleep like a baby as soon as he found something flat enough to lie down on . . .*

Here, following the stereotype of "coward nigger," Chick defines Lucas as a "nigger" based on the false allegation that Lucas has "*kill[ed] a man . . . [and shot] him in the back*" (which itself originates from the "word" of a white man). This

"nigger" tag in turn leads Chick to describe Lucas's sleep of the just as that of a "childish nigger" ("*like a baby*"), which reinscribes the old man's "nigger" identity to reconfirm the original definition. In this passage Faulkner also takes pains to represent the tension between chaotic reality and ordering language through his syntax; with the concessive preposition "*for all*," he presents the reductive "nigger" epithet ("*just a nigger after all*") as suppressing all the uncategorizable complexities of the real-life Lucas such as "*his high nose and his stiff neck and his gold watch-chain and refusing to mean mister.*"

Here Jacques Lacan's psychoanalytic theory on language and human subjectivity bears much relevance. The following passage elucidates, though not specifically in racial terms, the interplay between the lack of substantive, "real" signifieds corresponding to signifying words, the performative (i.e., at once descriptive and inscriptive) function of language which apparently covers the lack, and the "symbolic" construction of self which depends upon the empty signification:

> the function of language in speech is not to inform but to evoke.
>
> What I seek in speech is a response from the other. What constitutes me as a subject is my question. In order to be recognized by the other, I proffer what was only in view of what will be. In order to find him, I call him by a name that he must assume or refuse in order to answer me.
>
> I identify myself in language, but only by losing myself in it as an object. What is realized in my history is neither the past definite as what was, since it is no more, nor even the perfect as what has been in what I am, but the future anterior as what I will have been, given what I am in the process of becoming.

According to Lacan, language works to form human subjectivity not by signifying ("informing" of) something "real" about one's identity (which does not really exist). Rather, the speaker "evokes" a sense of difference from the addressed "other" (though, again, such difference does not have a substantial counterpart in the real world) who is to recognize the speaker as a subject by "assuming" or "refusing" the term of address. As a result, in identifying a person's self, language operates performatively, at the same time describing and inscribing "what I am in the process of becoming." Thus, the white men's frustration at labeling Lucas a "nigger"—and in turn defining themselves as opposed to that "nigger"—derives from the old man's transcending indifference to "assuming" or "refusing" the epithet, a transcendence that disrupts the whole system of racial identity construction. Tellingly, when his gold watch-chain and toothpick infuriate a white man with their out-of-place extravagance, Lucas responds only to the color-blind, familial part of the white's abuse ("You goddamn biggity stiffnecked stinking burrheaded Edmonds sonofabitch") but does not "assume" nor "refuse" the racially charged term "burrheaded": "I aint a Edmonds... I'm a McCaslin..."

As Faulkner critiques the ideologized language of the South in *Intruder in the Dust*, Lucas's silence, which Keith Clark criticizes as the author's "devoic[ing] [of] his 'strong' black protagonist," rather indicates a disruption of the reductive categories of the "black" and the "nigger" when it helps him evade responding to (i.e., "assuming or refusing") these epithets. Even when he does talk, Lucas's reticent words, such as the above-discussed remark that "I aint a Edmonds... I'm a McCaslin," work to defy the racializing function of the language. Tellingly, when the situation forces him to adopt a racially hierarchizing language, Lucas does so in such a way that he "said 'sir' and 'mister' to you if you were white but... you knew [he] was thinking neither and he knew you knew it"; thus exposing to the whites the emptiness of the honorific signifiers and the fictiveness of the "niggerish servility" which supposedly underlies their usage. On the whites' part too, in a somewhat different way, silence—in tandem with "Vocabulary"—can help liberate individuals if it provides a receptive space for ideologically unorthodox discourse. Thus, whereas white male adults resort to filling in Lucas's frustrating silence with the "murderous nigger" stereotype (as Gavin scolds him in jail, "if you just said mister to white people and said it like you meant it, you might not be sitting here now", Chick's capacity to "hear the mute unhoping urgency of [Lucas's] eyes" and accept his account against the ideological grain leads eventually to the old man's release. Symbolically, in accepting Lucas's rescuing "voice," the drowning twelve-year-old Chick unconsciously overcomes his already learned sense of racial difference which would have forbidden him to get help from a "nigger": "it didn't matter whose [voice it was]." In contrast, the white boy later resents the same "voice" which—saying, "Pick up his money... Give it to him"—refuses the money he offers for a dinner at Lucas's house. Back under the influence of racist

ideology, Chick cannot listen to the "voice" that hinders his ritualistic self-subjectification as a "superior white." According to Chick's ideologized sense of "honor," as Erik Dussere cogently argues, "having been given the gift of Lucas's hospitality, [Chick] is metaphorically in the position of social inferior to a 'nigger'" (46) ...

Intruder in the Dust dramatizes the interaction between Southern racist ideology and the racialized language of the South. Through his description of white Southerners' ideologically ritualized response to an alleged race murder, Faulkner makes the point that, in reducing the chaotic complexity of realities to simple notions, the racially clichéd language of the South denies people a discourse in which to think or act outside the scope of ideology. In contrast with the talkative white males who have "vocabulary" but not "Vocabulary," Lucas's silence, Miss Habersham's attentiveness to "truth" with her "Vocabulary," and Chick's willingness to listen to the discursively oppressed show a certain potential for escaping the control of ideologized discourse. At the same time, Faulkner's careful description of how the racist regime works subtly to hinder or even incorporate potentially subversive thoughts and actions suggests a predicament at a broader, literary-artistic level. As Toni Morrison elucidates in her *Playing in the Dark*, regardless of their attitudes toward the racial ideology, white writers' narrative conceptualization of the silenced African American body has necessarily entailed a certain ideological framing. Written in the racially charged mid-twentieth-century South, *Intruder in the Dust* shows the novelist's keen struggle to write against the linguistic-ideological grain. Not only do his lengthy and convoluted run-on sentences serve to complicate the differentiating operation of the language, Faulkner scrupulously depicts the problematics of the racist society which may even have extended to contain his own writing.

Source: Masami Sugimori, "Signifying, Ordering, and Containing the Chaos: Whiteness, Ideology, and Language in *Intruder in the Dust*," in *The Faulkner Journal*, Vol. 22, No. 1&2, Fall/Spring 2006, pp. 54–73.

SOURCES

Faulkner, William, *Intruder in the Dust*, Random House, 1948.

Fulton, Lorie Watkins, "Intruder in the Past," in *Southern Literary Journal*, Vol. 38, No. 2, Spring 2006, p. 65.

Gerstenberger, Donna, "Meaning and Form in *Intruder in the Dust*," in *College English*, Vol. 23, No. 3, December 1961, p. 223.

Sassoubre, Ticien Marie, "Avoiding Adjudication in William Faulkner's *Go Down, Moses* and *Intruder in the Dust*," in *Criticism: A Quarterly for Literature and the Arts*, Vol. 49, No. 2, Spring 2007, p. 183.

FURTHER READING

Blotner, Joseph, *Faulkner: A Biography*, University Press of Mississippi, 2005.

This quite recent biography has a reputation for being thorough; every known fact about Faulkner's life is here.

Brooks, Cleanth, *William Faulkner: The Yoknapatawpha Country*, Louisiana State University Press, 1963.

This collection by a well-regarded critic includes an essay on *Intruder in the Dust*.

Fadiman, Regina K., *Faulkner's* Intruder in the Dust: *Novel into Film*, University of Tennessee Press, 1977.

Fadiman describes the challenges involved in filming the book, and the choices made about what would have to be left out or changed.

Gresset, Michel, and Patrick Samway, *Essays on William Faulkner's* Intruder in the Dust, Saint Joseph's University Press, 2004.

This recent collection of essays by scholars is one of the only such collections to focus exclusively on this specific novel.

Kidnapped

ROBERT LOUIS STEVENSON
1886

Robert Louis Stevenson's *Kidnapped* (1886) is widely regarded as one of the finest boys' adventure novels ever written, although it is often overshadowed by the author's other major adventure tale, *Treasure Island* (1883). Still, many critics and scholars have agreed with Stevenson himself that the novel is, as he wrote in a letter to his father, "a far better story and far sounder at heart than *Treasure Island*."

Stevenson was inspired to write *Kidnapped* after researching an important murder trial that took place in Scotland in 1752—the Appin Murder, which figures prominently in the plot of the book. The novel tells the story of David Balfour, a poor Scottish teen who discovers upon his father's death that he is actually the heir to a wealthy estate. Before he can claim it, however, his greedy uncle has the boy kidnapped by sailors and taken to sea, to be sold into slavery in the American Colonies. The novel weaves fiction with the significant historical events of the time and includes detailed descriptions of various Scottish locales Stevenson had visited during his youth. Although the novel contains a great deal of phonetically rendered Scottish dialect and words specific to the region, the compelling story has helped the book remain a favorite among young readers for more than a century.

Robert Louis Stevenson (*The Library of Congress*)

AUTHOR BIOGRAPHY

Stevenson was born on November 13, 1850, in Edinburgh, Scotland, the son of a lighthouse engineer. He was an only child, and suffered from illnesses made worse by the damp weather and air pollution in their ever-expanding capital city. Much of his youth was spent reading books, although he also enjoyed exploring the outdoors when his health allowed. He worked briefly with his father as an engineer in training. Although he was not consistently healthy enough to make it a career, this period of travel with his father opened his eyes to many new places such as Erraid, the Scottish tidal island on which David Balfour becomes shipwrecked in *Kidnapped*.

Stevenson went to law school to please his father but never actually practiced law, preferring instead to write. His first books mainly concerned his travels, and are considered among the first and finest examples of what came to be called the travelogue. In *Travels with a Donkey in the Cévennes* (1879), Stevenson wrote not only of the sights he saw, but also the history of the region and the sharp divide between Catholic and Protestant cultures—

elements that would appear throughout much of his work, especially *Kidnapped.*

While traveling, he met and later married Fanny Osbourne, a woman from California with a young son named Lloyd. One day he and Lloyd began playfully creating a treasure map that showed the location of a pirate's gold. This eventually grew into Stevenson's first truly popular work and his first novel, *Treasure Island.* This marked the start of a creative period in which he produced his best-known works, including *Kidnapped, Strange Case of Dr. Jekyll and Mr. Hyde* (1886), and *The Master of Ballantrae* (1889).

In 1890, Stevenson moved to the Samoan Islands with the hope that the climate there would ease his still-chronic illnesses. He continued writing, and even produced a sequel to *Kidnapped* called *Catriona* (published in America as *David Balfour*) in 1893. However, both he and his readers found these books less compelling than his earlier works. Stevenson died of a stroke on December 3, 1894, at the age of forty-four.

PLOT SUMMARY

Chapters 1–4

Kidnapped begins in June of 1751, in a region of Scotland known as the Lowlands. David Balfour, an Essendean boy of sixteen, is left homeless when his seemingly poor schoolmaster father dies. With his mother already dead, David believes himself to be without inheritance or living relative until the local minister, Mister Campbell, gives him a letter prepared by David's father before his death. A note instructs David to take the letter to his heretofore unknown uncle, Ebenezer Balfour, at the house of Shaws in Cramond. The discovery that he hails from a wealthy family excites David, although Mister Campbell quickly reminds the boy—who has learned only simple country manners—to be on his best behavior when he arrives there. Mister Campbell gives David a Bible, a small amount of money, and a recipe for a healing drink, and David sets off on a two-day journey by foot to Cramond.

Along the way, David sees a regiment of the king's soldiers, known as "redcoats," marching past, and the sight fills him with pride. When he reaches the parish of Cramond, he asks local residents for directions to the Shaw house. He receives reactions both puzzled and negative,

MEDIA ADAPTATIONS

- A filmed adaptation of the novel was released by Walt Disney Pictures in 1960. Perhaps the most acclaimed film adaptation of the book, this version, starring Peter Finch, Peter O'Toole, and James MacArthur, is currently available on DVD.

- A film adaptation was directed by Delbert Mann for Omnibus-American International in 1971. The film, which combines elements from both *Kidnapped* and its sequel, *Catriona*, stars Michael Caine and Donald Pleasance, among others. The film is not currently available in the United States.

- A made-for-television adaptation of the book was directed by Ivan Passer in 1995. This version, starring Armand Assante and Brian McCardie, is currently available on DVD.

- A film adaptation of the novel was directed by Brendan Maher for BBC in 2005. This version, starring Iain Glenn and James Pearson, combines the first novel with its sequel, *Catriona*. It is currently available on DVD.

- An unabridged audio adaptation of *Kidnapped* was released on CD by Brilliance Audio in 2001. The book is read by Michael Page.

- An unabridged audiobook version of *Kidnapped* was released on CD by Monterey Soundworks in 2002. The work features a theatrical presentation of the book text, including music and sound effects.

- An unabridged audio adaptation of the book was released on CD by Commuters Library in 2002. The book is read by Ralph Cosham.

- An unabridged audio version of the book was released in MP3 format by In Audio in 2003. The files are stored on audio CD, but can only be played in a player that recognizes MP3 audio files.

- An audio adaptation of the novel was released on CD by Edcon Publishing Group in 2008.

- An unabridged audio version of the novel was released on CD by Audio Book Contractors Inc. in 2008. The book is read by Flo Gibson.

- *Kidnapped* was adapted as a short graphic novel by Alan Grant and Cam Kennedy in 2007 as part of a celebration of Edinburgh's selection as the first UNESCO City of Literature.

- The novel was adapted as a five-issue comic book series by Roy Thomas and Mario Gully, and released under the *Marvel Illustrated* imprint in 2009.

---

and begins to suspect that his family name and fortune may not be as grand as he had at first believed. When he finally arrives at the house of Shaws, he finds that "the house itself appeared to be a kind of ruin; no road led up to it; no smoke arose from any of the chimneys; nor was there any semblance of a garden." Indeed, the house seems unfinished, with exposed rooms on the upper floor and windows without glass.

After nightfall, David summons the courage to knock at the door, and is reluctantly greeted by an old man holding a gun. When the old man, Ebenezer Balfour, learns of David's identity—and presumably the death of his own brother—he agrees to let David inside. After a small meal of porridge, Ebenezer shows David to a bedroom, which the old man then locks from the outside. The next day, their relationship seems to improve slightly, and Ebenezer gives David thirty-seven gold guineas, each equal to one British pound, to fulfill a promise he says he once made to David's father. That evening, Ebenezer asks David to retrieve some papers from a trunk at the top of a tower several stories high. He sends David on the errand without so much as a candle to see by, and thanks only to the lightning from an approaching storm, the boy realizes that the staircase ends abruptly in front of him, high above the ground. After he safely climbs down, David accuses his uncle of trying to murder him and demands an explanation. The old man, surprised to see David still alive, falls victim to a weak heart and must lie down, although he promises to explain everything to David in the morning. David locks Ebenezer inside his room, just as Ebenezer had done to him the night before.

Chapters 5–8

The next morning, before Ebenezer explains himself—David assumes that "he had no lie ready for me, though he was hard at work preparing one"—a cabin boy knocks on the door with a letter for Ebenezer from his captain, Elias Hoseason. Ebenezer suggests to David that they go into the nearby port town of Queensferry, where Ebenezer can conduct business with the captain; after completing his business, he vows to take David to Mr. Rankeillor, a local lawyer, and straighten out matters of the boy's inheritance. David agrees, assuming the old man can do him no harm in such a public place.

The trio reaches Queensferry and meets Captain Hoseason at the local inn. David leaves the two older men alone to talk business, and while speaking with the landlord of the inn, David learns that his own father, Alexander, was actually the older brother of Ebenezer—contrary to what Ebenezer had claimed. From this, David realizes that he himself is the lawful heir to the entire family estate. Captain Hoseason and Ebenezer complete their business and the captain calls for David to join him briefly aboard his ship, the *Covenant*. David is wary to leave the safety of land in the company of one of his uncle's associates, but eventually he agrees. The captain, Ebenezer, and David board a rowboat and make their way to where the *Covenant* is anchored. Once David is aboard the ship, Ebenezer slips away and heads back toward shore. David realizes he has been betrayed and cries out for help, but he is struck from behind and knocked unconscious.

When David awakens, he finds himself tied up somewhere within the "ill-smelling cavern of the ship's bowels." He is visited by one of the captain's senior officers, Mr. Riach, who seems kind toward David and convinces the captain that the boy might die if he is left in such dismal conditions below decks. David is moved to the upper deck at the front of the ship, where he enjoys both sunlight and the company of the rough men who make up the ship's crew. David eventually pieces together his fate: he is to be taken to the Carolinas in the American Colonies, where he will be sold into slavery as part of Ebenezer's plan to keep the boy far away from his rightful claim on the family estate. Mr. Riach, whose kindness toward David appears only after he has been drinking, agrees to try and help the boy if he can.

Meanwhile, the cabin boy, Ransome, periodically relates to David terrible tales of his abuse at the hands of another of the ship's senior officers, Mr. Shuan. One night, David learns that Ransome has been severely beaten by Mr. Shuan; the boy is brought down to David's berth, and Captain Hoseason tells David that he is moving to the ship's roundhouse (a cabin that has one curved wall), where he will live and serve as the new cabin boy. Soon after, David hears that Ransome has died. The captain tells his officers that they will say the boy went overboard. Mr. Shuan changes starkly after the incident, becoming fearful of David and forgetful of Ransome's existence, as if the whole affair were just a nightmare. Despite this, and despite Mr. Riach's failure to deliver on his promise to help David return home, the boy settles rather easily into his new life aboard the ship.

Chapters 9–13

More than a week later, as David is serving Captain Hoseason and Mr. Riach their supper, the *Covenant* strikes another, smaller vessel in the fog and sinks it. By good fortune and brute strength, one member of the smaller boat manages to grab onto the *Covenant* and climb aboard. They bring the man into the roundhouse for a meal and a drink. The man, short and weathered but wearing fine French clothes and carrying a belt filled with gold coins, explains that he is a fugitive in his native Scotland. He tells the captain that he works in the service of a Highland chief who has been exiled by King George, and who is the rightful heir to the throne of England, Ireland, and Scotland. The money he carries is rent paid by the chief's still-loyal clan members. If he is discovered by the king's soldiers, the redcoats, he will surely be imprisoned or killed.

Captain Hoseason refuses to transport the man to France, but agrees to take him as far as Linnhe Loch on the west coast of the Scottish Highlands in exchange for sixty gold guineas.

The captain steps out with his officers, and David later overhears him planning to murder the man. They ask David to retrieve some pistols and gunpowder from the roundhouse, since most of the ship's weaponry is stored there and they do not want to raise the Highlander's suspicions by doing it themselves. David agrees, and returns to the roundhouse.

Instead of helping the captain and his men, David tells the Highlander, whose name is Alan Breck Stewart, of the captain's plot. Alan asks David to stand with him against the attackers, and David agrees. They secure the roundhouse and load as many guns as possible before the captain and his men have a chance to advance. Although they are outnumbered fifteen to two, David and Alan successfully fend off their attackers, killing several of the crewmen. Alan is so impressed with David's courage that he gives the boy one of the silver buttons from his coat, which were given to him by his own father.

David learns of Alan's hatred for a man named Colin Roy Campbell, also known as the Red Fox, from a Scottish Highland clan that supported King George and made enemies of other Highland clans. Colin Roy was chosen as the king's agent in the area, and was responsible for seizing possession of the Stewart clan's estates in the name of the king. David also learns that Alan once served in the English army as a redcoat, but changed sides when his conscience got the better of him. For this act of desertion, capture by the redcoats would mean certain death for Alan.

Captain Hoseason eventually calls for a truce so that David and Alan can help the short-handed crew navigate the *Covenant* through treacherous waters off the western coast of Scotland. Despite their best efforts, the ship crashes into a reef and David is thrown overboard. He manages to make it to shore, but can find no sign of the rest of the crew or Alan.

Chapters 14–16

David explores the beach and surrounding area where he has washed ashore, and comes to the conclusion that he is trapped on an island with very little food or water available. He sees signs of a town on the main island of Mull across the strait from his island, and notes that "it seemed impossible that I should be left to die on the shores of my own country, and within view of a church tower and the smoke of men's houses."

After four miserable days, David realizes that the body of water separating him from the main island all but disappears when the tide goes out, and that he can walk the distance without trouble.

David makes his way to the town he had seen from his previous location. He comes across an old gentleman who confirms that Alan and some of the other crewmen are still alive, and delivers a message: David is to travel to Torosay on the other side of the island, where he can then ferry to the mainland and meet up with Alan. The old gentleman and his wife offer David food and drink, and the man gives David a hat to wear on his journey.

At the end of the next day, David stops at another house and offers the poor man who lives there five shillings to let him stay the night and to guide David the following morning to Torosay. The man agrees, and after some delays caused by exchanging one of David's few remaining guineas for the smaller currency of shillings, they set off toward Torosay. The guide takes David part of the way, but demands more money to complete the journey. David agrees at first, but when the guide stops and asks for more money a second time, the two argue and the guide pulls a knife from his sleeve. David disarms the man and steals his knife and his shoes, and then continues on his way alone.

David soon encounters another traveler, a blind man who claims to be a man of religion. David is impressed by his ability to describe the nearby landmarks despite his lack of sight; as they walk, David realizes that the man carries a pistol and is acting suspiciously, and David threatens to shoot the man if he doesn't leave him alone. Upon arriving in Torosay, David discovers from a local innkeeper that the blind man is Duncan Mackiegh, known for being able to shoot accurately simply by sound, and also suspected of robbery and murder.

David takes the ferry from Torosay to Kinlochaline on the mainland. David shows the captain of the ferry, Neil Roy Macrob, his silver button from Alan's coat, and Neil delivers a message outlining the route David should take to reach the home of James of the Glens in Appin, where Alan will wait in safety among his clan. David spends the night at the inn at Kinlochaline, which he calls "the most beggarly vile place that pigs were ever styed in, full of smoke, vermin, and silent Highlanders."

The next morning, he sets out along the course Alan provided. He meets Henderland, a teacher of religion far more genuine than his traveling companions on Mull. Henderland provides David an evenhanded account of the history of conflict between the Campbells and the other clans in the area. The man also provides David with a meal, a sermon, and a very small amount of money to help him on his journey.

Chapters 17–19

David receives transport from a fisherman across the loch to Appin, Alan Breck's homeland. While resting on the roadside, the Red Fox himself—Colin Roy Campbell—approaches on horseback with some trusted cohorts and a group of redcoats marching behind. David stops the man and asks him for directions to the home of James of the Glens. As the two converse, Campbell is shot dead. Campbell's associates accuse David of being an accomplice who stopped the group so that Campbell could be killed. David runs away, and runs into Alan Breck hiding nearby. After the two escape the king's agents and soldiers, David accuses Alan of being the murderer. Alan denies it, and David acknowledges seeing another man flee from the area after the shooting. However, Alan refuses to identify the shooter, and argues that it is better for the two of them to be suspected as the killers, since this would draw the soldiers away from the guilty man—who is surely a member of Alan's clan. Although David disagrees with his reasoning, he goes with Alan to the home of James of the Glens in an attempt to effect an escape for both Alan and himself.

James is greatly distressed by the killing of Campbell, since he knows the blame will be put upon his people and his own family. He informs Alan that while he will help the two escape, he must also put out papers offering a reward for their capture. David is given a change of clothes so that his description will not match the one known to the king's men, and David and Alan set off for safer lands to the east of Appin.

Chapters 20–24

The two fugitives head eastward at a relentless pace, crossing mountains, rivers, and forests in an attempt to outrun the king's soldiers. At one point, they find themselves in the same open valley as a camp of redcoats, but the pair ultimately manages to escape unseen. They reach relative safety in a place called Corrynakiegh, and Alan uses the silver button he gave David

to send a message to a friend who lives there, John Breck Maccoll. Maccoll relays a message to James of the Glens, and brings back to Alan and David a small amount of money, a copy of the paper describing them as fugitives, and news that James himself has been taken prisoner by the king's men.

The pair continues eastward until they reach the moors, a flat, open area where it is nearly impossible to hide from soldiers. They spy a group of soldiers on horseback headed their way from the east, and change course to the north to reach Ben Alder, a mountain that can provide cover. As they approach Ben Alder, they encounter the clansmen of Cluny Macpherson, a rebel against the king and fugitive himself. David and Alan are invited to stay with Cluny in his hideout.

David, exhausted from their travels, falls ill for two days as Alan spends time playing cards with Cluny. Alan wakes David at one point and borrows the boy's small amount of remaining money. When David fully recovers from his illness and the pair prepare to head southward, he discovers that Alan has lost all of their money—both his own and David's—playing cards. Cluny is kind enough to return David's portion of the money, leaving very little for both men to spend during their travels.

Alan apologizes to David for the incident, but David refuses to accept his apology. This leads to a quarrel that nearly ends in a sword fight, but Alan refuses to fight. David, growing ever weaker, finally tells Alan that he cannot continue onward without his friend's help, and with that, their friendship is restored.

Chapters 25–30

David and Alan make their way southeast across Balquidder, a region filled with as many potential enemies as friends. Luckily, they arrive first at a home where Alan is known by name and well regarded, and the family—of the Maclaren clan—allows David to recover there for nearly a month. During that time, David is visited by Robin Oig, outlaw son of Scottish folk hero Rob Roy Macgregor. Robin and Alan clash when they meet, and almost draw swords before the host of the house, Duncan Dhu, suggests that they instead resolve their conflict by playing pipes. Alan plays impressively, but Robin is a master piper, and clearly wins the contest. All ill feeling disappears when Alan admits, "It would go against my heart to haggle a man that can blow the pipes as you can!"

When David and Alan finally leave Balquidder, it is near the end of August. They continue southeast toward the Firth of Forth, the body of water where David had been kidnapped two months before. The town of Queensferry and the home of the lawyer, Mr. Rankeillor, who David hopes will help him reclaim his rightful inheritance, both lie just across the water. However, David and Alan are unable to cross by bridge, where they would encounter soldiers. Instead, they reach Limekilns and gain the sympathies of a local innkeeper's daughter. She agrees to help, and under cover of night she steals a neighbor's boat and rows them across the water. Before they even have a chance to thank her, she rows away.

The next day, David finds Mr. Rankeillor and tells the man his story. Although David's tale is difficult to believe, the story fits with the small amount of information Mr. Rankeillor has received. Between them, the two devise a plan to get Ebenezer to confess his part in the kidnapping. They enlist Alan to help, and he tricks Ebenezer into admitting that he paid Captain Hoseason twenty pounds to take David away to the Carolinas to be sold into slavery. Mr. Rankeillor, his assistant Torrance, and David reveal themselves as witnesses to the admission, and Ebenezer agrees to pay David two-thirds of the yearly family income as his rightful inheritance.

With David's future secure, he and Alan head toward Edinburgh, where David plans to find a lawyer descended from the Appin Stewarts—and therefore trustworthy—to help Alan find a way out of the country. The two part ways, and Alan remains in hiding, awaiting David's further assistance. The story ends with David standing before his bank in Edinburgh, and concludes with an assurance from the author that from that point on, "whatever befell them, it was not dishonor, and whatever failed them, they were not found wanting to themselves."

CHARACTERS

David Balfour

The hero of *Kidnapped*, David Balfour is a sixteen-year-old boy from Essendean whose seemingly poor father, a schoolmaster, has just died. With his mother already dead, David has no choice but to leave the rented family home and find his way in the world. A letter left for him by his father sends him on a journey to Cramond, where he learns that he is actually from a wealthy family, the Shaws. An encounter with his devious uncle Ebenezer ends with David being kidnapped and taken aboard a ship bound for the American Colonies, where he will be sold into slavery. Aboard the ship, David meets Alan Breck Stewart and forms a friendship that keeps both of them alive through many perils, not the least of which include a shipwreck and being suspected of murdering a prominent agent of the king. David eventually returns to his rightful home, the estate of the Shaws, and claims his inheritance before departing for Edinburgh to help his friend Alan escape the country.

Ebenezer Balfour

The uncle of David Balfour, Ebenezer is the younger brother of David's father Alexander, rightful heir to the Shaws estate. As young men, the two quarreled over the love of a girl—David's mother—and Alexander gave up his claim to the Shaws estate in exchange for a life of happiness and family. Unfortunately, all the wealth of the house of Shaws could not make Ebenezer happy, and he became a bitter hermit within the ruined estate. His reputation among the locals of Cramond is poor, and his cruelty and greed have seriously tarnished the family name. When David shows up at his door, Ebenezer realizes that the only thing he has—his wealth—is in danger, since the estate belongs by law to Alexander and his descendants. He attempts to cause David to fall to his death while climbing an incomplete stairway, and when that ploy fails, he pays Captain Hoseason to kidnap the young man and take him to the Carolinas. After David returns and exposes Ebenezer's plan, Ebenezer agrees to give David the bulk of the estate.

Colin Roy Campbell

Campbell is a prominent member of a Scottish Highland clan who has become an agent of King George of England. His family's allegiance to the king has angered many other Highland clans, including the Stewart clan, of which Alan Breck Stewart is a member. A real-life historical figure, Campbell was entrusted with evicting the families of many Highland clans and taking control of their estates in the name of the king. In *Kidnapped*, David speaks briefly to Campbell and is a witness to his death by shooting—an actual historical event. In the novel, David and Alan Breck Stewart are accused of taking part in the murder.

Mister Campbell

The minister at Essendean, where David Balfour was raised, Mister Campbell is a close friend of David's father and looks after David until he leaves Essendean for Cramond. Mister Campbell is the one David's father entrusted to deliver a letter to David after his death; it is this letter that marks the beginning of David's adventures. Before David departs on his journey, Mister Campbell gives David some money, a Bible, and a recipe for Lily of the Valley water. Campbell also warns David of the temptations and dangers he may face along the way.

Jennet Clouston

A former tenant of Ebenezer Balfour, Jennet Clouston speaks with David on his journey to the house of Shaws. She has nothing good to say about Ebenezer, and says she has cursed him "twelve hunner and nineteen" times—according to Ebenezer, once for every day since he evicted her.

Mister Henderland

Mister Henderland is a religious teacher David meets while walking from Kinlochaline toward Appin. Henderland proves to be knowledgeable, fair-minded, and altogether pleasant traveling company for David. Henderland even invites David to stay at his house, offers him a small amount of money for his journey, and finds a fisherman to transport David across Linnhe Loch to Appin.

Elias Hoseason

Elias Hoseason is the captain of the ship *Covenant*, in the employ of Ebenezer Balfour. After David Balfour arrives at the house of Shaws, Ebenezer pays Hoseason twenty pounds to lure the boy to his ship, kidnap him, and sell him into slavery in the Carolinas. Hoseason later recruits David as his cabin boy aboard the *Covenant*. After David overhears Hoseason and his officers plotting to kill Alan Breck Stewart, he tells Alan and the two fend off the attackers. Hoseason eventually loses his beloved ship by crashing into a reef off the coast of Mull, but he survives.

Innkeeper at Queensferry

While in Queensferry for the first time, David speaks to an innkeeper who provides him valuable information about his father. David discovers from the innkeeper that his father was actually the older brother of Ebenezer, contrary to what Ebenezer had told him; this means that David, not Ebenezer, is the rightful heir to the house of Shaws.

Innkeeper's Daughter in Limekilns

In Limekilns, David and Alan encounter an innkeeper's daughter who proves instrumental in their safe passage to Queensferry. Unable to cross the Firth of Forth by bridge, the two must find a way across the water. They find an inn and play upon the sympathies of the innkeeper's daughter, telling her that David is likely to be killed if they cannot find someone to ferry them across the water. She agrees to help, and after nightfall she steals a boat and rows the pair across the water herself.

James of the Glens

See James Stewart

John Breck Maccoll

John Breck Maccoll is a good friend of Alan Breck Stewart's who lives in Koalisnacoan. When David and Alan are on the run as fugitives, Alan contacts John Breck and asks him to deliver a message to James Stewart. Although he initially refuses, John Breck delivers the message and returns to Alan and David with both some money and the information that James Stewart has been arrested by the king.

Duncan Mackiegh

Duncan Mackiegh is a blind religious instructor on the island of Mull. David encounters Mackiegh during his journey from Erraid to the ferry at Torosay. Although he is blind, he carries a silver pistol and can name every landmark along the road where he and David stand. While walking with Mackiegh, David grows to suspect that the man plans to harm or rob him, so he threatens Mackiegh and drives him away. David later discovers that Mackiegh, even though blind, is considered an excellent shot at close range, and is suspected of both robbery and murder.

Duncan Dhu Maclaren

Duncan Dhu Maclaren is a Balquidder resident whose family is friendly with the Stewart clan. David and Alan are fortunate enough to knock upon Duncan's door when David is ill and in need of help. The two remain in Duncan Dhu's home for nearly a month as David recovers, and Duncan frequently entertains everyone with his pipe-playing. When Robin Oig visits and a confrontation occurs between Oig and Alan, Duncan defuses the situation by asking them both to participate in a pipe-playing contest.

Cluny Macpherson

A Highland chief on the run from the British government, Cluny Macpherson hides out in a secret place near Ben Alder called "Cluny's Cage." David and Alan are brought to him by his men, who find the pair evading redcoats nearby. During their stay in Cluny's Cage, David is ill, but Alan keeps Cluny company by playing cards. Unfortunately, Alan loses all of his own money as well as David's. Cluny, being a gentleman, returns David's money.

Neil Roy Macrob

Neil Roy Macrob is the ferryman who transports David from Torosay to the mainland at Kinlochaline. Macrob is a friend of Alan Breck Stewart's, and after David shows him Alan's silver coat button, he gives David instructions for meeting Alan in Appin.

Robin Oig

Robin Oig is the son of Rob Roy, a legendary outlaw and hero to many Scots. Robin himself is also a fugitive from the law, having been part of a plot to kidnap a wealthy widow and force her to marry him. He meets David and Alan during their stay in Balquidder, and defeats Alan in a pipe-playing contest.

Mister Rankeillor

Mister Rankeillor is a lawyer in Queensferry familiar with the dealings between Ebenezer Balfour and his deceased brother, Alexander. Ebenezer promises to take David to see Rankeillor before having the boy kidnapped. When David returns from the Highlands, he finds Rankeillor and tells him what has transpired, including his uncle's devious plan. Rankeillor helps David get Ebenezer to admit his part in the kidnapping, and is instrumental in securing David's rightful inheritance.

Ransome

Ransome is the cabin boy aboard Captain Hoseason's ship, the *Covenant*. It is he who delivers a message from the captain to Ebenezer at the house of Shaws. David becomes somewhat friendly with Ransome while aboard the *Covenant*, and sees firsthand the abuse Ransome receives at the hands of Mr. Shuan. Ransome is eventually beaten to death by the drunken Mr. Shuan after offering the officer a dirty piece of dishware. Captain Hoseason and his officers agree to say that the boy simply fell overboard.

The Red Fox
See Colin Roy Campbell

Mister Riach

Mr. Riach is Captain Hoseason's second officer aboard the sailing ship *Covenant*. Riach is the one who knocks David unconscious after the young man boards the *Covenant*, and he later admits this freely to David. Riach's concern about David's well-being leads Hoseason to move the boy above-decks, where David's health improves. David later explains his situation to Riach, who agrees to help the boy return home. However, Riach never follows through on this promise, and is one of the crew members who attack David and Alan Breck Stewart after they block themselves in the roundhouse. David later learns that after the shipwreck, Riach takes arms against his fellow crewmen in an effort to protect Stewart from them.

Mister Shuan

Mr. Shuan is Captain Hoseason's first officer aboard the sailing ship *Covenant*. He also functions as the ship's main navigator. David at first has little contact with Shuan, but notes that he is pleasant enough during the rare times he is not drinking. When he drinks, however, he is cruel and physically violent—mostly to the ship's cabin boy, Ransome. One night, after Ransome brings Shuan a dirty piece of dishware, Shuan beats the boy so viciously that he dies. After he realizes what he has done, Shuan becomes haunted and barely able to grasp reality. Shuan is killed during the crew's assault on the roundhouse against David and Alan Breck Stewart. Because of this, the *Covenant* is navigated incompetently through the Torran Rocks, and is wrecked on a reef.

Alan Breck Stewart

Alan Breck Stewart is a Highlander who serves the heads of the Stewart clan in Appin. He is described as small in stature and rather fancily dressed, with a pockmarked face that was the result of smallpox. However, he proves himself to be both tough and a skilled fighter. A fugitive from English law because of his desertion from the army and his support of the Jacobite rebellion, Alan lives primarily in France. However, he makes periodic trips to and from Scotland to collect rents from loyal clan members for their exiled chieftain. While waiting in a small boat for his transport back to France, Alan and his clansmen are struck by the *Covenant*. Through luck and agility, Alan manages to survive the collision and climb aboard the *Covenant*. This is where he meets David Balfour, and the two become close companions and friends during their adventures.

James Stewart

James Stewart, also known as James of the Glens, is the functioning head of the Stewart clan in Appin. He is also a kinsman of Alan Breck Stewart, and the person Alan turns to after he and David are suspected of killing Colin Roy Campbell. James agrees to help, although he warns the two that he must also publicly condemn them for his own safety and the safety of his family. David and Alan discover days later that James has been arrested as an accomplice in the murder.

Mrs. Stewart

James Stewart's wife, Mrs. Stewart, is a kind woman who offers David her thanks for helping Alan and the Stewart clan. She later sends Alan and David all the money she can spare to help them escape.

Torrance

Torrance is Mister Rankeillor's clerk, and helps participate in the plan to trick Ebenezer into admitting his part in David's kidnapping.

THEMES

Justice

One of the main themes running through *Kidnapped* is the idea of justice, or the execution of what is right and fair, particularly in response to past wrongs. It serves as the driving force for many of the characters' actions, although their interpretations of justice vary widely, and some contradict each other. For David, justice means exposing his uncle's evil plot and claiming his rightful inheritance. For Ebenezer, justice means holding onto the estate that was relinquished to him by his brother as part of an agreement between them. For Alan, justice means the death of Colin Roy Campbell, the man responsible for evicting his brethren from their ancestral lands. For the Campbell family and other agents of the king, justice means the arrest and execution of those involved in Campbell's murder.

Related to this theme is the recurring idea that the justice system, as it exists in the real world, is imperfect. For example, although Alan and David are innocent of the murder of Colin Roy Campbell, Alan is certain that they would be convicted of the crime, since the judge and jury—sure to be made up almost entirely of members of the Campbell clan—would be looking for vengeance wherever they could find it. Similarly, although David has a legal right to claim the house of Shaws, Mister Rankeillor knows that dealing with the court, and having to prove David's identity, would take much time and work. For this reason, they devise the plan to get Ebenezer to confess his part in the kidnapping, and then get him to reach an agreement without the need for courts.

Exile and Homesickness

The theme of exile is central to both David's story and the larger story of the people of the Jacobite Highlander clans. At the beginning of the novel, David is essentially exiled from his family home, much like the many Highlanders he later encounters. His circumstances—being denied his rightful lands and set adrift in the world—mirror those of Alan Breck Stewart, Charles Stewart, and many others. For all of them, homesickness drives their actions, for better or worse. David uses his desire to return home as a source of strength when faced with a daunting journey. Alan, who could remain safe in France, returns periodically to his homeland in Scotland even though it means risking imprisonment and death. Cluny Macpherson, a fugitive chieftain exiled from his ancestral lands, lives in hiding in modest conditions just so he can remain near his home. Many of the novel's characters have an intimate connection to and understanding of their home environment; even the blind robber David encounters on Mull, Duncan Mackiegh, can identify and describe every element of his surroundings by sound and memory.

In contrast, Ebenezer is an example of emotional exile; although he remains in his family's estate, he has shut himself off from his family and the surrounding community. No one in Cramond has a kind word to say about him, and

TOPICS FOR FURTHER STUDY

- Music and song play a subtle but important role throughout *Kidnapped*. Different tunes serve as secret signals between clansmen, the singing of certain songs proves insulting or complimentary depending upon the circumstances, and a pipe-playing contest ultimately resolves a conflict between Alan Breck Stewart and Robin Oig. Research some of the traditional Scottish songs mentioned in *Kidnapped*, and write an essay about their importance in Scottish culture. Why do different clans have their own songs? What topics and themes do the songs focus on? How might these songs help a listener better understand the Scottish people?

- In *Kidnapped*, Stevenson uses dialect and Scottish Gaelic-flavored word choices to convey the unique speech of his characters. Go through the book and create your own glossary of difficult terms, writing down the word or phrase as Stevenson uses it and then defining it in plain, modern English. Use your library, the Internet, or other available resources to research any terms that are difficult to figure out.

- David Balfour is from the Scottish Lowlands, but spends much of *Kidnapped* traveling across the Highlands. Using a map and other geographical resources, compare the Scottish Highlands and Lowlands in a short report. Where is the boundary between the two? What makes the two areas different from a geographical standpoint? How do you think geography may have played a role in the formation of separate Highland and Lowland cultures?

- In *Kidnapped*, David Balfour is taken by force from his homeland, to be sent to the Americas and sold as a slave. Although David is ultimately spared this fate, millions of real-life captives were not. Watch the Steven Spielberg film *Amistad* (1997), based on the true story of an enslaved group of West Africans who took control of their captors' ship but ended up as prisoners in America as their fates were decided by the Supreme Court. Write a report comparing the two depictions. How are the conditions and treatment aboard the *Amistad* different from what is experienced by David Balfour? How are the captives' legal difficulties similar to those faced by David in the Highlands?

Jennet Clouston even curses him in front of David. The dilapidated state of the house of Shaws indicates that although Ebenezer lives there, he knows in his heart that it is not his rightful home.

Journey to Manhood

David's journey from Queensferry to the Highlands and back again is not just geographical; it is also emotional. He begins the novel as an arrogant boy with little understanding of the world he inhabits. Along the way, he learns courage, survival skills, the history of his family and his culture, and the importance of humility. This growth is first seen when he overcomes his fear of Captain Hoseason and his men, and chooses to warn Alan that the ship's crew is planning to murder him. David also experiences several other landmark events often associated with the passage into manhood. For example, he learns to fire a pistol and fends off the ship's crew alongside Alan. Soon thereafter, he becomes stranded on what he believes to be a desolate island, and must survive by his own wits for several days. Later, he holds true to his convictions about gambling in spite of temptation when he and Alan stay with Cluny Macpherson. Most importantly, he chooses to act selflessly and risk his own safety so that he might help Alan escape Scotland.

Scotsman in traditional Highland dress (After Robert
Ronald McIan | The Bridgeman Art Library | Getty Images)

STYLE

Historical Fiction

Kidnapped is an example of historical fiction, in
which an author tells a fictional tale set within a
realistically rendered historical time and place. For
this novel, the time and place is eighteenth-century
Scotland. Often, the author weaves actual historical events and people into the fictional narrative.
Stevenson uses several real-life figures in *Kidnapped*, including Alan Breck Stewart, James
Stewart, Robin Oig, and Colin Roy Campbell.
Although he uses artistic license in his depictions
of these characters, they are largely based upon
available descriptions from various historical
sources. In addition, one of the most significant
occurrences in the novel—the murder of Colin
Roy Campbell—is based closely on true events.
Sometimes an author uses historical events to
mirror or resonate with the happenings within
the story. In *Kidnapped*, Stevenson uses the plight
of Jacobite Highlanders during the eighteenth century as a direct parallel to his tale of a young man's
attempt to reclaim his rightful estate.

Local Color

"Local color" is the term used to describe literary
work that emphasizes the details of a specific
location. This may include realistic descriptions
of geography and plants and animals living in
the area, as well as dialogue or narration that
captures the speaking rhythms, dialect, and diction used by local people. Works of local color
may also focus on the beliefs or customs of the
people of the region, as well as their history. The
term is applied most frequently to American
authors such as Mark Twain, William Faulkner,
and John Steinbeck. Stevenson uses these same
local color techniques throughout *Kidnapped*.
Nearly every character, including the narrator,
speaks in a dialect unusual—and sometimes
potentially indecipherable—to American readers. Stevenson also spends a great deal of time
describing the route taken by David across Scotland, naming every landmark and describing the
topography and vegetation found in the area.
Finally, Stevenson introduces many elements of
Scottish custom and culture to David, and by
extension, to his readers.

HISTORICAL CONTEXT

The Jacobite Risings and Aftermath

One of the most significant events in the history
of relations between Scotland and England
occurred in 1688, when King James II of England—who also served as ruler of Scotland and
Ireland—was overthrown and replaced by his
Dutch son-in-law, William III. One of the main
reasons for the overthrow of James II was
his religion, Roman Catholicism, which had
become very unpopular in England during the
previous century and had led to the formation of
the separate Church of England. For this reason,
William III, who was not Catholic but Protestant, became the new king, and the laws were
changed so that the royal family line passed
down only through the Protestant portion of
the family.

This development was not well received by
many in Ireland or in Highland Scotland,
because Roman Catholicism was the prevailing
religion and James II himself was the leader of
the House of Stewarts (the clan from which Alan
Breck Stewart and James of the Glens hail in
Kidnapped). Many clans rebelled against the
new king, demanding that James II or his

COMPARE
&
CONTRAST

- **1750s:** Scottish Jacobite clans suffer after an unsuccessful rebellion against the British monarchy.

  1880s: Scotland and England together operate as a formidable center of world industry.

  Today: The Scottish National Party, whose goal is to gain status as a nation independent from England, maintains a minority control of the Scottish government.

- **1750s:** In the Scottish Highlands, the kilt—a traditional skirt-like garment worn by men—is banned by the British government, as are decorative fabric patterns specific to certain Highland clans.

  1880s: A reawakening of interest in Scottish culture, and an easing of tensions between England and Scotland, allow the kilt to

  be adopted as a symbol of traditional Scotland.

  Today: The kilt enjoys a limited resurgence both in and out of Scotland as a fashionable clothing item for men.

- **1750s:** Popular English literature consists of works like Henry Fielding's *Tom Jones* (1749), a comic novel broken down into several smaller books.

  1880s: Popular literature is dominated by periodicals that publish works of serial fiction, spread across multiple issues and filled with cliffhangers to maintain reader interest for the next installment.

  Today: Popular television shows such as *Lost* follow a format similar to serial fiction of the past, often ending each episode with a twist or cliffhanger.

descendants be returned to the throne. These rebels became known as "Jacobites," after the Latin word for "James." Two different rebellions occurred, in 1715 and in 1745; the second was led by Charles Edward Stewart, half brother to James of the Glens, and its failure led to his exile in France.

In response to this rebellion, King George II of England ordered his agents in the Highlands to strip the rebellious clans of their ancestral lands, which would come under control of the king and could be distributed or rented as he saw fit. Some chieftains fled to France, while others simply remained in the Highlands and lived as fugitives. Despite the efforts of the king, many members of the Jacobite clans continued to support their exiled chieftains, secretly aiding them with money or shelter as needed.

The Appin Murder
One of the key events in *Kidnapped* is the murder of the king's agent, known as the Red Fox. In 1752, Colin Roy Campbell—known as the Red

Fox because of his hair color—was working on behalf of King George II to remove rebellious Highland chieftains from their estates. He claimed the land in the name of the king and was largely disliked by the members of the clans he evicted, which included the Stewart clan. In the days or weeks leading up to Campbell's death, Alan Breck Stewart was reportedly heard to ask publicly, "Who will bring me the skin of the Red Fox?"

On May 14, 1752, while traveling along a road in Appin, Campbell was killed by a single shot. No other members of his party were fired upon or injured. Although no one could identify the shooter, and James Stewart—the putative head of the Stewart clan during his brother's exile—was seen by witnesses far from the scene of the crime, he was arrested for playing a part in the murder. Although there was no evidence against him, James was found guilty by a jury composed mostly of members of the Campbell clan, and was executed by hanging on November 8, 1752. His decomposing body was then put on display to send a message to other Jacobite

Waterfall and heather on a hillside in the Highlands of Scotland (*Ellen Rooney / Robert Harding World Imagery /* *Getty Images*)

rebels, and remained on display for three years. No other parties, including Alan Breck Stewart, were ever arrested or tried for the murder.

CRITICAL OVERVIEW

When *Kidnapped* was published in 1886, Stevenson was already established as a successful writer of popular fiction for children and adults. His novel *Treasure Island* (1883) was both critically acclaimed and a best-seller, and his novella *Strange Case of Dr. Jekyll and Mr. Hyde* (1886) proved his ability to craft more adult fare. Because *Kidnapped* was largely considered an adventure novel for boys, much like *Treasure Island*, it is not surprising that many reviewers compared the two, with *Treasure Island* often coming up the favorite. An unsigned reviewer from the *St. James Gazette* writes of the book, "Its incidents are not so uniformly thrilling [as

Treasure Island] . . . yet *Kidnapped* is excellent from end to end." R. H. Hutton, comparing the two in a review for *The Spectator*, notes, "*Kidnapped* is not so ideal a story of external adventure as *Treasure Island*." However, he also notes that *Kidnapped* has "perhaps even more of the qualities proper to all true literature." Author Arthur Conan Doyle expresses similar sentiments writing for the *National Review*: "*Treasure Island* is perhaps the better story, while *Kidnapped* may have the longer lease of life as being an excellent and graphic sketch of the state of the Highlands after the last Jacobite insurrection." Author Henry James, in an article for *The Century Magazine*, calls the novel "the finest of his longer stories," and considers the character of Alan Breck to be "a masterpiece."

Although critics at the time suggested that *Kidnapped* might outlast *Treasure Island* as enduring literature, the novel has remained less popular than Stevenson's earlier tale of treasure and pirates. Even worse, despite the continuous

WHAT DO I READ NEXT?

- Stevenson's *Catriona* (1893), originally published in the United States as *David Balfour*, picks up where *Kidnapped* ends. It continues the story of David and Alan Breck, focusing largely on their efforts to prove James Stewart innocent of the Appin Murder.

- *Treasure Island* (1883), Stevenson's first novel, is one of the best-known and most frequently adapted adventure tales ever written. In it, a poor young man discovers a pirate's treasure map and sets out to claim the booty, unknowingly bringing with him a bloodthirsty, one-legged pirate named Long John Silver who intends to keep the treasure for himself.

- *Waverley* (1814) by Sir Walter Scott is one of the earliest examples of historical fiction. The book takes place in Scotland during the Jacobite Rising of 1745—just six years before *Kidnapped*—and like Stevenson's novel, it offers a sympathetic view of the Jacobite Highlanders and their struggles.

- Patrick O'Brian's historical novel *Master and Commander* (1970) offers seafaring adventure of a different sort than *Kidnapped*. In the novel, the first in a series of over twenty books, a naval captain is given command of a new ship and hires on a physician friend as his naval surgeon. As in *Kidnapped*, the adventures of the captain and his crew are interwoven into actual historical events from the turn of the nineteenth century.

- *Twenty Thousand Leagues Under the Sea* (1872) by Jules Verne is a different kind of sea adventure. In it, a crew hired by the United States government takes to the sea in pursuit of a mysterious monster that turns out to be a technological marvel: a submarine piloted by the enigmatic Captain Nemo. Three crew members are taken prisoner by Nemo and travel the seas of the world, experiencing adventures ranging from an attack by a giant squid to a visit to the undersea ruins of Atlantis.

- Daniel Defoe's novel *Robinson Crusoe* (1719) is the "true autobiography" of a sailor who becomes shipwrecked alone on an island off the coast of South America. During his twenty-eight years on the island, he encounters cannibals and mutineers, and befriends a native man known only as "Friday," named after the day Crusoe first meets him.

---

popularity of his books, Stevenson's entire body of work was all but ignored by academics and literary scholars during the first half of the twentieth century. In recent decades, Stevenson has finally been acknowledged for his contributions to English literature, and *Kidnapped* remains extraordinarily popular among modern readers both young and old.

CRITICISM

Greg Wilson

Wilson is an author, literary critic, and mythologist. In this essay, he compares Stevenson's novel to the basic heroic myth structure described by Joseph Campbell in his landmark work The Hero with a Thousand Faces.

Robert Louis Stevenson's novel *Kidnapped* was first published as a serial in a boys' magazine in 1886. It was not until more than sixty years later that scholar and teacher Joseph Campbell wrote his landmark work *The Hero with a Thousand Faces* (1949), in which he suggests that many different myths from various religions and time periods could all be placed in a similar framework, broken down into distinct stages containing specific elements. He called this framework the "monomyth," and it has also been referred to as "the hero's journey." Although many modern

IN *KIDNAPPED*, DAVID IS IMMEDIATELY STRUCK UNCONSCIOUS AFTER BOARDING THE *COVENANT*, AND AWAKENS TO FIND HIMSELF IN THE "ILL-SMELLING CAVERN OF THE SHIP'S BOWELS." THIS DESCRIPTION IS ALMOST EERILY SIMILAR TO SOMETHING ONE FINDS IN ANCIENT MYTHS SUCH AS THAT OF JONAH, SWALLOWED BY A GREAT FISH."

adventure tales reflect the basic elements of ancient mythological quests, it is nonetheless somewhat surprising how well Stevenson's tale fits within the template Campbell later developed.

The monomyth cycle as described by Campbell consists of seventeen stages, and covers every important aspect of the heroic quest. It breaks the journey down into three basic parts: the departure, the initiation, and the return. In *Hero with a Thousand Faces*, Campbell remarks, "Many tales isolate and greatly enlarge upon one or two of the typical elements of the full cycle... others string a number of independent cycles into a single series (as in *The Odyssey*)." Campbell has also stated that some elements might appear in a different order than his framework describes. This concession of sorts has allowed scholars to apply the basic monomyth structure very loosely, or to pick and choose elements that support an author's particular viewpoint. For this exercise, *Kidnapped* will be viewed as a single monomythic cycle, start to finish, alongside Campbell's monomyth template.

The first stage of Campbell's monomyth is the Call to Adventure, which involves a removal of the hero from his normal place and way of existence. The entire journey of the hero is precipitated by this single event or summons. In *Kidnapped*, this occurs at the very start of the book, when David Balfour is essentially evicted from his family home after his father has passed away. True to Campbell's monomyth, David's adventure would never have occurred if it were not for this single event.

The second stage, which according to Campbell is found "not infrequently in the myths and popular tales," is the Refusal of the Call. Here, the hero decides not to change his normal course of existence, and generally suffers for this poor decision until deciding in the end to accept the call. In *Kidnapped*, David never completely refuses the call to adventure; after hearing several negative opinions about his uncle Ebenezer and the house of Shaws on his journey there, he does consider turning around and going home, and his doubts delay his arrival at the house until after nightfall. However, this occurs only after David has received special aid (stage three), so the order does not match precisely with Campbell's template. Still, even Campbell seems to acknowledge that this stage is not necessarily as prevalent as the other stages of the departure.

The third stage of the monomyth is Supernatural Aid, in which an elderly man or woman, usually recognized as a protector, provides the hero with some supernatural object or objects to use during his coming trials. In *Kidnapped*, David is given several objects by Mr. Campbell, the local minister, before he departs on his journey to see his uncle. Mr. Campbell is clearly portrayed as a protector or fatherly figure, and although the objects themselves are not overtly mystical, they are intended to protect David both physically (the money, which he can use for food and shelter) and spiritually (the Bible, which he can use for guidance and affirmation). The final item Mr. Campbell provides—a handwritten recipe for an elixir known as Lily of the Valley water—is the most mystical of all, since the plant itself is the subject of many legends and is potentially quite poisonous. Oddly, David never has occasion to use this recipe during his journey, and only reflects upon its usefulness in later years.

The fourth stage is the Crossing of the First Threshold, in which the hero passes from the familiar world into a land of the unknown. In *Kidnapped*, this occurs when David leaves the safety of land to board Captain Hoseason's ship, the *Covenant*. Hoseason himself can be seen as the guardian of this threshold, and it is only at his invitation—which turns out to be trickery—that David agrees to enter the unknown realm of sailors and the ocean.

The fifth and final stage of departure is the Belly of the Whale, in which the hero is literally or figuratively consumed by the unknown forces of the new realm. In *Kidnapped*, David is immediately struck unconscious after boarding the

Covenant, and awakens to find himself in the "ill-smelling cavern of the ship's bowels." This description is almost eerily similar to something one finds in ancient myths such as that of Jonah, swallowed by a great fish. This stage concludes with an emergence from the "whale," which symbolizes a rebirth. Indeed, when David emerges from the bowels of the ship, he regains his health and spirit.

The first stage of initiation is the Road of Trials, which Campbell describes as "a favorite phase of the myth-adventure." In this stage, the hero undergoes a series of difficult tasks, often with the aid of a supernatural protector. For David, that protector is Alan Breck Stewart, who, although not supernatural, seems to possess gifts of strength and luck seldom seen in mortal men. The trials David undergoes include a battle with the ship's crew, a shipwreck, a very long trek by foot across Mull and the Western Highlands, and more than one dishonest and dangerous traveling companion.

Where *Kidnapped* deviates most markedly from Campbell's monomyth is in the next stages: the Meeting with the Goddess, and Woman as the Temptress. In these stages the hero first encounters and becomes unified with a goddess or life-giving sacred force, and then is tempted to abandon his journey or becomes dismayed at the realities of the living world. In these stages, the "goddess" and "woman" are often, but not necessarily, female figures. In *Kidnapped*, David encounters precious few female figures, and there is little in the way of marriage or female temptation throughout the course of the work. This is perhaps expected for a tale meant for a boys' adventure magazine, but even a more symbolic representation of these stages is all but nonexistent in Stevenson's novel.

The next stage of initiation, Atonement with the Father, does not fare much better in a direct comparison between the monomyth template and the novel. One can argue that Alan Breck Stewart serves as David's symbolic father figure, portraying both the terrifying tyrant and the knowledge-giving protector. Ultimately, David has a falling-out with Alan that nearly leads to a duel, but the two become reconciled, much as in Campbell's template. However, this occurs far later in the story than in the monomyth framework—during stage thirteen, the Magic Flight.

The tenth stage of the monomyth is Apotheosis, in which the hero gains a larger view of the world, finds new abilities, and is even willing to sacrifice himself for a cause in which he believes. This is reflected in David's witnessing of the murder of the Red Fox, and his subsequent willingness to sacrifice his own safety and become a fugitive to protect both Alan and the mysterious gunman who actually committed the murder. By this point, David has gained a much fuller understanding of the conflict between the king's agents in Scotland and the members of the various Jacobite Highlander clans—better than those on either side of the conflict could hope to achieve.

The final stage of initiation, the Ultimate Boon, is the point at which the hero receives the thing he has sought during his journey. This may not seem at first a solid fit with the events of *Kidnapped*, in which David's only overt goal is to return home and claim his rightful inheritance. However, the boon David receives during his journey, and most notably after the murder of the Red Fox, is his maturity—or, perhaps more correctly, his loss of innocence and his entry into the adult world.

The final section of the Campbell monomyth is the Return, which begins with the Refusal of the Return. In this stage, the hero refuses to return to his normal world, and chooses instead to live in contentment away from his responsibilities to his fellow humans. Here the events of *Kidnapped* fail to match Campbell's model; although David considers going directly to the authorities to proclaim his innocence, this is more of an attempt to effect an easy return to the real world than it is a rejection of it.

Stage thirteen, the Magic Flight, is a remarkable fit with the chapters of *Kidnapped* collectively known as "The Flight through the Heather." In the Magic Flight, the hero is pursued during his journey back to the normal world by supernatural forces of opposition trying to stop his return. In *Kidnapped*, the king's redcoats take the place of supernatural forces, pursuing David and Alan across the Scottish Highlands as they make their way southward.

Stage fourteen of the monomyth is Rescue from Without. In it, the hero cannot complete his journey on his own; as Campbell himself puts it, "The world may have to come and get him." A key element of the Rescue from Without is a person from the "normal" world who aids the hero in returning at a time when the hero has exhausted all options of his own. In *Kidnapped*, when David and Alan are feeling completely defeated at their inability to cross the Firth of Forth and return David to Queensferry, the two call upon the sympathy of an innkeeper's daughter. She steals a boat and rows them across the water at great risk to herself, and never utters a word of the two fugitives to anyone else.

In stage fifteen, the Crossing of the Return Threshold, the hero returns to the normal world (in David's case, Queensferry) and makes the realization that the two worlds are part of the same whole. In *Kidnapped*, this realization is made especially clear because the two worlds are Highland Scotland and Lowland Scotland—literally, two parts of the same whole nation—and David's experiences convince him that the two are not so different after all. This leads to stage sixteen, Master of the Two Worlds, in which the hero gains the power to pass back and forth between the two realms. This holds true for David, who has learned the ways of the Highlanders and has made many lasting and devoted friends among people who would scarcely trust a Lowlander under any other circumstances.

The final stage of the monomyth, Freedom to Live, sees the hero assume a place of understanding and comfort in the world, not bound by fear of death or guilt for living. In *Kidnapped*, David assumes his place in the world by becoming the leader of the house of Shaws, and by traveling to Edinburgh to use his new wealth to help Alan secure safe passage to France.

Out of the seventeen stages of Campbell's monomyth, then, Stevenson's simple adventure novel for boys manages to match up with twelve stages quite nicely. What does this mean? It may suggest that narratives from all cultures and time periods share similar deep structures, which lends support to Campbell's idea of the monomyth. It may also explain why, in a culture increasingly focused on the journey of the hero as its primary storytelling structure, Stevenson's *Kidnapped* remains such a fresh and satisfying read for modern audiences.

Source: Greg Wilson, Critical Essay on Robert Louis Stevenson's *Kidnapped, Novels for Students 33*, Gale, Cengage Learning, 2010.

Anonymous

In the following excerpt, originally published in 1886, a reviewer for the St. James Gazette *compares Stevenson's work favorably to Sir Walter Scott's.*

Mr. Stevenson is the Defoe of our generation. Since the days when *Robinson Crusoe* first delighted English readers, no book of adventure has appeared that can pretend to rivalry with the story of *Treasure Island.* Beside the exquisite prose of Mr. Stevenson, his delightful quaintness of humour and his fertile inventiveness, the romances of Fenimore Cooper seem very poor performances. The simplicity which is the highest art, a mastery of language, and a subtle and sympathetic power of compelling attention, are all at the command of Mr. Stevenson. He is rarely dull, he is often slily humorous, and he is prone to weave into his narrative a fine and brilliant thread of suggestive reflection which is alike characteristic and alluring. The wave of his magician's wand is truly magical; but, while he draws his readers from a too prosaic world to one of aerial fancy, he lets them know in a sort of gravely jesting undertone that it is semblance and not reality. His writings inspire a pleasure which is all the more genuine and refreshing for their innocence; yet their fun, their effectiveness, their brilliancy would be much less striking were they not in part the result of a grave experience and understanding of human life, such as makes every man who is a man desire once more to become as a little child.

It is high praise, therefore, of this new volume to say that it is no unworthy companion of *Treasure Island.*

Its incidents are not so uniformly thrilling; there is no touch of art in it quite equal to the account of the blind sailor's visit to the country inn in the former story; yet *Kidnapped* is excellent from end to end. Two characteristics of Mr. Stevenson's last volume are in themselves worthy of notice. The first, that, as in *Treasure Island,* he has succeeded in telling a story in which women and feminine influence play positively no part. There is no love-making in *Kidnapped,* and, with one exception, no woman takes any share in the action. There are some pretty and touching passages illustrative of the unspoken love of man for man which has been a finer side of human intercourse since the days of David and Jonathan. But of the conventional heroine and the yet more conventional love scene, which are wont to appear even in so-called books for boys, Mr. Stevenson will have none. Not but that he indulges in delicate incidental references to the fair sex: as witness his ruffian sea-captain Hoseason, who never sails by his aged mother's cottage on the sea-shore of Fife without the compliment of a salute of guns. The second observation is that Mr. Stevenson has boldly and even wisely ventured into the field of Jacobite romance which has already been occupied by the genius of Sir Walter Scott. Different as is the character of his book, we feel that indirectly Mr. Stevenson owes a little of his general idea to the author of *Rob Roy* and *Waverley*. But although there is a perceptible parallel between the adventures of David Balfour and those that have immortalized the names of Osbaldistone and Bailie Jarvie, the parallel is too slight to be insisted on. The story of the Jacobite times is an inexhaustible mine for the writer of fiction, and the originality and literary skill of Mr. Stevenson is doubly welcome for this addition to the number of Highland stories. *Rob Roy* is inimitable; but it says much for Mr. Stevenson's powers that *Kidnapped* seems none the less charming for the very reason that it recalls the masterpieces of the greatest story-teller of our century.

Source: Anonymous, *"Kidnapped,"* in *Robert Louis Stevenson: The Critical Heritage*, edited by Paul Maixner, Routledge & Kegan Paul, 1981, pp. 233–235.

Anonymous

In the following excerpt, a critic for the Nation *discusses the place held by* Kidnapped *and its sequel* Catriona *in Stevenson's body of work, and their success as romantic fiction.*

The history of Stevenson's activity between 1881 and 1886 had made it clear that his permanent contribution to literature was not to be criticism, or vagabendizing, or fantasias in style or in narration—these were but the small talk of his genius—but serious romantic fiction of a high imaginative type. His own views, as expressed in "A Gossip on Romance" and "A Humble Remonstrance," form a sound Romantic creed, and he brought to his task a style which no English novelist has surpassed. It is superfluous to insist on the merits of *Kidnapped*. With its sequel or second part, *David Balfour* (1893), it is undoubtedly Stevenson's best book, and much of his inferior work will "live with the eternity of its fame." The second part suffers a little from the usual malady of continuations, but it has its own peculiar merits, too. The author, who had for the most part a pretty correct idea of the comparative excellence of his writings, wrote, not long before he died: "I believe the two together make up much the best of my work and perhaps of what is in me." The temptation to compare the adventures of David with some of the Waverley Novels is hard to resist; but the utility of such a comparison is not apparent. So far as it has been attempted, the result seems to be merely that Stevenson reached a kind of perfection in detail for which Scott never strove, and that, in addition, some scenes and characters in Stevenson are not unworthy of the great master, but that in those indefinable qualities which we vaguely suggest by the words "breadth" and "greatness" Scott still stands without a rival. The fact is, the hour for such a parallel has not yet come. By the middle of the next century, men may perhaps look at both writers from a sufficient distance of time to measure their comparative eminence. At present, Scott's supremacy in romantic fiction appears to be almost as unassailable as Shakspere's supremacy in dramatic poetry. It is not sufficient, however, to observe that Stevenson withholds his hand from great historical characters. This seems to be a rather artificial test of power, nor is it certain that Stevenson would not have succeeded as well with such characters as with his David or his Alan Breck, to say nothing of Prestongrange or Cluny Macpherson. True, his work fell off after the appearance of *Kidnapped*; but this, too, is not decisive of what he might have done if he had lived. It must not be forgotten that *David Balfour* and "The Beach of Falesá," which are hardly inferior to *Kidnapped*, were written shortly before his death, and that he left behind him the unfinished *Weir of Hermiston*, which Mr. Colvin rates very highly.

Source: Anonymous, "Robert Louis Stevenson," in *Nation*, Vol. 62, No. 1593, January 9, 1896, pp. 36–38.

A. Conan Doyle

In the following excerpt, Doyle compares the narrative and character styles of Kidnapped *and* Treasure Island.

A very singular mental reaction took Mr. Stevenson from one pole to the other of imaginative work, from the subtle, dainty lines of *Prince Otto* to the direct, matter-of-fact, eminently practical and Defoe-like narratives of *Treasure Island* and of *Kidnapped*. Both are admirable pieces of English, well conceived, well told, striking the reader at every turn with some novel situation, some new combination of words which just fits the sense as a cap fits a nipple. *Treasure Island* is perhaps the better story, while *Kidnapped* may have the longer lease of life as being an excellent and graphic sketch of the state of the Highlands after the last Jacobite insurrection. Each contains one novel and admirable character. Alan Breck in the one, and Long John in the other. Surely John Silver, with his face the size of a ham, and his little gleaming eyes like crumbs of glass in the centre of it, is the king of all seafaring desperadoes. Observe how the strong effect is produced in his case, seldom by direct assertion on the part of the story-teller, but usually by comparison, innuendo, or indirect reference...John himself says, "There was some that was feared of Pew, and some that was feared of Flint; but Flint his own self was feared of me. Feared he was and proud. They was the roughest crew afloat was Flint's. The devil himself would have been feared to go to sea with them. Well, now, I tell you, I'm not a boasting man, and you seen yourself how easy I keep company; but when I was quartermaster, *lambs* wasn't the word for Flint's old buccaneers." So by a touch here and a hint there, there grows upon us the individuality of this smooth-tongued, ruthless, masterful, one-legged devil. He is to us not a creation of fiction, but an organic living reality with whom we have come into contact; such is the effect of the fine suggestive strokes with which he is drawn. And the buccaneers themselves, how simple and yet how effective are the little touches which indicate their ways of thinking and of acting.

There is still a touch of the Meredithian manner in these [adventure] books, different as they are in general scope from anything which he has attempted. There is the apt use of an occasional archaic or unusual word, the short, strong descriptions, the striking metaphors, the somewhat staccato fashion of speech. Yet in spite of this flavor, they have quite individuality enough to constitute a school of their own. Their faults, or rather perhaps their limitations, lie never in the execution, but entirely in the original conception. They picture only one side of life, and that a strange and exceptional one. There is no female interest. We feel that it is an apotheosis of the boy's story—the penny number of our youth *in excelsis*. But it is all so good, so fresh, so picturesque, that, however limited its scope, it still retains a definite and well-assured place in literature.

Mr. **Stevenson**, like one of his own characters, has an excellent gift of silence. He invariably sticks to his story, and is not to be diverted off to discourse upon views of life or theories of the universe. A story-teller's business is to tell his

story. If he wishes to air his views upon other matters he can embody them in small independent works, as Mr. **Stevenson** has done. Where a character gives vent to opinions which throw a light upon his own individuality that is a different thing, but it is surely intolerable that an author should stop the action of his story to give his own private views upon things in general...Mr. **Stevenson** is too true an artist to fall into this error, with the result that he never loses his hold upon his reader's attention.

He has shown that a man may be terse and plain, and yet free himself from all suspicion of being shallow and superficial. No man has a more marked individuality, and yet no man effaces himself more completely when he sets himself to tell a tale.

Source: A. Conan Doyle, "Mr. Stevenson's Methods in Fiction," in *The National Review*, Vol. 14, No. 83, January 1890, pp. 646–657.

Henry James

In the following excerpt, James explains why he believes Kidnapped *to be Stevenson's best work.*

[James was a close friend of Stevenson and a critic and admirer of his work. In the following essay, James refutes William Archer's charge (1885) that Stevenson was more concerned with style than subject matter, and he identifies the author's major thematic interests as youth and personal heroism. Archer criticized Stevenson's work for its simple philosophy of good health and good spirits, a charge that James refutes by pointing to the difficult circumstances of Stevenson's life, asserting that he had earned the right to cheerful optimism. In addition, James discusses Stevenson's motive for writing, and his contributions to literature: "[Stevenson] would say we ought to make believe that the extraordinary is the best part of life even if it were not, and to do so because the finest feelings—suspense, daring, decision, passion, curiosity, gallantry, eloquence, friendship—are involved in it, and it is of infinite importance that the tradition of these precious things should not perish."]

I have left Mr. Stevenson's best book to the last...[There] are parts of [*Kidnapped*] so fine as to suggest that the author's talent has taken a fresh start, various as have been the impulses in which it had already indulged, and serious the hindrances among which it is condemned to exert itself. There would have been a kind of perverse humility in his keeping up the fiction that a production so literary as *Kidnapped* is addressed to immature minds, and, though it was originally given to the world, I believe, in a "boy's paper," the story embraces every occasion that it meets to satisfy the higher criticism . . . [The] history stops without ending, as it were; but I think I may add that this accident speaks for itself. Mr. Stevenson has often to lay down his pen for reasons that have nothing to do with the failure of inspiration, and the last page of David Balfour's adventures is an honourable plea for indulgence. The remaining five-sixths of the book deserve to stand by *Henry Esmond* as a fictive autobiography in archaic form. The author's sense of the English idiom of the last century, and still more of the Scotch, has enabled him to give a gallant companion to Thackeray's *tour de force.* The life, the humour, the colour of the central portions of *Kidnapped* have a singular pictorial virtue: these passages read like a series of inspired footnotes on some historic page . . . There could be no better instance of the author's talent for seeing the familiar in the heroic, and reducing the extravagant to plausible detail, than the description of Alan Breck's defence in the cabin of the ship and the really magnificent chapters of "The Flight in the Heather". Mr. Stevenson has in a high degree (and doubtless for good reasons of his own) what may be called the imagination of physical states, and this has enabled him to arrive at a wonderfully exact translation of the miseries of his panting Lowland hero, dragged for days and nights over hill and dale, through bog and thicket, without meat or drink or rest, at the tail of an Homeric High-lander. The great superiority of the book resides to my mind, however, in the fact that it puts two characters on their feet with admirable rectitude. I have paid my tribute to Alan Breck, and I can only repeat that he is a masterpiece. It is interesting to observe that though the man is extravagant, the author's touch exaggerates nothing: it is throughout of the most truthful, genial, ironical kind; full of penetration, but with none of the grossness of moralising satire. The figure is a genuine study, and nothing can be more charming than the way Mr. Stevenson both sees through it and admires it. Shall I say that he sees through David Balfour? This would be perhaps to underestimate the density of that medium. Beautiful, at any rate, is the expression which this unfortunate though circumspect youth gives to those qualities which combine to excite our respect and our objurgation in the Scottish character. Such a scene as the episode of

the quarrel of the two men on the mountainside is a real stroke of genius, and has the very logic and rhythm of life: a quarrel which we feel to be inevitable, though it is about nothing, or almost nothing, and which springs from exasperated nerves and the simple shock of temperaments. The author's vision of it has a profundity which goes deeper, I think, than *Doctor Jekyll.* I know of few better examples of the way genius has ever a surprise in its pocket—keeps an ace, as it were, up its sleeve. And in this case it endears itself to us by making us reflect that such a passage as the one I speak of is in fact a signal proof of what the novel can do at its best, and what nothing else can do so well. In the presence of this sort of success we perceive its immense value. It is capable of a rare transparency—it can illustrate human affairs in cases so delicate and complicated that any other vehicle would be clumsy. To those who love the art that Mr. Stevenson practises he will appear, in pointing this incidental moral, not only to have won a particular triumph, but to have given a delightful pledge.

Source: Henry James, "Robert Louis Stevenson," in *Partial Portraits*, Macmillan and Co., 1888, pp. 137–174.

SOURCES

Campbell, Joseph, *The Hero with a Thousand Faces*, MJF Books, 1949, pp. 59, 97, 246.

Doyle, Arthur Conan, "Mr. Stevenson's Methods in Fiction," in the *National Review*, January, 1890. Reprinted in *A Peculiar Gift: Nineteenth Century Writings on Books for Children*, edited by Lance Salway, Kestrel Books, 1976, pp. 391–403.

Hutton, R. H., Review of *Kidnapped*, in *The Spectator*, Vol. LIX, No. 3030, July 24, 1886, pp. 990–91, reprinted in *Nineteenth Century Literature Criticism*, edited by Laurie Lanzen Harris and Sheila Fitzgerald, Vol. 5., Gale Research, 1984, p. 400.

James, Henry, "Robert Louis Stevenson," in *The Century Magazine*, Vol. XXXV, No. 6, April 1888, reprinted in his *Partial Portraits*, Macmillan and Co., 1888, pp. 137–174.

Review of *Kidnapped*, in the *St. James Gazette*, Vol. XIII, July 19, 1886, reprinted in *Robert Louis Stevenson: The Critical Heritage*, edited by Paul Maixner, Routledge & Kegan Paul, 1981, pp. 233–235.

The Robert Louis Stevenson Website, http://dinamico2.u-nibg.it/rls/films-kidn.htm (accessed June 3, 2009).

Stevenson, Robert Louis, *Kidnapped*, revised edition, Penguin Books, 2007.

———, Letter written to Robert Stevenson, January 25, 1886, in *The Letters of Robert Louis Stevenson*, available from the University of Adelaide Library of Electronic Texts Collection, http://ebooks.adelaide.edu.au/s/stevenson/robert_louis/s848l/chap8.html (accessed June 3, 2009).

FURTHER READING

Herman, Arthur., *How the Scots Invented the Modern World*, Crown, 2001.
  This history book offers a unique hypothesis: that the modern world was largely shaped by the ideas and actions of the great Scottish thinkers, inventors, and political figures of the eighteenth and nineteenth centuries.

Harman, Claire, *Myself and the Other Fellow: A Life of Robert Louis Stevenson*, HarperCollins, 2005.
  This biography comprehensively examines every aspect of the author's short but productive life.

Tranter, Nigel, *The Wallace: The Compelling 13th Century Story of William Wallace*, Hodder & Stoughton, 1975.
  This historical novel focuses on a legendary Scot who lived centuries before the Jacobite Risings. Tranter's tale offers a realistic portrayal of the legendary Wallace's military accomplishments as leader of Scottish resistance forces fighting English soldiers during Scotland's war for independence.

Menikoff, Barry, *Narrating Scotland: The Imagination of Robert Louis Stevenson*, University of South Carolina Press, 2005.
  In this nonfiction work, Menikoff argues that Stevenson's varied writings, often dismissed as genre work, served a single unified purpose: to capture the experience, culture, and history of the Scottish people and preserve it for the sake of posterity.

A Lost Lady

WILLA CATHER

1923

Willa Cather's short novel *A Lost Lady*, published in 1923, is considered a minor work by this important American novelist and short story writer. Like a number of her other works, *A Lost Lady* is a modernist work (meaning it was written during a period of literary experimentation and expression in the early decades of the twentieth century). It realistically explores, with an austere yet effective and vivid prose style, the effects of the settlement of the Great Plains states on both the land and the people who live there. Also similar to some of her other novels, *A Lost Lady* focuses on a perceptive antagonist who must resolve an inner conflict, and emphasizes the effects of moral decay.

A Lost Lady is set in the late nineteenth and early twentieth centuries in the small town of Sweet Water, Nebraska. There, young Niel Herbert has an admiring friendship with the Forresters, especially Mrs. Forrester, the young wife of a much older husband, successful railroad builder Captain Daniel Forrester. Niel helps them both through personal crises as the Captain's life becomes more and more limited after a riding accident and two strokes. Niel, naive and idealistic, also tries to understand Mrs. Forrester and her sometimes adulterous behavior. Through this plot, Cather subtly explores ideas about generational moral differences, the settling of the American West, the sometimes claustrophobic nature of small-town life, and how young men like Niel of this era come of age.

Willa Cather (AP Images)

Widely praised at the time of its publication, critics were later divided over the importance of *A Lost Lady* in subsequent decades, but by the twenty-first century, its reputation had been restored. Writing about the novel in 2001, Eileen Battersby of the *Irish Times* notes, "This wonderful performance...displays her narrative technique at its sharpest, as well as her understanding of the eloquence of the slightest gesture, the simplest statement."

AUTHOR BIOGRAPHY

Willa Cather was born on December 7, 1873, in Back Creek Valley, Virginia, and was the daughter of a farmer. Until the age of ten, she was raised on the family farm with her six younger siblings. Hoping to find a better life, Cather's father moved the family to Red Cloud, Nebraska, where Cather went to school regularly for the first time. She enjoyed acting and performing for her family and with local theater groups. She also was interested in science and wanted to become a medical doctor. During her teen years she assisted a local physician on his house calls. For several years during this period,

Cather dressed as a male and called herself "William."

A gifted student, Cather entered the University of Nebraska in 1891. There, she put her medical goals aside once she realized that she had an aptitude for language and literature. As the editor of the school's literary journal, Cather published many of her own short stories, but journalism soon became her focus. Before graduating, she was already working as a reporter and critic for the *Nebraska State Journal*. After graduating in 1895, Cather took a job in Pittsburgh as the editor of the women's magazine *Home Monthly*, and later worked as an editor and reporter at the Pittsburgh *Daily Leader*. Cather published her first book, the poetry collection *April Twilights*, in 1903. In 1905 she released her first collection of short stories, *The Troll Garden*.

In 1906, Cather became the managing editor of the leading magazine *McClure's* and moved to New York City. For the next six years, Cather wrote for that publication while also working on her own fiction. After author Sarah Orne Jewett gave Cather profound advice about her writing, Cather left *McClure's* and focused on penning fiction. Although her 1912 novel *Alexander's Bridge* was unsuccessful, Cather soon found her voice writing from memories of her childhood in Nebraska, other incidents in her life, and her interest in art and artistic success. As an author, Cather was greatly influenced by Henry James.

After *Alexander's Bridge*, Cather wrote a series of popular novels. Among the best known are *O Pioneers!* (1913) and *My Ántonia* (1918). Another, less-admired novel, *The Song of the Lark* (1915), compared the artist to the pioneer. In her novels written after World War I, Cather expressed the disillusionment she felt with the social and political order of the world by expressing more hopelessness and a need to escape in such works as the Pulitzer Prize–winning *One of Ours* (1922), *A Lost Lady* (1923), and *The Professor's House* (1925). Such attitudes also seeped into her influential short story collections, including *Youth and the Bright Medusa* (1920) and *Obscure Destinies* (1932).

Cather's writing developed a more positive tone with two novels set in the distant past—the Howells Medal–winning *Death Comes for the Archbishop* (1927) and *Shadows on the Rock* (1931). Cather continued to write and publish until her death from a brain hemorrhage on April 24, 1947, in New York City.

PLOT SUMMARY

Chapter One

A Lost Lady opens with a description of how Captain Daniel Forrester became a prominent, rich man by building an extensive railroad network. While constructing his rail lines, he found a spot surrounded by creeks and meadows near the growing town of Sweet Water in Nebraska. There he eventually built a house, and, with his much younger second wife Marian Forrester, he provides hospitality for visiting friends, businessmen, and prominent local citizens. Although they also own properties in Colorado, the Forresters consider Sweet Water their primary home.

Chapter Two

When Niel Herbert is twelve years old and Mrs. Forrester is still young, Niel and a group of local boys from town enter the Forrester property one summer day. They ask Mrs. Forrester's permission to fish and eat lunch there. In part because Mrs. Forrester favors Niel, she gives her consent. At lunchtime, she brings them homemade cookies and spends a few moments talking to them. The boys appreciate that Mrs. Forrester treats them well.

The boys are sitting on the grass talking when an older boy, the teenaged Ivy Peters, joins them. They do not like Ivy and his condescending tone, and they believe he has poisoned several local dogs just because he disliked them. During the conversation, Ivy becomes annoyed by a woodpecker. Using a slingshot, he hits the woodpecker, stunning it, then slits its eyes with a small knife. When the bird comes to, it is unable to fly straight. With the help of Rheinhold Blum, Niel tries to retrieve the bird from the tree to put it out of its misery. Instead, Niel falls and breaks his arm. Mrs. Forrester comforts him until the doctor arrives.

Chapter Three

At first, the Forresters spend only May to Thanksgiving in Sweet Water, and live the rest of the year at their homes in Denver and Colorado Springs. However, their lives change completely when the Captain falls off his horse in Colorado. After spending the winter recuperating

MEDIA ADAPTATIONS

- *A Lost Lady*, adapted as a silent film by screenwriter Dorothy Farnum and director Harry Beaumont, was released by Warner Bros. in 1924. It starred Irene Rich and Matt Moore.

- *A Lost Lady*, adapted as a film by screenwriter Gene Markey and director Alfred E. Green, was released by Warner Bros. in 1934. It starred Barbara Stanwyck and Frank Morgan.

- *A Lost Lady* was recorded as an unabridged audio book with narration by Flo Howard. It was released by Audio Book Contractors, Inc., in 1998.

- The Willa Cather Foundation maintains a website at http://www.willacather.org with information on the author, her life, times, and works.

- The Willa Cather Archive at the University of Nebraska–Lincoln maintains a website at http://cather.unl.edu/ with information on the author, her life, community, and related scholarship.

in Colorado Springs, he and his wife come back to Sweet Water, where he is essentially forced to retire.

As the Captain's life changes, the town of Sweet Water also begins a downward spiral. Crop failures compel many farmers and ranchers, including Niel's father, to leave. At nineteen, Niel begins to read law with his uncle, Judge Pommeroy, and moves into a room behind his law offices. Niel decorates the offices and keeps them clean. The judge is proud of the young man Niel has become.

One winter day while both the judge and Niel are working, Mrs. Forrester pays a visit and invites them to a dinner party at her home. Mrs. Forrester asks Niel to help entertain one guest, Constance Ogden, who has just finished school in the East. At the party, Niel comments on how this is only the second Christmas the Forresters have spent in Sweet Water. Mrs. Forrester responds that the Captain has informed her they are having money trouble and cannot afford to go away this year. She also asks that Niel and his uncle keep an eye on the Captain when he is in town because he has become weaker.

Chapter Four

Niel and Judge Pommeroy are the only people from Sweet Water to attend the party because the rest of the guests are from Denver. Niel finds Constance somewhat attractive, but not easy to talk to. He has better luck with her mother, Mrs. Ogden, and notices that Mr. Ogden lights up when Mrs. Forrester passes by. Niel finds bachelor Frank Ellinger interesting, but senses that he has a dark side. Niel also notices that Constance is interested in Frank. While eating dinner, Niel sits across from Frank and is reminded of stories about Frank's wild side and loose morals.

After Captain Forrester gives his traditional "happy days!" toast, he tells the story of how he discovered the land for this home while working as a driver for a freighting company shortly after the American Civil War. Twelve years later, after marrying Mrs. Forrester, he built his house and moved there. Captain Forrester ends his speech by espousing his philosophy on life—that you will eventually get what you want in some form if you have goals and work toward them.

When the meal is complete, the group retires to the parlor to play card games. Although Mrs. Forrester tries to pair Constance and Niel, Niel senses that Constance would rather play with Frank and arranges it. Before he leaves, Niel promises to return the next day to entertain Constance, even though he knows she has other interests. While walking home, Niel reflects on how attractive and confident Mrs. Forrester is when compared to other women. After the rest of the group goes to bed, Mrs. Forrester and Frank are alone for a few moments before she goes to her room as well. It is clear they are attracted to each other.

Chapter Five

As Niel arrives the next afternoon, Mrs. Forrester and Frank are leaving in the cutter (a kind of sleigh) to find cedar boughs for Christmas. She asks Niel to go inside and amuse Constance.

There, Constance is cross and becomes more so when she learns that Niel cannot take her anywhere. In the cutter, Mrs. Forrester and Frank flirt and talk about their correspondence. She insists that he not write her love letters. She directs him to a deep ravine of cedars, and it is implied that they are intimate. When Frank and Mrs. Forrester leave the cedar grove wrapped in buffalo robes, they are observed by Adolph Blum, who is out hunting rabbits. Because of his social class and belief that the kind Mrs. Forrester is his superior, he plans on keeping her secrets to himself.

Chapter Six

After Christmas, Niel and his uncle spend several pleasant nights each week visiting the Forrester home. In March, a blizzard snows in the Forresters for three days. On the third day, Niel gathers their mail at the post office and takes it to them. Captain Forrester entertains him while Mrs. Forrester rests with a headache; both men believe she has been drinking. Captain Forrester instructs her to make them all tea and toast, and as they eat, he reads aloud from out-of-town newspapers.

After Captain Forrester falls asleep while reading, Mrs. Forrester insists that Niel walk the hills with her so she can escape the house. She laments the effect of staying the winter in Sweet Water has on her because she cannot dance or exercise. As they walk, Niel finds himself intrigued by Mrs. Forrester's relationship with her husband. He also reflects on the disparity of what her life is and could be.

Chapter Seven

That winter, when not at the Forrester home, Niel spends his time reading works of classic literature found in Judge Pommeroy's library. He finds such works as the *Heroides* quite enjoyable. Such books expand Niel's worldview in a way he deeply appreciates.

In the spring, Captain Forrester receives a telegram that distresses him. A savings bank in Denver that he has greatly invested in has failed, and Judge Pommeroy tells Niel that the Captain will probably lose a great deal of money. With his lawyer and the judge, Captain Forrester travels to Denver. At home, Mrs. Forrester seems to be in a state of denial. Three days after Captain Forrester's departure, Frank shows up in town and checks into the local hotel. Niel notices that Frank has been at the Forrester home, where Mrs. Forrester is still alone.

At dawn the next day, Niel gets up and heads to the Forrester place. As Niel walks, he cuts wild roses for Mrs. Forrester. Niel plans on placing them outside her bedroom window. As he places the flowers on the sill, he hears a woman laughing and a man's enthusiastic voice. Niel walks away bitterly and tosses the roses aside. His perspective on life and women has been altered.

Chapter Eight

Niel meets his uncle and Captain Forrester at the train station and drives them to the Forrester home. While sitting in the parlor, the Captain tells his wife that he spent all his money—save the house and his pension—to ensure the depositors at the bank receive all their funds back. A troubled Mrs. Forrester insists that they will get by; the Captain emphasizes that that is all they will do.

After the Captain goes to his room to have a nap, Judge Pommeroy explains what happened in Denver. He emphasizes that the Captain acted honorably toward the depositors and tells Mrs. Forrester how proud he is of the Captain's actions. While Mrs. Forrester organizes lunch plans, Judge Pommeroy commends his nephew for wanting to be an architect and not a tainted lawyer like Ivy Peters.

When Mrs. Forrester tries to wake up the Captain for lunch, she finds he has had a stroke. During his recovery, Niel spends much time at the Forrester home helping take care of the Captain. Cyrus Dalzell, the president of the Colorado & Utah Railway line, also comes to call. Niel notices that Mrs. Forrester is more alive than she has been for some time during Dalzell's visit.

Chapter Nine

Within three weeks, the Captain can move around again, but only with difficulty. The day before Niel is to leave to take the entrance exams for the Massachusetts Institute of Technology— where he is going to study architecture—he goes to the Forrester home to say good-bye. During the visit, Mrs. Forrester seems more confident in her role as mistress of the house, but her words indicate she is well aware of what she has lost. As he walks away, Niel ponders Mrs. Forrester's actions with Ellinger, and how they affects her persona.

Chapter Ten

Two years later, Niel is returning home to Sweet Water for summer vacation. He encounters Ivy Peters on the train and learns that in addition to

practicing law, Ivy now rents some of the marshland on the Forrester property, which he has drained and hired his brother to farm wheat on. Ivy informs him that the Forresters have come down in social standing because of their financial difficulties.

As Ivy talks, Niel realizes that Ivy has drained the marsh out of spite for him and Mrs. Forrester, because he knew they had been fond of the marshes. Ivy intensely dislikes Niel, and his actions demonstrate that he has no qualms about taking advantage of the Forresters' unfortunate situation to hurt him. Niel is troubled that the great men who settled the West are now at the mercy of ruthless men like Ivy.

Chapter Eleven

The next afternoon, Niel visits the Forresters. He finds the Captain in his chair in his rose garden looking at the sundial Cyrus Dalzell had made for him. Making his way to the top of the hill, Niel finds Mrs. Forrester resting in a hammock. She is happy to see him and he still appreciates her, even though he has lost some of his respect for her. As she questions him about his life, Niel notes that she has aged, and her personality overshadows her looks. He learns that the Forresters' financial situation has grown still more desperate, and the burden of maintaining the house weighs heavily on her. As they go into the house with Mr. Forrester, Niel is asked to take their mail, including a letter addressed to Frank, into town. Niel wonders what the Captain knows about his wife.

Chapter Twelve

Niel's summer plans to read regularly at the Forresters is ruined by Ivy Peters's frequent, and often annoying, appearances. Niel does not like the way Ivy treats both of the Forresters. He especially resents how familiar Ivy is with Mrs. Forrester. Niel shares his frustrations with the Captain, who agrees. One night in July, a restless Niel walks to the Forrester place. He finds Mrs. Forrester on the bridge over the creek, and learns that the Captain is already asleep. While they are standing there, Ivy emerges from the shadow of the house and discusses business with Mrs. Forrester. He rudely invites himself to lunch, and after he leaves Niel asks her why she puts up with him. Mrs. Forrester feels she has no choice because they need the money from his lease. She admits she is involved in a shady land investment with him that she hopes will soon fund a better life for herself, perhaps without the Captain.

Chapter Thirteen

After a late July flood, the Forresters are cut off from town. Their servant, Ben Keezer, is able to ride to them daily to help with chores and bring them mail. Niel sees him one day with the mail and asks to see their copy of the Denver newspaper. On the society page, Niel notices that Frank has married Constance Ogden.

Later that night, it is raining again when Niel is reading in his uncle's law offices. Near midnight, a drunken Mrs. Forrester shows up wanting to call Frank long distance. Niel tries unsuccessfully to dissuade her. When the call goes through, Niel tries to remind her that what she says will be heard by Mrs. Beasley, the town operator and gossip. The conversation is polite at first, but by the end, Mrs. Forrester is berating Frank.

After Frank hangs up on her, Mrs. Forrester cuts the phone line and begins to sob. She passes out, and Niel puts her in his bed. He then wakes his uncle and asks him to stay with her while Niel goes out to the Forrester place to stay with the Captain. In the morning, Niel tells the Captain that she had been called to town to receive a long-distance call. On his way to the stable to get a horse to take Mrs. Forrester home, Niel sees Mrs. Beasley telling another woman about what happened the previous night.

Chapter Fourteen

A short time later, Captain Forrester has another stroke and is further incapacitated. The pressure of caring for him breaks Mrs. Forrester. The town's women offer their help, but it is primarily an excuse for them to rummage through the house to satisfy their own curiosity about this formerly wealthy couple. Mrs. Forrester has ceased to care. In town, Niel overhears what these women say about Mrs. Forrester, her belongings, and her behavior. He tells his uncle he is going to drop out of school for a year and help the Forresters. With his uncle's support, Niel kicks the gossips out, and he and his uncle's servant, Black Tom, nurse the Forresters back to health. Within a few weeks, Mrs. Forrester is able to take charge of the household. Black Tom goes back to work for the judge, while Niel remains at the Forresters. He admits he misses school, but deeply appreciates their home and what it has meant to his life.

Chapter Fifteen

In early December, Captain Forrester dies. Dr. Dennison and Judge Pommeroy are the only close friends who serve as pallbearers at the funeral, which is packed with locals but lacks any out-of-town guests. Mrs. Forrester has the Captain's beloved sundial engraved as his headstone.

Chapter Sixteen

By April of the following year, Niel is taking care of his uncle's business while Judge Pommeroy is ill. One day, Orville Ogden appears at the law offices asking for the judge's help in getting the Captain's pension increased for Mrs. Forrester. He seeks to do this through government channels, without her knowledge. Niel informs him that his uncle is no longer her lawyer and she has hired Ivy Peters in that capacity. Niel tells Ogden that he does not trust the dishonest Ivy, and Mr. Ogden decides to leave the matter alone.

After Mr. Ogden leaves, Niel reflects on how Mrs. Forrester has changed since her husband's death. She acts indiscriminately, without direction and without the ability to be both gracious and proper. Ivy Peters now spends a lot of time at the Forrester home, and has changed the property. When Niel confronts her on the regular presence of Ivy and other young men in her home, she dismisses the talk of gossips and refuses to consider moving to California until she sells the home. She further reveals that she switched lawyers because she believes Ivy is smarter about business. Judge Pommeroy is greatly hurt by her actions, and Niel does not speak to her again for some time.

Chapter Seventeen

One day in May, Mrs. Forrester invites Niel to a dinner party. Although he does not want to go, he agrees and is the last to arrive among the guests—young men from town, Ivy, and Ivy's sister, Annie. Niel regards the young men with contempt, especially because of the way they kowtow to Ivy. The dinner is awkward; Annie and the young men have little to say to Mrs. Forrester. Niel attempts to draw them into conversation, but fails.

After dinner, the guests are more relaxed and Mrs. Forrester talks about living in California. Niel asks her to tell everyone how she met Captain Forrester. She relates that she was nineteen years old and still reeling over the tragic murder of her millionaire fiancé. To avoid publicity, she retreated to a cottage in the Sierras. One day, as she was climbing down the face of Eagle Cliff, she fell and suffered two broken legs. No one knew where to look for her, but a search party that included Captain Forrester eventually found her. He helped carry her out, and cared for her during her recovery. Niel realizes that she needs the right man to save her again.

Chapter Eighteen

By August, Judge Pommeroy is better and Niel makes plans to return to school. Niel is torn by leaving as he knows it will be a big break with his boyhood and his past. Niel does not say goodbye to Mrs. Forrester; he is still filled with contempt for her. He is happy that he helped the Captain in his last days, but feels betrayed by his widow, who allows Ivy Peters to touch her in a familiar way.

While Niel is back at school, Judge Pommeroy sends him news about Mrs. Forrester from time to time. She is publicly involved with Ivy but seems unhappy and broken. After his uncle's death, Niel learns that Ivy bought the Forrester home, married a woman from Wyoming, and Mrs. Forrester went West. Niel thinks of her occasionally, and his memory of her softens and becomes more positive over time.

One night years later, in a Chicago hotel dining room, Niel runs into Ed Elliott, an old friend. He tells Niel that twelve years after she left Sweet Water, Ed saw Mrs. Forrester in Buenos Aires, Argentina. She had married a wealthy but irritable Englishman named Henry Collins. Ed went to their home and Mrs. Forrester told him to give her love to Niel if he ever saw him again. Ed informs Niel that she subsequently died, three years ago. Both Niel and Ed are happy that she was taken care of until the end of her life.

CHARACTERS

George Adams

George Adams is one of the local boys who enters the Forrester property with Mrs. Forrester's permission to fish. He is the son of a gentleman rancher from Lowell, Massachusetts, and is the one who directly asks Mrs. Forrester for permission that day. Like Niel, George despises Ivy Peters and is upset that he disrupts their day

of fun. A few years later, George and his family return to Massachusetts after a number of crop failures.

Mrs. Beasley

Mrs. Beasley is Sweet Water's telephone operator. She overhears Mrs. Forrester's drunken call to Frank Ellinger after his marriage.

Black Tom

Black Tom is the African American servant of Judge Pommeroy. The judge lets the Forresters use him as a server during their dinner parties. Black Tom also helps care for the Captain after his second stroke.

Adolph Blum

The son of the German tailor in Sweet Water and the brother of Rheinhold Blum, Adolph is one of the boys who fish on the Forrester property. Like his brother, Adolph tries to sell the game he hunts and fish he catches to various local citizens, including Mrs. Forrester. Adolph also observes Mrs. Forrester and Frank Ellinger when they have an intimate moment in the cedar grove, but vows not to tell her secret, in part because of her respectful manner toward him. When Captain Forrester dies, Adolph brings Mrs. Forrester a box of yellow roses. The gesture deeply affects her.

Rheinhold Blum

The son of Sweet Water's German tailor, and brother of Adolph Blum. Rheinhold is another of the boys who play on the Forrester property. When Niel wants to retrieve the woodpecker Ivy Peters harms, he stands on Rheinhold's shoulders to get into the tree. It is implied that Rheinhold and his brother fish and hunt to make money.

Henry Collins

Henry Collins is the wealthy, miserly, and cantankerous Englishman who marries Mrs. Forrester some years after the death of the Captain. He lives with her in Argentina until her death.

Cyrus Dalzell

The president of the Colorado & Utah Railway, Cyrus Dalzell is a loyal friend to the Forresters. After Captain Forrester has his first stroke, Cyrus visits their home and offers his support. He continues to visit regularly and makes the Captain's beloved sundial for him.

Dr. Dennison

Dr. Dennison is the local physician in Sweet Water. He sets Niel's broken arm after Niel's fall from the tree, and he takes care of Captain Forrester during his illnesses.

Frank Ellinger

A resident of Denver, Frank Ellinger is apparently a man of means. He is known for his wild bachelor ways, and Niel does not trust him. Over the course of the novel, it is revealed that Mrs. Forrester has been having an affair with Frank. The two send letters to each other on a regular basis. The couple are alone, apparently on intimate terms, several times. Mrs. Forrester becomes distraught when she learns that Frank has married Constance Ogden.

Ed Elliott

Ed Elliott is one of the boys who plays on the Forresters' property. His father owns a shoe store in Sweet Water. As a young man, Ed attends the awkward dinner party Mrs. Forrester gives. At the end of the novel, Ed is working as a mining engineer when he runs into Niel in Chicago. Over dinner, Ed tells Niel how Mrs. Forrester lived her life after she left Sweet Water.

Captain Daniel Forrester

One of the novel's primary characters, Captain Forrester is symbolic of the men who built up the American West. After the Civil War, the young Forrester went West to work as a supply driver for a freighting company. While driving supplies from Nebraska City to Cherry Creek, he found the spot on the hill near Sweet Water, Nebraska, where he eventually made his home. Forrester bought the land from the railroad company and eventually made his fortune building the railroads that crisscrossed the country.

Twelve years after purchasing the property, Forrester was able to build his house on the land and settled there with his second wife, Marian Forrester. (His first wife was an invalid until her death.) When he first lived in Sweet Water, Forrester was still active in building railroads, and he and his wife spent part of the year living in Denver and Colorado Springs. After he had an accident in Colorado in which he fell off a horse, Forrester no longer took on new building contracts. He lived off his investments, which included a bank, mining interests, and other business concerns. As he traveled less, Sweet Water became his home and a place

where he found serenity growing flowers and enjoying nature.

Over the course of the novel, Captain Forrester grows weaker and suffers two strokes. While he still has significant friends like Cyrus Dalzell and Judge Pommeroy, the Captain, as both a builder and a man of honor, symbolizes a dying way of life. Forrester loses much of his income when a Denver bank he invested in fails, and he uses his own money to ensure that depositors get all their funds back. Because of these circumstances, Mrs. Forrester is compelled to take on a larger role in her husband's care. It is unclear if the Captain knows his wife has cheated on him with Frank Ellinger. When Niel reflects on their marriage, he realizes that the Captain is the one who kept his wife grounded—a fact he does not fully appreciate until Forrester's death.

Marian Forrester

See Mrs. Forrester

Mrs. Forrester

The woman at the heart of *A Lost Lady*, Marian Forrester is the much younger second wife of Captain Daniel Forrester. From Niel's point of view for much of the novel, she is an ideal woman, kind to everyone in the town, mindful of the social order, and a wonderful wife and hostess. She has a vitality and youthfulness about her that attracts many boys and men, even as she ages. Mrs. Forrester is depicted as needing the attention of men and making poor choices when she has been confronted with considerable responsibility.

Captain and Mrs. Forrester live in Sweet Water part of the year early in their marriage. Mrs. Forrester is especially fond of young Niel, but is nice to all the local residents. She finds her own identity in being socially and physically active, especially when she and Captain Forrester live in Denver and Colorado Springs for part of the year. Mrs. Forrester grows increasingly unhappy after the Captain's accident and subsequent strokes. She has an affair with Frank Ellinger and develops a noticeable drinking problem. When her husband loses his fortune, she continues to care for him but becomes more desperate as she is forced to take on more duties in the home. She breaks down several times, and Niel and his uncle help take care of her and the Captain.

After Captain Forrester's death, Niel watches Mrs. Forrester develop more serious problems, and he realizes that the Captain was her anchor.

She takes up with Ivy Peters and unceremoniously dumps Judge Pommeroy as her lawyer after years of his loyal service to her. She invites many young men to her home for dinner parties and basks in their attention. Niel later learns that she eventually went West, married a rich Englishman named Henry Collins, and lived in Buenos Aires for the rest of her life. Niel is not quite sure what to make of Mrs. Forrester at times, but he understands that she has greatly influenced his life and the way he views women. He is grateful that she was cared for at the end of her life.

Thaddeus Grimes

Thaddeus Grimes is one of the local boys who plays on the Forrester property. The red-haired son of the local butcher, he is grateful for Mrs. Forrester's kind treatment.

Niel Herbert

The primary character of *A Lost Lady*, Niel Herbert spends his youth and young adulthood fascinated by Mrs. Forrester. His parents were from Kentucky, and his mother died when he was five years old. The family moved to Sweet Water to make a fortune, but his father lost his property and worked in an office. When Niel is a teenager, his father moves to Denver to take a job and Niel moves in with his uncle, Judge Pommeroy, to read law. It is because of his uncle that Niel has social standing in Sweet Water, although Niel has friends across the social spectrum. He later decides he wants to be an architect; he leaves Sweet Water to attend the Massachusetts Institute of Technology. He returns for summer vacations but eventually lives elsewhere.

A kind, thoughtful, sensitive, and compassionate young man, Niel often puts the needs of others before himself. When Ivy Peters cuts the eyes of a woodpecker early in the novel, Niel goes up into a tree to put the animal out of its misery but falls and breaks his arm before completing the task. As a young adult, Niel helps his uncle run his business and assists the Forresters through their various crises and illnesses. For example, when Captain Forrester has his second stroke, Niel leaves school for a year to help take care of the Forresters. He also runs his uncle's legal office when the judge becomes ill. Although Niel never forgets the vivaciousness of Mrs. Forrester, he dislikes her dishonesty and lack of loyalty to both her husband and his uncle. Still, at the end of the novel, Niel is happy to hear that she was cared for by a husband until her death.

Ben Keezer

Ben Keezer is the Forresters' hired man. He helps them with chores, transportation, and other household tasks.

Maidy

See Mrs. Forrester

Mary

Mary works as a cook for the Forresters until her marriage to Joe Pucelik. She is a native of Bohemia.

Constance Ogden

A young lady from a family in Denver, Constance Ogden is a guest at the dinner party the Forresters throw early in the novel. At that point, she has just finished school in the East and is returning home. Although Mrs. Forrester tries to interest her in Niel, Constance becomes infatuated with Frank Ellinger, whom she eventually marries.

Mr. Orville Ogden

Mr. Ogden is the father of Constance Ogden. Although he is a faithful husband, he is also impressed by Mrs. Forrester. After the death of Captain Forrester, he asks Niel to speak to the judge about getting her government pension increased. Mr. Ogden is distressed when he learns how far she has fallen by allowing the shady Ivy Peters to take over her legal and business interests.

Mrs. Ogden

Constance's mother and Orville's wife, Mrs. Ogden is also a guest at the Forresters' dinner party. Although described as unattractive, Niel finds her friendlier and more sympathetic than her daughter.

Marian Ormsby

See Mrs. Forrester

Annie Peters

Annie Peters is the sister of Ivy Peters. She attends an awkward dinner party at Mrs. Forrester's home, along with Ivy, Niel, and a number of the town's young men.

Ivy Peters

Nicknamed Poison Ivy, Ivy Peters comes from a prominent local family and is a few years older than Niel and the other boys who play on the Forresters' property. As a young man, Ivy has a reputation for cruelty to animals. Early in the novel, he deliberately blinds a woodpecker that bothers him. The boys, including Niel and George, do not like Ivy, and a few fear him. Ivy eventually becomes a lawyer and shady businessman. Niel has several encounters with Ivy over the years, and does not respect him. After Captain Forrester has his first stroke and Niel goes away to college, Ivy leases part of the Forrester property, drains the marsh, and acts with impunity and privilege toward the Forresters. Mrs. Forrester will not let Niel interfere with Ivy, because she and the Captain are dependent on the income from the leased property. Upon the death of the Captain, Mrs. Forrester hires Ivy as her lawyer and becomes involved with him. Niel is disgusted when he observes Mrs. Forrester letting Ivy touch her intimately. Ivy eventually buys the Forrester place and marries a woman from Wyoming.

Judge Pommeroy

Judge Pommeroy is a prominent lawyer in Sweet Water, and he is cut from the same cloth as his friend Captain Forrester. He is the maternal uncle to Niel Herbert and takes charge of caring for him when Niel's father leaves to take a job in Denver. The judge gives Niel a place to live and a job working in his law offices until he goes to the Massachusetts Institute of Technology. He is very supportive of Niel's life choices. Judge Pommeroy values honesty and integrity, and is a loyal friend to people like Captain Forrester. The judge looks down upon lawyers like Ivy Peters, although he realizes that such men are emblematic of the future. After the Captain's death, Judge Pommeroy is extremely hurt by Mrs. Forrester's abrupt decision to drop him as her lawyer in favor of Peters.

Joe Pucelik

Joe Pucelik is the boyfriend of Mary, the Forresters' Bohemian cook. He eventually marries Mary.

Cousin Sadie

Cousin Sadie is a poor relation of Niel's family who comes from Kentucky to run his father's household some time after his mother's death. She is a spinster and Niel does not think she keeps the house in good order. However, Sadie is also described as helpful to neighbors.

Joe Simpson

A young man and local business owner, Joe Simpson is a guest at Mrs. Forrester's awkward dinner party.

Molly Tucker

Molly Tucker is Sweet Water's seamstress.

The Weaver Twins

The Weaver twins are two of the boys who fish on the Forrester property. They are the sons of Sweet Water's grocer, and are described as plump and brown. They always eat rye bread and hard cheese on these outings. This habit earns the contempt of Thaddeus Grimes.

THEMES

Conflict of Values between Generations

One concept that underscores much of the plot in *A Lost Lady* is how human values change over time. In the novel, Cather distinguishes between the generations and their different sets of principles. Men like Captain Forrester and Judge Pommeroy represent the old guard, the backbone of towns like Sweet Water in this period. The Captain helped build the railroads that crisscrossed the Plains States and linked the East to California and the Pacific Ocean, thereby fulfilling America's "Manifest Destiny." While the judge's exact role in building up Sweet Water is unclear, he is regarded as a leading citizen and upright lawyer. His respectable social standing extends to his beloved nephew, Niel Herbert, who shares many of his values despite his youth.

Mrs. Forrester's values contrast with those of her husband, who is twenty-five years older than she is. While the Captain loves his wife and her youthful vitality, she seems to feel limited by marriage. For much of the novel, Cather implies that she is having an affair with Frank Ellinger, a notorious bachelor from Denver. Mrs. Forrester garners attention from men and boys alike because of her friendly, always respectful, and sometimes flirtatious attitude. At times, this attitude manifests itself in friendships with younger men like Niel and the Blum brothers. As Captain Forrester's health deteriorates and he loses a significant portion of his wealth, Mrs. Forrester feels desperate and trapped. This leads to her affair with Ivy Peters and her decision to trust her business interests to this unscrupulous lawyer, who is involved in shady business deals.

When Mrs. Forrester is desperate, she does not care whom she hurts by her actions. In contrast, Captain Forrester cared for the welfare of

TOPICS FOR FURTHER STUDY

- Read both Cather's *A Lost Lady* and the classic novel *Madame Bovary* (1857) by Gustave Flaubert. Cather admitted to being influenced by Flaubert and this novel. In an essay, compare and contrast the novels and the primary female characters, whom many critics believe share several characteristics. How does each novel handle the women's adulterous relationships?

- Cather once said that she based *A Lost Lady* on her childhood memory of ex-governor Silas Garber and his young wife living in her childhood home of Red Cloud, Nebraska. Cather remembered how Mrs. Garber looked, the couple's big house on a hill, and a grove of trees on their property where the young Cather had gone for picnics. Write a short story based on your remembrances of someone from your childhood. You can research the Garbers to find links between the text of the novel and history that can inspire your own thought process.

- Watch the 1934 film version of *A Lost Lady*, which starred Barbara Stanwyck, and in an essay, compare and contrast the novel and the film version. Cather did not like the film and refused to allow any more films made of her works after seeing it. In your essay, speculate on why you think Cather felt this way. Do you think her feelings were justified?

- With a classmate, read both *A Lost Lady* and *The Great Gatsby* (1925), a novel by F. Scott Fitzgerald. Also, research the time period in which these books were written. Then stage a debate for the class about which novel best represents American society in the early twentieth century. You could also discuss the similarities and dissimilarities between Mrs. Forrester and Jay Gatsby, the tragic hero of Fitzgerald's classic novel.

- In *A Lost Lady*, there is little information about Niel and his biological family, but what is known is that his mother is dead, his father leaves, and his uncle becomes his father figure. He also develops a fascination with Mrs. Forrester, whom one could argue is his first love. Although Danny, the hero of Matt de la Peña's young adult novel *Mexican WhiteBoy* (2008), is of a different generation, he has many situations in his life that are similar to Niel's. In an essay, compare and contrast the characters of Niel and Danny. Read between the lines about Niel as needed for your essay based on what you know about the character.

---

others to the degree that he used nearly everything he owned to ensure that the depositors of his failed bank in Denver received their money back. Among Sweet Water's younger generation, only Niel is depicted as being this kind of upstanding citizen. (To a limited extent it is implied that the minor character of Ed Elliott shares Niel's values, but his role is small in the novel.)

Thus, for Cather, while the Captain is important, he, like the area where he chose to settle, becomes less relevant as he becomes more debilitated. Sweet Water started out with promise when the railroad was built there, but crop failures and other setbacks limited the town's growth. With Captain Forrester's death—a symbolic end to any chance Sweet Water has of being more than a small town—the values he represents in the town die a little with him. Because his widow does not like the advice Judge Pommeroy gives her on selling her home and other matters, Mrs. Forrester hires Ivy to represent her concerns. She does not care how she makes money or how her decisions will affect others; she simply fires the man who supported her and her husband through thick and thin. Ivy seems to win in one sense because he has an affair with Mrs. Forrester and eventually buys her home. However, Cather depicts Niel and Ed going out into the world and becoming good, respectable men. They are professionals who seem to live out the values of their elders and old Sweet Water in a way Ivy and Mrs. Forrester could not have understood.

Coming of Age

In some ways, *A Lost Lady* can be seen as a coming-of-age novel. Although written in the omniscient third person, much of the action and attitude is filtered through the perspective of Niel Herbert. The novel begins when Niel is a boy, playing with a group of boys on the Forrester property. At its heart are the experiences of Niel as he reaches adulthood. By the time he is nineteen years old, living in his uncle's law offices, he is still harboring his long-standing fascination with Mrs. Forrester. Cather wrote that this interest began when he was quite young, seeing Mrs. Forrester enter the Episcopal church one Sunday morning. Cather writes, "He was proud now that at the first moment he had recognized her as belonging to a different world from any he had ever known."

Cather uses Niel's infatuation with Mrs. Forrester as a vehicle for describing his maturation from boy to man. Guided by his uncle's values and support, Niel makes personal sacrifices to help the Forresters through the aftermath of the Captain's fall as well as his two strokes. Niel brings their mail during a blizzard, and takes walks and sleigh rides with Mrs. Forrester so she feels less trapped by her home and circumstances. When Niel leaves school for a year to help the Forresters following the Captain's second stroke, he takes charge when local women use the excuse of "helping" to rummage through the property contained in the Forrester home. Niel remains in Sweet Water after the Captain's death to run his uncle's law offices while the judge gets over his own bout with rheumatic fever.

During this time period, Niel has an epiphany that demonstrates he has reached maturity and an understanding of human complexities. While Niel is disappointed to learn that Mrs. Forrester has been having an affair with Frank Ellinger and thinks less of her for a time, he comes to be fascinated again by her and continues to help her. Later, Niel understands that it was Captain Forrester who grounded his wife, and not she who needed to be free from him to be herself. Cather writes, "For years, Niel and his uncle . . . had thought of the Captain as a drag

upon his wife; a care that drained her and dimmed her and kept her from being all that she might be. But without him, she was like a ship without ballast, driven hither and thither by every wind."

After this revelation, Niel feels more sympathy for Mrs. Forrester and no longer particularly infatuated with her. He does not want to go to the dinner party she gives for many of the local young men, including Ivy, but accepts the invitation and shows up nonetheless. Even then Niel understands she needs the right kind of man to restore her to a happy life, but he does not invest his time in helping her save herself from Ivy. Years later, a chance meeting with Ed Elliott brings news that Mrs. Forrester married again and seemed to have found what she was looking for before her death.

Strength and Weakness

Another key theme that underscores much of the action in *A Lost Lady* is the concept of strength and weakness. Cather distinguishes between the strong and the weak in a number of ways. Characters like Judge Pommeroy, Niel, and Captain Forrester are drawn as strong men with solid, upright, honest, respectable beliefs. Even when he becomes ill, the Captain remains dignified, bearing a type of inner strength. In contrast, characters like Mrs. Forrester and Ivy are depicted as weak. Cather implies that Mrs. Forrester needs affirmation, especially from men, to have self-esteem and direction. However, Cather allows Mrs. Forrester some leeway, suggesting that it might be forgivable for a woman to possess such weakness. The author does no such thing with Ivy Peters. From the first, Ivy is depicted as a weak young man who kills dogs and maims birds just because they annoy him. As he grows older, Ivy becomes a lawyer and has no qualms about engaging in shady business practices. He also begins some sort of affair with Mrs. Forrester while her husband is still alive. Cather emphasizes that Ivy uses the power he has over her—because he rents part of the Forresters' property and secretly invests some of her money in a land deal—to play a larger role in her life than he should. In the end, both the strong and the weak who are alive survive in their own way, but these aspects of their character do not seem to change.

Woodpecker in a tree (*Image copyright teekaygee, 2009. Used under license from Shutterstock.com*)

STYLE

Point of View

The point of view is the narrative perspective from which the author chooses to write. *A Lost Lady* is written in third person omniscient point of view. This allows readers to see the action from a perspective that allows them to understand the minds and actions of multiple characters without the restriction a single point of view might impose. Although much of the novel is filtered through Niel's thoughts and feelings, Cather also offers the perspective of characters like Adolph Blum, Mrs. Forrester, and others.

Setting

The setting is where, when, and the cultural environment in which a written work takes place. *A Lost Lady* is set primarily in the small town of Sweet Water, Nebraska, in an unspecified time period in the late nineteenth and early twentieth centuries. Although Cather does not specify the era, it is implied through such clues as the stories Captain Forrester tells about finding the plot of land on which he built his home in Sweet Water, the advent of local railroad building, the lack of automobiles, and the availability of telephones.

The setting is important to the novel as Cather uses images of this small town and the land around the Forrester property to emphasize how limited Sweet Water is compared to bigger cities like Denver. The author also notes that while Sweet Water was expected to grow into a thriving city, circumstances curtailed its growth, compelling some who were looking for a better life to move away, leaving it a small town. While some locals, like Judge Pommeroy, Niel, and the Blums thrive in Sweet Water, Mrs. Forrester only likes living there part of the year as she feels stifled by its limitations, especially as her husband grows more ill. Captain Forrester finds Sweet Water an ideal place to spend his last years, a place of rest after years of hard work.

At the end of the novel, Cather shifts the setting of *A Lost Lady* to Chicago, for even Niel has moved on. He received his education in Boston—although his experiences there are only talked about in limited fashion and never fully described—and left Sweet Water permanently after completing his schooling. In Chicago he runs into Ed Elliott and they discuss what happened to Mrs. Forrester after she left Sweet Water. There are few details about Chicago and the exact year, but both men are now adults and a bit nostalgic for the past in Sweet Water that included Mrs. Forrester.

Hero/Protagonist

Although *A Lost Lady* is written in third person omniscient, Niel Herbert is drawn as the hero and primary protagonist of the novel. A hero is the primary sympathetic character in a book, while the protagonist is the story's central character who serves as a focus for the story's themes and incidents as well as its development. Cather often describes Niel's perspective on events, including his infatuation with Mrs. Forrester, which drives the novel, as well as his helping both the Forresters through good times and bad. Cather often explores Niel's thoughts as he tries to understand why Mrs. Forrester acts the way she does. Readers only get limited insight into characters other than Niel. Judge Pommeroy, for example, rarely speaks for himself, and readers understand how the judge feels only due to Niel's actions and insights.

Antagonist

In *A Lost Lady*, Cather sets up several characters as antagonists. An antagonist is contrasted with the hero or protagonist, and usually works against him or stands in opposition to him. The antagonists in this novel include Ivy Peters and Frank Ellinger as well as Mrs. Forrester herself.

From his first introduction, Ivy Peters is drawn as a bully who bothers younger boys on their outing on the Forrester property, is believed to poison dogs, and maims a woodpecker. Ivy is often contrasted with Niel, who dislikes him intensely. This disgust increases when Niel meets Ivy on the train coming home from school, and later when he believes Ivy is taking advantage of the Forresters, especially Mrs. Forrester, while renting their property. The Denver-based Frank Ellinger is not as mean-spirited as Ivy, but Niel regards him as a bad person for having a long affair with Mrs. Forrester while her husband is still alive.

Because of Mrs. Forrester's actions in relation to these two men, she, too, can be regarded as something of an antagonist to Niel at certain points in the book. While Niel admires and ideal-izes her, these illusions are shattered when he learns that Mrs. Forrester is having an affair with Frank and when he sees Ivy touch her intimately. Niel is wounded by her actions after the Captain's death, when she drops his uncle as her lawyer in favor of Ivy. While Mrs. Forrester is not the clear-cut antagonist that Ivy and Frank Ellinger prove themselves to be, she becomes one over time and breaks all illusions that Niel had about her.

HISTORICAL CONTEXT

Western Railroads and the Settlement of Nebraska

During the second half of the nineteenth century, the westward expansion of the United States was driven largely by the establishment of railroad lines. Transcontinental rail travel—that is, rail-road travel from the Atlantic Ocean to the Pacific Ocean—first became possible in the United States in 1869, when the Pacific Railroad connected with the Eastern Railroad. Railroads drove industrial-ization and commerce across the country, and railroad owners made fortunes. The railroad line specifically mentioned in *A Lost Lady* is the Bur-lington Railroad, which ran through Nebraska. Cather was a child in Red Cloud during the expansion of the Burlington railroad, and makes frequent reference to the railroad in her works.

Not only did the growth of railroads spur industrialization, it allowed for increased settlement

of Nebraska, and the West in general. In 1860, the population of Nebraska was just under 30,000. The first large wave of settlers, taking advantage of federal land grants, arrived in Nebraska during the 1860s, taking the population to over 120,000 in just ten years. The Burlington railroad expanded through Nebraska in the late 1870s (in fact, tracks reached Cather's home town of Red Cloud in 1878), and became an important route from St. Louis and Kansas City west to Denver. The pop-ulation of the state boomed. By 1880, it reached nearly half a million, and by 1890 it doubled again to just over a million.

The time between 1860 and 1900 was clearly a period of enormous change in Nebraska. Cather is famous for capturing the lives of the hardy settlers of the prairie in such works as *My Ántonia* (1918) and *O Pioneers!* (1913), and is openly wistful about these lost "boom" days in Nebraska. By the time she wrote *A Lost Lady* in the early 1920s, Nebraska's growth had stag-nated (it held steady at about 1.3 million from 1920 to 1950, inching up to 1.7 million by 2000). As the twentieth century dawned, large urban centers like San Francisco and Chicago attracted more and more young people (like Niels, who ends up in Chicago), and smaller, rural com-munities faded, becoming, as Cather writes at the beginning of *A Lost Lady*, "so much greyer today than they were then."

The Panic of 1893

Ivy mentions in the novella that Captain For-rester's fortune was wiped out in "the panic." The panic he refers to was the so-called panic of 1893, a nationwide financial collapse that brought on one of the worst economic crises the United States had ever experienced (until the Great Depression of the 1930s). The panic caused many banks to fail. In fact, the First National Bank of Lincoln, which held the account of the Burlington railroad and the accounts of many Burlington railroad employ-ees, was close to failure in 1896. The bank's president asked the railroad to rescue it finan-cially. The First National Bank of Lincoln was the largest bank in the region, and its failure would have caused multiple smaller banks to fail and many businesses to go bankrupt. The president of the Burlington railroad, Charles Perkins, used his own money to prop up the bank until the end of the panic in 1899. Perkins, with whom Cather was acquainted, was likely a partial inspiration for the character of Captain Forrester.

COMPARE
&
CONTRAST

- **Pre-World War I:** Telephones were invented by Alexander Graham Bell in 1876. Over the next few decades, technology is put in place to allow telephone networks within cities, between cities, and overseas.

  1920s: Telephones in homes and businesses are becoming more common. In 1928, for example, there are 18.5 million telephones in use in the United States.

  Today: The use of landline telephones, which were common in the 1920s, is rapidly declining in favor of personal cellular telephones that can be carried anywhere.

- **Pre-World War I:** Established social norms limit women's roles in the United States to certain roles based on their social class.

  1920s: Flappers and other women challenge social norms about smoking, drinking, and personal appearance in the United States and face resistance from society.

  Today: It is now socially acceptable for women to smoke, drink, and dress as they choose in the United States. Social norms that are being challenged focus on issues such as gay marriage.

- **Pre-World War I:** The United States experiences regular boom and bust cycles that affect how Americans live, work, and consume.

  1920s: Prosperity gained from growing businesses and a booming stock market often leads to conspicuous consumption and materialism among the middle and upper classes in the United States.

  Today: Amidst one of the most severe economic downturns since the Great Depression, many Americans embrace concepts like saving and thriftiness.

- **Pre-World War I:** While the United States has significant urban areas, it is still primarily a rural country and farming is a common enterprise.

  1920s: Americans living in cities outnumber Americans living in rural areas for the first time. Yet a significant portion of Americans still make their full-time living from farming.

  Today: The United States Census ceased to count the number of Americans who live on farms in 1993, but it is believed that less than two percent of Americans make their full-time living from agriculture.

- **Pre-World War I:** The first film is created in 1888, but it is not until the early twentieth century that silent films become popular. One of the first movie stars is Mary Pickford, known as "America's Sweetheart."

  1920s: Movie star Clara Bow becomes a Jazz Age icon known as the "It Girl" after her appearance in the 1927 film *It*. She is considered the leading sex symbol in the United States in the 1920s and 1930s.

  Today: Movie stars like Angelina Jolie and Megan Fox are considered among the leading sex symbols in the United States, if not the world.

CRITICAL OVERVIEW

Over time, critics became divided on *A Lost Lady* as some considered it one of Cather's best novels while others believed it was among her weakest works. When first published, *A Lost Lady* was highly praised by critics, some of whom believed it was better than its Pulitzer Prize–winning predecessor, *One of Ours*. But even the critics who dismissed *A Lost Lady* found Cather's depiction of rural Nebraska worthwhile.

One early positive review came in the *Times Literary Supplement* in 1924. The critic writes,

Grove of cedar trees (*Image copyright Steve Slocomb, 2009. Used under license from Shutterstock.com*)

"In *A Lost Lady* . . . the blending of intuition and analysis is extremely subtle. Miss Cather attempts hardly a single direct observation on the mentality or temperament of her characters but yet reveals with the most unfailing exactness their individual characteristics and motives."

By the 1930s, critical tastes and mind-sets had changed. Thus, novels by Cather such as *A Lost Lady* were regarded more negatively because they lacked the elements that were considered in vogue among literary intellectuals of the time. Cather and certain of her novels were also dismissed because she condemned materialism, which was seen as implicitly endorsing Marxism at a time when such sentiments were unwelcome in American society.

By the 1960s, another edition of the novel was published, and critics were again recognizing the power of *A Lost Lady*. A *Times Literary Supplement* review notes of Cather, "She has never been generally appreciated as she deserves." Commenting on the novel itself, the critic writes, "A partial statement of the theme cannot indicate the economy and feeling with

which the story is told; nor the truthfulness of the vision, that never balks the evil or sordidness that haunt the action, without exaggerating them for easy sensational effects."

The novel continued to be popular among critics into the twenty-first century as well. Writing in the *New York Times* in 2003, Margo Jefferson admits both *A Lost Lady* and Cather's *My Mortal Enemy* impressed her. Jefferson comments, "What astonishing books! In the age of the New Woman, Cather was excavating the ladies and grande dames of the previous generation. So much of her work does this; she hunts for traces of a past that might be dismissed or forgotten. The tone is 'Once upon a time,' but that time was part of our history."

CRITICISM

A. Petruso

Petruso has a B.A. in history from the University of Michigan and an M.A. in screenwriting from the University of Texas at Austin. In this essay, she explores how the ideas of tragedy and loss underscore the themes and define the main characters of A Lost Lady.

Much of the plot of Willa Cather's *A Lost Lady* turns on incidents of tragedy, loss, and brokenness. From cracked limbs to strokes to personal and financial breakdowns, the author uses these difficult events to reveal the depth and breadth of her characters. Through it all, Niel, arguably the novel's primary character, must deal with the repercussions of his initial, idealized belief that Mrs. Forrester is a perfect example of womanhood. Cather draws everyone as very human, including Mrs. Forrester, something Niel comes to understand as he fully becomes an adult. An examination of how Cather depicts these dark incidents illuminates the reasons why Niel's idealization is so key to the novel and what affect it has on both him and Mrs. Forrester.

Cather often uses calamity and misfortune to define characters in *A Lost Lady*. She first employs the concept of loss in Part One, Chapter I when describing Captain Forrester's history and merits, then mentioning at the end that he had an accident that affected both him and Mrs. Forrester, his second wife. Referring to the couple's house in Sweet Water, Cather writes, "He grew old there—and even she, alas! grew older." Then, in Part One, Chapter II, Cather sets up another dynamic based on this idea. To prepare readers for how depraved and mean-spirited Ivy Peters is, Cather has the boys gathered for an outing on the Forrester property talk about how Ivy poisoned several local dogs he did not like. Ivy then uses a knife to slit the eyes of an innocent female woodpecker so that she cannot see or fly properly.

While Ivy's actions define his character, the incident paves the way for Cather to introduce more brokenness. Demonstrating Niel's sensitivity, he tries to get the woodpecker from her nest to put her out of her misery. In the process, he falls off the tree and breaks his arm. Niel becomes broken trying to do the honorable thing. Mrs. Forrester ensures he is taken care of by putting him in her bed and calling the doctor, adding to his idealization of her, but the break also provides a physical link between them. Near the end of *A Lost Lady*, at Mrs. Forrester's awkward dinner party, Niel asks Mrs. Forrester to share with her young guests how she met Captain Forrester. She tells them

AMIDST ALL THIS MISFORTUNE AND HEARTBREAK, NIEL—WHO HAS SO MUCH IN COMMON WITH MRS. FORRESTER—IDEALIZES HER, MAKING HER SEEM LIKE A ROSE BLOSSOMING IN THE SNOW OF A WINTER'S DAY."

how, while climbing down the face of Eagle Cliff in the Sierra Madres with mountain climber Fred Harney, their rope broke. Harney was killed while Mrs. Forrester suffered two broken legs and spent more than a day alone in pain before being rescued. The Captain helped find her, but she suffered even more pain as the fractures had started to heal and doctors had to break them again to re-set them.

These parallel breaks create an implicit bond between Niel and Mrs. Forrester: The Captain helped her walk again, and Mrs. Forrester nurtured Niel through recovery when he was still a boy. Cather links the characters through other tragedies in *A Lost Lady* as well. The Captain—who is twenty-five years older than his wife and the only family of her's that is ever mentioned—can be viewed as not just a husband who gives her high social standing, but also a father figure. While the couple lives well during the early part of their marriage, the Captain suffers a riding accident in Colorado that essentially forces him to retire to Sweet Water. There, he can still care for and provide stability for his wife, but cannot work building railroads. This situation grows more grave after he loses nearly all of his fortune when he covers the deposits in a failed Denver-based bank in which he is a major investor. The Captain does not really lose his social position, at least in Sweet Water, until his last days when he is forced to lease the marsh to arrogant Ivy. However, by then Captain Forrester is a broken man who relies on his much-younger wife for everything.

Thus, over the course of *A Lost Lady*, Mrs. Forrester goes from a subservient daughter/wife to a mother/wife of a gravely ill man. Niel's life is also implied to be littered with such tragedy. Cather talks about young Niel's home life as sad. Describing his boyhood home in Sweet

WHAT DO I READ NEXT?

- *One of Ours*, published in 1922, is Cather's Pulitzer Prize–winning novel. It is the first to explore the theme of hopelessness. The novel focuses on Claude Wheeler, a virtuous young man living in a Nebraska that has become increasingly materialist and prosperous. Because of his family's deteriorating values, he volunteers to serve in World War I and dies.

- *Don Juan*, published in 1819–1824, is an epic poem by Lord Byron. In *A Lost Lady*, Niel reads the poem even though his uncle tells him not to. Written in ottava rima (an Italian form of poetry), the poem offers a comic take on Don Juan's many adventures, including war, women, and pirates. Throughout the poem, Byron emphasizes the struggle between nature and civilization.

- *Dark Dude*, published in 2008, is a young adult novel by Oscar Hijuelos. This novel focuses on Rico, a light-skinned Cuban boy living in Harlem, who goes to rural Wisconsin where a friend is living. There, he finds his identity as a Latino challenging.

- *Heroides*, written some two thousand years ago, is a work of poetry by Ovid. The poems take the form of love letters written by the female mythological characters of Penelope, Medea, and Dido to their absent husbands or lovers. It is another work read by Niel in the course of *A Lost Lady*.

- *Daisy Miller*, published in 1879, is a short novel by Henry James. James was a major influence on Cather, and this novel, like *A Lost Lady*, explores what happens to a woman who breaks social norms and the social order.

- *The Last Exit to Normal*, published in 2008, is a young adult novel by Michael Harmon. This novel focuses on the journey of Ben Campbell, who goes to Montana with his father and stepfather to improve his life. There, Ben learns about small-town life and finds a love interest.

- *My Ántonia*, published in 1918, is considered one of Cather's best novels. Narrated by Jim Burden, he tells the story of his neighbors, the Shimerdas, a Bohemian immigrant family in Nebraska, who struggle to establish themselves. He is especially close to the daughter, Ántonia, who ends up leading a life very different from his.

Water, Cather writes, "Home was not a pleasant place to go to; a frail egg-shell house, set off on the edge of the prairie where people of no consequence live." Niel's parents moved to Nebraska to better their lives. Unfortunately, his mother died there when he was five years old and his father, like Captain Forrester, lost his property except for his house. Niel's father eventually took a job in which "he kept the county abstract books and made farm loans." An impoverished family cousin, the spinster Sadie, maintains their household haphazardly. By the time Niel is an older teenager, his father has sent Sadie home, shut up his house, and moved to Denver to take a new office job. Niel is left in the care of his beloved,

loving maternal uncle, Judge Pommeroy, who gives him a home, guidance, and social position in the community. The relationship between Niel and his uncle has a great deal in common with the Captain and Mrs. Forrester, especially before the Captain becomes seriously ill.

Amidst all this misfortune and heartbreak, Niel—who has so much in common with Mrs. Forrester—idealizes her, making her seem like a rose blossoming in the snow of a winter's day. Describing Niel's feelings about her, Cather writes, "How strange that she should be here at all, a woman like her among common people! Not even in Denver had he ever seen another woman so elegant.... Compared with her, other women were heavy and dull." Later, Cather has Niel reflecting on Mrs. Forrester's egalitarian nature, a quality he seems to share in his dealings with others. Cather writes, "One could talk to her about the most trivial things, and go away with a high sense of elation. The secret of it, he supposed, was that she couldn't help being interested in people, even very commonplace people." By imagining that she is ideal, it gives Niel credence to his way of life. Mrs. Forrester provides a motherless boy, who had only a poor housekeeping spinster cousin for a female role model, an ideal of what women should be.

Yet, like Niel himself, Mrs. Forrester is not really an ideal, but a troubled, messy, human woman, which leads to tragedy for both of them. Niel has his illusions about her shattered life. First, he struggles when he learns that Mrs. Forrester has been having an affair with Frank Ellinger during the first years she is trapped in Sweet Water after the Captain's accident and during his bank financial crisis. The affair ends badly when Mrs. Forrester, by then taking care of her husband after his first stroke, learns that Frank married Constance Ogden. Mrs. Forrester also over-consumes alcohol, leading to awkward situations with Niel and the Captain, among others. As the Captain gets sicker following his second stroke and dies, her behavior becomes even more erratic. She develops some kind of intimate relationship with Ivy Peters, alienating all who try to help her, including Judge Pommeroy and Niel himself. Niel does not fully grasp how she can be so self-destructive initially, but he comes to realize it was the Captain who grounded her—the Captain was not, as Niel initially believed, "a drag upon his wife"— while she, to some degree, brought needed youth to the Captain.

In the end, the tragedies of Niel and Mrs. Forrester force them out of Sweet Water in one way or another. Niel does not want to be a lawyer like his uncle or, more accurately, the kind of lawyer men of his generation like Ivy Peters have turned out to be. The changes in Mrs. Forrester also give him no reason to stay. To be his own man and escape his tragic past, the one who witnessed "the sunset of the pioneer," Niel goes away to attend the Massachusetts Institute of Technology and become an architect. Although he gives up one year of school to help the Forresters and his uncle through their illnesses, there is nothing in the story to indicate that he does not complete his degree, move away permanently

from Sweet Water, and have a successful career elsewhere. Niel has moved forward, and no further life tragedies are mentioned by Cather.

After Captain Forrester's death, Niel witnesses Mrs. Forrester's continued downward spiral and less than ideal behavior. Her emotional and social decline is evidenced by her inappropriate dinner parties, disloyalty to his uncle, and relationship with Ivy. Niel suggests she leave during this period, saying, "Mrs. Forrester, why don't you go away? to California, to people of your own kind. You know this town is no place for you." Mrs. Forrester admits to wanting to leave Sweet Water, but her inability to sell the house (with the alleged help of Ivy) keeps her in town for an extended period of time. Niel believes she needs the right man to ground her and provide a haven away from the tragedies of her life so she can be an ideal woman again. By the end of *A Lost Lady*, Niel learns that Mrs. Forrester did move away after selling the house to Ivy for his new wife, and she married well again. Upon learning of her marriage to an odd but wealthy Englishman until her death, Niel tells Ed Elliott, "So we may feel sure that she was well cared for, to the very end. Thank God for that!" It is clear at novel's end that tragedies did not define the whole of their lives.

Source: A. Petruso, Critical Essay on *A Lost Lady*, in *Novels for Students 33*, Gale, Cengage Learning, 2010.

Chad Trevitte

In the following excerpt, Trevitte examines how Cather draws Niel and relates this depiction to issues of art and modernity.

Yet the value of art in an industrial age is a problem that informs Cather's fiction in a much more complex fashion than was acknowledged by either her early critics or her response to them. In *A Lost Lady* Niel Herbert's narration already internalizes the tension between art as a self-contained object and as a socially mediated form. Through Niel, Cather incorporates her own concern with art as a thematic dimension of the book, yet in such a way that his experience also registers the inherent contradictions that Huyssen and other critics have traced in the concept of autonomous art. Just as one reads the novel both through and against Niel's vantage point, then, it is important to read it both through and against the concept of art that Cather received from her precursors. To do so allows for a much greater understanding of how the novel addresses the problem of aesthetic value in modern culture.

As noted by David Stouck, the role of Niel Herbert originated in Cather's attempt to resolve a stylistic issue. Having planned initially to write *A Lost Lady* in Niel's first-person voice, Cather subsequently decided to adopt a double perspective using both Niel's point of view and that of a third–person narrator. Such an approach, she thought, would allow her to convey Marian Forrester's qualities through their impact on another character's sensibility. Rather than limiting her focus to Niel's subjective standpoint or providing a relatively objective depiction of Marian via third–person omniscient narration, Cather situates the reader between these two angles of vision. In this way she departs from the personalized lyricism of *My Ántonia* for the sort of modulated perspective that characterizes Flaubert's *Sentimental Education* and the "impressionistic" style of narration she admired in Henry James. Yet precisely because this method establishes a measure of distance between the reader and Niel, it has raised interpretive questions regarding his motives. However one–dimensional he may seem initially, Niel's fluctuating vision reveals his highly ambiguous relationship with Marian, one that manifests both his own inner conflicts and his anxious response to a rapidly changing world. Niel thus functions as more than a mere narrative device: as the novel progresses, his romanticized standpoint demands substantive judgment from the reader.

Broadly speaking, Niel Herbert's development may be traced through three overlapping dimensions—the psychosexual, the sociohistorical, and the aesthetic. Corresponding to these are the three major roles that Niel's lost lady plays (and fails to play) in his imagination: Marian as maternal figure, Marian as emblem of a mythic frontier aristocracy, and Marian as self–contained object of beauty. Psychologically, *A Lost Lady* provides a highly nuanced depiction of Niel's uneasy initiation into the world of adult sexuality; read through this lens, the significance of the novel is rooted primarily in the individual ego of its male protagonist. Yet insofar as Niel's experience is also situated in the context of social transformation in the West, the "reality principle" that confronts him also involves an expanding sphere of industrialization and commercialism. In this light, Niel's troubled vision thus allows the novel to articulate a melancholic allegory of historical change: the passing of a previous, heroic era of Western settlement in the face of

capitalistic "progress." Finally, as a figure of the artist manqué, alienated from a world that violates his fantasies, Niel's particular form of bovaryisme introduces the thematic problem of truth and illusion in aesthetic experience. Through this lens, the novel may be read as a meditation on the meaning and value of art in a modern age.

While the last dimension is what concerns us here, it cannot be considered in strict isolation from the other two. Rather, these three dimensions operate within a comprehensive, dialectical structure in the novel, whereby Niel's view of Marian Forrester as objet d'art entails a failed attempt to contain the psychological and socioeconomic contradictions that he cannot resolve. His sexual neuroses and social perception thus not only serve as interpretive focal points but also provide the context for a complex genealogy of artistic consciousness—a genealogy that ultimately reflects on the status of the novel itself as an autonomous cultural artifact...

Source: Chad Trevitte, "Cather's *A Lost Lady* and the Disenchantment of Art," in *Twentieth Century Literature*, Vol. 53, No. 2, June 22, 2007, pp. 182–211.

Morris Dickstein

In the following excerpt, Dickstein looks at what makes A Lost Lady *a powerful novel.*

The casual, lifelike pattern of memory in *My Ántonia* foreshadows something decisive in *A Lost Lady*: a sense of character as mystery, a Wordsworthian way of seeing by glimpses that respects the "burden" of the mystery. Cather deliberately avoided telling us too much about a character; she believed in withholding character, as she once wrote in a letter to her friend Dorothy Canfield Fisher. The story of Mrs. Forrester's life preceding her marriage comes so late in the novel, and is so condensed and improbable, that it's almost a satire on our need to know, a deliberate piece of "fiction." The original Mrs. Garber was not one of Cather's contemporaries, like Ántonia, but a kind of Lady Bountiful to the young people of the town. We see Marian Forrester from young Niel Herbert's angle of vision: he is at first adoring, then bitterly disenchanted and at last grudgingly reconciled to her complex nature. Her impact on him is the heart of the novel, the key to its effect on the reader. Niel is not actually the narrator, since Cather needed to put things in the story that he could not have witnessed (and could not abide), but he enables Cather to evoke all that these people meant to her as a girl in Red Cloud, the town here called Sweet Water.

> CATHER TURNS THE RUGGED PIONEERS INTO
> MYTH, THE ANTITHESIS OF ALL SHE FINDS
> DETESTABLE IN THE NEW, MORE UTILITARIAN WEST.
> BUT HER TONE SIGNALS THAT SHE'S IDEALIZING
> THEM, REIFYING A LOST WORLD AS SHE REMEMBERS
> IT FROM CHILDHOOD."

For many years critics saw Niel simply as a window on the Forresters' world. Cather's first biographers, E. K. Brown and Leon Edel, wrote that Niel was "simply Jim Burden from *My Ántonia* renamed"; a later critic, Philip Gerber, carelessly described him as "the narrator of the novel" adding that "Niel exists chiefly to represent the author and her attitude." Cather herself once said in an interview that "he isn't a character at all; he is just a peephole into that world . . . He is only a point of view." But some recent critics have argued that because of his horror at Mrs. Forrester's adultery and his disgust at her refusal to "immolate herself" after her husband's death ("she preferred life on any terms"), Niel's point of view cannot be fully trusted. The question can be posed simply: Is Mrs. Forrester truly "a lost lady'" after her husband's death, "like a ship without ballast, driven hither and thither by every wind" as Niel thinks; or is she simply lost to him, because, like an unhappy adolescent robbed of his innocence, he cannot bear the sexual form of the vitality that first enthralled him. "Lilies that fester smell far worse than weeds" he mutters to himself, echoing the disillusionment of Shakespeare's Sonnet 94, with its lament that "sweetest things turn sourest by their deeds."

This issue can never be resolved, for what makes *A Lost Lady* such a rich and resonant work, as enchanting as its heroine, as ambiguous as its rifle, is that Cather has it both ways. She uses Niel as a delicate sensor to register the impact of Captain Forrester as a survivor of the frontier generation and of his wife as a beacon of graciousness, elegance, and beauty for Sweet Water. "*A Lost Lady* was a woman I loved very much in my childhood" Cather said in the same interview. "I wasn't interested in her

character when I was little, but in her lovely hair and her laugh which made me happy clear down to my toes." *A Lost Lady* conveys the magic of an impressionable child's point of view but also its inevitable limitations. The Captain himself pointedly rebukes Niel's implicit judgment of his wife; he makes it clear that he's aware of her affair and understands the complexity of her character, including her sexual needs, as Niel cannot; he shows Niel how much he values her.

Niel grows up in the course of the book, fired up at first by what the Forresters represent ("a different world from any he had ever known"), but then also educated by the troubles they undergo, the painful reverses that complicate their lives in a way he can only fathom as an adult (and barely even then). Cather drew inspiration from Flaubert's *Sentimental Education,* in which a young man is drawn by the beauty and charm of an older woman, only to find how disappointing, how commonplace, life can be, and to be left in the end with little more than a few early memories. But Cather added a generous dose of *Hamlet,* where another young man recoils from a woman's middle-aged sexuality, her insistence on surviving her husband and living life "on any terms." The novel's epigraph is from the disconnected ramblings of Ophelia, truly a lost lady. But the title phrase appears in the novel only as "his long-lost lady" with her "long-lost lady laugh," suggesting that despite the reverses in her life, she is lost only to Niel, who cannot keep from condemning her. But in the end, we hear, "he came to be very glad that he had known her, and that she had had a hand in breaking him in to life." After the idealizations that lit up his childhood, after his own failure to find the happiness her bright laughter had promised, he learns something about the mixed, ambiguous nature of the adult world.

If Niel's education were the whole story, the novel would be a sketchy example of the bildungsroman, the novel of personal culture or development. If Marian's adultery were the whole story, *A Lost Lady* would be a minor offshoot of works like Flaubert's *Madame Bovary,* Tolstoy's *Anna Karenina,* or Kate Chopin's *Awakening,* which Willa Cather reviewed caustically when it appeared in 1899. Like *My Ántonia, A Lost Lady* is a memory novel: by focusing on what the Forresters once meant to Niel, it conveys Cather's darkening sense of how the West has changed since she grew up. The settlers of *O*

Pioneers! and *My Ántonia* were homesteaders taming the land and making it fruitful by sweat and labor. But Daniel Forrester represents another kind of pioneer, the adventurer and entrepreneur; he and his powerful friends belong to the railroad aristocracy of "the road-making West." They "dreamed the railroads across the mountains" says the Captain, "just as I dreamed my place on the Sweet Water." They were the "men who had put plains and mountains under the iron harness."

There is a curiously abstract quality to Cather's reminiscence of the pioneer days in *A Lost Lady*. It feels disembodied, like a fairy tale of long ago. Where *My Ántonia*, written only five years earlier, gives us a vivid sense of the hardships of frontier life, in this novel the pioneers are remote figures, reduced to brilliant metaphor: they "dreamed the railroads across the mountains," they "put the plains and mountains under the iron harness." Those who built the railroads were not simply bold and hardy dreamers, as they appear here, but Gilded Age buccaneers, venturesome capitalists supported by cheap labor and vast federal subsidies. Here the Forresters and their friends take on the fabric of legend. "It had already gone, that age; nothing could ever bring it back. The taste and smell and song of it, the visions those men had seen in the air and followed,—these he had caught in a kind of afterglow in their own faces,—and this would always be his." These people and their stories added color, dash, and dreamy aspiration to Cather's childhood.

A Lost Lady weaves an elegiac myth about "the end of an era, the sunset of the pioneer" for Cather saw such people not simply as entrepreneurs and fortune-builders, not even as discoverers and nation-builders but as a local aristocracy of manners and moral responsibility. Now they are being replaced by new men whose conscience is not so fine, who cheat Indians out of their land and small bank depositors out of their savings. When a bank in which he has a major interest fails, Forrester impoverishes himself (and later his widow) by making good on every dime. "That was what a man of honour was bound to do" explains Niel's uncle, another man of the old school. Captain Forrester's "clumsy dignity covered a deep nature, and a conscience that had never been juggled with."

Despite the seeming casualness of the narrative, which at first appears to be no more than random memories punctuated by gaps and elisions, *A Lost Lady* is the most tightly organized novel Cather wrote, with hardly a spare word. The themes I've touched on here, the education of a young man and the dignity of the old order, are foreshadowed from the opening pages. The first two chapters form a prologue, set seven years before the main action begins, that shows us the Forresters' world at its zenith, when both their marriage and the town are still thriving. The story begins like a fairy tale, on "a summer morning long ago, when Mrs. Forrester was still a young woman, and Sweet Water was a town of which great things were expected." The Forresters' house "would probably have been ugly enough" but is made special by its lovely setting and the way of life of those who inhabit it. The prologue evokes the heyday of the pioneers, when Sweet Water was an important division point on the Burlington Railroad, and the house, set on a beautiful Indian site, was the place the railroad barons stopped to pay their respects and be graciously received. But now it has become a vestige of that earlier time. Mrs. Forrester extends her hospitality even to the boys of the town, including Niel (age 12), who fish and hike and play on the land.

The snake in this garden is an older boy named Ivy Peters—nicknamed Poison Ivy—who specializes in poisoning dogs and torturing birds. When Niel climbs a tree to put a blinded bird out of its misery, he breaks his arm and gets a luxurious taste of Mrs. Forrester's loving care. "He was in pain, but he felt weak and contented . . . The little boy was thinking that he would probably never be in so nice a place again." Ivy Peters, Niel's opposite number, is already the young upstart, the new man who feels that "I'm just as good as she is." For now he is expelled from the house by her "imperious courtesy." But eventually he will take revenge by draining the Forresters' lovely marsh, which stands not only for the children's Eden but also for the kind of impractical, unproductive beauty cultivated by the old order. As a young lawyer who amasses wealth by cutting corners, Peters will condescend to the Captain and, after the old man's death, have an affair with his wife and eventually take over her property.

All this is anticipated in the opening chapters. The Forresters, with their Sherwood Forest style of generosity, will give way to the Ivy Peters of the world, "this generation of shrewd young men, trained to petty economies by hard times" who exploit the fruits of the world the pioneers made. Ivy Peters is the great flaw in Cather's parable. Not only pragmatic but dishonest, disrespectful, gratuitously sadistic, he helps us notice how Cather idealizes the old order and demonizes the forces that shaped the modern world. Stepping outside the frame of her story, she cannot resist blazing out at all he represents when he drains the Forresters' marsh and puts their land to prosaic use:

> The Old West had been settled by dreamers, great-hearted adventurers who were unpractical to the point of magnificence; a courteous brotherhood, strong in attack but weak in defence, who could conquer but could not hold. Now all the vast territory they had won was to be at the mercy of men like Ivy Peters, who had never dared anything, never risked anything. They would drink up the mirage, dispel the morning freshness, root out the great brooding spirit of freedom, the generous, easy life of the great land-holders. The space, the colour, the princely carelessness of the pioneer they would destroy and cut up into profitable bits, as the match factory splinters the primeval forest.

In her next novel, *The Professor's House*, Cather would stay clear of the cardboard villainy of Ivy Peters and create a much more nuanced fable of decline, with the professor's student, Tom Outland, as the pure adventurer, who luckily dies in the war before he can fall into compromise, and the professor's son-in-law, the charming and ingratiating Louie Marsellus, as the enterprising Jew who knows how to market Outland's discoveries. Cather will build the story not around a single house, as in *A Lost Lady*, but around a series of houses, from the ancient cliff-dwellings of New Mexican Indians to soulless homes with all modern conveniences.

Yet even in *A Lost Lady* Cather qualified her moral when she describes the pioneers as "dreamers" and Ivy Peters as the man who "would drink up the mirage, dispel the morning freshness"; or when she tells us that the Captain, having no children of his own, is a man who "could afford to humour his own fancies." Dreams, mirages, fancies, and the morning dew are things that are inevitably dispelled, that evaporate of their own nature. Cather turns the rugged pioneers into myth, the antithesis of all she finds detestable in the new, more utilitarian West. But her tone signals that she's idealizing them, reifying a lost world as she remembers it from childhood. In Niel's painful disillusionment with

Mrs. Forrester, Cather takes the full measure of this disabling idealization ...

Source: Morris Dickstein, "The Magic of Contradictions: Willa Cather's *Lost Lady*," in *New Criterion*, Vol. 17, No. 6, February 1999, p. 20.

J. W. Krutch

In the following essay, Krutch offers a positive review of A Lost Lady.

Since American criticism is as tolerant as it is, only her own artistic conscience can explain the fact that Miss Cather has slowly and surely perfected herself in her craft. Easily pleased in general we are; we praise one writer for his interesting story, another for his satirical keenness, another for his philosophy, and still another for his realistic detail, without crying out much in protest when the defects are as glaring as the virtues. Obviously, Miss Cather has had her own counsel of perfection which has made her not so easily pleased. She has not been content to be praised justly for the vividness and freshness of the sketches which made up *My Ántonia* nor for the adroitness in the handling of plot which she exhibited in the stories composing *Youth and the Bright Medusa*. Instead, she has constantly struggled to achieve that synthesis of qualities which alone can make a novel really fine, and in *A Lost Lady,* short and slight as it is, she has achieved it. There would be no excuse for calling it a great novel—it is not that; but there would be equally little excuse for not recognizing the fact that it is that very rare thing in contemporary literature, a nearly perfect one. Miss Cather has come to the point where she can do the two or three things at once which a novelist must do. She can evoke by a few characteristic touches and by subtle suggestion a scene and a society without producing merely a "document"; she can present a character without writing a psychological treatise; she can point a moral without writing a sermon; and hence she is a novelist.

Memory is in a very true sense the mother of her muse, for in her youth she gathered a remarkable wealth of impressions, but instead of "pouring forth" this material in the approved contemporary fashion she has brooded upon it and formed it until her picture has both composition and meaning. Thus in the new book she has evoked again an epoch of the West, the epoch which she loves, when the land had been settled by "great-hearted adventurers who were unpractical to the point of magnificence" but had not yet passed from the hands of the pioneers into the hands of the swarm of exploiters and business men who came to "develop the country" with railroad, with factory, and with the hosts of thrifty hard-headed farmers who destroyed the "princely carelessness of the pioneer" and made the land populous and hence competitive and hence mean. But at the same time she has given us an original character completely integrated with the scene and a subtle problem in morals or aesthetics.

Miss Cather has been praised, and adequately praised, so many times during the last few years for her pictures of a civilization just past that in the case of the present book a fresher task will offer itself if the critic will turn from that aspect of her work and ask himself what she means by her story and what it reveals of the things to which her soul is most loyal. This lady, lost not upon the plains but lost to "ladyhood," who seemed in her big and gracious house an embodiment of the delicacies and refinements of a civilization which, save in her, had not yet reached the plains, but who was spotted within by a secret and unworthy passion—what does she mean to Miss Cather and what is the nature of her guilt? To the romantic boy through whose eyes we see her she is simply the problem as old as the time when women first were fair and false, but to Miss Cather, I think, the guilt is not moral but aesthetic, and aesthetic in a very particular way. The lady, though she did not write nor paint nor act nor sing, was essentially an artist. She was consciously a lady, and she had devoted her vitality to the creation of a person who was more than a person, who was The Lady as a type and as a work of art, so that when she failed she failed as an artist. In a completer civilization she might have found lovers worthy of her who would not have spoiled her creation but she failed because she was not artist enough to refuse to do at all what she could not do worthily. Her life on the frontier with her aging husband would have been dreary enough, and any mere private person might have been forgiven for seeking diversion wherever he could find it, but the artist must sacrifice himself for his work. The lost lady was guilty and lost because she put her own happiness before her art and betrayed her ideal to snatch at the joy of life.

When *One of Ours* was published many critics went into sackcloth and wept for a talented writer who seemed to have given her allegiance to a vulgar ideal, but *A Lost Lady* will serve to set

fears at rest. It makes clearer than any of her previous books has done the essentially aristocratic character of Miss Cather's sympathies and explains her choice of subjects. The artists and the pioneers whom she has always written about are united in their spirit of high adventure, in the romantic impracticability of their aims, and in their success in the creation of comely and rounded types—hence her interest. It is obvious that Miss Cather looks not only at her own craft but at life as well from the standpoint of one to whom fitness is all.

Source: J. W. Krutch, "The Lady as Artist," in *Nation*, Vol. 117, No. 3047, November 28, 1923, p. 610.

SOURCES

Battersby, Eileen, Review of *A Lost Lady*, in the *Irish Times*, March 10, 2001, p. 73.

Cather, Willa, *A Lost Lady*, 1923, Vintage Books ed., 1972.

Danbom, David B., *Born in the Country: A History of Rural America*, Johns Hopkins University Press, 1995.

Jefferson, Margo, "Not in Nebraska Anymore," in the *New York Times*, August 3, 2003, p. 23.

"Listening to Our Heartbeats," in the *Times Literary Supplement*, June 2, 1961, p. 344.

Parry, David. "Willa Cather and the Burlington Railroad." *The Willa Cather Archive.*http://www.unl.edu/Cather/scholarship/criticalstudies/burlington (accessed October 9, 2009).

Review of *A Lost Lady* in the *Times Literary Supplement*, September 4, 1924, p. 538.

FURTHER READING

Acocella, Joan, *Willa Cather and the Politics of Criticism*, University of Nebraska Press, 2000.
     This critical work seeks to address issues brought up in biography and criticism about the author and her works, including her alleged lesbianism.

Bohlke, L. Brent, ed., *Willa Cather in Person: Interviews, Speeches, and Letters*, University of Nebraska Press, 1986.
     This book gives voice to Cather through a collection of various published interviews, speeches she gave, and a selection of letters. Among the speeches is her radio address accepting the Pulitzer Prize.

O'Brien, Sharon, *Willa Cather: The Emerging Voice*, Oxford University Press, 1987.
     This interpretive biography focuses primarily on Cather's life from 1873 to 1913, when she

had her first literary success. O'Brien especially focuses on how Cather undermined the feminine ideal of the time by her lifestyle choices.

Rowse, A. L., "Tracing Willa Cather's Nebraska," in the *New York Times*, April 21, 1985.
    This travel essay focuses on the community of Red Cloud, Nebraska, Cather's home. The article offers both travel and biographical information about Cather.

Webb, Walter Prescott, *The Great Plains*, University of Nebraska Press, 1931.
    This classic work of American history describes the history of the central part of the United States, the people who settled there, and issues like railroads, water, and fencing.

Murder on the Orient Express

AGATHA CHRISTIE
1934

Although written somewhat early in a career that spanned almost six decades and over seventy novels, *Murder on the Orient Express* (1934; originally published in the United States as *Murder in the Calais Coach*) is still considered one of mystery writer Agatha Christie's greatest works. The book features her most enduring literary creation, the Belgian detective Hercule Poirot, and one of the trademark "twist" endings for which Christie was famous.

Murder on the Orient Express finds Poirot on his way back to England from Syria by way of the luxury rail transport known as the Orient Express. Along the way, a murder occurs in the very same passenger car in which Poirot is traveling, and the director of the rail line—a friend of the detective—asks Poirot to help solve the case. The more he investigates, the less the case seems to make sense, with the wide array of passengers—all from different backgrounds and seemingly strangers to each other—each providing a substantiated alibi for the night of the crime.

Christie drew inspiration for the novel from several sources, most notably her own experiences aboard the Orient Express while traveling between England and her archeologist husband Max Mallowan's dig sites in the Middle East. Christie also modeled the back story that connects the characters on the real-life kidnapping and murder of the son of famed aviator Charles

Agatha Christie (AP Images)

Lindbergh, which occurred just two years before the novel was published.

Although the novel is best remembered for its cleverly constructed mystery, it also contains themes seldom touched upon in previous works of detective fiction. One of the most surprising elements of the book is Poirot's brilliantly indirect participation in covering up the truth about the murder, since Poirot himself seems to agree that the killing is ultimately an act of moral justice.

AUTHOR BIOGRAPHY

Christie was born Agatha Mary Clarissa Miller on September 15, 1890, in Torquay, England, the third child of Clarissa Miller, an English woman, and Frederick Miller, an American living in England. Her childhood was somewhat unusual, in that she did not attend formal school. However, the family home contained an abundance of books, and her pursuit of knowledge was always encouraged.

Her father died when she was eleven, but her early years were shaped by another male influence:

author Eden Philpotts, who lived nearby and fostered in the girl a love of literature. In 1914, she married Archibald Christie, a lieutenant in the Royal Flying Corps. In the midst of World War I, Christie worked as a nurse and even passed the required test to become a pharmacist. Her only child, daughter Rosalind, was born in 1919.

Christie did not consider a career as a writer until she was challenged by her older sister to write a mystery in which the ending could not be guessed. That first novel, *The Mysterious Affair at Styles* (1920), was inspired by the knowledge of poisons Christie gained as a pharmacist, and was received well by both critics and readers. The novel, which earned the author a meager fee of twenty-five British pounds, also marked the introduction of a Belgian detective named Hercule Poirot. From that point on, Christie wrote and published at a pace of nearly a book a year, and continued to do so for over fifty years.

In 1926, Christie's mother passed away, and then Christie discovered that Archibald was having an affair; the couple divorced soon after. Despite these personal tragedies, her writing soared in both popularity and creativity. *The Murder of Roger Ackroyd*, one of her most audacious and controversial mysteries, was published in 1926. In 1930, Christie traveled to Baghdad, where she met archeologist Max Mallowan. The two quickly fell in love and married, and remained together until her death in 1976.

Christie made a habit of visiting her husband's archeological dig sites annually, and traveled back from the Middle East by way of the Orient Express on more than one occasion. On one particular trip in 1931, the Orient Express train on which she was a passenger became delayed; this delay planted the seeds of what would ultimately become *Murder on the Orient Express* (1934).

Although she was widely regarded by literary scholars as a writer of low caliber, she received several awards for her body of work during her lifetime. In 1954, Christie was honored as the recipient of the first Grandmaster Award from the Mystery Writers of America. In 1956, she received the rank Commander of the Order of the British Empire, the third-highest rank in the British order of chivalry; in 1971, she received the second-highest rank, Dame Commander—the equivalent of knighthood.

During the 1970s, Christie's health began to fail. However, she lived to see a filmed adaptation of *Murder on the Orient Express*, directed by Sidney Lumet in 1974, which earned six Oscar nominations and a win for Ingrid Bergman as Best Supporting Actress. In her final years, unable to continue writing, she produced from a bank vault two novels completed during World War II. One of these, *Curtain* (1975), relates Poirot's final case and even depicts his death. Christie herself died of natural causes just months after the book's publication, at the age of eighty-five.

PLOT SUMMARY

Part 1: The Facts

At the opening of *Murder on the Orient Express*, famous Belgian detective Hercule Poirot is preparing to depart from Syria on a winter's morning aboard the Taurus Express train line. He is on his way back to London, where he lives, with a short vacation planned in Istanbul, Turkey. He is escorted to the train station by Lieutenant Dubosc of the local police, with whom he has been working. Dubosc mentions that the number of travelers is generally light this time of year; Dubosc also expresses hope that Poirot's train will not be snowed in, as sometimes happens during the winter months.

Once aboard the train, Poirot discovers that there are only two other passengers: Mary Debenham, a young English woman traveling from Baghdad, and Colonel Arbuthnot, an English military man traveling from India. Poirot learns from their conversations with each other that she is a governess, and that both are traveling on to London. Poirot also overhears a hushed conversation in which the pair, who act as if they have just met for the first time on the train, seem to have a relationship that extends beyond their short time together on the Taurus Express.

The next day, when the train is delayed due to a fire under the dining car, Mary becomes very anxious that she might miss her connection with the Orient Express in Istanbul (or Stamboul, as it is called in the novel). The train is repaired in time, although Poirot makes a mental note of Mary's behavior. Arriving in Istanbul, Poirot learns he has been called back to London as soon as possible to assist with a case; unable to enjoy a few days of vacation, he books a compartment on the Orient Express leaving that night.

MEDIA ADAPTATIONS

- An unabridged audio recording of the novel was released in compact disc format in 2005 by BBC Audiobooks America. The book is read by David Suchet, who has starred as Hercule Poirot in a series of BBC adaptations of Christie's works.

- A full-cast dramatization of the book was released in audio CD format by BBC Audiobooks America in 2007. David Suchet serves as the narrator for this recording.

- A full-cast radio dramatization of the novel was released in audio CD format in 2004 by BBC Audiobooks Ltd. John Moffatt stars as Poirot in this dramatization.

- A film adaptation of the novel was directed by Sidney Lumet in 1974 and stars Albert Finney, Lauren Bacall, Ingrid Bergman, and Sean Connery, among many others. This version is currently available in DVD format from Paramount.

- A made-for-television adaptation was created in 2001 by director Carl Schenkel. The film stars Alfred Molina as Poirot, and the tale takes place in a modern, updated setting. A DVD version of the film was released by Allumination in 2005.

- A computer game adaptation of the book was released by The Adventure Company for Windows PC in 2006. The game retains most of the novel's plot, although the ending is altered and the player's character is an entirely new addition not found in the book. The game features the voice of David Suchet as Poirot.

- The novel was adapted as a French comic by Francois Rivière and illustrated by Solidor in 2003; an English-language version was published by HarperCollins in 2007.

Poirot is surprised to learn the Orient Express is completely booked in first class and second class—almost unimaginable during the slow season. However, he runs into his old friend

M. Douc, the director of the train line, who is also traveling on the Orient Express that night. Douc manages to secure for Poirot the only available compartment, a shared second-class space reserved to a man who fails to show up by departure time. Poirot's companion in the compartment is Hector MacQueen, an American who works for another American aboard the train named Ratchett—a man, Poirot observes, who seems to possess a certain wild savagery beneath his proper exterior.

The next morning, Poirot has breakfast with M. Bouc in the now-packed dining car. Poirot notes the new passengers, who include an American businessman, a boisterous Italian, an English servant, a loud American woman, a German or Scandinavian woman, an ugly and aging Russian princess, a Hungarian ambassador and his young wife, and a prim woman with a face like a sheep. Bouc observes of the passengers:

> All around us are people, of all classes, of all nationalities, of all ages. For three days these people, these strangers to one another, are brought together. They sleep and eat under one roof, they cannot get away from each other. At the end of three days they part, they go their several ways, never perhaps to see each other again.

After Bouc retires to his compartment, the American named Ratchett approaches Poirot and takes a seat. Knowing Poirot's reputation, Ratchett attempts to hire the detective as his protector during the train trip. Ratchett claims that he is a very wealthy man whose life has been threatened, and although he keeps a gun with him, he feels the need to hire extra protection, just to be safe. Because Poirot does not trust the man, he rejects the offer.

That evening, another coach is added to the train, and M. Bouc relocates to that coach, giving his first-class compartment to Poirot. The compartment is adjacent to Ratchett's, and in the middle of the night, Poirot is awakened by a loud groan next door, followed by a bell calling the conductor—Pierre Michel—for assistance. The conductor arrives at Ratchett's door and knocks, but eventually a voice from inside the room says, in perfect French, that it was a mistake.

Poirot finds that he cannot go back to sleep, and instead listens to the sounds of Ratchett using his washbasin next door. Another bell calls the conductor to the room just beyond Ratchett's, where the loud American woman is staying. Afterward, Pierre Michel brings Poirot some water, and explains that the woman insists a man was in her compartment, even though the door had been locked. The conductor also informs Poirot that the train has been stopped due to a snowdrift on the tracks, which might take days to clear. After he leaves, Poirot hears a heavy thud against his own compartment door; he opens his door and sees someone in a scarlet kimono hurrying away down the hall.

When Poirot rises the next morning, he finds the dining car filled with passengers upset about the train's continued delay. The only passenger who appears calm is Mary Debenham, whom Poirot remembers as being anxious about their previous delay before Istanbul. As breakfast winds down, Poirot is summoned by M. Bouc, who informs the detective that the American man named Ratchett was found murdered in his compartment that morning, stabbed several times. A doctor aboard the train, Dr. Constantine, estimates the time of death to be around 1:00 AM the previous night. M. Bouc asks Poirot to take charge of the investigation. Poirot agrees, and immediately narrows down the list of suspects to the passengers staying in the Orient Express coach—the one in which he himself resides.

Poirot is given each passenger's passport and ticket, and begins his investigation by speaking to Ratchett's employee, Hector MacQueen. He learns that MacQueen was Ratchett's secretary for the past year, and was tasked with helping the man get around in countries where he did not speak the language, and knows of threatening letters Ratchett received prior to his murder. MacQueen also suspects that Ratchett is not the man's real name, and that he left America to escape some sort of scandal.

Poirot then views Ratchett's body, still in his compartment. The window to the compartment is open, but the undisturbed snow outside suggests that no one could have escaped that way. The body itself, upon close examination, reveals twelve stab wounds of widely varying depth and force; the wounds even appear to be dealt by both a right-handed and a left-handed assailant. In addition, the relative lack of blood seems to indicate that the victim was dead before being stabbed. Poirot discovers other evidence left in the compartment: an empty glass containing the residue of some drug; a used match; a woman's handkerchief embroidered with the letter "H"; a pipe cleaner; a broken watch in the victim's pocket that stopped at a quarter past one; and a charred piece of paper containing the name "Daisy Armstrong."

From this last piece of evidence, Poirot determines that Ratchett was actually a man named Cassetti who was involved in the murder of a young girl in the United States. The girl, Daisy Armstrong, was the daughter of a Colonel Armstrong and his wife, both hailing from prominent and wealthy families. The girl was kidnapped by a gang led by Cassetti. After the parents had paid two hundred thousand dollars in ransom money, the little girl was found murdered. Her mother, pregnant with another baby, lost the child and died from complications related to the labor. Colonel Armstrong, having lost his entire family, killed himself. Cassetti was later arrested and tried for the murder, but, as Poirot states, he "was acquitted on some technical inaccuracy." He then left America, changed his name, and lived off his ransom earnings while traveling across Europe. Poirot suspects that Cassetti was murdered by someone connected to the Daisy Armstrong case—perhaps a former member of his own gang, or a member of the Armstrong family.

Part 2: The Evidence

Poirot establishes a Court of Inquiry with the intention of gathering evidence from each of the suspected passengers. He begins by questioning the conductor of the coach, Pierre Michel, who was in the best position to witness the comings and goings of each passenger at the time of the murder. The conductor cannot recall anything out of the ordinary, although he confirms the presence of an unidentified woman in a scarlet kimono at some point late in the night.

After that, Poirot once again interviews MacQueen. MacQueen confirms that he talked with Colonel Arbuthnot until two in the morning on the night of the murder. MacQueen also confirms that he does not smoke a pipe—which suggests the pipe cleaner found in the victim's room was not his. Poirot then questions Edward Masterman, Ratchett's valet. Masterman claims that before Ratchett was killed, he was upset about a letter he had received. He further states that he prepared a drug-laced drink for Ratchett to help him sleep, as he always did for his employer during train trips. This explains the empty glass containing drug residue in the victim's room. Masterman also states that he does not smoke a pipe.

Next to be interviewed is the loud American woman, Mrs. Hubbard. She immediately informs Poirot that the murderer was in her compartment the previous night. The compartment, adjacent to Ratchett's, is accessible from Ratchett's compartment through a door that can be locked on either side. Mrs. Hubbard describes how she had asked the Swedish woman whether the door was locked earlier that evening, and the woman replied that it was; Mrs. Hubbard could not see the lock from where she was, due to her spongebag hanging from the handle and obscuring her view. As evidence that someone was in her compartment, Mrs. Hubbard presents a button from a Wagons Lit conductor's uniform. Before she leaves, Mrs. Hubbard denies owning a scarlet kimono, and claims that the handkerchief found in Ratchett's room—which contains an embroidered "H"—does not belong to her.

Poirot then questions the Swedish woman, Greta Ohlsson. She confirms Mrs. Hubbard's version of the previous evening's events, and states that neither she nor her compartment mate, Mary Debenham, left their room after around eleven that evening. She also confirms that neither of them wear a scarlet kimono.

Poirot takes a moment to ask Pierre Michel about the button found in Mrs. Hubbard's room. Pierre shows that he has not lost a button, and cannot explain where the button came from. Next Poirot speaks with Princess Dragomiroff, who admits that she was friends with members of Daisy Armstrong's family, but offers no useful information about the previous night. Poirot then summons Count and Countess Andrenyi of Hungary, although only the Count appears. He claims that neither he nor his wife saw anything the previous evening, and is reluctant to allow Poirot to speak to his wife. Finally, however, he relents, and the Countess confirms that she knows nothing about the murder. She also states that her dressing gown is not a scarlet kimono.

Poirot next interviews Colonel Arbuthnot. The Colonel admits to smoking a pipe, but offers no other useful information related to the murder. Poirot then questions another American passenger, Cyrus Hardman. Hardman, who initially claims to be a salesman, rather quickly admits to being a detective hired by Ratchett. Ratchett, according to Hardman, was concerned for his safety after receiving threatening letters, and even offered a description of the person he believed was trying to harm him: a small, dark man with a feminine voice. Despite remaining on the alert throughout the evening, however, Hardman admits to seeing nothing of the murderer. After he leaves, Poirot notes that the description of the suspected murderer does not match any of the passengers in the Orient Express car.

Poirot next questions the Italian passenger, Antonio Foscarelli, who shares a compartment with Ratchett's valet, Masterman. The detective discovers that Foscarelli actually lives in Chicago, where he sells cars. Although he offers no new information about the crime, he validates Masterman's account of the evening. M. Bouc strongly suspects that the crime was committed by Foscarelli simply because he is Italian, but Poirot insists, "It is a crime that shows traces of a cool, resourceful, deliberate brain—I think an Anglo-Saxon brain."

Poirot then interviews Mary Debenham, who claims she saw a woman wearing a scarlet kimono earlier that morning, but did not see the woman's face. After she leaves, Poirot tells M. Bouc and Dr. Constantine of the suspicious conversation he overheard between Mary and Colonel Arbuthnot while on the Taurus Express. However, each of them has an alibi for the time of the murder established by an independent person. Poirot continues his interviews with Hildegarde Schmidt, the maid of Princess Dragomiroff. Although she does not have a scarlet kimono dressing gown and denies being the owner of the handkerchief found in the victim's room, Mrs. Schmidt notes that she saw a conductor other than Pierre Michel walking down the hall late that night. She describes the conductor as a small, dark man with a moustache who speaks with a feminine voice. Poirot asks her to examine the other train conductors, but she insists that none of them are the man she saw.

As Poirot summarizes the statements they have heard, Mrs. Hubbard appears and presents the detective with the murder weapon, a dagger discovered in her spongebag. The detective guesses that the murderer slipped it into her bag after entering through the door that connects her compartment with Ratchett's. Poirot explains how the killer opened the locked door quite simply: the door was locked, but only from the other side (in Ratchett's compartment). When Greta Ohlsson checked the door for Mrs. Hubbard, she simply pulled on it and, when it did not budge, assumed it was properly locked from Mrs. Hubbard's side. The killer could easily have unlocked the door on Ratchett's side and entered Mrs. Hubbard's room.

The detective and his cohorts begin a search through the luggage of every passenger aboard the Orient Express car. In one of Hildegarde Schmidt's suitcases they find a conductor's uniform with a missing button. Poirot guesses the killer placed it in Mrs. Schmidt's luggage after she spotted him in the hallway the previous night. Poirot then returns to his own compartment to retrieve cigarettes. Inside his own suitcase, someone has left the elusive scarlet kimono.

Part 3: Hercule Poirot Sits Back and Thinks

As Poirot attempts to reconcile the facts of the case, he notes that the voice that came from Ratchett's room on the night he was killed—the voice telling the conductor that ringing the bell had been a mistake—most likely did not belong to Ratchett. MacQueen had previously mentioned that Ratchett was not knowledgeable about foreign languages, and the response was issued in perfect French.

Poirot also guesses that the fancy handkerchief found in the victim's room belongs to Countess Andrenyi. Although she stated that her first name is Elena and the handkerchief contains an embroidered "H," the beginning portion of her first name as listed on her passport is obscured by a spot of grease. Poirot suggests that her real first name is Helena, and that someone has deliberately tampered with the passport to hide this fact.

After piecing together the facts of the crime, Poirot is led to believe that the murder was planned to look like it was committed by an unknown, outside assailant. If the train had not been stopped by a snowdrift, the plan would have succeeded, and the true murderer would have escaped without suspicion. However, the stoppage of the train interfered with the perfectly constructed plot. This fact, along with the fact that the burnt note found in Ratchett's room was lit by a match that came from somewhere else, leads Poirot to a simple conclusion: someone on the train is intimately connected to the Daisy Armstrong murder, and that person killed Ratchett out of vengeance.

Poirot confronts the Countess about her handkerchief and her real identity: Helena Goldenberg, the aunt of Daisy Armstrong. She admits her true identity, but still denies that the handkerchief is hers. Poirot then correctly guesses that the handkerchief belongs to Princess Dragomiroff, whose first name is Natalia—which, when written in Russian letters, begins with "H." However, she claims to have no knowledge of how the handkerchief ended up in Ratchett's compartment.

As Poirot investigates further, he finds more connections between the Daisy Armstrong case and the passengers on the train: Mary Debenham admits to being governess of the Armstrong house at the time of the kidnapping; Antonio Foscarelli was the chauffeur for the Armstrong family; Greta Ohlsson was the nurse in charge of Daisy; and Edward Masterman was Colonel Armstrong's valet. From this abundance of suspects with motive for the murder, Poirot reaches a conclusion that he offers as the second of two theories explaining the crime.

In his first solution, Poirot proposes that the killer had boarded the train at a prior stop and killed Ratchett an hour earlier than everyone had assumed. This explanation results in many questions that can only be answered with fanciful explanations. However, the crime itself can be attributed well enough to the mysterious figure described by several witnesses.

In his second solution, Poirot suggests that every other passenger aboard the Orient Express was connected to the Armstrong case. In addition to the relationships already confirmed, he proposes that Colonel Arbuthnot was Colonel Armstrong's friend; Mrs. Hubbard is actually Daisy Armstrong's grandmother, accomplished actress Linda Arden; and even the conductor, Pierre Michel, was the father of the Armstrong's nursery-maid, who had killed herself after being accused of participating in the kidnapping.

The gathering of passengers, then, was not at all by chance—it was planned as an act of delayed justice against Ratchett. Twelve people from different backgrounds, all connected to the Armstrong household but pretending not to know each other, came together as a symbolic jury to finally deliver the punishment Ratchett deserved. All twelve participated, with each one stabbing Ratchett's drugged body once; this explained the different degrees of wounds he received. No one would know which blow killed him, since they all acted together. If the remnants of the note connecting Ratchett to the Daisy Armstrong case had not survived burning, or if the train had not been stopped by a

snowdrift, the plan would have gone completely undiscovered. Because of the complication presented by the train's delay, the group decides to plant false clues to deepen the mystery, such as the pipe cleaner, the handkerchief, and the woman in the scarlet kimono.

Poirot's second solution fits every known fact of the case perfectly, and Mrs. Hubbard admits to the entire plot. She asks Poirot to lay the blame solely on her. Poirot, convinced of Ratchett's guilt in the Daisy Armstrong case and sympathetic with the conspirators, leaves the decision in the hands of his friend, M. Bouc. Bouc decides that Poirot's first explanation is, after all, the correct one, and suggests that they stick with that story for the sake of true justice.

CHARACTERS

Count Andrenyi

Count Andrenyi is a Hungarian diplomat traveling with his young wife, Elena. Although he cooperates with Poirot's investigation into the murder of Ratchett, he attempts to keep his wife shielded from questioning as much as possible. Although the Count himself has no direct connection to the Daisy Armstrong murder, he participates in the plot against Ratchett on behalf of his wife, the Countess.

Countess Elena Andrenyi

Countess Elena Andrenyi is the wife of a Hungarian diplomat, a quiet young woman whom Poirot finds charming nonetheless. She claims to have taken a sleeping aid on the night of the murder, and therefore did not see or hear anything of importance. However, Poirot later discovers that her name has been altered on her passport, and that she is actually Helena Goldenberg, the aunt of Daisy Armstrong—the girl kidnapped and murdered by Ratchett years before. Although her motive is compelling, Poirot ultimately finds Countess Andrenyi to be the one passenger who is not guilty of participating in Ratchett's murder; instead, her husband acted on her behalf.

Colonel Arbuthnot

A stiffly formal Englishman, Arbuthnot is one of the first passengers Poirot encounters while traveling by train from Syria to Istanbul. He is tan and lean, having spent time in India, and although he pretends not to know Mary Debenham prior to boarding the train, Poirot sees indications that the two have some sort of close relationship. Arbuthnot is ultimately revealed to be a close friend of the Armstrong family, and although he prefers the idea of trial by jury to vigilante justice, he participates in the murder of Ratchett as a member of a symbolic jury of twelve, carrying out the sentence that the courts could not.

Linda Arden
See Mrs. Hubbard

M. Bouc
Bouc is the director of the Compagnie Internationale des Wagons Lits, the company that runs the Orient Express. A fellow Belgian, he has known and been friends with Poirot for many years. It is he who secures a sleeping compartment for Poirot on the fully booked Orient Express, and it is he who asks Poirot for his assistance in solving Ratchett's murder.

Cassetti
See Samuel Ratchett

Dr. Constantine
Constantine is a Greek doctor who happens to be traveling aboard the train when Ratchett is murdered, although he is not a passenger in the Orient Express car. M. Bouc asks for his assistance in determining the time of death, which he estimates to be between midnight and 2:00 in the morning. Dr. Constantine ends up becoming part of Poirot's investigative team, accompanying Poirot during passenger interviews and examinations of the crime scene. He also becomes a sounding-board for Poirot to discuss different scenarios regarding the murder, although he always appears to be several steps behind the detective when evaluating the clues.

Mary Debenham
A tall, thin English woman with a cool demeanor, Mary Debenham is one of the first passengers Poirot meets while traveling from Syria to Istanbul. Upon first inspection, Poirot considers her "the kind of young woman who could take care of herself with perfect ease wherever she went." Although she pretends to be newly acquainted with another passenger, Colonel Arbuthnot, Poirot overhears a conversation between the two

that suggests they have a much closer relationship. The detective eventually discovers that Debenham had served as companion governess in the Armstrong household at the time of Daisy's kidnapping. Later, Mrs. Hubbard acknowledges that Debenham was one of two people who came up with the detailed plan to exact revenge upon Ratchett.

Princess Natalia Dragomiroff
Described as an ugly old woman with a "yellow, toad-like face," Princess Dragomiroff is a member of Russian royalty who inspires respect and fear among the staff of the Orient Express, including M. Bouc. Early into the investigation of Ratchett's murder, she admits to being friends with the Armstrong family. However, Dr. Constantine insists that a woman of her frail state could not have administered most of the stab wounds to Ratchett's body. In the end, Poirot guesses that she dealt one of the more superficial blows to Ratchett's body.

Lieutenant Dubosc
Dubosc is a member of the French Army in Syria. He is entrusted with accompanying Hercule Poirot to the train station after the detective has finished helping the French Army with a case. At the beginning of *Murder on the Orient Express*, Dubosc secretly laments having to make conversation with Poirot as they await the detective's departing train.

Antonio Foscarelli
An Italian American car salesman, Foscarelli shares a compartment with Edward Masterman on the Orient Express car. Although he is one of M. Bouc's favorite suspects following the murder of Ratchett—simply because he is Italian, and Bouc considers stabbing to be an Italian type of crime—Masterman insists that Foscarelli did not leave their compartment at all during the night. Poirot eventually discovers that Foscarelli was the chauffeur for the Armstrong household at the time of Daisy Armstrong's kidnapping and murder.

Helena Goldenberg
See Countess Elena Andrenyi

Cyrus Hardman
Cyrus Hardman is an American aboard the Orient Express who initially claims to be a typewriter ribbon salesman. When questioned by Poirot, however, Hardman quickly admits to

being a detective hired by Ratchett to protect him. Poirot later discounts this as false, and guesses that Hardman was the boyfriend of the Armstrongs' nursery-maid, who killed herself after being accused of participating in Daisy Armstrong's kidnapping and murder.

Mrs. Hubbard

Mrs. Hubbard is a somewhat elderly American woman who continually tells the other passengers stories about her daughter. Her compartment is located immediately adjacent to Ratchett's, and she claims that a man was in her compartment on the night of Ratchett's murder. Mrs. Hubbard is ultimately revealed to be famed actress Linda Arden, grandmother to Daisy Armstrong. When Poirot exposes the passengers as conspirators in Ratchett's murders, Mrs. Hubbard explains the background of their plan in detail, and offers herself to be presented as the killer to the authorities so that the others may be spared.

Hector MacQueen

Hector MacQueen is Ratchett's secretary, entrusted primarily with handling his boss's foreign business and travel affairs. At the start of the journey aboard the Orient Express, MacQueen shares his second-class compartment with Poirot, because it is the only available space. MacQueen is later revealed to be a friend of Sonia Armstrong, and is exposed as part of the group that exacts revenge upon Ratchett for the murder of Daisy Armstrong. MacQueen also tells Poirot that his father was the district attorney in the original case against Ratchett.

Edward Masterman

A restrained Englishman, Edward Masterman is Samuel Ratchett's personal valet. During Hercule Poirot's investigation of Ratchett's murder, Masterman admits to being Colonel Armstrong's personal valet prior to Daisy Armstrong's murder at the hands of Ratchett. Masterman was able to get himself hired as Ratchett's valet as part of the plot to murder the man as punishment for his crimes.

Pierre Michel

Michel is the conductor of the Orient Express car at the time of Ratchett's murder. At first he appears concerned that he will be blamed for not seeing the murderer, because the passengers of the car are his responsibility. Later, however, Poirot reveals that Michel is one of those

involved in Ratchett's murder. Michel's daughter had been the nursery-maid of Daisy Armstrong; when Daisy was kidnapped, she was accused of participating in the crime. She was so overcome with shame over the accusations that she killed herself, even though she was later cleared of any wrongdoing in Daisy's kidnapping and murder.

Greta Ohlsson

A Swedish woman described as having the appearance and demeanor of a sheep, Greta Ohlsson is a matron in a school run by missionaries in Istanbul. According to the passenger statements, she was the last person to see Ratchett alive the night he was murdered. It is later revealed that Ohlsson was the nurse in charge of Daisy Armstrong before she was kidnapped and murdered.

Hercule Poirot

Poirot is a Belgian detective famed for his ability to solve seemingly impossible crimes. He is a small man with an egg-shaped head and an enormous moustache. At the beginning of *Murder on the Orient Express*, Poirot is on his way back to England from Syria after helping out the local authorities with a case. He is called to duty while riding home aboard the Orient Express passenger train, when an American named Ratchett is murdered on the same train.

Because Poirot is trapped on the snowbound train, he gladly accepts the challenge of the case, stating, "In truth, this problem intrigues me. I was reflecting, not half an hour ago, that many hours of boredom lay ahead whilst we are stuck here. And now—a problem lies ready to my hand." His investigative method involves carefully surveying the crime scene for clues, interviewing anyone who might possibly be involved in the crime, and, most importantly, simply thinking through every aspect of the crime in his head. He creates lists and maps to aid him in his mental reconstruction, making sure that even the smallest detail can be explained by any possible solution he considers.

However, despite his obsession with cracking the case, Poirot demonstrates that he is not simply a cold, rational man of the law. Because he feels certain that Ratchett was guilty of Daisy Armstrong's murder and yet escaped punishment on a technicality, Poirot conceives of an alternative explanation for Ratchett's murder that allows his killers—who appear to be otherwise decent people seeking justice—to remain free from suspicion.

Samuel Ratchett

Samuel Ratchett is a wealthy American traveling aboard the Orient Express with his secretary, Hector MacQueen, and his valet, Edward Masterman. Upon first seeing him, Poirot senses a savagery in the man's character and describes it to his friend M. Bouc: "The body—the cage—is everything of the most respectable—but through the bars, the wild animal looks out."

After Ratchett is murdered during the night in his own compartment, Hercule Poirot begins a search for the man's killer. Poirot discovers that Ratchett was actually a man named Cassetti, who had led a gang that kidnapped and murdered a young girl named Daisy Armstrong years before. Although he was arrested and tried for the murder, he was ultimately released on an unspecified technicality. His own murder is an act of vigilante justice carried out by a group of people connected to the Armstrong family.

Hildegarde Schmidt

Hildegarde Schmidt is Princess Dragomiroff's lady's-maid, responsible for taking care of her employer's basic daily needs such as preparing her clothing or attending to her medications. Schmidt claims to have seen an unknown person in a conductor's outfit walking along the Orient Express car on the night of Ratchett's murder. Poirot later guesses correctly that Schmidt was the cook in the Armstrong family household at the time Daisy Armstrong disappeared.

THEMES

Justice

The nature of justice is a pervasive theme in *Murder on the Orient Express*. Although Poirot is dedicated to finding Ratchett's killer as a matter of justice, his discovery of Ratchett's true identity raises difficult questions about the possible gap between moral justice and legal justice. According to Poirot, Ratchett had kidnapped and murdered a young girl, and not only was he allowed to go free on a legal technicality, he was also made rich by keeping the ransom he collected for the girl. For reasons not offered to the reader, Poirot is certain of Ratchett's guilt in the matter. When Poirot discovers that the passengers who

murdered Ratchett were all connected to the Armstrong family, and were all deeply affected by Daisy's murder, he has a difficult choice: side with legal justice, exposing the murderers and allowing them to be tried for their actions; or side with moral justice, supporting an alternative explanation for the murders that would leave the conspirators free from suspicion. In the end, Poirot allows M. Bouc and Dr. Constantine to choose which solution to present to the police, and they choose in favor of moral justice.

Colonel Arbuthnot is also shown to be conflicted about the idea of committing murder as an act of justice for Ratchett's many crimes, both known and unknown. Arbuthnot prides himself on being a man of law and procedure, and even tells Poirot that the trial by jury system is a sound one. Although the justice system fails Ratchett's victims, and Arbuthnot agrees to the murder plot, he insists upon having twelve accomplices to constitute a symbolic "jury" condemning Ratchett for his misdeeds.

Class and Cultural Differences

Differences between class and culture also play a key role in *Murder on the Orient Express*. Although the Orient Express is a car reserved for first-class and second-class passengers, the group that surrounds Poirot is a mixture of people from all walks of life, from servants to royalty. Hungarian, Swedish, German, British, American, Italian, French, Greek, and Belgian passengers all, as M. Bouc puts it, "sleep and eat under one roof, they cannot get away from each other." Poirot is also struck by the variety of passengers, and it is precisely this variety that helps him solve the case:

> I agreed with him, but when this particular point came into my mind, I tried to imagine whether such an assembly was ever likely to be collected under any other conditions. And the answer I made to myself was—only in America. In America there might be a household composed of just such varied nationalities—an Italian chauffeur, an English governess, a Swedish nurse, a German lady's-maid, and so on."

The class and cultural differences are emphasized by the various passengers as a way of deflecting suspicion regarding their plot. For example, the British Colonel Arbuthnot claims that he does not like Americans, while the Italian, Foscarelli, refers to the English as "a miserable race." Yet Arbuthnot provides an alibi for MacQueen, an American, and Foscarelli provides an alibi for the English valet, Masterman. Even the

TOPICS FOR FURTHER STUDY

- Like most of Christie's works, *Murder on the Orient Express* is a "whodunit," in which the central mystery revolves around pinpointing the person or persons who committed a crime. Create your own version of a whodunit story, providing a cast of suspects and clues that might help the reader solve the mystery. Remember, your whodunit does not have to deal with murder; it could be something as simple as catching a bicycle thief, or discovering who has been tracking mud onto the living room carpet.

- Christie's mysteries have often been likened to literary puzzles. How does Christie's presentation resemble that of puzzles such as logic games? How does it differ? Write a short essay comparing and contrasting the two, providing examples from specific Christie stories to support your points.

- At the end of *Murder on the Orient Express*, Poirot gives M. Bouc the option to allow the murderers to go free, implying that their act was one of moral justice that should not be prosecuted in the courts. Do you think there are certain circumstances in which breaking the law might make moral sense? For example, would speeding on the highway be excusable if someone were trying to transport an injured person to the hospital? Write a persuasive essay supporting either side of the issue, providing reasons and specific examples to support your argument.

- At the time the novel was written, the Orient Express was the finest mode of passenger transportation available to most people. Using your library, the Internet, or other available resources, find detailed images and descriptions of the passenger and dining cars aboard the Orient Express. Create a multimedia presentation that recreates the experience of an Orient Express passenger. Do you see the appeal of luxury rail travel? What do you think the advantages and disadvantages of such travel would be?

investigators allow cultural divisions to cloud their objectivity: M. Bouc insists throughout much of the investigation that the Italian man must have done it, because stabbing is the type of murder one would expect an Italian to commit.

STYLE

The Mystery Novel and the Serial Detective

Murder on the Orient Express is considered a mystery novel. Most mystery novels contain a central dilemma or crime, usually a murder, which must be solved by the main character, who is generally a detective or investigator in some form. Throughout the course of the story, clues are provided to the reader that might allow the perpetrator of the crime to be revealed, even though mystery writers often try to trick readers with false clues so that the ending of the story will remain a surprise.

The earliest story widely recognized as a modern mystery tale is "The Murders in the Rue Morgue" (1841) by Edgar Allan Poe. Poe also began the tradition of using a detective character who reappears in multiple stories, a tradition carried on by Arthur Conan Doyle with his Sherlock Holmes tales, and Christie herself with her stories of Hercule Poirot and Miss Jane Marple. In early serial detective stories, the main character is generally rather static—he or she does not undergo dramatic changes or developments, but serves simply as a keen processor of evidence and clues, which are shared with the reader. As the mystery genre grew in popularity throughout the twentieth century, newer generations of writers began to

Albert Finney as Hercule Poirot in the 1974 film adaptation of the novel (Paramount Pictures / Hulton Archive / Getty Images)

explore grittier and more realistic characters and crimes. Even in these more modern tales, however, the central mystery and recurring detective are enduring characteristics.

Omniscient Point of View

An omniscient point of view is one in which the author can reveal the thoughts of any and all characters to the reader at different points of the story. It is sometimes referred to as the "all-knowing" point of view, although authors such as Christie frequently restrict the amount of information provided to the reader for dramatic effect. For example, when Mary Debenham is first introduced to the reader in *Murder on the Orient Express*, the omniscient narrator details Mary's trip up until that point, provides a description of her feelings, and even includes her thoughts upon first seeing Poirot. However, the narrator reveals nothing of the murder plot in which she is involved and will soon carry out.

HISTORICAL CONTEXT

The Heyday of the Orient Express

The Orient Express train service existed in various forms as early as 1883, originally conceived as a luxury passenger train that transported travelers between Paris, France, and Istanbul, Turkey. The train offered something relatively new to rail passengers: the comfort of sleeping quarters and full-service restaurant cars. These amenities were popular with wealthy European travelers, and the Orient Express line continued to grow in both popularity and number of destinations. In 1906, the Simplon Tunnel through the Alps, which connected Switzerland and Italy, was opened. It measured over twelve miles in length, at the time the world's longest railway tunnel. The tunnel significantly reduced the travel time for the Orient Express between Paris and Venice.

The popularity of the Orient Express continued through the 1920s, when Christie herself rode the train and was inspired to write a murder mystery set upon it. During World War II, however, fractious relations between the nations of Europe meant that cross-continental travel was all but impossible. When the war was over, the economies of Europe had been devastated, and luxury travel was therefore less popular. By the time European passengers were once again ready to travel, commercial airlines had begun to offer long-distance passage in a fraction of the time that trains required. Still, the Orient Express from Paris to Istanbul remained in operation through 1977, and has continued to operate in various forms—and under various names—to this day.

The Lindbergh Baby Kidnapping

In *Murder on the Orient Express*, Ratchett is discovered to be an American who allegedly kidnapped and murdered a three-year-old girl from a prominent family. Christie borrowed many details for this back story from the real-life tragedy that befell aviator Charles Lindbergh's family just two years before the novel was published.

Charles Lindbergh became famous around the world for being the first pilot to successfully complete a nonstop flight between New York and Paris in 1927. As a celebrity, much media attention was lavished upon Lindbergh when he married Anne Morrow two years later. The couple had their first child, Charles Jr., in 1930. On March 1, 1932, Charles Jr. was taken from his second-floor room in the Lindbergh family home in New Jersey. A ladder was found propped against the second-story window to the room, and a ransom note demanding fifty

COMPARE & CONTRAST

- **1930s:** The wealthy elite of Europe travel across the continent by way of luxury passenger trains such as the Orient Express, traveling at an average of about twenty-five miles per hour.

  Today: Even those with modest incomes can travel across Europe in a passenger jet, with an average speed over twenty times faster than the original Orient Express.

- **1930s:** The murder trial of Bruno Hauptmann, alleged kidnapper of the Lindbergh baby, results in a media circus previously unseen in the history of journalism.

  Today: Murder trials involving celebrities such as O. J. Simpson and Robert Blake continue to result in media frenzy characterized by nonstop coverage by various news outlets.

thousand dollars in exchange for the baby was left as well.

The case of the missing child became the most important media event of the year, and several branches of law enforcement set to work trying to locate the Lindbergh baby. After a month of fruitless searching, Lindbergh paid the ransom through an intermediary; however, the information the kidnapper provided to Lindbergh to locate his son was false. Over a month later, a truck driver happened upon the decomposing body of young Charles Lindbergh Jr. located in the woods just a few miles from the Lindbergh home. The doctor who examined the body stated his belief that the child was killed on the night he was abducted.

During the search for the murderer, a maid who worked for Anne's mother became a suspect due to her unconvincing alibi for the night of the murder. She ultimately killed herself by drinking poison, although authorities were never able to connect her to the kidnapping and murder. This parallels the fate of Susanne, the nursery-maid in the Armstrong household in *Murder on the Orient Express*.

Unlike Christie's Samuel Ratchett, the alleged kidnapper and murderer of Charles Lindbergh Jr.—a German construction worker named Bruno Hauptmann—was found guilty of the crimes and was executed by electrocution in 1936.

CRITICAL OVERVIEW

Christie was already considered to be one of the world's premier mystery writers when *Murder on the Orient Express* was first published in 1934. Reviews of the book were generally quite favorable, although her works were carefully distinguished as entertainment and not serious literature. Will Cuppy, in his review for the *New York Herald Tribune*, calls the novel "your best mystery bet at the moment by quite some distance—a thoroughly up-to-snuff Christie that ought to go down in history as one of the author's slickest." Although Cuppy acknowledges that the novel may strain the reader's credulity, he calls it "a tour de force in the way of an artificial and no less gripping riddle." An unnamed reviewer for the *Times Literary Supplement* comments on the work, "Mrs. Christie makes an improbable tale very real, and keeps her readers enthralled and guessing to the end."

In the years following its first publication, many within the mystery genre had come to regard Christie, and *Murder on the Orient Express* in particular, with a certain level of scorn. As other mystery writers began to tend toward realism and depth of character over ingenious plotting, the novel was perceived as antiquated in style. Mystery author Raymond Chandler, writing in his "Casual Notes on the Mystery Novel" (1949), criticizes the book as one "in which the whole set-up for the crime

Charles Lindbergh, Jr., son of the famous pilot, just months before he was kidnapped and murdered. The case helped inspire Murder on the Orient Express. *(BIPS | Hulton Archive | Getty Images)*

reveals such a fluky set of events that nobody could ever really believe them."

Still, while many writers and readers of the mystery genre began to regard her work as old-fashioned and contrived, others were finally beginning to appreciate her work on a more literary level. In a 1967 issue of *Life*, famed novelist and critic Anthony Burgess states,

> Agatha Christie has been entertaining us so long and so relentlessly that she has soared above the level of the entertainer. There are scholars who are prepared to take her art, the skill of devising fresh and insoluble puzzles, with the seriousness proper to a Joyce or James or Lawrence.

Regardless of critical opinion, Christie remains one of the most popular writers of all time, with over two billion copies of her works in print in over forty-five different languages. Of those works, *Murder on the Orient Express* remains one of the most beloved by readers around the world.

CRITICISM

Greg Wilson

Wilson is an author, literary critic, and mythologist. In this essay, he examines Christie's use of culturally insensitive and stereotypical ideas in her novel, concluding that they detract from the work's literary merit.

Agatha Christie is an author whose body of work is prodigious, yet her reputation in both popular and academic circles seems to rest largely upon a handful of works. *Murder on the*

IN *ORIENT EXPRESS*, CHRISTIE ACTUALLY TOUCHES UPON THEMES THAT BRING THE WORK TO A LEVEL OF ARTISTIC MERIT THAT FEW OTHER MYSTERY TALES ACHIEVE. UNFORTUNATELY, SHE TRIVIALIZES THESE THEMES WITH HER USE OF DELIBERATELY STEREOTYPICAL VIEWPOINTS."

Orient Express is arguably her most enduring work as far as the average reader goes, due to the daring gimmick the author was able to pull off: *they all did it.* But the work is shot through with ideas and character viewpoints that to modern readers come across as, at best, culturally shallow, and at worst, ethnically biased and stereotypical. Should these characteristics be allowed to diminish the work as a piece of literature? Did Christie include these elements because they were a necessary part of the narrative? And is it fair to judge the author based on the views she bestows upon her characters?

It is not difficult to find examples of stereotyping or culturally insensitive ideas in *Murder on the Orient Express.* Christie was not widely known for sensitivity in that regard; for example, when her 1939 novel *Ten Little Niggers* was published in the United States the following year, American public opinion regarding the "N-word" was already such that the publishers wisely decided to rename the book *And Then There Were None.* However, while that book merely contained a questionable title, *Orient Express* is jam-packed with references to people of various ethnic and cultural backgrounds, due primarily to its multinational cast of characters.

Italians seem to fare the worst in the book. The very nature of Ratchett's murder—a stabbing—immediately evokes suggestions that the killer must be either a woman or an Italian. (The train's chef, who appears only briefly in the novel, seems to exist solely so that he can insist the murderer is a woman, stating, "Only a woman would stab like that.") M. Bouc clings dearly to the idea that the lone Italian man aboard the train must be the killer, even before the man has been properly interviewed—and

indeed, still holds to the notion even after the man has been cleared through an independent alibi. Bouc points out, as if it were accepted fact, that "an Italian's weapon is the knife, and he stabs not once but several times." Colonel Arbuthnot later reinforces this stereotype when he states that "you can't go about having blood feuds and stabbing each other like the Corsicans or the Mafia."

British and American people also receive some negative stereotyping, although it is comparatively mild and even occasionally borders on complimentary. British people are routinely characterized as cold and unsympathetic, while Americans are described as brash and crude. However, the British are also credited as rational and orderly, while Americans are "criticized" by Arbuthnot for being sentimental and idealistic. Other cultural putdowns abound, but perhaps the simplest and most forgivable—thanks to its humor—is Mrs. Hubbard's summation of Greta Ohlsson: "Poor creature, she's a Swede."

One might argue that Christie uses the shallow, ethnocentric comments of the characters as a crucial part of the murder plot. Indeed, the participants in the murder play up their differences so that no one else aboard the train suspects that they are somehow connected. Thus when the Italian Foscarelli refers to the English as "a miserable race," it is much more compelling that his English compartment mate, Masterman, provides for him a secure alibi during the time of the murder. In the same way, Colonel Arbuthnot makes it clear that he does not like Americans, yet he provides an alibi for Ratchett's American secretary, Hector MacQueen. And MacQueen, who refers to the British as "a stiff-necked lot," nonetheless vouches for Arbuthnot's activities on the night of the murder. Taken on its own, this appears to be a clever sort of theatricality carried out by the murderers, perfectly in keeping with the logic of the story.

However, Christie does not restrict such comments to the conspirators. As mentioned previously, M. Bouc and other staffers aboard the train make similar comments throughout the investigation. In addition, information conveyed straight from the author to the reader is even subject to such stereotyping. The first time Foscarelli is heard to speak, his words sound like a cartoon version of an Italian man: "That whatta I say alla de time." This has the net effect of rendering all the characters in the novel

WHAT DO I READ NEXT?

- *The Murder of Roger Ackroyd* (1926) is another of Christie's most popular mystery novels. The tale is narrated by a doctor named Sheppard as he follows and assists Poirot in his attempts to solve the murder of a widower in the village of King's Abbott. The book is considered a landmark in the mystery genre for its shocking twist ending.

- The Christie novel *And Then There Were None* (1939) echoes *Murder on the Orient Express* in its prevailing theme of vengeance enacted for crimes unpunished. In the book, ten strangers of various backgrounds are invited to an island estate off the coast of England, where they are systematically killed off, one by one, as punishment for murders each had previously committed and escaped punishment for.

- *Death on the Nile* (1937) is another classic Poirot mystery by Christie. Poirot takes a vacation to Egypt, but cannot escape intrigue and murder. A new bride is killed during her honeymoon cruise up the Nile, and her former best friend—who also happens to be her new husband's ex-fiancée—seems to be the obvious suspect. But deception runs deep aboard the cruise ship, and the case is enough to challenge even Poirot's keen powers.

- *Curtain: Poirot's Last Case* (1975) was the last of Christie's books published during her lifetime, and does indeed feature the final case of Hercule Poirot. The detective ends his literary adventures as he began, at the Essex manor of Styles Court, where he claims to be on the trail of a serial killer who has managed to avoid suspicion in every murder he or she committed. Although the novel features a Poirot at the edge of death from old age, it was actually written by Christie during World War II and kept locked away for over thirty years.

- *The Hound of the Baskervilles* (1901) by Arthur Conan Doyle features the most famous literary detective of all time, Sherlock Holmes. In the novel, Holmes investigates the death of a wealthy man who, some believe, was cursed and hunted down by a supernatural hound. The novel is set in the county of Devon, near where Christie was born and lived for many years.

- *The No. 1 Ladies' Detective Agency* (1999) by Alexander McCall Smith is the first in a series of novels about the first female private detective in Botswana, Mma Precious Ramotswe. In the book, Precious sets up shop and begins taking cases helping local citizens; she relies largely upon her own good sense and memory of the works of Agatha Christie to help her along the way.

- *Dance Hall of the Dead* (1973) by Tony Hillerman is the author's second novel featuring Joe Leaphorn, a Navajo Tribal Police lieutenant in charge of investigating crimes committed in the Navajo Nation, an American Indian reservation in the southwestern United States. In the book, two boys disappear—one Navajo, one Zuni—and the only evidence left behind is blood from one of the boys. The book was awarded the 1973 Edgar Award for Best Novel.

superficial—a complaint not unfamiliar to Christie, who emphasizes the mechanics of mystery solving over depth and verisimilitude. It may seem pointless to harp on Christie's weaknesses when her intent was clearly to create something more along the lines of light cerebral entertainment. For this book, though, her stylistic choices—if indeed they can be called choices and not unconscious habits—are all the more disappointing because of how close she comes to greatness. In *Orient Express*, Christie actually touches upon themes that bring the work to a level of artistic merit that few other mystery tales achieve. Unfortunately, she trivializes these themes with her use of deliberately stereotypical viewpoints.

Should these characteristics be considered when evaluating Christie's work as literature? Most certainly. Allowances are too often made for the circumstances of a literary work's creation, forgiving this fault or that weakness, because the author was a product of a different era or worked only within a specific, accepted formula. Great literature remains great not because modern readers bother to forgive its faults, but because it speaks clearly across generations and cultures without the need for apologetic footnotes. Even though Christie's intent may not have been to create literature, her work should not receive a handicap because of its modest aims.

If someone were truly, desperately grasping at a way to secure Christie's artistic redemption, one could argue that Christie's cast of characters are meant to represent the state of European relations at the time the novel was written. Indeed, Europe was a continent fractured along geographic, social, and philosophical lines, with friction increasing between, for example, German and British citizens. Just five years later, they would find themselves on opposite sides in World War II. It is telling that Poirot cracks the mystery when he realizes that only in America would such a varied assembly of people normally be found together. However, attributing such depth to Christie's motives is fanciful, because none of the characters exhibit similar depth, and there are no hints within the text that the author is attempting anything more meaningful than creating a literary puzzle-box.

But the most incriminating bits found in the novel are not, for example, M. Bouc pigeonholing an entire nation of people by asking, "Do not Italians stab?" The fundamental problem with the novel can be found in the great detective Poirot's response to Bouc's question: "Assuredly," said Poirot. "Especially in the heat of a quarrel." Poirot is the hero of not only this novel but of a wildly successful series of novels and stories; without a doubt, readers are intended to marvel at his thought processes. And here he is, agreeing wholeheartedly with the idea that Italians as a whole not only quarrel passionately, but also stab more readily than people of other ethnic

backgrounds. To add further insult to injury, Poirot states his reason for thinking an Italian could not be responsible for the murder: "It is a crime that shows traces of a cool, resourceful, deliberate brain—I think an Anglo-Saxon brain." In other words, the crime was committed too cleverly for an Italian to have done it. Yet Poirot insists equally that "it is *im*possible—quite impossible—that an honourable, slightly stupid, upright Englishman should stab an enemy twelve times with a knife!" Poirot, then, bases his entire investigation on generalizations and stereotypes, and counts on them to reach his conclusion, which turns out to be correct—an implicit validation of such questionable methods.

Moments like this, where the author insists that the reader accept culturally biased ideas as truths within the world of the story, seriously damage the inherent literary value of the work. Even if Christie did not believe in these ideas herself, she still uses them as the foundation upon which she constructs her literary framework. This does not mean the author as carpenter is inherently inept—many of the smaller architectural details are crafted with precision, care, cleverness, and humor. But it does mean the house is irreparably slanted, which is bound to affect its perceived value as the years pass by.

Source: Greg Wilson, Critical Essay on *Murder on the Orient Express,* in *Novels for Students 33*, Gale, Cengage Learning, 2010.

Nicholas Birns

In the following excerpt, Birns and Birns analyze Christie's techniques with regard to her depiction of her detectives and their suspects.

The pretense, disguise, play-acting, and outward show that are essential to the mystery genre are given a special intensity in Christie's work by her constant emphasis on and reference to the "theatricality" of her character's actions. A well-known example is *Murder on the Orient Express* (1934), in which Hercule Poirot comes to realize that he has been an audience of one for a careful series of performances. In this book, Christie is at the furthest extreme from the romanticization of the criminal as a solitary outlaw; Christie's criminal is far less often a rogue psychotic (her few attempts at this sort of portrait, as in *Endless Night* [1967], are, though not uninteresting, uncharacteristic) than somebody who is manipulating the known and tolerable conventions of English society to his or her own advantage.

Aboard the **Orient Express**, the solution to the crime, that "they were all doing it," foregrounds a persistent feature of Christie's characterization: she is less probing the souls of her characters than seeing how their enactment of roles implicates them in carceral circumstances that are sometimes apprehended as "criminal," sometimes not.

Christie's detectives operate crucially in orchestrating these plots. Miss Marple and Hercule Poirot delight in assuming ridiculous, caricature like disguises only to reveal a surprising potency as the books move on. They depend on an innocuous facade not only to lull those about them into a false sense of security but also to surprise the reader with their almost ruthless perspicacity. Because disguised as a harmless old English tabby, or as a humorously Belgian rather than dangerously French elf, Christie's detectives astonish the reader and the other characters with their mental and imaginative powers. The grotesque exaggeration involved in the characterization of, say, Poirot (for one thing, it is very unlikely that a Belgian emigré could ever become the leading practitioner of a method of critical investigation conducted in the English language) means that his character is more or less fixed. Again, this need not be counted as a defect. For indeed, Miss Marple and Hercule Poirot are not just empty containers, but central plot-functions operating in a legitimate and interesting mode of discourse. Both detectives take as their characteristic mode acting a part that protects and serves the detecting self hidden "inside," a subterfuge which persuades the criminal as well as the reader into believing that the detective will present no significant challenge, has no convincing authority—an illusion always pierced by book's end, when the authority of the detective is subtly, but thoroughly affirmed. Both of Christie's major detectives become, as their careers unfold, more stylized, more purely plot functions; unlike many later detectives, their lives do not particularly change from story to story.

Christie found the masked quality of her detectives' selves somehow fascinating, this intriguing quality having less to do with the souls of the detectives than with their minds. The classical model is, preeminently, a cerebral, ratiocinative one. Most critics have denounced this cerebrality as being in some way oppressive and limited. But Christie, instead of focusing on the cerebral or rational as structures of normative containment, as they are portrayed by the advocates of the Romantic celebration of the expressive will, calls attention to precisely the way in which the cerebral and the ratiocinative are unusual, weird, preternatural. In doing this, she is only following the tradition of Poe, the explorer of the turbid underside of the psyche who was also lured by the strangely similar obverse presented by the intellect in the shining excess of its power. Possessed of a cerebrality that is as out-of-the-ordinary as any criminal impulse, Christie's detectives function not only to discover crime, but to possess a peculiar empathy with the criminal sensibility.

The emotional undercurrent of this central revelation in Christie's work always suggests an element of the uncanny. Like Christie's detectives, Christie's villains employ the "typical" selves they present to others in order to conceal what they prize as their true nature, relying on what Goffman has called "normal appearances" to allay suspicion. Christie's villains are shown to hide an incivility, an "imperfect socialization" that amounts to a truncated humanity and indicates a dangerous fragility in the social nexus that had heretofore been an important ingredient in creating the fully human self. The "surprise ending" of a Christie mystery turns not only on the discrepancy between role and "real self," but on our trust (always misplaced) that people are fully identical with the repertoire of roles which constitute their participation in society. On the contrary, people who appear to be generic figures, such as the Sweet Little Old Lady, the Fetching Young Mother, the Helpful Policeman, the Adorable Child, the Good Doctor, not to mention the Great Detective himself, are exposed in Christie's fiction as deliberately flattened by roles that trick us into discounting them as murder suspects. A characteristic Christie embodiment of this surprise is the plot device called "the double bluff," in which a character is initially suspected of the murder, exonerated, and then turns out in the end to have committed the crime, or, alternately, where a character who has been seen by the reader exclusively as a potential victim of a crime, is in fact the perpetrator.

Source: Nicholas Birns and Margaret Boe Birns, "Agatha Christie: Modern and Modernist," in *The Cunning Craft: Original Essays on Detective Fiction and Contemporary Literary Theory*, Western Illinois University, 1990, pp. 120–134.

Ina Rae Hark

In the following excerpt, Hark analyzes Christie's storytelling techniques as they relate to character and revelation of information to the reader, concluding that it was necessary for director Sidney Lumet to make fundamental changes to adapt the story for the screen.

The first time Sidney Lumet teamed with screenwriter Paul Dehn to adapt an English thriller for the screen, the book was John Le Carré's *Call for the Dead* and the style of the resulting film, *The Deadly Affair,* was, as Leslie Halliwell comments: "deliberately glum, photographed against the shabbiest possible London backgrounds in muddy colour." Le Carré's complex, psychically tortured characters, gray moral ambivalence, and naturalistically detailed settings meshed well with the predilections of the director who would explore the pressures of urban life in such films as *The Pawnbroker, Dog Day Afternoon,* and *Prince of the City.* When Lumet and Dehn collaborated again, they had exchanged Le Carré for Agatha Christie, and the style of *Murder on the Orient Express* had been chosen by producers John Brabourne and Richard Goodwin as one of all-star cast glamor and glittering period detail. Many reviewers agreed with Paul Zimmerman that Lumet was out of his element in the plush, stylized ambience of the film: "But a rough, scrappy, hustling inventiveness, full of gritty textures, has always characterized his best work. He simply has no feel for high style." After completing the film, Lumet himself admitted the stylistic difficulties it had presented: "I did *Murder on the Orient Express* because I love melodrama. That's all. I wanted to have fun. It turned out to be some of the hardest work I've ever done, because the piece was highly stylized."

The stylistic differences involved not only *mise en scène* but significant variations in the concept and revelation of character. In Christie's novels, the efforts of the detective and the unfolding of the narrative produce gradual revelations of previously concealed information about characters. The process, moreover, is constantly circumscribed by the structural necessities of the mystery genre. As Charles Derry remarks: "Thus the omniscience is rhetorically selective in regard to which characters it can reveal as well as in regard to the comprehensiveness with which it can reveal them. Of course, if any character were to be revealed completely, he could no longer be a suspect." In a Lumet film, on the other hand, vey little stands in the way of a character's steady and full psychological disclosure, and the way characters reveal themselves and the factors that compel their revelations are crucial.

When Poirot puts his little grey cells to work on the suspects' stories in the novel of *Murder on the Orient Express*, he remarks: "The passengers have sat here, one by one, giving their evidence. We know all that can be known—*from outside...*" Our view as Christie readers is similarly extrinsic. David Grossvogel has observed that in Christie's world "the people in that landscape are as tautological as the landscape itself: an adjective or two are sufficient to call their identity to mind." Although the fact of the murder having been committed means that "the tautological evidence can no longer be trusted," the author provides little direct evidence of any other kind by which the "true" character can be known. Indeed, Christie's novels derive much of their narrative energy from the suspects' dissembling resistance to the sleuth's probing. While the innocent may sometimes explode under questioning, it usually serves the culprits to preserve a calm facade and to give away as little as possible. The author does not lead the reader toward the secrets, as Lumet does, but throws up smokescreens between the reader and the emerging clues.

Christie depends on three devices to block perception of the extent of the conspiracy. She first counts on the reader's familiarity with detective story conventions that dictate that some suspects must be innocent. She trusts that the reader will say to himself, as Poirot reports having done, "They can't all be in it." She secondly delays sketching in a complete picture of the Armstrong household at the time of the tragedy for as long as possible. Indeed, the Armstrong case itself is never mentioned until a quarter of the way through the book, when Poirot deciphers the burnt fragment of the last threatening letter Ratchett received. When he recounts the case to Bouc and Dr. Constantine, he mentions only Linda Arden in addition to those who died. We do not learn that Mrs. Armstrong had a younger sister until page 87. The nurse, governess, the vague "servants" are only considered when Poirot questions Countess Andrenyi for a second time on page 168. Christie thirdly plays up the international diversity of the passengers, making it seem unlikely that the members of such a polyglot group could possibly be linked in any way.

Source: Ina Rae Hark, "Twelve Angry People: Conflicting Revelatory Strategies in *Murder on the Orient Express,*" in *Literature/Film Quarterly*, Vol. 15, No. 1, 1987, pp. 36–42.

Stewart H. Benedict

In the following essay, Benedict studies Christie's growth as an author, from her early imitations of Arthur Conan Doyle's mysteries to what he calls "the genuine Christie novel."

Just as in politics the British offspring of an American mother became the symbol of Empire in a time of need, so too the most typically English mystery novels have come from the pen of an authoress who, although she can boast of almost a hundred million sales, cannot boast of one hundred percent pure U.K. blood. The lady in question is of course Agatha Christie, whose heraldry bears a transatlantic bar sinister, but who in her books has out-Harrowed the Harrovians and out-Blimped the Blimps.

Miss Christie launched her criminal career in 1920, *The Mysterious Affair at Styles*, and, since this first case, has finished almost seventy others and has dispatched close onto two hundred fictional victims, incidentally becoming the world's best-selling authoress in the process.

Evidently fully convinced that nothing succeeds like success, Miss Christie at the start of her career relied on Sir Arthur Conan Doyle about as whole-heartedly as, say, V. I. Lenin did on Karl Marx. Her debt to the Sherlock Holmes stories can be seen in her choice of titles for novels (like *The Secret Adversary* and *The Big Four* and short stories (like "The Adventure of the Cheap Flat," "The Tragedy at Marsdon Manor," and "The Mystery of Hunter's Lodge").

Indeed, the team of Hercule Poirot and Captain Hastings, as originally conceived, is a virtual carbon copy of Holmes and Watson. Poirot, like Holmes, is a convinced and convincing spokesman for the human rational faculty, has an unshakable faith in his own reason, uses his long-suffering Boswell as a sort of echo-chamber, and even has a mysterious and exotically named brother who works for the government. Captain Hastings, like Watson a retired military man, has much else in common with his prototype: he is trusting, bumbling, superingenuous ex-soldier whose loyalty is touching but whose intellectual abilities, especially when turned loose on a problem of deduction, are so feeble as to be risible. Occasionally, though, the amanuensis wins applause from the master by making an observation which by its egregious stupidity illuminates some corner previously dark in the innermost recesses of the great mind.

Nor does the fumbling and ineffectual Inspector Lestrade lack a copy: Inspector Japp of the Christie novels is equally tenacious, incorruptible, and uninspired.

But the Baker Street influence permeates far deeper than these superficial features would indicate. Many scenes from Agatha's earlier works, especially those presenting conversations between the two principals, are considerably more Holmesian even than the literary collages constructed in imitation of the master by Adrian Conan Doyle and John Dickson Carr.

At the same time as she was writing by formula, Miss Christie was experimenting with a second type, in which she tried out various assorted detectives and crime-chasers, professional, semi-professional, and amateur.

In these novels she introduced a whole gallery of new sleuths: Tuppence and Tommy, Colonel Race, Superintendent Battle, Mr. Harley Quin and Mr. Satterthwaite, Parker Pyne, and Jane Marple. Some of the newcomers starred once and subsequently reappeared in supporting roles, some never moved out of short stories, while Miss Marple joined Poirot as a Christie regular.

Tuppence and Tommy Beresford, whose specialty was ferreting out espionage, made their debut in *The Secret Adversary*, showed up again in *Partners in Crime* and were resurrected in 1941 for *N or M?* Their frivolous and insouciant approach to detection, if something of a relief-giving contrast to the Holmes-Poirot methodology, nonetheless must have made them seem to their creatress too unreliable to cope with any subtle or complicated crime.

The enigmatic, laconic Colonel Race appeared first in *The Man in the Brown Suit* and sporadically thereafter. The Colonel, whose *locus operandi* was the colonies, did make it back to England for the fateful bridge party in *Cards on the Table*, but clearly his chief interest lay in shoring up the house that Rhodes built. Further, although not precisely what Miss Christie customarily refers to as "a wrong 'un," the Colonel gave the distinct impression of being willing to temporize on questions of ends and means, a point of view, we must assume, acceptable in the colonies but not in the Mother Country.

Superintendent Battle, stolid, dependable, hard-working, came onto the scene in *The Secret of Chimneys* and solved *The Seven Dials Mystery*, but his lack of color and elan must have been responsible for his being relegated to a subordinate role of later cases.

The most atypical product of the Christie imagination was the weird pair consisting of the other-worldly Harley Quin and his fussbudgety, oldmaidish "contact," Mr. Satterthwaite. The short stories in which they figured marked the authoress' closest approach to the occult.

Another unusual character who debuted during this experimental period was Parker Pyne. The ingenious Mr. Pyne specialized not in solving murders, but in manipulating the lives of others so as to bring them happiness and/or adventure. In some of these cases he was fortunate enough to have the assistance of Mrs. Ariadne Oliver, the mystery novelist. Just as it could not be proved that Willie Stark is Huey Long, so too it could not be stated flatly that Ariadne Oliver is Agatha Christie, but many of the clues seem to point in that direction. Mrs. Oliver's incessant munching on apples, her sartorial disorganization, and above all her theories on the art of the mystery novel make it difficult to avoid that conclusion.

It was in 1930, in *Murder at the Vicarage*, unquestionably the best-written Christie novel, that she first presented the character who became one of her two favorites. The attraction to Jane Marple is not hard to understand: she is one of those personified paradoxes in whom both authors and readers delight. Behind the antique, Victorian, tea-and-crumpets, crocheted-antimacassar facade, is a mind realistically aware of the frailty of all human beings and the depravity of some.

About 1935 there began to appear the third type, or what might best be called the genuine Christie novel, with its numerous unique features.

Most publicized among these features, of course, is the use of an extraordinary gimmick: in *Murder in the Calais Coach* the **murder** is done with the connivance of a dozen people; in *The ABC Murders,* the highly suggestive suspect believes himself guilty of a series of crimes of which he is innocent and convinces the reader of his guilt; in *And Then There Were None*, the reader is led to believe that the killer has been a victim in a series of murders.

Less discussed, but really more significant, is the Christie ability to manage what may be called (to pirate a phrase from Sarcey) "the optics of the mystery." The successful mystery novel involves a special problem: the death(s) of the victim(s) must be made of interest, but not of deep concern, to the reader. The conventional, or, by now, hackneyed, methods of developing this special attitude in the reader are two: either the prospective corpse is presented so briefly that, living, he makes no impression at all, or he is depicted as so vicious that the audience looks forward eagerly to his demise.

Miss Christie, however, has evolved a completely different formula: she arranges a situation which is implausible, if not actually impossible and into this unrealistic framework places characters who act realistically for the most realistic of motives. In *Easy to Kill,* for example, four murders are committed in a minuscule town without any suspicions being aroused; in *A Murder Is Announced* the killer advertises in advance; in *What Mrs. McGillicuddy Saw*! the witness to a murder is a pasenger in a train which travels parallel to another train just long enough for Mrs. McGillicuddy to see the murder. And, of course, some of the Christie Classics, especially *Murder in the Calais Coach, And Then There Were None,* and "Witness for the Prosecution," really test the ducility of coincidence.

As for the realistic elements, in only one instance (the short story "The Face of Helen") does a murderer have recourse to a bizarre weapon; in every other case a completely pedestrian one is used: the poison bottle, the knife, the gun, the garrote, the bludgeon. The motive is always equally pedestrian: it is invariably either money or love.

The single characteristic which most stamps a whodunit as a Christie product, however, is the fate of the killer. Miss Christie sees murderers as being either good or bad individuals; the good ones dispose of evil victims, and vice versa. Further, the bad murderer is distinguished because he unvaryingly preys on people with inadequate defenses: he may be a doctor (and therefore *ipso facto* to be trusted, as contemporary folklore teaches us); or a handsome and clever lover who first uses, then kills, a woman who has been unlucky enough to fall in love with him; or an old and respected friend and confidant; or a man who selects a child, an old person, a physical or psychological cripple as a victim. This element, the victim's inadequate defenses against the criminal, puts the murderer beyond the pale—he is unsportsmanlike and consequently despicable. Over and over reference is made to the viciousness of those who betray faith and trust. Says Dr.

Haydock in *Murder at the Vicarage* after he learns that the murderer has attempted to pin his crime on an innocent young curate who suffers from sleeping sickness and is not really sure of his own innocence: "The fellow's not fit to live. A defenseless chap like Hawes." In an analogous situation Hercule Poirot says to Franklin Clarke, who has actually succeeded in getting the suggestible epileptic Alexander Bonaparte Cust to believe himself a murderer: "No, Mr. Clarke, no easy death for you ... I consider your crime not an English crime at all—not above-board—not sporting—..." He adds later, in analyzing the crime, "It was abominable—... the cruelty that condemd an unfortunate man to a living death. *To catch a fox and put him in a box and never let him go. That is not le sport.*"

Conversely, when the victim is completely unsympathetic and the murderer a decent person, it is very possible that the culprit will be revealed to be a sufferer from a far-advanced case of some incurable disease. If he is healthy, he usually has or is presented with the opportunity to commit suicide. On rare occasions such a person escapes any punishment at the hands of the law: in *Murder in the Calais Coach*, for instance, the victim turns out to have committed an especially unsportsmanlike crime and the otherwise tenacious Hercule Poirot simply steps out of the case, leaving it unsolved.

It is very clear, then, that Miss Christie is no moral absolutist where **murder** is concerned. In *Mr. Parker Pyne, Detective* Ariadne Oliver, speaking, we suppose, for the authoress, asks Poirot, "Don't you think that there are people who ought to be murdered?" The view that there are indeed such people seems to be sustained in *And Then There Were None*, in which no less than ten preeminently sleazy slayers are dispatched by a retired judged who escapes legal justice through suicide. The entire tone of this book gives the strong impression that Miss Christie is not sorry to see them go. It also suggests that there is a stratification of murderers, with special punishment due those whose crimes have been particularly un-British, i.e., heinous, even though the later Miss Christie can hardly be accused of advocating unrestrained *laissez-tuer*.

Since Miss Christie's prestige among her fellow mystery writers is towering, and since she has by implication espoused the quaint theory that a sportsmanlike murder doesn't really count, it is interesting to speculate as to whether this latitudinarian attitude has in any way influenced the writers of the hard-boiled school with their philosophy that it is all right to kill a killer. Paradoxical as it may seem, perhaps the literary godmother of bone-crushing Mike Hammer is none other than genteel Jane Marple.

Source: Stewart H. Benedict, "Agatha Christie and Murder Most Unsportsmanlike," in *Claremont Quarterly*, Vol. 9, No. 2, Winter 1962, pp. 37–42.

SOURCES

Burgess, Anthony, "Murder Most Fair by Agatha the Good," in *Life*, December 1, 1967, p. 8.

Chandler, Raymond, "Casual Notes on the Mystery Novel," reprinted in *Raymond Chandler Speaking*, edited by Dorothy Gardiner and Kathrine Sorley Walker, University of California Press, 1997, p. 63.

Christie, Agatha, *Murder on the Orient Express*, Berkley Books, 2004.

Cuppy, Will, Review of *Murder on the Orient Express*, in *New York Herald Tribune Book Review*, March 4, 1934.

"The Great Age of Train Travel: 1883–1977," Venice Simplon Orient-Express website, http://www.orient-express.com/web/vsoe/history_great_age.jsp (accessed June 27, 2009).

Manning, Lona, "The Lindbergh Baby Kidnapping," in *CRIME Magazine* website, http://www.crimemagazine.com/07/lindbergh,0304-7.htm (last updated March 4, 2007; accessed June 27, 2009).

"The Queen of Crime: Biography," AgathaChristie.com, http://www.agathachristie.com/about-christie/the-queen-of-crime/biography/ (accessed June 27, 2009).

Review of *Murder on the Orient Express*, *The Times Literary Supplement*, January 11, 1934, p. 29.

FURTHER READING

Burton, Anthony, *The Orient Express: The History of the Orient Express Service from 1883 to 1950*, Chartwell Book Sales, 2001.

This nonfiction chronology of the Orient Express line contains detailed information and photos of the luxury cars during their heyday in the early twentieth century.

Chandler, Raymond, *The Big Sleep*, Vintage, 1988.

Originally published in 1939, this novel introduced readers to Philip Marlowe, a tough, hard-living private detective who operates out of Los Angeles. The novel, a complex tapestry of deception and double crosses, is also one of the most enduring examples of hard-boiled detective fiction.

Christie, Agatha, *An Autobiography*, HarperCollins Publishers Ltd, 2001.

Originally published in 1977, almost two years after her death, this generally wistful account of the author's life was written primarily during the 1950s and 1960s. It focuses largely on her youth and life outside the writing world rather than discussing her own works in great detail.

Fisher, Jim, *The Lindbergh Case*, Rutgers University Press, 1987.

This nonfiction study of one of the most famous kidnapping and murder cases of all time is written by a former FBI agent and professor of criminal justice. In it, Fisher argues that Bruno Hauptmann, the man convicted and executed for the crimes, is indeed the one who did it.

Nicholas Nickleby

CHARLES DICKENS

1839

Charles Dickens wrote *Nicholas Nickleby* between February 1838 and October 1839. It was commissioned to appear in monthly installments by the London publisher Chapman and Hall, a contract Dickens received based on the tremendous popularity of his previous novel, *The Pickwick Papers*. Dickens was offered a payment of 150 pounds per month, an amount ten times higher than what he received for *The Pickwick Papers*. And unlike the previous novel, copyright was to revert to the author after five years. Dickens met every deadline, although he was at no time even one number ahead of the publication schedule. On April 1, 1938, fifty thousand readers bought the first number of Dickens's new novel.

Nicholas Nickleby is considered one of Dickens's minor works. While it paved the way for his more thematically and technically complex novels, it is essentially a light romantic comedy. However, the novel contains a remarkable roster of 117 speaking characters, and every one of its nearly nine hundred pages has its own heading. Nicholas himself is a classic romantic hero, and his journey from boyhood to manhood, through all of the social strata of Victorian London, allows Dickens to develop tools for social critique that he will wield with greater precision in later works. In *Nicholas Nickleby*, Dickens sharpens these critiquing tools by taking on one of the social scourges of his day: the infamous "Yorkshire schools," institutions for poor,

Charles Dickens

deformed, illegitimate, or otherwise unwanted boys.

Dickens's genius for creating believable characters from all walks of life, especially villains and outsiders, was already in evidence when he published *Nicholas Nickleby* at the age of twenty-six. His villain here, Ralph Nickleby, uncle to the title character, remains one of his most subtly and completely developed characters. Dickens's talent for developing complex plots and writing hilarious dialogue is also clearly in evidence in the novel, as is his commitment, new in the English literary world, to present poor people in a realistic light, giving their struggles and hopes as much serious attention as books of that era generally accorded only to the educated classes.

AUTHOR BIOGRAPHY

Charles Dickens was born on February 7, 1812, in Portsmouth, England—a port city near London. He was the first son of John and Elizabeth Dickens. Elizabeth Dickens was a vivacious woman who loved to dance; in fact, she went dancing on the night before Charles was born. In Dickens's early youth his father held steady employment as a clerk in the Navy Pay Office, but the family lived beyond their means, and when Dickens was twelve years old, the entire family was forced to take up residence at the Marshalsea, an infamous debtors' prison in London that was to figure darkly in several of Dickens's novels. The boy was forced to leave school to work in a "blacking shop," where he pasted labels on bottles of shoe polish. This interlude led to his lifelong concern about the living and working conditions of poor children.

The success of *The Pickwick Papers*, published in serialized form in 1836 and 1837 when Dickens was only twenty-four, made him the most successful writer of his era. In many ways, he became the first modern celebrity. Two years later, in 1838 and 1839, Dickens published *Nicholas Nickleby*, again in serialized form. Over the next thirty years, Dickens produced a staggering quantity of work: fifteen major novels and numerous pieces of short fiction and journalism, while editing a magazine and conducting speaking tours across Britain and America. His writing created the template for many British authors who followed him.

Dickens regarded himself as an outsider to bourgeois society because of his working-class upbringing, and most of his books contain overt critiques of the British class system. He had an outgoing, convivial personality and loved to converse with people of all classes while on the long walks he took around London daily. His private life was less than idyllic. After producing ten children with his wife of twenty-two years, Catherine Hogarth, the couple divorced in 1858, scandalizing Victorian England. Subsequently, some literary scholars suggest, he may have had a lengthy affair with actress Ellen Ternan, and the couple may have had at least one child who died in infancy. But no concrete proof exists. Dickens devoted his later years to giving public readings of his works, often as fund-raisers for people in need. Dickens had himself wanted to be an actor in his youth, and this belated immersion in the theater was satisfying but exhausting. He died of what was probably a stroke on June 9, 1870, in Gad's Hill, England.

PLOT SUMMARY

Chapters 1–3

Nicholas Nickleby opens with Nicholas's grandfather Godfrey Nickleby, who has been driven by poverty almost to the point of suicide, inheriting money from an uncle. He buys a farm and raises two sons, Nicholas and Ralph. Cold and miserly Ralph becomes a rich money-lender, while the kinder Nicholas remains poor, eventually investing badly in the stock market and losing what little he has. He dies a broken man, leaving his wife and two children, Nicholas and Kate, penniless.

The scene shifts to the office of the children's uncle, Ralph Nickleby, in Golden Square, where readers first meet Ralph's assistant, Newman Noggs, another former gentleman who was ruined through bad investments. Newman is the first of many characters in the novel who is deformed in some way. In Newman's case, it is due to his "two goggle eyes, of which one was a fixture" [made of glass], his absurdly small clothes, and his incessant knuckle-cracking. Ralph himself is dressed in a manner suggesting financial stability, and there is "something in his very wrinkles, and in his cold restless eye, which seemed to tell of cunning that would announce itself in spite of him." This chapter also mocks the British Parliament as it debates the merits of the Muffin Trade, Muffin Boys, and the Muffin System, eventually voting in favor of a muffin monopoly.

Meanwhile the eponymous hero, Nicholas, his sister Kate, and their mother, Mrs. Nickleby, have come to London from their home in the country and are renting rooms while they wait for an audience with Ralph, who, they hope, will help them. The family's first meeting with Ralph goes badly. Mrs. Nickleby is weak-minded and easily influenced by anyone with authority. Ralph, while perceiving Kate's beauty, takes an instant dislike to Nicholas because he resembles his late father (Ralph's brother), for whom Ralph feels a scornful envy.

Chapters 4–6

In Chapter 4, we are introduced to Mr. Wackford Squeers, headmaster of Dotheboys School for Boys in Yorkshire. Squeers, like Noggs, also has only one eye and is of freakish appearance. Ralph brings Nicholas to the Dotheboys School for Boys in Yorkshire, having learned from a newspaper advertisement that the headmaster is seeking a "first assistant master." Dotheboys is a fictionalized version of a type of institution infamous in that era as a "Yorkshire school," the eradication of which was Dickens's goal in writing the novel. Illegitimate, deformed, or otherwise unwanted boys from poor families were consigned to these places, where insufficient food and harsh treatment led to injuries, as well as many premature deaths. Squeers, a past business associate of Ralph's, agrees to hire Nicholas, who is overjoyed at what he naively believes is his uncle's kindness. On the way home, Ralph asks Nicholas to drop off some papers at his office, and Nicholas meets Newman Noggs, who understands Ralph's true motives and takes pity on Nicholas. Nicholas leaves for Dotheboys the next morning by coach, amid sad farewells from his mother and sister, whom Nicholas believes will be looked after by his uncle. Noggs appears at the leave-taking, pressing a letter into Nicholas's hand. On the journey Nicholas is shocked by Squeers's harsh treatment of his young charges, denying them food or a safe place in the coach.

Chapters 7–9

Nicholas arrives at Dotheboys Hall and is horrified by the cruelty Mr. Squeers and his wife exhibit toward the children. He is also astounded by the appearance of Smike, a longtime inmate who acts as an unpaid servant to the Squeers family. Although Smike is clearly at least eighteen years old, he is dressed in a "skeleton suit" usually worn by little boys, and an old, shredded, linen frill around his neck. Smike is also lame, and is so "dispirited and hopeless" that Nicholas can scarcely bear to look at him. Nicholas opens the letter from Newman Noggs, who offers him a place to stay in London if he should ever need one.

On Nicholas's first day at the Dotheboys, he encounters sad, broken boys, prematurely aged and starving. He also discovers that Squeers steals the boys' letters from home, including any enclosed money or belongings. Nicholas meets Squeers' daughter Fanny, who resembles her father in both appearance and temperament, and who promptly falls in love with Nicholas. She arranges a tea party for Nicholas, her best friend Tilda, and Tilda's fiancé, the large and hearty Yorkshireman John Browdie. Tilda flirts with Nicholas to enflame both John and Fanny. Nicholas flirts back, as Tilda is a distraction from his own predicament. John threatens Nicholas, and Fanny is furious. Nicholas, his mind occupied with other matters, is surprised by the

MEDIA ADAPTATIONS

- *Nicholas Nickleby*, like many of Dickens's novels, has been produced on stage and in film. The Tony Award–winning 1981 stage production *The Life and Adventures of Nicholas Nickleby* by the Royal Shakespeare Company played to sold-out crowds in London and New York and is considered the greatest Dickens adaptation of all time. It was nine hours long and was presented in four two-hour acts. Parts 1 and 2 could be seen either in one day or over two consecutive nights. The play was recorded by A&E and released on VHS in 1983. This film of the play features thirty-nine actors playing 150 roles and stars Roger Rees as Nicholas. It is available on DVD and is considered the definitive screen version of the novel.

- The British production company Ealing Studios released a 1947 film adaptation of *Nicholas Nickleby* directed by Alberto Cavalcanti. The film starred Derek Bond as Nicholas, Sally Ann Howes as Kate, and Cedric Hardwicke as Ralph. The film is considered true to the period and very effective at conveying the squalor of Dickensian England. It is available on DVD.

- In 2002, Hart-Sharp Entertainment released another film adaptation of *Nicholas Nickleby* written and directed by Douglas McGrath. It features American movie star Anne Hathaway as Madeline and Charlie Hunnam, star of the British version of *Queer as Folk*, as Nicholas. The stellar supporting cast includes Christopher Plummer, Nathan Lane, and Alan Cumming. This version is lighter than other adaptations and glosses over some of the worst hardships endured by the characters. It is available on DVD.

- Stephen Whittaker directed a made-for-TV version of *Nicholas Nickleby*, produced by Britain's Channel Four in 2002. James D'Arcy stars as Nicholas, Sophia Myles (*Mansfield Park*) plays his sister, and veteran dramatic actor Charles Dance plays Ralph. It is available on DVD.

- Many audio cassettes of the book exist, including one featuring Roger Rees, star of the Royal Shakespeare Company version. It was produced by A&E.

---

vehemence of all parties, and blames himself for not paying attention. "Well, it is a just punishment," he concludes, "for having forgotten, even for an hour, what is around me now!"

Chapters 10–12

Ralph has also procured a job for Kate, at the establishment of a milliner, Madame Mantalini. Kate is to work from nine in the morning until nine at night for five to seven shillings a week. Madame Mantalini has a lewd and flirtatious husband, the first of many such brutes Kate will contend with. Ralph tells Kate he has an empty house she and her mother can live in temporarily until he rents it. Newman Noggs, who Kate recognizes as having a kind spirit,

conducts them to their new lodging, an awful place with animal bones on the floor. It stands near a wharf on the Thames River. Kate's life is now as cheerless and frightening as her brother's.

Nicholas realizes that not only is Fanny in love with him, but she also believes that he is in love with her, a misapprehension he attempts to correct immediately. He believes that his only hope is to leave Dotheboys Hall without looking back. This is one of many times when Nicholas speaks or acts from his emotions, one sign in Dickens of a true hero, and a behavior that differentiates him from Ralph, who acts only from cold calculation. Nicholas confides in Smike and tells him that he plans to leave the school as soon as possible.

Chapters 13–15

Smike escapes from Dotheboys but is soon caught and brought back. As Squeers prepares to beat the feeble boy, Nicholas intercedes for the first time in Squeers's brutal treatment of his charges, shouting, "'Stop!' in a voice that made the rafters ring." Squeers strikes Nicholas first, and Nicholas, "concentrating into that one moment all his feelings of rage, scorn, and indignation" beats Squeers until "he roared for mercy."

Nicholas then sets out on foot for London. On the road he meets John Browdie, who, hearing of the treatment meted out to the schoolmaster, bellows with approval and presses money on Nicholas, so that he can have lodging for the night. On the second night, Nicholas takes shelter in a barn. On waking he finds Smike, who has followed him and who begs to be allowed to stay with him. Nicholas agrees. The two set out for Newman Noggs's boardinghouse, arriving there at two in the morning. A jolly party is going on in the lodgings of the Kenwigses, a family with modest means and many daughters. It is a comic scene, and it underscores the importance of girls' wealth in making good marriages—a theme that will recur later in the romances of both Kate and Nicholas. When two "queer-looking people, all covered with rain and mud" are announced to Noggs, Newman grabs a candle and a cup of hot punch and runs to welcome them. Newman advises Nicholas not to see his mother and sister until he has first seen his uncle, and produces a copy of a letter Ralph has already received from Fanny Squeers. The letter greatly exaggerates her family's injuries at Nicholas's hands and accuses him of also stealing their jewelry.

Chapters 16–19

Nicholas visits the General Accounting Office, an employment agency, seeking work. While there he becomes smitten with a beautiful girl who is also looking for work, but he fails to learn her name. The clerk refers Nicholas to the office of a member of Parliament, Mr. Gregsbury, who needs a secretary. Here Dickens has another chance to ridicule the British government, because Gregsbury refuses to do even one of the things he promised to do during his campaign, but also refuses to resign. Gregsbury enumerates the endless responsibilities the secretary's job entails, which include all the work that would normally be expected of a member of Parliament himself, and names the paltry salary. Nicholas, already less naive than he was when he agreed to work at Dotheboys, declines this job. But the Kenwigses, hearing of his need for work, engage him as a French tutor for their daughters. They believe this nicety will add to the girls' marriageability.

In the meantime, Kate toils through difficult days at Madame Mantalini's millinery shop. The shop forewoman, the nosy middle-aged spinster Miss Knag, at first champions Kate, then becomes jealous when Kate rather than she is requested as a model. The unemployed Mr. Mantalini makes improper advances to Kate. Kate consoles herself with the thought that at least Nicholas is faring better at his place of employment—or so she imagines.

Kate encounters Ralph as she is leaving work one night. He invites her to dinner at his house; there she meets the vile aristocrats Sir Mulberry Hawk and Lord Frederick Verisopht. She is the only female present at the dinner, a situation that invites scandal and could compromise her reputation. The men are vulgar and in debt to her uncle. They bet on whether Kate is wishing one of them will court her. She hurries from the room to hide, crying. Hawk follows her; they are completely alone, a situation that can ruin her chances to make a good marriage. Ralph appears, and Hawk accuses him of using Kate to lure Verisopht, the richer and younger of the two, into greater debt. Ralph acknowledges the truth of the accusation. He then takes Kate home, and seeing her tear-stained face brings back a memory of her father. He "staggered while he looked and went back into his house, as a man who had seen a spirit from some world beyond the grave." This is the first of several occasions in which Kate's misery provokes a fleeting feeling of guilt in Ralph.

Chapters 20–22

Nicholas decides to visit the lodgings of his mother and sister. However, Ralph gets there first and recounts Fanny Squeers's version of Nicholas's beating of her family and the alleged theft. Nicholas bursts in. He explains the facts of the case, admitting he beat the deserving Squeers and left with Smike. Ralph tells them that neither Nicholas nor anyone who helps him will ever have a penny of Ralph's money. Nicholas naively leaves his mother and sister again in Ralph's care, warning him that if any harm should befall them, he will face a heavy reckoning. Nicholas then joins Smike to go seek his fortune outside of London until his name is cleared.

Kate loses her job when Madame Mantalini goes bankrupt due to the extravagant behavior of her husband. Kate is set up again by Ralph, this time as companion to a pampered rich woman named Mrs. Wititterly. Nicholas and Smike, meanwhile, head toward the coast to sign on as seamen. Instead they fall in with a theatrical company run by Vincent Crummles, who offers Nicholas and Smike employment as actors and offers Nicholas extra work as a writer of theatrical adaptations of novels. The two gratefully accept.

Chapters 23–25

Nicholas and Smike meet Crummles's family—his wife, several boys, and the Infant Phenomenon, a girl of perhaps fifteen whose growth has been stunted by an unknown means, possibly alcohol, so that she can continue to play children's roles. The theater people are kind, but silly; they seem, like children, always to be playing. Nicholas sees their current production the next evening and is very impressed by its quality. The magic of the theater affects him strongly, and he throws himself into writing a new piece for the company. He receives great acclaim from both the company and the audience for this new piece, which we writies and acts in under the name of "Johnson." This is the alias he has given the Crummleses because he is still in flight from the law. Nicholas helps Smike learn his part as an apothecary (pharmacist) in the play, and after much gentle help, Smike is able to remember his few lines.

Chapters 26–30

Kate continues to be harassed by the loathsome boors Sir Mulberry Hawk and Lord Frederick Verisopht. The men go to her residence and meet Mrs. Nickleby, who assumes they are honorable gentlemen vying for Kate's hand. Meanwhile, Ralph suppresses feelings of remorse for his actions. "Selling a girl—throwing her in the way of temptation, and insult, and coarse speech. . . . Pshaw! Match-making mothers do the same thing every day." He arranges a "chance" meeting between the scoundrels and Kate at the theater. Kate narrowly escapes another compromising scene with Sir Mulberry, in which he attempts to touch her. Next, the men hound her at her place of employment, having impressed the status-seeking Mrs. Wititterly with their titles. Kate appeals to her employer for help, but winds up getting fired. Kate next appeals to Ralph for help, but he refuses. Kate says she will ask no more of him and instead will

appeal to God for help. Newman Noggs, overhearing, vows that "someone else" shall hear of it soon, too.

Nicholas continues to receive rave reviews at the theater. He receives a letter from Newman saying that he may need to return to London. After guessing that Newman's letter implies further treachery by Ralph, Nicholas has one final triumphant performance and bids adieu to the world of the theater.

Chapters 31–33

Upon arriving in London, Nicholas goes to Noggs's residence, and, finding Noggs out, goes to a tavern to wait. Nicholas hears Hawk and Verisopht in the tavern discussing his sister in very disrespectful terms and understands at once the breadth of Ralph's villainy against his family. After giving the men his card, Nicholas demands to know Hawk's name, but Hawk will not divulge it, nor will Verisopht. Nicholas says he will follow Hawk until he learns it; Hawk gets into his carriage, beating Nicholas away with his whip. Nicholas grabs the whip and strikes Hawk a heavy blow, opening a gash in his face. Nicholas proceeds to remove Kate and his mother from the dismal house in which Ralph has installed them; they all go to live in the friendly lodging house where they had first stayed in London. Nicholas sends a letter to Ralph, stating that the family renounces him and leaves him to his grave.

Chapters 34–36

Ralph reads Nicholas's letter again and again. He is visited by Squeers, who asks for financial recompense for Nicholas's beating. Ralph begins to plot revenge against Nicholas, using Smike as a weapon. Ralph recognizes that his hatred for Nicholas is grounded in the boy's likeness to his dead brother, thinking, "He was open, liberal, gallant, gay; I a crafty hunks of cold and stagnant blood."

Jobless again, Nicholas returns to the General Accounting Office where he saw the mysterious, beautiful girl; this time he has another important encounter. He meets an amiable older gentleman, Charles Cheeryble, who, upon listening sympathetically to Nicholas's sad story, conducts him immediately to the offices of the Brothers Cheeryble. Here Nicholas meets Charles's identical twin, Ned, and their clerk, Tim Linkinwater, who has been with them for forty-four years. The kindly brothers offer Nicholas a job keeping their books at a respectable salary of

120 pounds per year, and install the family in a lovely cottage they own at no charge. The benevolent twin brothers embody a miracle of generosity after the harsh treatment the family has endured.

Chapters 37–39

The Brothers Cheeryble throw a party in honor of Tim Linkinwater's birthday. All the house staff is invited—porters, warehousemen, cooks, butlers and maids—there is no class discrimination here. In stark contrast to every other servant in the book, the employees of the Brothers Cheeryble almost cry with happiness as they express their gratitude to be working there.

Meanwhile Smike is failing in health and feeling deep sorrow. Sir Mulberry Hawk is reported to be in bad condition, bruised and scarred after his encounter with Nicholas. Ralph visits the recuperating scoundrel, and stokes his desire for revenge. When Ralph leaves, Sir Frederick Verisopht, who is now revealed to "really have a kind heart," comes to Nicholas's defense, saying Hawk was in the wrong. Smike, out for a walk, is accidentally discovered by Squeers, who captures him. The genial farmer John Browdie, who is visiting London with his new bride, Tilda, subsequently rescues him.

Chapters 40–42

Smike returns to Newman's home, where he cries to hear that the Nickleby family, especially Kate, have been worried about him. Meanwhile, Nicholas is amazed to discover the beautiful girl from the General Accounting Office meeting with the Brothers Cheeryble at his place of work. She is crying, and upon seeing a stranger enter the room immediately faints. The brothers Cheeryble refuse to tell Nicholas who she is, and he becomes unable to think about anything else. He enlists Newman to discover her name and address. Newman follows her, reporting her name is Cecilia Bobster. After swallowing his surprise at her lack of a genteel name, Nicholas attends a secret meeting set up for him by Newman and discovers that Miss Bobster is in fact the wrong girl. Mrs. Nickleby, in another comic scene, is being pursued romantically by a mysterious older gentleman over the garden wall, who throws cucumbers and turnips as a way to court her. Squeers confronts John Browdie, and John and Nicholas threaten Squeers with legal action should he ever harass Smike again.

Chapters 43–45

Nicholas meets Frank Cheeryble, a nephew of the Cheeryble brothers. Frank is a younger version of his amiable uncles, and Nicholas is immediately worried that the mysterious girl may be intended for him in marriage. The brothers bring the young Frank along when they pay a visit on the Nicklebys. Frank is immediately smitten with Kate.

Ralph is approached by a man named Brooker, who, professing to know some secret about Ralph, tries to bribe him. Brooker asks, "Are those of your own name dear to you?" and Ralph answers, "They are not," assuming Brooker refers to Nicholas and Kate. Newman Noggs follows Brooker and listens closely to Mr. Brooker's story.

The Nickleby household hosts a tea party for John Browdie, Smike's savior on two occasions, and his new wife Tilda. Ralph suddenly appears, accompanied by Squeers and another scoundrel, Snawley, who has brought what Ralph says are documents proving that Smike is actually Snawley's son. Nicholas and John refuse to give Smike up, although Ralph threatens Nicholas with legal proceedings that will ruin his future prospects and "make this house a hell."

Chapters 46–49

The Cheeryble brothers tell Nicholas that Ralph has been to see them regarding Smike, and that they told Ralph to leave. They also relate the story of the beautiful girl, whose name is Madeline Bray. She is the daughter of the woman Charles Cheeryble himself hoped to marry in his youth, but who instead had married a scoundrel and soon died. The girl works night and day to support her sick father. The Cheerybles enlist Nicholas in their plan to help her. He agrees to participate, although he worries that his own interest in the girl may cloud his abilities. He goes to her house, pretending to be interested in buying her paintings, but blurts out that he would die to serve her. Madeline weeps with gratitude. Ralph, it turns out, has plans to marry Madeline off to an old miser named Arthur Gride in return for money he needs to pay off an old debt of Madeline's father. Gride and Ralph also know that Madeline will inherit property when she marries and plan to trick her out of it.

Kate, meanwhile, has romantic feelings for Frank Cheeryble, who has become a regular visitor to the cottage. Smike sits alone in his room and continues to seem very melancholy, although he will not tell Nicholas the cause. Smike is diagnosed with consumption, a disease that "so prepares its victim, as it were, for death."

Chapters 50–53

Sir Mulberry Hawk, mostly healed, swears to murder Nicholas. Lord Frederick Verisopht vows to prevent this. The two duel; Verisopht dies and Hawk flees to France.

Meanwhile, Nicholas learns from Newman about Madeline's upcoming marriage to Gride and bolts from the house with Newman chasing him. Nicholas begs Madeline to postpone the marriage for one week, in which time the Cheerybles will have returned from abroad. She protests that she cannot delay, for her father will surely die if not restored to affluence by this marriage. Nicholas staggers to the home of Arthur Gride, offering him money to put off the wedding and hinting that he knows of the plot to defraud Madeline of her inheritance. Gride, assuming he is bluffing, refuses.

Chapters 54–56

Ralph and Arthur go to the Bray home on the wedding morning. Walter Bray, feeling guilty for what he is about to do to his daughter, tells Ralph of a dream he had: "The floor sank with me. . . . I alighted in a grave." Nicholas and Kate barge in, intending to prevent the marriage by any means possible. Nicholas threatens Ralph with what he knows of the plot.

The three hear a crash. Bray's premonition has been realized; he has died just in time to spare his daughter from her awful fate. Nicholas carries Madeline out to a waiting coach. Madeline subsequently falls ill, but Kate lovingly nurses her back to health.

Mrs. Nickleby tells Nicholas that Frank Cheeryble and Kate are in love. Nicholas declares that a marriage between them would be impossible due to Kate's poverty and the appearance it would create of the penniless Nicklebys taking advantage of the wealthy Cheerybles. Smike grows alarmingly sicker, and he and Nicholas leave for a stay in the peaceful country environs where Nicholas and Kate grew up. Arthur Gride, meanwhile, discovers he has been robbed by his maid, Peg Sliderskew, of papers relating to Madeline's inheritance that he and Ralph had themselves previously stolen. Ralph discovers that Nicholas has told certain important persons about Ralph's plot to ensnare

and defraud Madeline Bray. This has caused Ralph's stocks to collapse. Ralph, swearing revenge against Nicholas, hires Squeers to recover the papers stolen from Gride.

Chapters 57–59

Squeers does his dirty work with Peg Sliderskew, getting her drunk so that she will reveal the papers she has stolen. As she at last produces the right one, Newman Noggs emerges from the shadows and knocks Squeers senseless.

Smike and Nicholas, meanwhile, revisit many beloved places of Nicholas's and Kate's childhoods. Smike asks to be buried under a tree where Kate napped as a girl. Finally at peace—having now known real love with the Nickleby family, and admitting he loves Kate—Smike dies.

Ralph, anxious and unable to sleep, worries about Noggs's absence, little suspecting that his own servant is in on Nicholas's plot to destroy him. He is surprised by a visit from Charles Cheeryble, who urges Ralph to ask Nicholas's mercy. Ralph scoffs at the idea. Ralph visits Snawley's home. His wife informs Ralph that Snawley is now being pursued by the law for pretending to be Smike's father at Ralph's request. Ralph next looks for Gride, who hides from him. Ralph finally visits the Cheerybles, because no one else will talk to him. He finds to his astonishment that Newman is there. Newman and the Cheerybles explain how they uncovered Ralph's plots and reveal that Gride, Snawley, and Squeers had all confessed their parts in Ralph's schemes. They tell Ralph that the world knows what he has done, and that he ought to go away from London to hide and "become a better man." Ralph again ignores their advice.

Chapters 60–62

Ralph visits Squeers in jail. Squeers has told the authorities that Ralph had hired him. He, like all of Ralph's former accomplices, has no respect or even interest in Ralph anymore. Ralph returns home and is summoned by Tim Linkinwater to the Cheeryble house. Once there, the brothers reveal the man Brooker, who tells Ralph that his only son, whom Ralph believed died as a child, had indeed lived a starved and wretched life and died in the arms of his cousin Nicholas. In other words, Smike was in fact Ralph's son. Ralph smashes a lamp to the ground and disappears without a word.

Kate, meanwhile, refuses the marriage proposal of Frank Cheeryble because of her poverty. Nicholas resolves to move Madeline to some other lodgings so that he is not tormented by his own romantic feelings for her. Nicholas and Kate imagine a chaste future together, growing old and kindly like the Brothers Cheeryble. After telling all this to Charles, Charles tells Nicholas that Ralph wants them to both visit him that afternoon. Ralph, meanwhile, alone in his house, imagines the happy life he might have had with his son; the thought that his son died in Nicholas's arms tortures him. Ralph realizes he has lost his fortune and can never ply his trade again. Thinking of a final way to hurt his family, Ralph hangs himself, crying as he does so, "Throw me on a dunghill and let me rot there to infect the air!"

Chapters 63–65

The Brothers Cheeryble convene a meeting. Charles tells Kate and Nicholas that they are the children of a worthy gentleman, whereas the Cheerybles themselves were once only "two poor simple-hearted boys, wandering, almost barefoot, to seek our fortunes." He insists that Madeline loves Nicholas and the two must marry; their nephew, Frank, can marry Kate. Nicholas travels to John Browdie's house to tell him the great news. While there he learns that Dotheboys Hall broke up after news of Squeers's imprisonment.

Nicholas buys his childhood home when he becomes a prosperous partner in the firm of Cheeryble and Nickleby, and he and Madeline have many lovely children. Kate and Frank live in a house nearby, and Mrs. Nickleby divides her time between her two sets of grandchildren. The book's last words are devoted to Smike, buried beneath a nearby tree. His grave is ringed by garlands of flowers made by the children, who "spoke low and softly of their poor, dead cousin."

CHARACTERS

Madeline Bray

Nicholas falls in love with Madeline Bray after seeing her at an employment agency. Not knowing her name, Nicholas despairs of ever meeting her until he discovers she is having secret evening meetings with the Brothers Cheeryble. Like Nicholas, she is from the gentler classes but has fallen on hard times and must now support herself and her family. Much drama ensues, including Nicholas's ingenious and heroic plot to save her from a forced marriage to elderly miser Arthur Gride, yet another association brokered by Ralph for his own financial gain. Unbeknownst to Madeline, she will get an inheritance upon marrying, which will then become Gride's, as a wife's property becomes her husband's. Ralph plans to force Gride to give it to him to pay Ralph back for Madeline's father's debts.

Walter Bray

Walter Bray is Madeline's father. Once a dashing man who swept Madeline's mother off her feet, he is now a selfish invalid who forces his daughter to support him financially. He agrees to Ralph's plan to force Madeline to marry Gride. Dickens's portrayal of this narcissistic, self-deluded man is one of the most subtle depictions of evil in all of his works.

John Browdie

John Browdie is a jovial giant of a man who lives in the vicinity of Dotheboys Hall. He is the only kind inhabitant of the area, it seems, and he helps Nicholas and Smike get free of Squeers's clutches on two separate occasions. As the book progresses Nicholas come to regard him as a good friend.

The Brothers Cheeryble

The jolly and rotund Brothers Cheeryble, Charles and Ned, are mirror images of one another. They represent the first example of unselfish kindness Nicholas has seen. The two brothers, twins made wealthy after years of honest hard work, adopt Nicholas after hearing of his troubles, installing his entire family in a lovely cottage and giving Nicholas a full-time job at their happy place of business. Their primary work, however, seems to be giving away money, and Nicholas is soon drawn into that as well. The obese brothers are as freakish in their own way as any of the evil characters, and Dickens has been faulted by critics for making them caricatures as he did with so many of his "good" characters.

Frank Cheeryble

Frank Cheeryble is the nephew of the Brothers Cheeryble, recently returned to London from representing the interests of their firm abroad. Frank soon falls in love with Kate, and in doing so he presents a dilemma for the Nicklebys. Although Kate loves him too, she realizes that she cannot marry him both because she is poor and because it would represent a conflict of interest with Nicholas's employers, the Brothers Cheeryble.

Mr. Vincent Crummles

Mr. Vincent Crummles runs the theatrical company Nicholas and Smike join while escaping from Squeers. Crummles and his troupe embody exactly the type of melodramatic posturing expected from actors in the era. Dickens is often faulted for creating unnaturally dramatic characters, but with the Crummles' theater family he has license to go all out.

Arthur Gride

Arthur Gride is a repulsive old miser whom the beautiful young Madeline Bray is almost forced by her father and Ralph Nickleby to marry.

Sir Mulberry Hawk

Sir Mulberry Hawk is a villain: a lecherous, greedy money-lender who forces himself on Nicholas's sister, Kate. Nicholas beats him, and Hawk vows revenge.

The Kenwigses

The Kenwigs family lives in the same lodging house as Newman Noggs, where Nicholas and Smike come to stay upon their escape from Dotheboys Hall. The Kenwigses mainly provide comic diversion, but their obsession with inheriting money from their one wealthy relative so that their many daughters can catch wealthy husbands illustrates one of the novel's central themes of the family being primarily a financial unit.

Tim Linkinwater

Tim Linkinwater has been the employee of the Brothers Cheeryble for over forty years. The kindly brothers fuss over him and praise him, demonstrating in the process how thoroughly they can take others into their happy family circle, as they soon do with Nicholas and his relatives.

Mr. Mantalini

Mr. Mantalini is the unemployed husband of Kate's employer at the millinery shop. He makes lewd advances toward her.

Madame Mantalini

Madame Mantalini owns the millinery shop where Ralph first secures employment for Kate. Although not as dangerous as Dotheboys Hall, the factory is a grim place for Kate to work, demanding twelve-hour days and subjecting her to the envy of the other women who work there.

Kate Nickleby

Kate Nickleby, the sister of Nicholas, is the second hero of the novel. She is in every way a female version of her brother—noble and self-sacrificing, a second moral compass for the reader in the unstable world of the novel. She is hard-working and always proper to the point of refusing to marry the man she loves because his family has more money than hers.

Mrs. Nickleby

Mrs. Nickleby is Nicholas and Kate's mother. She is quite different from her sensible and smart children, and is given to long rambling monologues that wander wildly from one topic to another. Dickens's portrayal of the workings of Mrs. Nickleby's romance-muddled and utterly disorganized mind is considered to be one of the greatest achievements of *Nicholas Nickleby*. She is a precursor to similar characters in later literature, including Molly Bloom in James Joyce's masterpiece *Ulysses*.

Nicholas Nickleby

Nicholas Nickleby, the hero of the novel, is a handsome, capable, and intelligent young man. He has been raised in a genteel manner in the countryside, and is often referred to as the son of a gentleman (valuable currency in the world of the novel), but he has no employment experience yet. He is, like many of Dickens's "good" characters, rather featureless. Nicholas excels, however, at every job he turns his hand to, and throughout the novel he matures noticeably, becoming able to acknowledge not only good but evil in the actions of those around him, losing his innocence as he grows from a boy into a man able to provide for and protect his family.

Ralph Nickleby

Ralph Nickleby, the uncle of Nicholas and Kate and brother of their deceased father, is a rich miser and money-lender. He is the dark villain of *Nicholas Nickleby*. Infinitely more complex as a literary creation than any of the "good" characters in the novel, Ralph is fully three-dimensional in his evil. Dickens shows the reader, without any moralizing, how Ralph came to be the way he is and fleshes out his thought processes more fully than any of the book's other characters. Ralph is unremittingly vile in his actions, but the reader occasionally gets a momentary glimpse of him softening emotionally, especially toward his niece, Kate, although these impulses are quickly submerged. Ralph judges others solely on their ability to earn money and scoffs at any imputation of good deed-doing, or any motive other than purely selfish gain. Ralph's unraveling into madness at the novel's conclusion is as complex as any psychological depiction Dickens ever attempted.

Newman Noggs
Newman Noggs is Ralph's employee, a formerly well-to-do fellow who was ruined by causes unspecified but probably including alcohol and gambling. Ashamed of his fallen condition, Newman works for Ralph so that he can hide from the world. Newman takes an immediate interest in young Nicholas, and helps him in ways both large and small throughout the novel.

Smike
Smike is an unfortunate inmate of Dotheboys Hall, where he has grown from a small boy into a physically stunted and feebleminded young man of nineteen. He is used as the unpaid servant of the Squeers family. Nicholas takes pity on the boy and takes him with him to London when he leaves Dotheboys Hall. Smike is adopted by Nicholas, Kate, and their mother. In the book's tragic conclusion Smike is revealed to be none other than Ralph's only son, whom Ralph had long presumed dead.

Snawley
Snawley is a weak-willed lackey of both Squeers and Ralph. He is first seen delivering boys into Squeers's possession. Later he pretends to be the father of Smike to wrest him away from Nicholas and Kate.

Mr. Wackford Squeers
Wackford Squeers is the proprietor of Dotheboys Hall, the school for poor boys at which Ralph secures employment for Nicholas. He is a sadistic buffoon with one eye who will stop at nothing to maximize the profit he can gain from his charges, including stealing from them,

beating them, starving them, and neglecting every aspect of their welfare. His is a provisional evil rather than the kind of total evil embodied by Ralph; when circumstances change, Squeers pursues another, less criminal path.

Lord Frederick Verisopht
Lord Frederick Verisopht, while younger than his mentor, Sir Mulberry Hawk, appears to be that man's equal in venality in his immoral behavior toward Kate. However, he has a change of heart toward the novel's conclusion, proving himself to be honorable despite his previous conduct.

THEMES

Class and Privilege
Nicholas Nickleby, like most of Dickens's novels, is explicitly concerned with the human costs of the class system. Nicholas and Kate suffer a tremendous loss of privilege when they lose their father's fortune and sink from the genteel class status of their birth to a sort of purgatory class of the educated poor who must find paying work. They are no longer in charge of their own destinies, but must rely on the kindness of their one relative, Ralph, or on the kindness of strangers to procure work.

Both siblings are forced to do work that is beneath their accustomed class status—work that requires none of their talents or education, but rather hard physical labor and a willingness to abandon all ethical qualms in return for a paycheck. Ralph, in procuring these jobs for the siblings, makes it clear that this is the level appropriate to their new, lower-class status. Nicholas must work for the brutal and dishonest Squeers, helping him brutalize and rob boys even more unfortunate than Nicholas himself. Kate must labor twelve hours per day in the millinery shop of Madame Mantalini, whose husband makes obscene remarks to her, and where she is subjected to the ridicule of the upper-class ladies who patronize the shop.

Exploitation
Nicholas Nickleby is, at heart, a story of exploitation. Kate and Nicholas are unaccustomed to being used in this way for someone else's own advantage, having grown to adulthood in a privileged middle-class family. But with the financial

TOPICS FOR FURTHER STUDY

- Watch the 1947 and 2002 film adaptations of the novel. Discuss these questions as a class: Which film was truer to the novel? Which film gave a more realistic portrayal of Dickensian England? Which film did students enjoy more? Why?

- Nicholas finds the London theater world exciting and rewarding. Using your library and the Internet, find out more about popular theatrical productions in England in the 1830s. Who were the most successful playwrights? What types of audiences did they write for? What did audiences like about their plays? Read a popular play of this period, and present a summary of it to your classmaters.

- *Nicholas Nickleby* was one of the first novels in English to depict the lives of working-class and poor people. Dickens wanted poor people themselves to read his work. Was this possible? Why or why not? Research the subject of literacy in nineteenth-century England to support your answer. Produce a graph or chart examining the rise of literacy among the working classes in England in Dickens's era.

- In *Nicholas Nickleby*, marriages between men and women are based as much on economic necessity as on love. Upon marrying, a woman's entire property and wealth, including inheritances payable upon marriage, became the sole property of her husband. Write a research paper on marriage laws in the United States. Did these marital property laws exist in the United States? If so, when and how were they changed?

ruin of their father, everything changes. Nicholas is thrust into Dotheboys Hall, where miserable, abandoned boys are mistreated and used by the unscrupulous Squeers. Kate is forced to work long hours for low pay and endure the lewd advances of adult men, all for the benefit of the owners of the establishments where she works. Only the most powerful persons, those who depend on no one for money, such as Ralph and the Cheeryble brothers, escape being exploited themselves. These hard lessons are learned by Nicholas and Kate as they come of age and realize that, with very few exceptions, people will exploit others who have less power. Ralph lives by this rule, and although the siblings defeat him in various ways by the end, Ralph seems to have actually won by imbuing them with this worldview.

Coming of Age

Nicholas Nickleby is a coming-of-age story of Nicholas and his sister, Kate. In a coming-of-age story, also called a *bildungsroman*, a young protagonist undergoes several challenges that help strengthen his character and move him along the path to maturity. Nicholas starts out the novel as a handsome and intelligent young man with no experience of life other than a privileged childhood in a pastoral locale. He is all untried potential. This seems to be precisely what his uncle, Ralph Nickleby, hates about him. Ralph sets out to ruin Nicholas by getting hired at Dotheboys Hall, where he will work long hours at miserable tasks, and moreover he will be exposed to people possessing exactly the type of selfishness Ralph believes all people possess.

Nicholas rises nobly to each task set before him, and copes honorably with all of the dishonorable situations into which he is thrown. After the book's first section, in which Nicholas obediently does what he is told to do by his uncle and by his employer, the sadistic schoolmaster Squeers, he shows his first sign of adult maturity by stopping Squeers from abusing a boy entrusted to his care. A true romantic hero, instead of attempting to reason with Squeers or threaten him with legal consequences, Nicholas takes actions he knows will get results: He yells, "Stop!" after which he beats Squeers with a stick and then departs, taking the abused boy Smike along with him.

After this episode, Nicholas shows his increasing maturity when he admits that his uncle is untrustworthy and may be in fact dangerous to his sister and mother, whom he has left in Ralph's care. Nicholas is also now cautious about whom he chooses as an employer, rejecting a job with an impossibly demanding member of Parliament and quitting the Crummles' theater when he senses that Kate may be in danger. His coming of age is complete when he is no longer shocked at how low people will stoop to get what they want.

Kate Nickleby presents a second, parallel coming-of-age story in the novel. She too must come to accept the fact of human evil in the form of her uncle, Ralph, as he sets her up with unendurable work, installs her and her mother in unsafe lodgings, and, worst of all, compromises her reputation (and with it her chance to make a good marriage), all for his own financial gain. Kate, a second romantic hero, proves herself to be honorable and good, refusing to be compromised by either her own poverty or by the grasping and selfish people around her.

STYLE

Romance

Nicholas Nickleby is often described as Dickens's first romance (he had previously been primarily a journalist). The novel has all the hallmarks of a romantic novel, with an unabashedly idealized hero (and heroine) and a coming-of-age story that contains many theatrical, almost melodramatic, scenes and important themes. Nicholas nobly overcomes all the painful trials set before him, finding his way in the world despite tremendous setbacks. He discovers a creditable way to earn a living to support his family, defeats a powerful villain, rescues the girl of his dreams, and, essential to a romance, lives happily ever after with her.

Antihero

Nicholas Nickleby is filled with numerous heroes and antiheroes. Antiheroes are characters who have some of the qualities of a villain but are at heart motivated by some of the good impulses of a conventional hero. This novel contains several traditional antiheroes, characters who are physically weak or deformed, have no ideals to live up to, and feel they can have no real effect on the world. Newman Noggs is a prime example, with his bulbous nose, spasmodically twitching limbs, and hopeless life as Ralph's underpaid, abused employee. Noggs works for Ralph even though he hates him, but secretly helps Nicholas on his

1839 illustration from Nicholas Nickleby. *Original caption reads "Mr. Ralph Nickleby's first visit to his poor relations."* (Hablot Knight Browne / The Bridgeman Art Library / Getty Images)

journey. Another antihero is the wealthy Lord Frederick Verisopht, the protégé of Sir Mulberry Hawk. Verisopht seems content to drift along in his venal mentor's shadow, echoing his inanities and imitating Hawk's cruel exploitation of poor, unprotected Kate Nickleby with no awareness of how his actions will affect her. In the end, however, he dies honorably. Because Dickens tended to create more multidimensional, interesting villains than he did heroes, even the villain Ralph displays some characteristics of an antihero, especially when he feels pangs of guilt over his treatment of Kate.

The Character as Foil

Nicholas Nickleby is also filled with figures who serve as foils for other characters. A foil is a character whose physical or psychological qualities contrast with, and therefore highlight, the corresponding qualities of another character.

The primary examples in *Nicholas Nickleby* are the many characters who play this role for Nicholas himself. First, Ralph is his foil. While Nicholas thinks of the safety and happiness of others, Ralph thinks only of his own material gain. Sir Mulberry Hawk also serves as Nicholas's foil. While Nicholas is willing to give up Madeline, the girl he loves, because their respective financial situations would create discomfort for others, Hawk pursues Kate with no awareness of the irreparable damage he is doing to her reputation or even of the fact that she detests him. The Cheeryble brothers also serve as powerful foils for Ralph in their bottomless generosity and compassion—even for him.

HISTORICAL CONTEXT

Reform in England

Dickens wrote *Nicholas Nickleby* in 1838 and 1839, at the end of a turbulent decade in Britain. British workers had fought for an extension of the right to vote early in the decade, but the Reform Act of 1832 in actuality disenfranchised some workers. The Poor Law Amendment Act, passed in 1834, all but ended "outdoor relief," or payments to supplement the income of the poor, and created harsh workhouses meant to be an alternative only for those facing starvation. Then in 1837 unemployment spread through industrial districts as a result of an economic depression that gripped the country. A large-scale workers movement called the Chartist movement emerged from all of these causes to push for universal manhood suffrage, the secret ballot, the abolition of property requirements to be elected to Parliament as well as pay for its members, and annual elections. While the Chartist movement ultimately failed to achieve its goals, it was the first large-scale workers' political movement—a prospect that middle- and upper-class Britons found deeply threatening.

Dickens, with his own family history of time spent in debtor's prison, must have had these developing workers' movements in mind as he explored issues of work and class in *Nicholas Nickleby*. He portrayed his protagonists sympathetically as they worked for long hours in abysmal conditions. For example, he condemns the conditions under which Kate Nickleby works: six twelve-hour days each week, with no control over her work or conditions and employed only at the whim of her managers and employers.

The existence of the infamous "Yorkshire schools" was another social problem that preoccupied Dickens as he wrote *Nicholas Nickleby*. These institutions were located in the countryside some distance from London. There poor boys were sent to live. Dickens, who began his career as a journalist, was indignant upon hearing about the conditions the boys endured—scanty food, cold and filthy lodgings, physical beatings and other humiliations, and no real education. Approximately twenty of these schools existed, and many of them had been in operation for over a hundred years when they came to Dickens's attention. In advertisements in London papers, they boasted "no vacations" for the young inmates. A schoolmaster named William Shaw, who became the model for Squeers, the sadistic schoolmaster in the novel, had been sued in 1823 by the parents of two boys who went blind under Shaw's care. At the trial, it was revealed that at least ten boys had gone blind there due to lack of medical treatment.

In 1838, just prior to beginning *Nicholas Nickleby*, Dickens visited Shaw's school. Dickens posed as a man seeking such a school for a widowed friend's children, but Shaw was evasive. Dickens then went to the graveyard, where he found the graves of twenty-five boys who had died from Shaw's mistreatment during the past twenty years. *Nicholas Nickleby* has the rare distinction of being a novel that actually changed the world: due to its enormous popularity, the book single-handedly caused the Yorkshire schools to close.

Realistic Novels of the Working Class

In the decade during which Dickens began publishing, there was a lull in the great writing produced in Britain. This lull contributed to Dickens's enormous and immediate popularity, and also allowed him the freedom to write in a way that was new in both style and content. Instead of writing about the upper classes, Dickens wanted to represent working-class people; he sought to reproduce their speech and dialect and filled tens of thousands of pages with their hopes, fears, and triumphs. British novelists who followed Dickens in the 1840s, 1850s, and 1860s—including George Eliot, Trollope, Wilkie Collins, and both Brontë sisters—all owed a direct debt to Dickens for the pathways of acceptable subject matter he opened before them. They were each by turns grateful and resentful, but they were always keenly aware of his influence.

COMPARE
&
CONTRAST

- **1830s:** Charles Dickens is among the first authors in English to write about and for poor people, whose experiences had previously been considered unworthy of serious literary attention.

  Today: Hundred of thousands of English-language novels depict the hopes, struggles, and triumphs of poor and working-class people, whose lives are considered by many to be as important as the lives of those with more wealth and power.

- **1830s:** The working class agitates for the development of workers' unions in Britain, to regulate working hours and conditions, but few unions exist.

  Today: British law gives all workers the right to join a union. Nearly seven million workers are represented by the Trades Union Congress. Working conditions and work

hours are regulated by law. Laws also ensure that workers will receive insurance, overtime pay, vacations, and retirement benefits.

- **1830s:** Tens of thousands of people die of "consumption" (known in modern times as tuberculosis). It is called "the wasting disease" because of the way it very slowly eroded its victims' health. At this time there is no cure for consumption.

  Today: Antibacterial drugs are today very effective at eradicating all symptoms of tuberculosis. With a full regimen of treatment, a patient can be fully cured in approximately six weeks. However, an estimated three million people die from tuberculosis worldwide every year, particularly in developing countries where access to the lifesaving drugs can be limited.

CRITICAL OVERVIEW

Nicholas Nickleby sold fifty thousand copies of its first installment and maintained steady sales throughout its full run. Its popularity, however, has not held up over time. The book is not regarded as one of Dickens's great novels but only, as novelist Jane Smiley puts it in her biography of Dickens, "the first truly characteristic novel of the most characteristic novelist of the Victorian period."

Nicholas Nickleby was Dickens's first romantic novel, a definitive move away from the journalism background that had been reflected in the more sketchlike form of his two previous novels, *The Pickwick Papers* and *Oliver Twist*. "'The Pickwick Papers'," writes critic G. K. Chesterton, "may be called an extension of one of his bright sketches. 'Oliver Twist' may be called an extension of one of his gloomy ones." *Nicholas Nickleby* was itself an extension of his two previous novels. In his introduction to the Knopf

Everyman edition of the novel, Dickens scholar John Carey writes, "Dickens wanted his new novel to combine the strengths of *Pickwick* and *Oliver*, and to do something larger than either of them. *Nicholas Nickleby*, then, gives us a bookload of Dickens's art at its most dynamically youthful, ambitious, abundant and optimistic. It allows us to identify the factors that shaped and limited him as a novelist."

In fact, in *Nicholas Nickleby* Dickens first adopts the form he will use in all of his future masterpieces: a coming-of-age story about a protagonist's search for fulfillment both in romance and in livelihood. In this sense, the novel was a definitive break from his earlier work and a roadmap of the works that came later. Jane Smiley sees the novel as a transitionary one: "[*Nicholas Nickleby*] became one of Dickens's least read works, a high-spirited but not quite successful transitional novel in which Dickens began to try out the ideas and methods that would bear fruit a few years later."

David Threlfall and Roger Rees in the Royal Shakespeare Company's production of Nicholas Nickleby *in London, 1980* (*Nobby Clark | Hulton Archive | Getty Images*)

CRITICISM

Melanie Bush

Bush is a writer and journalist. In this essay, she discusses Dickens's evolution from journalist to novelist and explores some of the possible reasons Dickens chose fiction as his means of fighting social injustice.

Nicholas Nickleby was Dickens's third novel, after *The Pickwick Papers* and *Oliver Twist*, and it is considered his first classic romantic novel. This latter point is important because *Nicholas Nickleby* marked an important turning point for Dickens, the definitive fork in the road at which he became a writer of fiction rather than journalism, and thereby changed the face of literature forever.

Dickens had been a successful journalist in his so far rather short writing career. (He was only

> DICKENS WAS GAMBLING ON HIS BELIEF THAT THE PUBLIC WAS READY FOR A NEW KIND OF NOVEL, ONE THAT ADDRESSED SOCIAL PROBLEMS AND DEPICTED THE LIVES OF THE POOR IN A REALISTIC WAY."

twenty-six when *Nicholas Nickleby* was published in 1838.) A collection of his journalistic pieces from London newspapers, *Sketches by Boz*, had been published to enormous acclaim two years earlier. The two novels that followed, *The Pickwick Papers* and *Oliver Twist*, are characterized by critics as having the quality of stories stitched together, as literary rather than journalistic "sketches." *Nicholas Nickleby* would change that pattern.

The novel was born, however, from Dickens's journalistic instinct. Dickens had read in the newspapers about the infamous Yorkshire schools. These were institutions located in a rural area outside of London where boys, poor, illegitimate, or otherwise unwanted by their families, were sent to live. Dickens was incensed upon hearing about the lives of these children: scant food, cold and filthy lodgings, physical beatings—and no real education. London papers had followed the story of a schoolmaster named William Shaw, who had been sued by the parents of two boys who went blind under his care. At the trial it was revealed that at least ten boys had gone blind there due to lack of medical treatment. In 1838, just prior to beginning *Nicholas Nickleby*, Dickens visited Shaw's school, posing as a man seeking such a place for a widowed friend's children. Shaw was evasive. Dickens then proceeded to the graveyard, where he discovered twenty-five graves of boys who had died at Shaw's establishment. As a writer, Dickens felt compelled to do something.

What was it that led Dickens to the decision to draw the public's attention to the Yorkshire schools through fiction rather than through journalism? Using the form of a novel to discuss the plight of the poor was a new idea at the time. Dickens was gambling on his belief that the public was ready for a new kind of novel, one that addressed social problems and depicted the lives

WHAT DO I READ NEXT?

- Charlotte Brontë' *Jane Eyre* (1847) was published nine years after *Nicholas Nickleby* and concerns many of the same social issues, including the plight of poor children and romances foiled by discrepancies in the class status of the lovers. Although unremittingly serious in tone, as opposed to the lighter *Nickleby*, *Jane Eyre* offers the point of view of a female protagonist making her own way in a difficult world.

- *David Copperfield*, published in 1850, is considered by many critics to be Dickens's finest novel. It, too, is a coming-of-age story. A young man, thrown into poverty by his father's death, travels through the many levels of Victorian society to find his place. This book, more than most of Dickens's other works, takes as its central theme the qualities a man needs to develop for true success in life and also the importance of choosing an appropriate marriage partner.

- Another classic Dickens novel, *Great Expectations* (1861), follows the story of a young boy from a poor family who acquires a mysterious wealthy benefactor. The book details Pip's journey through the social strata of Victorian England. This is one of the jewels in Dickens's string of masterpieces that use a poor child as the hero.

- Daniel Pool presents many fascinating facts about daily life in Victorian England in his book *What Jane Austen Ate and Charles Dickens Knew*, published in 1993. The book, which categorizes information under headings such as "The Public World," "The Private World," and "The Grim World" (the latter covering such issues as orphans, jail, and death), is a great resource for understanding the many differences between daily life in Dickens's era and today.

- *Emma* (2006), by Kaoru Mori, is a Japanese *manga*, or comic book, set in Victorian England. It presents a romantic tale of love between an upper-class boy and a maid. Manga allows the author great power in depicting emotional changes with subtle shifts of line and tone, and Mori has clearly studied the period in great detail.

- In Michael Livi's young adult novel, *The Whispering Road* (2005), two impoverished children search for the mother who abandoned them. On their journey, they encounter many colorful characters and experience the harsh conditions and cruelty often meted out to poor children in Dickens's time.

---

of the poor in a realistic way. This was partly based on the rising rate of literacy among the working class, who had helped make his two previous novels a huge financial success. But perhaps it was also based on his belief that fiction might be a better way to tell the truth about social issues than journalism. Maybe Dickens realized that a writer could explore these issues more effectively in a novel than he could by using what might seem the more direct form of journalism.

In nearly nine hundred pages, Dickens had an unparalleled chance to delve very deeply into

whatever aspects of Yorkshire schools that he chose; he could not only describe the conditions at the schools in great detail but he could create enormous sympathy for the boys interred there by personalizing their stories through characters such as Smike. In a novel, Dickens could make the experiences of a single boy real to a reader in a way that journalism, with its generalizing tendencies, its extreme brevity of form, and its insistence on an "objective" tone, could never accomplish.

The emotional as well as intellectual understanding of the boys' plight that readers took away from *Nicholas Nickleby* spurred such wide-spread indignation and public outcry that the Yorkshire schools were rapidly shuttered. Dickens's gamble paid off. *Nicholas Nickleby* has the rare distinction of being a novel that actually changed the world. Could a journalist, even one with as profound a writing talent as Charles Dickens's, have created the same result through the medium of journalism? Perhaps the novel was Dickens's literary equivalent of Nicholas's heroic attempt to single-handedly end the abuse of boys at Dotheboys Hall. Instead of threatening legal action or invoking moral precepts, Nicholas simply yells "Stop!" and beats the schoolmaster with a stick. The nine hundred pages of *Nicholas Nickleby* are Dickens's outraged cry of "Stop!" The whole novel is Dickens's stick.

Another social issue of the time that Dickens explores thoroughly—one might say relentlessly—in *Nicholas Nickleby* is the family as an essentially economic structure. Throughout the novel, individual family members are depicted as units of income, either potential income, produced income, or lost income. This was a staple trope of Victorian literature, as it was a reality of Victorian life, and other British writers of the period based their dramas around this issue, including the Brontë sisters, George Eliot, and Jane Austen.

In *Nicholas Nickleby* readers are made to understand the economic basis for the family from multiple perspectives, something that again would be difficult to do in journalism form. At the beginning of the novel, Nicholas and his sister, accompanied by their mother, have arrived in London to seek financial help from their Uncle Ralph after their father has literally died of grief over the loss of his wealth. As the book progresses Nicholas believes he cannot marry Madeline, the girl he loves, because she is to be married to a rich miser to support her father's flamboyant lifestyle. Later Kate comes to the agonizing realization that she cannot marry the man she loves because of differences in their financial status, and also because he is the nephew of Nicholas's employers, which could interfere with Nicholas's livelihood, essential to support their mother.

There is also an elaborate subplot involving a family called the Kenwigses that Dickens seems to have added simply to reinforce this idea of the family as an economic unit. During repeated visits to the Kenwigs home, the reader is made privy to the family's fervent hope, almost an obsession, that their one wealthy relative, the middle-aged yet unmarried Mr. Lillyvick, will leave his fortune to the Kenwigs daughters for use as dowries to catch rich husbands. When Mr. Lillyvick abruptly marries an actress the family is devastated; they had shared their food and drink with Mr. Lillyvick for years in the most explicit hopes of inheriting his fortune. When the actress just as abruptly leaves Lillyvick, the Kenwigses receive him back only after he solemnly promises that no such frivolities will occur again. "I shall, tomorrow morning, settle upon your children, and make payable to the survivors of them when they come of age and marry, that money which I once meant to leave 'em in my will," Lillyvick swears. Only then is he received back into the bosom of his loving family.

Nicholas Nickleby, in the view of Dickens scholar G. K. Chesterton, represents the precise point at which Dickens decided to write novels rather than journalistic "sketches." Chesterton believes that Dickens reached this decision because he realized he wanted to write "a seminal and growing romance" that only a novel could contain. In his own life Dickens had reached a thrilling moment: He had just married Catherine Hogarth, the pretty eldest daughter of a family whom Dickens passionately admired, and he was also, according to Chesterton, "for the really first time, sure that he was going to be at least some kind of success." Chesterton asserts that *Nickleby* represents the "supreme point of Dickens's spring.... This book coincided with his resolution to be a great novelist and his final belief that he could be one."

And *Nicholas Nickleby* is a novel, rather than a collection of sketches, by virtue of many typically romantic characteristics. It is Dickens's first novel, Chesterton observes, to include "a proper and dignified romantic hero; which means, of course, a very chivalrous young donkey." The young donkey, Nicholas, goes on to slay more than one fearsome dragon on his way to winning the princess. The book contains many dragons—Ralph, Squeers, Hawk, Madeline's father—all of them older men whom Nicholas must forcibly remove from his path toward manhood. And this coming-of-age story also rewards the reader with multiple happy endings; all of the good characters live happily ever after while the bad ones meet fates commensurate to their wickedness.

None of this, of course, could be accomplished through journalism. While Dickens used the novel to explore themes that had concerned him as a journalist, he could never have used journalism to express the ideas that consumed him as a novelist. *Nicholas Nickleby* marks the moment this transition occurred. Had it not, says Chesterton, "we might have lost all Dickens's novels; we might have lost altogether Dickens the novelist."

Source: Melanie Bush, Critical Essay on *Nicholas Nickleby*, in *Novels for Students*, Gale, Cengage Learning, 2010.

G. K. Chesterton

In this piece, Dickens scholar Chesterton discusses Nicholas Nickleby *as Dickens's first romantic novel.*

Romance is perhaps the highest point of human expression, except indeed religion, to which it is closely allied. Romance resembles religion especially in this, that it is not only a simplification but a shortening of existence. Both romance and religion see everything as it were fore-shortened; they see everything in an abrupt and fantastic perspective, coming to a point. It is the whole essence of perspective that it comes quickly to a point. Similarly, religion comes to a point—to the point. For instance, religion is always insisting on the shortness of human life. But it does not insist on the shortness of human life as the pessimists insist on the shortness of human life. Pessimism insists on the shortness of human life in order to show that life is valueless. Religion insists on the shortness of human life in order to show that life is frightfully valuable—is almost horribly valuable. Pessimism says that life is so short that it gives nobody a chance; religion says that life is so short that it gives everybody his final chance. In the first case the word brevity means futility. In the second case the word brevity means opportunity. But the case is even stronger than this. Religion shortens everything. Religion shortens even eternity. Where science, submitting to the false standard of time, sees evolution, which is slow, religion sees creation, which is sudden. Philosophically speaking, the process is neither slow nor quick, since we have nothing to compare it with. Religion prefers to think of it as quick. For religion the flowers shoot up suddenly like rockets. For religion the mountains are lifted up suddenly like waves. Those who quote that fine passage which says that in God's sight a

> IF IN THE SAME WAY THERE IS A SUPREME POINT OF SPRING, 'NICHOLAS NICKLEBY' IS THE SUPREME POINT OF DICKENS'S SPRING."

thousand years are as yesterday that is passed and as a watch in the night, do not realize the full force of the meaning. To God a thousand years are not only a watch but an exciting watch. For God time goes at a gallop, as it does to a man reading a good tale.

All this is equally true for romance. Romance is a shortening and sharpening of the human difficulty. Where you and I have to vote against a man, or write (rather feebly) against a man, or sign illegible petitions against a man, romance does for him what we should really like to see done; it knocks him down; it shortens the slow process of historical justice. All romances consist of three characters. Other characters may be introduced; but those other characters are certainly mere scenery as far as the romance is concerned. They are bushes that wave rather excitedly; they are posts that stand up with a certain pride; they are correctly painted rocks that frown very correctly; but they are all landscape—they are all a background. In every pure romance there are three living and moving characters. For the sake of argument they may be called St George and the Dragon and the Princess. In every romance there must be the twin elements of loving and fighting. In every romance there must be the three characters; there must be the Princess, who is a thing to be loved; there must be the Dragon, who is a thing to be fought; and there must be St George, who is a thing that both loves and fights. There have been many symptoms of cynicism and decay in our modern civilization; there have been many indications of an idle morality cutting up life to please itself, and an idle philosophy doubting first whether truth is accepted and then doubting whether truth is at all. But of all the signs of modern feebleness, of lack of grasp on morals as they actually must be, there has been none quite so silly or so dangerous as this: that the philosophers of today have started to divide loving from fighting and to put them into opposite camps. There could be no worse sign than that a man, even Nietzsche, can be found to say that we should go in for fighting instead of loving. There can be no worse sign than that a man should be found, even Tolstoy, to tell us that we should go in for loving instead of fighting. The two things imply each other; they implied each other in the old romance and in the old religion, which were the two permanent things of humanity. You cannot love a thing without wanting to fight for it. You cannot fight without something to fight for. To love a thing without wishing to fight for it is not love at all; it is lust. It may be an airy, philosophical and disinterested lust; it may be, so to speak, a virgin lust; but it is lust, because it is wholly self-indulgence and invites no attack. On the other hand, fighting for a thing without loving it is not even fighting; it can only be called a kind of horse-play that is occasionally fatal. Wherever human nature is human and unspoilt by any special sophistry, there exists this natural kinship between loving and fighting, and that natural kinship is called romance. It comes upon a man especially in the great hour of youth; and every man who has ever been young at all has felt, if only for a moment, this ultimate and poetic paradox. He has felt that loving the world was the same thing as fighting the world. It was at the very moment that he offered to love everybody he also offered to fight everybody. To almost every man that can be called a man this especial moment of the romantic culmination has come. In the first resort the man wished to live a romance. In the second resort, in the last and worst resort, he was content to write a romance.

Now there is a certain moment when this element enters independently into the life of Dickens. There is a particular time when we can see him suddenly realize that he wants to write a romance and nothing else. In reading his letters, in appreciating his character, this point emerges clearly enough. He was full of the afterglow of his marriage; he was still young and psychologically ignorant; above all, he was now, for the really first time, sure that he was going to be at least some kind of success. There is, I repeat, a certain point at which one feels that Dickens will either begin to write romances or go off on something different altogether. This crucial point in his life is marked by 'Nicholas Nickleby'.

Everything has a supreme moment and a crucial; that is where the poor old evolutionists go wrong. I suppose that there is an instant of midsummer as there is an instant of midnight. If

in the same way there is a supreme point of spring, 'Nicholas Nickleby' is the supreme point of Dickens's spring. I do not mean that it is the best book that he wrote in his youth. 'Pickwick' is a better book. I do not mean that it contains more brilliant characters than any of the other books in his youth. The 'Old Curiosity Shop' contains at least two more brilliant characters. But I mean that this book coincided with his resolution to be a great novelist and his final belief that he could be one. Henceforward his books are novels, very commonly bad novels. Previously they have not really been novels at all. There are many indications of the change I mean. Here is one, for instance, which is more or less final. 'Nicholas Nickleby' is Dickens's first romantic novel because it is his first novel with a proper and dignified romantic hero; which means, of course, a very chivalrous young donkey. The hero of 'Pickwick' is an old man. The hero of 'Oliver Twist' is a child. Even after 'Nicholas Nickleby' this non-romantic custom continued. The 'Old Curiosity Shop' has no hero in particular. The hero of 'Barnaby Rudge' is a lunatic. But Nicholas Nickleby is a proper, formal and ceremonial hero. He has no psychology; he has not even any particular character; but he is made deliberately a hero—young, poor, brave, unimpeachable and ultimately triumphant. He is, in short, the hero. Mr Vincent Crummles has a colossal intellect; and I always have a fancy that under all his pomposity he saw things more keenly than he allowed others to see. The moment he saw Nicholas Nickleby, almost in rags and limping along the high road, he engaged him (you will remember) as first walking gentleman. He was right. Nobody could possibly be more of a first walking gentleman than Nicholas Nickleby was. He was the first walking gentleman before he went on to the boards of Mr Vincent Crummles's theatre, and he remained the first walking gentleman after he had come off.

Now this romantic method involves a certain element of climax which to us appears crudity. Nicholas Nickleby, for instance, wanders through the world; he takes a situation as assistant to a Yorkshire schoolmaster; he sees an act of tyranny of which he strongly disapproves; he cries out "Stop!" in a voice that makes the rafters ring; he thrashes the schoolmaster within an inch of his life; he throws the schoolmaster away like an old cigar, and he goes away. The modern intellect is positively prostrated and flattened by this rapid and romantic way of righting wrongs. If a modern philanthropist came to Dotheboys Hall I fear he would not employ the simple, sacred and truly Christian solution of beating Mr Squeers with a stick. I fancy he would petition the Government to appoint a Royal Commission to inquire into Mr Squeers. I think he would every now and then write letters to newspapers reminding people that in spite of all appearances to the contrary there was a Royal Commission to inquire into Mr Squeers. I agree that he might even go the length of calling a crowded meeting in St. James's Hall on the subject of the best policy with regard to Mr Squeers. At this meeting some very heated and daring speakers might even go the length of alluding sternly to Mr Squeers. Occasionally even hoarse voices from the back of the hall might ask (in vain) what was going to be done with Mr Squeers. The Royal Commission would report about three years afterwards and would say that many things had happened which were certainly most regrettable; that Mr Squeers was the victim of a bad system; that Mrs Squeers was also the victim of a bad system; but that the man who sold Squeers's cane had really acted with great indiscretion and ought to be spoken to kindly. Something like this would be what, after four years, the Royal Commission would have said; but it would not matter in the least what the Royal Commission had said, for by that time the philanthropists would be off on a new tack and the world would have forgotten all about Dotheboys Hall and everything connected with it. By that time the philanthropists would be petitioning Parliament for another Royal Commission; perhaps a Royal Commission to inquire into whether Mr Mantalini was extravagant with his wife's money; perhaps a commission to inquire into whether Mr Vincent Crummles kept the Infant Phenomenon short by means of gin.

If we wish to understand the spirit and the period of 'Nicholas Nickleby' we must endeavour to comprehend and to appreciate the old more decisive remedies, or, if we prefer to put it so, the old more desperate remedies. Our fathers had a plain sort of pity; if you will, a gross and coarse pity. They had their own sort of sentimentalism. They were quite willing to weep over Smike. But it certainly never occurred to them to weep over Squeers. Even those who opposed the French war opposed it exactly in the same way as their enemies opposed the French soldiers. They fought with fighting. Charles Fox was full of horror at the bitterness and the useless bloodshed; but if any one had insulted him over the matter, he would

have gone out and shot him in a duel as coolly as any of his contemporaries. All their interference was heroic interference. All their legislation was heroic legislation. All their remedies were heroic remedies. No doubt they were often narrow and often visionary. No doubt they often looked at a political formula when they should have looked at an elemental fact. No doubt they were pedantic in some of their principles and clumsy in some of their solutions. No doubt, in short, they were all very wrong; and no doubt we are the people, and wisdom shall die with us. But when they saw something which in their eyes, such as they were, really violated their morality, such as it was, then they did not cry 'Investigate!' They did not cry 'Educate!' They did not cry 'Improve!' They did not cry 'Evolve!' Like Nicholas Nickleby they cried 'Stop!' And it did stop.

This is the first mark of the purely romantic method; the swiftness and simplicity with which St. George kills the dragon. The second mark of it is exhibited here as one of the weaknesses of 'Nicholas Nickleby'. I mean the tendency in the purely romantic story to regard the heroine merely as something to be won; to regard the princess solely as something to be saved from the dragon. The father of Madeline Bray is really a very respectable dragon. His selfishness is suggested with much more psychological tact and truth than that of any other of the villains that Dickens described about this time. But his daughter is merely the young woman with whom Nicholas is in love. I do not care a rap about Madeline Bray. Personally I should have preferred it to have Cecilia Bobster. Here is one real point where the Victorian romance falls below the Elizabethan romantic drama. Shakespeare always made his heroines heroic as well as his heroes.

In Dickens's actual literary career it is this romantic quality in 'Nicholas Nickleby' that is most important. It is his first definite attempt to write a young and chivalrous novel. In this sense the comic characters and the comic scenes are secondary; and indeed the comic characters and the comic scenes, admirable as they are, could never be considered as in themselves superior to such characters and such scenes in many of the other books. But in themselves how admirable they are. Mr Crummles and the whole of his theatrical business is an admirable case of that first and most splendid quality in Dickens—I mean the art of making something which in life we call pompous and dull, becoming in literature pompous and delightful. I have remarked before that nearly every one of the amusing characters of Dickens is in reality a great fool. But I might go further. Almost every one of his amusing characters is in reality a great bore. The very people that we fly to in Dickens are the very people that we fly from in life. And there is more in Crummles than the mere entertainment of his solemnity and his interrupted tedium. The enormous seriousness with which he takes his art is always an exact touch in regard to the unsuccessful artist. If an artist is successful, everything then depends upon a dilemma of his moral character. If he is a mean artist success will make him a society man. If he is a magnanimous artist, success will make him an ordinary man. But only as long as he is unsuccessful will he be an unfathomable and serious artist, like Mr Crummles. Dickens was always particularly good at expressing thus the treasures that belong to those who do not succeed in this world. There are vast prospects and splendid songs in the point of view of the typically unsuccessful man; if all the used-up actors and spoilt journalists and broken clerks could give a chorus, it would be a wonderful chorus in praise of the world. But these unsuccessful men commonly cannot even speak. Dickens is the voice of them, and a very divine voice; because he was perhaps the only one of these unsuccessful men that was ever successful.

Source: G. K. Chesterton, "Appendix," in *Nicholas Nickleby*, Knopf, 1993, pp. 835–843.

John Carey

In this excerpt, Carey, a Dickens scholar, discusses the use of deformity as a metaphor in Nicholas Nickleby.

When Dickens started writing *Nicholas Nickleby* on 6 February 1838—the day before his twenty-sixth birthday—he was riding the crest of a wave. Two years earlier he had been a comparative nobody—just a fairly successful journalist who had recently bundled together some of his magazine and newspaper articles to make a book, *Sketches by Boz* (1836). It was *Pickwick Papers* that catapulted him to fame. Within a twelvemonth of its first number appearing, on 31 March 1836, each monthly instalment was selling 40,000 copies, and Pickwick and Sam Weller had become household names.

During the same triumphant twelve months Dickens had married pretty Kate Hogarth, had

> THE FACT THAT PHYSICAL DEFORMITY IS SO WIDELY USED IN *NICHOLAS NICKLEBY* TO AROUSE COMIC INTEREST, AND THAT IT IS NOT A REAL HANDICAP, HAS AN UNFORTUNATE EFFECT FROM THE VIEWPOINT OF THE NOVEL'S INTEREST IN SOCIAL REFORM."

been appointed editor of the prosperous *Bentley's Miscellany*, had moved into a substantial family house in genteel Doughty Street, and had become a father—his first son, Charley, was born on 6 January 1837. Next month the first number of his new story, *Oliver Twist*, came out, and it was soon clear that he had another phenomenal success on his hands.

He was still writing regular monthly episodes of *Oliver* when he set to work on *Nicholas Nickleby*. It had been hanging over him since he signed the contract for it with the publishers Chapman and Hall back in November 1837, and he was glad to break the ice. 'I *have* begun!' he announced jubilantly to his friend John Forster, on 7 February 1838, 'And what is more I can go on.' His confidence is reflected even in his handwriting. In mid-February 1838 it undergoes a major change—the capital 'M' (as in the self-approving pronouns 'Me' and 'My') drops its old schoolboy form and becomes more flamboyant. He was right to feel on top of the world. *Nicholas Nickleby's* first number sold almost 50,000 copies on its first day (1 April 1838). The next evening Dickens and Kate met Forster for a gala dinner at the Star and Garter in Richmond to celebrate the book's success and their second wedding anniversary.

Dickens wanted his new novel to combine the strengths of *Pickwick* and *Oliver*, and to do something larger than either of them. *Nicholas Nickleby,* then, gives us a bookload of Dickens' art at its most dynamically youthful, ambitious, abundant and optimistic. It also allows us to identify the factors that shaped and limited him as a novelist.

A good starting-point, if we want to locate what he could already do supremely well, is the description in Chapter 2 of Golden Square, where

Ralph Nickleby lives. Golden Square was, and is a real place, just north of Piccadilly Circus, to the west of Soho. Watching Dickens the journalist demarcate it, we can understand why Walter Bagehot was to dub him 'a special correspondent for posterity'.

> Although a few members of the graver professions live about Golden Square, it is not exactly in anybody's way to or from anywhere. It is one of the squares that have been; a quarter of the town that has gone down in the world, and taken to letting lodgings. Many of its first and second floors are let, furnished, to single gentlemen; and it takes boarders besides. It is a great resort of foreigners. The dark-complexioned men who wear large rings, and heavy watchguards, and bushy whiskers, and who congregate under the Opera colonnade, and about the box-office in the season, between four and five in the afternoon, when they give away the orders [free tickets],—all live in Golden Square, or within a street of it. Two or three violins and a wind instrument from the Opera band reside within its precincts. Its boarding-houses are musical, and the notes of pianos and harps float in the evening time round the head of the mournful statue, the guardian genius of a little wilderness of shrubs, in the centre of the square. On a summer's night, windows are thrown open, and groups of swarthy mustachioed men are seen by the passer-by lounging at the casements and smoking fearfully. Sounds of gruff voices practising vocal music invade the evening's silence; and the fumes of choice tobacco scent in the air. There, snuff and cigars, and German pipes and flutes, and violins, and violincellos, divide the supremacy between them. It is the region of song and smoke.

The assurance of Dickens' writing here is apparent. It seems extraordinarily mature, when we compare it with much of the later writing in *Nicholas Nickleby*. It looks back to *Sketches by Boz*, but it also strikes a note of fascination with, and wistful detachment from, the urban scene that was to go on reverberating in literature up to the modernist period. The atmosphere of T. S. Eliot's 'Portrait of a Lady', with its street piano and attenuated violins, its tobacco smoke and its 'evening yellow and rose', seems redolent of Golden Square.

But if we analyse the factors that make the Golden Square passage at once so precise and so evocative, we find that they are not entirely congenial to a novel. The stance is that of an outside observer or passer-by. He glimpses other people's lives through open windows on summer evenings. We notice that he does not hear what they say.

He hears their gruff voices practising vocal music. He hears their musical instruments. But he is cut off from their conversation by language as well as by distance. They are foreigners. Though he is extremely attentive to their external features—their rings, watchguards, the tobacco they smoke—they remain unknown. Also, the passage reveals an imagination that is fascinated by the chance and the transitory—by the variegation that goes with the shabby and down-at-heel: houses let off into lodgings, musicians practising, moth-eaten shrubs in a town square. In other words, this is a writer for whom interest lies in oddities and incidentals, and who may find it hard to tackle the sustained and developed strategies of narration that a novel demands.

The problem for Dickens, at this early stage in his career, was, I would suggest, how to retain the intriguing, varied quality that he finds in Golden Square when he looked at people rather than at a locality—when he looked at people, that is, more closely than just through house windows on a summer evening. How could he make people meet his imaginative needs when they were no longer eye-catching bits of a townscape, but characters engaged in a narrative?

The first answer that seems to have come to Dickens was that he should make them deformed. Physical deformity could give them, he seems to have felt, some of the intriguing irregularity that Golden Square possessed. Several prominent characters in *Nicholas Nickleby* suffer from physical handicaps, which are exhibited to amuse us. Almost the first thing we learn about Wackford Squeers is that he has only one eye, and no ordinary eye: 'The eye he had was unquestionably useful, but decidedly not ornamental, being of a greenish grey, and in shape resembling the fanlight of a street door. The blank side of his face was much wrinkled and puckered up, which gave him a very sinister appearance, especially when he smiled.' Squeers is physically odd in other ways. His hair stands on end, his clothes do not fit: 'His coat sleeves being a great deal too long, and his trousers a great deal too short, he appeared ill at ease in his clothes, and as if he were in a perpetual state of astonishment at finding himself so respectable.'

The other members of the Squeers family are also physically imperfect. The son, Wackford Squeers junior, is grotesquely fat: 'Pretty well swelled out,' as his father boasts. When we first meet Squeers' daughter Fanny, her strange physique is what we are chiefly asked to notice: 'She was not tall like her mother, but short like her father; from the former she inherited a voice of harsh quality, and from the latter a remarkable expression of the right eye, something akin to having none at all.' This is an odd piece of writing, because it is difficult to conceive how someone can have an eye that makes it look as if there is no eye there. What Dickens is trying to do is to give Fanny the effect of a physical handicap without actually making her handicapped, which would interfere with the part he wants her to play in the narrative.

The fact that the Squeers family are deformed might suggest that deformity is an attribute of the evil characters—their outer ugliness matching their inner, as it were. But that is not the case. For one of the novel's most virtuous characters, Newman Noggs, is spectacularly deformed as well. His part in the narrative is rather dull, though useful, and Dickens seems to have felt the need to compensate by giving him a mass of physical oddities. He has a red nose, a cadaverous face, and two goggle eyes—'whereof one was a fixture' (i.e., glass). His clothes, like Squeers' are 'very much too small', and he has a habit of rubbing his hands together 'cracking the joints of his fingers, and squeezing them into all possible distortions ... The incessant performance of this routine on every occasion, and the communication of a fixed and rigid look to his unaffected eye, so as to make it uniform with the other, and to render it impossible for anybody to determine where or at what he was looking, were two among the numerous peculiarities of Mr Noggs, which struck an inexperienced observer at first sight.'

Precisely: and striking an observer is just what Noggs is concocted for. He keeps up the finger-cracking and fixed eyes like a clockwork toy, even when he has nothing more coherent to contribute to the dialogue. In his interview with Nicholas in Chapter 4: 'Newman Noggs made no reply, but went on shrugging his shoulders and cracking his finger-joints, smiling horribly all the time, and looking steadfastly at nothing out of the tops of his eyes, in a most ghastly manner.' As the novel unwinds, Newman acquires other deformities. He develops facial spasms—though whether these spasms are 'of paralysis or grief or inward laughter, nobody but himself could possibly explain'. His nose becomes redder, until during Nicholas' adventure with Miss Bobster it glows 'like a red-hot coal'. In Chapter 31, when he is talking to Miss

La Creevy, he glances, we are told, at his 'paralytic limb'. This is the first time we have been told he has one, and it is hard to believe, for it does not seem to restrict his movement in any way. At the end of Chapter 57 it is Newman Noggs who creeps into Peg Sliderskew's room and lays Squeers out with a pair of bellows. How could he manage this with a paralytic limb? Similarly we might note that Squeers' lack of an eye never seems to trouble him. It is clearly not part of Dickens' purpose, when he creates these grotesques, to interest himself in, the problems that the physically handicapped actually encounter. Deformities in *Nicholas Nickleby* are not real in this way. They are more in the nature of a theatrical costume that can be put on and taken off at will.

In this respect Smike is the most theatrical of the *Nicholas Nickleby* grotesques. When we first meet him in Dotheboys Hall his mental and physical deformities are virtually the sole components of his character. He is lame, and dressed in a bizarre assortment of clothes—a little boy's suit, much too short in the arms and legs, a huge pair of boots, 'too patched and tattered for a beggar', and a 'tattered child's frill' round his neck. The word 'tattered' keeps recurring, as if Smike were coming to pieces. He tries to read from a 'tattered book ... vainly endeavouring to master some task which a child of nine years old, possessed of ordinary powers, could have conquered with ease, but which to the addled brain of the crushed boy of nineteen was a sealed and hopeless mystery'. So Smike, we gather, is mentally retarded, on top of everything else. The narrator calls him a 'poor half-witted creature'.

But when Smike escapes from Dotheboys Hall with Nicholas, moves in with the Nickleby family, falls in love with Kate, and starts to die pathetically of consumption, a transformation takes place. The suggestion of comic oddity that has distinguished him in the earlier part of the novel is banished. He becomes capable of coherent thought and moving eloquence. He is, as Dickens frankly puts it in Chapter 40, 'quite a different being'. He has taken off his Smike costume.

The fact that physical deformity is so widely used in *Nicholas Nickleby* to arouse comic interest, and that it is not a real handicap, has an unfortunate effect from the viewpoint of the novel's interest in social reform. The book was intended, in part, as an attack on one of the scandals of early Victorian England, the Yorkshire boarding schools. There were about twenty of these establishments, dating from the eighteenth century, and situated in the Barnard Castle area. They were notorious for negligence, cruelty and incompetence, being, in effect, little more than private juvenile prisons to which unwanted and illegitimate children could be permanently sent. They advertised regularly in quality newspapers such as *The Times*, often mentioning, as a special attraction, that their pupils were allowed 'no vacations'.

In the Preface to the first cheap edition of *Nicholas Nickleby* (1848), Dickens recalls that these schools, or rumours of them, had already been familiar to him when he was 'not a very robust child, sitting in bye-places near Rochester Castle'. His impressions were 'somehow or other connected with a suppurating abscess', which a Yorkshire schoolboy had suffered from, and a Yorkshire schoolmaster had ripped open with an inky penknife (an incident Dickens transfers to Squeers' school in Chapter 34).

William Shaw, the model for Squeers, kept a school called Bowes Academy at Greta Bridge, and back in 1823, fifteen years before Dickens took up the subject, he had been sued by the parents of two children who became totally blind there through infection and neglect. During the trial it was testified that the boys were given maggotty food, that as many as five usually slept in a single flea-infested bed, that they were often beaten, that ten boys had lost their sight there and been given no medical treatment. Shaw was convicted and paid £300 damages in each case, but continued to run his school.

Dickens knew of the Shaw case, and on 30 March 1838, just before starting work on his novel, he travelled up to Greta Bridge. He met Shaw, who was suspicious and would say little, on 2 February. Then he visited the churchyard, which contained the graves of twenty-five pupils, aged between seven and eighteen, who had died there in the previous twenty years.

When Dickens depicts the inmates of Dotheboys Hall, he modifies these facts. He does not, for example, show any child blind or going blind—presumably because it would be almost impossible to reconcile that with the predominantly comic treatment of Squeers and his school. It is Squeers, not the boys, who is visually handicapped. However, Dickens does give a list of the boys' physical deformities when we are first introduced to Dotheboys Hall: 'Pale and haggard faces, lank and bony figures, children

with the countenances of old men, deformities with irons upon their limbs, boys of stunted growth, and others whose long meagre legs would hardly bear their stooping bodies; ... there were the bleared eye, and harelip, the crooked foot, and every ugliness or distortion that told of unnatural aversion conceived by parents for their offspring.'

These deformities are quite different from those we have got used to in *Nicholas Nickleby*. These are real and serious. They make their possessors ugly, not funny. They maim and cripple. They cannot be ignored by their possessors, as Squeers' or Newman Noggs' deformities can. Deformities 'with irons upon their limbs' inhabit a different sphere of reality from Noggs, although he is supposed in theory to be twisted and paralysed. It is as if we have stepped momentarily out of a pantomime into a hospital. And it is because the deformities of the Dotheboys Hall boys are authentic medical deformities that they cannot, in fact, be accommodated in Dickens' novel, where deformity, as we have seen, serves a theatrical and comic purpose. After this initial list of the Dotheboys' deformities, we hear no more of them. We never see a boy with a hare lip or an iron on his leg. At the end of Chapter 63, when the scholars rebel, break up the school, and punish the Squeers family, they seem quite strong and able bodied.

Dickens' dependence on deformity for narrative interest, then, combines uneasily with his reformist campaign against the Yorkshire schools, according to which deformity is a shocking thing, and those who fail to sympathize with it should be punished by law. I have suggested that he was attracted to deformity because there was something about it—its irregularity, its foreignness, its visual value—that chimed with his imaginative interest in places like Golden Square. In both cases the watcher's gaze turns what it sees into a curiosity. At the same time the watcher registers his own separation from what he sees, his own difference, superiority and loneliness. He represents normality, surrounded by aliens.

This theme of loneliness threads through *Nicholas Nickleby*. Several moralizing passages dwell on it. On the very first page we are told 'It is extraordinary how long a man may look among the crowd without discovering the face of a friend.' In Chapter 4 there is a troubled, intrusive passage about Newgate, and the executions that have taken place there, and the crowds that gathered, and how 'in the mass of white and upturned faces' the dying man would not see one 'that bore the impress of pity or com = passion'. The same preoccupation with the isolated individual, and the callous disregard of the crowd, inspires the end of Chapter 50, when Lord Frederick Verisopht has been killed at dawn in a duel, and Dickens describes his dead body: 'the leaves quivered and rustled in the air, the birds poured their cheerful songs from every tree ... all the light and life of day came on, and, amidst it all, and pressing down the grass whose every blade bore twenty tiny lives, lay the dead man'. This allusion, singular for Dickens, to the lives of birds and insects, does not indicate a sudden interest in biology. He simply wants to foreground the lonely, disregarded individual.

From one angle *Nicholas Nickleby* is the story of a sensitive, delicate boy who is isolated—forced to seek his fortune in a corrupt and malicious world. His isolation is intensified by the grotesques and deformities that surround him. By comparison with him they are monsters, visual curiosities. At times they even seem to pride themselves on their curiosity value. Take Miss Knag, Madame Mantalini's assistant. In Chapter 17 she boasts about her physical refinement, and certifies, to this end, that the Knag family has always been celebrated for its small feet—'ever since—hem—our family had any feet at all ... I had an uncle once ... who lived in Cheltenham, and had a most excellent business as a tobacconist—hem—who had such small feet, that they were no bigger than those which are usually joined to wooden legs.' Though it is not what Miss Knag intends, this suggestion of deformity is enough to recruit her family into the misbegotten freak-show that surrounds Nicholas.

Nicholas' distinction as an undeformed person is spelt out in Chapter 9 when Fanny Squeers questions the servant-girl about the new arrival at Dotheboys Hall. Describing Nicholas, the girl mentions his straight legs, 'upon which last-named articles she laid particular stress, the general run of legs at Dotheboys Hall being crooked'. Fanny, after her first sight of Nicholas' legs, is likewise impressed: '"I never saw such legs in the whole course of my life!" said Miss Squeers, as she walked away.' When Nicholas first meets Madeline Bray, the young woman he is to marry, it evidently matters that we should be assured of her exemption from the deformity that attacks so many of the other characters. This guarantee

is given in Chapter 16, the moment Madeline enters. She is small—'of very slight and delicate figure', but—reader, rejoice!—perfectly formed—'exquisitely shaped'.

Source: John Carey, "Introduction," in *Nicholas Nickleby*, Knopf, 1993, pp. xi–xxix.

Sylvere Monod

In this excerpt, Monod discusses the novel's effect on the Yorkshire schools of which Dickens was so strongly critical

Every mark of an evolution, toward the end of *Nickleby*, concurs in showing that, once he had completed *Oliver Twist*, Dickens resolved to devote himself more methodically to the practice, though not to the theoretical study, of his art. Nevermore would he attempt to write two novels at the same time. His dawning consciousness of the duties devolving upon a conscientious artist would preclude it. Unfortunately, his perceptible technical progress is not paralleled by a similar improvement in psychology. During the sixteenth number, Lord Frederick Verisopht is too suddenly transfigured. He had been both a simpleton and a rake: he no longer is either the one or the other. A number of other characters undergo similar changes. Miss La Creevy, the miniature painter, loses at one blow all her ridiculous conceit. John Browdie, the Yorkshire miller, sheds all his churlishness to become a jovial Quixote. Nor are such transformations preceded by any psychological evolution that might justify them. The only thing that evolves is the author's attitude to his characters: he becomes fonder of his creations. Dickens' sympathy with an increasing number of characters as the novel proceeds toward its close redounds to the credit of his sensibility and generosity, but it makes light of psychological verisimilitude.

In *Nickleby*, generally, characters are stiff and all of a piece. Psychological analysis is perfunctory. The case of Sir Mulberry Hawk and his companions is characteristic. They belong to a class that Dickens is unfamiliar with: he cannot therefore apply to them his usual method, which consists of making real beings live and talk in front of the reader, of recording the combined results of his observations. This method, whenever it is employed, as it is in the case of Mrs. Nickleby and a few others in the same novel, endows the tale with matchless life and truth. But nothing could be more labored than the author's explanations of Hawk's motives. It is

> EVERY MARK OF AN EVOLUTION, TOWARD
> THE END OF *NICKLEBY,* CONCURS IN SHOWING THAT,
> ONCE HE HAD COMPLETED *OLIVER TWIST,*
> DICKENS RESOLVED TO DEVOTE HIMSELF MORE
> METHODICALLY TO THE PRACTICE, THOUGH NOT
> TO THE THEORETICAL STUDY, OF HIS ART."

most embarrassing to the reader to find Dickens stressing the fact that Hawk is preparing "to execute a plan of operations concerted by Sir Mulberry himself, avowedly to promote his friend's object, and really to obtain his own" (chap. xxvi). Nor could double-dealing be more crudely expressed than in "'What a happiness this amiable creature must be to you,' said Sir Mulberry, throwing into his voice an indication of the warmest feeling" (chap. xxxvi). When he thus launches into psychological analysis, Dickens clearly gets out of his depth, and his explanations detract from the value of his observation. Hence the limitations of Dickensian psychology in the days of *Nickleby.* He is able to create a larger number of truthful and lively characters than almost any other writer, when he takes them from the social classes he knows well, from paupers to the middle middle class, but the aristocracy and the higher middle class are beyond his scope. And though he can convincingly reproduce gestures, speech, and attitudes, he cannot as yet explore souls. It takes him another ten years to become the equal of the truly great psychological novelists: this he does when his genius reaches full maturity in *David Copperfield.*

In the final numbers of *Nickleby,* psychology is almost out of the question. Event now follows event in quick succession, and the plot thickens tragically. Nicholas makes up his mind to see Madeline and prevent her from marrying Gride (chap. lii). He cannot persuade her, or Gride either (chap. liii). On the morning of the day appointed for the wedding, Madeline's father dies opportunely and Nicholas provides a home for the orphaned girl. He goes to Devonshire with Smike, who is alarmingly ill. Gride's housekeeper has disappeared and taken away

some compromising documents, among others Madeline's grandfather's will, which Squeers must attempt to recover on behalf of Ralph (chap. lvi). The moment he is possessing himself of the paper, Noggs and Frank Cheeryble burst into the room (chap. lvii).

That is the end of the eighteenth and last but one number, published on September 1, 1839. Dickens devoted the month of September to the composition of the final installment, supposedly of double size—it is called *Nos. XIX & XX*—which must disentangle all the difficulties and ensure the happiness of the worthy and the punishment of the wicked. The task is not an easy one. The first chapter of that number is entitled: "In which one scene of this History is closed" (chap. lviii). This phrase adequately sums up the novelist's attitude from that time on. Hemmed in by the episodes and characters he has so lavishly created, he resorts to young Horace's strategy in Corneille's play, and endeavors to tackle each of them separately. "I am hard at it," he was writing to Forster, from Broadstairs, on September 9, 1839, "but these windings-up wind slowly, and I think I shall have done great things if I have entirely finished by the twentieth." On the eighteenth, he could confirm this date: "I shall not finish entirely before Friday, sending ... the last twenty pages of ms by the night-coach. I have had pretty stiff work as you may suppose, and I have taken great pains. The discovery is made. Ralph is dead. The loves have come all right, Tim Linkinwater has proposed, and I have now only to break up Dotheboys Hall and the book together. I am very anxious that you should see this conclusion before it leaves my hands ... and we will devote [Saturday] night to a careful reading." His letter alludes to the last events in the narrative. Smike is dead (chap. lviii). The "discovery" is that of Smike's identity: he is Ralph's son (chap. lx). Ralph kills himself when he has lost every kind of hope (chap. lxii). The "loves" are Nicholas' for Madeline and Frank Cheeryble's for Kate, which result in a twofold wedding after overcoming imaginary obstacles, made up once again of unclear scruples. Tim—the Cheerybles' aged clerk—marries Miss La Creevy. Dotheboys Hall is dissolved after Squeers has been sentenced.

Almost simultaneously with the final number, the first edition in book form was published, preceded by the original preface. The bulk of the preface is devoted to the Yorkshire schools question and asserts that they are truthfully described in the book. Besides this, the author expresses his regret at leaving his beloved readers and the hope that they will experience regret also and regard Dickens' works "as the correspondence of one who wished their happiness and contributed to their amusement." The volume was inscribed to the actor W.C. Macready, to whom Dickens also dedicated, a few weeks later, his second daughter, born in October. The actor standing godfather to her, she was christened Kate Macready Dickens. When he asked his friend to play that part, the prospective father described the forthcoming child as destined to be "the last and final branch of a genteel small family of three." He was a little out in his calculations, however, since the genteel small family was to be adorned with seven additional branches in the next dozen years.

At the end of 1839, the Dickenses left their small house in Doughty Street, in which half of *Pickwick* and nearly the whole of *Oliver Twist* and *Nickleby* had been composed, to occupy Devonshire Terrace, a glamorous house, close to Regent's Park and more in keeping with the income of a great popular novelist. For that is the title which his contemporaries were prepared to grant him after *Nickleby*. Perhaps the critics of today would be more reluctant to concede that he was a great novelist on the strength of his first three works of fiction alone.

He had certainly not completely mastered his art. The structure of his narratives had made slow progress, and he was still often carried away by inspiration or led astray by incidental circumstances and needs foreign to his central purpose. When he moved from one scene to another, when he turned back to an earlier period, the vagaries of his narrative were often ponderously stressed, rather than justified or excused by phrases like these:

> This narrative may embrace the opportunity of ascertaining the condition of Sir Mulberry Hawk (chap. xxxviii), this history may pursue the footsteps of Newman Noggs, thereby combining advantage with necessity ... (chap. li), [or what discloses yet more clearly the lack of a firm grasp of events on the author's part] the course which these adventures shape out for themselves, and imperiously call upon the historian to observe, now demands that they should return to the point they attained previous to the commencement of the last chapter (chap. lvi).

He still had much to learn. It has been seen that in the final section of his novel, he had made

an attempt to write more artistically and thus given evidence at least of his desire to learn and progress.

Yet Dickens' chief purpose in *Nickleby*—apart from the permanent need of earning money—remained sentimental rather than artistic. He wished above all to be in sympathy with his readers and to be loved by them. When he sent Macready the first copy of the original edition, he defined *Nickleby* as "the book itself, my whole heart for twenty months." He felt he must gain the affection of the people to whom he was thus surrendering his whole heart. The finest tribute he ever received must have been the most gratifying to him: it was paid by Thackeray, who said:

> All children ought to love him. I know two that do, and read his books ten times for once that they peruse the dismal preachings of their father. I know one who, when she is happy, reads "*Nicholas Nickleby*"; when she is unhappy, reads "*Nicholas Nickleby*"; when she is tired, reads "*Nicholas Nickleby*"; when she is in bed, reads "*Nicholas Nickleby*"; when she has nothing to do, reads "*Nicholas Nickleby*"; and when she has finished the book, reads "*Nicholas Nickleby*" over again. This candid young critic, at ten years of age, said, "I like Mr. Dickens's books much better than your books, papa," and frequently expressed her desire that the latter author should write a book like one of Mr. Dickens's books. Who can?

Dickens was quite prepared to content himself with being an inimitable enchanter, even if, in point of technical mastery, he was not yet a great novelist. In fact, he did not himself lay claim to the latter title. On the contrary, in the preface to *Nickleby*, he represented himself, not as the successor of Fielding and Smollett or of Scott and Jane Austen, but as the emulator of Henry Mackenzie, the author of *The Man of Feeling* as well as of several magazines analogous to Addison's and Johnson's, made up of essays and miscellaneous articles. At the close of a lengthy quotation from Mackenzie about the right enjoyed by the author "of a periodical performance" to be loved by his readers, he concluded with a description of himself—in spite of the recent development of his own technique in the direction of more solid and methodical construction—as "the periodical essayist, the author of these pages."

Source: Sylvere Monod, "Towards the Dickensian Novel: *Nicholas Nickleby*," in *Dickens the Novelist*, University of Oklahoma Press, 1968, pp. 139–165.

SOURCES

Carey, John, "Introduction," in Charles Dickens, *Nicholas Nickleby*. Alfred A. Knopf, 1993.

Chesterton, G. K, Introduction to the Original Everyman Edition of *Nicholas Nickleby*, 1907, in Charles Dickens, *Nicholas Nickleby*. Alfred A. Knopf, 1993.

Dickens, Charles, *Nicholas Nickleby*. Alfred A. Knopf, 1993.

Smiley, Jane, *Charles Dickens*. Penguin Putnam, 2002.

FURTHER READING

Collins, Philip, *Dickens and Education*, Macmillan, 1963.
Dickens was a tireless advocate for educational reform. He not only criticized bad schools mercilessly in his fiction but also in journalism, speeches, and other public forums. In this study, the author details Dickens's campaigns against the Yorkshire schools, as described in *Nicholas Nickleby*, and also his attempts to either eliminate or improve other educational institutions of the era, such as Ragged Schools, Dame Schools, Public Schools, and Mechanics' Institutes.

Coolidge Jr., Archibald C, *Charles Dickens as Serial Novelist,* Iowa State University Press, 1967.
Coolidge argues that the serialized form in which *Nicholas Nickleby* and other early novels of Dickens were published helped Dickens become one of the world's great novelists.

Monod, Sylvère, *Dickens the Novelist*, University of Oklahoma Press, 1968.
Dickens scholar Sylvère Monod explores Dickens's development as a writer, from his earliest days as a journalist through his late masterpieces. The book includes a section about *Nicholas Nickleby*.

Pool, Daniel, *What Jane Austen Ate and Charles Dickens Knew: From Fox Hunting to Whist-The Facts of Daily Life in Nineteenth-Century England*, Touchstone, 1994.
This handy guide describes and defines the terms and customs of everyday life in nineteenth-century England, including topics such as clothing, money, etiquette, jobs, slang, pastimes, and transportation.

No Longer at Ease

CHINUA ACHEBE

1960

No Longer at Ease is the second novel by Nigerian author Chinua Achebe. It was published in London in 1960, two years after Achebe's groundbreaking debut, *Things Fall Apart*, a work often cited as the first great novel written in English by an African artist. *No Longer at Ease* is a sequel to *Things Fall Apart*, although set two generations later. Its protagonist, Obi Okonkwo, is the grandson of the hero of the prior book, the Ibo (Igbo) warrior Okonkwo. Obi's father is Okonkwo's estranged son Nwoye, known in this book as Isaac. Like his grandfather, Obi Okonkwo suffers a tragic fate, although the circumstances and the actions (and failures to act) that cause his demise are profoundly different.

No Longer at Ease was released in the same year that Nigeria attained its independence from the British Empire. The novel is set in modern Nigeria on the cusp of independence, after a half century of colonial rule. Where *Things Fall Apart* depicts the origins of the colonial enterprise, the initial subjugation of the Ibo people and their traditional way of life, *No Longer at Ease* reveals the extent of the damage done to African society. The corruption that pervades the modern world Achebe presents—a major theme of the novel—stems ultimately from the weakening of tribal culture under colonialism. In *Things Fall Apart*, Okonkwo confronts an overt clash between indigenous Africa and colonial Europe. By the time of *No Longer at Ease*, the

Chinua Achebe (*AP Images*)

nature of that clash has changed. It now takes the form of a contest between two incompatible value systems within the mind of young Nigerians such as Obi Okonkwo. The result is a moral crisis that vanquishes the hero's divided soul.

AUTHOR BIOGRAPHY

Albert Chinualumugo Achebe was born November 16, 1930, in the eastern Nigerian village of Ogidi. His parents were devoted advocates of the Christianity brought to the region by British missionaries, and as a child he attended mission schools. He showed academic promise early, beginning to learn English at the age of eight. At fourteen, he was admitted to an elite school in the city of Umuahia, with classes conducted in English, and at eighteen he joined the founding class of the University of Ibadan on a scholarship. He intended to proceed to medical school but, like Obi, switched his major to English literature. While at university he wrote his first short stories. Achebe drew on his own personal history when he created Obi Okonkwo, the main character of *No Longer at Ease*.

After receiving his degree, Achebe began working for the Nigerian Broadcasting Corporation, where he became a radio producer and was later put in charge of the Voice of Nigeria shortwave service. He traveled to England in 1957 to train with the British Broadcasting Corporation (BBC), bringing his manuscript-in-progress with him. When it was finished in 1958, the British publisher Heinemann released the novel, titled *Things Fall Apart* after a line from the poem "The Second Coming" (1919) by the Irish poet W. B. Yeats.

Things Fall Apart remains the most well known and widely read work in the entire body of African literature. No African writer had created such a powerful, complex portrait of precolonial African civilization, or of the encounter with European missionaries and colonial administrators. Achebe's achievement was profound: writing in the colonial language (English), he managed to convey the textures of oral culture and communal life among the Ibo people.

Achebe then turned his sights on contemporary Nigeria and the challenges facing its educated youth in *No Longer at Ease* (1960). His third novel, *Arrow of God* (1964), takes place in the 1920s, after British rule had been well established. The story of a village priest who loses the support of his clan, the novel once again reveals the detrimental effect of colonialism on the integrity of Ibo life and customs. Both *A Man of the People* (1966) and *Anthills of the Savannah* (1987), although published twenty years apart, are pungent political satires that treat the close relationship between power and corruption.

Achebe is frequently thought of as the originator of modern African literary fiction. His five novels, each set in a different time period, span nearly a century of history. Collectively, they provide an insightful portrait of Nigeria's uneven path to modernity, and the pitfalls along the way. Achebe is also the author of numerous poetry collections, children's books, and political essays.

Achebe and his family moved to the United States in the 1970s. He has been on the faculty of Bard College in Annandale-on-Hudson, New York, since 1993. Achebe was nominated for the Nobel Prize in Literature in 2000 and received the Man Booker International Prize in 2007. An automobile accident in 1990 left him paralyzed from the waist down.

PLOT SUMMARY

Chapter 1

No Longer at Ease reveals its ending at the beginning: Obi Okonkwo is on trial for accepting a bribe. The trial is the talk of Lagos and the courtroom is crowded. Obi has maintained a demeanor of indifference throughout, but at the judge's summation tears come to Obi's eyes. The scene shifts to a British club, where Obi's boss, Mr. Green, cites the case as proof of his conviction that "the African is corrupt through and through." The Umuofia Progressive Union, an association of Ibo from Obi's home village, meets to discuss Obi's case. This group has raised funds to send select young men from Umuofia to study in England. Obi Okonkwo, a brilliant student, won the first scholarship, but disappointed his sponsors by studying English instead of law.

The flash-forward ends, and the narrative backtracks to reveal how Obi's disgrace came about, beginning with a prayer meeting and feast held at the Okonkwo family home before Obi's departure for England. The guests sing, pray, and make speeches. The Reverend Samuel Ikedi thanks Obi's father, Isaac Okonkwo, and urges Obi to take his studies seriously, deferring the pleasures of the flesh.

Chapter 2

Obi gets his first brief view of the Nigerian capital of Lagos before flying to England. He stays with his childhood friend Joseph Okeke, but must walk around the neighborhood when Joseph brings a woman back to his apartment. The story then flashes forward several years, as Obi drives through the Lagos slums with his girlfriend, Clara, recalling his first impressions of the city. The couple's mild quarrel reveals that their relationship is well established. Earlier that day, the pair had gone to lunch with Obi's friend Christopher. The two men, who enjoy debating each other, engage in argument about bribery in the civil service. Obi espouses the view that bribery is routine to the older generation, but younger officials can afford to remain virtuous.

Chapter 3

Obi and Clara's relationship begins when they meet at a dance in London. Obi admires Clara's beauty but is at a loss for words and steps on her toes on the dance floor. Eighteen months later,

MEDIA ADAPTATIONS

- *Bullfrog in the Sun* (1971), a film directed by Hans Jürgen Pohland and produced by Francis Oladele is based on both *Things Fall Apart* and *No Longer at Ease*. It is set in postcolonial Nigeria, with flashbacks depicting scenes from the earlier novel. Actor Johnny Sekka portrays both Okonkwo from *Things Fall Apart* and his grandson Obi Okonkwo. The film also stars Princess Elisabeth of Toro. Achebe was not happy with the film, which took liberties with the material, venturing into the issues behind the Biafra War. The film was retitled *Things Fall Apart* for distribution in the United States, but never had a commercial release there.

they happen to be returning to Nigeria on the same boat. Obi is invigorated by the sea in the morning and sits down to breakfast with the other passengers, avoiding Clara's eyes. Later in the day the sea becomes choppy and Obi declines to eat his dinner. Clara, a nurse, comes to Obi's cabin door with medicine for seasickness.

Obi befriends a young Englishman, John Macmillan. In the evening, the boat anchors in the Madeiras and Obi disembarks with Macmillan and Clara. The three of them drink wine and return to the ship holding hands. When Macmillan goes to his cabin, Obi kisses Clara passionately and declares his love for her. Clara says she will hate herself in the morning, but returns his kiss.

Chapter 4

On Obi's arrival in Lagos, a young customs officer offers to reduce his duty payment in exchange for a bribe. Obi dismisses him coldly. The Umuofia Progressive Union (U.P.U.) holds a reception for Obi. The guest of honor shows up in his shirtsleeves, displeasing his hosts who expected him to dress formally. The union secretary introduces him with a rather pretentious address; Obi's plainspoken speech fails to impress the crowd. Afterward, Obi and Joseph dine at the Palm Grove. The U.P.U. has paid for Obi to stay at a hotel, but Obi insists on staying at Joseph's flat. A handsome young politician, Hon. Sam Okoli, enters the hotel lounge, and Obi spies Clara waiting outside in Okoli's car.

Chapter 5

At his job interview, Obi impresses the chairman of the Public Service Commission by discussing modern literature. When another man asks him directly whether his interest in the civil service relates to taking bribes, Obi's response is heated. Obi sets out aboard one of the ubiquitous mammy-wagons—rickety pick-up trucks fitted out with brightly painted wooden roofs and benches that were West Africa's principle means of public transportation—for the long journey to Umuofia. Police stop the wagon. One officer is about to take a bribe from the driver's mate (someone who travels with the driver of a truck and helps them load and unload goods) when he sees Obi and stops. The other officer finds fault with the driver's papers and ends up accepting an even larger bribe. The driver blames Obi for intervening and the other passengers mock the "too know" young man.

After riding through the night, Obi stops at the market in Onitsha before a car takes him to Umuofia. The entire village has turned out to welcome him home. During the reception at the family compound, Isaac Okonkwo states that since his is a Christian house, no customary ceremony must be made over a kola nut. A quarrel ensues until an elder, Ogbuefi Odogwu, resolves matters by blessing the kola nut "in the name of Jesu Kristi."

Chapter 6

Obi notices that his mother and father are frail from insufficient food and advancing age. He lies in response to his father's inquiry whether he had read his Bible while abroad. He recalls the loneliness of his strict Christian upbringing: he was never allowed to dine in his neighbors' homes and never learned the folk stories his mother knew as a child. Obi lies awake calculating how much of his earnings he can afford to give his parents; he has already agreed to pay his younger brother's school fees. He also wonders why Clara did not want him to tell his parents about their relationship.

Chapter 7

At his new job, Obi takes an immediate dislike to his boss, Mr. Green. Once officially appointed, he buys a brand-new Morris Oxford car. He and Clara have drinks at the home of Hon. Sam Okoli, then go out to a celebratory dinner. Clara is upset and they do not touch their food. Clara cries and tells Obi she cannot marry him because she is an *osu*—a member of an untouchable caste. Obi recounts the story to Joseph, and insists that he will marry Clara despite her status. Joseph is aghast, but his reaction serves only to strengthen Obi's conviction. The next day he buys Clara an expensive engagement ring and a Bible. Joseph reminds Obi of his special position amongst his people and warns him that his family will not consent to the marriage, but Obi remains confident that he can overcome his mother's objections.

Chapter 8

Joseph accompanies Obi to the meeting of the Umuofia Progressive Union. All are ecstatic when they arrive in Obi's new pleasure car. Midway into the agenda, Obi rises to speak. He is obligated to repay the union the money it has loaned for his education, but he asks for a four-month delay before beginning his repayments. The group grants Obi's request, yet the president warns him not to fall into bad ways, for he has heard that Obi is involved with "a girl of doubtful ancestry." Obi becomes enraged, revokes his request, and storms out of the meeting.

Chapter 9

Obi works as secretary to the Scholarship Board alongside an English secretary, Marie Tomlinson. Obi is wary of Miss Tomlinson at first, but warms toward her after she expresses genuine delight upon meeting Clara. An Ibo man named Mr. Mark visits Obi in his office. His sister has applied for a scholarship. It becomes clear that he seeks to offer a bribe. Obi sends him away; afterward, he feels victorious. Elsie Mark herself, an attractive girl of about eighteen, appears later at the door of Obi's apartment, pleading for his help. While they are talking, Clara enters. Obi and Clara drive the girl back to town. After hearing the whole story, Clara says Obi was too hard on Mr. Mark, because offering money is not as bad as offering oneself.

Chapter 10

Obi's annual car insurance payment comes due, and this fact awakens him to the precarious nature of his finances. He obtains an overdraft from the bank and begins to economize in his apartment by removing extra lightbulbs and instructing his steward, Sebastian, to turn off the water heater and refrigerator. When Clara hears about the bank overdraft, she is angry that Obi didn't think to tell her about his troubles. He says the troubles are not serious, but they part with the matter unresolved.

Chapter 11

Obi and Marie discuss Mr. Green. Obi dislikes his boss, but inwardly admires his sense of duty. A small parcel arrives from Clara, containing an apologetic note and fifty pounds in cash. Obi wants her to take back the money, but does not want her to be hurt. Obi and Clara go out dancing with Christopher and his girlfriend, Bisi, until two o'clock in the morning. When Obi and Clara return to his car, they discover that the fifty pounds have been stolen from the glove compartment.

Chapter 12

Obi receives a letter from his father, hoping he will visit soon to discuss an urgent matter. Obi suspects his parents have received word that Clara is an *osu*. Obi and Christopher drive to a convent to play tennis with two Irish women, teachers at a local convent school, newly arrived in Nigeria. The four have already gotten to know each other and played on two previous occasions, but this time the women say they cannot socialize with Obi and Christopher anymore because the head nun at the convent warned them not to go out with African men. While driving home, Obi brings up his visit from Elsie Mark, and he and Christopher discuss the incident. Once again Christopher takes a more easygoing stance than does Obi on the ethics of bribery.

Chapter 13

Obi prepares to travel home on his local leave. The night before his departure, Clara, in tears, says they should break off their engagement, because she does not want to come between him and his family. Obi has decided to spend one week at home rather than two, so that he won't run out of money. When he arrives home, he is eager to see his mother and aggrieved at how ill she looks.

Chapter 14

On his first night home, Obi sits down to talk with his father. Hearing the name of Clara's father, Isaac Okonkwo understands that she is *osu* and tells his son he cannot marry her. *Osu* is like leprosy, the elder Okonkwo says, and to marry one would shame his family for generations. Obi argues that they are Christians and that the ignorant superstitions of the past will soon disappear. His father is unmoved. The next day, his mother tells him of a bad dream she had, in which termites devoured the bed in which she slept. She connects the dream with the news of her son's intention to marry an *osu*. If he insists on marrying her, she demands that he wait for her to die; if he does not, she tells him, she will kill herself. Obi is undone by her words and shuts himself in his room, spurning visitors and absenting himself from family prayers. His father speaks to him of his own past: how his own father had placed a curse on him after he ran away with missionaries in his youth. Because he suffered, he tells Obi, he understands Christianity more deeply than his son ever will.

Chapter 15

Driving back to Lagos in a stupor, Obi avoids a head-on collision with a mammy-wagon by making a last-second swerve into a bush. He and the car survive with minimal damage; onlookers aver that he is extremely lucky. He tries to persuade Clara that all will work out in the end, but she returns her engagement ring. Clara hints, without admitting, that she is pregnant. Obi becomes alarmed. He asks Christopher if he knows a doctor. Obi and Clara visit two doctors; the first refuses to perform an abortion, but the second agrees to for a fee of thirty pounds in cash. Both doctors ask Obi why he doesn't marry Clara.

Chapter 16

Facing the need to find thirty pounds by the afternoon, Obi thinks of asking Hon. Sam Okoli. Obi brings Clara to the doctor. Alone in his car, Obi has a premonition of doom and is unable to drive away. When Clara and the doctor get into a car, Obi wants to jump out and stop them, but he does not. He drives after them but is unable to find them in the traffic of Lagos. That evening, the doctor tells him to return in the morning. The next morning, Obi pushes past the attendant to see the doctor, who tells him Clara is at a private hospital. A patient berates him for jumping ahead and accuses him of arrogance.

Chapter 17

Back at his job, Obi sees the administrator, Mr. Omo, about a salary advance. He has visited Clara at the hospital, but she turned away and refused to look at him. Vowing to return Clara's fifty pounds, Obi decides to stop repaying his loan to the Umuofia Progressive Union. He writes a letter to Clara, asking her to give him one more chance. She returns the letter by messenger, unopened.

Chapter 18

Clara leaves the hospital after five weeks and departs from Lagos without seeing Obi. A messenger brings Obi a telegram bearing news that his mother has died. His grief is deep, yet he decides not to travel to Umuofia for the funeral, but merely to send money. The Umuofia Progressive Union finds that Hannah Okonkwo's funeral was cheaper than she deserved, and Obi is roundly criticized for skipping it. One man reminds the group that Obi's father did the same when his father died. Nevertheless, a contingent of Obi's kinsmen from Umuofia pay him a condolence call at his flat. All are embarrassed when one of them tells a story about a tortoise who seeks to avoid his mother's funeral.

Chapter 19

After a period of sadness and guilt, Obi comes to feel a strange sort of inner peace. His ideals and illusions have passed away, leaving his heart lighter. As scholarship season arrives, Obi accepts a bribe for the first time. More bribe money comes his way, allowing him to pay off his debts. When a young woman comes to see him seeking a scholarship, he accepts her advances. One day, after a man has left him twenty pounds, Obi feels he can no longer stand it. A moment later, he is caught and placed under arrest.

CHARACTERS

Bisi

Bisi is a girlfriend of Obi's friend Christopher. She and Christopher go out one Saturday night with Obi and Clara; Bisi wants to go to the movies, but agrees to go out dancing instead. They stay out until two in the morning, and Bisi is reluctant to leave; she says the dance is just starting to heat up.

Christopher

Christopher is a good friend of Obi Okonkwo. He has a degree from the London School of Economics, and has recently been transferred to Lagos from the city of Enugu. Christopher and Obi enjoy lively intellectual debates, especially on the topic of corruption in the Nigerian civil service. Christopher invariably opposes Obi's point of view, perhaps for the sheer pleasure of playing the devil's advocate. Christopher's attitude is much looser than Obi's on the ethical questions concerning bribery. Obi admires Christopher's flexibility in moving between standard English and pidgin, or "broken" English, depending on the context. Christopher does not support Obi's choice to marry Clara, but helps Obi find a doctor willing to perform an abortion.

Mr. William Green

William Green is Obi's supervisor at the Scholarship Board. Mr. Green is a stern, demanding boss who insists that the Africans working under him address him as "sir." His attitude toward Africans in general, and educated ones in particular, is contemptuous. He frequently proclaims that the Nigerian people are selfish, irresponsible, and not equipped to govern themselves. However, he is capable of generosity on an individual level; for example, he pays the school fees for the sons of his African steward. Although Obi dislikes Mr. Green personally, he admires his devotion to duty, noting that he often works until the evening, even putting off personal obligations like dental appointments because of constantly pressing work. Obi finds it paradoxical that Mr. Green should work so hard for a country he does not believe in.

Charles Ibe

Charles Ibe, an Ibo, works as a messenger for the Scholarship Board in Lagos. He writes a letter to Obi asking for a loan of thirty shillings, saying his wife has just borne their fifth child.

Reverend Samuel Ikedi

Reverend Samuel Ikedi, pastor of St. Mark's Anglican Church in Umuofia, leads a prayer meeting for Obi Okonkwo at his parents' home before his journey to England. At the end of a long speech, he advises Obi to take his studies seriously and not to be drawn into the pursuit of pleasure.

Lorry Driver

The lorry driver takes Obi from Lagos to Onitsha aboard a mammy-wagon christened "God's

Case No Appeal." He smokes and chews kola nuts to stay awake, but nevertheless nearly falls asleep at the wheel. When the lorry is stopped by the police, Obi's watchful presence prevents the policeman from accepting a two-shilling bribe. Moments later, out of view, the policeman charges the driver's mate ten shillings. The driver then berates Obi for sticking his nose in business that does not concern him and for being "too know." Other passengers echo the driver's rebuke.

John Macmillan

John Macmillan, a young Englishman working as an administrator in Nigeria, sails there from Liverpool on the same boat as Obi. The two become friends and go ashore for the evening, along with Clara, when the boat docks in the Madeira Islands.

Elsie Mark

Elsie Mark, a girl of seventeen or eighteen years of age, hopes to obtain a scholarship to study in England. She comes to see Obi at his home and pleads for his help, saying "I'll do whatever you ask." Obi feels for her but tells her he can make no promises. He and Clara give her a ride back to town.

Mr. Mark

Mr. Mark pays a visit to Obi at the office of the Scholarship Commission. Speaking in Ibo, so as not to be overheard by Miss Tomlinson, he tells Obi his sister is applying for a scholarship to study in England. When Obi understands that he means to offer a bribe, he abruptly sends Mr. Mark away.

Nora

Nora is one of two Irish nuns who have recently come to Nigeria. Obi meets them at his friend Christopher's apartment. Obi tries several times to kiss Nora, who politely declines his advances. The four of them meet twice to play tennis, but on the men's third visit to the convent, Nora tells them the Mother Superior has asked them not to go out with African men.

Ogbuefi Odogwu

Ogbuefi Odogwu, an elder of Umuofia, attends the reception to celebrate Obi Okonkwo's return from "the white man's land." Although he is not a Christian, he respects Isaac Okonkwo's insistence that no "heathen sacrifice" take place under his roof. Odogwu says a brief, quasi-Christian

blessing over the kola nut, to the satisfaction of the entire party. He praises Obi by saying he is the return of the spirit of his grandfather, Okonkwo the warrior.

Clara Okeke

Clara Okeke, a young, beautiful nurse, is Obi Okonkwo's girlfriend. She meets Obi briefly at a dance in London; eighteen months later, they meet again on the way home to Nigeria and become romantically involved. She asks Obi not to tell his family about her. The reason becomes clear when she reveals to him that she is an *osu*. Among the Ibo, the *osu* are considered the property of the gods, and their descendants are permanent outcasts. However, Obi's modern sensibility leads him to defy the traditional taboo. He immediately buys Clara an engagement ring. Before Obi goes on leave to visit his family, Clara tells him she wants to break off their engagement, perhaps already aware that despite his words, Obi's bond with her will not survive his parents' disapproval. After he comes back, she returns the ring and hints that she is pregnant. She and Obi then go together to a doctor to seek an abortion. The operation is botched and Clara is hospitalized for five weeks. She refuses to look at him when he visits or read the letter he writes. When she is discharged she leaves Lagos and Obi's life.

Joseph Okeke

Joseph Okeke was a childhood classmate of Obi Okonkwo now living in Lagos and employed as a government clerk. Obi stays in Joseph's small apartment before embarking for England, and again after he returns several years later. Joseph is the first person who voices an objection to Obi's plan to marry Clara, but his arguments serve only to embolden Obi. Joseph accompanies Obi to a meeting of the Umuofia Progressive Union, and privately tells the union president about Obi's engagement. Obi considers this a betrayal, and Joseph falls out of his favor. Months later, however, after Obi's mother dies, Joseph appears at his door, bringing bottles of beer to help entertain those who come to offer their condolences.

Hon. Sam Okoli

Hon. Sam Okoli is a young government minister. He is handsome, well dressed, and has a reputation as the most eligible bachelor in Lagos. Obi sees Clara sitting in Sam's car, but later learns that they are not romantically involved. Later, Obi borrows thirty pounds from the minister to pay for Clara's abortion.

Eunice Okonkwo

Eunice Okonkwo is Obi's youngest sister, and the only one still living with their parents in Umuofia.

Hannah Okonkwo

Hannah Okonkwo is Obi Okonkwo's mother. During the four years of Obi's absence in England, her health has suffered and she has grown frail. For years she has been a devout Christian, fulfilling her duty as the wife of a catechist. However, she still enjoys "heathen" music and she used to tell Obi folk stories while her husband was out at prayer meetings. Obi feels a strong bond with his mother, and he is her favorite child. After becoming engaged to Clara, Obi is confident that he can persuade his mother to accept his choice. When he visits her again, however, her outrage is so powerful that it overwhelms him. She demands that her son not wed the *osu* woman until after her death, otherwise she will kill herself. From this point on, Obi is sapped of will. Shortly afterward, while Obi is in the midst of a crisis after Clara's abortion, he receives word of his mother's death. He chooses not to travel to Umuofia for her funeral.

Isaac Okonkwo

Isaac Okonkwo is Obi's father. He was for many years a catechist of the Church Missionary Society in Umuofia. Now retired, he is one of the most prosperous men in the village, known for entertaining lavishly. He has a stern, stubborn personality, and is especially serious about maintaining a Christian home, free of what he calls "heathen" influences. Isaac refuses to give permission for his son to marry Clara; he is unimpressed by Obi's appeal to Christian ethics. Late in the novel, he speaks to Obi about his past. Readers of *Things Fall Apart* will be familiar with the story of how Isaac (known then as Nwoye) ran away from the home of his father, Okonkwo, to become a Christian, and later refused to grieve his father's death.

Obi Okonkwo

Obi Okonkwo is the main character of *No Longer at Ease*. He is the first young man from the village of Umuofia to travel to England for his studies; in the parlance of the Ibo people, he goes there to "learn book." He is twenty-five years old when he returns to his home country with a degree in English literature. He settles in Lagos and gets a senior civil service job as secretary to the Scholarship Board. His personality is reserved, passive, intellectual, and somewhat haughty. At first he is idealistic and disdains the routine corruption of Nigerian life. As a young, cosmopolitan leader in the era just before Nigerian independence, Obi believes his generation is bound to change the country dramatically. He dismisses all criticism of his involvement with Clara, confident that the taboo against the *osu* is an antiquated superstition that will soon disappear.

The events of the novel reveal the weakness of Obi's moral fiber. He cannot overcome his mother's fierce objection to his engagement to Clara and lacks the personal strength to move forward with Clara anyway. He allows Clara to break off their engagement despite her pregnancy. In the end, his emotional and financial difficulties lead him to compromise his principles and begin accepting bribes, resulting in his arrest.

Mr. Omo

Mr. Omo is the administrative assistant of the Scholarship Board. He has worked there thirty years. When Obi comes to him to see about a salary advance, his manner implies that he may demand a bribe.

President of Umuofia Progressive Union

The president of the Umuofia Progressive Union in Lagos is considered the father of the sons of Umuofia now living in the capital city. He is willing to accept most requests for help that come from individuals. He approves a ten-pound loan to Joshua Udo, and is willing to grant Obi a four-month postponement of his debt to the union. However, he reserves the right to offer personal advice. For example, he confronts Obi about his relationship with Clara, whom he calls "a girl of doubtful ancestry."

Sebastian

Sebastian is Obi Okonkwo's steward. He is somewhat confused by Obi's orders to turn off the refrigerator at night, but to buy foods at the market only once a week.

Miss Marie Tomlinson

Miss Marie Tomlinson, a young Englishwoman, is Mr. William Green's secretary and shares an office with Obi at the Scholarship Board. Although she is attractive, Obi is at first wary of her, suspecting that she may be reporting on him, but gradually he lets down his guard and the two become friendly. They speak frequently about their coworker Mr. Green, whom Marie views as a good man, although somewhat odd.

THEMES

Colonialism

The social and psychological effects of European colonialism in African life is a central theme in all of Achebe's writing. *No Longer at Ease* is set toward the end of the colonial period; two generations have passed since the white man's initial disruption of Ibo society, the period depicted in *Things Fall Apart*. Blatant racial prejudice remains quite alive in the world of the latter novel. For example, the two Irish nuns are discouraged by their Mother Superior from socializing with African men. The patronizing attitudes expressed by Mr. Green reveal another dimension of the clash between cultures.

However, *No Longer at Ease* illuminates a subtler, deeper effect of colonialism, and that is the division and confusion of values—the conflict between tradition and modernity, between indigenous and Christian religion, between village communalism and urban materialism. Obi Okonkwo exemplifies this division. His upbringing, with his father's devout Christian faith and his mother's reluctant abandonment of folk culture, left Obi with one foot in each world, with neither world claiming his allegiance. His European education only deepens his alienation from his own society. Through his engagement to Clara, Obi intends to break away from the restrictions of traditional beliefs. He knows he will have to face opposition to his decision and he steels himself for battle. However, he is ultimately unable to defy the demands of custom when expressed forcefully by his mother. Unable to reconcile the conflicting values within him, Obi's character collapses at its foundations. He betrays Clara and drifts away from his moral principles. Obi's tragedy, Achebe implies, can be attributed to the subtle but pernicious effects of colonialism.

Political Corruption

Corruption is clearly key to the plot of *No Longer at Ease*. Right from the start, the author makes clear that Obi Okonkwo has been prosecuted for accepting a bribe. It soon becomes clear that bribery and corruption are pervasive in the social world depicted in the novel. The author hints at this early in the opening chapter by revealing that some people paid money to

TOPICS FOR FURTHER STUDY

- Achebe wrote *No Longer at Ease* as a sequel to *Things Fall Apart*. Read *Things Fall Apart*. How are the two novels related? Viewed together, how do the two works augment each other's meaning?

- Write a 3–5 page research paper on the political history of Nigeria since independence. Consider to what degree Nigeria's post-colonial history reflects the ideals of the young Obi Okonkwo, or the failure of those ideals. Use examples to support your ideas. (You may want to supplement your research by reading Achebe's essay *The Trouble with Nigeria*, 1983.)

- Prepare a report on the status of the *osu* in contemporary Nigeria. Has the caste system changed since the generation of "pioneers" such as Obi?

- Read Buchi Emecheta's *The Bride Price* (1976). In small groups, discuss the ways in which Emecheta's portrayal of the *osu* caste system differ from Achebe's. What do you think accounts for the difference?

- In the years since Obi Okonkwo's sojourn in England, it has become more common for a young Nigerian to travel abroad and return with the identity of a "been-to." What effects would you predict this trend would have on cultural life in Nigeria? How can you research whether your predictions are accurate? Develop a research plan for this topic that identifies the specific sources you would use to find information.

receive a phony doctor's note so they could skip a day of work and attend Obi's trial. References to corruption recur frequently, demonstrating that the disease has penetrated deep into the social fabric of colonial Nigeria. Even before Obi disembarks from the boat that has taken him home from England, a customs official suggests a bribe to reduce his duty. "Dear old Nigeria," he

Lagos, Nigeria *(Dan Kitwood / Getty Images)*

chuckles to himself. When he interviews for a public service job, Obi is shocked when one man asks him directly, "Why do you want a job in the civil service? So that you can take bribes?"

Achebe suggests that the ubiquity of political corruption in pre-independence Nigeria is due, in large part, to widespread alienation from the government—another result of the colonial presence. As Obi begins his adult life in Lagos with an idealistic outlook, certain that he can uphold his scruples and avoid temptation. But the novel makes clear that he is swimming against the current. As a government official, he is expected to take bribes. When his friend Joseph describes Obi in this way: "Him na gentleman. No fit take bribe," a colleague replies with obvious doubt. Obi's friend Christopher expresses a looser, somewhat jaded view of the ethics of bribery, and this cynical perspective seems closer to the prevailing sentiment. Obi eventually succumbs to the pressure; when he gets caught accepting a twenty-pound bribe, few people are surprised. One of

Obi's kinsmen in fact finds it shameful that the offending bribe was for such a small amount. Another chalks it up to inexperience, saying, "Obi tried to do what everyone does without finding out how it was done." Their objections, in other words, are not at all ethical in nature. These remarks illustrate the debasement of values that are the target of Achebe's satire.

Individualism

Before the advent of colonialism, African societies such as the Ibo were centered on the clan or tribe. All individuals were expected to subordinate their personal interests and behave according to the best interests of the group. The coming of modernity brought changes to the meaning of tribal identity and strains to the bonds of kin and clan. At the same time, it gave rise to a new, more European concept of individual rights and privileges. Obi Okonkwo's kinsmen in the village of Umuofia raised a large sum of money to pay for his overseas education. They expected, with good reason, that Obi would return and serve the people of the village, thus justifying their investment. To their consternation, Obi immediately asserts his own will. Instead of studying law, he majors in English literature. When he returns to Nigeria, he settles in the metropolis of Lagos instead of Umuofia. At his reception, he foils his kinsmen's expectations by dressing and speaking informally. To the tribe, Obi's self-will bespeaks impudence, but from Obi's point of view, he is a sophisticated "been-to" and a pioneer.

The conflicting claims of the individual and the group come to a head in Obi's decision to marry Clara, despite the long-standing social taboo against the *osu* caste. Obi finds the taboo archaic and out of place in the mid-twentieth century, but he underestimates the opposition his "pioneering" decision will provoke. He approaches the Umuofia Progressive Union to ask for relief from his debt to them, but then leaves the meeting in a huff when the union president publicly raises his relationship with Clara. This incident brings to light the viewpoint of communal responsibility: Obi comes seeking further financial support from the group, but will tolerate no interference in his personal affairs. He cannot have it both ways. In the end, Obi stops repaying his debt to the U.P.U. altogether. With the ties of clan no longer binding, Obi cements his status as a modern, isolated urban individual.

STYLE

Irony

Irony is a classic literary device that employs apparent paradox or double meaning to convey profound messages indirectly and through humor. In dramatic irony, an event or phrase reveals meaning to the audience that could not be known to the characters involved. Irony is a prominent feature of Achebe's literary style, particularly in *Things Fall Apart* and *No Longer at Ease*.

Achebe creates an ironic framework in *No Longer at Ease* by revealing his main character's fate at the outset and then returning to the beginning of the story. Because the reader knows that Obi Okonkwo is ultimately convicted of taking a bribe, all his subsequent efforts to resist corruption are cast in an ironic light. For example, Obi tells Christopher that the young generation of civil servants, in which he includes himself, "can afford to be virtuous." Eventually, however,

Obi's pressing financial problems are among the factors causing his virtue to erode. The final irony is that it is just when Obi becomes unable to bear his moral decline, and it appears possible that he will reform himself, that he is arrested.

Language and Diction

Achebe is famous for the innovative way he uses the English language to convey an African sensibility and African speech patterns. In *No Longer at Ease*, Achebe creates an intricate arrangement in which his characters alternate between three different languages: standard English, Ibo, and pidgin, or "broken" English. All these languages communicate different attitudes or ways of seeing the world. The Ibo language, which Achebe renders in English, is languid and formal. Its many proverbs and parables contain the accumulated wisdom of an oral tradition. Obi asserts that Ibo speakers "make a great art of conversation." The spoken English of this novel, by contrast, appears cold, crisp and businesslike; it is the tongue of the colonizer, spoken by Africans on public business or in the presence of Europeans. Pidgin is a hybrid language, spoken not only by the urban working class but also occasionally by Obi and other middle-class Africans. Although the use of pidgin suggests a lack of fluency in English, its musical rhythms also deliver a witty folk perspective and a sense of brotherhood among Nigerians.

The linguistic choices the characters make from moment to moment often reveal their motivations and allegiances. For example, when Obi realizes that Mr. Mark seeks to bribe him, he switches from Ibo to English to create distance: "'I'm sorry, Mr. Mark, but I really don't understand what you are driving at.' He said this is English, much to Mr. Mark's consternation." Also, Obi begins to hope that Clara could care for him when she addresses him in Ibo for the first time. It is significant that Obi is self-conscious about his use of Ibo; at several key moments, he fails to find an appropriate proverb. His lack of mastery over his mother tongue is a crucial indication that Obi is out of step with Nigerian culture.

Allusion

Obi earns his degree in English, and he uses literature as a lens for viewing the world. The novel contains many literary references, especially to modern English writers. The first such reference is the epigraph from T. S. Eliot's poem "The Journey of the Magi," (1922) which furnishes the book's title:

We returned to our places, these Kingdoms,
But no longer at ease here, in the old
dispensation.
With an alien people clutching their gods.

The Eliot passage highlights Obi's feeling of disconnectedness in Nigeria. Other key references are to two modern novels set in Africa: Graham Greene's *The Heart of the Matter* (1948), which Obi discusses at length in his interview with the Public Service Commission, and Joseph Conrad's *Heart of Darkness* (1899). Both works center on the moral changes, or slow corruption, of European men after they are sent to work in Africa.

Obi himself had tried his hand at writing poetry while studying in England. His nostalgic poem about rural life in Nigeria is clearly influenced by the British pastoral tradition. When he returns to Lagos, he finds reality far removed from his own idyllic verses: "'I have tasted putrid flesh in the spoon,' he said through clenched teeth. 'Far more apt.'" Even his new observations allude to modern poetry, in this case Eliot's *Murder in the Cathedral*. Achebe reveals the literary influences on Obi's thinking to illustrate the degree to which he has absorbed the worldview of a foreign culture and lost his intuitive feeling for his own country. Although Obi "knows book," his book learning is as much a hindrance as a help in navigating contemporary Nigeria. Like Eliot's magi, he is no longer at ease.

HISTORICAL CONTEXT

In the first half of the twentieth century, the empires of Europe controlled most of the African continent. Achebe depicts the roots of British rule over the Ibo people of the Niger Delta in *Things Fall Apart*. As colonial administrators were setting up the machinery of government, European industrialists exploited the country's natural resources, and Christian missionaries introduced Western religion. Economic development, and the imposition of taxes, led many young men from the countryside to enter the cities in search of wage labor. Tribal unions, resembling the fictional Umuofia Progressive Union in *No Longer at Ease*, sprang up to keep the bonds of clan affiliation alive and provide mutual aid amid the anonymity of the city. A select few Africans received a European education, and gradually an African professional class emerged. Nevertheless, the changes imposed during the colonial era

undermined African tribal existence on every level, from the logistics of village life to spiritual practices and belief systems. Obi's attempts to be "modern" in choosing an *osu* wife, living in the city, and refusing bribes ultimately fail because of the strong pull of traditional values, but his struggles exemplify the conflicts individuals sometimes felt between traditional and colonial or European belief systems.

Because of the devastation of Europe caused by World War II, and also because of the rise of pan-African and African nationalist movements, decolonization became all but inevitable after 1945. Between 1946 and 1954, Britain gradually increased the level of autonomy and political representation granted the Nigerian people. *No Longer at Ease* is set on the eve of Nigeria's independence, when a generation of leaders such as Obi Okonkwo was preparing to take over from the British. Oil was discovered in the Niger Delta in 1956, sparking hopes of a rapid rise to prosperity. A relatively well-trained middle class entered a competitive scramble for civil service jobs, development contracts, and political advantage.

Nigeria had no history as a nation. It was, in fact, an invention of the British colonial authorities. Within the borders they drew lived hundreds of tribes and ethnic groups with their own languages and customs. Some of these tribes, such as the Yoruba and the Ibo, had a history of antagonism. Rather than a unified movement for national independence, Nigeria developed a number of separate political groupings organized along regional and ethnic lines. The British attempted to create a federal system of government in Nigeria, and conferred autonomy on a regional basis, first to the western and eastern regions in 1957, then two years later to the mostly Islamic northern region. By a vote of the British parliament, Nigeria became an independent state, still within the British Commonwealth, on October 1, 1960. The new nation was immediately beset by several serious difficulties, including the culture of political corruption, vividly illustrated in *No Longer at Ease*.

CRITICAL OVERVIEW

Achebe's first novel, *Things Fall Apart*, was largely responsible for bringing African literature to the world's attention, and was immediately recognized as the first modern African "classic." *No Longer at Ease* took much longer to receive critical recognition. While widely

COMPARE
&
CONTRAST

- **1950s:** Most of Africa is still under the control of such European colonial states as Britain, France, and Portugal; only nine African states achieve independence before 1960.

  Today: The decolonization of Africa is complete, with fifty-three sovereign members of the African Union, including the island nation of Madagascar.

- **1950s:** With the Cold War raging worldwide, most newly independent African states align with either the United States or the Soviet Union.

  Today: While socialist and communist parties still govern a handful of African states, all

of Africa belongs to the Non-Aligned Movement. An "African renaissance" and democratic movement has gained ground on the continent since South Africa eliminated its race-based apartheid system in 1994.

- **1950s:** Achebe is among the first African literary artists to reach a worldwide audience.

  Today: Africa's contributions not only to literature but all the arts have vastly increased. Achebe's countryman Wole Soyinka was the first African writer to win the Nobel Prize in Literature, in 1986.

reviewed, its initial reception was uneven. Many reviewers praised Achebe's control of language and deft juxtaposition of city and country scenes, but the overall view held that *No Longer at Ease* was a less satisfying novel than its predecessor. A key objection was to the character of Obi Okonkwo, who struck some reviewers as difficult to sympathize with and too weak to hold the novel together. Critic David Carroll articulates this view: "Because [Obi] does not come alive as a unique individual, we are never encouraged to see in his predicament the more universal theme it implies." Other critics, such as Philip Rogers, take a contrary view, arguing that the emptiness at the heart of Obi's character is in fact an essential aspect of the novel's meaning.

Over time, critical estimation of the novel has risen considerably. *No Longer at Ease* is now seen as an important link in the historical cycle comprising Achebe's first four works. *Arrow of God*, published four years after *No Longer at Ease*, is set in an earlier time, between the generations of Okonkwo and his grandchild Obi. For this reason, some scholars treat the four novels together as a historical chronology. Such an analytical strategy may obscure the links

between *Things Fall Apart* and *No Longer at Ease*, its sequel. In addition to the significance it carries in conjunction with its author's other work, *No Longer at Ease* has received ample scholarly attention in its own right. Commentators have studied the work for, among other aspects, its use of setting and location as a subtle influence on character; its sophisticated combination of Ibo, standard English, and pidgin; its relation to modern European literature; its layers of comic and tragic irony; and its exploration of the class structure and social mores of Nigeria in the late colonial period.

CRITICISM

Roger K. Smith

In this essay, author and writing professor Roger K. Smith takes the measure of the character of Obi Okonkwo, a "modern African nowhere man."

With great subtlety and economy, *No Longer at Ease* creates an intricate psychological portrait of a modern African nowhere man. Outwardly, Obi Okonkwo appears a model of success and uplift, a local boy from the bush who rises into the elite to lead a glamorous life in the

The "Mammy Wagon," as it is known in Nigeria, is primarily a large estate car, and each has its own slogan painted on the side. This one with "Safe Journey" written on its side obviously didn't live up to its name. *(Keystone | Hulton Archive | Getty Images)*

city with an enviable post in the senior civil service. But by probing, almost systematically, into the thought and behavior of his protagonist, Chinua Achebe reveals the weak foundations on which Obi's character rests. Like a sapling unable to take nourishment from depleted soil, Obi is on his own with few resources on which he can draw. Yet it is not enough to pity this character, or scorn his bad judgment. Beneath Obi's tragedy lies a more complex one, the tragedy of a society so vitiated by decades of foreign domination that its best and brightest are as strangers in their own land.

Achebe provides enough clues for the reader to discern that a great deal of Obi's later difficulties stem from his upbringing. His father, Isaac Okonkwo (or Nwoye, as he is called in *Things Fall Apart*), has built his life around Christianity, spurning his own father and the "heathen" ways of his people. Obi's mother, Hannah, has set aside many of the customs with which she was raised to live as the wife of

a catechist. There are clear hints that Hannah has some regrets over the compromises she has made:

> She was a very devout woman, but Obi used to wonder whether, left to herself, she would not have preferred telling her children the folk stories that her mother had told her. In fact, she used to tell her eldest daughters stories. But that was before Obi was born. She stopped because her husband forbade her to do so.

Thus the conflicted legacy of colonial Nigeria has sown discord in the heart of Obi's family life. As a result, Obi has no culture he can truly call his own; he grows up estranged from both tribal and Christian ways. He declines to identify with Christianity, and is unable to receive nurture from traditional Ibo culture. He is deprived of the oral tradition his mother could have imparted to him, so much so that he is humiliated at school because he knows no folk story to tell when called upon. (His mother finally teaches him a story on the sly.) Furthermore, his father so fears Obi's

WITHOUT THE SUPPORT OF A CLEAR CULTURAL IDENTITY AND A STABLE SET OF VALUES, WITHOUT A STRONG BOND TO EITHER HIS FAMILY OR HIS CLAN, WITHOUT A COMMITMENT TO ANYONE'S INTEREST BUT HIS OWN, WHAT DOES OBI OKONKWO HAVE GOING FOR HIM?"

exposure to tribal ritual that he forbids the boy to eat in his neighbors' houses. These strictures are more than enough to keep the young Obi at a remove from his Ibo kinsmen.

The consequences of this alienation from his native culture become apparent on close examination of the adult Obi's behavior. For one thing, he is portrayed as having less than full mastery of the Ibo language. When he makes a speech to his town union, he begins in Ibo but falls back on English midway through. When he asks Clara to explain a proverb, she replies, "I have always said you should go and study Ibo." For an accomplished student with a college degree in English, such an educational deficit is somewhat shocking.

Not only the Ibo language, but also the prevailing mind-set and mores of his fellow Ibo elude Obi's intuitive grasp. This becomes clear soon after he returns to Nigeria from England. Obi arrives at a reception held in his honor—a major event covered by the press—dressed in his shirtsleeves; everybody else is turned out in formal attire. He proceeds to disappoint the crowd still more with his speech, which is also too informal and fails to flaunt the prestigious education he has received. It could be said that Obi's casual behavior reflects the mentality of a cosmopolitan "been-to" still under the influence of British culture. But it is equally plausible, given his upbringing, that he simply overlooks, or disdains, the respect for formality and ceremoniousness that is engrained in Ibo customs.

Lacking this instinctual sense of belonging within his clan, Obi reveals little awareness of his place in either his family or his community. The reader learns that Obi has six sisters and one brother, but he hardly interacts with them, and

they do not seem to figure largely in Obi's life. He does become aware of a responsibility to contribute a share of his salary to his parents' upkeep, and he volunteers to pay his youngest brother's school fees. These acts are appropriate given Obi's high income and status. Soon, however, Obi's growing feelings for Clara, and the complications caused by her caste position, lead to an inner conflict: "Family ties were all very well as long as they did not interfere with Clara," Obi thinks to himself. He tries to convince himself that he can convince his mother to put aside her objections, so he will not be forced to choose between his blood and his heart. But he is deluding himself; he cannot avoid this choice, and it is his undoing. It is characteristic of Obi that he is not fully conscious of the depth of his connection to his mother. He is more closely bonded to her than any other person, but he takes that bond for granted until it is threatened by his stubborn passion for Clara.

Hannah Okonkwo's revulsion at the idea of her son marrying an *osu* is in keeping with her identification with Ibo culture and values, an identification her husband's Christianity could never erase. Obi is blind to his mother's predictable reaction. No doubt his wishful thinking is caused, in part, by the blindness of love; but there is another explanation, his other blind spot—his disconnection from the values of his people.

This lack of tribal solidarity also reveals itself in Obi's dealings with the Umuofia Progressive Union. It is because of this group's largesse that Obi has received the opportunity to study overseas and become a big man. What do the Umuofians deserve from Obi in return for their investment in him? The union hoped Obi would study law, so when he returned he could help the village settle land claims. Traditional tribal values would imply that any valuable resource—such as, in this case, Obi's expensive education—should serve the interest of the clan as a whole. Yet Obi shows no sign of subscribing to such values. He pursues only his own individual interests. He reads English instead of law. He appears to offer nothing back to the community, apart from his financial commitment to repay the scholarship loan—and by the novel's end, he is even reneging on that. Moreover, he dismisses the idea that he has a responsibility to set a good example in his conduct. He becomes furious when the union president comments during a meeting about Obi's affiliation with "a girl of

WHAT DO I READ NEXT?

- Achebe originally planned *Things Fall Apart* and *No Longer at Ease* as a single novel. He published *Things Fall Apart* in 1958, and after half a century it is still the most famous of all African novels. Its portrait of the beginning of British colonialism in Nigeria, and its impact on the Ibo community of Umuofia, is considered an insightful work of anthropology as well as a beautifully crafted work of fiction.

- Achebe's fourth novel, *A Man of the People* (1966), continues his relentless investigation of greed and political corruption in modern Nigeria. At the climax of the novel, an economic crisis leads to military intervention in the government. Achebe's satire was amazingly timely: just as it was published, Nigeria experienced its first military coup.

- The novel *Mister Johnson* (1939) by British author Joyce Cary, set in Nigeria, was an important influence on Achebe's early writing. Despite its author's liberal views, the novel's depiction of Africans remains mired in negative stereotypes.

- *The Bride Price* (1976) by Buchi Emecheta explores sensitive issues of women's lives in Nigeria. Its heroine, Aku-nna, refuses to enter into an arranged marriage. She chooses to pay the price for pursuing her own dreams and passions.

- *Efuru* (1966), by Nigeria's Flora Nwapa, was the first novel published in English by an African woman. Efuru is a beautiful, successful businesswoman. When her husband deserts her, however, she begins to lose her status in the community and must call upon the assistance of Umahiri, the Goddess of the Lake.

- The title character of Bernard Binlin Dadié's autobiographical novel *Climbié* (1956) has much in common with Obi Okonkwo. The novel follows him from a rural childhood in the Ivory Coast, through his education in elite colonial schools, to adult life in Dakar, the capital of Senegal. Climbié slowly learns that by forsaking village life for the city, he has given up an essential part of himself.

- *The Palm-Wine Drinkard and His Dead Palm-Wine Tapster in the Dead's Town* (1952), by Amos Tutuola, provides a fascinating glimpse into Nigeria's literary art before Achebe. This richly imaginative adventure fantasy is loosely based on traditional Yoruba folk tales.

- For a highly informative account of Africa's transition from colonialism to independence, see *Africa Since 1940: The Past of the Present* (2002), by Frederick Cooper.

---

doubtful ancestry." The elder Umuofian clearly believes he has the prerogative to offer frank advice to the young man who has received the group's help (and has already asked for further help at this meeting). The president is displaying the values of the tribe. Obi, on the other hand, reveals an individualistic mind-set when he interprets the president's comments as an unjustified intrusion into his personal affairs. The exchange underscores the essential truth that modernization causes the ties of community to become

thinner and more attenuated—indeed, Obi doesn't seem to feel the least bit bound by them.

The confusion in Obi's thinking leads him to identify in a materialistic sense with European culture, an essentially inaccurate assessment of his social status. Once ensconced in his senior service job, he does not hesitate to buy a car he can scarcely afford, and even to hire a driver. He takes a flat in an expensive European suburb of Lagos and employs a steward. Because of such profligate choices, even though he is earning far above the norm, he soon finds himself unable to pay his car insurance, and later his income tax. He realizes that it will be difficult to explain his financial problems to his fellow Umuofians whose sacrifice made his education possible:

> Obi admitted that his people had a sizable point. What they did not know was that, having labored in sweat and tears to enroll their kinsman among the shining élite, they had to keep him there. Having made him a member of an exclusive club whose members greet one another with "How's the car behaving?" did they expect him to turn round and answer: "I'm sorry, but my car is off the road. You see I couldn't pay my insurance premium"? That would be letting the side down in a way that was quite unthinkable. Almost as unthinkable as a masked spirit in the old Ibo society answering another's esoteric salutation: "I'm sorry, my friend, but I don't understand your strange language. I'm but a human being wearing a mask."

The reference to esoteric Ibo rites in this passage appears somewhat strained; much more revealing of Obi's thought process is the phrase "letting the side down," a British sports expression. Because Obi does not want to "let the side down," or is afraid to, he eventually succumbs to the temptation to square his debts through ill-gotten gain.

Without the support of a clear cultural identity and a stable set of values; without a strong bond to either his family or his clan; without a commitment to anyone's interest but his own, what does Obi Okonkwo have going for him? He appears to have two strong assets, one being his intellectual prowess. But this is highly abstract, and tooled in the European fashion, through the study of the printed word. Obi "knows book." He flaunts his book-smarts in his employment interview, and this appears to be the central way he earns his "European" job posting. But the novel repeatedly reveals that his European education is of limited use for getting along in modern Nigeria. It needs to be complemented with street smarts and common sense, both of which are somewhat deficient in Obi's case. As a case in point: why does he not know that it is unwise to leave fifty pounds cash in the glove box of his car in a nightclub parking lot with "half a dozen half-clad little urchins" trolling around?

His other major strength—until it gives way—is his sense of morality. But this too proves to be a liability at times, such as when he silently interposes himself into the exchange between the

> OBI CANNOT BE OKONKWO BECAUSE HE LACKS THE MORAL CHARACTER BASED ON SOLID VALUES THAT SUSTAINED THE "GIANTS" OF OLD."

police and the mammy-wagon driver. Obi's vigilant gaze, it turns out, costs the driver eight shillings, and earns him the derision of the other passengers, who correctly peg him as "too know." Once again, he is out of step with the goings-on around him.

More importantly, for all the reasons discussed above, Obi's individual ethical stance lacks a firm foundation. He is unwittingly prophetic when he says to Christopher, speaking of his generation: "It's not that they're necessarily better than others, it's simply that they can afford to be virtuous." Later, when circumstances press him, he can no longer afford the cost of virtue. Like the benighted, colonial society around him, he drifts passively into corruption and decay.

Source: Roger K. Smith, Critical Essay on *No Longer at Ease*, in *Novels for Students*, Gale, Cengage Learning, 2010.

Romanus Okey Muoneke
In the following excerpt, Muoneke looks for potential remedies to the social problems raised in No Longer at Ease.

The Nigeria of *No Longer at Ease* is perverted through and through. Bribery is common practice among the Police, the Customs, and the Civil Service.

Corruption in the Nigerian society is ubiquitous according to Achebe. Why would he lay so much emphasis on corruption in this novel? Roderick Wilson attributes the conflicts in the novel to the fragmentation of the individual and the society as a whole (162–66). For example, the Umuofia Progressive Union is a victim of the conflict of expectations. They grant a loan to Obi to enable him to earn a university education in England, and they also expect to benefit the Umuofia society, especially in winning land cases, acquiring education and employment for their sons and members. The Union anticipates a return from Obi also. They expect him to repay his loan, maintain a high standard of living commensurate with his new status, and fulfill all his financial obligations to his extended family, for example, to pay his brother's school fees and to bear the financial responsibility for his mother's funeral. They insist on Obi's maintaining a European life style, but at the same time, expect him to be traditional on the question of *osu*. The fragmentation extends to individuals; for example, Obi's friend and townsman, Joseph is both modern and traditional. In education, employment, and life style, Joseph is Westernized, but he is fiercely opposed to Obi's relationship with Clara because she is an *osu*. Obi's parents too are divided between their strong Christian belief and their traditional belief. The fragmentation in this society is explained by the so-called cultural collision.

What Achebe repeatedly insists upon in this novel is that the lack of a solid grounding in both traditional and Western values is largely responsible for the moral and cultural crises in the pre-independent Nigeria. The novel implies that the solution to the crises demands true adaptation, which involves exploiting the good in each culture. Commenting on the positive aspect of colonialism, Achebe once said:

> I am not one of those who would say that Africa has gained nothing at all during the colonial period, I mean this is ridiculous—we gained a lot. But unfortunately when two cultures meet, one might expect if we were angels we could pick out the best in the other and retain the best in our own. But this doesn't often happen. What happens is that some of the worst elements of the old are retained and some of the worst of the new are added ... (Quoted by Killam, *The Writings of Chinua Achebe*, 4–5).

Obi Okonkwo therefore needs the affirmative values of Western education and the positive values of the traditional society to build a wholesome character. The fragmented society needs a blending of the positive values from both cultures to achieve wholesomeness.

To press this point, Achebe contributes concrete examples of what values should be possessed by those Nigerians who will be assuming the duties of their colonial counterparts. Hard work and devotion to duty are two outstanding qualities shown by the officials. Marie, the expatriate Secretary to Mr. Green, shows a remarkable combination of cheerfulness and efficiency in her work. As for Mr. Green, Obi's boss, his great devotion to duty, as well as his kindly heart, is deserving of honor and respect. Mr. Green, on the other hand, does not believe that Africans, including well-educated ones, could run modern institutions. Obi marvelled at the paradox he finds in his boss:

> Obi had long come to admit to himself that, no matter how much he disliked Mr. Green, he nevertheless had some admirable qualities. Take, for instance, his devotion to duty. Rain or shine, he was in the office half an hour before the official time, and quite often worked long after two, or returned again in the evening. Obi could not understand it. Here was a man who did not believe in a country, and yet worked so hard for it ...

The irony in the case of Mr. Green is biting. His continuing commitment and devotion at a time when the British are about to handover the reins of government is contrasted with the lack of serious commitment on the part of those Nigerians preparing to take over power. On the one side, this contrast raises considerable doubt regarding the readiness of the people for independence. On the other side, it suggests a solution to the general ethical depravity in the country. Achebe is therefore inferring that Western culture, as well as the colonial experience, possesses an immense treasure of values that should be implemented for responsible nation-building. The grim irony is that the people are more attracted to the "materialistic" (if not venal) elements of Western tradition. Umuofia Progressive Union's infatuation with meaningless bombastic English expressions, and "the Honourable" Sam Okoli's over-indulgence in petty, fanciful Western gadgets, are indicative of the kind of imitation of colonial governance that Achebe finds supercilious in light of the substantive offering of Western culture.

Obi's lot is that of many Nigerians who return from overseas equipped with technical knowledge and filled with goodwill in the hope of improving their country. However, they are soon disillusioned and frustrated by the rampant corruption of Nigerian society and the stagnation of its economy. Their enthusiasm dampens, and their slogan shifts from "I will change society" to "if you can't beat them, join them." As a representative of the educated elite that would replace the colonial elite, his fall becomes more resounding and tragic. In Achebe's proverbial language, "the [country's] only palm-fruit ... [has got] lost in the fire." "I cannot comprehend how a young man of your education and brilliant promise could have done this," said the presiding Judge during Obi's trial. This could equally be said to the whole of the failing generation of educated Nigerians on the "eve" of Nigeria's independence.

Corruption has received a lion's share of treatment in this novel, and it will be interesting to examine Achebe's hints toward its solution. A consideration of possible solutions is found in Obi's contemplation of the prevalent corruption in his society. He considers mass education to be one corrective measure but dismisses this resolution because such a remedy will take centuries to accomplish. Enlightened dictatorship is a scary solution. What about finding a meeting point between democracy, corruption, and ignorance? Achebe's suggestion is that the surest way to rid society of corruption is through individual effort. This redemptive "one man," whose example would stand out for others, is the singular figure Obi aimed to be but failed.

Obi needs the fortitude of his grandfather to succeed. Achebe deliberately refers us to the period in Umuofia's history when traditional values held sway. The old man Odogwu recalls the period of greatness when "giants" lived in Umuofia. Odogwu sees the spirit of Okonkwo in Obi; he equates Obi's academic achievement with Okonkwo's heroic achievement of the past. This is, of course, Achebe's irony, for the reader knows well that Obi does not stand comparison with his forebear. The point however is that, had Obi been as strong and determined as Okonkwo, he would not have compromised his high principles. He would never have taken bribes nor would he have failed to marry Clara because of the hullabaloo about her being an *osu*. Obi cannot be Okonkwo because he lacks the moral character based on solid values that sustained the "giants" of old.

An incident situated in Isaac Okonkwo's house points to the solution of the problem of culture-conflict in the country. Obi had returned from England and paid a visit to Umuofia. Friends and kinsmen gathered in his father's house to rejoice with his family. An old man had asked Isaac to bring a Kola nut "to break for this child's return." Isaac, often "uncompromising in conflicts between church and clan," and sometimes tending toward fanaticism, refused to bring the kola nut that would be "sacrificed to idols in a Christian house." The old man left the room in protest and chose to sit outside. This

conflict is a microcosmic representation of the larger conflict between the traditional and the Western cultures. Odogwu's solution of the conflict in Isaac's house reflects the kind of solution Achebe is advocating. Odogwu was known to be at peace with the two traditions. He offered to produce the symbolic kola nut, and, as he searched his goat-skin bag, "things knocked against one another in it—his drinking-horn, his snuff-bottle and a spoon." The items in his bag signify a blending of cultures—the new and the traditional. His kind gesture worked the miracle on Isaac who changed his mind and served three kola nuts in a saucer. Odogwu insisted on adding his, thus making sure that the saucer contained a mixture of "Christian" and "heathen" kola nuts. Odogwu was the type of "heathen" who went to church at harvest, and one thing he was fascinated with was the Christian expression, "as it was in the beginning, it will be in the end." In blessing the kola nuts, Odogwu said a prayer that cheered every heart, Christian or "heathen": "'Bless this kola nut so that when we eat it, it will be good in our body in the name of Jesus Kristi. As it was in the beginning it will be at the end. Amen.'" Achebe is advocating a redemption after the spirit of Odogwu, which is at once open to Christian and traditional cultures. Kola nut among the Igbo signifies peace and friendship. The form and content of Odogwu's blessing brings together Christian and traditional elements, and the result is a union of hearts. Achebe is implying, therefore, that the problems caused by the culture conflict can be solved by exploiting the positive and efficacious elements from both cultures. This again calls for compromise and balancing. Isaac Okonkwo's near-fanaticism will not permit a balance, nor will the old man's uncompromising reaction. Odogwu's reconciling spirit is an index to peace, unity, and progress.

Source: Romanus Okey Muoneke, "Redemption: *No Longer at Ease*," in *Art, Rebellion and Redemption: A Reading of the Novels of Chinua Achebe*, Peter Lang, 1994, pp. 130–135.

Umelo Ojinmah

In the following excerpt, Ojinmah assesses the novel's political implications by viewing Obi Okonkwo as a representative of Africa's young leadership class.

At the period just before independence the destiny of many of the new nations of Africa were in the hands of the emergent black administrative

> OBI EXHIBITS A MARKED IGNORANCE OF HIS
> SOCIETY'S WORLD-VIEW. THIS IGNORANCE IS FURTHER
> COMPOUNDED BY HIS SENSE OF INDIVIDUALISM
> RESULTING FROM HIS WESTERN EDUCATION."

class, represented by Obi Okonkwo. In this class were vested the authority and privilege of shaping and mapping out the course that these colonies would take on independence, and of laying the foundations on which democracy could be built.

Achebe, at the time of writing *No Longer at Ease*, was concerned that, as heirs of the new order, this new emergent black administrative class might not have been adequately equipped for the task of self governance (since it is assumed that democratic processes demand very high standards of commitment, honesty and, above all, responsibility in those vested with authority, to be productive, meaningful and sustained). Mr Green tells Obi:

> You know, Okonkwo, I have lived in your country for fifteen years and yet I cannot begin to understand the mentality of the so-called educated Nigerian. Like this young man at the University College, for instance, who expects the government not only to pay his fees and fantastic allowances and find him an easy, comfortable job at the end of his course, but also to pay his intended [fiancee]. It's absolutely incredible. I think Government is making a terrible mistake in making it so easy for people like that to have so-called University Education. Education for what? To get as much as they can for themselves and their family. Not the least bit interested in the milllions of their country-men who die everyday from hunger and disease.

Granted, Mr Green, as John Povey says, "is not an agreeable man to represent a moral stand point", but despite his sarcastic tone, or even because of it, Achebe uses him to point at underlying problems of both the emergent black administrative class represented by Obi, and to Nigeria as a country in transition: "There is no single Nigerian who is prepared to forgo a little privilege in the interest of his country. From your Ministers down to your most junior clerk. And you tell me you want to govern yourselves."

Ironically, the antagonism of Obi Okonkwo for "the Greens" and the stereotypical picture of Mr Green, dims the poignancy of his message - "that a country that is born on a cesspool of bribery and corruption" was not mature enough to value democracy. I should hasten to say that the Nigeria of *No Longer at Ease*, on the verge of transiting from a colony into an independent nation, is not unlike a villager from a rural community in his first journey to an urban environment. Both demand tentative, almost hesitant steps and constant vigilance, or else, just as the villager is liable to be run-over by a moving vehicle in the unaccustomed bustle of the city if he is not careful, or miss his way, the country is also liable to collapse or be destroyed, if those vested with authority are not honest, responsible, and careful.

It is my contention that Achebe portrays this Nigeria in terms that are similar to the way he portrays the main character, Obi Okonkwo. The problems that beset both are similar, and their solutions or lack of solutions are also similar. Achebe's analysis of the problems and challenges that this emergent black administrative class, which Obi represents, face as a result of both societal and family demands and expectations, and how they respond to these, shows why he indicts them of irresponsibility.

Achebe believes that members of this class did not seem to comprehend the enormity of the responsibility asked of them as representatives of the people at large. They are depicted as having adopted the common attitude which sees the government as an amorphous, unquantified establishment to which they owe no personal commitment: "'Have they given you a job yet?' the Chairman asked Obi over the music. In Nigeria the government was 'they'. It had nothing to do with you or me. It was an alien institution and people's business was to get as much from it as they could without getting into trouble."

Even the education which the society makes possible for this class, becomes for them, a means to material acquisition:

> A University degree was the philosopher's stone. It transmuted a third-class clerk on one hundred and fifty a year into a senior Civil Servant on five hundred and seventy, with car and luxuriously furnished quarters at nominal rent. And the disparity in salary and amenities did not tell even half the story. To occupy a 'European post' was second only to actually being a European. It raised a man from the

masses to the elite whose small talk at cocktail parties was: "How's the car behaving?"

As Mr Green remarks, education, to Obi and his class, is a means "to get as much as they can for themselves and their family." None of them is shown to be "the least bit interested in the millions of their country-men who die every-day from hunger and disease." Neither were they prepared, as Mr Green also says, "to forgo a little privilege in the interest of [their society]".

Achebe views maturing for an individual as having a lot in common with a country on the verge of attaining independence, both demand more than the average sense of responsibility. Obi and his class are shown to be interested only in the material perquisites of their positions: "Obi bought a Morris Oxford a week after he received his letter of appointment. Mr Green gave him a letter to the dealers saying that he was a senior civil servant entitled to a car advance. Nothing more was required. He walked into the shop and got a brand-new car." Earlier in the day Obi had been given sixty pounds as 'outfit' allowance. "'You think Government give you sixty pounds without signing agreement?' It was only then that Obi understood what it was all about. He was to receive sixty pounds outfit allowance." Even this early in Obi's career, he is shown to embody the perverse corruption which he criticises, as he falsifies his statement of expenditure after receiving another allowance because he "had not realised that the allowance was not a free gift to be spent as one liked."

The scramble, for Obi and his class, is for the distribution of what Nigerians call "the national cake." This metaphor likens the economic resources of the nation to a cake which exists so that anyone in a position to do so, might carve from it as big a piece as he possibly can for himself and his family and, by extension, for his tribe or ethnic group.

Achebe thus identifies Nigeria's tragedy as the fact that the country, even at birth, already carried the germs of decay, through the still-born idealism of such people as Obi Okonkwo.

It is my view that to Achebe, the term "responsibility" is central to the resolutions or understanding of the tensions and problems of Obi Okonkwo, the Nigerian elite class he represents, and the Nigerian state.

If we organise the "evidence" which Achebe presents to us, and if we treat Obi as a real person, as Achebe's kind of social realism invites us to do, then we find that a lot of Achebe's criticisms and his stern reproof of this class begin to make sense.

Achebe, foreshadowing Obi's financial irresponsibility, had said through Mr Green, "You will do well to remember ... that at this time every year you will be called upon to cough up forty pounds for insurance... It is, of course, none of my business really. But in a country where even the educated have not reached the level of thinking about tomorrow, one has a clear duty." When the insurance letter came, Obi "had just a little over thirteen pounds in the bank", thus proving Mr Green's assessment of him, and the class he represents, to be correct. For a civil servant who has no other source of income, but his monthly salary of forty-seven pounds and ten shillings (£47.10), to be spending about seventy-four pounds, three shillings and seven pence indicated financial imprudence and lack of planning and foresight—or an anticipation of illegal means of getting the difference.

Having looked at the financial demands on Obi Okonkwo, it is necessary to also assess the societal expectations and demands on him. This is important as both demands cannot really be divorced from each other. Society expects Obi and his class to reflect their pioneer status in their behaviour. Paradoxically, the same society expects them to live like elites, with all the trappings that the type of life demand—a car, driver, steward and other such luxuries:

The society also expects that they use their positions to the benefit of their own people. Umuofia Progressive Union's discussion on Joshua's plight, reflects this:

> Joshua is now without a job. We have given him ten pounds. But ten pounds does not talk. If you stand a hundred pounds here where I stand now, it will not talk. That is why we say that he who has people is richer than he who has money. Everyone of us here should look out for openings in his department and put in a word for Joshua ... Thanks to the Man Above,' he continued, 'we now have one of our sons in the senior service. We are not going to ask him to bring his salary to share among us. It is in little things like this that he can help us. It is our fault if we do not approach him. Shall we kill a snake and carry it in our hands when we have a bag for putting long things in?'

The society, represented in this instance by Umuofia Progressive Union, expects Obi to use his position to the advantage of the immediate family represented also in this context by the people of the same tribe or kindreds—to find jobs for his people irrespective of whether the applicants are qualified for the jobs or not. No one questions the morality of the expectations. The prevailing feeling is that as long as he is doing it for "us" it is all right, "us" referring to people from his tribe, clan, or kindred.

As has been mentioned, Achebe considers the issue of both personal and collective "responsibility" as central to the whole concept of self-governance, and he sees Obi Okonkwo as typical of the average Nigerian graduate of the period who were the inheritors of the new nation . . . As has also been illustrated, society expects Obi, by virtue of his position, to demand and accept bribes as his due. As Joseph's friend tells him in respect of Obi: "'E go make plenty money there. Every student who wan' go England go de see am for house. "E no be like dat," said Joseph. "Him na gentleman. No fit take bribe." "Na so," said the other in unbelief.' The society also expects those who indulge in such dishonest activities, as Obi does, to be clever enough not to be caught: "Obi tried to do what every-one does without finding out how it was done." Paradoxically the same society, as exemplified by Joseph's implicit defence of Obi, believes that he [Obi] and his class should be gentlemen of honour, and that they should refuse such corruptive influences, and thus usher in a new era. It is therefore these contradictions, and Achebe's comments about no one understanding why Obi succumbs to corruption, that No Longer at Ease tries to explicate.

Achebe sees the resolution of these conflicting demands as only possible through the actions of people who are exposed to both worlds, as Obi and his class are.

Unfortunately, Achebe characterises Obi as both naive and having no proper sense of history.

Obi's alienation stems both from his upbringing and his liberal western education. Traditionally, a child in Igboland belongs to the community and his obeisance to the culture and tradition of his people rests as much on what the child picks up instinctively by association with other children and the community at large, as on the parent's teachings. By depriving Obi of this second and fundamental part of his 'childhood lessons,' his parents had helped alienate him from his roots:

Isaac Okonkwo was not merely a Christian; he was a catechist. In their first years of married life he made Hannah see the grave responsibility she carried as a catechist's wife. And as soon as she knew what was expected of her she did it, sometimes showing more zeal than even her husband. She taught her children not to accept food in neighbours' houses because she said they offered their food to idols. That fact alone set her children apart from all others, among the Ibo, children were free to eat where they liked.

This childhood upbringing has not only estranged Obi from his culture, it has also made him ignorant of his responsibility to the community. Obi exhibits a marked ignorance of his society's world-view. This ignorance is further compounded by his sense of individualism resulting from his western education.

The society had trained Obi with the expectations that he would return to them "with the boon of prophetic vision." But Obi returns with an acquired and heightened sense of his individuality, plus an inclination to benefit from the traditional communal sense of solidarity and kinship. Obi seeks the benefit of the communal solidarity which made his education possible along with the liberal notion of individuality which has no place in the traditional society. It is evident that Obi cannot have the best of both worlds. His insubordination to Umuofia Progressive Union is only an expression of the desire to be his own man, but viewed from the cultural perspective, Obi is seen as an ingrate.

The individualism which Obi expresses: "I am not going to listen to you anymore . . . But don't you dare interfere in my affair again," is not compatible with the society that makes it the duty of elders to advise and when necessary admonish the young.

In No Longer at Ease, therefore, Achebe through Obi Okonkwo illustrates the lack of reponsibility, among other things, exhibited by the inheritors of the new nations of Africa, whose primary functions should have been to lay the concrete foundations for post-colonial developments but who, instead, "like the absurd man who was pursuing rats while his house was in flames", preferred to allow their houses to be razed rather than salvage what they can, by institutionalising corruption, graft, and tribalism.

Source: Umelo Ojinmah, "A Legacy Squandered: Achebe's Disillusionment at Post-colonial Irresponsibility in No Longer at Ease and A Man of the People," in Chinua Achebe: New Perspectives, Spectrum Books Limited, 1991, pp. 37–60.

OBI'S RELATIONSHIP WITH HIS PEOPLE IS
PARALLELED IN HIS ATTITUDE TOWARDS HIS NATIVE
LANGUAGE. HE HAS LOST CONTROL OVER IT."

Felicity Riddy

In the following essay, Riddy explores the theme of language in No Longer at Ease.

A year before war broke out in Nigeria the novelist Chinua Achebe wrote, to a group of people concerned with English teaching in Nigeria, that he knew of

> ... no serious weight of opinion today against the continued presence of English on the Nigerian scene. This is fortunate for our peace of mind for it means we can believe in the value of English to the very survival of the Nigerian nation without feeling like deserters. Thus we can use our energies constructively in the important task of extending the frontiers of the language to cover the whole area of our Nigerian consciousness while at the same time retaining its world-wide currency.

Nor was this a new theme. On a previous occasion, for example, Achebe had spoken of the need for '... a new English, still in full communion with its ancestral home, but altered to suit its new African surroundings.' The implications of these remarks are obvious, and are not entirely invalidated by the current plight of the Federation: the vernacular tongues of Nigeria lack universality in a country made up of diverse peoples and orientated towards the rest of Africa and the world at large; and yet English, though as an international language essential to Nigerian nationhood, has not yet fully adapted itself to the Nigerian scene. Less obvious perhaps is the relevance of all this to Achebe's second novel *No Longer at Ease*, and yet it is precisely this situation that confronts Obi Okonkwo: none of the languages available to him is adequate to express the urban experience.

Furthermore, in this book languages are closely related to values; English and Ibo are not merely different ways of saying the same thing, but vehicles for expressing completely different attitudes to life. Where one language or the other proves inadequate, so for the same

reasons do the values it represents. The tension between 'traditional' and 'modern' in the educated West African has been described elsewhere by the poet and playwright John Pepper Clark:

> The great complication, perhaps, for the West African elite brought up in a system not quite British is that he swims in a stream of double currents, one traditional, the other modern. Both currents do not completely run parallel; in fact, they are often in conflict. Accordingly, you are likely to find him at church or mosque in the morning and in the evening taking a title at home that carries with it sacrifice of some sort to his ancestors and community gods. In the same manner, a man however 'detribalized' and successful in his city career and profession, will not outgrow the most backward member of his family.

Obi Okonkwo is what Clark calls 'a citizen of two worlds'. As the first person in his village to receive a university education and a post in the senior service, his future seems assured in a Nigeria approaching independence. The difficulties which confront and finally overcome him stem from his inability to identify himself wholly with either the traditional or the modern way of life, and his lack of a sense of identity is most clearly reflected in his speech.

Achebe uses on occasion two different styles, particularly in conversation, to distinguish between the Ibo and English tongues. On the one hand, Ibo is represented by a cadenced, proverb-laden style similar to that in *Things Fall Apart* and *Arrow of God*, to which Professor Eldred Jones has drawn attention, rich in images drawn from traditional rural life. It is the rhetorical manner of 'men who made a great art of conversation':

> Here is a little child returned from wrestling in the spirit world and you sit there blabbing about Christian house and idols, talking like a man whose palm-wine has gone into his nose.

> If a man returns from a long journey and no one says *nno* to him he feels like one who has not arrived.

> Greatness has belonged to Iguedo from ancient times. It is not made by man. You cannot plant greatness as you plant yams or maize. Whoever planted an iroko tree—the greatest tree in the forest? You may collect all the iroko seeds in the world, open the soil and put them there. It will be in vain. The great tree chooses where to grow and we find it there, so it is with the greatness in men.

They are also men who make an art of living, and the 'Ibo' style not only stands for a mode of speech but also symbolizes a whole way of life: ceremonial, ordered, governed by traditional wisdom and rooted in the soil. It is the way of life practised by the Christians and the adherents of the old religion of Umuofia alike. Both retain, for example, an element of ritual in daily living in the ceremonial breaking of kola. In fact, Christianity has not swept aside the traditions of Umuofian society as completely as it seemed about to do in *Things Fall Apart*; in certain areas it has accommodated itself to them. The most obvious example of this is in the scandalized reaction of Isaac Okonkwo, the catechist, to his son's proposed marriage to an *osu* or outcast; his wife had long since come to a compromise over the matter of teaching pagan folk-tales to her children.

The element of syncretism in Umuofian Christianity finds expression, fittingly enough, in a syncretic style half 'Biblical', half 'Ibo'. This is displayed early in the novel, when Hannah Okonkwo's friend Mary leads the prayers at the meeting held before Obi's departure to England:

> 'Oh God of Abraham, God of Isaac and God of Jacob,' she burst forth, 'the Beginning and the End. Without you we can do nothing. The great river is not big enough for you to wash your hands in. You have the yam and you have the knife; we cannot eat unless you cut us a piece. We are like ants in your sight. We are like little children who only wash their stomach when they bath, leaving their back dry ...'

After this glimpse into the nature of Umuofian Christianity it is not altogether surprising when, much later on, Isaac Okonkwo not only draws naturally on the Biblical analogy of Naaman to defend the *osu* system, but also describes the consequences of marriage to an *osu* in a manner which reveals a less conscious identification of Christian and pagan thought:

> *Osu* is like leprosy in the minds of our people. I beg of you, my son, not to bring the mark of shame and of leprosy into your family. If you do, your children and your children's children unto the third and fourth generations will curse your memory.

If, as Dr Abiola Irele has suggested, the paramount virtue in *Things Fall Apart* was manliness, in *No Longer at Ease* the main emphasis has shifted on to what might be termed 'brotherlines', a sense that one's primary obligations are to one's kinsmen, both within the family circle and beyond it in the clan. The proverb, 'anger against a brother is felt in the flesh, not the bone',

is quoted on more than one occasion, and the theme is repeated in the pagan song that Obi hears outside his father's house:

> He that has a brother must hold him to his heart,
> For a kinsman cannot be bought in the market,
> Neither is a brother bought with money.

The Umuofia Progressive Union is itself a product of this sense of kinship; it was as a result of communal effort that Obi was sent to England in the first place, and when he has gained his post in the senior service it is assumed that his prestige will reflect (in a strictly practical way) on his kinsmen. The sense of brotherliness takes an external form in the sharing of a common language, as Obi realizes at an early stage in his relationship with Clara: 'But then she had spoken in Ibo, for the first time, as if to say, "We belong together: we speak the same language."' In attempting to bribe Obi, Mr Mark addresses him in Ibo to establish the same point. But there is a moment when brotherliness becomes exclusiveness (as with the treatment of the *osu*), and an incident like that in which a hostile policeman's manner changes abruptly when he realizes that Obi and Clara are, like himself, Ibo, reveals how kinship may be abused in a larger society not based on kin.

Just as the Ibo language is strictly limited in its currency, so the traditional way of life has parallel limitations, as Achebe's occasionally overt satire reveals:

> Mr Ikedi had come to Umuofia from a township, and was able to tell the gathering how wedding feasts had been steadily declining in the towns since the invention of invitation cards. Many of his hearers whistled in unbelief when he told them that a man could not go to his neighbour's wedding unless he was given one of those papers on which they wrote R.S.V.P.—Rice and Stew Very Plenty—which was invariably an over-statement.

This minor incident serves to illuminate a larger truth, that urban life has complexities of which traditional society has no comprehension. Obi cannot begin to explain his financial predicament to his clansmen when, faced with a fifty-pound debt to Clara and the bill for an abortion, he has to simplify his situation into terms they can understand in order to be relieved of his obligations to them:

> He would just stop paying and, if they asked him why, he would say he had some family

commitments which he must clear first. Everyone understood family commitments and would sympathize. If they didn't it was just too bad. They would not take a kinsman to court, not for that kind of reason anyway.

His education seems to have emancipated Obi from the restricted world of the clan, and he continually flouts its conventions, not only by planning to marry an *osu* but in smaller things as well. He turns up to the welcome meeting in the wrong kind of clothes; he sleeps at Joseph's rather than at a hotel; he announces his intention to Joseph of ignoring the bride-price tradition, and so on. Finally he proposes to challenge the whole basis on which the clan rests, the bond of kinship:

> Obi knew better than anyone else that his family would violently oppose the idea of marrying an *osu*. Who wouldn't? But for him it was either Clara or nobody. Family ties were all very well as long as they did not interfere with Clara.

But he over-estimates his own resources. He is ultimately unable to reject the strongest tie of all, with his mother, and through her with the clan.

Obi's relationship with his people is paralleled in his attitude towards his native language. He has lost control over it. He stumbles over the prayers in his father's house. When he is searching for an apt proverb, Clara tells him, 'I have always said you should go and study Ibo.' The second time he addresses the Umuofia Progressive Union he begins in Ibo but is unable to sustain it. Nevertheless he still derives a sense of pride from his language and the way of life it represents:

> Let them come to Umuofia now and listen to the talk of men who made a great art of conversation. Let them come and see men and women and children who knew how to live, whose joy of life had not yet been killed by those who claimed to teach other nations how to live.

He takes no such pride in English, which, as his second language and the subject he studied for his degree, is available to him in two forms: in the intercourse of colonial society and in English literature.

English conversation, in contrast to Ibo, has no distinctive rhetoric. It is laconic, almost abrupt:

> 'Come in, Clara. Come in, Obi,' he said as if he had known both of them all his life. 'That is a lovely car. How is it behaving? Come right in. You are looking very sweet, Clara. We haven't met, Obi, but I know all about you. I'm happy

you are getting married to Clara. Sit down. Anywhere ...'

> 'Hello, Peter. Hello, Bill.'

> 'Hello.'

> 'Hello.'

> 'May I join you?'

> 'Certainly.'

> 'Most certainly. What are you drinking? Beer? Right Steward. One beer for this master.'

> 'What kind, sir?'

> 'Heineken.'

> 'Yes, sir.'

> 'We were talking about this young man who took a bribe.'

> 'Oh yes.'

The unceremoniousness of this kind of talk coincides with the casualness of relationships in colonial urban society and its lack, for Obi at least, of the genuine sense of community out of which ceremony grows. European corporate life finds its only manifestation in the club; in the first chapter of the book the club and the Progressive Union are portrayed as two parallel groups of exiles striving to preserve their identities. In fact European Lagos as a whole is symbolized for Obi by the club (a club that is more like a secret society) whose members are all engaged in an elaborate masquerade. It has a language of its own; one must either speak it or consider oneself expelled.

Having laboured in sweat and tears to enrol their kinsman among the shining élite, they had to keep him there. Having made him a member of an exclusive club whose members greet one another with 'How's the car behaving?' did they expect him to turn round and answer 'I'm sorry, but my car is off the road. You see I couldn't pay my insurance premium.'? That would be letting the side down in a way that was quite unthinkable. Almost as unthinkable as a masked spirit in the old Ibo society answering another's esoteric salutation: 'I'm sorry, my friend, but I don't understand your strange language. I'm but a human being wearing a mask.' No, these things could not be.

Obi has been admitted to the club because of his talents, but his membership is precarious. When he endeavours to speak its language he is in a sense acting out a part; his financial difficulties are exacerbated, if not caused, by his attempts to maintain his role and supply the answers expected of him. Language is no longer a tool but a master. Even the Hon. Sam Okoli, who seems so much at ease among the trappings of colonial society, and who gives the esoteric salutation with such urbane assurance ('That's a lovely car, How is it behaving?') reveals himself on occasion as less than certain about his own predicament. 'White men done go far. We just de shout for nothing', he says to Obi at their first meeting. Momentarily he speaks not as a member of the club but as an outsider, and it is significant that in doing so he drops its language and switches into pidgin, the *lingua franca* of the uneducated. In a somewhat similar fashion Obi deliberately uses an unEnglish pronunciation in order to dissociate himself from expatriate attitudes, when, at a restaurant with Joseph, he is served European instead of Nigerian food:

> Then he added in English for the benefit of the European group that sat at the next table: 'I am sick of boiled potatoes.' By calling them boilèd he hoped he had put into it all the disgust he felt.

The uncertainty of both Obi and the Hon. Sam Okoli about their position in colonial society stems largely from its exclusiveness.

Nigerians may take their degrees, gain places in the senior service and learn to talk the right language, but they are still open to insults from Mr Green and Irish girls are still warned away from them by the nuns.

European values are directed towards maintaining external appearances. The cardinal sin is 'letting the side down', being found out. When Obi is finally arrested and tried it is the Union, not the club, that stands by him; colonial society closes its ranks against him, even though—'You think white men don't eat bribe? Come to our department. They eat more than black men nowadays.'

But spoken English is not the only form of the language that 'fails to cover the whole area of . . . Nigerian consciousness', since in writing his own poetry Obi draws on the tradition of English literature in which he has been educated. Joseph Warton's *The Charms of Nature* and Wordsworth's *The Prelude* lie somewhere behind 'How sweet it is to lie beneath a tree', but in Obi's poem nature is merely a means of localizing nostalgia.

The tone of naive optimism is not only invalidated by Obi's experience but also fails to take account of his own far more tentative and contradictory attitudes towards his native land.

With his sharply critical turn of mind, Obi is well aware of the feebleness of his own creative efforts, but as F. R. Leavis has pointed out in another context:

> To invent techniques that shall be adequate to the ways of feeling or modes of experience of adult sensitive moderns is difficult in the extreme.

It is a task for which Obi has the training but not the strength of character. When his mother threatens to kill herself if he marries Clara he is made aware for the first time of his own lack of a sense of identity and purpose:

> His mind was troubled not only by what had happened but also by the discovery that there was nothing in him with which to challenge it honestly. All day he had striven to rouse his anger and his conviction, but he was honest enough with himself to realize that the response he got, no matter how violent it sometimes appeared, was not genuine.

He cannot after all reject the claims of the blood-tie, and in failing Clara acquiesces, however unwillingly, in the values of the clan. Nevertheless it is only a temporary capitulation: on his mother's death his bond with the clan, which his relationship with her has symbolized, is relaxed and he immediately outrages Umuofian morality by not attending the funeral. He writes in his diary at this time that he feels 'like a brandnew snake just emerged from its slough', but he discovers that this rebirth is also a death:

> He no longer felt guilt. He, too, had died. Beyond death there are no ideals and no humbug, only reality. The impatient idealist says: 'Give me a place to stand and I shall move the earth.' But such a place does not exist. We all have to stand on the earth itself and go with her at her pace.

Coming to terms with reality in this sense is an invitation to compromise. Stripped of 'ideals and humbug', including his vision of a Nigeria freed from corruption, owing allegiance to nothing and having lost all self-respect, Obi finally succumbs to the financial pressures upon him. His decision to take bribes is at once a confirmation of that loss of a sense of identity of which he is already aware and the defeated gesture of a man who has been unable to find the means of expressing himself.

Source: Felicity Riddy, "Language as a Theme in *No Longer at Ease*," in *Critical Perspectives on Chinua Achebe*, edited by C. L. Innes & Bernth Lindfors, Three Continents Press, 1978, pp. 150–159.

SOURCES

Achebe, Chinua, *No Longer at Ease*, Heinemann, 1960.

Bengoechea, Mercedes and Gema S. Castillo Garcia, "The Semantics of Solidarity and Brotherhood in Chinua Achebe's *No Longer at Ease*," in *Journal of English Studies*, Vol. 2, 2000, pp. 19–34.

Carroll, David, *Chinua Achebe: Novelist, Poet, Critic*, Twayne, 1970.

Rogers, Philip, "*No Longer at Ease*: Chinua Achebe's 'Heart of Whiteness'," *Research in African Literature*, Vol. 14, No. 2, Summer 1983, pp. 165–83.

FURTHER READING

Booker, M. Keith, *The Chinua Achebe Encyclopedia*, Greenwood Press, 2003.
> This book is a comprehensive, alphabetical guide to everything related to Achebe and his work.

Champion, Ernest A., *Mr. Baldwin, I Presume: James Baldwin–Chinua Achebe, A Meeting of the Minds*, Press of America, 1995.
> An imaginative work of comparative literature, this book focuses on two famous black writers of the twentieth century, finding important similarities in their thinking and literary techniques.

Innes, Catherine Lynette, *Chinua Achebe*, Cambridge University Press, 1990.
> This critical study argues that Achebe reshaped the genre of the novel to serve African purposes, laying the groundwork for a new African literary tradition.

Killam, G. D., *The Novels of Chinua Achebe*, Heinemann, 1969.
> One of the first full critical treatments of Achebe's fiction, this book focuses attention on the literary achievement, as opposed to the cultural or anthropological interest, of his novels.

Wren, Robert M., *Achebe's World: The Historical and Cultural Context of the Novels of Chinua Achebe*, Three Continents, 1980.
> This work is designed to provide important background information to readers of Achebe's fiction.

Ordinary People

1980 In 1976, Viking Press published a manuscript plucked from the slush pile, Judith Guest's *Ordinary People*, and it succeeded in garnering critical success. In this best seller, the Jarrett family struggles to heal emotionally after the oldest son's tragic death in a boating accident. The story begins following the suicide attempt of troubled younger son Conrad and builds around themes of alienation, the search for identity, and coming of age. Young Conrad learns to face his feelings with the aid and friendship of a psychiatrist. This reflects a popular trend in the 1970s that valued the idea of self-exploration and psychological discovery.

In 1980 Robert Redford, in his directorial debut, adapted Guest's novel into an Academy Award–winning film starring Timothy Hutton as Conrad, Mary Tyler Moore as his mother Beth, Donald Sutherland as his father Calvin, and Judd Hirsch as Dr. Tyrone C. Berger. In 1981, Redford won an Oscar for Best Director, Timothy Hutton won for Best Supporting Actor, and the film won Best Picture. Mary Tyler Moore was honored with a nomination for Best Actress. *Ordinary People*, both the novel and film, has been praised for its universal appeal, particularly in its portrayal of grief and realistic family dynamics.

Robert Redford accepts the Best Director Oscar for Ordinary People *at the 53rd Annual Academy Awards in 1981.* (Ron Galella | WireImage | Getty Images)

PLOT SUMMARY

The novel, *Ordinary People*, takes place in Lake Forest, Illinois, during the 1970s. The story centers on the Jarrett family—Calvin, Beth, and their son Conrad. They are mourning the older Jarrett son, Buck, who was killed in a boating accident. Conrad felt so guilty about Buck's death that he attempted suicide by slashing his wrists before the novel begins. Guest uses three points of view to tell the story, allowing Calvin and Conrad to narrate their own internal conflicts in alternating chapters and also occasionally using an omniscient narrator. Beth's character is developed through the point of view of her husband or her son.

Screenwriter Alvin Sargent meticulously adapted *Ordinary People* for the screen. Director Robert Redford, in contrast to Guest, adheres to a traditional onscreen storytelling style with an omniscient point of view and a focus on characterization through action. Redford cuts and combines certain scenes and rearranges the order of certain plot points, altering the chronology of Guest's original story.

Opening Scenes
The film version of *Ordinary People* opens with several quick camera shots to set the scene. First, the camera pans over a serene setting: empty winding roads, fallen leaves over a small bridge, a pier jutting out over calm water. Next the scene cuts to an imposing school, where inside a student choir sings "Hallelujah." Next Conrad Jarrett, a boy from the choir, wakes up in bed in a sweat.

Viewers next see a stage play in which a husband and wife are having a conversation. The husband tells his wife that he doesn't know a thing about her—especially little things, like what perfume she wears—but he has always been in love with her. The camera pans to the audience, where Beth and Calvin Jarrett are sitting. Calvin is asleep. In the car on the way home, Beth remarks on Calvin's quiet mood. When they get home, Beth sees Conrad's bedroom light on, but ignores it. Calvin goes in to talk to his son and asks if he is okay. Later that night in bed, Calvin makes love to his wife.

The next morning, Beth makes breakfast, while upstairs in his bedroom, Conrad appears anxious. He finally goes downstairs, but declines the French toast Beth offers. She dumps it down the sink even though Calvin tells her not to waste it. Beth rushes out. Calvin assures his son that they just want him to get stronger and suggests he start bringing friends home again. Calvin also asks if Conrad has called the doctor.

The novel opens with similar domestic scenes, but focuses more on internal conflict. In his room, Conrad dreads the day before him and sees routine tasks as daunting. Calvin and Beth are also beginning their day. Calvin, who was raised in an orphanage, thinks about how his fatherless childhood has affected him as a father. Calvin seems lost as his son. Calvin, Beth, and Conrad spend a tense breakfast together.

Family and Friends
Conrad waits outside for his friends to pick him up for school. They tease him about the fact he has to repeat eleventh grade because he missed final exams. The car stops for a train, and Conrad flashes back to a cemetery. After the train passes they continue on; when they see Jeannine Pratt walking to school, they harass her a bit.

FILM TECHNIQUE

- In the film adaptation of *Ordinary People*, Robert Redford gives "objective treatment" to Guest's original story, written in the points of view of Conrad and Calvin. In other words, when watching the film, the viewer observes what happens from an omniscient viewpoint. Though Redford often ratchets up the drama by cutting one scene quickly to the next, the film unfolds for the most part in a narrative style called "invisible editing," a technique usually adopted for realist approaches to storytelling. Although the editing is not truly invisible, the term refers to the way in which a cut from one scene to the next emphasizes character and plot development and gives a sense of following "real" events as they occur. These cuts also force a sense of "compressed time," compelling the viewer to presume a specific amount of time has passed between scenes. This compressed time can be seen at the start of *Ordinary People*, when Conrad and other students are singing in the choir and the scene quickly jumps to Conrad waking up in his bedroom in the middle of the night, sweating from a bad dream. The viewer assumes time has elapsed between those two events.

- Redford doesn't use any type of voice-over to put events in context, though at times he uses music and silence to draw out the emotions of certain scenes and sequences. During the opening sequence of the movie, for example, Pachelbel's Canon plays behind serene scenic shots. An empty pier, a deserted park, a bridge cluttered with autumn leaves, and winding roads offer a feeling of peace and, at the same time, of isolation and loneliness, major themes in the film. The pier, park, bridge, and roads could be anywhere, and the music—a theme most people recognize but cannot name—seems universal.

- Redford also manipulates time in the film through "flashbacks," as experienced by Conrad and Calvin. In a "flashback," past events are revealed or remembered. In *Ordinary People*, flashbacks take the viewer out of the present-day narrative and offer glimpses of what happened both during the boating accident and the night of Conrad's suicide attempt. Flashbacks also provide details of the relationship between Conrad and Buck. Only through flashbacks can the viewer put together what happened on the night of the boating accident as well as understand relationships between family members before the tragedy. A flashback serves as a catalyst for the climax of the film when Conrad recalls the boating accident and realizes he is furious at Buck for letting go of the boat. After remembering what happened, Conrad races across town to meet with Berger and unleashes his sorrow, anger, guilt, and blame. This scene marks a major triumph in Conrad's healing process.

In English class, Conrad's teacher asks him for his theory on Thomas Hardy's "Jude Frawley," and inquires if Conrad thinks he is a "powerless" character. Conrad eats lunch alone on the bleachers outside and later nervously calls Dr. Berger to set up a meeting. At swim practice, Coach Salan pushes Conrad to perform better. Later, Beth, Calvin, and Conrad have dinner together. The mood is tense and quiet. Beth talks only about superficial things, and does not address the tension in the room. She tells Calvin about a party they have to attend, but Calvin doesn's want to go.

The film illustrates the internal conflict Guest portrays in the novel through visuals, while the novel strives for a balance of "showing and telling." Similar to the film, the novel demonstrates Conrad's uncertainty and unease with his life through tense conversations with his parents, his swimming coach, and his old friends. But the novel also allows the reader inside Conrad's emotional state. For example, in the novel, as Conrad waits for his friend Lazenby to pick him up for school, the reader is privy to Conrad's anxiety. He fears his mental instability is creeping back and feels guilty about worrying his parents. The reader also gets an inside view of Conrad's crush on a new girl at school, Jeannine Pratt, as well as his insecurities about swimming.

Flashbacks and Therapy

Conrad dreams about being caught with his brother Buck in a storm. The film cuts to Conrad standing in front of a building and contemplating whether to go inside. In the elevator Conrad looks nervous and practices small talk aloud. He enters the office; Dr. Berger tells him to sit. Conrad does not. Berger asks why he was in the hospital. Conrad says, "I tried to off myself." Berger inquires about the method and begins questioning him about his feelings. Conrad admits he wants to be more in control. He also confesses he does not like the idea of seeing a psychiatrist. Berger says he knows Conrad had a brother who died in a boating accident. Berger also says he is "not big on control." Conrad decides to see Berger instead of attending swimming practice.

The scene cuts to Beth and shows how extremely organized her kitchen drawers are. Conrad tells Calvin that he went to see Dr. Berger, and an encouraging Calvin asks how the therapy went. The scene then jumps to Conrad at swim practice, where Salan dresses him down and grills him about the therapy methods used in the psychiatric hospital. The scene changes again to Conrad in the school hallway with friends. He meets Jeannine, who compliments him on his singing in choir.

The film omits a detail about Berger that the novel uses as a form of character development. When Conrad meets Berger, the doctor's office has just been robbed. Despite the incident, however, Berger is unconcerned. He seems rather indifferent to the fact that someone broke in, but wonders what to do about the mess left behind. Conrad asks if Berger is going to call the police, but the doctor dismisses the idea because he is certain that calling them would not do any good. This scene between Conrad and Berger establishes Berger as a man who doesn't think too highly of doing things the conventional way. In contrast, the film version of

Berger comes across in a more serious, straight-forward manner.

Memories

In the film, Beth answers the door to greet trick-or-treaters with homemade treats. She mentions spending Christmas in London, but Calvin does not think a holiday is a good idea. Beth wants to get back to normal. The scene jumps to Beth coming home to an empty house. She opens a closed bedroom door and goes inside. She sits on the bed and gazes at her deceased son's belongings. The camera pans around the room to the awards and trophies. Conrad pokes his head in the room, startling his mother. Beth gasps and Conrad apologizes profusely. He tries to make small talk and reaches out to her, but she avoids him.

Rather than focusing on Beth, the novel reaches deeper into Calvin's psychological conflicts as he thinks about the argument with his wife and why he feels tempted by his attractive secretary, Cherry. For example, he wonders who he really is, and recalls his youthful dreams of becoming a soldier or an athlete. He questions his career choice, remembering how he took up a law career after his mentor, the famous tax attorney Arnold Bacon, offered him advice and a clerkship. Calvin also realizes that he never learned how to deal with grief.

Privacy, Dreams, and the Past

Calvin and Beth drive to their friends' party, despite the fact that Calvin does not want to go. Party guests make small talk about business, golf, and money. Calvin retreats to a staircase with friend Annie Marshall. The two talk about their kids, and Calvin tells her about Conrad's therapy with Berger. Beth overhears, and on the drive home lashes out at Calvin for speaking about what she considers a "very private matter."

Conrad asks Berger if he should tell him about his dreams and wonders if he should be taking tranquilizers, because he feels "jumpy." Berger does not have much faith in dream analysis or tranquilizers. Conrad thinks the hospital was easier because "nobody hid anything there." In the next scene, Conrad sees Karen, a friend from the psychiatric hospital. They are awkward and tense with each other as they discuss seeing doctors. Before the scene ends, she turns around and, in a loud voice that startles other patrons in the restaurant, says, "Hey, would you cheer up?"

The novel includes the scene in which Conrad meets up with Karen. He tells Karen that he is seeing a psychiatrist, and she admits that she once saw one too, but stopped. She tells him that he must help himself, with faith in God. The film omits Karen's religious commitment. The novel also shows Calvin as drinking more in response to his problems. He tries to connect with Conrad and tells Beth that the family should postpone their vacation until the spring. He and Beth argue about their holiday on the way to a neighbor's cocktail party, and in the novel, the event is depicted in a much more intimate fashion than the way it is portrayed in the film. In the novel, when the Jarretts' friends ask Calvin and Beth about Conrad, the situation seems close, claustrophobic, almost as if Calvin and Beth feel they are under a microscope. In contrast, the party portrayed in the film is large, and when Calvin talks to a friend about Conrad, he seems to be divulging their business in a much more public forum.

Furthermore, in the novel, Guest describes Conrad's upsetting dreams as another way for the reader to see a different level of Conrad's fear and anxiety. For example, Conrad dreams that he is at the ocean and wanders into a drainage tunnel with walls that close in on him. Dr. Berger, whom he visits the next day, tells him the dream does not mean anything. Berger tells Conrad to lie on the floor for a "change in perspective." Conrad admits he is nervous all the time and does not want to swim anymore. At the same time, he fears quitting because he does not want to seem like a failure.

Tension in the Family

The film highlights the tension between Beth and Conrad. Conrad is in the backyard staring up at the sky. Beth comes outside to see if he needs a sweater and wonders what he is thinking about. Conrad tries to bond with her by mentioning how Buck once wanted a dog. Beth changes the subject, but to get her attention, he loudly barks. Their conversation ends abruptly. Back inside the house, Beth sets the table and Conrad offers to help. She declines and tells him that he can clean the closet upstairs in his room instead, insisting that it "really is a mess." The phone rings and Beth answers it, ignoring Conrad to talk with a friend. Her laughter prompts Conrad to remember Buck making

his mother laugh. Conrad later talks with Berger about his problems connecting with his mother.

The scene shifts to Calvin and Ray, his law partner of many years, walking down the street. Ray says Calvin is "losing it" and wonders what's wrong with him. He uggests that he stop worrying about Conrad. Calvin flashes back to a memory of his sons fighting over a sweater, then to a disjointed memory of him pounding on a door, a stretcher, and an ambulance. These flashbacks are not included in the novel, but heighten the drama and emotional development in the film.

At swim practice Coach Salan tells Conrad that he has a bad attitude and is messing up his life. The action moves to Conrad at his school locker, where Lazenby says Salan told the swim team that Conrad quit and presses Conrad for a reason. Conrad avoids him. At a therapy session, Conrad tells Berger that he cannot relate to his mother. He also admits that he wants to keep control and stop feeling "lousy."

The novel explores Conrad's anxiety about the swim team and his conflict with his friends on a deeper level, as the reader is actively engaged with Conrad's point of view. For example, as Conrad watches swimming practice and fears getting back into the pool, he repeats the mantra, "Doesn't matter doesn't matter I didn't really want to swim." Though the viewer sees that reaction in the film, the novel allows a glimpse directly inside Conrad's mind.

The novel also provides more dimension to Calvin's feelings. When Calvin runs into Lazenby's mother Carole and asks her to have lunch with him, the reader understands how Buck's death has made Calvin feel as if nothing is the same as it was before the tragedy: "because she looks so real and so alive, he is absurdly glad to see her; asks her to go to lunch with him on the spot." Calvin longs to connect physically and emotionally with someone.

Family and Budding Romance

The tension between Beth and Conrad comes to a head in a scene involving Conrad, Calvin, Beth, and Beth's parents. Conrad's grandmother is taking photos of Conrad, Calvin, and Beth. When Calvin asks to snap a picture of Conrad and Beth, she tries to avoid having her picture taken with her son by saying she will take the pictures. Conrad lashes out and tells Calvin to "give her the goddamn camera." Beth later speaks to her mother about Conrad, wondering out loud if they should send him to boarding school.

After choir practice, Conrad catches up to Jeannine in the hall, where she compliments his singing. They walk together, talking about music. After seeing her to the bus, Conrad walks home elated. When he gets home, he calls Karen, but talks to her mother who says Karen is not home. Conrad looks through the phone book for Jeannine's number, but has difficulty mustering the nerve to make the call. When he finally does, the conversation is a bit shaky, but she accepts when he asks her out on a date.

While the film portrays the family tension in more straightforward and simple manner, the novel layers internal and external conflicts and builds the plot along with the character development. For example, the novel shows Conrad beginning to heal as he fills his time with studies, birdwatching at the park, and Christmas shopping for his family. He makes a "Life List" and sets goals. In a session with Berger, Conrad confesses that he hasn't told his father about quitting swimming because he doesn't want him to worry. He continues to talk about his lack of connection with his mother. Berger encourages Conrad to allow himself to feel bad and to stop thinking so much. Conrad runs into Jeannine after school and invites her to have a drink with him. Their date boosts his self-esteem. On the way home, a display window prompts him to remember a skiing trip he took with Buck.

Christmas and Forgiveness, Flashback and Family Therapy

Calvin and Conrad bring home a Christmas tree but Beth arrives home angry after hearing from a friend that Conrad quit the swim team. Calvin asks why Conrad did not tell them. Conrad says that "the only reason she cares is because someone else knew about it first." After Beth leaves the room, Conrad confesses his resentment that his mother did not visit him in the hospital, telling his father that he is certain she would have visited Buck in the hospital. Conrad flees to his bedroom.

Calvin asks Beth to speak to Conrad with him, but she refuses. Calvin talks to Conrad alone. Conrad doesn't want his father to be angry. He also confesses to Calvin that he believes Beth hates him and will never change. Conrad later tells Berger about the argument, but says he doesn't really blame his mother because he caused the problems

in her life. He describes the bloody mess in her tidy bathroom after he attempted suicide. Berger wants him to recognize his mother's limitations and to let himself off the hook. Conrad realizes he needs to forgive himself.

Calvin goes jogging with a friend, but when they part, Calvin continues to run, thinking back to the family argument while decorating the Christmas tree. Calvin later meets with Dr. Berger and admits he feels responsible for Conrad's suicide attempt. He also feels as though his family is drifting away from him. He confesses that he thinks Beth cannot be close to Conrad because the two are too much alike—neither of them cried at Buck's funeral.

Calvin returns home. Beth finds him sitting outside in the car and asks what is wrong. Calvin wants to discuss Buck's funeral. Beth had made a fuss about the shirt he had chosen, and he had always wondered why the shirt mattered. Beth hugs him but says nothing. This scene is not included in the novel, but provides visual character development and shows the disconnect in the relationship between Calvin and Beth.

Later, Beth meets Calvin for lunch. He suggests they see Berger together as a family. Beth refuses, insisting problems need to be solved in private. She wants Calvin to go away with her and tells him she has already talked to her parents about staying with Conrad.

Conrad and Jeannine go on a date. They go bowling, then out to eat. Jeannine asks Conrad about his suicide attempt. He tells her that she is the first person who has asked him. She asks why he did it, and he says he "fell into a hole that got bigger and bigger." Conrad's friends from the swim team come into the restaurant acting raucous, making Jeannine laugh. Conrad becomes upset by her reaction. She apologizes, but he shuts down.

The novel delves further into Conrad's sexuality than the film does. While Conrad visits the library, a pretty young woman admires him openly. Conrad is surprised and tells Berger about the encounter at their next therapy session. He also opens up to Berger about his sexual feelings for girls and about his masturbation habit. Berger says his behavior is normal, and suggests he ask a girl out on a date. Later in the novel, Conrad makes love with Jeannine.

The novel provides more opportunities to illustrate Conrad's growing relationship with his father. For instance, on his eighteenth birthday, Conrad clears out the garage with Calvin and the two bond.

Beth and Calvin Go Away; Conrad has an Epiphany

Calvin and Beth take a trip to Houston alone. In the meantime, Conrad goes to a swim meet and watches from the bleachers as his friends lose the meet. After the meet, Stillman asks Conrad if he has had sex with Jeannine. This leads to a fistfight. Everyone but Lazenby walks away, calling Conrad crazy. Lazenby asks Conrad if he wants to talk and offers his help, but Conrad says it hurts too much to be around him.

Conrad returns to his grandparents' house and phones Karen. A man tells him that she has killed herself. Horrified and upset, he flashes back to his brother's boating accident and tears out of the house. He runs to a pay phone and calls Berger, who immediately meets him at the office. In an emotional scene, Conrad tells Berger that he blames himself for the accident, but also blames Buck for not holding on to the boat or turning back at the first sign of bad weather. Berger asks him, "How long are you going to punish yourself?" and demands to know, "What was the one wrong thing you did?" Conrad admits that he blames himself for living.

Conrad loiters outside Jeannine's house. She comes out and apologizes for her behavior at the restaurant and invites him for breakfast. Meanwhile, Calvin and Beth are golfing in Houston. Calvin mentions Conrad and thereby upsets Beth. She accuses Calvin of being controlled by Conrad. On the return trip, Calvin thinks about the early, simple days of his relationship with Beth.

Calvin and Beth arrive home. Conrad hugs his mother and tries to reach out, but she resists. That night Beth wakes and finds Calvin gone. She goes downstairs and finds him crying at the dining table. He accuses her of being weak and cold, with the inability to love anyone. He also confesses that he does not know if he loves her anymore. She goes upstairs and packs a suitcase. She only allows herself one sob, but true to her character, prevents herself from crumbling.

In the novel, Guest offers more character development than does the film in this section. Beth and Calvin discuss the trip to Houston. Calvin remembers the early years of his marriage and other trips they took. In the novel, by getting inside Conrad's head, the reader is able to experience the gradual change in Conrad and sees firsthand when he finally considers how the loss of Buck affected his friends and family.

Also in the novel, Guest gives Jeannine Pratt a more developed narrative. Conrad plans for a date with Jeannine, but she has to stay at home and take care of her brother. Jeannine reveals to Conrad that her parents have a messy relationship but she wants them to reconcile. When she becomes upset, Conrad comforts her. Conrad gains more confidence through his relationship with Jeannine.

The scene in which Conrad discovers Karen has committed suicide plays out differently in film and novel. In the novel, when Conrad reads the newspaper, he finds an article reporting the suicide of his friend Karen. Reeling from the news, he retreats to his bed where he drifts in and out of dreams and memories. He remembers his relationship with Karen and his own treatment in the hospital. He thinks of the day he tried to commit suicide. He wakes in the middle of the night and goes for a walk, but a policeman encourages him to go home. He tries to sleep, but has nightmares about the boating accident. Conrad believes Buck would have survived if he had held on to the boat.

Conrad awakens and calls Dr. Berger in the middle of the night. They meet at the office, where Berger encourages Conrad to release his pent-up emotions. Conrad admits to Berger that he needs to be let off the hook for not saving Buck. Berger suggests that Conrad might be subconsciously striving to be Buck and encourages Conrad to be himself. Berger mentions the death of Karen, which prompts Conrad to weep. Berger reassures Conrad that feeling horrible about certain things can be a good thing. He advises Conrad to stop punishing himself for things that were out of his control. Conrad returns to his house in Lake Forest where he flashes back to a horrible childhood incident when he and Buck were playing a game of torture, and to the time he spent with Karen.

Ending

Conrad watches his mother drive away in a taxi. He finds Calvin in the backyard and asks what happened. Calvin says Beth is going to Houston for a while and tells Conrad not to blame himself. He admits he never worried about Conrad, because he always appeared in control, but should have worried more. Conrad tells his dad he loves him, a sentiment Calvin reciprocates. The camera pulls back to show the house, with the two on the steps in an embrace.

The ending of the novel is a bit less dramatic, visually speaking, than the ending of the film.

Beth leaves Calvin and does not say good-bye to Conrad. Calvin tells Conrad his mother has gone and plans for the two of them to live in a rented house in Evanston, where Conrad will finish high school. Conrad begins to criticize his mother for her departure, but Calvin turns the tables on his son and suggests Conrad needs to learn how to take criticism himself. Conrad agrees and advises his dad to criticize him more often. Conrad tells his father he loves him. The novel also includes an epilogue, which takes place in the new house where Conrad and Calvin live. Conrad finishes his therapy with Dr. Berger but insists they will remain friends. He also goes to Lazenby's house to make amends. Conrad is slowly healing.

CHARACTERS

Karen Aldrich

Karen is Conrad's friend from the psychiatric hospital. Conrad tries to reconnect with her after they leave the hospital, but they are no longer close. When Conrad learns she has committed suicide his discovery precipitates a crisis. Exploring his emotions about her death helps Conrad to finally heal the pain from his brother's tragic death. In the film, Karen is played by Tony Award–winning actress Dinah Manoff, best known for her sitcom roles.

Dr. Tyrone C. Berger

Dr. Berger is Conrad's therapist. In the novel, he is quirky and eccentric. In the film, Berger is more low-key and focused. Berger teaches Conrad that expressing his feelings is vital to good mental health. He helps Conrad recognize that he is not responsible for his brother Buck's death and that he needs to forgive himself for both surviving the boating accident and attempting suicide. In the film, Dr. Berger is played by Judd Hirsch, who received an Academy Award nomination and a Golden Globe nomination for Best Supporting Actor for his performance.

Beth Jarrett

Beth Jarrett, Conrad's mother, is a perfectionist and expects those around her to be perfect as well. She views Conrad's suicide attempt as punishment directed at her and cannot understand her son's emotional problems. She resists sharing her feelings and wants life to return to the way it was

before Buck's death. In the end, she distances herself from her husband Calvin, blaming him for becoming depressed about what has happened to their family. Calvin sees that Beth's perfectionism and practicality function to cover up her fears about losing control. In the novel, Beth's character is developed through the points of view of her husband and son. In the film, Beth is played by Mary Tyler Moore, who won a Golden Globe for Best Actress in a Motion Picture (Drama) and received both an Academy Award nomination and a British Academy of Film and Television Arts nomination for Best Actress in a Motion Picture for the role.

Buck Jarrett

Buck, Conrad's, brother, dies in a boating accident before the story begins. Throughout the story, Conrad's need to be in control and feelings of guilt and responsibility are contrasted with Buck's easygoing manner. In the film, Buck is played in flashbacks by Scott Doebler.

Calvin Jarrett

Calvin, Conrad's father, battles his grief over his son Buck's death and his sense of guilt about Conrad's suicide attempt. Calvin tries to hold the family together, but his overwhelming concern for his son causes a rift between he and his wife. In the end, he becomes closer to Conrad when he realizes he needs to accept his emotions, rather than control them as his wife does. He finally puts his son first. In the novel, Calvin Jarrett provides one of the main points of view. In the film, Calvin is played by Donald Sutherland.

Conrad Jarrett

Ordinary People opens after seventeen-year-old Conrad attempts suicide in the wake of his brother Buck's death in a boating accident. It follows his personal development as he works through his guilt with his therapist, Dr. Berger, over surviving the accident. In the process, he deepens his relationship with his father, Calvin, and learns to accept and forgive himself for his suicide attempt. Much of the novel is told from Conrad's point of view. In the film, Conrad is played by Timothy Hutton, who won an Oscar and a Golden Globe for Best Supporting Actor, as well as a Golden Globe for New Star of the Year in a Motion Picture for his debut performance.

Jordan Jarrett

See Buck Jarrett

Ray Hanley

Ray is Calvin's law partner of many years. He tries to advise Calvin on his marital troubles. Calvin feels misunderstood by Ray, who, like Beth, does not understand the depth of his grief over the loss of his son, Buck, and the worry and concern he feels for his troubled son, Conrad. In the film, Ray is played by James B. Sikking, best known for his role as Lieutenant Hunter on the popular 1980s television series *Hill Street Blues*.

Joe Lazenby

Before *Ordinary People* begins, Lazenby had been one of Conrad's best friends; both boys were on the swim team. However, Conrad finds the friendship difficult to sustain after Buck's death. Their friendship crumbles until Conrad can once again appreciate Lazenby's genuine concern. In the film, Lazenby is played by Fredric Lehne, whose career spans television, film, and theater.

Jeannine Pratt

Jeannine is Conrad's first serious girlfriend. Both she and Conrad have a personal history of depression and family difficulties. Because Jeannine can relate to Conrad's personal struggles, she makes him feel less isolated and alone. He is attracted to her compassion and empathy. In the film, Jeannine Pratt is played by Elizabeth McGovern.

Coach Salan

Salan coaches the swim team. He is very hard on Conrad when his performance on the team suffers after Buck's death and his own suicide attempt, even grilling him about his hospitalization. Conrad's feelings of guilt and shame are triggered by this confrontation and lead him to quit the swim team. In the film, Salan is played by M. Emmet Walsh, who has acted in over one hundred film and television productions.

Kevin Stillman

Stillman is a diver on Conrad's swim team whose irritating remarks and insensitive behavior lead Conrad into the first fight of his life. In the film, Kevin Stillman is played by Adam Baldwin.

THEMES

Grief

Grief is a central theme in *Ordinary People*. Each surviving member of the Jarrett family—Beth, Calvin, and Conrad—battles to cope with Buck's tragic death. Their grief, collective and individual, greatly exacerbates problems in the family dynamic and serves as the catalyst for both emotional healing and the family's breakup.

Each family member marks Buck's death in a different way. Conrad blames himself for Buck's death; his unbearable guilt and emotional pain causes him to attempt suicide. Only when he begins to work through these emotions with Dr. Berger can he properly grieve. Calvin's grief prompts him to examine his relationships with both his wife and his surviving son. In mourning Buck and learning to understand Conrad's pain, Calvin takes stock of his tightly controlled life and decides to make healthy changes. On the other hand, Beth grieves because she cannot accept the fate of her favorite son.

The conclusion of *Ordinary People* illustrates power of grief to both bring people closer together and to tear them apart. Calvin and Conrad both stop blaming themselves for Buck's death and Conrad's suicide attempt, fully feeling their grief and in the process, embracing each other. Beth, however, flees her family rather than descend into the grief that would force her to accept Buck's death.

Identity

Both Conrad and Calvin struggle with figuring out what kind of people they want to be in the wake of Buck's death. In both novel and film, Conrad is portrayed as feeling lost once his brother, who he idolized, is gone. In therapy with Berger, Conrad recognizes that his suicide attempt stemmed from thinking of himself as worthless compared to Buck (who was a star athlete) as well as from his inability to measure up to Buck's legacy. As Conrad comes to feel valued by Jeannine and more loved by his father for who he is, and as he uncovers and accepts his feelings, he becomes more true to himself.

Calvin, too, struggles with coming to terms with his identity, although the novel, with its more detailed character development, explores this theme more fully. Calvin's controlled relationship with Beth and his adherence to social expectations have buried his true desires. His grief over Buck's death and worry over Calvin's suicide attempt force him to reevaluate his priorities, however. He grows into a more loving and connected father as a result, although he loses his wife, Beth, who refuses to accept the changes stemming from the family's tragedy.

READ. WATCH. WRITE.

- Watch Redford's adaptation of *Ordinary People* and read the novel written by Judith Guest. Learning how to express his emotions physically is an important part of Conrad Jarrett's personal development and healing process. Write a short essay comparing Redford's portrayal of Conrad's emotional and physical expression to Guest's portrayal. Pay attention to his relationship with his mother, his father, Jeannine, Berger, and Stillman. Use quotations from the film and novel to support your ideas.

- As a film, Redford's adaptation of *Ordinary People* must translate the internal complexities of Conrad's suicide attempt into action. With a small group of your classmates, choose one or two key scenes and discuss how Redford showed Conrad's inner conflict through Timothy Hutton's behavior. Pay attention to gestures, expressions, movement, and dialogue.

- Write a short essay comparing the treatment of Redford's version of Beth with Guest's version. Discuss how Redford showed Beth's inner conflict through Mary Tyler Moore's behavior, as well as how Guest depicted Beth's conflict through the points of view belonging to Conrad and Calvin. Use dialogue from the film and book to support your ideas.

- Redford's adaptation of *Ordinary People* has a different point of view than Guest's novel. Write a short essay discussing how Redford's cinematic point of view changes the novel's original narrative. Does the film accurately reflect the novel's plot and characterization? Does the film capture the conflict in the same fashion? Which medium pulls the reader deeper into the story and why: film or novel? Do you lose anything in translation from novel to film?

Isolation

Conrad, Beth, and Calvin all struggle with feelings of isolation even as they live as a family unit. After being released from the hospital, Conrad feels alone and misunderstood. He has a difficult time connecting with friends and family and struggles to open up to Dr. Berger. Conrad cannot see that others grieve for Buck as he does. By the end of the film, however, Conrad has built fulfilling and honest relationships with Jeannine, Dr. Berger, and his father and realizes that sharing his pain with them will help him heal. Similarly, Calvin tells Berger that he feels like he's drifting, an image that definitively marks the disconnectedness between him, Beth, and Conrad. He sees himself as standing alone and cannot even turn to Beth, who purposely withholds her emotional support. Calvin tries to reach out to Beth by asking her to talk to him about Buck's death, but she refuses. Beth also tries to prevent Calvin from reaching out to others. While Calvin and Conrad turn to one another by the end of

both the film and the novel, Beth remains isolated, packing up her things and leaving Calvin and Conrad behind.

Forgiveness

A central theme in both the film and novel versions of *Ordinary People* is forgiveness. Neither Conrad nor Calvin can begin to heal until they forgive themselves for the roles they think they played in the tragedy. Conrad blames himself for not saving his brother and for surviving the boating accident. His guilt is compounded by his suicide attempt. He cannot forgive himself and feels his parents cannot forgive him either. Calvin blames himself for not paying more attention to Conrad, thus missing the signs of his son's depression and hopelessness. He also blames himself for not showing Conrad the love he deserves. Both characters, to some degree, fear that the other blames him; however, the final scene in which Conrad and Calvin embrace

The Kobal Collection. Reproduced by permission.

marks both their forgiveness of themselves and their love and acceptance of the other.

In contrast, Beth cannot forgive Conrad or Calvin for their need to grieve Buck's death and move on. Her failure to see her own part in the family dynamic and her inability to accept and forgive her husband and son leaves her alone in the end.

STYLE

Characterization

The themes that emerge from *Ordinary People*— grief, identity, isolation, and forgiveness—rely upon character development. In the novel, Guest tells the story through the alternating points of view of Conrad and Calvin, allowing the reader to get an inside look at each character's thoughts. In the film, however, director Redford uses an omniscient or "objective treatment" approach. As a result, the film relies on characters' actions, rather than thoughts, to develop each character and explore the central themes of the film.

In the novel, Guest relies on the internal conflict of her characters to build sympathy, compassion, and understanding in the reader. While Redford cannot use a character's thoughts to show conflict, he has other cinematic techniques at his disposal. He often uses quick cuts from one scene to the next, a technique which does not lend itself to character development, but does increase the drama and sense of tension in the film. Redford also uses music, specifically the haunting, fragile Pachelbel's Canon, to underscore the emotions of certain characters and scenes.

Use of Flashbacks

Both the film and novel versions of *Ordinary People* use flashbacks. In the novel, Guest relies on them to build drama, show character development, and provide a sense of mystery that keeps the reader turning the page. With every flashback, Guest provides clues as to the tragedy surrounding Buck's death and shows Conrad getting closer and closer to facing his inner demons and forgiving himself. The flashbacks are often woven into Conrad's dreams, and Guest indicates flashbacks with italics. In the film, Redford also uses flashbacks, but they vary in clarity and mood. Some are fragmented and nightmare-like, while others contain clear memories of the past. Both Guest and Redford use flashbacks to take the viewer out of the present-day narrative and to offer glimpses of what lies at the bottom of the characters' emotional struggle. The reader and viewer begin to see the truth behind the Jarrett family's grief and remorse. The most significant flashback comes toward the end of the film when Conrad remembers the boating accident and, in reliving the events, realizes that he blames his brother both for taking them out in the storm and for drowning.

CULTURAL CONTEXT

Both the novel and the film versions of *Ordinary People* reflect the growing interest in both psychotherapy and the quest for personal fulfillment in the 1960s and 1970s. In earlier decades, family problems were considered private, and people suffering from depression did not commonly seek a doctor's help. By the 1970s, many people began to reject what they saw as the pointless stoicism and emotional emptiness of the previous generation. They came to see personal fulfillment as something that was their right, and they used new methods to achieve it. Psychotherapy, which had been far too expensive for any but the wealthy, became accessible to middle-class people when major health insurance companies began covering psychiatric treatment and counseling during the 1970s. "Popular psychology" books such as *How to Be Your Own Best Friend* (1974), and *I'm OK, You're OK* (1969) became huge bestsellers. The fact that one of the top rated television shows in the United States, *The Bob Newhart Show* (1972-1978), featured a main character who was a psychiatrist further demonstrates just how popular psychotherapy had become.

In the context of psychiatric healing and personal fulfillment, Beth comes across not as strong and brave as she might have been seen by an earlier generation, but as repressed and cold. Calvin's decision to leave his marriage, which might have seemed like a unmanly failure to earlier generations, is instead shown as a move that is necessary for Calvin's happiness, and therefore perfectly understandable.

Ordinary People focuses on personal evolution and growth as it explores the emotional upheaval resulting from a family tragedy. Though the wardrobe and set design undoubtedly position the film in the 1970s, the realistic dialogue and conflict, not to mention Redford's direct cinematic style, give the film a universality which still appeals to today's audiences.

A Shift in Tradition

The late 1960s and early 1970s also produced the term "generation gap," as traditional morals, values, gender expectations, and notions of sexuality began to shift. Guest's version of *Ordinary People* weaves narratives about three distinct generations. Though the film does not dwell on this through line, Redford does include scenes that show the disconnect between the generations. Both Beth and Calvin struggle with the conservative values they inherited from their parents' generation. Controlling one's behavior and maintaining a sense of social propriety at all times was the deep-seated norm. Beth and Calvin both adhere to the rigidity of cultural expectations with which they were raised in order to deal with their emotions. Though Redford offers plenty of interaction between the characters to illustrate their struggle with self-control, he also reveals this element of their characters through the subtleties of wardrobe choice and gesture. Before Buck died, Beth wore bright colors and her hair long, as shown through flashback. After his death, she grows more conservative, with shorter hair and darker clothing. Calvin is also conservative, wearing a buttoned-up suit when he meets with Berger. Redford also shows Beth carefully setting the table for dinner, putting everything neatly in its place. The napkins are tightly rolled in rings, even when they are put away inside kitchen drawers.

A Revolution in Gender and Sexuality

Though neither the film nor the book blatantly mention the influence of feminism, Redford picks up on Guest's allusion to effects of the movement which began in the 1960s with the Civil Rights movement and gained force in the 1970s. Women publicly fought for legal equity and for the restructuring of gender roles and social institutions. In 1966, the National Organization for Women (NOW) was formed and, under the leadership of Betty Friedan, campaigned for equal opportunity and an end to sex discrimination. The film leaves out details from the book that show the women moving past their traditional housewife roles and reclaiming their independence—for example, the fact that Carole Lazenby, a housewife, is taking a college course to further her education and the fact that Jeannine's mother

The Kobal Collection. Reproduced by permission.

is divorced, a marital status that at the time was just starting to become socially accepted. In the film, Redford keeps the focus on Beth, showing how she must break free from the conventional role of the passive housewife in order to do what she must for personal survival. At the end of the movie, rather than confess her deepest feelings, Beth packs a bag and leaves her husband and son, choosing to escape rather than demonstrate weakness. Ironically, the men in the book take on what was seen during that time as the more traditionally "female" traits: they share their emotions and open themselves up emotionally. Calvin is left to raise his son alone as Beth pursues a new life on her own, a radical ending that befits the wave of new ideas about gender.

Character development in both novel and film also includes allusion to the sexual revolution of the 1970s. At the time, as gender notions were being reevaluated, traditional ideas about sexuality were also being reexamined. In the book, Guest pays more attention to Conrad's sexuality than Redford does in the film. While Guest frequently refers to Conrad's masturbation habit and categorizes it as a release of emotional and physical tension, Redford merely touches on that habit in therapy sessions between Berger and Conrad. In the novel, Guest also confronts the issue of teenage sexuality by having a sexual relationship progress naturally between Conrad and Jeannine. In the film, however, Redford picks up on the romance between Conrad and Jeannine, but does not show the couple engaging in sexual activity. Redford also chose to leave out the romantic issues between the young single secretaries and their boyfriends, as well as the affair between Cal's friend Ray and one of the secretaries. Furthermore, in the novel, when Calvin and Beth attend their friends' party, Guest suggests a certain level of physical flirtation and admiration between the couples, implying a particular sense of marital openness. Redford's party scene is a bit more impersonal and revolves mostly around business conversation.

CRITICAL OVERVIEW

Ordinary People was a critically acclaimed novel. Redford's adaptation was perhaps even more well received; it garnered Academy Award wins and nominations. In 1981, Redford won an Oscar for Best Director, Timothy Hutton won an Oscar for Best Supporting Actor, and the film took Best

Picture honors. Mary Tyler Moore received a nomination for Best Actress.

Jay Scott of *The Globe and Mail* was one of the few critics of the film. He declared that the film was "earnestly boring," calling it a "manipulative domestic tearjerker" in the vein of *Kramer vs. Kramer*. According to Scott, the adaptation didn't seem rich enough for film, but rather more like an "overwritten, overprocessed TV drama."

But the majority of film reviewers found the movie to be a powerful portrayal of a family in crisis. Critics praised Redford for his ability to draw out his characters' motives, emotions, strengths and flaws. Roger Ebert of the *Chicago Sun-Times* credited Redford with allowing each character "the dramatic opportunity to look inside himself, to question his own motives as well as the motives of others, and to try to improve his own ways of dealing with a troubled situation." Richard Schickel of *Time Magazine* applauded Redford for creating "an austere and delicate examination of the ways in which a likable family falters under pressure and struggles, with ambiguous results, to renew itself." Schickel argued that "the power of *Ordinary People* does not lie in originality but in the way it observes behavior, its novelistic buildup of subtly characterizing details."

CRITICISM

Michelle S. Lee

Lee has taught courses in composition, rhetoric, film adaptation, and literature. In this essay, she discusses how director Robert Redford uses extra scenes in his film remake of Judith Guest's Ordinary People to raise the emotional stakes and to dramatically portray each character's inner turmoil.

Both Judith Guest's novel and Robert Redford's film adaptation of *Ordinary People* stay true to the same narrative: an upper-middle-class family struggles to cope with the loss of its eldest son following a boating accident. Before the tragedy, the Jarrett family prided themselves on appearances. They lived by propriety, living in a neat, comfortable home, wearing the right clothes, involving themselves in socially acceptable activities, and saying the perfect thing at the perfect time. Their lives were tidy, as much in the privacy of their own home as at school, the office, or lunch with friends. But this self-control successfully hid their deeply rooted fears—fears that Conrad, Beth, and Calvin each resist after Buck's untimely death, fears they

> BY DEPICTING BETH SOLELY AS "STONY AND CALM THROUGHOUT," REDFORD REINFORCES THE IDEA THAT BETH WILL FOREVER KEEP HER EMOTIONS IN CHECK, EVEN IN THE DARKNESS OF HER OWN GARAGE, EVEN FROM HER OWN FAMILY."

must confront in order to grieve and heal. In the film version of *Ordinary People*, Redford adds a few key scenes to Guest's original to further emphasize this thematic through-line, to take advantage of an omniscient, rather than limited, point-of-view, and to ramp up the drama.

One scene Redford chooses to alter occurs in the third chapter of Guest's novel. Conrad comes home from swimming to an empty house and, in his room, finds a photograph in a desk drawer of the "First Place Medley Relay Team." His brother Buck stands in the middle of the team, "all confidence." He quickly stuffs the picture back into the drawer and leaves his room, startling his mother. They have a stilted conversation about her golf game and his swim practice until she begs off with a headache. In the film, Beth arrives home to the empty house first. She is compelled to enter Buck's room, where she gazes at his photos, medals, and trophies. She sits on his bed, obviously grieving for her lost son. At the same time, she does not cry or outwardly display her mourning. Conrad comes home unbeknownst to her and sticks his head in the door of the bedroom, scaring her. She tells him never to do that again, and the viewer wonders what her words mean exactly: don't scare her, don't make her feel something unexpectedly, don't intrude? Mary Tyler Moore, who plays Beth, keeps her facial expressions and gestures tightly controlled, but the viewer senses a chaos beneath the rigidity. Richard Schickel notes this quality in Moore's portrayal, marking "the coldness that can sometimes be found at the heart of those all-American girls she often plays." Roger Ebert echoes Schickel in saying that Moore as Beth "masks her inner sterility behind a façade of cheerful suburban perfection." Beth is not cheerful in this scene, but rather held together by a thread. Timothy Hutton, playing Conrad, both captures what Roger Ebert calls the "sulks, rages, and panics of adolescence"

WHAT DO I SEE NEXT?

- Like *Ordinary People*, *Kramer vs. Kramer* was a hugely successful film. At the 1979 Academy Awards, Dustin Hoffman and Meryl Streep won Oscars for their performances, and the film also earned honors for Best Picture, Best Director and Best Screenplay. Ted, played by Hoffman, is an ambitious urban professional who discovers his wife, played by Meryl Streep, plans to leave him and their six-year-old son. After some adjustment, Ted realizes he loves being a full-time parent, but a battle ensues when his wife returns to reclaim the boy.

- Another drama with an emphasis on emotional recovery, *The Prince of Tides*, was adapted in 1991 from a best seller by Pat Conroy. The film was nominated for a host of Academy Awards in 1992, and Nick Nolte won a Golden Globe for his role. Inspired to help his suicidal sister, Nolte, a Southern schoolteacher, goes to New York City and reveals horrific, repressed memories to a psychiatrist played by Barbra Streisand, who also directed the film.

- Robert Redford directed *A River Runs Through It* in 1992, the story of two fly-fishing brothers at the turn of the century. Uptight scholar Norman, played by Craig Sheffer, and risk-taking gambler Paul, played by Brad Pitt, struggle to reach the high moral standards and keen fishing ability of their Presbyterian preacher father, played by Tom Skerritt. The movie won an Oscar for Best Cinematography in 1993.

and the vulnerability of a boy needing his mother. Redford's choice to have Conrad catch Beth in Buck's bedroom raises the stakes for both characters and for the narrative itself. Conrad is trespassing on Beth's private moment, Beth fears being caught in a vulnerable state, and Conrad blames himself for his mother's private anguish and withdrawal, not to mention the fact that his brother is

gone. Though the scene is not in Beth's or Conrad's point of view, the viewer realizes that this empty, yet emotionally loaded room lives between the two characters, a room they cannot share.

Another scene Redford changes unfolds in the twenty-sixth chapter of the novel. Conrad reads the newspaper only to discover an article reporting the suicide of his friend Karen. Stunned by the news, he retreats to his bed into a night of dreams and memories: his relationship with Karen, his own treatment in the hospital, his attempted suicide, the boating accident. He even carries on an imaginary conversation with Buck about the accident. Upset, he awakens and phones Dr. Berger. Berger meets with him and says he needs to release his pent-up emotions. In the film, however, Conrad phones Karen, wanting to see her. When he calls, a man answers and tells him she killed herself. The personal delivery of the horrifying news sends Conrad into an emotional tailspin. Devastated, he remembers his brother's boating accident, which Redford shows in a flashback, and runs out of the house. He phones Berger, who agrees to meet him at the office. Similar to Guest's version of the scene, Conrad tells Berger that he blames himself for the accident, but also blames Buck for not holding on to the boat or turning back at the first sign of bad weather. Berger asks him how long he will punish himself, and Conrad confesses that he blames himself for living. In making Karen's suicide the impetus for Conrad's action—desperately asking for Berger's help and finally releasing pent-up emotions—Redford actively marks the moment of Conrad's emotional shift, the moment when Conrad chooses to connect to another human being and is not rejected. In Guest's novel, Conrad works through his memories and spends the night in his head before he is driven to reach out.

A third scene Redford reconfigures does not fully appear in Guest's novel. Toward the end of the novel, Calvin remembers how he had cried at Buck's funeral, but Beth had not. Both she and Conrad had been "stony and calm throughout." Calvin recalled that she had only cried after Conrad had attempted suicide. In the film, Beth's "stony" demeanor at the funeral becomes the crux of an argument between Calvin and Beth. Calvin returns home from talking with Berger, where he mentions the fact that Beth never cried at Buck's funeral, and sits in the car, thinking. Beth comes outside to see what is wrong. Calvin urges her to talk about Buck's funeral, where

Beth had made a fuss about the shirt he had chosen to wear. Calvin tells her he had always wondered why the shirt mattered. Beth hugs him, but says nothing. She shows compassion and connection to Calvin, yet resists answering him. By putting this scene early in the film, Redford builds the stakes for Calvin and Beth and generates questions for the viewer: Will their marriage survive? Will Beth ever share her feelings with Calvin? The scene continues to reinforce a simple line of dialogue from the novel—as Audrey, a friend of both Beth and Calvin, tells Calvin in the novel, "[E]motion is her enemy." Redford neglects to mention how Beth reacted after Conrad's attempted suicide. By depicting Beth solely as "stony and calm throughout," Redford reinforces the idea that Beth will forever keep her emotions in check, even in the darkness of her own garage, even from her own family. Redford also portrays Calvin as a man who wants to change, to heal, to share his feelings so he can move on. He wants to connect with his wife, but begins to realize that she doesn't have the ability.

Although Redford's vision of *Ordinary People* faithfully follows Guest's novel, the director creates a few extra scenes to highlight themes prominent in the narrative and increase the dramatic stakes. Redford adds scenes that emphasize each character's need for self-control, as well as each character's fear of, and desire for, connection and intimacy. Redford's added scenes illustrate Guest's emotional arc through action and reaction and rely on the expressions and behaviors of the actors to make Guest's internal conflicts come to life.

Source: Michelle S. Lee, Critical Essay on the film adaptation of *Ordinary People* in *Novels for Students*, Gale, Cengage Learning, 2010.

Karen Beyard-Tyler

In the following essay, Beyard-Tyler discusses Guest's involvement with the film adaptation of her novel.

Because she was involved from the beginning, Guest came to know the actors who portrayed her characters. In the novel, Conrad Jarrett is a deeply troubled seventeen-year-old whose suicide attempt makes it impossible for his family to deny the changes brought about by his brother Buck's accidental death. Timothy Hutton was selected to play Conrad in a debut which won an Academy Award. Judith Guest loves him.

He is beautiful. He's the sweetest kid, gentle like Conrad, very sensitive and yet funny. He's got a good sense of humor and he's bright, but he always struck me as being vulnerable. You fantasize about all actors being like the characters they play. Sometimes you think, if I just knew that guy, I know I'd love him. You would really love Timothy Hutton. He's very much like Conrad.

Audiences seem to know this and are doubly affected by the character Hutton plays and the person Hutton seems to be.

Mary Tyler Moore's performance as Conrad's mother is different. The audience must see her in a role unlike their expectations of her. Nonetheless, Guest feels it is Moore who "really brings off" the character of Beth Jarrett, the mother who could not accept changes in her family. Perhaps it is because Beth is a person who cannot talk about herself that Guest found her to be a very difficult character to write about.

> I felt when I saw Mary Tyler Moore acting that she really brought the character to life. And yet, she remains as enigmatic as before—something about her portrayal. The first couple of times I saw the movie, I cried a lot, but the only scene that I consistently cry in still is the scene in Texas with her on the golf course, the only time she really opens up and tells people what's going on inside her. I find it so moving, I can hardly bear it.

Another deeply moving scene occurs near the end of the film when Beth's husband Calvin (played by Donald Sutherland) confronts her with his despair. This scene is one of the few major departures the film makes from Guest's novel.

> I've had a lot of discussions with a lot of different people about that scene, and I've pretty much come around to thinking I have a personal quarrel with it that has little to do with the overall quality of the movie or the scene. I've just always felt that the point I was trying to make is that when one person starts changing in a family, everybody has to change. There is no way you can keep responding to a person in a given way if the person's reactions and responses to you are changing. And so, I think that the conflict should be her unwillingness to change. If that's true, her only option is to get out. Neither Beth nor Calvin wants her to go, but since she can't face staying and fighting it out, she has to leave. In the movie, however, he seems to be kicking her out when he says to her "I don't think I love you anymore."

When Guest discussed this difference with Redford, he agreed but felt the scene worked well for the movie. And it does. As Guest points out, "It's a really subtle difference, one that probably isn't important to anyone but me." As her many viewings of the movie imply, it's also not a difference that interferes with her appreciation of the movie.

Source: Karen Beyard-Tyler, "Judith Guest on 'Ordinary People'," in *The English Journal,* Vol. 70, No. 5, September 1981, pp. 22–25.

Jay Scott
In the following essay, Scott finds several problems with the movie version of Ordinary People.

Judith Guest's 1976 novel Ordinary People, in which an affluent WASP high school student named Conrad Jarrett attempted to take his life (razors and wrists), was spare and lean and vigorously unsentimental. In the film adaption, written by Alvin Sargent and directed by Robert Redford, what was spare seems stingy, what was lean seems thin and what was unsentimental has franchised a Kleenex concession: *Ordinary People* (at the Plaza) has all the earmarks of an earnest hit, *Kramer Vs. Kramer* division.

The only thing that could keep it from box-office bingo is the fact that it is earnestly boring.

The setting is Lake Forest, Ill., Chicago's Rosedale, where the luggage is suede, the cars overpowered, the lipstick pale, the swimming pools aquamarine and the autumns auburn. These are not Ordinary People: they are Ordinary Rich People, and John Cheever, worst luck, is nowhere in view. Into their careful yet paradoxically carefree existence (wealthy WASPs in Hollywood movies have earned the right to be carefree because they have been careful) comes Conrad (Timothy Hutton) and his dripping wrists. They ooze all over monster mummy's carpets (Mummy is played, and played very well, by Mary Tyler Moore) and they burn like acid through plastic poppa's facade (Poppa is played, equally well, by Donald Sutherland).

Mum, a snooty soul with a large circle of golfing friends, discovers that she cannot forgive Conrad for having bled on her carpets and she's not too happy about his failing to save the life of her favorite son, either (a boating accident). Pop, on the other hand, wants to get to know his boy: he wants to be rid of masks, to be Real, to Understand.

Naturally, knowing how to be Real and how to Understand do not come easy in Lake Forest—

which Redford records with the same libellously slick condescension Mike Nichols brought to the "plastics" party scene in *The Graduate*—and Pop sends Conrad to Dr. Berger, a godlike if not god-fearing shrink (Judd Hirsch, in the Robert Redford role).

Dr. Berger is the one character in the film who really does have all the answers, including the big one: there ain't any. He is the one character who does not want to be in control of his surroundings ("I'm not big on control," he says). He is the one character who believes emotions should be expressed. He is the one character whose environment—his office—is a mess. He is the one character who is wise beyond his income and profound beyond his syntax. (He is the one character who sounds like Jack Webb on *Dragnet*—after est.) And he is the one character who is Jewish.

This final fact is absolutely essential to exposing the myths by which *Ordinary People* operates: its WASPs are as colorless as the WASPs in Woody Allen's Interiors (Miss Moore's Mum is no more than a younger version of Geraldine Page) but its Jew is a brand new stereotype: to Dr. Berger goes the Sidney Poitier Pristine Pedestal Award.

In his debut as a director, Redford has treated his cast lovingly. Within the boundaries of their wizened roles, his actors perform competently, although Timothy Hutton's Conrad can be caught calculating his effects, and his big *Night Must Fall* tour de force, when he regresses psychologically to the scene of his suicide trauma, is a psychiatric and esthetic embarrassment. If the problem is neither in the acting nor in Redford's direction (workmanlike), where is it? The film-makers have said repeatedly that they have been "true" to Miss Guest's novel, which is not entirely accurate. Where, for instance, is the Epilogue, in which she graciously acknowledged the essential banality and ephemerality of her tale? But they have treated her words with more reverence than might have been necessary. Or wise.

That other manipulative domestic tearjerker, *Kramer Vs. Kramer*, was also based on a novel of merit but, when the story reached the screen, it had shifted tone and altered allegiance; it had been reconceived for the movies. The problems of adapting *Ordinary People* are greater—its predominant virtue cannot be transferred to the screen. How do you pictorialize an author's analysis of the psychic states of people notable for refusing to articulate their thoughts, or even to feel their feelings? How do you communicate in images an omniscient psychological dissection? Redford and Sargent sidestep the conundrum and settle for blindly reproducing Miss Guest's dialogue.

Unfortunately, out of Miss Guest's precisely composed context, the words are archly literary: *Ordinary People's* people are ordinary, ordinary TV people in an ordinary, overwritten, overprocessed TV drama. The most this sincere little movie expects of you is tears; it would be modestly pleased if its mirror reflects a little sliver of your life; it does not want to shock you, provoke you, frighten you, intellectually stimulate you, or even teach you anything you do not already know. If the hero of *Leave It to Beaver* had grown up, gone to high school and taken it into his head to off himself, the made-for-TV-movie that could have ensued—*Leave It to Beaver Tries to Leave It*—might have been a lot like *Ordinary People*.

Source: Jay Scott, "Redford's *Ordinary People* Earnestly Boring," in *Globe and Mail* (Canada), September 27, 1980.

Roger Ebert

In the following review, Ebert reviews director Robert Redford's cinematic interpretation of Guest's novel.

There's the surviving son, who always lived in his big brother's shadow, who tried to commit suicide after the accident, who has now just returned from a psychiatric hospital. There's the father, a successful Chicago attorney who has always taken the love of his family for granted. There's the wife, an expensively maintained, perfectly groomed, cheerful homemaker whom "everyone loves." The movie begins just as all of this is falling apart.

The movie's central problems circle almost fearfully around the complexities of love. The parents and their remaining child all "love" one another, of course. But the father's love for the son is sincere yet also inarticulate, almost shy. The son's love for his mother is blocked by his belief that she doesn't really love him—she only loved the dead brother. And the love between the two parents is one of those permanent facts that both take for granted and neither has ever really tested.

Ordinary People begins with this three-way emotional standoff and develops it through the autumn and winter of one year. And what I admire most about the film is that it really does develop its characters and the changes they go

through. So many family dramas begin with a "problem" and then examine its social implications in that frustrating semifactual, docudrama format that's big on TV. *Ordinary People* isn't a docudrama; it's the story of these people and their situation, and it shows them doing what's most difficult to show in fiction—it shows them changing, learning, and growing.

At the center of the change is the surviving son, Conrad, played by a wonderfully natural young actor named Timothy Hutton. He is absolutely tortured as the film begins; his life is ruled by fear, low self-esteem, and the correct perception that he is not loved by his mother. He starts going to a psychiatrist (Judd Hirsch) after school. Things are hard for this kid. He blames himself for his brother's death. He's a semi-outcast at school because of his suicide attempt and hospitalization. He does have a few friends—a girl he met at the hospital, and another girl who stands behind him at choir practice and who would, in a normal year, naturally become his girlfriend. But there's so much turmoil at home. The turmoil centers around the mother (Mary Tyler Moore, inspired casting for this particular role, in which the character masks her inner sterility behind a facade of cheerful suburban perfection). She does a wonderful job of running her house, which looks like it's out of the pages of Better Homes and Gardens. She's active in community affairs, she's an organizer, she's an ideal wife and mother—except that at some fundamental level she's selfish, she can't really give of herself, and she has, in fact, always loved the dead older son more. The father (Donald Sutherland) is one of those men who wants to do and feel the right things, in his own awkward way. The change he goes through during the movie is one of the saddest ones: Realizing his wife cannot truly care for others, he questions his own love for her for the first time in their marriage.

The sessions of psychiatric therapy are supposed to contain the moments of the film's most visible insights, I suppose. But even more effective, for me, were the scenes involving the kid and his two teen-age girlfriends. The girl from the hospital (Dinah Manoff) is cheerful, bright, but somehow running from something. The girl from choir practice (Elizabeth McGovern) is straightforward, sympathetic, able to be honest. In trying to figure them out, Conrad gets help in figuring himself out.

Director Redford places all these events in a suburban world that is seen with an understated matter-of-factness. There are no cheap shots against suburban lifestyles or affluence or mannerisms: The problems of the people in this movie aren't caused by their milieu, but grow out of themselves. And, like it or not, the participants have to deal with them. That's what sets the film apart from the sophisticated suburban soap opera it could easily have become. Each character in this movie is given the dramatic opportunity to look inside himself, to question his own motives as well as the motives of others, and to try to improve his own ways of dealing with a troubled situation. Two of the characters do learn how to adjust; the third doesn't. It's not often we get characters who face those kinds of challenges on the screen, nor directors who seek them out. *Ordinary People* is an intelligent, perceptive, and deeply moving film.

Source: Roger Ebert, "Review: *Ordinary People*," in *Chicago Sun Times*, January 1, 1980.

SOURCES

Beyard-Tyler, Karen, "Judith Guest on *Ordinary People*," in *The English Journal*, Vol. 70, No. 5, September 1981, pp. 22–25.

Clemons, Walter, "Out of the Ordinary: *Ordinary People*," in *Newsweek*, July 12, 1976, p. 71.

Ebert, Roger, Review of *Ordinary People*, in *Chicago Sun-Times*, January 1, 1980, http://rogerebert.suntimes.com/apps/pbcs.dll/article?AID=/19800101/REVIEWS/1010325/1023.

Guest, Judith, *Ordinary People*, Penguin Books, 1976.

———, "How I Wrote *Ordinary People*: The Author of the Bestselling Novel Discusses How She Handled the Challenges of Establishing a Point of View, Avoiding Sentimentality, and Finishing a Piece of Writing," in *The Writer*, Vol. 8, No. 120, August 2007, p. 24.

Janeczko, Paul, "In Their Own Words: An Interview with Judith Guest," in *The English Journal*, Vol. 67, No. 3, March 1978, pp. 18–19.

Mitgang, Herbert, "Reading and Writing, Literary Vigilantes," in *New York Times*, October 23, 1983, p. 24.

Ross, Jean, "An Interview with Judith Guest," in *Contemporary Authors New Revision Series*, Vol. 15, edited by Linda Metzger, Gale Research. 1985.

Schickel, Richard, "Cinema: Nuclear Explosion in Chicago," in *Time*, September 22, 1980, http://www.time.com/time/magazine/article/0,9171,952759,00.html.

Scott, Jay, "Redford's *Ordinary People* Earnestly Boring," in *The Globe and Mail*, September 27, 1980, p. E5.

Seger, Linda, *Creating Unforgettable Characters*, Henry Holt and Company, 1990.

FURTHER READING

Campbell, John and Stephen Hunt, "Sundance: The Kid's Fest is Hip, Hot, and Here to Stay, *Moving Pictures Magazine*. Jan./Feb. 2005, http://www.movingpictures-magazine.com/departments/belowtheline/sundance.

    Moving Pictures Magazine, available online, is a magazine devoted to articles about filmmakers and filmmaking. This long article contains details on Redford's growing influence in Hollywood as a director, producer, and founder of the influential Sundance Film Festival.

Mintz, Steven, *Hollywood's America: United States History through Its Films*, Wiley-Blackwell, 2001.

    Mintz offers a thorough historical grounding for American films of the twentieth century.

Quart, Leonard and Albert Auster, *American Film and Society Since 1945*, Praeger, 2001.

    This cultural history of American film provides a detailed social and political context through which films of different periods can be interpreted. The book is divided into chapters by decade, and provide a detailed discussion of *Ordinary People*.

"Robert Redford," *Internet Movie Database* (IMDb), http://www.imdb.com/name/nm0000602.

    IMDb provides comprehensive information on the projects of people involved in the film industry. Redford's entry contains a complete list of films in which he acted, directed, or produced, along with links to further information on each film.

Le Père Goriot

HONORÉ DE BALZAC

1834

Honoré de Balzac's *Le Père Goriot* is one of the most enduring novels of world literature, a chronicle of ambition and despair to touch any but the stoniest heart. Initially criticized as poorly written because it did not conform to rigid standards of poetic style, the novel has nonetheless been continuously in print since its serial publication in the *Revue de Paris* in the winter of 1834 and 1835. Balzac wrote the novel in the autumn of 1834 to satisfy his creditors—from whom he was literally in hiding. Perhaps as a consequence, *Le Père Goriot* is above all else concerned with money: specifically, the vast social and economic changes that occurred in France between the French Revolution of 1789 and the July revolution of 1830. These were tumultuous decades in France, marked by high political intrigue, wild swings of economic fortune, and level of social mobility never before seen.

Set in Paris in 1819, only four years after the restoration of the Bourbon monarchy, *Le Père Goriot* focuses on the intertwined characters of Eugène de Rastignac, an ambitious young man from the poorer rural nobility; Vautrin, a criminal mastermind; and Jean-Joachim "Père" Goriot, an old man eking out his last years in increasing poverty. The novel involves characters from a variety of economic classes competing for money, power, and social recognition—much as in the real France of the time. *Le Père Goriot* is just one small part of Balzac's massive

Honoré de Balzac (*International Portrait Gallery. Reproduced by permission.*)

lifework, *La Comédie Humaine,* or *The Human Comedy,* which includes well over one hundred interwoven novels, stories, and essays. Nonetheless, this small part is a particularly important one; it was with *Le Père Goriot* that Balzac first began systematically to write about the same characters from novel to novel and story to story. Rastignac, here a young man, had appeared previously in *La Peau de chagrin* (1831) as an elderly man. His mode of social climbing resonated so deeply with readers that his name became literally synonymous with "social opportunist."

AUTHOR BIOGRAPHY

Honoré de Balzac was born May 20, 1799, to Bernard-François and Anne-Charlotte-Laure de Balzac, in what was then the small town of Tours in France's Loire Valley. His parents put him out to nurse (that is, sent to a lactating woman who nursed him until he was past infancy) within hours of his birth. Hence Balzac's earliest experiences of the world were, by and large, not with his parents at their home, but rather with a nurse

whom he later described as a *gendarme,* a policeman, with whom he was left until he was four years old. Certainly, troubling encounters with nurses appear with some frequency throughout his fiction, and mothers tend—as in *Le Père Goriot*—to be absent in one way or another, either physically or emotionally. Biographer Graham Robb writes, "As Balzac suggests, the root of his problems was his mother—anxious to impose her authority, prone to interpret intelligence as insubordination and, disastrously, wanting some suitable recompense for her trouble."

After returning home at age four, Balzac's life was far from happy. The young Honoré was soon sent off to boarding school, where he was to spend a number of difficult years before his family's 1814 move to Paris. In Paris, Balzac finished school and followed in his father's footsteps by taking a law degree. Thereafter, however, he began pursuing his own interestes. Deciding, to his parents' dismay, that he wanted to be a writer, he prevailed upon them to set him up with a small allowance, enough to stay in his own apartment and read and write. From 1819 to 1824, he honed his writing skills, publishing several short, anonymous works.

In 1829, the year of his father's death, Balzac experienced a rebirth as a writer. He published a novel under his own name for the first time. *Les Derniers Chouans,* later titled *The Chouans,* chronicled peasant resistance to the French Revolution, and met with modest success. This was also toward the end of his first long love affair, with Laurie de Berny. After this initial breakthrough, Balzac published prolifically. In 1831, he completed *La Peau de chagrin,* or *The Magic Skin,* and in 1833 he published *Eugénie Grandet,* widely regarded as two of his masterworks. After *Le Père Goriot* was published in 1834 and 1835 (it was published in installments in a magazine), Balzac published dozens more books, engaged in dozens of get-rich-quick schemes, and threw himself into various love affairs. He married his longtime Polish mistress, Madame Evelina Hanska, in 1850. The fifty-one-year-old Balzac died only five months later, on August 19, 1850, in Paris, leaving Evelina to deal with his many creditors. In the century and a half since his death, innumerable biographies have been written of Balzac. As early as 1904, biographer Mary Sandars was able to write, "Books about Balzac would fill a fair-sized library." There is ample reason for this biographical interest. Self-deluding, piercingly honest, and grandiose, Balzac treated his own life as a story to be written—with the same sorts of dramatic contradictions, scandals, great alliances, and cheerful acceptance of the best and the worst that readers find in his dozens of novels.

PLOT SUMMARY

Le Père Goriot has been divided in several different ways by its various translators in the nearly two centuries since its original publication in French; the sections here follow the helpful divisions in the Franklin Library's 1980 edition of an anonymous 1897 translation generally attributed to Jane Minot Sedgwick.

Part One: The Vauquer House
The novel begins with an extended description of the Maison Vauquer, a shabby boardinghouse run by the even shabbier Mme Vauquer, and of its inhabitants. The year is 1819, and the novel's three protagonists, Eugène de Rastignac, Vautrin, and Jean-Joachim "Père" Goriot, are lodgers at this boardinghouse in one of the grimier corners of Paris's Latin Quarter, as are the young Victorine Taillefer and her guardian, Mme Couture. Also residing at the Maison Vauquer, which Balzac introduces directly after asking whether it is "more horrible to look upon a withered heart or an empty skull," are an "old maid," Mlle Michonneau, and "an old man," M Poiret. Balzac informs the reader how much each boarder is paying for lodging, and takes pains to contrast Taillefer and Rastignac with the rest of the occupants. While "the boarders were all oppressed by poverty more or less apparent," and most "suggested dramas that had already been completed or were still in action," Taillefer and Rastignac are different: they at least are still young, their dramas yet scarcely begun. Telling the reader that "the happiest of these afflicted souls was Mme Vauquer, who ruled in this free prison," Balzac traces out Vauquer's particular history with Goriot, whom she had initially hoped to marry because of his wealth. In the process, we learn also that Goriot has been getting progressively poorer since his arrival at the Maison Vauquer in 1813. His two daughters have spent much of his retirement money. Worse still for him, the other boarders do not believe "the women whom he called his daughters" really are his daughters, because they are so obviously rich and he is increasingly only

"a ruined man to whom poverty has taught submission."

Part Two: First Glimpses of Society
In contrast to the much-ridiculed Père Goriot, young Rastignac is presented as a dashing, clever student. Balzac follows him through his ambitious entrance into Parisian society, supported by his aunt, Mme de Marcillac, at a ball given by his rather distant cousin Mme de Beauséant, and his return to the boardinghouse. Once home from the ball, Rastignac sees two odd things: evidence of Goriot's wealth in the form of a silver breakfast set, which Rastignac assumes has been stolen, and Vautrin counting coins with a nighttime visitor.

Goriot, it transpires, is selling silver to pay the bills of a woman he claims is his daughter and whom the others believe must be his mistress. This woman, however, is indeed Goriot's daughter, Mme Anastasie de Restaud, with whom Rastignac felt he had fallen in love at the ball the previous night. Vautrin, meanwhile, declares his intention of helping young Victorine Taillefer secure her inheritance, which her father is wrongfully withholding.

The next afternoon, Rastignac calls upon the Restaud household, where he is received with some coolness by the Mme de Restaud and her lover Comte Maxime de Trailles. Still, he meets with success in making himself welcome with her husband, the Comte de Restaud. The success is short-lived, however, as Rastignac accidentally offends the count. Later, his cousin, Mme de Beauséant, advises him to be ruthless in his social interactions.

Rastignac resolves to pursue not Anastasie de Restaud, but her sister—Goriot's other daughter—Delphine de Nucingen, the wife of a German capitalist and an outcast from true Parisian aristocracy. To this end, he promptly writes to his mother and younger sisters for money, threatening to "blow out my brains in despair" if his mother will not aid. This fresh-faced young law student from the country, son of an impoverished branch of the rural aristocracy, appears here as a changed person: a determined social climber.

Rastignac turns his attention to learning the history of Goriot, Delphine's father and the man he hopes to use to make his fortune. Here, Goriot appears as a doting father, an opportunist who has profited by the 1789 Revolution and subsequent Napoleonic empire, and also as a casualty of the return of the old aristocracy to Paris in 1815. His debased condition and his daughters' scorn of him is due in large part to the aristocracy's disdain for business (they believed working for a living, even if one earned a lot of money, was vulgar) and to the deep unpopularity of the friends of the Revolution after the Restoration of the Bourbon monarchy.

Part Three: The Debut

A letter arrives from Rastignac's mother, and though he weeps to read that she has sold her jewels, a second letter, from his sister, revives his spirits. His sister's innocent faith in him leaves him determined that "every coin must tell to the utmost advantage," and he immediately begins spending the money as planned, though it has not yet arrived, on new clothing, meals out, and the other goods that he feels will help him make his way into society. Forced to borrow a franc from Vautrin a short while later, Rastignac makes haste to return it immediately. As he acknowledges, he does not trust "the sphinx in

a wig." This distrust, though, and his way of communicating it, are insulting to the point that the other boarders believe Vautrin and Rastignac will have a duel. Later Vautrin tells Rastignac his idea: he will kill Victorine's brother in a duel, in exchange for Rastignac's giving him two hundred thousand francs of Victorine's once she inherits. He does this on the presumption that Rastignac will court and win the young girl's heart.

However, Rastignac is already courting Goriot's second daughter, Delphine de Nucingen. And Goriot, for his part, is only too obliging, falling over himself to help Rastignac. Likewise, Rastignac's cousin Mme de Beauséant, despite an initial reluctance brought on by her heartache at the prospect of losing her lover (the Marquis d'Ajuda-Pinto), takes pains to help Rastignac. Bringing him with her to the opera, she points out Mme de Nucingen, whom Rastignac meets by the Marquis d'Ajuda-Pinto's good graces. When left alone together, Rastignac quickly makes a move, giving "sweet speeches" that "a woman likes nothing better than to hear." All, however, has not gone quite so swimmingly as he thinks. At the end of the opera, "The poor fellow [is] quite unaware that the Baroness [Nucingen] had paid no attention to him and was expecting a delusive and agonizing letter from De Marsay," the lover who has deserted her.

No one in all this is happier than old Goriot, whose hideous little room at the Maison Vauquer makes quite a contrast to the grandeur of even his daughter's carriage at the opera. The extent of Goriot's delusions becomes apparent as Rastignac tells the old man about his evening with Delphine. At one point, he cries, "Mme de Restaud is fond of me too, I know, for a father sees into his children's hearts and judges their intentions just as God does ours." To Rastignac's objection that it is odd that daughters who love him so much should allow him to live in poverty while they enjoy immense luxury, Goriot explains that he cannot explain—but that he "live[s] three lives," his own and his daughters'.

All this has stirred Rastignac's own ambition still further, and he begins to give serious thought to Vautrin's offer. Rastignac's need for funds becomes all the more apparent in a subsequent encounter with Mme de Nucingen. She invites him to her house, and then goes with him to a gambling den, where she asks him to bet with her money. Fortunately, Rastignac does well, though he is completely ignorant of the rules of the game he is playing. He returns to Delphine with seven thousand francs—enough to pay off her ex-lover's debts, with a thousand francs to spare. This transaction solidifies their affair. But the high living to which he is now committed takes its toll, and Rastignac finds himself heavily in debt. Vautrin's offer looms ever-present in the background, promising Rastignac a way out of his financial difficulties.

Part Four: Shadows of Intrigue

Rastignac toys more and more with the idea of courting Victorine Taillefer. Meanwhile, M Poiret and Mlle Michonneau are approached by a policeman, M Gondureau, who seeks their help in capturing the man they know as Vautrin. Vautrin, he explains, is actually "Jacques Collin, surnamed Trompe-la-Mort [Cheat-death or Beat-death]," a criminal of the highest order. Moreover, he tells the mindless Poiret and the canny Michonneau, they will need to drug Vautrin into sleep, because he is a homosexual and cannot be distracted by Michonneau. Gondureau promises to pay Michonneau three thousand francs to drug Vautrin.

However, Vautrin's actions soon sour Rastignac on the idea of dueling with Victorine's brother. Vautrin enters a room where Rastignac and Victorine are sitting together to "suddenly disturb their happiness by singing in a loud jeering voice." Later he discusses with Rastignac the murder-to-be of Victorine's brother in an extremely callous manner. Indeed, so disturbed is Rastignac that he "resolve[s] to go that evening to warn M Taillefer and his son." It is at just this moment that Goriot enters, brimming with good cheer. He draws Rastignac aside to inform him that he has secured a nice apartment for the young man and Delphine—as long as they consent to his living just above them. Vautrin subsequently overhears Rastignac telling Goriot about the plan to kill Victorine's brother in a duel, and Rastignac's good intentions go for naught. Vautrin slips a sleeping potion into the other men's drinks to keep them from warning M Taillefer of the impending duel.

Only a short while later Mlle Michonneau, on instructions from the police, slips a drug into Vautrin's own drink. News arrives that Victorine's brother is near death from wounds sustained in a duel, and Victorine and Mme Couture leave

to attend to this surprising turn of events. A short while later, Vautrin falls down as though dead. Rastignac goes out to fetch his friend Bianchon, and is struck during his solitary wanderings—for the first time in the novel—by pangs of conscience regarding the sanctity of marriage. He works to convince himself that an affair with Delphine will not be wronging her husband, and has more or less succeeded by the time he returns to the boardinghouse. The police arrive moments later; Vautrin offers no resistance to arrest. Instead, he makes a grand speech. In speaking to the assembled company (only Goriot is absent), he becomes "no longer a single man, but the epitome of a degenerate nation, of a people at once savage, logical, brutal, and facile." His courage and powerful personality, his intensity and authenticity, leave the rest of the boarders awed. As Sylvie puts it, "Well, he was a man all the same!" Accordingly, the rest of the company insists that Michonneau and Poiret, now branded as police spies, leave the Maison Vauquer immediately. Goriot returns to whisk Rastignac away to his new apartment, and only ten of the usual eighteen are left to dine at Mme Vauquer's establishment.

In the new apartment, Rastignac has qualms about accepting so much from Delphine and her father. Balzac writes, "the arrest of Vautrin, which showed him the depths of the abyss into which he had so nearly fallen, had strengthened his delicacy and better feelings... powerfully." Goriot reveals that he is prepared to lend Rastignac all he needs; however, Goriot must absurdly deprive himself to make it possible. He tells the couple, "I can live like a king on two francs a day, and I shall have something left over." All is not necessarily well, though, as Goriot acts almost as though *he*, not Rastignac, is his daughter's lover:

> They behaved like children all through the evening, and Père Goriot was not the most sensible of the three. He sat at his daughter's feet and kissed them; he gazed long into her eyes, rubbed his head against her dress and, in short, was as foolish as the youngest and most tender lover could be.

Part Five: Confrontation

Much has been settled, but one great event remains: Mme de Nucingen's introduction into the upper echelons of Parisian high society at a grand ball thrown by Rastignac's cousin, Mme de Beauséant. Delphine is overjoyed to see the invitation, which clearly notes that her husband, the Baron de Nucingen, is not to attend. The following day, though, as he is gathering the very last of his effects from the Maison Vauquer, Rastignac overhears a troubling conversation between Goriot and Delphine. The Baron de Nucingen, it seems, has all of her money tied up in shady investments, and she has little truly available to her. Meanwhile, Anastasie de Restaud enters and begs help from her father. She has sold the Restaud family jewels to a money-lender in order to support her cheating lover Maxime de Trailles and been found out by her husband, who is dispossessing her of all that she has—even of her children—and threatening to dramatically curtail her movements. All this is too much for Goriot: "It is the end of the world," he cries, "I am sure the world is going to pieces. Go and save yourselves before it happens!" The two women begin to argue, and Goriot becomes increasingly hysterical.

Rastignac rushes in with a bill of exchange—much like a present-day bank check—that Vautrin had given him when he tried to persuade him to swindle Victorine out of her family money. Anastasie accepts the money without gratitude, and heaps insults upon her sister until Goriot cries out repeatedly, "They are killing me." And indeed the old man does seem to be dying, which does not stop Mme de Restaud from leaving as soon as she has secured his signature on the bill of exchange. Bianchon arrives and confirms that Goriot is dying. Rastignac recalls "how the old man's two daughters had worked upon their father's heart without mercy" although he chooses to believe that Delphine at least loves her father. That evening, at the opera, he takes "precautions to avoid alarming Mme de Nucingen," but these prove unnecessary. She is not inclined to believe her father is truly dying, though she does hold him in part responsible for her unhappiness over the past years. She is much more interested in being courted by Rastignac and in gossiping about the Marquis d'Ajuda-Pinto's impending marriage, which will take place on the day his former mistress, Mme de Beauséant, holds her grand ball.

Part Six: The End Approaches

Caught up in the pleasure of being alone together, neither Delphine nor Rastignac think of Goriot until late the next day. When Rastignac arrives at the Maison Vauquer, he finds that Goriot had gone out to sell the very last thing of value that he had—the first set of silver cutlery he ever owned, and which he has kept to

this moment as a reminder of happier times—and subsequently collapsed. Bianchon tends to the old man, who has sold the silver to pay a final debt for Anastasie and who now talks irrationally of returning to business, of buying grain abroad and selling it for a profit in France. With Bianchon, Rastignac keeps watch over Goriot, whose condition improves somewhat as the day of the ball approaches. Neither daughter visits, with Mme de Restaud, far too focused on the ball, sending only a messenger to pick up the money her father has procured for her and Mme de Nucingen.

At the ball itself, Mme de Beauséant is glad to see Rastignac, the only person there whom she feels she can truly trust, and gives him a letter for the Marquis d'Ajuda-Pinto. Rastignac is deeply affected by Beauséant's grief. Back at the Maison Vauquer, the dying Goriot is himself tormented by a feverish grief and a tragic awareness of his own previous blindness regarding his daughters' supposed devotion to him.

Torn at the thought of the old man dying alone, Rastignac goes to find Mme de Restaud, but her husband will not let her leave. She, for her part, is a changed person: "Before turning to Rastignac, her timid glance at her husband told of the prostration of a will, crushed by moral and physical tyranny." Rastignac is also unsuccessful with Delphine. Delphine does not at first believe her father is deathly ill, and once she has been convinced, she is willing to come but is also held back by her husband. Upon Rastignac's return to the boardinghouse, Mme Vauquer presses him for money for Goriot's rent and a shroud in which to wrap him. When paid, she sends Sylvie to collect a set of moldy sheets to use as a shroud. Goriot's final words are "My darlings!" Mme de Restaud, at least, is there for his death; Delphine never arrives, and neither woman's family is willing to pay funeral expenses or even to receive Rastignac when he calls on them. At the Père-Lachaise cemetery, Rastignac and the servant Christophe are the only mourners, and Rastignac must borrow a franc from Christophe in order to pay the grave-diggers their fee. Still, in the end he is able to look out over the evening lights of Paris from the cemetery on its hill, and to see in the city his future. The novel closes with a foreshadow of this future: "Then, as a first challenge offered to Society, Rastignac [goes] to dine with Mme de Nucingen."

CHARACTERS

Marquis d'Ajuda-Pinto

Though he appears only briefly, the Spanish Marquis d'Ajuda-Pinto occupies an important structural role in the novel. In leaving Mme de Beauséant for a younger and, more importantly, wealthier woman, he signals not only his former lover's social demise but also foretells the end of an era.

Mme de Beauséant

Rastignac's distant cousin is his ticket into Parisian high society, but she is more than that. Mme de Beauséant represents an idealized version of the French aristocrat, and her nobility, grace, and beauty are meant to inspire not only admiration but sorrow. As her troubles in love and eventual self-banishment to the rural provinces suggest, she is a member of a dying breed.

Bianchon

Occupying a somewhat similar position in society to Rastignac, Bianchon is a young medical student who takes his meals at the Maison Vauquer. Unlike Rastignac, however, he is shown throughout the novel as being quite devoted to his studies, and there is no evidence that he comes from an aristocratic background.

Christophe

Christophe is a server at the Maison Vauquer, where he plays a minor role in keeping Vautrin's intrigues hidden from the other boarders—for a fee. It is significant that he is included in the plot at all; during Balzac's lifetime it was unusual for French novelists to concentrate on the thoughts, experiences, and conversations of the lower classes. Hence, Christophe's presence at Goriot's funeral, and his thoughts on the proceedings are of particular note.

Mme Couture

Scarcely present as a personality in her own right, Mme Couture nonetheless has an important charge to keep: the shepherding of young Victorine Taillefer. She lives with Victorine in one of the nicer suites at the not terribly agreeable Maison Vauquer.

M Gondureau

Gondureau is the Chief of Police who convinces Poiret and Michonneau to help him capture Vautrin.

Père Goriot

The title character of the novel, Père Goriot—or Old Goriot, as he is called in some translations—is a quiet man of odd excesses. Almost a hermit in the boardinghouse, scarcely ever drawn out of himself by even the cruel taunts of the other boarders and diners, Goriot is nonetheless fiercely passionate when it comes to his daughters. Goriot sacrifices everything for his daughters. Having worked his way up from humble origins, and having made some politically savvy choices during the Revolution that produced ample economic benefits, Goriot is shown as having been the capitalist extraordinaire, the quintessential member of the bourgeoisie. His primary passions in life, Balzac makes clear, are and were his daughters and his grain business. The former, however, forced him to relinquish the latter. With the fall of the quasi-democratic Republic and the return to power and social prominence of the aristocracy, Goriot became an embarrassment to his daughters Delphine and Anastasie—and to their husbands, one of whom was a banker and marginal member of the aristocracy, and the other a count.

Duchesse de Langeaise

Mme de Beauséant's "best friend" is far from friendly; the first thing she does upon learning that the Marquis d'Ajuda-Pinto is leaving Mme de Beauséant for another woman is go over to the other woman's house to gloat.

Mlle Michonneau

Mlle Michonneau, though advanced in years, is unmarried because she spent her youth in Paris's intrigues and sexual power plays. In the boardinghouse itself, she is scarcely a figure at all, but she takes on new significance when deciding whether or not to help the police apprehend Vautrin. While her companion, M Poiret, dithers and has no real thoughts about the matter, Michonneau does not hesitate to bargain with the police inspector. She hopes to make as much of a profit as possible on selling—or not selling—Vautrin to the police. Her complicity in Vautrin's downfall eventually earns her the scorn and abuse of the other denizens of the Maison Vauquer.

Baron de Nucingen

Delphine's husband, the Baron de Nucingen, acquired his title under Napoleon—which meant that other members of the aristocracy considered him less than authentic nobility. In actuality, he is a dishonest German banker. His unsuitability as a husband is one of the things Delphine holds against her father. She feels he should have protected her from such a poor choice of a partner.

Baroness Delphine de Nucingen

The Baroness Delphine de Nucingen is, despite her aristocratic title, a relative outsider to Parisian high society. She is as guilty as her sister of using and ignoring their father, old Goriot, and for the same basic reason: he detracts from her prestige. Delphine is, however, more sympathetically presented than Anastasie, her sister, and eventually serves as Rastignac's love interest

M Poiret

M Poiret serves throughout the novel as comic relief, both because other characters make fun of him and because he has a rather mindless air about him.

Eugène de Rastignac

Rastignac serves as protagonist of the novel. His initiation into Parisian high and low society, his mercenary dealings with mother and sisters, his convenient habit of falling in love with women who will be well placed to help him succeed socially: all these mark Rastignac as a young man of ambition.

Anastasie de Restaud

More entrenched in scandal than her sister Delphine, Anastasie de Restaud is utterly callous with her husband and father as well as with Rastignac. Rastignac's hopes of courting Mme de Restaud are disappointed when he mentions that he knows her father, of whom she is deeply ashamed.

Comte de Restaud

The Comte de Restaud, Anastasie's husband, has been partially responsible for her rejection of her father, Goriot. A middle-ranking member of the aristocracy, he cannot afford to be connected so closely with a bourgeois shopkeeper. Eventually, he deprives Anastasie herself of her income and social status.

Sylvie

Like Christophe, Sylvie is a server at the Maison Vauquer. She also serves, however, as a confidante of sorts to Mme de Vauquer, and helps out to some extent in the day-to-day running of the boardinghouse. She is present at Goriot's deathbed, though not at his actual passing.

Victorine Taillefer

Victorine Taillefer might be the novel's only true innocent. Apart from participating in a brief romance initiated by Rastignac after he has despaired of making his way in high society otherwise, Victorine does nearly nothing of note. And yet, she is a crucial character all the same. Renounced by her wealthy father (who is apparently mistaken in believing that she is not his real daughter), and living on a small fixed income with no friends in the world save the blandly maternal Mme Couture, Victorine is as pathetic a figure as can be found in *Le Père Goriot*. This makes her the perfect centerpiece of Vautrin's offer to Rastignac: he, Vautrin, will arrange to have Victorine's brother killed in a duel, Victorine will inherit her father's fortune, and Rastignac will pay him two hundred thousand francs after marrying Victorine for that money.

Comte Maxime de Trailles

Comte de Trailles is Anastasie de Restaud's spendthrift lover, whose gambling debts are keeping her—and even more so her father, who gives her the money to pay the debts off—perpetually on the brink of bankruptcy.

Mme Vauquer

Though not herself a part of any of *Le Père Goriot* main plot lines, Mme Vauquer—like the boardinghouse she runs, the Maison Vauquer—frames them all. Also like her boardinghouse, Mme Vauquer is older and somewhat run-down. A stingy and not particularly scrupulous landlady, she is an interesting choice of character in a novel rich with ambition, great crime, and tragic familial love.

Vautrin

In *Le Père Goriot*, Vautrin is from the very start a dark figure, of uncertain aspect. The other boarders at the Maison Vauquer both fear and respect him. Early in the novel it becomes clear that he is hiding something. In fact, Vautrin is an alias for Jacques Collin, the famous criminal known as Trompe-la-Mort (often translated as "Cheat-death," but perhaps more closely rendered as "Beat-death"). He challenges many of French society's notions of morality, but he does so in a way that cannot be simply dismissed. Though a criminal, he is in the end more respected than the law-abiding citizens who betray him in exchange for a reward.

TOPICS FOR FURTHER STUDY

- Consider the sections into which *Le Père Goriot* has been divided, both here and in your own copy of the text. Why might the translator have chosen to divide the book in this manner? Are there problems with this way of categorizing the different sections of the novel? How would you divide the novel differently, and why? Where would you make the section breaks, and how would you title those sections? To what extent is it important that a novel be broken into clear sections or chapters?

- Divide your class into two groups. Have one group develop an argument to support the idea that Balzac portrayed Vautrin as a hero; have the other group develop an argument supporting the idea that Balzac portrayed Vautrin as a villain. Each group should use examples from the novel to support its position. Have one or two people from each group present their argument to the class as a whole. Afterward, discuss as a class which argument is more convincing.

- *Le Père Goriot* is filled throughout with frequent references to specific sums of money, and with statements about relations among and between different social classes. Using your library and the Internet, research the historical and economic context of the novel—the 1789 Revolution, the rise of Napoleon, the restoration of the House of Bourbon, and the July Revolution. Write a short paper in which you explain what you think Balzac felt about these massive social and political changes. Ground your argument in both a careful analysis of the novel and historical research.

- Rastignac faces a moral dilemma that has since become famous in literary history. He must choose whether to accept Vautrin's offer to be morally complicit in the death of Taillefer's brother—a death that will benefit both Rastignac and Taillefer, and will help right a wrong. Divide the class into small groups and ask them to come up with three examples of situations where it might be the morally right choice to break a law or rule. Have each group present one of their "moral dilemmas" to the class as a whole, and then debate what choice is right or wrong in each example.

- Literature and film are full of tales of ambitious social climbers, some sympathetic, some not. Choose one of the following films or books, and watch or read it: *Sister Carrie* (1900) by Theodore Dreiser; *Vanity Fair* (1847–1848), by William Makepeace Thackeray; *Stella Dallas* (1937), a film directed by King Vidor; *The Great Gatsby* (1925), by F. Scott Fitzgerald. Write a paper in which you compare and contrast the protagonist with Rastignac.

THEMES

The Influence of Environment on Character

Balzac's portrayal of various social climbing characters in *Le Père Goriot* examines how one's environment shapes one's character. As A. J. Krailsheimer puts it in the preface to his 1991 translation of the novel, "What interests Balzac is cause and effect, environment more than heredity, and behavioral rather than ethical categories," Many readers see in Balzac's realism the precursor to the naturalism of Émile Zola and Thomas Hardy. These later writers saw individual character as a product of social and physical environment, drawing heavily on biologist Charles Darwin's theories of evolutionary adaptation in their examinations of human nature. Balzac himself, though, seems to believe that environment influences, but does not determine, behavior. Hence, the novel's extended descriptions of a wide variety of scenes, and the narrator's frequent suggestions about various tendencies associated with different environments, cannot dispel the essential tensions: Will Rastignac succeed or fail in society? Which would be better for him morally? Will Vautrin escape or will he be caught? Again, which would be better? Will Goriot's daughters at last return his love, or are there good reasons for their rejection of him? Environment will in any case influence a given character's actions, but it can neither predict them surely nor tell us the outcome of those actions.

Social Change

Rastignac, Vautrin, and Goriot represent three classes whose struggles with one another were changing the balance of power in France as Balzac wrote *Le Père Goriot*. Rastignac is a member of the rural aristocracy that in large part is excluded from Parisian high society, the urban aristocratic class that had returned to prominence with the ouster of Napoleon and the restoration of the Bourbon monarchy. His own struggles to enter the urban elite occur against the backdrop of the monied bourgeoisie's same struggles. Having failed to supplant the aristocracy permanently, as evidenced by the fall of first the Republic and then Napoleon, many members of the bourgeoisie—that class made up of people, like Goriot, who own factories and businesses—were eager to enter that aristocracy. Père Goriot's daughters and husbands reject him in part because he is so clearly bourgeois. To a large extent, the question of social change is a question of what one ought to value. Balzac seems to ask if the beauty and nobility of spirit of the aristocratic classes should be most highly valued more than the loyalty and work ethic of the bourgeoisie. Or perhaps instead he suggests with the ambiguous figure of Vautrin that radical disruption of the status quo should in fact be most highly valued. Balzac himself claimed to be a staunch royalist, determinedly in favor of rule by the aristocracy and the conservation of a grand social tradition, but *Le Père Goriot* appears to be far less clear in its political philosophy.

STYLE

Realism

La Père Goriot is, along with Stendhal's 1830 *Le Rouge et le Noir* (*The Red and the Black*), considered one of the fundamental pieces of French realism. Realism is generally understood as a movement in fiction writing (continuing up to the

An engraving of Mme. Vauquer from the 1850 edition of Le Père Goriot *(Bertall (Charles Albert d'Arnoux) | The London Art Archive | Alamy)*

present day, in various forms) that attempts to faithfully portray the world as it actually is. Such practitioners as Henry James and W. D. Howells have tended to write in careful detail about the concrete world. In doing so, they embodied the idea that material reality could be more or less adequately shown in words. As Auerbach writes of Balzac's characters, "What we see is the concrete individual figure with its own physique and its own history, sprung from the immanence of the historical, social, physical . . . situation." The opening scene of *Le Père Goriot*, with its careful description of the unpleasant Rue Neuve-Ste-Geneviève and its phony monument to love, is one of the classic moments in realist fiction.

Anti-Stylistics

One of the most historically common criticisms of Balzac's novels has been that they are inattentive to questions of style. Early biographer Mary Sandars, for instance, writes of both "the bitter dislike Balzac had evoked in the literary world" and his "occasional obscurity and clumsy style." A later biographer, Graham Robb, complains of the

COMPARE & CONTRAST

- **1810s:** The disruption of a system of aristocracy begun during the 1789 Revolution loses momentum with the rise and fall of Napoleon.

  1830s: The French aristocracy begins to change. It becomes more bourgeois in nature—in other words, it discovers modern ways of making money.

  Today: In France, as in the United States and elsewhere throughout the world, social class is largely determined by wealth, not by parentage.

- **1810s:** The French novel is defined by its attention to the lives of members of high society, and by its flowery, "high" style.

  1830s: Stendhal and Balzac redefine the French novel by ushering in the era of realism in fiction—with a "plain" style and a focus on a wide spectrum of characters.

  Today: French literature covers a wide variety of content matter and styles, with many prominent writers in French coming from former colonies. As of 2009, more Nobel Prizes have been awarded to French nationals than to citizens of any other country.

- **1810s:** France is at war with nearly all of Europe. This era of confrontation comes to an end with Napoleon's defeat at Waterloo in 1815.

  1830s: France enjoys a period of relative external peace, with most of its difficulties involving internal political factions.

  Today: France has troops deployed in various countries under United Nations and NATO (North Atlantic Treaty Organization) auspices, but it is not at war with any other state.

---

similarity of Balzac's "descriptive passages to an auctioneer's catalogue." And, at the very least, it seems that Balzac is sometimes simply rude. A short way into *Le Père Goriot*, he directly addresses his readers, and in not a very friendly manner. He writes, "You who hold this book in your lily-white hand, as you lounge in your soft armchair, thinking, perhaps it will amuse me." However, Balzac does attend to style; this narrative intrusion, for instance, is far from accidental or careless. Rather, as Richard Bolster notes in his critical guide, *Balzac: Le Père Goriot*, it is actually "one of the main narrative traditions in the novel," helping readers "to reflect at times on certain social or psychological realities." Balzac, in fact, uses such stylistic devices to encourage the reader to think.

HISTORICAL CONTEXT

Balzac's short life was intertwined from start to finish with one of the most turbulent periods in French history, and *Le Père Goriot* reflects these great changes. The French Revolution, which began in 1789 with the uniting of wealthy capitalists and starving workers and peasants against the monarchy, had resulted in the formation of a republic by 1792. The French Republic itself, with its rejection of a social order founded in the privilege of aristocracy and its formulation of a new hierarchy based on an odd combination of capitalism and revolutionary fervor, ended with the rise of Napoleon Bonaparte. He was a fabulously successful general who conquered most of Europe in the name of France (after most of Europe's monarch declared war on the French Republic). Ironically, the hero of the French Republic had himself crowned emperor in 1804. In only fifteen years, the entire social order of France had flipped twice, first with the fall of the House of Bourbon and again with the establishment of an empire under Napoleon. Emperor Napoleon's reign was short, however. He was defeated by British and Prussian forces at the Battle of Waterloo in 1815—four years before the action of Balzac's novel begins.

In the twenty-six years between the beginning of the French Revolution and Napoleon's final ouster and supervised exile on the island of Saint Helena in 1815, power in France had changed hands many times. At the start of Balzac's novel, the Bourbon monarchy that had been overthrown by the French Revolution has been restored. This restoration would also be short-lived. While *Le Père Goriot* was set during the restoration of the Bourbon monarchy, the novel was written a full fifteen years after this moment, and three years after France's next moment of Revolution.

The July Revolution of 1830 ousted the autocratic Charles X of Bourbon and installed the more modern, democratic King Louis-Philippe. The accession of Louis-Philippe to the throne came as the result of a comparatively bloodless revolution, heralding a new era in French history. The July Revolution lasted only three days, and replaced the former absolute monarchy with a constitutional monarchy, which gave the king more limited power.

CRITICAL OVERVIEW

Le Père Goriot's most positive early reviews came from its author itself. In a January 26, 1835, letter to his longtime lover Evelina Haska—before the final installment of the book had even come out in the *Revue de Paris*, he wrote, "*Le Père Goriot* is a raging success; my fiercest enemies have had to bend the knee. I have triumphed over everything, over friends as well as the envious." If immodest, Balzac's crowing was nonetheless accurate. While none was more convinced of the book's genius than he, nearly everyone in Paris of the time seemed to agree that it was important—including those who thought it quite bad.

Within a few months of its publication, *Le Père Goriot* had received reviews, often quite lengthy ones, in every Parisian newspaper and journal of note. Many of these, however, were critical of the novel's technique; the *Courier français*, for instance, "objected to what it saw as Balzac's obsession with 'microscopic' descriptions conducted with 'endless patience'," and to the novel's immorality. Balzac's critics in the early nineteenth century criticized the novel's failure to describe the world in the elegant, high-minded manner of French novels prior to

1922 illustration from Le Père Goriot *(Quint | The Bridgeman Art Library | Getty Images)*

this point. By the turn of the twentieth century, however, American-British novelist Henry James described Balzac as "really the father of us all." For James, Balzac's importance to the novel was precisely his indifference to matters of style as traditionally understood, the fact that "the lyrical element is not great, is in fact not present at all." James viewed Balzac's stylistic clumsiness—James imagined Balzac "with huge feet fairly ploughing the sands of our desert"— appears here as crucial to be able to realistically describe the world.

Contemporary scholarly responses tend to be less interested in the stylistic "success" or "failure" of *Le Père Goriot*, although it remained common in literary critics to talk about such matters well into the latter half of the twentieth century. Instead, the focus now is often on reading novels philosophically or historically—less for what they say about an author's "greatness" or lack thereof, and more for what they reveal about historical moment in time or about tendencies in novel writing in particular or human behavior more broadly. Attention to *Le Père Goriot* has been no exception to this trend, with recent works to treat the novel historically including Sharon Marcus's *Apartment Stories: City and Home in Nineteenth-century Paris and London* (1999), and David Harvey's *Paris: Capital of Modernity* (2003). Probably the most significant work of literary theory to directly address *Le Père Goriot* has been Erich Auerbach's monumental *Mimesis: The Representation of Reality in Western Literature* (1953), which continues to shape contemporary understandings of the relationship between what is presented as reality in a work of fiction and what we take to be reality in the world outside that fiction. Also crucial have been Marxist critics such as Georg Lukacs and Frederic Jameson, who find in the novel's form itself a helpful lens on the belief systems of Balzac's—and our own—time.

CRITICISM

Ira Allen

Allen is a doctoral candidate in Rhetoric and Composition at Indiana University, Bloomington. He has published previously on Thomas Hardy and naturalism, the arts community and censorship in Singapore, and medical ethics in the European Union. Here, he considers the relationship between rhetoric and literary realism in Le Père Goriot.

Socially conscious literary critics have made much of Balzac's realism: his gritty depictions of actual life, in which the sentiments of a social moralist crop up here and there amidst the careful accounts-keeping of a bourgeois citizen (who would rather have been an aristocrat); his troubled portrayal of the decline of the aristocracy and the rise of the bourgeoisie; his focus, for all that, on the voices of the underclasses, of the poor and the downtrodden as well as the beautiful and the wealthy. Literary theorist Fredric Jameson offers one particularly compelling version of such criticism in his description of "the novels of Balzac . . . as reflecting the reactionary ideology of a dying class." Another, conflicting strand of criticism, however, follows Karl Marx's collaborator Friedrich Engels in seeing Balzac's realist approach to literature—which uses the novel as a tool for re-presenting a total social reality—as "further[ing] the class struggle by bringing out, with fidelity to detail, the essential aspects of society in a particular place and at

> ...WE CANNOT SEE BALZAC AS UNAMBIGU-
> OUSLY REJECTING RHETORIC. ... HE IS NEGOTIATING
> HIS WAY THROUGH THE QUESTION OF WHAT CONSTI-
> TUTES THE PROPER BOUNDS FOR RHETORIC—TESTING
> IT AS AN APPROACH TO MORALITY."

a particular time." Resolving this tension, between Balzac's realist fiction as reactionary and as politically radical, requires of us a question: How is one to decide just which aspects of society are truly essential? If society as a whole is always larger than any individual's imagination, it would seem that this is a matter of and for rhetoric—a question of persuasion, where attitudes are formed through the limited free play of symbols and fantasies. Oddly, given the extraordinary rhetorical fertility of Balzac's mind and moment both, *Le Père Goriot*'s particular focus on rhetoric has received relatively little scholarly attention, though it intersects in important ways with the more frequently discussed matrix of class struggle and literary realism. The critical indifference to *Le Père Goriot*'s non-indifference to rhetoric is perhaps a product of the generally held view that realism emerged as a literary movement in opposition to the more 'rhetorical' style of early nineteenth-century French fiction.

Indeed, Yuri Lotman expresses the critical consensus when he writes that the realist novel is marked by its "rejection of rhetoric"—its exclusion of overtly persuasive or flowery writing in favor of a straightforward representation of reality. Balzac's curiously unstable attitude toward rhetoric in *Le Père Goriot*, however, suggests otherwise. In the figure of Vautrin, rhetoric, radicalism, and realism combine in a way that the novel frequently rejects—but almost as frequently embraces. In *Le Père Goriot*, it is Vautrin who calls Rastignac again and again to question assumptions about who and what is truly moral. Though Vautrin is a "criminal mastermind," sometimes portrayed as unacceptable or even evil, Balzac's treatment of him is uneven and shifts back and forth between identification and rejection. At one moment, he is a devil, "displaying his chest, shaggy as a bear's back, but with

WHAT DO I READ NEXT?

- Balzac's *Cousine Bette* (*Cousin Betty*), published in 1846, is another often-read novel from the *Human Comedy* series. The title character is vengeful and greedy, and the novel itself is considered Balzac's last great work.

- Although Karl Marx's most frequently read text is *The Communist Manifesto*, coauthored with Friedrich Engels, his *The Eighteenth Brumaire of Louis Napoleon* (1852) makes natural follow-up reading for *Le Père Goriot*. Like Balzac, from whom he drew inspiration, Marx is concerned in this text with the plight of France's working poor; *The Eighteenth Brumaire of Louis Napoleon*, however, seeks to understand political events in France leading up to the revolution of 1848, the final revolution of several during Balzac's lifetime.

- Stendhal's 1830 *Le Rouge et le Noir* (*The Red and the Black*) is, along with *Le Père Goriot*, one of the classic works of French realist fiction. Stendhal's protagonist, Julien Sorel, resembles Rastignac in his ambition and questionable morality, but differs in coming from a nonaristocratic background.

- Jane Smiley's 1991 novel, *A Thousand Acres*, is like *Le Père Goriot* a reinterpretation of William Shakespeare's *King Lear*. In Smiley's Pulitzer Prize–winning novel, Lear is examined from a feminist standpoint.

- Sally Gardner's 2008 novel for young adults, *The Red Necklace: A Story of the French Revolution*, deals with the French, exploring the evils of the revolution itself as though they were part of a series of magical struggles.

hair that was of a reddish hue both repulsive and startling to behold," but he was first introduced as "not disagreeable...cheerful and obliging... [and] prompt to offer his services." Granted, even in that initial moment, there is something disquieting about Vautrin; but what is important is that he is a complex figure, neither easily accepted nor easily rejected. It is fitting, then, that *Le Père Goriot*'s greatest attention to rhetorical power is reserved for this Vautrin, a.k.a. Trompe-la-Mort, a.k.a. Jacques Collin: a man whose words are so powerful he needs three different names to mark which sorts of words he's using with (or *on*) whom. Vautrin's use of language is thus presented at times as usefully questioning social norms and at other times as evil plain and simple, and Balzac's apparent ambivalence on this score is of a piece with his complex portrayal of Vautrin's overall role in society. This ambivalence toward rhetoric, though, marks a break from the dismissal of the norms of persuasion generally held to be a key component of literary realism. Indeed, *Le Père Goriot*'s back-and-forth on the moral

status of Vautrin's symbol use helps clarify the link between realism and the domain of rhetoric: rather than a simple rejection of the latter by the former, this is a relationship of inclusion-of-the-thing-excluded.

But what is this 'rhetoric' that is being included while also excluded? As rhetorical scholar and philosopher of language Kenneth Burke puts it, "the basic function of rhetoric [is] the use of words by human agents to form attitudes or to induce actions in other human agents." It is a bridge between physical coercion and powerlessness, a way of approaching control over others without ever quite getting there. "Rhetorical power," as exercised by Vautrin and others, refers then to the *potential* for persuasion in a given use of symbols. Unlike the coercive force of physical power, the persuasive force of rhetoric is always only potential, and it is the relatively conscious negotiation of this particular potential that makes *Le Père Goriot* a realist novel. So, to say that literary realism founds itself as a discourse not by *rejecting* rhetoric, but rather by *negotiating* its inevitable presence is to say that realist novels—and *Le Père Goriot* in particular—try on different attitudes toward powerful symbol use. As we might then expect, throughout the novel, different characters are shown considering how best to harness symbols for their use; and we the readers are encouraged to take various moral attitudes toward the particular choices they make.

Shortly after Rastignac's mother has sent him the money he requested of her, so that he may make his way in society (though he has not told her that, she has intuited it), Vautrin applauds the decision, but also warns the young man that he must learn to duel. Rastignac must then borrow a franc from Vautrin to tip the messenger, and doing so leads him to reflect on what has become a somewhat hostile relationship between the two. Here, though, Balzac's often-intrusive narrator barges in, going off on a seemingly unrelated tangent about the power of ideas. With no preamble whatsoever, we as readers are led from Eugène de Rastignac "idly wonder[ing] why it was" that he watched Vautrin so closely, to the statement, "Ideas are, no doubt, projected with a force in direct ratio to that with which they are conceived." Drawing on the metaphor of the cannonball, Balzac's narrator continues, "Ideas are very different in the effects they produce . . . there are limp and flimsy minds into which other people's ideas drop slowly as a spent cannonball sinks into the soft earth"—while Rastignac's, in contrast, "head was filled with explosive material ready to ignite at the least touch." This brief introduction to the power of "that contagion of thought, whose odd phenomena influence us so often without our knowledge," would seem proof positive of the realist novel's need to reject rhetoric. The narrator warns of the power other people's words and ideas have to influence people without them knowing it. Balzac seems so keen, in fact, to warn readers of this threat that he breaks the narrative flow of the story entirely, allowing his narrator to push in without regard for even the reader's comfort.

Only a few pages later, Vautrin suggests that the young Victorine Taillefer has "put an idea into [his] head," but that this is an idea that will make both her and Rastignac "very happy." The idea, of course, is the one behind Rastignac's later moral dilemma: Vautrin will arrange to have Mlle de Taillefer's unpleasant brother killed in a duel, so that she may receive monies

from her father that are, though this father and her brother refuse to acknowledge it, her birthright. If not rhetoric in itself, it would seem here that an idea—the starting point of all rhetoric being the formation of some idea as a symbol or set of symbols—may after all be a positive thing, or at least potentially positive. The moral status of this particular idea remains fuzzy throughout the course of the novel. Likewise, in the same scene, though Rastignac wants to duel with Vautrin right that moment, the latter persuades him otherwise, no doubt saving his life (since Vautrin is an accomplished marksman and Rastignac is not). Vautrin speaks in a knowing way, calculated to stir Rastignac's interest; and the young man, as though a puppet, lets go his insistence on dueling and sits "down at the table, *overcome* by his curiosity that was now raised to the highest pitch by the sudden change in manners of this man, who had just talked of killing him." Vautrin's rhetorical power now comes to seem unambiguously positive; he has just saved one or perhaps even two lives merely by changing the way he spoke.

In contrast, Balzac offers for our clear censure Mme de Restaud, who gains power in her marriage by attending closely to such actions as will symbolize her acceptance of her husband's mastery. Her close study of "her husband's character in order that she may behave herself as she pleases" makes possible her "morganatic" union or ongoing affair with Comte de Trailles, but that affair proves utterly disastrous for her. Mme de Restaud serves throughout the novel as an example of symbolic power-use at its worst, and comes to no very good end in either her love affair or her marriage. *Her* rhetoric, Balzac rejects, though he may not reject rhetoric itself.

Far less negative is the narrative treatment of Rastignac's cousin Mme de Beauséant, from whom he learns to use a woman's interest in him as a symbolic tool, a wedge with which to make his way into society. In a dark moment in her own life, Mme de Beauséant urges the use of rhetorical power as a way of taking an ethical middle ground in an inevitable struggle for power. "Then [once you have made your way into society with this power]," she tells Rastignac, "you will know that the world is made up of dupes and rogues, but try yourself to be neither one nor the other." Here, it as though one may be inducted into rhetorical knowledge as into a knowledge of good and evil—the suggestion being that one must thereafter be "fallen," but need not be evil because of that. Thus, Rastignac subsequently "saw the world as it is; he understood that law and morality have no power over the rich," and "his imagination, transported to the high levels of Parisian society, filled his heart with evil thoughts." He is presented as having inside him now an evil that was not previously there. And yet, as literary critic Bruce Robbins notes, this moment itself has only been made possible by rhetorical calculation on Rastignac's part, by a supportiveness of his cousin in her distress that has been both sincere and manipulative. Rastignac, then, has actually brought with him the (rhetorical) knowledge of good and evil that he might be supposed to be learning here for the first time; we might say he is being formally made a citizen of a state that he already inhabits, the state of rhetoric. And thus it is, in the pages to follow, that he is able to wrestle successfully with his conscience, to resist what the novel presents as the greatest temptation—Vautrin's offer—all the while following his cousin's advice so well that one might wonder whether he has really been any better than Vautrin, after all.

Indeed, even Vautrin's offer itself is far from unambiguously evil. To the contrary, it seems to shift shapes. Leading up to the offer, we may read Vautrin as a sort of stand-in for Balzac himself, and at the same time as the consummate rhetorician. Beginning with his tour-de-force presentation of Rastignac to himself, Vautrin is both relentlessly realistic in his detailed descriptions of the young man's desires and deeply rhetorical in the way he calls Rastignac's attention again and again to the gap between those desires and his ability to fulfill them. He suggests, all before making his offer, that Rastignac has in fact "already chosen" one of the "only two courses to take: either blind obedience or open revolt"—and this emphasis on binary opposition is tailor-made to persuade the young man to do as Vautrin wishes, as are various pieces of flattery throughout. But he also says, sounding now like Balzac himself when talking of his realist novels, "You may draw your own conclusions; I have shown you life as it is. It is no less ugly than a kitchen and quite as evil smelling."

Rather than rejecting rhetoric in all this, Balzac is calling attention to the helpless rhetoricality of his own realism. He is acknowledging that yes, indeed, whatever else might be the case, his depiction of society must pick and choose,

must for all his own protests to the contrary select some portion of reality and present that as more real than the rest. Consider here the Roman law scholar and orator Cicero, who writes in the first century *BCE*—in the service of rhetoric—"The narrative will seem to be plausible if it seems to embody characteristics which are accustomed to appear in real life." So far, then, Vautrin sounds close to Balzac, and both sound closer to Cicero, known for his insistence on rhetoric's status as a highly moral activity, than either do to the figure of the devilish rhetorician. But this is shortly to change. In explaining his offer to Rastignac, Vautrin claims, like Milton's Lucifer, the ultimate figure of devilish eloquence, "I take upon myself to play the part of Providence, and I will direct the will of God," urging his target to "Care no more for your opinions than you do for your words.... There is no such thing as principle; emergency is everything." This figure of the rhetorician as indifferent to morals is even older than Cicero, tracing its way back at least to Plato, who complained that rhetoric was a mere "knack ... for producing a certain gratification and pleasure": like pastry-making, indifferent to the question of the good, of principle. And yet, once more, we cannot see Balzac as unambiguously rejecting rhetoric here. Instead, he is negotiating his way through the question of what constitutes the proper bounds for rhetoric—testing it as an approach to morality.

It is in this context that the immediately apparent evilness of Vautrin's offer to Rastignac becomes disturbingly unclear upon further consideration. As philosopher Iddo Landau argues in an article titled "To Kill a Mandarin"—based on Rastignac's discussion of his dilemma with Bianchon in terms of anonymous complicity in the killing of a Chinese mandarin—"The thought experiment suggests that we pretend that we are more moral and autonomous than we actually are, not only to others, but also to ourselves." That is to say, as Rastignac's conversation with his friend Bianchon shows, Vautrin's proposition is far less outrageous in practice, in the context of the decisions we actually do make, than it is in theory. Bianchon's initial response, when Rastignac puts the question to him, is a joke that is no joke at all: "Pooh!" he says, "I have already come to my thirty-third mandarin."

To recap, at first glance it might seem obvious that Balzac is offering a negative vision of rhetoric in *Le Père Goriot*, a classic rejection of rhetoric such as Lotman describes: "The aesthetics of realism ... was characterized mostly by a negative feature of anti-romanticism and was perceived against a projection of romantic norms, so creating a 'rhetoric of the rejection of rhetoric'." On this vision, it was only in distancing itself from such romantic, rhetoric-focused ideas about what language was and ought to be that the realist novel carved out a space for itself in readers' hearts. And that distance is achieved, in *Le Père Goriot*, in part through the vilification of Vautrin.

Except that, as we have seen, Vautrin is not simply vilified. Apart from the passages here discussed, it is worth keeping in mind that—though Rastignac ends up rejecting his offer—Vautrin follows through on the plan and in the process does well by poor Victorine Taillefer. Likewise, it becomes increasingly apparent that Vautrin's illegal plotting is not terribly different from the plotting carried out by the representative of the law, who "count[s] upon some violence on his part tomorrow morning that will allow us to make an end of him." It is as though Balzac, royalist though he was, simply could not bear not to show as many sides of society as possible. In so doing, however, he could not help but at least partially redeem Vautrin, his devilish rhetorician who wasn't. And it is this version of realism, a realism that asks us to confront our own potential for hypocrisy, to confront the contradictions in our systems of values, that has radical rhetorical power. If we can be persuaded to re-engage with our own, often easy and thoughtless notions of morality, change in the world may well be possible.

Source: Ira Allen, "Rhetorical Realism in Balzac's *Le Père Goriot*," in *Novels for Students*, Gale, Cengage Learning, 2010

Ruth Amossy

In the following excerpted essay, Amossy urges readers to understand Le Père Goriot *as a symbolic meditation on social, political, and economic change.*

To seek out the essential reality beneath the surface in order to expose the internal mechanism of society: such, according to Georg Lukács, is the principal goal of realistic art. Thus Balzac, in *Old Goriot*, does not simply mimic a preexistent world already endowed with meaning, nor is he content to show things as they appear. If, as some

> BEYOND THE PSYCHOLOGICAL DIMENSION, THE NOVEL DENOUNCES A SOCIETY WHERE ALL FAMILIAL AND PERSONAL TIES ARE MEDIATED BY MONEY. THE BLESSED TRANSPARENCY OF HUMAN RELATIONSHIPS BASED NEITHER ON POWER NOR ON WEALTH IS NOTHING BUT A NOSTALGIC DREAM."

writers and critics would have it, the novel is a mirror, it is a mirror that reveals the hidden logic of human and social formation. While creating an illusion of reality through detailed description and true-to-life characters, *Old Goriot* in effect provides us with an in-depth analysis of French society in the first half of the nineteenth century.

Balzac constructs a fictional world that might usefully be decoded on at least two levels. On the first level, the novel constitutes a true-to-life representation, replete with vivid detail. On the second level, all the elements that advance the representation are woven into a web of complex relations through which they acquire symbolic meaning. The composition of *Old Goriot* thus allows for a significant distribution of its material: the Vauquer boardinghouse is one of three Parisian spheres staged by the novel; Goriot is related to a series of father figures, among whom are Taillefer and Vautrin; Rastignac and Bianchon embody two of the options open to youthful ambition. This combination of verisimilitude and symbolic organization, of mimesis and carefully crafted structure, is at the very core of Balzac's realism. It offers a comprehensive scheme for both describing and interpreting the social formation. Formal patterns yield social meanings; more or less explicit configurations of elements such as characters, places, and scenes uncover the logic of postrevolutionary France. These principles are illustrated by a close reading of the father-son relationships in *Old Goriot*.

Although Goriot's drama of paternity derives from his neglect by his two daughters, who are his sole and absolute passion, clearly his paternal function is not confined to these painful relationships. It has often been observed that

Eugène de Rastignac nourishes filial sentiments toward Goriot, who in turn looks on Rastignac as a son and is delighted when the young man has a love affair with Delphine de Nucingen, Goriot's daughter. "So you wish to be my dear child too?" says Goriot to Rastignac. On another occasion, the two men express their feelings in a significant exchange: "[D]ear Father Goriot, you know very well that I am fond of you," says the student to the old man, who answers: "Yes, indeed, I can see that you are; you are not ashamed of me! Let me embrace you." Admiring Father Goriot's qualities and appreciative of his immense generosity and self-sacrifice, Rastignac willingly accepts the old man, uneducated as Goriot is, while his own daughters, in shame, hide him from the world. "He says nothing about what he has endured, but anyone can guess it. Well, I will look after him as though I were his son; I will fill his life with happiness," thinks the young student to himself. The adoptive son even takes on himself the duties Delphine and Anastasie fail to perform. When the old man is on his deathbed, Rastignac is constantly at his side, trying to comfort him in his anguish while Goriot's daughters claim to be delayed by personal concerns. Deeply moved by Goriot's despair, Rastignac spares no effort to induce Anastasie and Delphine to pay one last visit to their dying father: "Well, then, promise me," he says to M. de Restaud, Anastasie's husband, "you will tell her that her father has not a day to live; that he looked for her at his bedside, and cursed her when she did not come." M. de Restaud, "impressed by the fierce indignation expressed in Eugène's voice," answers, "You may tell her that yourself." It is Rastignac who takes charge of the funeral arrangements, and he and the Vauquer servant are the only mourners present at a burial ceremony that the daughters decline to attend. This painful ordeal is a significant factor in the hero's apprenticeship and constitutes the final stage in the process of his disillusionment: "He looked at the grave, and in that place the last tear of his youth was shed."

What, then, is the meaning of a symbolic paternity bestowed on a man unable to play the role of a spiritual father? Goriot is deprived of all paternal attributes, since he has no knowledge and no power. Rastignac rapidly acquires in Paris experience of the world and a capacity to behave according to the rules of society—a capacity the old man will never have. Rastignac begins to grasp the hidden mechanisms that move people in familial and social situations, while Goriot remains forever unable to analyze, and thus to master, the world around him. Moreover, in the Vauquer boardinghouse, Rastignac protects the old man, who has become the laughingstock of his fellow boarders: "'Anyone who annoys old Goriot shall answer for it to me from now on,' said Eugène, looking at the old vermicelli-maker's neighbour. 'He's worth more than all of us put together [...].' Balzac's novel thus presents a striking reversal of the traditional roles. The man endowed with understanding and savoir faire, the benevolent protector, the parental caretaker is not old Goriot, but young Rastignac. The novel stages the fall of the father and the rise of the son.

What, then, is the knowledge acquired by the son that completely escapes the father? One of the main things Rastignac learns during his Parisian apprenticeship is never to confuse the principles of law with their practical application in real-life situations. To conquer a position in the world, the young man has not only to study law but also to become proficient in the ways of the world. He has to understand how laws are adapted to the needs of influential people and thus enabled to serve money and power. The distinction between legality and legitimacy remains beyond Goriot's understanding. A close and solid connection between law and justice is at the base of the reforms pursued by the Revolution and intended to put an end to the arbitrary power of an absolute monarch and to ensure the equality of all citizens. The "old '93" believes in the efficiency of law to protect defenseless citizens against illegitimate measures. When Delphine reveals that her husband, the banker Nucingen, has invested all his money in a questionable business concern and has offered her personal freedom in return for placing her fortune at his disposal, Goriot naively protests: "But there are such things as laws! [...]. There's a Place de Grève for that sort of son-in-law! I would guillotine him myself if there were no public executioner to do it for me!" Delphine responds, "No, no, Father, the law can't touch him."

It is the daughter who teaches the father that morality and family respectability cannot be protected by laws. She reveals to him the crooked ways in which Nucingen has built a fortune, "swindling poor people out of their money" behind a lawful facade. She tells Goriot that the banker has straw men who build houses on his land, pay the contractors with postdated bills, sell the properties to him for small sums, and then "slide out of their debt to the duped contractors by going bankrupt." The wisdom of the son-in-law, as explained by the daughter, is something that the father can neither understand nor admit. To fight it, he sees no other recourse than turning to the tribunal and applying the letter of the law.

This appeal to a law designed to protect natural rights, that is to say, moral principles enshrined in nature, reappears in hyperbolic form when the old man lies on his deathbed. Seeing that his two ungrateful daughters do not care enough to sustain him in his final moments, Goriot cries out in a terrible instant of despair, "My daughters! My daughters! Anastasie! Delphine! I must see them. Send the police to fetch them, compel them to come! Justice is on my side, [...] natural affection, and the law as well. I protest!" Later he cries out, "Pass a law for dying fathers. It is shocking! It cries for vengeance!" Rastignac has no answer for the unfortunate man. Did he himself not abandon his studies in law when he understood that law and morals do not apply to the wealthy, since money is the world's ultima ratio?

In short, the father, who symbolically stands for the law, no longer represents its power, does not know its real use, and calls in vain for its support. The breakdown of paternal authority and the increasing gap between law and natural rights threaten the very existence of the new society.

Family seems to survive only as an archaic memory in the distant provinces. Thus Rastignac takes pleasure in a warm family where relationships between parents and children, brother and sisters, are based on true love and devotion.

The young hero's relationship with his family expresses a nostalgia for a lost harmony, a nostalgia shared by other characters. Old Goriot often recalls his former life with his two daughters when they were still young and lived with him in a loving home. He tries to revive it by setting up a love nest for Delphine and Rastignac. The old man dreams of sharing the happiness of the young couple and restoring a lost family cell dominated by true feeling. Taking Rastignac to the apartment he has furnished, he is thrilled at the idea that they are going to have dinner with Delphine: "The three of us are

dining together, together! do you understand? [...] Ah! it's a long, long time since I've had such a peaceful happy time with her as we shall have now." Goriot's desperate efforts thus produce a parody of the original family unit...

Beyond the psychological dimension, the novel denounces a society where all familial and personal ties are mediated by money. The blessed transparency of human relationships based neither on power nor on wealth is nothing but a nostalgic dream. "Money buys everything, even daughters," says the dying father to Rastignac in a moment of horrible lucidity. From beginning to end, the text implicates the personal and the socioeconomic levels. Emotional or spiritual planes have no self-sufficiency in Balzac's novels: love, lust, parental affection are all subordinated to material components. The hero's love for Delphine cannot be separated from his social ambitions. Delphine's beauty and the desire Delphine arouses in the young man greatly derive from the luxury surrounding her and the splendor of her dress. Rastignac does not fall in love with Victorine Taillefer, although she is naturally pretty, because she does not have the seductive qualities of a sophisticated Parisian socialite. Rastignac himself, in order to seduce Delphine, has to spend his money on fashionable clothes, since "[o]ne glance at Monsieur de Trailles had made Rastignac realize the influence that tailors exercise in young men's lives." Moreover, he has to be introduced as Mme de Beauséant's relative to attract the attention of the ladies. The intimate relationship between Delphine and Rastignac starts with the young woman's confession of her financial problems. It develops thanks to the apartment that old Goriot brings as a present to his protégé, laying out his last franc. Money runs the world; it gives life and love, as Goriot aptly puts it in his misery.

Viewed from this perspective, the lesson of the novel is no less cynical than that offered by Vautrin. The hero's apprenticeship begins with the initial steps taken by an impoverished law student anxious to make his way in the world through university studies. He soon discovers that hard work is by no means the only way to succeed and that knowledge of the world is of far greater value than knowledge itself. At first he is "resolved to open two parallel lines of attack on Fortune, to lean on Knowledge and on Love, to be a learned doctor of law and a man of the world". Eventually, however, he is obliged to concede, together with the narrator, that the two lines are "asymptotes" that can "never meet". Abandoning the classroom, Rastignac serves his entire apprenticeship in the world, learning more between the blue boudoir of Mme de Restaud and the pink boudoir of Mme de Beauséant than he could ever have done at university. What he aims to study is Parisian law—without which no fortune can ever be made.

Thus in *Old Goriot*, parallels and oppositions between symbolic sons and fathers and their relation to the law are designed to reveal the hidden meanings of the new French society's sociopolitical and economic dimensions. The novel raises problems without trying to provide solutions or even unequivocal answers. It exposes the various and often contradictory attitudes adopted by its fictional characters in accordance with their individual perceptions of society at large. Readers, then, are invited not to pass judgment based on moral precepts already in place but rather to analyze, to configure the elements in meaningful patterns, to compare viewpoints, and to reflect on a fictional world intended to equip them with a better understanding of their own.

Source: Ruth Amossy, "Fathers and Sons in Old Goriot: The Symbolic Dimension of Balzac's Realism," in *Approaches to Teaching Balzac's Old Goriot*, edited by Michael Peled Ginsburg, Modem Language Association of America, 2000, pp. 45–53.

Carol Mossman

In the following excerpted essay, Mossman examines Le Père Goriot *for what it can tell us about how music functions in novels.*

No one would dispute opera's heavy debt to the novel. Nor is this a coincidence for, as musicologists Donald Grout and Susan McClary have both pointed out, the beginnings of opera as a form which tells stories with and through music can be situated at that point in history when the conventions of musical composition are shifting away from the "architectural" (to use Grout's expression) toward a linear and teleological unfolding not unlike the conventions governing narrative closure.

In fact, the gradual modulation toward tonality in music occurring in the late sixteenth century parallels the rise of the novel form. So there is some sense in which opera and the novel are siblings, the one destined, perhaps, to be the public projection of what the other is murmuring in private. Thus, beyond the public/private divide,

> VAUTRIN HAS NOW FALLEN INTO HIS OWN TRANCE, AND HIS BODY IS FORCED INTO BETRAYING HIS CRIMINAL PAST. IN ONE READING, THE MASTER SEMIOTICIAN HAS HIMSELF BEEN DECIPHERED. BUT, IN ANOTHER READING (OR HEARING), IT IS THE POWER OF HIS OWN REFRAIN WHICH COMES BACK TO PERFORM ITSELF UPON HIM."

opera and the novel stand in a relation to each other which is at once historical and formal.

Prose works which have been shaped into opera libretti are almost too numerous to count . . . However, transformation of the private discourse characteristic of the novel into the highly public musical text is rarely accomplished without violence to the prose text. Massive excisions may be necessary in the fashioning of an opera libretto which must be sufficiently tight to be performed within a limited time frame and textually concise enough to allow for play of the lyrical. Additions, too, may be in order: a well-known case in point is Halévy and Meilhac's invention of the Micaëla character in Bizet's *Carmen*.

One might say that what is lost in the passage from prose to music theater is the discursive armature of novelistic mediation. Drawing on Bakhtin, this armature encompasses narrative voice, the dialogue between present and past with the consequent relativization of traditional hierarchies, a temporality both subtle and variegated, intersecting "planes" of language, and, more pertinently for my purposes here, a certain capacity to import, naturalize, and domesticate discourses and genres alien to the novel itself (Bakhtin 3–40).

In Bakhtin's reading, the novel, as a genre whose business it is to ingest every imaginable form of literary and social discourse, sets these up in strange and perhaps strained conversations with one other, conversations which, because they are multilateral and relational, tend to the flattening out of discursive hierarchies . . . Bakhtin goes on to suggest that: "After all, the boundaries between fiction and nonfiction, between literature and nonliterature … are not laid in heaven" (Bakhtin 33). Thus, the novel is the unholy of unholies precisely because it desacralizes cultural essences.

It is the second of these unheavenly borders—that separating literature and another aesthetic discourse—which I wish to cross here by investigating not what occurs when prose is adapted into libretto and matched up with the story as it is told in terms of the musical composition, but rather what is the fate of music and its text when these are imported into the novel. Does novelistic appropriation of the acoustic text somehow flatten out musical discourse, or does the performative retain its peculiar power in spite of the domesticating tendencies Bakhtin alleges of the novel as genre? For purposes of demonstration, I shall focus on Balzac's *Le Père Goriot*.

What, then, are some of the features of the acoustic text which might defy incorporation into the novel? There are at least three which stand as fundamentally inimical to novelistic discourse. First, opera and music theater constitute a discourse which is public in its essence. Second, the acoustic enjoys greater proximity to the body. Finally, to the extent that it is performative, and thus reiterative, music theater stands in a different relation both to time and space…

Let me now explore the above concepts by turning to *Le Père Goriot,* listening particularly to the voice of the very versatile Vautrin. Much has been written about Vautrin's function as a master semiotician, deciphering and managing the myriad codes in play whilst himself remaining illegible until at last his body is tricked into revealing its eloquent truth. Yet Vautrin is far more than a manipulator of codes and people: he is himself a singer, who, at strategic moments of the narrative, is wont to burst into songs which he generally takes from the light opera or vaudeville repertory.

In *Le Père Goriot* it is Vautrin who does most of the singing, although on two occasions other characters do sing. The first of these occasions follows on Eugène de Rastignac's social gaffe committed through the mention of the name "Goriot" in the presence of the latter's daughter, the comtesse de Restaud. Turning to the piano, she inquires as to whether Eugène sings. To his "no," she responds, "That's a pity for you've deprived yourself of a great means of success," [my translation] croons the comtesse, borrowing from Cimarosa's *Il Matrimonio segreto.* [The Secret Marriage]

The art of song, she implies, is one of the keys unlocking those doors Eugène so ardently desires opened. Nonetheless, in this narrative, it is Vautrin who is the lead singer. More often than not, he announces his entrances by singing. This type of entrance is certainly operatic. Moreover (and this is what I wish to examine in detail), these entrances are performative in the context of the novel. By this I mean that they shift the modalities of narrative representation to the point where an operatic spatialization is produced on the one hand even as the reader is, by implication, situated as an audience. For instance, in the first such entrance, Vautrin sings what will turn out to be his refrain. Bellowing ("in his bass voice"): "Long have I wandered o'er the earth, / And I've been seen in every part" [adapted from p. 54 in the Jane Minot Sedgwick 1897 translation—one of many still in current circulation] from the light opera, *La Joconde ou les courers d'aventures* [Joconde, or the Riders of Fortune] The song is understood by Mme Vauquer as pure frivolity and, when Vautrin continues with "Courting the girls, brunette and fair, / Loving and sighing … [p. 54 ibid.]," she giggles girlishly at his attentions.

Mme Vauquer is not an initiated listener. However, this episode occurs early in the novel and while the seasoned reader of Balzac might suspect that Vautrin is imparting some kind of knowledge, any allusion contained in the acoustic text remains opaque. Taking Vautrin's brief insertion into an operetta at face value, we stand to conclude that he is a man of broad experience (certainly true) much given to womanizing (certainly not true). When subsequently he sings this refrain, the blondes and brunettes have been excised. When Victorine Taillefer, the story's damsel in distress, begs him to intercede with her estranged father on her behalf, Vautrin belts out the by now familiar "J'ai longtemps parcouru le monde," [Long have I wandered o'er the earth] which, once again, passes as sound signifying nothing in that setting. In fact, it is only at the *finale* that the real power of this refrain will reveal itself.

There is a sense in which Vautrin's recourse to song in the midst of an appreciative if uncomprehending cast reconstructs certain peculiarly operatic conventions according to which, for instance, singers may perform for the sole benefit of advancing audience understanding whilst others on stage appear to remain as if entranced in some other zone of existence. There is also the convention—again, a purely operatic one—of the duet or quartet where singers simultaneously utter different texts, surely not transmitting knowledge to each other but rather communicating ostensibly to the audience, although verbal communication under these circumstances is next to impossible unless one is already familiar with the libretto.

What is being suggested here is that in *Le Père Goriot*, the acoustic word functions to delimit spaces and fields of understanding to a degree which novelistic discourse would be hard-pressed to achieve through other means. I hope to show that invoking the operatic creates 1) zones of trance and unknowing, 2) as a corollary, privileged spaces of cognition and complicity, and 3) intersecting spaces which create mis/understanding and *malentendu* [another word for misunderstanding, emphasizing in this article that misunderstanding is *bad* understanding]. As *mise-en-scène*, [a manner of staging] the operatic also situates readers in that space and at that distance wherein as audience, they, unlike any of the characters, are privy to *all* information. This is the space of synthesis, perspective, and power which ultimately enable a level of cognition encompassing and exceeding that of Vautrin himself: it is here that cognition becomes recognition.

I would further like to entertain the notion that importing the acoustic word into this novel carries a particular performative spin because it spatializes that temporality associated with novelistic representation. By spatialization, I am not referring to descriptions such as the celebrated one which opens this novel, but instead spatialization which serves purposes which are functional narratologically. The following interlocking scenes which are central to the novel's *dénouement* [the final unraveling or tying up of a fiction or drama's various threads—comes after the climax and falling action] tend to disrupt the temporal by positioning the cast of characters operatically—that is, into privileged spaces of cognition and complicity, corollary zones of trance and unknowing and intersecting planes of mis/understanding and *malentendu*.

These three scenes include Eugène's *tête-à-tête* [private conversation, literally "head-to-head";] with potential bride Victorine, the interruption of this scene by Vautrin with Eugène's subsequent attempt to wriggle out of his Faustian contract with Vautrin, all this leading into the boisterous dinner which is to be Vautrin's Last Supper before his coffee is spiked, he is betrayed and delivered over to the law.

These scenes follow in rapid sequence and form a whole under the aegis of the operatic since Vautrin enters strategically singing the same lines with which he will later exit in the company of the police. The acoustic word is thus what frames the novel's *dénouement* itself.

In the first of the three scenes, Eugène de Rastignac is engaged in sweet discussion with his future dowry, Victorine Taillefer. Enter Vautrin singing: "My Fanny is charming / In her simplicity" [my translation] (vaudeville air from *Les Deux jaloux* [Both Jealous men]). Complicity is immediately established between Eugène and Vautrin to the exclusion of the all-too-simple Victorine, who, listening to this performance, is positioned in the zone of unknowing. However, (scene two) Eugène's conscience has been pricked, and besides Old Goriot and daughter Delphine have mustered enough cash to secure an apartment in which Eugène can nestle as a kept woman with his integrity intact. As the desperate Eugène (out loud) plans to avert M. Taillefer of the upcoming "accident" scheduled to befall his son and heir, Vautrin, nearby, overhears, and entering, bursts into a lamentation: "Oh Richard, oh my king, / All the world doth leave you" [my translation] (from Grétry's *Richard Cœur de Lion* [Richard the Lionheart]).

As earlier with Victorine, this singing entrance organizes a space of cognition and complicity between Vautrin and his would-be protegé, while the zone of trance and unknowing encompasses Goriot who remains ignorant of Vautrin and Eugène's shady partnership. Yet the spring has been wound and the plot is unstoppable; this inexorability is signified once again by Vautrin's appeal to the power of performance. Undaunted by Eugène's betrayal, he intones his refrain: "J'ai longtemps parcouru le monde / Et l'on m'a vu." This refrain continues to function as a soliloquy to the extent that the other listeners present (and possibly the audience) do not seize its meaning. The spotlight is on Vautrin, while the rest of the assembly falls into the penumbra.

Hereupon Christophe announces dinner and the three descend to the awaiting company (scene three) which includes nearly the entire *pension* [boardinghouse]: Mlle Michonneau, the snitch; Bianchon, the medical student; Mme Couture, Victorine's confidante and chaperone; Victorine; and M. Poiret, whose name sums it up.

The scene which ensues is essentially choral with joking, punning, and imitating of animals—in short, a boisterous din, "a veritable opera whose orchestra Vautrin led like a conductor" [my translation]. The *chef d'orchestre* [conductor] is here also a chef *tout court* [as such] since he spikes the wine consumed by Eugène and Goriot with sleeping potion to prevent them from alerting M. Taillefer of the disaster to come. They then fall into their trance as Vautrin, poised for his exit, sings: "Sleep, my dear loves, sleep, / For you I'll always my watch keep" [adapted from p. 241 ibid.] whereupon he kisses his sleeping beauty, Eugène.

Here again, recourse to song organizes the company into the zones of trance and unknowing, with the reader/spectator now positioned in complicity with the knowledge of Vautrin's homosexuality *and* his intentions to carry on with his sinister plot. On this tender note, he exits, still singing—this time a kind of hymn to the sun: "Sunlight, sunlight, divine sunlight, / That mak'st the mellow pumpkins bright" [p. 242 ibid.]. This is hardly a line from the repertory of high opera, but as if not to break with the tone, and as if conveyed by the performative itself, Vautrin is off to his box in the *Théatre de la Gaieté* [a theater or the Boulevard du Temple in Paris].

On his return, as we know, it is announced that the Taillefer son has been killed in a duel. It is at this point that Mlle Michonneau spikes Vautrin's coffee and it is here that Vautrin's cognition is superseded by audience and cast recognition for Vautrin has now fallen into his own trance, and his body is forced into betraying his criminal past. In one reading, the master semiotician has himself been deciphered. But, in another reading (or hearing), it is the power of his own refrain which comes back to perform itself upon him. For, the ultimate irony of Vautrin's refrain, "J'ai longtemps parcouru le monde / Et l'on m'a vu de toute part," is that, when he in his turn falls into that trance—and it is his body being read—he is indeed seen everywhere. The acoustic text, besides organizing the novelistic/temporal into discrete spaces of understanding comparable to those of music theater, overflows its context, and ends up performing itself on its erstwhile performer, Vautrin.

Source: Carol Mossman, "Sotto Voce-Opera in the Novel: The Case of *Le Père Goriot*," in *The French Review*, Vol. 69, No. 3, February 1996, pp. 387–93.

Stanley L. Galpin

In the following essay, Galpin emphasizes the importance of contrasting environments for Rastignac's development in Le Père Goriot.

The Influence of Environment in *Le Père Goriot*

Emile Faguet in his volume on Balzac criticizes the novelist for his lengthy descriptions, while assenting to his theory (as set forth in the preface of *La Comédie Humaine* [*The Human Comedy*, Balzac's novelistic corpus in nearly its entirety], 1842) that character is the product of environment so far as to say (p. 60) that to introduce the human animal, it is essential for me to describe its habitat and how the home explains its inhabitant. [my translation] He goes on to say, however, that often Balzac's descriptions of dwellings do not explain characters, taking as an illustration *Le Père Goriot* and its extended description of Mme. Vauquer's boarding-house . . .

But it is not the correspondence of Mme Vauquer with her environment that is the most important application of Balzac's theory in this novel. The Maison Vauquer and its inmates are a portion of the environment of young Eugène de Rastignac, whose changing fortunes divide with the sorrows of Old Goriot the attention and sympathy of the reader. Balzac's older characters do not change when once their habits of life have become fixed. In the novel in question it is not Mme Vauquer, Old Goriot and Vautrin who develop, it is Eugène. Arriving unspoiled from the provinces, he has his eyes opened to Parisian life, and his life purposes and interests change as he becomes aware of the luxuries of life and the accepted means by which they were procured in the society of which he had recently become a part. It is by contrasting his home life and the Maison Vauquer with the elegance and comfort in which Mme de Beauséant, Mme de Restaud and Mme de Nucingen lived that he came to make his definite resolve to make his way in the world and procure for himself the same material satisfactions they possessed.

Eugène began, like other students, by envying the luxury of the occupants of the carriages on the Champs-Élysées, and by comparing it with the simplicity and financial distress of his own family in the provinces. The first result, a very transitory one, was to arouse him to work: still under the spell of an illusive energy caught from the splendors of fashionable society. [p. 44

in the Jane Minot Sedgwick 1897 translation—one of many still in current circulation] It was at Mme de Beauséant's that he caught his first glimpse of a luxurious interior: He was now to see for the first time the wonders of personal elegance that reflect the mind and habits of a lady of rank [p. 87 ibid.] Its effect upon him was immediate: The demon of luxury gnawed at his heartstrings, and the lust of gain took possession of him; his throat was parched with the thirst for gold. [p. 90 ibid.] Returning to the Maison Vauquer, the importance of whose detailed description is now apparent, he was struck by the disagreeable contrast, and his ambition received a new impulse:

> After reaching the rue Neuve-Ste-Geneviève, he ... went into the loathsome dining room, where he found, like so many cattle at a trough, the eighteen boarders in the course of feeding themselves. The spectacle of their misery and the squalor of the room were horrible to him. The transition had been too abrupt, the contrast too complete, to do other than develop his ambition beyond all measure. On one side of him were the fresh and charming images of life in high society, young and living faces framed by the marvels of art and luxury, passionate minds filled with poetry; on the other, sinister pictures edged with sludge, countenances to which the passions had left nothing but their strings and their mechanisms... Rastignac resolved to open upon fortune with two parallel lines of attack, to trust both to study and to love, to be at the same time a learned doctor and a man of fashion. [adapted from p. 107 ibid.]

Mme de Béauseant invites Eugène to dinner, and the contrast again overwhelms him:

> Still, as he looked at the embossed silver and the thousand refinements of the sumptuous table, as he admired the silence, quite new to him, with which dinner was served; it would have been difficult for a man of such ardent imagination as his not to prefer a life of continual elegance to the privations he had been willing to embrace in the morning. His thoughts carried him back to his bourgeois boardinghouse for a moment, and he was overcome with such profound revulsion that he swore he would leave it ... [adapted from p. 161–62 ibid.]

His final conversion to the doctrine of material success comes with his establishment as Delphine's lover in the apartment which her father has furnished for them:

> He had always hesitated to cross the Parisian Rubicon [as Caesar, too, had hesitated to cross this Italian stream; the phrase franchir le Rubicon, or "to cross the Rubicon," came in French

to express a sudden, strong resolve] ... Nevertheless, his last scruples had vanished on the previous evening when he found himself in his new apartment. Upon actually enjoying the material advantages of fortune, ... he had shed the skin of a provincial and had established himself in a position from which he could descry a great future. [adapted from p. 293–94 ibid.]

It was therefore the effect of the contrast between his humble provincial home and impossible Parisian boarding-house, and the life of comparative luxury of which he had glimpses, that aroused the worldly ambition of Eugène de Rastignac and inspired him to utter the challenge expressed in his final words, spoken from the heights of the Père-Lachaise cemetery as he gazed down upon the fashionable quarter of the city: *A nous deux maintenant!* [It's down to you and I, now!]

"The Influence of Environment" in Le Père Goriot (Stanley Galpin—1917)

Source: Stanley L. Galpin, "The Influence of Environment in *Le Père Goriot,*" in *Modern Language Notes*, Vol. 32, No. 5, May 1917, pp. 306–308.

SOURCES

Arendt, Hannah, *On Revolution*, Penguin Classics, 1990.

Auerbach, Erich, *Mimesis: The Representation of Reality in Western Literature*, translated by Willard R. Trask, Princeton University Press, 1953.

Balzac, Honoré de, *Le Père Goriot*, translator anonymous, The Franklin Library, 1980.

Bolster, Richard, *Le Père Goriot*, Grant & Cutler Ltd., 2000.

Burke, Kenneth, *A Rhetoric of Motives*, University of California Press, 1969.

Cicero, *De Inventione; De Optimo Genere; Oratorum Topica*, translated by H.M. Hubbell, Loeb Classical Library, Harvard University Press, 1949.

Habermas, Jürgen, *The Structural Transformation of the Public Sphere: An Inquiry into a Category of Bourgeois Society*, translated by Frederick Lawrence, MIT Press, 1989.

Harvey, David, *Paris: Capital of Modernity*, Routledge, 2003.

Herman, Luc, *Concepts of Realism*, Boydell & Brewer, 1996.

James, Henry, *The Question of Our Speech; The Lesson of Balzac: Two Lectures*, Houghton Mifflin, 1905.

Jameson, Fredric, *Marxism and Form: Twentieth-century Dialectical Theories of Literature*, Princeton University Press, 1974.

Kanes, Martin, *Père Goriot: Anatomy of a Troubled World*, Twayne Publishers, 1993.

Krailsheimer, A. J., Preface to *Père Goriot*, in *Père Goriot*, Oxford University Press, 1991.

Landau, Iddo, "To Kill a Mandarin," in *Philosophy & Literature*, Vol. 29, No. 1, 2005, pp. 89–96.

Lotman, Yuri, *Universe of the Mind: A Semiotic Theory of Culture*, translated by Ann Shukman, Indiana University Press, 2000.

Lucey, Michael, *The Misfit of the Family: Balzac and the Social Forms of Sexuality*, Duke University Press, 2003.

Marcus, Sharon, *Apartment Stories: City and Home in Nineteenth-century Paris and London*, University of California Press, 1999.

Plato, *Gorgias*, translated by Donald J. Zeyl, Hackett Publishing Company, 1987.

Robb, Graham, *Balzac: A Biography*, W.W. Norton and Co., 1996.

Robbins, Bruce, *Upward Mobility and the Common Good: Toward a Literary History of the Welfare State*, Princeton University Press, 2007.

Sandars, Mary Frances, *Honoré de Balzac, His Life and Writings*, Dodd, Mead & Company, 1905.

Taggart, Malcolm George, "Old Goriot," in *Encyclopedia of Literary Translation into English*, edited by Olive Classe, Taylor & Francis, 2000, 104–105.

FURTHER READING

Hunt, Lynn Avery, *Politics, Culture, and Class in the French Revolution*, University of California Press, 2004.
>   This twentieth-anniversary reprinting of Hunt's seminal work on the social structure and lasting impacts of the French Revolution is essential reading for anyone who wants to understand the world in which Balzac wrote.

Pasco, Allan H, *Balzacian Montage: Configuring "La Comédie Humaine,"* University of Toronto Press, 1991.
>   This book offers a clearly laid out argument for viewing all of Balzac's writings, as Balzac himself intended but as few readers do, as a unified work. In working through the various principles underlying that unified work, *La Comédie Humaine* (The Human Comedy), Pasco can help readers understand *Le Père Goriot* more fully.

Prendergast, Christopher, *The Order of Mimesis: Balzac, Stendhal, Nerval, Flaubert*, Cambridge University Press, 1988, pp. 83–118.
>   In this well-regarded text, Prendergast examines the way understandings of *mimesis*, the textual re-presentation of a world, are and are not shifted by the critical movement of poststructuralism. His chapter on Balzac (83–118) helps situate the author in terms of both his historical and critical contexts, and offers a reasonable (if somewhat difficult) introduction to poststructuralist theory.

Tocqueville, Alexis de, *The Old Regime and the Revolution, Volumes 1 and 2*, edited by François Furet, translated by Alan Kahan, University of Chicago Press, 1998 and 1999.
>   Tocqueville's classic, and final, work of political science examines the ways in which the French Revolution was, after all, not as revolutionary as it initially seemed. Written in 1851, a year after Balzac's death, the book has been translated anew by scholar of French and European history Alan Kahan.

Sense and Sensibility

1995

Sense and Sensibility, published in 1811 under the author's pseudonym "A Lady," was Jane Austen's debut novel. She had begun writing the novel in epistolary form—or as a series of letters—at age nineteen in 1795, with a working title of *Elinor and Marianne*. Later she changed the title to focus on the book's main theme. After rewriting the novel, Austen paid for the book to be published sixteen years after she had begun writing it and gave the publisher a commission on sales. The novel was printed in three volumes by Thomas Egerton at the Military Library publishing house. The stakes for Austen were high, as the cost of publication was more than a third of her household's 460-pound annual income. But the first edition of the novel—a run of 750 copies—sold out by July 1813 and launched Austen's career as a respected writer.

A 1995 film adaptation of the novel, written by Emma Thompson and directed by Ang Lee, stays close to the narrative of Austen's original, which is, at heart, about late-eighteenth-century and early-nineteenth-century courtship and marriage. Sisters Elinor and Marianne get caught up in a social dance of suitors, secret engagements, and financial concerns. However, because Thompson also starred as Elinor, the main character's age was changed from nineteen to twenty-seven, which was more plausible for contemporary audiences. *Sense and Sensibility* was Lee's first venture into Hollywood film; he partnered with Columbia TriStar. The film won numerous accolades,

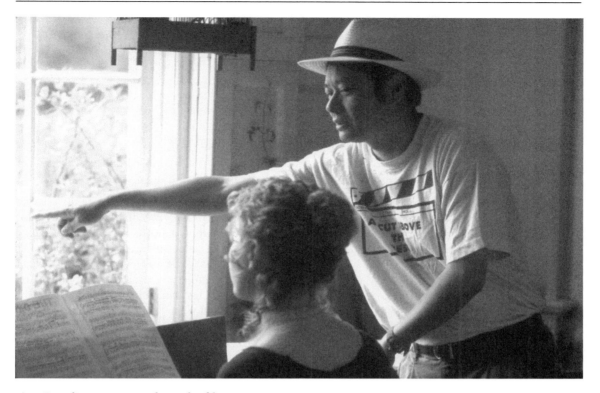

Ang Lee directs a scene from the film. (© Sygma / Corbis)

including an Oscar for Best Adapted Screenplay and Golden Globe awards for Best Motion Picture-Drama and Best Screenplay.

Lee's adaptation is but one of many made of *Sense and Sensibility* for television and the big screen. The most recent was a BBC-produced television series that was adapted by Andrew Davies and directed by John Alexander in 2008, nearly two hundred years after the novel's publication.

PLOT SUMMARY

Opening Scenes

The film adaptation of *Sense and Sensibility* directed by Ang Lee and written by Emma Thompson opens with the impending death of Henry Dashwood, an old bedridden man who explains to his son John that he will inherit the family estate, Norland, upon Henry's death. The old man wants John to promise to take care of Henry's wife and daughters. Although the film does capture the essence of the novel's opening and conveys the difficult financial circumstances of the Dashwood

women, the novel provides a more detailed version of the story of the Dashwood inheritance. In the novel, Mr. Henry Dashwood, his wife, and three daughters come to live at Norland when Henry Dashwood's mother dies. His mother was the sister of the owner of the "old" Mr. Dashwood. Henry, his wife, and his daughters take good care of the elderly Mr. Dashwood and live happily at Norland, visited occasionally by John Dashwood (Henry's grown son from an earlier marriage), his wife Fanny, and their young son Harry. When old Mr. Dashwood dies, he bequeaths his estate to Henry, but in such a way that gives him little control over it financially. Norland is secured to John and to Harry in the event of Henry's death. Because of the terms of the bequest, Henry Dashwood is left with no way of financially providing for his wife and daughters after his death. He asks John to care for them after his death, he leaves ten thousand pounds to secure a future for his family.

In both the novel and the film, the son agrees to help his stepmother and half sisters, but after his father dies, John and his wife Fanny do not want to be that liberal with their money (although they have ample). Austen provides several detials that

FILM TECHNIQUE

- Austen's novel *Sense and Sensibility*, Austen uses free indirect discourse to express her characters' feelings and thoughts. Free indirect discourse or free indirect speech describes a style of third-person narration, which blends characteristics of third-person omniscient with first-person direct speech. In other words, the reader cannot easily discern between commentary offered by the omniscient narrator and the thoughts of a character. The reader must ultimately determine if the contemplation, judgment, or emotion can be authentically attributed to a particular character or to an objective, third-person party. This narrative strategy enables the reader to sympathize with the character but still allows narrator control and distance.

- In the film, Director Ang Lee, using an "objective treatment," that allows the viewer to observe what happens from an omniscient viewpoint that resembles Austen's narrative technique. Though Lee sometimes moves the camera through a scene using what feels like first person point-of-view (as in the ball), he most often depicts scenes as if the viewer is an observer of the world created on film. He makes certain to capture the entirety of the setting, as exemplified in the scene in which Edward and Elinor take a horseback ride through the hills during an intimate discussion. The camera is pulled back to show the riders, the lush curves of green field, a shepherd leading his sheep across the pastures. Another example of this technique occurs in the scene in which Marianne wanders over the hills toward Willoughby's home. She is a lone figure in the rain, the sky is gray and vast, and Willoughby's home is shown, dark and imposing, in the distance.

- Lee shot the film in a narrative style called "invisible editing," a technique usually adopted for realist approaches to storytelling. Although the editing is not truly seamless or invisible, the term points to the way a cut from one scene to the next emphasizes character and plot development. This technique tends to mimic the pace of following "real" events as they occur. These cuts also inspire a sense of "compressed time," making it feel like a specific amount of time has passed between scenes. This compressed time can be seen at the end of *Sense and Sensibility*, when Margaret, in her treehouse, sees Edward propose to Elinor before the film quickly moves on to a wedding, with children running down the road in celebration, waving colorful flags. The viewer assumes time has passed between those two events. Lee transitions between scenes by easing into the action with a slow pan across the setting or with a quiet beat before the actors speak.

- Lee uses music to emphasize the emotions underlying certain scenes. The score of the film was composed by Patrick Doyle, with songs titled to reflect the mood of the scene. For example, the song titled "To Die for Love," played during Marianne's heartbreak, is somber and heavy on violin, while "Throw the Coins," played when the Colonel tosses the coins at the end of the film, is full and rich to reflect the tender conclusion to the film.

---

make Fanny seem especially disagreeable. For example, Fanny persuades John to give his stepmother and half sisters only five hundred pounds apiece. Immediately after Henry Dashwood's death, Fanny acts as mistress of the estate; John's stepmother Mrs. Dashwood and his half-sisters Elinor, Marianne, and Margaret "are degraded to the condition of visitors" in their own home. In the film, Lee conveys Fanny's stinginess and sense of superiority in a scene in which she rides through the city streets perched in a carriage with her husband. They discuss the family finances, all the while looking disdainfully at the working class.

The teenaged Marianne Dashwood first appears in the film playing somberly on a pianoforte (a forerunner of the modern piano); she is in mourning for her father's death. Her older sister Elinor encourages her to play something more cheerful. Their mother, Mrs. Dashwood, is upset by her husband's passing and also about being treated like a visitor in their own home. Elinor is determined to find them all a new house. The film stays true to Austen's characterizations of these two women, with the exception that Elinor is described as nineteen years old in the novel, and Emma Thompson, the actress playing Elinor, is clearly older. In the film, her character is twenty-seven.

Margaret in the Treehouse and Meeting Edward

Elinor calls her little sister Margaret down from an elaborate treehouse. Margaret asks why Fanny and John are living at Norland, the family estate. Elinor explains that the law dictates that a property must pass from father to son, not father to daughter. With the scene, Lee provides an unobtrusive explanation of British inheritance law. He also underscores how painful it must be for Henry's widow and daughters to be essentially forced from their home due to laws that favor men over women, and what a large change in financial circumstance the women will have to face. Margaret's treehouse is clearly the kind of thing only enjoyed by privileged girls with wealthy families. In the treehouse scene, Lee quickly demonstrates the comfort and status to which the Dashwood women had become accustomed. In the novel, the Dashwood women remain at Norland for several months after Henry's death at John's invitation. Austen provides multiple examples of Fanny's unpleasantness and unkindness, and makes it clear that it is Fanny who ultimately pushes the Dashwood women out of Norland.

After the treehouse scene in the film, Elinor goes inside to tell a fairly large gathering of servants that the family can retain only two of them—Thomas and Betsy—when they leave Norland. Again, Lee underscores the coming change in financial status of Elinor, her mother, and sisters by showing the size of their household staff. Dinner that night is awkward. Elinor asks about Fanny's mother and two brothers, Edward and Robert Ferrars.

At breakfast, the family has another tense moment together. Elinor asks about Edward's arrival at the house. Fanny inquires if Margaret can give up her room for Edward, because it has the best view. Edward arrives, and both Mrs. Dashwood and Fanny vie for the role of mistress of the house in greeting him. Fanny wonders why Margaret is never around and deems her a wild child. Mrs. Dashwood declares that Margaret is just shy. Later, Fanny tells Edward that the Dashwood daughters are spoiled, but Edward is compassionate and does not agree with his sister's assessment. Fanny gives him a tour of the house. When they reach the library, it is obvious Margaret is hiding beneath a table. Edward does not reveal her hiding place to Fanny. After the tour, Edward tells Elinor and Mrs. Dashwood that he found Margaret. Elinor and Edward go to the library and coax the young girl out by debating about geography. Smitten by Edward, Elinor watches him play swords with Margaret on the lawn.

Edward comes into the house and sees Elinor with her head leaning against a doorframe, crying at the lovely piece of music her sister is playing on the pianoforte. He offers Elinor a handkerchief, and she thanks him for being nice to Margaret. Elinor asks if her younger sister showed him her treehouse. Edward says no and wonders if Elinor will show him. As they walk out, Mrs. Dashwood sees them and is pleased, but Fanny stands on the landing above and is not happy with the pair growing close.

Edward and Elinor walk the grounds and ride horses. Edward tells her of his dream to have a country life, but his mother's dream of him having a grand important life. Later, with the family, Edward reads aloud, but Marianne corrects his boring delivery. She thinks he should be more passionate.

Another day, Marianne comes in with a message from Sir John Middleton, Mrs. Dashwood's cousin. He offers to let them stay in Barton Cottage on his estate. Mrs. Dashwood holds off telling Elinor or the others, because she believes Edward and Elinor have "formed an attachment." Marianne finds Edward too sedate and the pair's affections not passionate enough. Mrs. Dashwood accuses her of "taking her romantic sensibilities a little far." Before going to bed, Elinor and Marianne discuss the possibility of Elinor marrying Edward, but Elinor remains cautious. The next day, Elinor and Edward walk together, under the keen eye of Fanny and Mrs. Dashwood. Fanny says their mother, Mrs. Ferrars, has great hopes for her son and would disown him if he married beneath his station. Mrs. Dashwood understands her meaning—that Elinor is not of sufficient social standing to be a suitable wife for Edward. At dinner, Mrs. Dashwood tells everyone about Sir John's invitation to live at Barton Cottage. Margaret invites Edward to visit, and Edward agrees, but Fanny insists he cannot, because he is expected in town. In the novel, Austen makes it explicit that Mrs. Dashwood is especially glad to leave for Barton Cottage because it is quite distant from Norland, in Devonshire country, and she wishes to be as far as possible from her objectionable daughter-in-law Fanny.

As the Dashwoods get ready to leave, Edward asks to speak with Elinor in the stables. He begins to explain something about his education with a Mr. Pratt, but Fanny interrupts to say he must leave at once for London. The novel delves more deeply into Edward's character, which is influenced by the fact his mother controls his considerable fortune.

Sir John and Mrs. Jennings

The Dashwoods arrive at Barton Cottage to a warm welcome from Sir John, his dogs, and Mrs. Jennings, his mother-in-law. The house is drafty, and life is not as they knew it. They dine with Sir John and Mrs. Jennings, and Mrs. Jennings jokes with Elinor about having a secret love. Margaret plays along and says his name begins with "F." Marianne saves Elinor from further embarrassment by playing the pianoforte. As she sings and plays, Colonel Brandon arrives. He is attracted to her. Sir John and Colonel Brandon served in the East Indies together.

When they are alone, Sir John and Brandon discuss Marianne. Sir John thinks the Colonel and Marianne would make a good match, but the Colonel does not think he has a chance with her. On a later occasion, when the Dashwoods, Mrs. Jennings, Sir John, and the Colonel are spending another lovely afternoon outdoors, Mrs. Jennings tells Elinor that she sees the Colonel is infatuated with Marianne. She tells Elinor about the Colonel's tragic history: how he once loved the young ward of his family, but his parents had not permitted them to marry. Instead, the girl was flung out of the family, and he was forced into the army. When he returned from India, he searched for her and found her dying in a poorhouse. Mrs. Jennings shifts topics and insists on conducting an experiment: as the Colonel and Marianne walk up the incline together, she tries to show the Colonel's good side by praising his pianoforte-playing skills and suggesting he play a duet with Marianne. Marianne dismisses the idea. She later confides in Elinor that she finds the Colonel unappealing. They suddenly receive a parcel from Edward: the atlas Margaret was using at Norland. Margaret wonders why he did not come to the house himself to deliver the atlas. Mrs. Dashwood tells Elinor that Edward loves her, but Elinor brushes the notion aside. In the novel, Marianne and her mother discuss the fact that Edward has not visited at length, and worry about what this might mean for Elinor. The novel also gives Marianne's frank assessment of Colonel Brandon: she finds him so old (in his mid-thirties) as to be out of the question as a suitor.

The film offers vivid visuals to show how life changes for the Dashwood women at Barton Cottage—for example, Elinor is shown practically freezing because the house is not as well heated as their previous residence, and the sisters are depicted taking on more chores than they are used to. The novel also establishes the change in their lifestyle, but more so by "telling" and not "showing."

Twisted Ankles and Willoughby

Marianne drags Margaret outside for a walk during a rainstorm. In her passion to "chase the blue sky," Marianne runs ahead, slips, falls, and hurts herself. In running back to the house, Margaret encounters a man on horseback, who immediately comes to Marianne's rescue. He asks if he can feel her foot for breaks and removes her shoe. Marianne is smitten. He carries her home and asks if he might call on them the next day. Before he leaves, the Dashwoods ask his name, which, it turns out, is John Willoughby. Marianne is besotted by the romance, spirit, and feeling of the man.

The next day, the Dashwoods ask Sir John about Willoughby, but he only knows about his dogs. The Colonel arrives with flowers for Marianne, which she almost completely ignores. Willoughby is on the way to the house, and Sir John tells the Colonel they must leave him to be alone with the women. Willoughby is charming and brings wildflowers for Marianne. He praises their home and notices Marianne is reading Shakespeare's sonnets. He happens to carry a tiny book of sonnets with him everywhere. He gives her the book as a "talisman." When he leaves, Elinor thinks Marianne should be cautious, but Marianne thinks concealing her feelings is not the way to act.

One evening, Marianne spends her time drawing Willoughby's portrait; he is seated behind a lit drawing screen. Colonel Brandon watches them with envy. While Elinor is mostly occupied by running the household, she also notices her sister and Willoughby growing closer. She witnesses the latter cutting a lock of Marianne's hair and kissing it. This also happens in the novel, but it is Margaret who witnesses it—and quickly reports the incident to Elinor as proof that Willoughby must be close to proposing to Marianne.

In the film, Marianne and Willoughby go on a wild carriage ride one afternoon as the village looks on. Elinor scolds her about impropriety. In the novel, Austen goes into more detail about the growing concern Elinor feels about her sister's attachment to Willoughby. She feels that Marianne's actions and emotions are immoderate and impractical. For example, Willoughby offers Marianne a horse as a gift. Marianne is flattered and excited until Elinor wisely comments on how inconvenient and expensive the horse will be to maintain. Elinor also notes the impropriety of receiving such a generous gift from a man Marianne hardly knows. Marianne believes time is not a measure for getting to know people well, but admits that owning a horse would put a burden on their mother and their household finances.

In both film and novel, the Colonel grows increasingly attached to Marianne, but receives no encouragement from her. In the film, he arrives at the cottage to invite them to a picnic at his estate. Marianne looks away to see Willoughby arriving, so the Colonel quickly says he will invite Willoughby. Marianne goes for a carriage ride with Willoughby, leaving Elinor and the Colonel to discuss Marianne and her future.

Secret Business and Abrupt Exits

Although Colonel Brandon arranges a picnic on his estate, the event never occurs. As the party—including Lucy Steele, a flighty and manipulative cousin of Lady Middleton; Charlotte Palmer, the daughter of Mrs. Jennings; and Charlotte's husband—gathers to wait for their conveyances, a messenger rides up to give the Colonel a note. The Colonel must go away to London at once, and although Sir John protests, the Colonel rides away. The party is dismayed, but Lucy tells Elinor she wants to become fast friends with her. In the novel, Mrs. Jennings speculates that the Colonel's errand has something to do with his "natural daughter," a Miss Williams. Also, in the novel the Palmers and Lucy Steele are introduced later.

The afternoon of the cancelled picnic, Marianne and Willoughby complain about the Colonel's actions. Elinor asks why Willoughby is being so hard on the Colonel, and Willoughby suggests it is because the Colonel spoiled his fun. In the novel, Sir John steps in, orders carriage rides for everyone, and throws a dinner and dance at his home for the whole party. Marianne and Willoughby take a walk unaccompanied by others, and Willoughby tells Marianne he wants to say something important to her tomorrow, alone. She agrees to stay home from church and meet him. It is clear that she expects a proposal. In the novel, Willougby and Marianne visit what will one day be his estate—again, giving the distinct impression to Marianne that she is being shown her future home and can expect a proposal of marriage.

The next day, the Dashwood women come home from church to find Marianne crying and Willoughby looking piqued. He says his aunt wants him to go to London right away and will not return to the country for quite some time. He leaves abruptly. Marianne is upset and wants to be alone. She will not explain exactly what is wrong. Elinor asks Marianne if Willoughby has proposed to her. Mrs. Dashwood says Elinor believes the worst of the man, however, they should give him the benefit of the doubt. All the Dashwood women, except Elinor, end up sobbing in this scene behind closed doors. In the novel, Mrs. Dashwood makes it clear that she fully believes that Willoughby and Marianne are engaged, and that Willoughby's aunt has sent him away because she does not approve. Elinor is not convinced, however, because of the simple fact that neither Marianne nor Willoughby has ever said they were engaged. Austen lightly mocks the immensity of Marianne's grief in the novel, noting that she considers it almost a point of honor not to sleep at all the night after Willoughy's departure.

In the novel, Austen adds a few more plot points and social events to provide additional character development. For example, a week or so after Willoughby leaves, the three Dashwood sisters are out walking when a man approaches on horseback. The rider is Edward Ferrars, on his way to visit them at Barton. He stays with them for several days. Edward seems more distant and reserved than they remember, but Marianne still thinks he has feelings for Elinor. Marianne comments on his ring that contains a lock of hair, and Edward tells her the hair belongs to his sister. Marianne, however, believes the hair is Elinor's, even when Elinor denies this.During his visit, Edward talks to the Dashwoods about wanting a simple life despite his mother's expectations. Marianne reassures him about his future and says that happiness does not require wealth or status to be happy. Elinor, however, argues that wealth and happiness are interconnected. In omitting Edward's visit from the film, Lee builds more drama as the viewer wonders what could be keeping Edward from Elinor. This provides more tension in later scenes when Edward and Elinor see each other again.

After a week of frantic social activity, Edward decides to leave. Elinor tries to convince herself that he is leaving because he has an important task relative to his demanding mother. When he leaves, she cannot stop thinking of him. In the novel, it is at this point that Austen introduces Charlotte Palmer and her husband, who visit Barton Cottage with Sir John, Mrs. Jennings, and Lady Middleton; in the film, the Palmers have already been introduced. Austen also introduced Lucy Steele at this point.

On a rainy day the Dashwoods, Lucy, Charlotte, and Mrs. Jennings are playing cards and conversing in the sitting room. Mr. Palmer makes snide remarks but is attentive only to his newspaper. Lucy approaches Elinor to talk and wants to ask her something. Lucy asks if Elinor knows Fanny's mother. They walk about the room for privacy and Lucy suggests that she may be "connected" to the woman soon, since she has a relationship with Edward. She proceeds to tell a shocked Elinor that Edward was educated by her uncle, Mr. Pratt, and she and Edward have been secretly engaged for five years (four years in the novel). They had a young passion, though they only see each other twice a year at best. Lucy notices that Elinor seems out of sorts. Mrs. Jennings grows curious about their whispers. The two young women lie and say they are talking about London. Mrs. Jennings invites Lucy, Elinor, and Marianne to stay at her home in London. Elinor says they cannot but she is overruled. Marianne is

thrilled. Elinor worries about seeing Edward. Marianne wonders what Lucy said to her.

The Dashwoods in London

The Dashwood sisters go to London with Mrs. Jennings. (In the novel they are later joined by Sir John, his wife, and Lucy.) Lucy admits to Elinor that she wants to see Edward. Marianne gives the manservant a message to deliver to Willoughby. Colonel Brandon arrives and tells Elinor that he heard about Marianne and Willoughby being engaged. Elinor insists they have mutual affection, but does not define their relationship further. Marianne keeps asking for messages from Willoughby and grows impatient when she receives nothing. Mrs. Jennings tells her not to worry. She also says that Edward will make an appearance at a ball that they plan to attend.

At the ball, Robert Ferrars, not Edward, appears. He tells her that his brother "had no special acquaintance to make his attendance worthwhile." In dancing with Robert, Elinor encounters Willoughby, who asks about the family. Marianne sees Willoughby across the room and dashes to greet him. He receives her awkwardly. She asks why he has not visited and if he received her letters. He leaves abruptly and joins another woman who behaves snidely toward Marianne. Marianne is stunned and hurt. Robert offers to escort Lucy home when Mrs. Jennings and Elinor take Marianne back to the house.

Marianne impulsively writes a letter and Elinor urges her to confide her feelings to her. Marianne dismisses the request, because Elinor does not confide her feelings in Marianne. Later, Lucy tells Elinor she likes Fanny and they get along famously.

Elinor checks on Marianne after some time has passed. She finds that Marianne has received a note from Willoughby, which informs her that he did not mean to lead Marianne on and that he had affections elsewhere. Marianne confesses that she and Willoughby never were engaged and he had never declared his love. Elinor says that he betrayed the whole family by his actions. Mrs. Jennings confirms Willoughby's engagement to Miss Sophia Grey, a very wealthy woman, and professes herself appalled at his behavior. Thompson's screenplay highlights Austen's dry humor in her presentation of Mrs. Jennings' confirmation of Willoughby's engagement. As opposed to the novel, in which Elinor overhears Mrs. Jennings and her friends discuss how Willoughby misspent his fortune and quickly became engaged to Miss

Grey, Mrs. Jennings is seen in the film dashing down the street toward home, anxious to spread her gossip. This portrayal of her excitement at passing on the news illustrates the way relationships were treated as vital public information, particularly for women looking to make a match.

The Colonel arrives and Elinor wonders if he will help see them back to Barton. The Colonel confesses more of his past: the young ward he loved had a child named Beth, and he had offered to look after the latter by having her live with a nice family in the country. He indulged her whims as she grew up, but she ultimately ran away. On the day of the picnic, he found out she was pregnant. Willoughby was the father of her child. Apparently, Willoughby's aunt, upon hearing the news, threw him out of the house and disinherited him, so he went to London in search of a woman of means whom he could marry. Colonel Brandon wonders if he could help Marianne by telling her this information. Willoughby actually did intend to propose, but money came first with him. Elinor reveals the story to Marianne.

Lucy arrives with dramatic news for Elinor: she was introduced to Fanny's mother. Edward arrives unexpectedly as well, and Elinor asks him in, remarking, "You know Miss Steele, of course." She invites him to sit, but he does so awkwardly. Lucy says he must be surprised. Edward is stunned into silence. Marianne joins the party, glad to see him. But Edward remains quiet and finally leaves. Marianne asks Elinor why she let him go so coldly.

Lucy talks to Fanny about marriage. Fanny insists that she will marry well. Lucy reveals her secret engagement to Edward. Fanny is infuriated (she clearly feels Lucy is not worthy of her brother) and physically attacks Lucy. Mrs. Jennings runs home with the gossip that Edward's mother demanded he break the engagement to Lucy but he refused, being too honorable. His mother decided to disinherit him. Marianne asks Elinor how long she knew about Edward and Lucy and wonders why Elinor said nothing. Elinor says that she must accept Edward's decision. Marianne suggests that Elinor lacks feeling, and Elinor erupts emotionally and reveals all she has endured by keeping her love a secret and suffering in silence.

The Colonel takes a walk with Elinor and they discuss Edward and his dire financial situation. The Colonel has a proposal for Edward for her to deliver. She asks why the Colonel cannot deliver

it himself, and he suggests the offer would better come from a friend. Elinor agrees and tells Edward that the Colonel wants to offer Edward a parish on his estate so he and Lucy can marry. Edward is astonished by the Colonel's kindness, and Elinor agrees that the Colonel is a kind person. Edward confesses to Elinor: "Your friendship has been the most important of my life."

Austen includes a few scenes that Lee does not include in the film. For example, Elinor and Marianne go to Gray's, a jeweler, where they run into their half brother John, who has been in town for two days but has been too busy to visit. The next day, he goes to Mrs. Jennings's home where he spends time with Elinor. He advises her to marry Colonel Brandon, and informs her that Mrs. Ferrars expects Edward to marry a wealthy Miss Morton.

Thompson's screenplay omits details of Charlotte Palmer giving birth. Mrs. Jennings is thrilled when Mrs. Palmer produces a son and heir, but Mr. Palmer acts as indifferent as always. Though Mr. Palmer is indifferent to the news, the detail about the birth of a son reflects the financial importance of being a male heir in that society, especially given the fact that the Dashwood daughters could not inherit anything from their father.

Marianne Takes Ill and Finds a New Love

Elinor and Marianne visit Charlotte Palmer's home. Charlotte talks incessantly. Marianne walks in the garden after an exhausting journey and ends up wandering to Willoughby's estate, which is nearby. She stands in the pouring rain, reciting Shakespeare. Elinor is concerned that Marianne has apparently disappeared in such terrible weather. The Colonel rushes out to find Marianne, and carries her home. She is drenched and in shock. Elinor wants Mr. Palmer to send for a doctor. The Colonel worries about Marianne, who has an infectious fever. Mr. Palmer is sympathetic, but, on the doctor's orders, he, his wife, and his child leave their home to avoid contracting the illness. The Colonel asks Elinor to give him something to do to help Marianne. She tells him to go fetch their mother. Marianne's condition is very grave and Elinor is distraught. She is afraid that Marianne will die and she will be left alone.

Thompson's screenplay and Lee's direction makes the Dashwoods' time at the Palmers' more dramatic. While in the film, Marianne purposefully wanders across the moors to Willoughby's home in the driving rain, in the novel Marianne, still depressed over the whole Willoughby incident, spends her time taking long walks and catching a nasty cold a bit more gradually. When she grows feverish, Colonel Brandon volunteers to get Mrs. Dashwood from Barton. One evening, before Brandon has arrived with Mrs. Dashwood, Willoughby arrives to apologize. He tells Elinor that he had always known that he could never marry Marianne because of financial matters, but he learned the meaning of love by being with her. He admits to marrying Miss Grey for money, not love. Willoughby asks Elinor to relay this to Marianne, and Elinor agrees, only when her sister's condition improves.

In the film version, Marianne regains consciousness after being delirious with fever. Mrs. Dashwood arrives. Marianne acknowledges the Colonel's presence and thanks him. After Marianne has recovered, the Colonel and Marianne begin courting. One day, as the Colonel reads to her, he tells her he "must away" on secret business. She tells him that she hopes he will not stay away too long.

Thomas, the Dashwood's manservant, relays the news to the Dashwoods that Mr. Ferrars has married Lucy Steele. Elinor leaves the room, upset. Thompson's screenplay simplifies Austen's plot somewhat, particularly as it nears the end. In the novel, Elinor learns from Anne Steele that Edward will not dissolve his engagement to Lucy. Additionally, Edward reveals plans to obtain a curacy and to live a modest life. Lucy pledges her heart to him no matter their financial situation. Lucy conveys the details in a letter to Elinor. Furthermore, when Colonel Brandon asks Elinor to express the offer of a curacy to Edward, Elinor planned to give Edward the details in a letter, but Edward arrives at Mrs. Jennings's home where she talks with him in person. Elinor also pays a visit to Fanny, who is still upset by Edward and Lucy's engagement.

The Colonel has a pianoforte delivered to the Dashwood home, to the delight of Marianne, who plays it and sings. Elinor and Mrs. Dashwood see a man coming down the lane. Recognizing Edward, they hurriedly prepare for his visit. He inquires after their health, and they awkwardly make small talk, inquring about Mrs. Ferrars. Edward tells them that they have misunderstood—his brother Robert married Lucy. Elinor is overcome

with emotion upon hearing the news. Her mother and sisters leave the room. Edward tries to explain that he was very young when he met Lucy, and that he has come to realize that Elinor is his true love, and he asks her to marry him. Margaret spies on them from her treehouse and tells Marianne and Mrs. Dashwood that he proposed on one knee.

The film ends with a wedding scene: the bride Marianne and her groom, the Colonel, come out of the church, Elinor and Edward happily behind. Willoughby watches from the hills and rides away. The film does not clarify whether Elinor and Edward are married yet.

Austen ends the story differently. In the novel, Edward proposes to Elinor, who accepts. When Colonel Brandon hears the news of their engagement, he offers to renovate the parsonage at Delaford as a gift to them. Mrs. Ferrars accepts Edward's life direction, but still favors Robert over her eldest son. Married, Elinor and Edward invite both Marianne and Colonel Brandon to visit, hoping to foster a relationship between the two. Colonel Brandon and Marianne marry, and are exceedingly happy. In the end, "instead of falling sacrifice to an irresistible passion," Marianne tempers her fate with a bit more sense and less sensibility.

CHARACTERS

Colonel Christopher Brandon
A retired army officer and a friend of Sir John Middleton, the kind and honest Colonel Brandon falls in love with Marianne Dashwood and marries her at the end of the film. In the novel, the Colonel is thirty-seven-years old. Alan Rickman, best known for his role as Professor Severus Snape in the Harry Potter films, plays Brandon in the Lee-Thompson film adaptation.

Elinor Dashwood
The twenty-seven-year-old eldest daughter of Mr. and Mrs. Henry Dashwood, Elinor restrains her passion in favor of reason and decorum. She is the character who represents the "sense" of the title. She falls in love and ultimately marries Edward Ferrars. Emma Thompson plays Elinor in the Lee-Thompson film and won an Academy Award for the role. Elinor in the Austen novel is only nineteen.

Fanny Dashwood

Self-centered, arrogant, and manipulative, Fanny is the wife of John Dashwood and the sister of Edward and Robert Ferrars. Harriet Walter plays Fanny in the Lee-Thompson film adaptation. The character in the film is portrayed a bit more flamboyantly than in the novel.

Henry Dashwood

The father of John Dashwood and, by a second marriage, of Elinor, Marianne, and Margaret Dashwood, Henry dies early in *Sense and Sensibility*. He leaves his estate at Norland to John Dashwood. Tom Wilkinson, whose illustrious career includes *Michael Clayton* and *Eternal Sunshine of the Spotless Mind*, plays Henry in the Lee-Thompson film.

John Dashwood

John Dashwood inherits Norland estate after his father dies. His wife Fanny persuades him into leaving his stepmother and half sisters with little money to secure their future. James Fleet, who starred in the British television series, *The Vicar of Dibley*, plays John in the Lee-Thompson film.

Margaret Dashwood

Thirteen-year-old Margaret takes after older sister Marianne in her energy, good humor, and romantic ideals. This role in the Lee-Thompson film was the debut role for Emilie Francois. Margaret figures into the film plot more than the novel, particularly as Thompson plays up her playful friendship with Edward Ferrars.

Marianne Dashwood

Spontaneous Marianne lives for romantic idealism and "sensibility." She falls in love with John Willoughby, who deceives her and causes her heartbreak. In the end, she marries and learns to love Colonel Brandon, who has admired her from the moment he met her early in the story. Kate Winslet played this role in the Lee-Thompson film, two years before her award-winning performance in the film *Titanic*.

Mrs. Dashwood

The mother of Elinor, Marianne, and Margaret and second wife to Henry Dashwood, the loving Mrs. Dashwood possesses no wealth of her own, but seeks better financial situations for her daughters by looking to match them with well-off husbands. Gemma Jones, best known among Harry Potter film fans as Madam Pomfrey, plays this role in the Lee-Thompson film.

Edward Ferrars

Affable and rather awkward, Edward is the older brother of Fanny Dashwood and Robert Ferrars. Edward becomes friends with Elinor (and Margaret) while staying at Norland, although he is secretly engaged to Lucy Steele. In the end, he marries Elinor, after escaping from his obligation to Lucy and choosing the simple life he has always wanted for himself. In the film, Edward is portrayed as more endearing than the version in the novel, mostly due to his kind treatment of Margaret. Hugh Grant played this role in the Lee-Thompson film at the height of his popularity in the 1990s. He had previously appeared in *Four Weddings and a Funeral* and *The Remains of the Day*, among other films.

Robert Ferrars

Conceited and arrogant, Robert is the younger brother of Edward and Fanny. Robert marries Lucy Steele, the woman who once was engaged to his brother. Richard Lumsden plays this role in the Lee-Thompson film. The role in the film is more marginal than in the book, where Robert is given further characterization.

Mrs. Jennings

A gossip who possesses the best intentions, Mrs. Jennings is Sir John's mother-in-law. Throughout the film, she is preoccupied with marrying off every single woman she knows. Elizabeth Spriggs, who had a vast career in British television and film, plays this role in the Lee-Thompson film.

Sir John Middleton

Gregarious and generous, this distant relation of the Dashwoods invites Mrs. Dashwood and her three daughters to stay at Barton Cottage when Mr. and Mrs. John Dashwood inherit Norland. Robert Hardy plays this role in the Lee-Thompson film.

Charlotte Jennings Palmer

Chatty and at times silly, Charlotte Palmer is Mrs. Jennings's daughter. She invites the Dashwood sisters to stay at her home in Cleveland. Imelda Staunton plays the role of Charlotte in the Lee-Thompson film.

Mr. Palmer

Mr. Palmer is Charlotte Palmer's husband. He is fairly indifferent to the goings-on around him and displays a dry sense of humor. Hugh Laurie,

Sense and Sensibility

known to television fans as the lead role in the medical series *House*, plays the role of Mr. Palmer in the Lee-Thompson film.

Lucy Steele
Lucy is Mrs. Jennings's cousin. She is manipulative and opportunistic. Although she was secretly engaged to Edward Ferrars for four years, she marries his brother Robert instead when Edward loses his fortune. Imogen Stubbs, who had much success on stage with the Royal Shakespeare Company, plays the role of Lucy in the Lee-Thompson film.

John Willoughby
Charismatic and handsome, Willoughby charms Marianne into falling in love with him, but dumps her in favor of the wealthy Miss Sophia Grey when he gets a third young woman pregnant and is disowned by his aunt. Greg Wise plays this role in the Lee-Thompson film.

THEMES

"Sense" and "Sensibility"
The title of Austen's novel and the Lee-Thompson film adaptation identifies one key theme of the story: the contrast between good sense and untrustworthy emotions. The moral of *Sense and Sensibility* is that rational thought, not strong emotions, should guide one's actions and decisions. Those who get carried away by strong feelings—their sensibilities—must conquer their emotions or else continue to be hurt by their impulsiveness. In both novel and film, Elinor ultimately finds love with Edward through her consistent "sense," while Marianne's sensibility leads her through heartache before she adopts a bit of good "sense" and settles down with Colonel Brandon.

The dichotomy of "sense" and "sensibility" in Austen's novel reflects the early eighteenth century, when two cultural movements—classicism, dominant during the seventeenth and eighteenth centuries in Europe, and romanticism, which emerged during the late eighteenth and early nineteenth centuries. Elinor's rational leanings, keen insight, and tendency toward moderation typify classicism, while Marianne's lofty ideals, imagination, and idealism typify the romantic "cult of sensibility." Like Austen's portrayal of Elinor and Marianne, the cinematic interpretation demonstrates the changing cultural trends of the

READ. WATCH. WRITE.

- Watch the Lee-Thompson's film adaptation of *Sense and Sensibility* and read Austen's novel. Choose one character and write a short essay comparing the film portrayal of that character with the portrayal of the character in Austen's work. Pay attention to physical description, emotional development, and the character's role in the narrative. Is the casting effective in the film? Use quotations from the film and novel to support your ideas.

- Watch the BBC's *Sense and Sensibility* (2008). How does it compare to the Lee-Thompson film? With a small group of your classmates, choose one or two key scenes from the two films to compare and contrast. Develop an audiovisual presentation detailing your findings.

- As a class, discuss how marriage is portrayed in the film. Does marriage mean the same thing for men and for women? Is marriage portrayed positively or negatively? How are marriage ideals today similar or different to those depicted in the film?

- Select a scene from the Lee-Thompson film adaptation of *Sense and Sensibility* that is radically different than the novel. Write a brief essay detailing the scene and discussing how the cinematic interpretation of the scene changes Austen's original intention.

eighteenth century and suggests a need for balance between rational thought and emotions. While Elinor is shown doing practical things like balancing the household budget, Marianne is shown wandering across the hills lamenting her lost love.

The Lee-Thompson film emphasizes Austen's approach to sense and passion, or romance. In the film, as in the novel, Elinor's sense of reason, decorum, and propriety keeps her from following her own desires or pursuing romance. She keeps the household running smoothly, plays the diplomat in explaining away Marianne's behavior, goes

2 7 4   *Novels for Students, Volume 3 3*

to London to help Marianne even though the trip may dredge up uncomfortable feelings for her, and acts as go-between on numerous awkward occasions. Believing that it is better to conceal her emotions from the world, Elinor smothers her own feelings for Edward when Lucy reveals her secret and designates her as confidante. Instead of fighting for the man she loves, Elinor looks to acceptance and sacrifice. In contrast, Marianne looks to romance as the basis for love and life. She allows her own desires to control her, as exemplified when she wanders off to Willoughby's home in a storm and risks her life. She is taken by Willoughby because of the tiny book of sonnets he keeps in his pocket and the way he seems to embrace life without any thought to propriety. Marianne, in contrast to her sister, wears her heart on her sleeve.

Appearance vs. Reality

In many Austen novels, things are not as they seem, and the film adaptation of *Sense and Sensibility* also emphasizes the differences between how things appear and reality. Willoughby serves as the main example of this theme. To Marianne—and to the audience—he appears romantic, dashing, and genuine. His charming behavior and thoughtful gestures lead Marianne to believe he is in love with her and intends to marry her. Yet he flees Marianne at the news that he has gotten another woman pregnant in order to find a wealthy wife. In doing so he reveals himself to be a secretive, self-centered, and thoughtless cad. Lucy Steele is another example of this theme—she appears devoted and loyal to Edward, but in fact she is selfish and conniving. When Edward loses his fortune, she quickly transfers her affections to his suddenly wealthy younger brother, Robert.

In her novels, Austen often makes characters quick to judge people on first impressions. Emma Thompson also made certain to retain this trait when she adapted the original story. Each character judges another, as they try to make friends, foster romantic relationships, and determine who might hurt them. Characters are frequently quick to judge others positively and negatively, as Marianne does with Willoughby or as Fanny does with the Dashwood sisters. Elinor judges people's behavior and level of propriety, as exemplified in her judgment of Marianne's relationship with Willoughby. Elinor finds her sister too impassioned and wishes Marianne would be more cautious, and they argue about their differing approaches to life. In the end, Elinor's prudent judgment leads her and her sister

Liaison Agency | Getty Images

to a happy end. Elinor's first impressions tend to be the most reliable in the story.

Money and Marriage

Austen is known for her "marriage plots" in which some marry for love and others for money. True to the novel, Emma Thompson's screenplay focuses on how marriage plays a key role in defining social status and solidifying the financial futures of Austen's young characters. Marianne and Elinor will not inherit much money from their mother and must take the wealth of their potential suitors into account, although they both also want to find love. The adaptation shows Elinor often concerned about household financial matters and worried about how to feed the family properly. Willoughby sacrifices his affection for Marianne to marry Miss Grey for money, while Lucy turns her back on Edward to marry his brother Robert for what he stands to inherit. Elinor marries Edward for love, yet his position in the rectory, a gift from Colonel Brandon, will provide them both with security and comfort. At the end of the film, after the Colonel and Marianne marry, he tosses coins into the celebrating crowd of guests, signifying their riches of happiness as well as their monetary riches.

STYLE

The Merchant-Ivory Connection

Many critics compare the Lee-Thompson film adaptation of *Sense and Sensibility* to a Merchant-Ivory film. Films made by the production team of James Ivory and Ismail Merchant were often period pieces set in the early twentieth century, usually in Edwardian England, and were often based upon novels or short stories written by Henry James and E. M. Forster. Films by Merchant-Ivory include *A Room with a View* (1985) and *Howard's End* (1992). These films featured lush, romantic shots of the English countryside and English cities, with careful attention to period detail. *Sense and Sensibility* shares the same attention to detail, high production quality, and beautiful English scenery.

The Marriage Plot, the Melodrama, and the "Chick Flick"

Novels centered on a courtship or marriage plot grew popular in the eighteenth and nineteenth centuries. The main narrative of these novels focuses on who will marry whom and for what reasons. In writing *Sense and Sensibility*, Austen followed in the literary footsteps of authors like Samuel Richardson and Frances Burney and inspired a generation of authors including George Eliot and the Brontë sisters to put their own spin on the genre. In these novels, marriage is often not a choice, but a requirement for a prosperous future, yet at the same time, a truly happy marriage is equated with love, not financial security. Those who marry for money ultimately reside in comfort, but lead empty lives, while those who marry for love are rewarded with joy.

Often in the eighteenth and nineteenth centuries, novels centered on the marriage plot fell into the genre of melodrama. The genre is marked by "stock" characters, or characters that evoke a particular type, like villain, hero, or crone. Melodrama also uses sentiment to evoke a personal response and connection with the reader. Chris Hicks of the *Deseret News* called the Lee-Thompson film adaptation of *Sense and Sensibility* an "utterly winning comic melodrama." Contemporary critics usually consider films melodramatic if they are characterized by plots that play on the emotions of the audience and deal with universal conflicts that emerge in relationships like failed romance, strained familial situations, illness, or physical hardship. Melodramatic films are typically formulaic and usually end happily. Ang Lee and Emma Thompson pared down Austen's original work to its basic narrative, emphasizing its melodramatic qualities, though the novel cannot be categorized as a pure melodrama. The depth and variety of Austen's characters, the fact that Austen does not position her characters in extreme situations, and the way she avoids the use of stock plot devices keeps her novel from settling into a genre that can be considered cliché and over-the-top.

The film version of *Sense and Sensibility*, with its emphasis on the marriage plot is often categorized as a "chick flick." Supposedly designed to appeal to a female audience, a chick flick is a film genre usually heavy on emotion and features relationship-based themes and stock characters like the romantic hero and the best friend. Often, chick flicks are patterned after fairy tales like Cinderella and canonical work, such as the novel, *Sense and Sensibility*. Given that the lead characters in the film are young women with their minds toward matrimony and domestic matters, the film adaptation fits squarely in the chick flick genre. However, because of its positioning in literary history, as the novel genre was just growing popular, Austen's novel is considered a classic work, rather than Chick Lit, the literary equivalent to the cinematic chick flick.

CULTURAL CONTEXT

Jane Austen was born a year before the start of the American Revolution, became a teenager at the beginning of the French Revolution, and grew up during the Napoleonic Wars, the height of the English Empire, and a time of rapid industrial development. Yet global politics do not dramatically affect the narratives of her original novel, *Sense and Sensibility*, or the film versions. The events of the world neither intrude on Austen's English idyll and social drama nor the interpretation of that idyll and social drama in the 1995 film adaptation, remaining on the periphery in the form of military characters or other subtle references.

Inheritance and Marriage

Instead, Austen's works deal with domestic matters, particularly the lives and futures of women of

Liaison Agency | Getty Images

her time. One issue that she returns to throughout her canon is the matter of inheritance. In Austen's day, as in the world of her novels, women could not inherit their father's estate, as it was "entailed" to the closest male relation. Another issue important to Austen's plots is marriage. Marriage, for most upper-middle class women, was the only option for a secure future. While men could pursue careers in the military, the clergy, law, or medicine, women were encouraged to make a "successful" match with one of these professional men, or even "landed" gentry. Members of the landed gentry owned property and rarely had to work for a living. In families of the landed gentry, the eldest son inherited the estate and the younger sons joined the professional class to earn their keep. In "Sense and Sensibility," Elinor and Marianne socialize with and ultimately marry landed gentry. Luckily, the sisters are fortunate in both financial matters and love.

Industrial Revolution
In 1811, as King George III was diagnosed with porphyria and was going insane, his eldest son George, the Prince Regent, inherited the throne.

During this time, Britain sought territories and resources overseas, extending its reach into Africa, Asia, and across Pacific Islands. When Napoleon was finally defeated in 1815, British sea power was unchallenged. Though Britain had lost control of the American colonies, the English East India Company was taking control of India. This conquest completed by 1858, when the British Crown took direct rule under a government system called the "British Raj." In India, the British found wealth in the booming trade markets of cotton, silk, indigo, tea, and opium. In the film, when the Colonel is first introduced, he has a humorous exchange with Sir John and Margaret about his military tour in India, "full of spices." The worldwide expansion of trade, improved methods of transportation (including canals, roads, and railroad systems), and the development of technological inventions like the steam engine inspired more factories and created employment opportunities beyond the agricultural sector. With the Industrial Revolution came a rise in the middle class, which began to encroach on the power of the landed gentry. References to the Industrial Revolution only appear tangentially in Austen's novel and in the Lee-Thompson film adaptation. In the book, references are only made in relation to a character's fortune or circumstance, a character's future prospects, or certain social interactions or relationships. In the film, the working class is only shown from a distance. Austen's characters were those who passively reaped the material reward from Britain's imperial involvement and industrial growth, and the elegant feel of the Lee-Thompson film evokes this luxury and class.

CRITICAL OVERVIEW

When Austen began her literary career, her novels received little attention from critics. In 1870, James Edward Austen-Leigh's *Memoir of Jane Austen* promoted his aunt's work. It became very popular with middle- and upper-middle-class audiences nostalgic for what they saw as the simpler times of the early nineteenth century. Austen's world represented a certain ideal "Englishness," a certain reason, decorum, and propriety beneficial to upholding the British Empire.

The Ang Lee–Emma Thompson film adaptation of *Sense and Sensibility* brought that "Englishness" to the big screen and received positive reviews for its period portrayal. Todd McCarthy of *Variety* praises Lee and Thompson for their elegantly dramatic vision: "Thompson's script manages the neat trick of preserving the necessary niceties and decorum of civilized behavior of the time while still cutting to the dramatic quick."

Marjorie Baumgarten of the *Austin Chronicle* agrees with McCarthy, suggesting that Ang's "sensibilities turn out to be in perfect accord with Austen's." Baumgarten also homes in on the actors who bring this film to life: "Not enough can be said about this fine cast, each of whom chisels a vibrant, one-of-a-kind characterization."

Barbara Shulgasser of the *San Francisco Examiner* also compliments the way the Lee-Thompson team treat the canonical material, particularly its wit: "Emma Thompson has adapted the novel to include all the Austenesque humor and some of the Thompsonesque variety as well."

Critic Chris Hicks of the *Deseret News* also appreciates the humor, calling the film an "utterly winning comic melodrama," one that "unfolds casually, Merchant-Ivory style, with all the lush trappings of late eighteenth-century rural England."

CRITICISM

Michelle S. Lee

Lee has taught courses in composition, rhetoric, film adaptation, and literature. In this essay, she discusses how the 1995 film adaptation of Sense and Sensibility, directed by Ang Lee and written by Emma Thompson, exemplifies the canonical literature that has infused twenty-first-century "Austenmania," with a universal appeal that continues to resonate with audiences in its portrayal of the ideal nineteenth-century "Englishness."

AustenBlog declares that "She's everywhere." Laurie Brown's time-travel novel published in 2009 is titled after the question the heroine constantly asks herself: "What Would Jane Austen Do?" More than a decade ago, Austen scholars and readers started their own Republic of Pemberley online (named after Darcy's estate in *Pride and Prejudice*) as a clearinghouse of Austen information and gathering place for discussion. Austen fans travel the globe, from Bath to San Antonio, to dress in Regency period costumes and attend balls similar to those in Austen novels. Year after year, Austen novels are remade for television and film, are transformed into contemporary novels, and serve as inspiration for online fanzines and journals. How do the worlds of Jane Austen's fiction spark such an avid following and translate across different mediums and genres, even today?

Austen's debut novel, *Sense and Sensibility*, began two centuries of this type of Austen mania. The novel has been adapted a number of times, from the BBC miniseries in 1981 and the more recent BBC television remake written by Andrew Davies in 2008 to *Kandukondain Kandukondain* (*I Have Found It*), a South Indian adaptation transformed into a romantic musical written in the Tamil language (2000). In 1995, the film adaptation directed by Ang Lee and written by Emma Thompson and including a stellar cast received critical acclaim and numerous awards and honors, including an Academy Award for Best Adapted Screenplay and nominations for Best Actress, Cinematography, Costume Design, and Original Score. Lee and Thompson captured Austen's tone, rhetorical intention, and literary themes and created an

WHAT DO I SEE NEXT?

- Austen's second book, *Pride and Prejudice*, was made into a successful 1995 BBC miniseries, adapted by Andrew Davies and starring Colin Firth and Jennifer Ehle. The critically acclaimed miniseries received a multitude of awards, including a BAFTA Television Award for Best Actress and an Emmy for Outstanding Individual Achievement in Costume Design for a Miniseries or a Special.

- *Northanger Abbey* was the first novel Jane Austen completed, but the last to be published, after her death in 1817. In 2007 the UK channel ITV produced the novel as a television drama. This is the second adaptation of this Austen novel.

- Released in 2007 by BBC Films and the Irish Film Board, *Becoming Jane* stars Anne Hathaway as Jane Austen and depicts the early life of the author and her supposed relationship with Thomas Langlois Lefroy. Some Austen scholars question the historical accuracy of the movie.

- *The Jane Austen Book Club*, released in 2007 by Sony Pictures, was based on a novel by Karen Joy Fowler and stars Emily Blunt, Amy Brenneman, and Hugh Dancy. Women form a book club to discuss the six novels written by Jane Austen, but as the women discuss the texts, they find themselves struggling with personal conflicts that reflect the literary themes.

- *A Room with a View*, a Merchant-Ivory film produced in 1986, was based on a novel written by E. M. Forster and tells the story of a young woman, played by Helena Bonham Carter, struggling with her individuality in the early twentieth century as well as with her love for a charming young man, played by Julian Sands.

- *Howard's End*, a Merchant-Ivory film produced in 1992, chronicles the story of three families who represent three social classes: rich Victorian capitalists who are displacing the aristocracy; the enlightened bourgeois class; and the lower middle class. The film is based on a novel by E. M. Forster and begs the turn-of-the-century question, "Who will inherit England?" through the uncertain ownership of a house, Howard's End.

- An adaptation of Jane Austen's *Emma* was released in 1996 by Miramax. The film stars Gwyneth Paltrow as Emma, the affable young woman who makes it her life's business to meddle in other people's love lives, and an all-star cast that includes Toni Collette, Ewan McGregor, and Alan Cumming.

---

exuberant world with which mainstream film-goers could identify. As Barbara Shulgasser of the *San Francisco Examiner* remarked in her review of the film, "Lee and Thompson create a world so believable in its absurd rigidity that we feel we have known these characters all our lives. We are unshakably interested in everything that happens to them." Most critics agree that the Lee-Thompson film version of *Sense and Sensibility* provides a rich insight into the world Austen created in her novel, one that continues to make an undeniable impact on our popular

culture and still speaks to our contemporary desires. The Lee-Thompson remake keenly acknowledges that Austen is "everywhere," particularly in light of the fact that the adaptation was released by a major Hollywood motion picture company worldwide. The commercial and critical success of the film shows that the characterization, conflicts, and elegance of Austen's *Sense and Sensibility* still have the power to hold our contemporary interest. But ultimately, the simplicity of English idyll from another time—the fact that love and romance seem to

AT THE CENTER OF *SENSE AND SENSIBILITY* IS THE CHARACTERS' QUEST FOR THEIR HEART'S DESIRE."

be the only real problem in this period and place—is what draws us in and keeps us there.

For the most part, the characters of the film adaptation of *Sense and Sensibility* fit the descriptions detailed in Austen's novel. They have strong traits, making it easy for viewers to immediately understand and identify with the role each plays or will play in the narrative. For example, Thompson's Elinor Dashwood stands on strong morals, a deep sense of propriety, and social restraint. As Karen Stohr notes in her article on "Practical Wisdom and Moral Imagination" Elinor "fulfills every major social duty without ever being obsequious or false. Always conscious of the demands of gratitude and family relationships, she defends people according to, but not beyond, their true merits." Though Stohr speaks to the Elinor written by Austen, her observation accurately pinpoints the Elinor in the Lee-Thompson adaptation. As in the novel, the film version of Elinor is not cold, but rather thoughtful in the way she conducts herself, a woman of passion tempered by reason. After all, as Austen writes, Elinor possessed "a strength of understanding, and a coolness of judgment, which qualified her, though only nineteen, to be the counsellor of her mother," as well as "an excellent heart." Elinor's proper demeanor, though given to a twenty-seven-year old in the film rather than the teenager of the novel, hides a core of intense feeling and compels the viewers—and readers—of *Sense and Sensibility* to sympathize with her as she tries so hard to serve as the touchstone for everyone else's drama. Her moral code tells her to consider others' needs before her own, and this selfless manner, expertly portrayed by Emma Thompson, prompts viewers to hope Elinor receives her own happy ending. Viewers want to see Elinor get a just reward for her kindness, her thoughtful restraint, and her unrequited longing—namely a happy ending with Edward Ferrars.

At the center of *Sense and Sensibility* is the characters' quest for their heart's desire. Elinor and Marianne must navigate upper-middle-class society and, in different ways, attempt to secure love despite the machinations and secrets of others. These obstacles generate conflict that makes the viewer wonder: will the sisters get what they want? Will they find true love? Will they find happiness? The viewer sympathizes with Elinor when Lucy reveals her secret, since they witnessed Elinor and Edward sharing sweet moments of longing and a budding romance. The viewer falls in love with Willoughby right along with Marianne as Lee makes certain to capture the lovestruck expressions on Kate Winslet's face every time he is around. The personal quest of the Dashwood sisters for love, happiness, and security is a basic, human quest that undeniably resounds with the viewer, no matter their decade or generation. As Edward Shoben argues, the work of Jane Austen reflects "a universal and fundamental experience that is at once affective and cognitive, emotional and intellectual, in its character." Lee and Thompson build anxiety and anticipation about the future for the Austen characters, allowing the viewer to identify with and understand their emotions, as well as their intense longing for a certain outcome. The viewer can easily experience the characters' desires, pain, grief, and personal restraint.

The world of Jane Austen is uncomplicated: girl meets boy, girl cannot have boy because of certain social dictates or because boy is a cad in disguise or because boy must marry for money, and finally, girl ultimately ends up with the best man for her. In the Austen world, no one (of major consequence to the narrative) is employed, and characters have time for long conversations, long walks, and long carriage rides. Every window looks out onto wide, sweeping vistas, every face is clean and rosy. The Lee-Thompson adaptation brings this English fantasy to life. Viewers get the chance to spend a few hours in a place where the biggest concern is who is marrying whom or where the next picnic is or who will attend the ball. Certainly, the film shows Elinor worrying about domestic matters, but at its core, the cinematic *Sense and Sensibility* portrays a setting in which working folk are shown only on the periphery, while the main characters are allowed to think and roam and take care of their personal lives as needed. In the twenty-first century, when people are reachable anywhere, anytime, by phone, e-mail, or text, when working does not necessarily stop when one is away from the workplace, this film depicts a simple existence where the minute details are taken care of, leaving characters plenty of time to focus on emotions amidst their pursuit of pleasure. In the nineteenth century, when religion and nationalism went hand in hand, this rural idyll represented a sort of English paradise, an idea of Eden that obviously still exists and appeals to many people.

The 1995 film adaptation of *Sense and Sensibility* is but one of many successful Austen remakes; these films are in large part successful due to Austen's textured settings, clearly defined themes, and her unfettered narrative style. In her review of the 1995 film adaptation of the novel, Jeanne Aufmuth wonders, "Enduring love, heartbreak, undying passion and bitter betrayal. What more could you ask from Jane Austen, and for that matter, from a film?" Douglas McGrath, scriptwriter of Miramax's version of Austen's *Emma*, says Austen writes "superb dialogue, she creates memorable characters, [and] she has an extremely clever skill for plotting." Indeed, the "superb dialogue," "memorable characters," and sharply defined romantic conflicts, not to mention the struggle to fulfill innermost desires and the pursuit of happiness, have allowed Austen to become successfully translated across genres, definitively positioning Austen "everywhere" in our social and cultural consciousness.

Source: Michelle S. Lee, Critical Essay on *Sense and Sensibility*, in *Novels for Students*, Gale, Cengage Learning, 2010.

Richard Alleva

In the following review, Alleva argues that Ang Lee's Sense and Sensibility *deserves a place on the "honor roll" of fine film adaptations of classic novels.*

The only way to turn a classic novel into a vivid movie is to bring a lot of tough love to the project. Reverence alone won't do (as witness Visconti's paralyzed and paralyzing version of *Death in Venice*), and brisk assurance without tact produces such vulgarities as Kenneth Branagh's *Mary Shelley's Frankenstein* and Richard Brook's *Lord Jim*. But boldness in the service of love can result in films like the Noel Langley-Alistair Sim *Christmas Carol,* Eric Rohmer's poignant rendering of Kleist's *The Marquise of O,* John Huston's great expansion of Kipling's *The Man Who Would Be King.*

> ANG LEE TRIUMPHS. HE NEVER PERMITS HIS CAMERA TO BE A TOURIST OF THE ENGLISH COUNTRYSIDE BUT USES THE SETTINGS TO SUPPORT THE EMOTIONS OF ANY GIVEN SCENE."

Add one more film to the honor roll. Judging by her adaptation of Austen's *Sense and Sensibility*, Emma Thompson is the toughest of tough lovers, the most disciplined of Janeites. Lovingly directed by Ang Lee, the movie doesn't send you scurrying back to the original to find out why Character X did this or that, or how Character Y really felt, because what's up there on screen is satisfying in itself. But if you do return to the book, you may be astonished by Thompson's expansions and curtailments. And you will certainly be struck by her complete understanding of what this novel is really about.

Sense and Sensibility is a tale of two sisters: the reserved, sensible Elinor, who finds Mr. Right apparently too late; and the romantic Marianne, who finds a Mr. Right who turns out to be Mr. Wrong. It's a good novel, but I wonder if it would enjoy classic status if Jane Austen hadn't written anything else. Just as *Barnaby Rudge* has ridden to immortality on the coattails of *Pickwick Papers* and *Bleak House,S&S* has survived the depredations of time mainly because it is boxed, in complete sets of Jane Austen, with the true masterpieces, *Pride and Prejudice, Persuasion,* and *Emma*. Its plot is serviceable yet seems a little overloaded with breathless messengers riding posthaste on frothing steeds. The two protagonists are poignantly drawn and some of the supporting players are richly comic. But the faithful lovers of the sisters, Edward Ferrars and Colonel Brandon, are two sticks walking about in frock coats. (On the other hand, Willoughby, the cad who betrays Marianne, is alive precisely because he is a cad, and the author, casting a cold eye on him, sees him clearly and from more than one angle.) And there are too many minor characters whom we cannot really see in our minds' eyes as they perform what are purely functional roles.

Yet *Sense and Sensibility* has something no other Jane Austen novel—with the exception of

Persuasion—has: naked emotion. We smile at Elizabeth Bennet and Darcy, we laugh at Emma Woodhouse, we are disturbed by the sexual predators of *Mansfield Park*, but when Marianne runs across a ballroom to the man she is obsessed by, and who is ignoring her, and exclaims "Good God! Willoughby, what is the meaning of this?" only to be met by cold looks and even colder words, we may feel tears coming to our eyes and the hairs on our forearms rising. *Sense and Sensibility* is a very direct book.

How well Emma Thompson and Ang Lee have understood this and how cleanly they have cut to the core of Austen's comedy and drama! Thompson doesn't hesitate to turn the book's happily married Sir John Middleton into a widower because she understands that Sir John's comicality registers most vividly when he appears in tandem not with his starchy wife but with his mother-in-law, Mrs. Jennings, the great supergossip of English literature. As written by Thompson and as played, to the hilt, by Robert Hardy and Elizabeth Sprigg, the two good-hearted meddlers become a great comic team.

But that is a masterstroke of excision. As an example of creative enlargement, look at what the scriptwriter has done with Edward Ferrars. In the book, Elinor's choice of such a dull man as her life's companion diminishes her. But Thompson makes it clear from the start that what Elinor cherishes in Edward is not his self-effacement but his generosity and the tact by which that generosity enacts itself. When the film's Edward finds that his visit to the Dashwood house has deprived the youngest sister, eleven-year-old Margaret, of her bedroom, he tacitly claims a less agreeable guest chamber. When the child hides herself from all visitors, Edward brings off a playful ruse that coaxes Margaret back to civilization. Although Hugh Grant's performance is the only faulty one in the movie—too much squinting and shoulder-hunching—he does render Edward's diffidence as pure charm and courtesy. We believe Elinor is right to love this man, and that's what counts.

But what counts most of all is that the screenwriter comprehends the theme of the novel. Like much of Austen's fiction (and much of Henry James's) *S&S* is about honor. Not the sort of honor defended in duels but the kind all men and women defer to when they honor their commitments. Jane Austen, pace George Eliot or Doris Lessing fans, remains the supreme feminist of fiction because her major female characters are always presented as moral agents, not as fortresses of virginity determining which males will be allowed to breach the gates nor as bluestockings preoccupied by the bees of idealism buzzing in their bonnets. When Elinor understands that Edward may be unable to marry her because he has already pledged himself to a Miss Steele, she not only approves of his scruples but tries to expedite the dreaded marriage because she'd rather see her lover retain his honor than be with her in dishonor. Not exactly a modern girl, this Miss Dashwood, but Thompson makes us understand that she is as chivalrous as any knight on a white charger.

Jane Austen was a genius at characterization and plotting but physical description was never her forte. That's not a defect, just a negative attribute of her special art. But this puts a burden on the director to supply the visual equivalent of the novelist's sensibility. Ang Lee triumphs. He never permits his camera to be a tourist of the English countryside but uses the settings to support the emotions of any given scene. He and cameraman Michael Coulter have drawn upon the paintings of Vermeer for certain of the quieter domestic scenes and (I think) Constable for some of the outdoor passages, but the lighting of Marianne in agony on her sickbed is pure Caravaggio, and justly so. Lee's subtle directorial touches can be relished at second, even third viewings. Let me cite only one shot: the overhead view of Elinor sitting on a landing and holding a cup of 3tea that nobody wants while—to Elinor's left, front, and right—every other member of the all-female household locks herself in her bedroom to howl over Willoughby's hasty departure. Elinor's heart is breaking, too—for Edward's sake. But how can a girl weep when the rest of her family holds the monopoly on grief and she is expected to be the dry-eyed pillar of common sense? So she just sits and thinks and sips the tea that nobody wants while we, perched by Lee high above the landing, gaze down on her in admiring pity, in smiling commiseration. It's a very poignant and very funny shot, and has perfect Austen pitch.

Greg Wise, as Willoughby, had the teen-aged girls four rows down from me swooning through the first half of the movie and hissing him in the second. Way to go, Greg. They then transferred their swooning to Alan Rickman as noble Colonel Brandon. Way to go, Rickman. Imogene Stubbs is amazing as the steely Miss Steele. Simultaneously laughable, smarmy, and frightening, she leans right into her rival's bosom, flutters her eyelashes, and verbally batters away at the mid-section with a relentlessness that Joe Frazier would have envied. Kate Winslet, as Marianne, is both formidable and pitiful in the coils of passion, and, in those scenes which require vocal fireworks, Winslet unleashes a voice that might do justice to Shakespeare.

To Emma Thompson's performance as Elinor I would like to raise a monument of words, but I can only toss a pebble onto the pile already heaped by fellow critics. In passages of wit, she is the driest of clarets, in scenes of grief and yearning, the most full-bodied of Burgundies. My metaphors are drawn from wine because I wish to offer a toast to the finest actress (and now, apparently, one of the best scriptwriters) currently working in the English-speaking cinema.

I regret that circumstances didn't permit me to review *Persuasion* last year. Let me just state that I think it a very good adaptation but that certain elements in it—the drizzly (and lovely) photography, the anachronistic music (Chopin, among others), the generally hushed quality of the soundtrack, and the almost self-effacing performance of Amanda Root (of, to be sure, a self-effacing heroine), nudge it a little further into the nineteenth century than the sensibility of Jane Austen belongs. Nevertheless, this movie's style does capture the tenderness and melancholy of a book written by a woman who probably sensed her impending death.

The little I saw of *Pride and Prejudice* on the Arts and Entertainment channel repelled me. Here was a cuddly Elizabeth Bennet, and how in the name of F. R. Leavis can a Jane Austen heroine be cuddly? Here was a Darcy who dived into cold lakes to quench his sexual appetite. Was the fellow educated in Jesuit boarding schools? Here was a camera that looked at the English countryside as if it were a National Trust guide showing yuppie Yank tourists the Stately Homes of England. ("And over here, ladies and gentlemen, the servants' quarters. Note the ruddy faces of our healthy, happy yeomen.") If the film *Persuasion* steers Austen close to Bronte country, this *Pride and Prejudice* dumped her right into the land of Regency Romance paperbacks.

Source: Richard Alleva, "Sense and Sensibility," in *Commonweal*, v. 123, no. 5, March 8, 1996, pp. 15–17.

SOURCES

Aufmuth, Jeanne, Review of *Sense and Sensibility*, in *Palo Alto Online*, 1995. http://paloaltoonline.com/movies/moviescreener.php?id=001428&type=long (accessed June 16, 2009).

Austen, Jane, *Sense and Sensibility*, Penguin Books, 1998.

Austenblog.com, http://www.austenblog.com (accessed June 16, 2009).

Baumgarten, Marjorie, Review of *Sense and Sensibility*, in *Austin Chronicle*, December 15,1995, http://www.austinchronicle.com/gyrobase/Calendar/Film?Film=oid%3a138305 (accessed June 16, 2009).

Benedict, Barbara, "Jane Austen's *Sense and Sensibility*: The Politics of Point of View," in *Philological Quarterly*, Vol. 69, No. 4, Fall 1990, p. 453.

Copeland, Edward and Juliet McMaster, eds., *The Cambridge Companion to Jane Austen*, Cambridge University Press, 1997.

Galperin, William, *The Historical Austen*, University of Pennsylvania Press, 2003.

Hicks, Chris, Review of *Sense and Sensibility*, in *Deseret News*, January 24, 1996, http://www.deseretnews.com/article/700001617/Sense-and-Sensibility.html (accessed July 21, 2009).

"Jane Austen Biography," *JaneAusten.org*, http://www.janeausten.org (accessed June 19, 2009).

McCarthy, Todd. "Austen Makes Big Screen 'Sense'," in *Variety*, December 4, 1995, http://www.variety.com/review/VE1117910516.html?categoryid=31&cs=1 (accessed July 21, 2009).

Nokes, David, *Jane Austen: A Life*, Straus & Giroux, 1997.

Parrill, Sue, *Jane Austen on Film and Television*, MacFarland, 2002.

The Republic of Pemberley, http://www.pemberley.com (accessed June 16, 2009).

Shulgasser, Barbara, "A Austenesque-Thompsonesque Experience," in *San Francisco Chronicle*, December 13, 1995, http://www.sfgate.com/cgi-bin/article.cgi?f=/e/a/1995/12/13/STYLE2770.dtl (accessed July 21, 2009).

Shoben Jr., Edward, "Impulse and Virtue in Jane Austen: "Sense and Sensibility" in Two Centuries," in *The Hudson Review*, Vol. 35, No. 4, Winter 1982–1983, p. 521.

Stohr, Karen, "Practical Wisdom and Moral Imagination in "Sense and Sensibility" in *Philosophy and Literature*, Vol. 30, 2006, p. 378–394.

Tomalin, Claire, *Jane Austen: A Life*, Knopf, 1997.

FURTHER READING

Cahir, Linda Costanzo, *Literature into Film: Theorty and Practical Approaches*, McFarland & Company, 2006.

Cahir presents a detailed discussion, with an emphasis on film theory, of the relationship between original works of literature and their film adaptations.

Dilley, Whitney Crothers, *The Cinema of Ang Lee: The Other Side of the Screen*, Wallflower Press, 2007.

Lee provides an excellent overview of Lee's career, written with the needs of serious film students in mind. The book provides thorough consideration of each of Lee's films as well as dicusisons of recurring themes throughout Lee's body of work.

"Emma Thompason," *Internet Movie Database* (IMDb), http://www.imdb.com/name/nm0000668.

IMDb provides comprehensive information on the projects of people involved in the film industry. Thompson's entry contains a complete list of films in which she acted, directed, or produced, along with links to further information on each film.

Parrill, Sue, *Jane Austen on Film and Television: A Critical Study of the Adaptations,* McFarland & Company, 2002.

This scholarly, but very readable, critical study analyzes the many different film and television versions of Jane Austen works. There is a full chapter devoted to various interpretations of *Sense and Sensibility*.

The Street

ANN LANE PETRY

1946

Published in 1946, *The Street* was the first novel by a female African American writer to sell over one million copies. Inspired by her experiences working in the ghettos of Harlem, Ann Petry's first book joined the growing number of African American voices that called attention to the horrific impact of racial and gender inequality in the United States—a chorus whose message was ignored by many until the civil rights movement of the 1960s. Unlike the works of her contemporaries, Petry's novel paints a picture of urban ghetto life from a female perspective. Until publication of *The Street*, novels written about urban African American women, such as Nella Larsen's *Quicksand* (1923) or Jessie Fauset's *Plum Bun* (1929), focused primarily on the experiences of middle-class protagonists. Other famous works that did focus on the experiences of poor, urban African Americans often neglected the female experience.

Set in Harlem in the 1940s, Petry's novel paints a grim picture of life for African Americans in the ghettos of New York. Speaking to the inextricable relationship between racial inequality and poverty, *The Street* follows one working-class woman, Lutie Johnson, as she struggles desperately to find a safe place to raise her only son. As readers learn early in the novel, eight-year-old Bub is at risk of falling prey to the many traps that often ensnare the African American youths of the inner city—violent crime, substance abuse, and prostitution, among others. Believing

Ann Petry *(AP Images)*

that hard work and determination will ultimately enable her to alter what seems increasingly like an inevitable spiral downward, Lutie labors tirelessly to achieve the American Dream of financial stability. Despite her remarkable resilience and commitment to not sell her body for money, Lutie not only fails to achieve her goals but is consumed by rage and abandons her son completely, leaving readers to wonder what, if anything, could have been done to change the story's devastating outcome.

While the majority of Petry's novel is concerned with the interior experiences of its characters, it does paint a realistic picture of life in Harlem during the 1940s, including occasional descriptions of violence and instances of profanity that may be disturbing to some readers.

AUTHOR BIOGRAPHY

The youngest of three daughters, Ann Lane was born on October 12, 1908, into one of only two black families in the small town of Old Saybrook, Connecticut. Ann never knew her oldest sister, who died at the age of two. Ann grew up at

a time in the United States when African Americans were considered by many to be inferior to Anglo Americans—racism and discrimination were rampant. In contrast to the poverty-stricken characters of Petry's fiction, the Lanes were relatively comfortable and solidly middle-class by the time Petry had achieved success as writer. Despite their economic stature, the Lanes suffered from the widespread racism and discrimination that existed in the predominantly white town of Old Saybrook. Not surprisingly, racial discrimination features prominently in much of Petry's fiction and is the focus of much of the criticism written about her major works including *The Street.*

Ann's mother, Bertha James Lane, was a strong African American woman who owned a small shop and worked simultaneously as a hairdresser, licensed chiropodist (foot doctor), and entrepreneur. Having earned his pharmacy license in 1890, Petry's father, Peter Clark Lane, owned a local drugstore and worked as a pharmacist, as did her aunt and uncle, who owned a pharmacy in the nearby town of Old Lyme.

In 1925, Ann was the only African American in the graduating class of Old Saybrook High School. While she had expressed interest in writing during her younger years, Ann decided to follow in the footsteps of the many chemists in her family and subsequently elected to attend the Connecticut College of Pharmacy in New Haven, where she was one of only a few African Americans. In 1931, Petry graduated with a Ph.G. (Graduate in Pharmacy) and returned home, where she worked in the family drug store for a total of seven years—the first five at her father's store in Old Saybrook and the last two at her aunt and uncle's store in Old Lyme. Both towns appear briefly in *The Street.* During this time, Petry wrote fiction but did not publish her work.

In 1938, Ann married George D. Petry and moved to New York, where she worked as a newspaper writer for *The People's Voice* and *Crisis* magazines in addition to working as a teacher in Harlem. During her work as a reporter, Petry became intimately familiar with the lifestyles of African Americans living in Harlem. It was while taking a creative-writing class at Columbia University that Petry began to transform her observations of life in Harlem into fiction.

Petry published her first short story, "Marie of the Cabin Club" (1939), in a Baltimore newspaper. A few years later, she published another story, "On Saturday Night the Sirens Sound" (1943), which caught the eye an editor who suggested Petry apply for a writing award. She followed the advice and in 1945 won the Houghton Mifflin Literary Fellowship in fiction—the funds of which allowed her to write and publish the opening chapters of her first novel, *The Street* (1946). The work was an immediate success and launched her career as a professional fiction writer.

Hailed as a master of urban American realism, Petry went on to write *Country Place* (1947), *The Drugstore Cat* (1949), *The Narrows* (1953), *Harriet Tubman: Conductor of the Underground Railroad* (1955), *Tituba of Salem Village* (1964) *Miss Muriel and Other Stories* (1971), as well as numerous poems and essays of social criticism. Over the course of her writing career, Petry received widespread recognition, numerous honorary degrees, and became well respected in literary circles for her contribution to African American literature.

Ann Petry died on April 28, 1997 near her home in Old Saybrook.

PLOT SUMMARY

Chapter 1

The Street opens with the story's main character, Lutie Johnson, braving a bitter, cold wind as she walks through Harlem in New York City. The wind Lutie faces is personified as a hostile character, mirroring the aggressive attitude of many white Americans toward African Americans during the pre-civil rights era. More generally, the wind represents the oppressive forces of poverty and racial inequality and the chilling impact they have on the urban-dwelling African Americans of Petry's novel. Lutie is on her way down 116th Street to look at an apartment she is interested in renting for her and her eight-year-old son Bub. In addition to wanting to shelter her son from a life of poverty and violence, Lutie seeks to protect Bub from the influence of Lil, her father's current girlfriend, a promiscuous woman who gives Bub alcohol and has him light her cigarettes for her. At first Lutie thinks that anything would be better than continuing on with her father and Lil. But as she inspects the poverty-stricken street in Harlem, the dilapidated building, and the apartment itself, she is not so sure. In addition to the depressing state of

the building and the proximity to domestic violence and alcoholic men, moving to this apartment would mean living under the management of William Jones, the "super" (building supervisor), who eyes Lutie lustily as she inspects the apartment. Despite her reservations, Lutie decides that she will take the apartment.

Two other important characters appear in the opening chapter. As she weighs her options, Lutie reflects on the advice of her deceased grandmother, Granny, whose "nonsense" Lutie often dismisses but also uses to guide herself. The first person Lutie meets at the apartment building, which will eventually become her home, is Mrs. Hedges, a woman who is revealed to be the madam of a prostitution operation that takes advantage of impoverished women and depressed men looking for an escape from the dark reality of life in the ghetto.

Chapter 2

The next chapter takes readers back in time to the events that led up to Lutie's separation from her husband, Jim. Wanting to provide for her family, Lutie takes a job working as a live-in maid and nanny for a white family, the Chandlers, in Lyme, Connecticut. While she initially takes it out of desperation—Jim is unemployed and this is the only job she can get—she ends up staying for two years. Among her many responsibilities, Lutie is the primary caregiver for the Chandler's son, who is the same age as Bub. During her stay at the Chandlers, she endures constant discrimination and racism because she is black. On Christmas Eve, Mr. Chandler's brother, Jonathan Chandler, commits suicide in front of the whole family—an event that the Chandlers pass off as an accident to the public. Lutie receives a message from her father informing her that her husband is now living with another woman, and this prompts Lutie to quit her job and return home. Enraged, she kicks the other woman out of the house, takes Bub, and moves in with her father. Years go by and Lutie works menial jobs while studying for civil-service examinations. Eventually she gets a position as a file clerk. Chapter 2 ends with Lutie resolving never to stop fighting against the negative forces of the street.

Chapter 3

Lutie walks down the street worrying about money and Bub. She has an encounter with a white butcher that causes her to reflect on her struggle to gain power. After buying groceries, she returns home to find Bub shining shoes for money. Angered because she feels the work is conditioning Bub to accept a low status in society, Lutie slaps him across the face, bewildering him. She tries to explain why she is angry and then reflects on the ways in which African Americans are trapped in the ghetto of Harlem. Determined not to stay trapped herself, Lutie resolves to fight her way out. After reflecting on how poverty and racism affected her father and husband, Lutie heads out for a drink at a local bar, owned by Mr. Junto, a white man.

Chapter 4

Here, the narrative perspective shifts from Lutie's to that of William Jones, the supervisor of her apartment building. Jones sees Lutie going out all dressed up and he feels lonely: "It was a loneliness born of years of living in basements and sleeping on mattresses in boiler rooms."

He feels an attraction to Lutie and schemes about how to possess her. Readers learn that it was his idea for Bub to shine shoes—the first of many attempts to get to Lutie by manipulating her son. The super's newfound attraction to Lutie disrupts the stability of his living situation with Min, a woman he resents for her helplessness. While pondering his previous interactions with Lutie, the super reveals that he was fantasizing about raping her while she was inspecting the apartment, thus confirming Lutie's intuition about his predatory intentions. While Lutie is out, the super visits her apartment, plays cards with Bub and goes through Lutie's personal belongings, even going so far as to steal her lipstick for his sexual gratification. The super plans to throw Min out as soon as possible.

Chapter 5

Chapter 5 is told from Min's perspective. Ever since Lutie moved in, William Jones has treated her like he treats the dog, kicking and verbally abusing her when he is angry. She no longer feels safe in the apartment, so she goes to Mrs. Hedges to ask if she knows where she can find a root doctor (a person who uses traditional and supposedly magical plant preparations to help others). Following the advice of Mrs. Hedges, Min consults with the Prophet David, who treats her like a human being. The consultation is significant because it is the first time Min has acted in defiance of the men in her life. The Prophet gives Min a cross, some candles, and small vial of red liquid.

Min declares that her interaction with the Prophet was the most satisfying experience of her life.

Chapter 6

After letting Bub go to the movies, Lutie visits Mr. Junto's bar, where many people go to escape the problems that plague their lives in the ghetto. While she is there drinking beer, she sings along to the music from the jukebox and everyone stops to listens to her. One of the wealthier black men at the bar, Boots Smith, hears her and asks her to sing in his band with him. Boots and Lutie go for a night drive outside the city, prompting Lutie to contemplate the relationship between money and power.

Chapter 7

Lutie and Boots return to the city because Boots is late for work. They are pulled over for speeding by a white policeman and Lutie is afraid because the man's face changes when he sees they are black. Boots gives him money with his driver's license and the policeman lets them go without a ticket. In her mind, Lutie compares Boots unfavorably with her husband, who had always struggled to have enough money. Unlike Boots, her husband had warm, open eyes. She begins to feel like Jim's cheating on her was partly her fault. Lutie reflects on the events that led to her taking work away from the family, including a brutal fight where Jim slapped her across the face and she broke a chair.

Chapter 8

Lutie returns home thinking about life on the street. When she enters her apartment, she notices that the ashtray has been used. Bub tells her that the super had come by and played cards with him. Lutie falls asleep that night thinking of the super as less than human and has terrible nightmares. The next day Lutie reflects on the horrible things she has seen while living in Harlem and resolves once again to keep fighting the pressures of life on the street. Inside she feels rage and hatred, but Lutie forces negative thoughts out of her mind because they do not lead anywhere. As she goes to her closet to pick out her clothes, she notices a blouse has been crumpled. After questioning Bub, she realizes that the super was in her bedroom fondling her clothing.

Chapter 9

The first part of chapter 9 is told from Bub's perspective. When Lutie goes out to sing with

Boots's band, Bub is afraid to stay at home alone. He is lonely when she is away and in the dark the furniture turns into monstrous shapes. Bub hears couples fighting, women being beaten up, and people crying through the thin walls. Bub falls asleep. The narration then shifts to Lutie's perspective as she enters the dance hall at the Casino where Boots's band is playing. Lutie performs very well and receives a standing ovation from the orchestra. Boots tells Lutie that she won't have to worry about money anymore. Lutie is glad because she believes that

> No one could live on a street like this and stay decent. It would get them sooner or later, for it sucked the humanity out of people—slowly, surely, inevitably.

Chapter 10
William Jones continues to lust after Lutie, while also becoming increasingly disgusted with the presence of Min in his apartment. He wants to throw her out, but he cannot because the Prophet David's tricks have worked. When Lutie returns home from singing at the Casino, Jones apprehends her in the hallway and tries to drag her to the cellar to rape her. He is interrupted by Mrs. Hedges, who rescues Lutie and brings her back to her apartment to recover from the traumatic experience. The narration shifts to Mrs. Hedges's perspective, revealing the painful events of her past and the details of her long-standing relationship with Mr. Junto. Readers are given a window into the function of prostitution on the street and the threat it poses to Lutie and her son.

Chapter 11
After being summoned by Mr. Junto, Boots assumes, incorrectly, that someone found out how Mr. Junto helped Boots avoid being drafted into the army. Boots recalls his conversation with Mr. Junto about his deep-seated hatred for white folks and his feelings about the war. Instead of talking with him about the war, Mr. Junto tells Boots not to pursue Lutie Johnson romantically because he wants her for himself. Boots weighs the benefits of pursuing Lutie against the risk of losing Mr. Junto's power and influence; he decides Lutie is not worth it. He remembers the time he caught his partner, Jubilee, sleeping with a white man. He beat her up and she cut him across the face with a knife, leaving a prominent scar. Boots agrees to Mr. Junto's request and Mr. Junto tells Boots not to pay Lutie for her work singing in the band.

Chapter 12
William Jones is enraged because Mrs. Hedges and Min have ruined his plan to rape Lutie in the cellar. He wants to punish Mrs. Hedges by turning her over to the police for operating a whorehouse but knows that she is protected by the power of Mr. Junto, a white man. In a cloud of delusional thinking, he imagines that if he gives Lutie a present she will want to be with him. He also imagines that the only reason she does not want to be with him is that she wants Mr. Junto. Angry, he comes up with a plan to hurt Lutie through her son, Bub. He gets Min to copy a master mailbox key he has designed. He tells Bub that he will pay him to steal letters from people's mailboxes as part of a secret operation to catch crooks. Bub does not think his mother will approve and runs away from Jones.

Chapter 13
Back at the Casino, during an intermission in the show Lutie finds out that Boots is not going to pay her for singing in the band, at least not for several months, because Mr. Junto thinks she is not ready yet. She tells him she is not interested in singing for free. Boots gives her a pair of rhinestone earrings sent by Mr. Junto. Filled with a sense of loss and trying to control her anger, Lutie blames herself for being unrealistic with her planning. She returns home to the misery of her Harlem apartment complex and resolves once again that she will never become resigned to staying in the ghetto. She tells Bub about her financial worries but then feels badly for the way she harps on him to keep their costs low. Responding to an advertisement she had found in an African American newspaper, Lutie travels to the Crosse School for Singers to audition for a Broadway and nightclub singing job. Mr. Crosse tells her she has a good voice and that she can earn seventy-five dollars a week if she pays one hundred and twenty-five dollars for this school to train her. She gets up to leave because she does not have nearly enough money to pay for the training. Mr. Crosse stops her by grabbing her arm. He tells her that if she "gets together" with him several times a week, the lessons will be free. Lutie picks up an inkwell and hurls ink at his face before slamming the door and rushing out of his office. On her way home, she reflects in anger on the oppression of African Americans. At home, Bub thinks Lutie is mad at him. She tells him that she is only worried about money, prompting Bub to return to the super and tell him he has changed his mind about stealing the letters for money.

Chapter 14

Bub's schoolteacher, Miss Rinner, is a white woman who has worked in Harlem for many years. She cannot stand the smell of Harlem or the children she teaches and is so ashamed of where she works that she does not tell her white friends the exact location of her job. On the weekend, Miss Rinner dreams of being transferred to a school where she can teach healthy white children who have a bright future. During the week, she travels to and from work feeling an irrational and excessive fear of black people. In reaction to her attitude, the children do not respect her and make fun of her with accusatory rhymes. One day, Bub tells Miss Rinner he needs to use the bathroom and uses his time to leave school early and beat the other children to the candy shop, where he buys his mother a pair of earrings. One of the members of a gang known as "the big six-B boys" sees that he has money and the boys chase Bub through the streets. Bub outruns them and feels a rush of excitement at his own daring. Feeling confident, Bub easily steals letters from an apartment block on a different street. He tells lies to the residents to explain his presence and feels a thrilling sense of success. He thinks he is playing an important part of a larger plan to catch crooks for the police. On his way home Bub gets so distracted watching some men gamble that he does not see the big six-B boys. The boys grab Bub and taunt him that his mother is a whore. Bub is rescued just in time by Mrs. Hedges, who tells the leader of the group, Charlie Moore, not to mess with Bub anymore. Bub meets the super down in the cellar and asks if they have caught any criminals yet. The super says they have not but assures him that they will soon.

Chapter 15

Feeling unbearably uncomfortable living with William Jones and his hostility, Min decides that it is time to move. She loads her belongings, including her bird Dickie Boy and an ornately carved table given to her by a previous white employer, into a hired pushcart and sets off in search of a new place to live. Before she leaves the apartment, Min notices several stolen letters on the desk and knows Jones has been doing something crooked. She knows she can never return to Jones because she will never be safe with him. Knowing that a single black woman cannot live alone without being exploited by her landlord, Min wonders if she would have a chance with the pushcart man—indicating that she intends to continue her pattern of moving from man to man in order to protect herself.

Chapter 16

Jones learns from Mrs. Hedges that Min is gone. When he goes upstairs to confirm this for himself, he notices the stolen letters that Min had seen. He looks around the apartment to see if Min has taken any of his things. When Jones looks at the bed, he thinks he sees the cross that Min brought home from the Prophet, only to find out shortly later that the cross he had seen was only an outline of dust where the cross had hung. Jones feels trapped and worries about not knowing what is real and what is imaginary. He fantasizes about quitting his job and feels free. Two post-office investigators, both white, come looking for the supervisor of Lutie's building because it is the only one in the area where people have not made complaints about letters being stolen. Jones happily points them to Bub, who is caught red-handed bringing stolen letters back to Jones. In turn, Jones is gratified by thoughts of hurting Lutie. Lutie returns home and the investigators, who assume negative things about her character, are waiting for her. They give her paperwork and explain that Bub has been taken to the children's shelter and will appear in Children's Court. Lutie cries and blames herself for what has happened to Bub. She sets out in search of a lawyer, who tells her it will take two hundred dollars to free Bub.

Chapter 17

Desperate to save Bub, Lutie wonders where she can find two hundred dollars. After dismissing several options, she phones Boots Smith and asks to see him right away. While visiting Boots at his expensive apartment, Lutie explains what has happened to Bub and asks to borrow the money. He is surprised to learn she has a son but quickly agrees to give her the money. Lutie leaves and goes home, where she reflects on growing up with Granny. The next day, Lutie visits Bub at the Children's Shelter. She knows that she has pushed him away with her anger, resentment, and hate. Lutie goes home and cleans her apartment, trying to get through the day until she will go collect the money from Boots. Looking for an escape from her thoughts, Lutie goes to a movie but leaves partway through the picture. Next, she goes to the beauty parlor but it is unusually quiet. Lutie senses an inescapable stillness near her.

Chapter 18

On her way out to see Boots, Lutie speaks briefly to Mrs. Hedges, who hints that Lutie can earn the money she needs by prostituting herself to Mr. Junto. Lutie turns away from her before she is finished, perplexing Mrs. Hedges. Lutie realizes that the inescapable stillness that has provoked her fear is actually Mr. Junto. Even when he is not around, she can feel his presence. When Lutie arrives at Boots's apartment, Mr. Junto is there waiting to meet her. Boots takes Lutie into the bedroom and tells her to "be nice " to Mr. Junto (in other word, to sleep with him) so that Mr. Junto will give her the money. Sensing that if she accepts this deal she will be completely trapped, Lutie demands that Boots get Mr. Junto out of the apartment. Boots complies and then decides that he will let Mr. Junto have sex with Lutie but he will have her first, thereby getting revenge against Mr. Junto for pushing him so hard about Lutie. Boots locks the door behind Mr. Junto and puts the key in his pocket. After pouring two drinks, one for Lutie and one for himself, Boots makes advances to Lutie. Sensing the danger she is in, Lutie tries to leave, but Boots protests. While looking at the scar on Boots's face, Lutie sees everything she abhors about life on the streets of Harlem. Boots has come to represent all the traps she has been trying desperately to avoid. Boots kisses her and Lutie feels a surge of rage. She realizes that he has trapped her with the lure of money. Lutie yells at Boots and he slaps her across the face, triggering an explosion of suppressed rage. She grabs an iron candlestick from the mantel and murders Boots. Afterward, realizing what she has done, Lutie decides to buy a one-way train ticket for Chicago so that Bub will never know that his mother is a murderer.

CHARACTERS

Jonathan Chandler

Jonathan Chandler, also referred to as Mr. Chandler, commits suicide on Christmas Eve in front of the whole Chandler family, including live-in maid Lutie and Little Henry Chandler. Afterward, the Chandlers pay off a number of officials to make sure the incident is recorded as an accident in the public records. This episode makes Lutie realize how money shapes reality.

Little Henry Chandler

Little Henry Chandler is the young son of Mr. and Mrs. Chandler. Lutie takes care of Little Henry while she is living away from her own son of the same age. Little Henry grows attached to Lutie and is devastated when she leaves. For Lutie, his wealth and privilege represent all that she wants to give her son but cannot because she is poor and black.

Mr. and Mrs. Henry Chandler

Mr.and Mrs. Henry Chandler, parents of Little Henry Chandler, employ Lutie as a maid and nanny. Their interactions with Lutie reveal their unconscious racism toward African Americans.

Mr. Crosse

Mr. Crosse trains singers for Broadway and nightclub appearances. Lutie auditions at his studio and throws an inkwell in his face when he propositions her. He had offered to give her singing lessons for free if she sleeps with him several times a week.

Granny

Granny is Lutie Johnson's grandmother. Her intuition about people—particularly men with bad intentions—conforms to Lutie's own experience. Lutie grew up with Granny's company and was never afraid of the dark because Granny made her house feel known and familiar.

Mrs. Hedges

The madam of a house of prostitution, she has a close relationship with Mr. Junto, a powerful white man. Many years ago, she narrowly escaped a burning building. The fire left her permanently disfigured. Her appearance is a source of immense insecurity for the woman and a barrier to intimacy with Mr. Junto, who appears to like and respect her. Mrs. Hedges intervenes to protect both Lutie Johnson and her son Bub at key moments in the novel. She is a strong woman who intimidates William Jones and the local bullies who harass Bub.

Bub Johnson

Bub Johnson is Lutie's eight-year-old son. He desperately wants to gain his mother's approval and love. While much of the novel concerns Lutie's attempts to take care of her son, she shows little warmth toward him and often lashes out at him under the pressure of trying to survive in the awful conditions of the Harlem ghetto.

Bub does not understand why his mother is so concerned about money and tries to please her by earning money from the super, who in turn manipulates him into stealing letters from people's mailboxes. Bub is eventually caught by the police and sent to jail, where his mother visits him once, promising him she will be back soon. Lutie never returns and Bub is left abandoned at the jail with a bleak future ahead of him.

Jim Johnson

Jim Johnson is Lutie's husband. He cheats on her while she is away working for a white family, the Chandlers, in Lyme, Connecticut. Unable to find work because he is black, Jim grows depressed because he cannot provide for his family. After Lutie finds out about the affair, Jim moves away and neither Lutie nor Bub hear from him again, although Lutie eventually comes to understand the despair he felt while she was away.

Lutie Johnson

Lutie Johnson is the main character in the novel. She has been estranged from her husband, Jim Johnson, ever since she returned home from working at the Chandlers' to find another woman living in their house. Although she and her son Bub no longer have any contact with Jim, she remains married to him. Lutie is a strong woman who works hard to provide for her son. Her primary concern is that she make enough money to move out of the ghetto. Unlike many peripheral characters in the novel, Lutie refuses to sell her body for money. It is the one compromise she is completely unwilling to make—a fact that stands in strong contradiction to the expectations of many people around her who assume that all black women welcome to the advances of white men. Despite many setbacks, Lutie remains determined to fight her circumstances for the sake of her son. Unfortunately, during the many years Lutie has endured racial and gender inequality, oppression, and hardship, her anger at "the street" has reached an unbearable level. By the novel's devastating conclusion, Lutie has been consumed by her rage. Blinded by her anger, she murders Boots after he traps her in a hotel room. Not wanting Bub to know that his mother is a murderer, Lutie abandons him completely, buying a one-way ticket for Chicago.

William Jones

William Jones is the superintendent of the apartment building into which Lutie Johnson moves with her son Bub. Jones lives with a dog, which he physically abuses when he is angry, and a woman, Min, who is so submissive to Jones that she is virtually invisible to Lutie when she comes to rent the apartment. As the story progresses, Jones becomes increasingly obsessed with physically attractive Lutie and tries in various ways to reach her through Bub.

Mr. Junto

Mr. Junto is a wealthy and powerful business owner in Harlem who is good friends with Mrs. Hedges. Mr. Junto takes an interest in Lutie Johnson after he hears her sing at a bar he owns. He tells one of his employees, Boots, to let her sing in Boots's band but not to pay her, presumably so that she will remain economically desperate. He tells Boots not to pursue Lutie because he wants her for himself. After learning that she is not interested in sleeping with him for money, Mr. Junto becomes angry.

Lil

Pop's promiscuous girlfriend, who provides the motivation for Lutie to find a new place to live. In addition to having a "loose bosom," Lil offers Bub alcohol behind Lutie's back and asks him to light her cigarettes for her.

Charlie Moore

See Gray Cap

Charlie Moore is the leader of a gang of older boys, the "big six-B boys," who live on the street and bully Bub.

Mom and Pop

Lutie's parents, referred to only as Mom and Pop, are minor characters in the novel. However, Pop's role in Lutie's history is significant. It is because of him and his girlfriend Lil that Lutie decides to escape to Harlem.

Min

Min is a meek yet intuitive woman who lives with William Jones. Her relationship with the super was stable until Lutie Johnson moved into the building. Min is so submissive toward the super that she becomes invisible to Lutie. Once the super begins to desire Lutie, his feelings toward Min turn increasingly hostile. Sensing that she is in danger, Min consults a witch doctor, the Prophet David, who tells her how to prevent the super from being violent toward her. His tricks work and Min keeps herself safe until she eventually moves to another apartment on a nearby street.

The Prophet David

The Prophet David is a root doctor (a herbalist purported to have magical powers) who serves women who seek protection from the abusive men in their life. He helps Min to protect herself from William Jones.

Miss Rinner

Miss Rinner is Bub's white teacher at school. She has worked in Harlem for many years and cannot stand the smell of black children. She does not think there is any point to teaching them and dreams of the day she will be transferred to a school of blond-haired and blue-eyed children.

Boots Smith

Boots Smith, who has a long scar on his face, is a wealthy African American man who works for Mr. Junto and meets Lutie Johnson after she sings at Mr. Junto's bar. Boots takes an interest in Lutie Johnson and invites her to sing in his band. Hw lures her with the promise of money he knows that she desperately needs, assuming she will sleep with him in return. Much to his disappointment, Boots is unable to pursue Lutie further because Mr. Junto tells him he wants her for himself. Sensing their motivations, Lutie trusts neither man and has no desire to sleep with either of them but plans simply to make money by singing. After Bub is jailed for theft, Lutie comes to Boots in desperation and asks to borrow money for Bub's bail. Boots agrees and tells her to come to a hotel room where Mr. Junto is waiting, assuming she will sleep with him for the money. Enraged, Lutie ends up kicking Mr. Junto out of the room and then murdering Boots with a candlestick when he makes sexual advances toward her. After he is dead, Lutie finds the door locked, indicating that Boots had intended to rape her.

THEMES

Pursuit of the American Dream

While working for the Chandlers, a white family of considerable wealth, Lutie is exposed to the idea that success and financial freedom are the guaranteed outcomes of hard work and perseverance—the American Dream. Determined to transcend her impoverished circumstances in Harlem, Lutie adopts this mentality and worries about money constantly. Her son, Bub, does not understand why Lutie is so concerned about money but wants to please her, so he tries to make money too. This leads to his imprisonment when William Jones takes advantage of his desire to earn his mother's love and tricks him into stealing letters. Unfortunately, as Petry successfully demonstrates in her novel, America was not a place of equal opportunity for African Americans or women in the 1940s. Lutie faces barriers of racial and gender discrimination as she tries to make money. Ultimately, she fails to achieve her dream of winning the fight against the street.

Racism and Discrimination against African Americans

As a single mother and African American woman, Lutie Johnson is discriminated against in every sector of her life—both personal and professional. Regarded as belonging to an inferior race, Lutie and the other African Americans in the story are unfairly denied many privileges and opportunities that are afforded to Anglo Americans. At the time Petry wrote her novel, housing in New York City was segregated by race and only certain buildings would rent apartments to black tenants—a form of institutional racism that severely limited the choices of African Americans. Like the other black residents of New York, Lutie wants desperately to get out of crowded Harlem but cannot because she lacks the financial resources to live elsewhere. The African American characters in Petry's novel are inextricably tied to Harlem by the rampant poverty and institutional racism that existed prior to (and to a certain extent after) the civil rights movement of the 1960s. This causes them to feel anger and frustration, as they are denied the rights and privileges that are afforded to others. These sentiments are exacerbated by the expectation that African Americans should fight alongside other Americans in World War II, for freedoms that differentially benefit white Americans.

Gender Disparities and Sexism

Equally salient in Petry's novel is the portrayal of sexism in the United States during the 1940s. In her search for a decent job, Lutie is treated as an object by men, who do not value her as a person. She feels she must hide the fact that she has a son because potential employers, like

TOPICS FOR FURTHER STUDY

- Discuss the impact Lutie's belief in the American Dream has on her life in *The Street*. How do her beliefs change over the course of the novel? Explain your view using examples from the novel. How is your view of the American Dream relevant to the sociopolitical climate of the United States today?

- In several places throughout *The Street*, Lutie alludes to Benjamin Franklin. What role does this serve in furthering the novel's themes and why does the author choose him? Write a persuasive essay explaining why Petry chooses to include this particular historical figure in the novel.

- Analyze the ending of *The Street*. Explain why Lutie abandons her child in *The Street*. Are her actions justified? Support your opinion with a close reading of the text.

- Compare and contrast the character of Lutie Johnson of *The Street* with the protagonist of Richard Wright's *Native Son* (1941). In what ways are their struggles similar? How can you account for the differences between them?

- Using a variety of sources, compare and contrast the opportunities available to African Americans living in New York City during the 1940s with those available today. Where have improvements been made? What work still needs to be done? Looking at your community or school, can you identify any ways in which people are discriminated against based on their race, ethnicity, or gender?

Boots, are only interested in her because of her potential as a romantic partner. As evidenced by the tragic outcome of the novel, hard work alone is not enough to transcend the barriers of race, gender, and class that exist in American society.

STYLE

Literary Naturalism

Literary realism is a style in which events are portrayed as they occur in real life. This style originated in France during the nineteenth century and made its way to America in the twentieth century. An outgrowth of the movement that accompanied the popularity of realism was a literary movement called naturalism. Naturalistic writers diverge from their realist counterparts in that naturalism seeks to understand the underlying reasons why things are the way they are, whereas realism aims only to describe them accurately. Many scholars consider Petry's work strongly naturalistic because her focus is on racism as an environmental force adversely affecting the lives of the African American characters in her work. Like Theodore Dreiser, Jack London, Stephen Crane, and Frank Norris, Petry trained in journalism, and characteristic of her work from this period is a detailed documentary style. Her short stories and *The Street* parallel the naturalistic work of other prominent Afro-American authors who published during the 1940s, including Richard Wright, Chester Himes, William Attaway, and Willard Motley.

Third-Person Omniscient Point of View

Petry's narrative mode in *The Street* is well suited to her naturalistic style. By writing in a third-person omniscient point of view, Petry gives readers a window into the thoughts and feelings of various characters as she shifts between events in the characters' memories of the past and experiences in the present. With this technique, Petry deftly demonstrates a nuanced understanding of the tense racial and gender relations that existed in the 1940s. She conveys a sense that no one individual is at fault for the disparities of privilege that exist between people, but rather that larger systemic forces such as poverty and institutional racism are to blame.

HISTORICAL CONTEXT

Rise of the Harlem Renaissance

After the abolition of slavery in 1865, the racial climate in the South became increasingly hostile toward African Americans. Lynch mobs and

Harlem *(© Bettmann / Corbis.)*

widespread violence posed a constant threat to the physical safety and well-being of these individuals and, as a result, many African Americans chose to migrate to northern states. Urban areas like New York City provided better access to jobs and schooling opportunities, and so they attracted the majority of the migrants. Some of these jobs were created by the American involvement in World War I, which generated a need for increased industrial production. While the Northern cities did provide increased opportunities for African Americans, racial discrimination was still ubiquitous and only certain areas of the cities, such as Harlem in New York, were available to black renters. As a result, African American communities were concentrated in densely populated neighborhoods that brought talented artists into close contact with one another.

During the early twentieth century, the artistic and intellectual work of African Americans blossomed, as many people strove to understand and express the black experiences of hardship and resilience. This surge in creative output was referred to as the Harlem Renaissance, and it grew steadily until the stock market crash of 1929, which drastically reduced the financial resources available to such artists. Petry arrived to work in Harlem as a journalist in the 1930s. While she was not in New York City during the height of the Harlem Renaissance, she was inspired to express her own impressions of the ghetto and drew upon the naturalistic tradition of her contemporaries.

World War II and the Drafting of African American Soldiers

Given the gross disparity in opportunities that were available to white and black Americans in the 1940s, it is not surprising that some African American men questioned the value of fighting a war to protect freedoms that were preferentially

COMPARE & CONTRAST

- **1940s:** As a result of the Harlem Renaissance, a flowering of artistic activity in the African American community of Harlem during the 1920s, the area was known as the black capital of America.

  Today: The population of Harlem remains predominantly black and is often pointed to by equal-rights activists as evidence that the quality of life for African Americans is still not equal to that of their white counterparts.

- **1940s:** The close living quarters made tuberculosis the number-one killer of African Americans living in Harlem, with rates almost four times as high as that of their white New York counterparts.

  Today: Chronic health problems continue to plague the residents of Harlem at rates disproportionately higher than those of residents of the rest of New York City.

- **1940s:** About 37 percent of African American women are employed. About 60 percent of working black women were domestic servants.

  Today: Almost 80 percent of African American women were employed in 2000, and most of them worked in government jobs, health-care-related jobs, or education.

afforded to white citizens at the expense of their black counterparts. In Petry's novel the character of Boots exemplifies the sentiments of black men who believed they were being drafted into a "white man's war."

CRITICAL OVERVIEW

Compared to books by Petry's female contemporaries, *The Street* enjoyed considerable popularity following its publication in 1946 and was the first novel by a female African American writer to sell over one million copies. Unfortunately, this popularity was relatively short-lived. In contrast to Richard Wright's *Native Son* (1941), Ralph Ellison's *Invisible Man* (1953), or James Baldwin's *The First Next Time* (1963), Petry's work received little critical attention between 1950 and 1985, when it was finally reissued. It then drew renewed interest from literary scholars. After reaching this pivotal point in its reception history, *The Street* and other works by Petry have become staples of African American literature courses—particularly those that emphasize feminist perspectives on the black experience.

CRITICISM

Laura K. Noll

Noll is a literary scholar with research interests in comparative literature and psychoanalytic theory. In the following essay, she argues that the persuasive power of Petry's work can be traced to the changing perceptions of her characters as their experience of space shifts in response to their experiences of oppression.

While often treated as a realist novel about the interior lives of its characters and their internal experiences of oppression, Ann Petry's *The Street* may also be read as a powerful protest novel—one with the potential to provoke specific political and social changes for the benefit of African Americans and women. Like the other black characters in Petry's work, the novel's protagonist Lutie Johnson and her son Bub are victims of an institutional racism that grants privileges to Anglo Americans while denying them to African Americans. By crafting Lutie as beautifully human, while simultaneously paying close attention to the relationship that exists between physical space and freedom, Petry persuades readers that white people bear the ultimate responsibility for the fate of her characters.

Harlem street (*UPI* / *Corbis-Bettmann*)

To make her protest against institutional racism rhetorically compelling, Petry must successfully dispel the misguided notion that problems of the ghetto may be attributed to some failing on the part of its residents. For this purpose her determined protagonist, Lutie Johnson, is perfect. Willing to do anything short of selling her body for money, Lutie makes every effort to escape the physical walls of her apartment in Harlem and overcome the many racial barriers to opportunity that press in on her with increasing force as she moves closer to her tragic fate. While certainly misguided in her belief that the pursuit of the American Dream will be fruitful, Lutie works with integrity to feed and clothe her only son. As a strong, beautiful woman, she evokes the sympathy of readers, who cannot help but admire her strength and perseverance while those around her insist that she succumb to the lure of easy money by prostituting herself—a proposition that Lutie rejects in spite of her

desperation. With Lutie's uncompromising attitude toward her body, Petry insists to readers that black people are human. In his famous essay "Everybody's Protest Novel," writer James Baldwin critiques the genre of protest fiction popular with African American authors, arguing that the "failure of the protest novel lies in its rejection of life, the human being, the denial of beauty." With the very human, sympathetic Lutie, Petry appears to succeed where her contemporaries fail.

Intimately tied to the success of her protest is Petry's treatment of space. In the beginning of the novel, Petry introduces the idea that Lutie's perception of space is tied to her life journey: "As the train gathered speed for the long run to 125th Street, the passengers settled down into small private worlds, thus creating the illusion of space between them and their fellow passengers." Implying that everyone has a need for a private psychological world, Petry's description

UNFORTUNATELY, AS BECOMES
INCREASINGLY OBVIOUS THROUGHOUT THE NOVEL,
THE ESCAPES AVAILABLE TO AFRICAN AMERICANS,
ESPECIALLY WOMEN AND CHILDREN IN HARLEM,
ARE NO MORE THAN DANGEROUS TRAPS THAT SEAL
THEIR FATE. "

of the crowded train suggests that a relationship exists between the need for physical and psychological space. The train is in motion, serving as a metaphor for Lutie's life journey and the processes of changing race relations in the inner-city. By introducing Lutie's experience of changing physical and psychological spaces in a neutral context relevant to all people regardless of race, Petry builds a foundation onto which she can build an argument with universal appeal:

> She noticed that once the crowd walked the length of the platform and started up the stairs toward the street, it expanded in size. The same people who had made themselves small on the train, even on the platform, suddenly grew so large they could hardly get up the stairs to the street together.

The crowd that Lutie observes is implicitly diverse but moves together, suggesting from the start that Lutie's journey concerns us all.

As the story progresses, Lutie's experience of a need for space grows in its specific relevance to the black experience of the impoverished ghettos in Harlem. No longer describing the details of an experience to which all New York City residents can relate, Petry writes about the inadequate living conditions of the inner city neighborhoods, explaining, "The trouble is that these rooms are so small. After she had been in them just a few minutes, the walls seemed to come in toward her, to push against her." Likewise, Lutie's desire to find a better place to live is framed in terms of a need for space: "Now that she had this apartment, perhaps the next thing she ought to do was to find another one with bigger rooms." Again keeping the prejudices of white readers at bay, Petry conveys Lutie's experience in terms that are not racially specific while simultaneously evoking sympathy for Lutie's

struggle. By keeping the focus in the beginning of the book on Lutie's experience of Harlem's poverty, rather than on race, which was extremely controversial during the 1940s (the United States Army was still segregated racially during World War II and in the occupation of Germany thereafter, for instance), Petry invites white readers to empathize with the need for escape, "No matter what it cost them, people had to come to places like the Junto ... so they could believe in themselves again," and with the powerful relief provided by the illusion of increased space:

> The big mirror in front of her made the Junto an enormous room. It pushed the walls back and back into space. ... It pushed the world of people's kitchen sinks back where it belonged and destroyed the existence of the dirty streets and small shadowed rooms.

Unfortunately, as becomes increasingly obvious throughout the novel, the escapes available to African Americans, especially women and children in Harlem, are no more than dangerous traps that seal their fate. Like the adult characters in Harlem who are lured by the illusion of space at Junto's bar, Bub—an innocent child—is lured by the space William Jones inhabits in the cellar of their apartment building, since "there was so much space down here, too." In the warmth of the fire and the attention of Jones, Bub's perception of reality shifts dangerously into line with that of the malicious superintendent,

> This was real. The other was a bad dream. Going upstairs after school to a silent, empty house was not real either. This was the reality. This great, warm, open space was where he really belonged. Supe was captain of the detectives and he, Bub, was his most valued henchman.

Only, Supe is not the captain of detectives. He is a desperate man acting like a caged animal in his devious ploy to hurt Lutie and Bub. "He had been chained to buildings until he was like an animal," a fact that Petry underscores through the cruelty of his subsequent actions.

Like Lutie's, the parallel struggles of other adult women in the novel are tragic. Lutie's unsuccessful attempts to find more space for herself and Bub are not unlike Mrs. Hedges's escape from a burning building, "determined that she would force her body through the narrow window." Like Mrs. Hedges, Lutie survives the novel physically, escaping on a train to Chicago; however, also like Mrs. Hedges, she withdraws from the people who love her.

WHAT DO I READ NEXT?

- *Iola Leroy* (1892), a novel by Frances Harper. The protagonist of this story, a biracial woman who is the child of a slave owner and a slave, refuses to conceal her racial identity and instead chooses to fight for racial equality.

- *The Autobiography of an Ex-Colored Man* (1912), an autobiography by James Weldon Johnson. In this work, the biracial author struggles in post-Reconstruction America to choose between expressing his racial identity as half-African American and hiding in obscurity by pretending to be white.

- *Not without Laughter* (1930), a novel by Langston Hughes. In this story about the reality of being black in a small Kansas town during the 1920s, the protagonist, Sandy, struggles to live life in the face of racial prejudice and discrimination.

- *Native Son* (1940), a novel by Richard Wright. This book tells the story of an African American man living in a Chicago ghetto under conditions of racism and violence. He accidentally kills a white woman, rapes and kills his girlfriend, and then must come to terms with the consequences of his crimes.

- *Black Boy* (1945), an autobiography by Richard Wright. This book tells the story of the author's difficult experiences growing up in the racially prejudice South.

- In *The Narrows* (1953), Petry tells the story of love between a Negro man and a married white woman, giving readers a window into the relationships that exist between race, class, and gender in the 1950s.

- *Invisible Man* (1952), a novel by Ralph Waldo Ellison. Because of racial prejudice and inequality, the narrator of this story, an African American man, feels socially invisible to mainstream culture.

- *Harriet Tubman: Conductor of the Underground Railroad* (1955), is Petry's biography of the slave girl who escaped to freedom, returned, and led three hundred other slaves to the North by way of the Underground Railroad.

- *Beloved* (1987), a novel by Toni Morrison. Based on the life of Margaret Garner, a slave, this Pulitzer Prize–winning story follows Sethe and her daughter after their escape from slavery.

Where Mrs. Hedges withdraws from Mr. Junto, who genuinely admires and respects her, Lutie withdraws from her son when she abandons him at the Children's Shelter. By aligning the plights of her characters, Petry bridges the gap between her feminine ideal, Lutie, and those characters who gave up the futile fight against institutional racism long ago, thereby extending the implications of Lutie's story to all African Americans who are forced to live in the ghettos of the inner city by unfair governmental and business lending practices.

In contrast to the insight she develops later in the novel, Lutie's early view is relatively limited: "[Lutie] hummed as she listened to it, not really aware that she was humming or why, knowing only that she felt free here where there was so much space." As she continues to come up against the forces of institutional sexism and racism, her perspective begins to shift into a deeper understanding of her own oppression—encouraging readers, who have come to sympathize with her, to shift their perspective on race relations as well. As Lutie discovers after noticing the disparity between her own observations of an event and the way it is presented in the newspaper, "it all depended on where you sat how these things looked." Viewing her situation from a new vantage point after experiencing multiple setbacks in her attempt to find decent work, Lutie begins to recognize that her situation is not unique: "It was a bad street. And then she thought about the other streets. It wasn't just this street that she was afraid was bad. It was any street where people were packed together like sardines in a can. And it wasn't just this city." Here, Lutie begins to understand and clarify for the reader the relationship between housing segregation (a situation created in part by unfair mortgage lending practices) and the poverty of African Americans, thinking,

> It was any city where they set up a line and say black folks stay on this side and white folks stay on this side, so that black folks were crammed on top of each other—jammed and packed and forced into the smallest possible space until they were completely cut off from the light and air.

By the time Lutie comes to the conclusion that it is white people who are responsible for the situation in Harlem, readers are so invested in Lutie's perspective that they cannot help agreeing with her when she declares, "No one could live on a street like this and stay decent. It would get them sooner or later, for it sucked the humanity out of people—slowly, surely, inevitably."

As the novel careens toward its devastating conclusion, Lutie herself becomes less able to feel human. After her audition with Mr. Crosse for a position as a singer, Lutie feels trapped, and comes to realize that her attempts to escape have been futile because "from the time she was born, she had been hemmed into an ever-narrowing space, until now she was very nearly walled in and the wall had been built up brick by brick by eager white hands." Nor can she control the anger she feels in response to being trapped: "She was neatly caged here on this street and tonight's experience had increased this growing frustration and hatred in her." To preemptively counter those readers who are inclined to disagree, Lutie's perspective is immediately juxtaposed with that of Bub's white teacher, Miss Rinner, who incorrectly attributes the erratic animal-like behavior of her black students to their lack of morality rather than differences in privilege that existed between white and black residents of New York.

The persuasive power of Petry's carefully crafted work can be traced to the changing perceptions of *The Street*'s characters as they experience changes in the space available to them in response to their experiences of oppression. By quietly earning the readers's sympathy for Lutie as a human being and then gradually introducing readers to the idea that white people are to blame for the one-way train Lutie boarded at

birth, Petry gives herself a chance to be heard by white and black readers alike and succeeds in protesting the status quo.

Source: Laura Noll, Critical Essay on *The Street*, in *Novels for Students*, Gale, Cengage Learning, 2010.

Heather J. Hicks
In the following article, Hicks explores Petry's rhetorical choices in The Street.

> She stood there thinking that it was really a pity they couldn't somehow manage to rent the halls, too. Single beds. No. Old army cots would do. It would bring in so much more money. If she were a landlord, she'd rent out the hallways. It would make it so much more entertaining for the tenants. Mr. Jones and wife could have cots number one and two; Jackson and girl friend could occupy number three. And Rinaldi, who drove a cab nights, could sublet the one occupied by Jackson and girl friend.
>
> She would fill up all the cots—row after row of them. And when the tenants who had apartments came in late at night, they would have the added pleasure of checking up on the occupants. Jackson not home yet but girl friend lying in the cot alone—all curled up. A second look, because the lack of light wouldn't show all the details, would reveal—ye gods, why, what's Rinaldi doing home at night! Doggone if he ain't tucked up cozily in Jackson's cot with Jackson's girl friend. No wonder she looked contented. And the tenants who had apartments would sit on the stairs just as though the hall were a theater and the performance about to start—they'd sit there waiting until Jackson came home to see what he'd do when he found Rinaldi tucked into the cot with his girl friend.

In this early passage from Ann Petry's novel, The Street, protagonist Lutie Johnson muses with both irony and indignation on the violations of privacy that segregation and its attendant over-crowding engender in 1940s Harlem. Because in this scene Lutie is confronting both severe financial difficulties and the grim prospect of renting an apartment in the tenement that she is scrutinizing, one might interpret her arch fantasy of beds in the halls as nothing more than a bitter indictment of slumlordship and the social ills it breeds. Students of literary realism, however, will recognize in this passage a familiar self-reflexive gesture toward the complex scopic politics of that genre. As Mark Seltzer has demonstrated, writers from Charles Dickens to sensationalist social commentator George R. Sims have figured their representations of urban spaces

> PETRY CHALLENGES THE VERY INTEGRITY OF
> THE "KNOWLEDGE" THE REALIST NOVEL SEEMS TO
> OFFER READERS, ULTIMATELY SUBVERTING THE
> VISION-KNOWLEDGE-POWER FIELD THROUGH THE
> RHETORICAL FORM OF THE QUESTION"

in such "theatrical" terms, characterizing their very act of describing life in the modern city as a "taking down of the fourth wall" (33). In this case, Lutie's cynical vision of exposing beds and their occupants' indiscretions can be read as a moment of self-scrutiny by Petry herself. Petry seems to ask whether, in her attempt to dramatize the traumas of racism and segregation, she is actually exploiting those she wishes to champion, turning the intimate dramas of their lives into a public spectacle for her own gain. Is she, in short, a slumlord of the imagination, creating through literature a space that exposes the lives of African Americans to public scrutiny in a way few slumlords in the material world would dare?

In his meditation on the novels of Henry James, Seltzer argues that the realist and naturalist project of enjoining readers to a position of spectatorship is fully implicated in another mode of seeing, that of "surveillance and policing" (45). The passage from The Street I have quoted above certainly shows traces of such a collaboration, traces of the "twin operations of vision and supervision, of spectatorship and incrimination" that Seltzer locates in realist and naturalist novels (34). For Lutie not only imagines a scene in which the lives of Harlem denizens become theater; she also characterizes the arrangement as one in which the tenants "check up" on one another. Such surveillance, Petry implies, would be motivated by a sense that wrongs are going to be committed, that a norm or standard of conduct, which Foucault suggests always underwrites acts of supervision, will be violated and that that violation must be somehow registered (*Discipline and Punish* 177–84). If we accept the correspondence that I sketched above between the scene this passage depicts and Petry's own project of exposing the complexities of Harlem life to public scrutiny, then here we can imagine

that Petry is acknowledging the degree to which her book not only sells the spectacle of Harlem, but polices it as well.

Indeed, as I will show, Petry's novel does in fact persistently question its own practices of surveillance. It is here, however, that my reading of Petry's realist project parts company with Seltzer's treatment of James's work. For in the course of reviewing James's self-conscious examinations of practices of spectatorship and surveillance, Seltzer concludes not only that James's defiance of the policing functions of realism fails, but that resisting "power" through acts of realist writing is itself an essentially fruitless enterprise. Conversely, I want to suggest the ways that Petry's self-conscious negotiation of these issues produces a commentary on the (racial) politics of realism that effectively exposes and dismantles the power structures encoded into that genre. Specifically, I will suggest the ways that Petry challenges the very integrity of the "knowledge" the realist novel seems to offer readers, ultimately subverting the vision-knowledge-power field through the rhetorical form of the question, a mode of discourse that neither resists nor cooperates but instead leaves open a possibility that cannot be neatly classified as either the order or disorder that Foucault and his admirers understand as the pistons of power.

James, of course, was a very different writer than Petry; while much of Seltzer's effort is given to countering the work of critics who have contended that James eschewed politics in his novels, no critic could fail to miss the overt political work Petry undertook, not only in The Street, but also in her later short stories and novels, especially The Narrows. Despite their different approaches to matters of politics, however, the parallels between the work of James and Petry make Seltzer's discussion an excellent sounding board for Petry's first novel. Seltzer has demonstrated that in James's *The Princess Cassimassima*, a "reciprocal watchfulness... invests every relation" between characters; it is a text, that is, in which characters are constantly described in the act of regarding one another. I would suggest that Seltzer's claim that *The Princess Cassimassima* reflects "a generalized extension of the power of watching and policing" (40, 44), is equally appropriate for The Street. Virtually every page of Petry's novel is suffused with images of characters watching one another, suggesting that Petry, like James, is deeply interested in the "power of watching."

Seltzer ultimately argues that, by rejecting the practice of omniscient narration, James attempts to separate "'mere' seeing, consciousness, and knowledge [from]... an exercise of power" (55). Yet, according to Seltzer, James fails to achieve this separation. Indeed, Seltzer claims that James's effort should be understood as a "ruse" that remystifies "the realist policing of the real" by "recuperat[ing it] as the 'innocent' work of the imagination" (56). And within his larger project, Seltzer argues that this failure to disarm realism is, from a Foucauldian perspective, a consequence of the very pervasiveness of power:

> The 'literary' contradiction between autonomy and regulation (between 'liberation' and 'repression') has the circular efficiency of the normalizing operation. The very instability and oscillation between the terms of the double reading deploy the power such a reading seems to deplore. This exit from power is a revolving door. (184–85)

It is here that I believe that Petry's novel can be productively read against the grain of Seltzer's work. For while Seltzer treats the "techniques of the novel" as inescapably implicated in regulatory power dynamics, through her discourse on race and knowledge, Petry succeeds where, according to Seltzer, James fails. Petry, that is, both critiques looking relations within the content of her text and self-consciously resists the narrative techniques of realism that reinforce the policing effects of acts of looking.

Before delineating how Petry critiques the realist genre she is deploying—how she "disown[s] the policing that it implies," to borrow Seltzer's phrase (54)—I must briefly return to the stakes of such resistance for a black realist writer. Twigg, in his Foucauldian reading of Jacob Riis's *How the Other Half Lives,* trenchantly formulates how acts of surveillance have had particular repercussions for non-whites: "Techniques of surveillance," he writes, "such as the gathering of statistics, monitoring living conditions, collecting census data—in short, making immigrant and working classes visible—could transform 'alien' populations into an exploitable labor and consumer force" (308). Twigg argues that realism enacted a particularly pernicious form of this scopic management: "In subtle, yet ideologically powerful ways, documentary realism poetically transformed the surveyed Other into a manageable, containable,

and usable fiction who, in the process, was politically marginalized" (309).

While Twigg is specifically referring to photography in his account, his emphasis on the double function of realism both to contain and to construct racialized others suggests, in a way that Seltzer's discussion does not, how, precisely, realism could be undervise the common designation of Lutie as a "blind" character, and then explore how precisely one might better understand Lutie's relationship to seeing and knowing in the text.

According to most critics, Lutie is blinded by an American ideology of individualism and self-making that renders invisible the insurmountable barriers created by racial prejudice. And indeed, Petry certainly depicts Lutie as profoundly influenced by her contact with the Chandlers, a wealthy white family who had employed her in their suburban Connecticut home prior to the central action of the novel. In the course of the second chapter, Petry offers an extended flashback to the insidious and lasting impact that the Chandlers' value system has had on Lutie. Dazzled by their wealth and the ease of their lives, Lutie comes to believe that such a life might be attainable for her and her husband:

> After a year of listening to their talk, she absorbed some of the same spirit. The belief that anybody could be rich if he wanted to and worked hard enough and figured it out carefully enough... She and Jim could do the same thing, and she thought she saw what had been wrong with them before—they hadn't tried hard enough, worked long enough, saved enough. There hadn't been any one thing they wanted above and beyond everything else. These people had wanted only one thing—more and more money—and so they got it. Some of this new philosophy crept into her letters to Jim.

This sensibility about hard work and equal opportunity will surface again and again as Lutie battles the obstacles that foil her attempts to move away from 116th Street. Yet while other critics treat Lutie's adherence to the "American Dream" as blindness, I would situate it in terms of Petry's interest in the fundamentally local character of ideas that are naturalized as universal truth.

Importantly, Petry arranges this flashback chapter so that Lutie's memories of the Chandlers are triggered by an image she sees while riding on the train:

Like some of the other passengers, she was staring at the advertisement directly in front of her and as she stared at it she became absorbed in her own thoughts. So that she, too, entered a small private world which shut out the people tightly packed around her.

For the advertisement she was looking at pictured a girl with incredible blond hair. The girl leaned close to a dark-haired, smiling man in a navy uniform. They were standing in front of a kitchen sink—a sink whose white porcelain surface gleamed under the train lights. The faucets looked like silver. The linoleum floor of the kitchen was a crisp black-and-white pattern that pointed up the sparkle of the room. Casement windows. Red geraniums in yellow pots.

This image, which she turns to look at once more at the conclusion of the chapter, links the ideology of possessive individualism that Lutie has internalized to a visual arena in which material wealth and whiteness enjoy a normative status of "truth" that racial others can only labor futilely to realize. Neither the construction of white femininity nor the material abundance made plainly visible in this image is Lutie's "reality." Petry's choice to access Lutie's memory of the Chandlers through such a visual image becomes one of the first of many instances in which Petry challenges the reliability or universality of knowledge derived from visual information.

It is not that Lutie cannot see, then; rather, she underestimates the degree to which the meaning of what she sees is contingent on her marginalized position. Certainly, as a consequence of such images, Lutie attempts to live her life according to principles that she has no real hope of effectively deploying in a racist and segregated society. Yet, overall, Petry represents Lutie as anything but blind; rather, Lutie is more often depicted as an apt observer of the several levels on which the street functions. Indeed, I would argue that Petry is intent on suggesting *how much* Lutie sees in order to question the degree to which the knowledge she gleans from vision can empower her.

In fact, in its very first scene The Street establishes Lutie's ability to see and interpret her world. In this remarkable opening, which reflects her debt to naturalism, Petry fuses the activities of seeing, reading, and knowing, setting the key terms for the remainder of the novel. As Lutie approaches the building that will become the setting of the novel, she spies a sign advertising an available apartment. As she looks up a violent wind whips the sign back and forth,

so that "Each time she thought she had the sign in focus, the wind pushed it away from her so that she wasn't certain whether it said three rooms or two rooms." What is striking about this passage is precisely Lutie's ability to see and interpret her world in spite of the hostile climate through which she moves. Defying the wind, Lutie immediately begins to discern information from the sign:

Even with the wind twisting the sign away from her, she could see that it had been there for a long time because its original coat of white paint was streaked with rust where years of rain and snow had finally eaten the paint off down to the metal and the metal had slowly rusted, making a dark red stain like blood.

She then sees even more: "The wind held it still for an instant in front of her and then swooped it away until it was standing at an impossible angle on the rod that suspended it from the building. She read it rapidly. Three rooms, steam heat, parquet floors, respectable tenants. Reasonable." In the paragraphs that follow, Lutie produces a gloss of these few words, reflecting that the meaning of the words on the sign are specific to their context on this street:

She looked at the outside of the building. Parquet floors here meant that the wood was so old and so discolored no amount of varnish or shellac would conceal the scars and the old scraped places, the years of dragging furniture across the floors, the hammer blows of time and children and drunks and dirty slovenly women. Steam heat meant a rattling, clanging noise in radiators early in the morning and then a hissing that went on all day.

With this scene, the novel establishes Lutie's more typical adroitness: her "street knowledge," which is highly developed and precise. The exegesis that she produces proves to be entirely accurate once she has entered the building itself.

Yet equally striking and poignant in this opening scene is the uselessness of Lutie's perceptiveness. The building's interior is indeed nightmarish, and she senses the rapacious madness of the Super. Yet even as she thinks that, "No, she didn't want to see the apartment—the dark, dirty three rooms called an apartment," she answers, "Yes," to the Super's invitation to view it. Moreover, after seeing the apartment and realizing that the menacing Super wants her to take the apartment "so badly that he's bursting with it," she thinks, "no... not that apartment," yet ultimately, "grimly," says that she will take it. While this sense of entrapment reflects the influence of naturalism on The Street, the degree to which Lutie self-consciously sees and analyzes her predicament takes the text beyond the usual terms of determinism.

Indeed, by establishing both that Lutie sees and understands the complex layers of meaning that comprise the world around her—explicitly in this case through reading—and that such knowledge is of little value, Petry merges elements of naturalism with a critique of realist epistemology. Throughout the remainder of the text, Lutie again and again astutely reads the behavior and circumstances of those with whom she interacts. Yet in a key passage early in the text, Petry formulates even more explicitly the possibility that seeing and knowing might provide no justice or other benefits to the residents of Harlem, localized as that knowledge is within the disempowered realm of a segregated ghetto. As Lutie walks through her neighborhood observing the inequities of wealth and poverty, she muses:

> This world was one of great contrasts, she thought, and if the richest part of it was to be fenced off so that people like herself could only look at it with no expectation of ever being able to get inside it, then it would be better to have been born blind so you couldn't see it, born deaf so you couldn't hear it, born with no sense of touch so you couldn't feel it. Better still, born with no brain so that you would be completely unaware of anything, so that you would never know there were places that were filled with sunlight and good food and where children were safe.

Even as the central consciousness of the text scans and registers the environment around her on behalf of Petry's readers, that same consciousness challenges the usefulness of the knowledge that is being transmitted to readers. What, Petry's novel asks here, is the value of recognizing or understanding racism in a profoundly racist society?

The relevance of this question to Petry's own project becomes even more apparent in the two sections of the novel where the text most overtly shifts to a realist mode. In each, Petry produces muck-raking accounts of some of the most virulent effects of racism with the apparent intent of enhancing the knowledge of her readers; yet built into each of these passages is an overt challenge to the reliability of any such reporting and an insistence that racism itself perfectly exemplifies the situated nature of all knowledge.

In the first of these passages Lutie reflects on a number of scenes of injustice that she has witnessed in the streets of Harlem. As a reporter, Petry actually observed a number of these episodes herself. Yet regardless of their actual status as incidents she documented during her years as a reporter, the events she narrates, in which a young indigent black man is stabbed by a white store owner, and two women are knifed by jealous lovers, are distinguished by a precise attention to detail that marks them as expressions of a realist current in the text. Petry carefully describes the remembered scene of the young stabbing victim, sprawled on the street:

> But the thing she had never been able to forget were his shoes. Only the uppers were intact. They had once been black, but they were now a dark dull gray from long wear. The soles were worn out. They were mere flaps attached to the uppers. She could see the layers of wear. The first outer layer of leather was left near the edges, and then the great gaping holes in the center where the leather had worn out entirely, so that for weeks he must have walked practically barefooted on the pavement.

Having constructed this almost microscopically detailed account of the man's shoes, Petry moves from the technology of transparency constituted by such realist prose to a more self-conscious interrogation of whether the event she has reported is objectively knowable. Lutie recalls reading an account of the incident in the newspaper the following day:

> She held the paper in her hand for a long time, trying to follow the reasoning by which that thin ragged boy had become in the eyes of a reporter a 'burly Negro.' And she decided that it all depended on where you sat how these things looked. If you looked at them from inside the framework of a fat weekly salary, and you thought of colored people as naturally criminal, then you didn't really see what any Negro looked like. You couldn't, because the Negro was never an individual. He was a threat, or an animal, or a curse, or a blight, or a joke.

> It was like the Chandlers and their friends in Connecticut, who looked at her and didn't see her, but saw instead a wench with no morals who would be easy to come by. The reporter saw a dead Negro who had attempted to hold up a store, and so he couldn't really see what the man lying on the sidewalk looked like. He couldn't see the ragged shoes, the thin, starved body. He saw, instead, the picture he already had in his mind: a huge, brawny, blustering, ignorant, criminally disposed black man who

had run amok with a knife on a spring afternoon
in Harlem and who had in turn been knifed.

Here, by dismissing the possibility of seeing
outside of a historically and socially constructed
subject position, Petry's novel disassembles the
"rigorous continuity" between seeing and knowing that Seltzer associates with realism. The rec-
iprocity between seeing and knowing ("He saw,
instead, the picture he already had in his mind")
destabilizes the notion that realism transforms a
visible reality into objective knowledge for
readers.

Equally important to Petry's critique of the
interface between sight and knowledge in relation
to race is a later chapter of the text, in which Petry
depicts the public school system in Harlem. By
depicting the public school as an institution
where the "knowledge" that is being dispersed is
racial prejudice, Petry again challenges the integrity of knowledge itself even as she implements the
epistemological technologies of realist prose. Petry
herself worked as a volunteer in an elementary
school in Harlem and clearly had firsthand knowledge of the conditions in the schools. Once again,
however, the formal details of the chapter project a
visual "reality" that demand a reader's trust,
regardless of their origins in Petry's own experience. Petry presents the chapter through the consciousness of Miss Rinner, a white, racist teacher
who finds her black pupils unbearably repugnant:
"when the class assembled, the sight of their dark
skins, the sound of the soft blurred speech that
came from their throats, filled her with the hysterical desire to scream." It is the "sight" of the children that informs all of Rinner's responses to
them, but as in her other metadiscursive passages,
here Petry refuses to locate vision as simply the
origin of racism; instead it is represented as part of
a set of reciprocal, mutually generative relations.
What Rinner sees, that is, is not an objective reality, but instead a perception always already shaped
by her subject position as an embattled, racist
white woman.

To convey the contaminated nature of the
"knowledge" Rinner disseminates to her students,
The Street details her daily encounters with the
population of Harlem and the almost infinite
forms her hatred for them takes. She sees African
Americans as "a people without restraint, without
decency, with no moral code." She then carries this
view into her interactions with her students, whom
she regards as incorrigible and unteachable:

> And now, as she watched the continual motion
> of the young bodies behind the battered old

desks in front of her, she thought, They're like
animals—sullen-tempered one moment, full of
noisy laughter the next. Even at eight and nine
they knew the foulest words, the most disgust-
ing language. Working in this school was like
being in a jungle. It was filled with the smell of
the jungle, she thought: tainted food, rank,
unwashed bodies.

The reference to blacks as animals here echoes the earlier moment when the reporter produces a racist account of the young slain man.
Knowledge production and dissemination are
again represented as fully implicated in racist
social dynamics from which they cannot be extri-
cated. Petry resists realism's simple continuum
between sight and knowledge by once again inti-
mating that there are infinite, often competing,
ways to see a given person or event.

In the final scene of Petry's novel, she again
issues this challenge as Lutie at last grasps the
enormity of the forces against which she has
been battling. When one of Junto's employees
attempts to rape her, her despair becomes rage,
and she beats her attacker to death, destroying
her own dreams of a better life in the process.
Importantly, the implement Lutie uses to lash
out against Boots—the man onto whom she
projects all of the destructive forces of which
she has become aware—is a candlestick. The
candlestick becomes in part an answer to the
phallic flashlight with which the Super terrorized
Lutie in the opening pages of the novel. Lutie's
counter-assault on Boots is itself a rape—an act
of power in which Boots stands in for the larger
dynamics over which Lutie cannot exercise any
control. Yet introduced as it is at the moment in
the narrative when Lutie finally acquires knowledge of Junto's plotting, the candlestick also
symbolizes the phallogocentric knowledge that
is reified by white power. Consistent with the
theme that Petry has developed throughout the
text, this form of knowledge harms and entraps
Lutie even as she wields it.

In her meditation on vision and epistemology, "The Persistence of Vision," Donna Haraway argues that "a usable, but not innocent,
doctrine of objectivity" can emerge from
embracing "the particularity and embodiment
of all vision." Again and again, Petry captures
this notion of situated knowledge, not merely by
changing the perspective from which the text is
narrated, but by aggressively dislocating knowledge from an abstract arena of truth and utility.
As Lutie remarks early in the text, "perhaps

because she was born with skin that color, she couldn't see anything wrong with it." Such is the dilemma of all of the characters in the text who attempt to arrive at unified knowledge in a society riven by a racism that fragments consciousness. While Seltzer argues that realist writers, in offering resistance to the policing effects of their prose, are merely complying with "the 'double *discourse*' of disavowal and reinscription" that fuels "modern power arrangements of discipline and normalization" (174 emphasis mine), Petry asserts double *consciousness* as a means of neutralizing the stable, regulatory effects that serve such power. Haraway writes:

> I am arguing for politics and epistemologies of location, positioning, and situating, where partiality and not universality is the condition of being heard to make rational knowledge claims. These are claims on people's lives. I am arguing for the view from a body, always a complex, contradictory, structuring, and structured body, versus the view from above, from nowhere, from simplicity.

It is this view that Petry provides by denying the simplicity of the vision-knowledge axis that realism typically underwrites.

Ultimately, however, Petry does not simply reject the stability of knowledge, and in doing so dismiss the very project she has undertaken as useless. Instead, Petry constructs her text as a question, a riddle for the reader that resituates knowledge in their own bodies. As she flees from the city, leaving Bub still incarcerated in the Children's Home, Lutie ponders the events that have led her to such devastation. At last, the question that the text has asked again and again is articulated for readers:

> As the train started to move, she began to trace a design on the window. It was a series of circles that flowed into each other. She remembered that when she was in grammar school the children were taught to get the proper slant to their writing, to get the feel of a pen in their hands, by making these same circles. Once again she could hear the flat, exasperated voice of the teacher as she looked at the circles Lutie had produced. 'Really,' she said, 'I don't know why they have us bother to teach your people to write.'
>
> Her finger moved over the glass, around and around. The circles showed up plainly on the dusty surface. The woman's statement was correct, she thought. What possible good has it done to teach people like me to write? (435–36)

Here Petry seems to indict her own inability to escape from the circular logic of racism that is fed by the differential looking relations she has mapped in her novel. What good has it done to teach *Ann Petry* to write, the reader must reflect. Yet, I maintain that the answer lies in the question itself: precisely by posing such a question, Petry escapes from the "normalizing operation" of what Seltzer describes as the "'literary' contradiction between autonomy and regulation." In place of the "exit from power [that] is a revolving door" (184–85), Petry opens the possibility of subverting the policing function of the realist form by replacing the pretense of any definitive mode of knowledge with an open invitation to the reader to question the very essence of the text she has constructed—that is, its claim to provide the reader with objective knowledge of the place and time she describes. The rhetorical form of the question, placed at the very conclusion of the text, punctuates the entire novel with a question mark. Satisfied with neither complicity nor resistance, Petry reimagines realism as the liberating act of interrogation itself.

Source: Heather J. Hicks, "Rethinking Realism in Ann Petry's 'The Street,'" in *MELUS*, Vol. 27, No. 4, Winter 2002, pp. 89–105.

Barbara Christian

In the following article, Christian traces out key moments in Petry's career and compares the success of her work to that of her contemporaries.

Last February Houghton Mifflin reissued Ann Petry's first novel, The Street, which it was fortunate enough to publish to much acclaim in 1946. This work was the first novel by an African American woman to focus on the struggles of a working-class black mother in an urban ghetto, and a reissue in a quality edition is long overdue.

In the 1920s and 30s, African Americans published novels centered on urban women. But these—Jessie Fauset's *Plum Bun* (1929), for example, or Nella Larsen's *Quicksand* (1923)—portrayed middle-class female protagonists usually childless, whose lives, despite their class status, are gravely constrained by the sexism and racism of urban America. African American male writers—Richard Wright in *Native Son* (1941), or William Attaway in *Blood on the Forge* (1941)—wrote protest novels to dramatize how the lower-class or working-class status of their black male characters determined their tragic fate. Zora Neale Hurston built *Their Eyes*

Were Watching God (1937) on a black woman's search for fulfillment in a rural community. But few African American writers in the first half of this century attempted to gauge the effect of the urban ghetto on the sexism and racism that African American women had always confronted.

Ann Perry's graphic portrayal of the inevitable downfall of her character, Lutie Johnson, is remarkable for its intensity of focus. By constructing a proletarian protest novel from the point of view of a black woman, Petry both criticized and developed that genre. Given the fact that millions of African American women live in conditions like those of The Street, and when one considers the emphasis on urban racial issues in the sixties and on women's issues in the seventies, one has to wonder why this novel is not better known, more accepted.

I first saw a copy of The Street in the early seventies. I'd been teaching supposedly "uneducable" Harlem blacks and Puerto Ricans at City College in New York, and had learned what might now seem obvious but was then considered radical—that if my students were presented with books that related to their lives, they "miraculously" became passionate about reading and writing. Because in those times only a few books by blacks were regularly available at "normal" bookstores, I periodically combed Harlem's thrift stores for discarded books.

It was in one of those unintellectual places that I found a dingy copy of The Street. I was drawn to its cover—a brash photograph of an attractive black woman in wintry urban clothing framed by bold print: "She was a soul on ice in a brutal ghetto"—words which gave me the mistaken impression that the novel was influenced by that literary blockbuster of 1968, Eldridge Cleaver's *Soul on Ice.* Unconsciously registering the fact that a woman's book was being authenticated by a man's, I wondered how I could have missed such a rare event—a new novel by a black woman.

I would soon discover that the much-used paperback I'd bought for ten cents was the eighth printing of a 1961 reissue of a novel originally published in 1946. Ann Perry was not a new writer: my Pyramid reissue had been cleverly packaged to take advantage of the country's then intense interest in the black ghetto, particularly its raging male inhabitants, a result of the response to "race riots" that swept major US cities in the 1960s. That interest was too short-lived to keep many such books in print. The few

that did survive were written by men: Richard Wright's *Native Son* (1941), James Baldwin's *The Fire Next Time* (1963), Ralph Ellison's *Invisible Man* (1953). Nor were even these books usually taught in literature classes, since African American literature apparently did not exist; they were more likely to turn up on sociology class lists, where blacks were seen as appropriate objects of inquiry.

No wonder then that The Street has had its ups and downs. In print and acclaimed in the late 1940s, it was ignored for much of the 50s. Reissued in the early 1960s, it was difficult to obtain for much of the 1970s and 80s. In 1985, it was reissued under Deborah McDowell's editorship in a series of black women's novels that had been long out of print but were brought to light through the efforts of African American women critics. Now Houghton Mifflin has not only reissued The Street but intends to add Petry's other works for adults: two novels—The Narrows (1953) and A Country Place (1947)—and her collection of short stories, Miss Muriel and Other Stories (1971).

In tracing critical response or the absence thereof towards this novel from the fifties through the eighties, I mean not only to underline its significance but also to sound a cautionary note about our own biases when we read and study African American women's writing: it still seems difficult for readers and critics in this country to comprehend and appreciate that black women can have differing visions at one and the same time.

In the few literary analyses of African American fiction published in the 1950s, The Street was usually mentioned, but almost always as a foil to Richard Wright's *Native Son,* whose alienated, angry, male protagonist was seen as more emblematic of the black ghetto than Petry's industrious, upwardly mobile black woman. These novels do have much in common. Both Bigger Thomas and Lutie Johnson are trapped by the physical and social space which their race and poverty condemn them to move in. At a pivotal point in the novel, each is employed as a servant to a wealthy white family whose racial or sexual stereotypes influence their tragic fate. Both Thomas and Lutie Johnson kill in the course of each novel as a result of the racial or sexual myths imposed on them.

But there are also major differences between the two novels—in their respective authors' philosophical concerns and their delineation of their major characters. While Bigger Thomas does not care about his family or believe in the American Dream, Lutie Johnson, like many other poor mothers, believes—one is tempted to say, *must* believe—that if she works hard enough, is thrifty, follows Benjamin Franklin's example, she might be able to save her son from the degradation of those streets that attempt to destroy or at least entrap anyone who is black and poor. While Wright adopts major Western philosophical frameworks—Existentialism, Marxism—to articulate the psychology of Bigger Thomas, Lutie Johnson is worried not so much about her womanhood as she is about the mundane: about food (for example, the red dye in the meat she and other Harlem mothers are forced to buy); about housing—not only the rent she can barely afford but the claustrophobia of her three tiny rooms; about her son, and whether her attempts to protect him from the dangers of his own street are futile; about her own body as she maneuvers in the terrain of male desire where both black and white men see her as sexual prey.

Perhaps the most telling disparity between these two protest novels arises out of their parallel plots: both protagonists kill, but the conditions and the effects of their acts are very different. Bigger Thomas accidentally kills Mary Dalton, a white woman in whose bedroom he is trapped, because of his fear (a well-founded one) that he will be accused of having raped her. Lutie Johnson, defending herself against being raped, kills Boots, a black man. Bigger is psychologically liberated by breaking the Great American Taboo (that of a black man having sexual relations with a white woman); he is defended by a Marxist lawyer in a trial that is as much about the meaning of oppression as it is specifically about his crime; and he comes to some self-knowledge just before his execution by the State.

In contrast, Lutie Johnson flees to another ghetto after her act of self-defense, leaving her child behind to the white world of the juvenile hall, because she is convinced that he is better off there than with her, his powerless and now criminal mother. Lutie does not draw the attention of Marxist lawyers. She does not become a *cause célèbre*. After all, how could a black woman be raped? And even if she were, after all, all she did was to kill a black man. While Wright's novel employs the outlines of the crime story intact with a murderer on the run, Petry's novel is not about adventure so much as it is about cramped space, about doors of opportunity that shut one after another in Lutie Johnson's face.

No wonder then that Wright's novel overshadowed Petry's in the 1950s and 60s. The civil rights and Black Power movements emphasized the muscular path of black manhood. Since the US was clearly a patriarchal society, how else could blacks achieve equality? One result of that assumption was the much-touted belief that black men had been castrated—not only by white society but by the overpowering black matriarch, the female head of household so domineering she prevented her sons from growing up to be responsible men. It was she who was to blame for the "breakdown" of the black family, for the epidemic of black juvenile delinquents who threatened the order of society.

That perspective was to culminate in the Moynihan Report of 1966. But as public policy it had been circulating among intellectuals and popular commentators since the 1940s. In writing *The Street*, Petry used the mass of detail gathered in the investigative reporting she'd done for the Harlem weekly *The People's Voice* on urban ghetto housing, on black male unemployment and its relationship to "broken" marriages, on education, childrearing and sexual violence in the ghetto, to demonstrate that juvenile delinquency and the breakdown of black urban communities were due not to domineering black mothers but to rampant institutional racism. Petry underlined this point when at the end of the novel Lutie Johnson ironically asks whether there is really any difference between the Southern slave plantation and the urban ghetto.

In the fifties the prospect of integration raised hopes among many that US racism might be eliminated once blacks finally "legally" gained access to the American Dream. But neither Benjamin Franklin's philosophy nor her own literacy, beauty, intelligence and morality save Lutie Johnson. In its scathing critique of the benefits of access, The Street might have been seen as a throwback to a less enlightened decade. Too, protest as a literary form was becoming unpopular, not only because it dwelt so heavily on the "grim side of black life," but also because it reduced black characters to types, as James Baldwin would argue so eloquently in his essay "Everybody's Protest Novel."

But what about the sixties the decade that dwelt so much on urban black America and fostered so much protest? Why didn't The Street receive more attention when it was reissued then, since it, perhaps more than any other African American novel I've read, details so completely the conditions that a person encounters every day in the ghetto: the crowded tenements, the smelly streets, the grimy food markets, the hostile police, the indifferent, tired educational system? Why didn't cultural nationalists celebrate this "realistic" novel as they did the philosophical *Native Son*?

Though they valued literature as protest, the Black Power movements of the 1960s portrayed women as adjuncts to men, a perspective that Alice Walker, June Jordan and Audre Lorde would later come to criticize. One has only to consider the killing of Boots—a black rapist, not a white one—to see the ideological difficulties that cultural nationalists might have with the novel. At a time when Black Unity meant that women should not protest their conditions as women, Petry's analyses of the ways in which black men routed their frustrations on black women must have seemed (at best) strategically incorrect.

When I taught The Street for the first time in 1971, many of my students who lived in Harlem were alert to that point—what they called Petry's fostering of disunity. However, as the women's movement gained momentum, students from the same background were intrigued by the fact that a novel written well before the explosion of African American women's literature in the 1970s had attacked sexism in the African American community. Now they objected instead to the way in which the black community was represented as a ghetto, an alienated place where there is no indication that community ties exist. Many of them pointed to Petry's own small-town New England background as a way to justify their sense that a different moral and social ethos was at work: Petry was an outsider who saw the ghetto only as a place of material deprivation, and not as a community with deep cultural vitality.

But why hadn't these same students raised this objection to *Native Son?* Didn't Wright also focus on the black urban environment as a deprived ghetto? Unlike Petry, he came from a devastatingly poor family and had suffered intense racism in his childhood, so what did background have to do with it? Might not Petry's as well as Wright's emphasis on the destructiveness of the ghetto have more to do with the intention of the protest novel—that its goal is to

demonstrate the effects of oppression? Would these novels be as effective as protest if rich cultural vitality was their focus? June Jordan pointed out in an essay on *Native Son* and *Their Eyes Were Watching God* that novels of affirmation *and* novels of protest are necessary to African American intellectual and social expression: doesn't that also apply to The Street?

As my students examined their criticisms, it became increasingly clear that while they could accept, even applaud, Wright's representation of an urban black man as alienated and angry, they could not accept Petry's representation of an urban black woman as disconnected from the community and angry at the limitations of her environment. Black women, whatever their class or condition, had to be community-oriented, or how would the community survive? What they applauded was Janie in *Their Eyes Were Watching God*, a woman who desired community, was clearly sensual, and achieved her voice. Ironically, while Hurston's novel had been rejected for decades because it was *not* a protest novel, now The Street was being criticized because a woman's novel should be affirmative.

While my students' opinions are not exactly a definitive explanation of why The Street failed to attract more attention in the woman-centered seventies, I think their responses do indicate the discomfort this novel might have caused in the last two decades among readers who yearned (as we should have) for rebels like Morrison's Sula, or her wise Pilate in *Song of Solomon* (1977), or for political activists like Alice Walker's Meridian or Toni Cade Bambara's Velma in *The Salt Eaters* (1981). Although I do not share Hazel Carby's assessment of our idealization of *Their Eyes Were Watching God* as a return to a pastoral past, I do think we ought to reflect on why so few novels about working-class urban black women were published or celebrated during the 1970s—and why so many prominent African American women's novels of that period were set in small towns, villages of the past.

In the fiction of the 1980s the issue of class became more focal. Yet except for Gloria Naylor's *The Women of Brewster Place* (1980), most of these novels emphasized middle-class black women: Jadine in Morrison's *Tar Baby* (1981), Celie in Alice Walker's *The Color Purple* (1983), Sarah Phillips in Andrea Lee's 1984 novel of the same name. Whether or not that trend was due to a social climate in which working-class lives were less central to intellectual inquiry or to the perceptions of publishing companies, it is nonetheless true that African American women were then and are now a majority of the Black urban ghetto.

In the 1990s a new trend is beginning to emerge. Films like *Boyz N the Hood* and *New Jack City* indicate that the new black ghetto, the "hood," is causing the rest of American society much consternation. Perhaps The Street will receive more attention in this era, and find the place it deserves in the literary history of the US. For as Petry pointed out in a recent interview, the world it portrays is as real now as it was in 1946.

Source: Barbara Christian, "A Checkered Career," in *The Women's Review of Books*, Vol. 9, No. 10–11, July 1992, pp. 18–19.

Arthur P. Davis

In the following article, Davis reviews Petry's The Street *and discusses her place among authors of Hard Boiled Fiction.*

With her first novel, The Street, Ann Petry joins that fast-growing school of hard-boiled Negro fiction writers—the school of William Attaway, Charles Offord, Chester Himes, and Richard Wright.

This school specializes in depicting the sordidness and the social degeneracy one finds in the modern city slum, particularly in the black ghettos of these various slums. Emphasizing the brutality of a social order geared to crush the unfortunate Negro within its clutches, these writers delineate in harsh detail the helplessness of the victim and the warping and distorting influence on his personality wrought by this hostile social scheme. The writers of this group say in effect: here is what the prejudiced American system does to the Negro. All he asks is a chance to live a decent life. You not only deny him that chance, but you also make of him a brutal caricature of humanity.

Primarily writers of social criticism and protest, these authors make frequent use of filth and obscenity, a fact which has alienated many Negro readers. The latter tend to forget, however, that this objectionable material is not inserted wholly for sensational effect. Another weapon in the arsenal of protest, it is used to shock the American conscience into an awareness of the inequalities and injustices in our system. And these Hard Boiled writers are doing a good job in this respect. Though futilitarian in their own works and attitude, they, by the very intensity of their attacks, have done much to enlist the aid of liberal America to the cause of the Negro.

The Street tells the story of the pathetic but futile efforts of Lutie Johnson to provide a decent home for her only son—a nine-year-old Harlem "key-child"—on 116th Street. Neither the child nor Lutie has a possible chance in the fight with 116th Street, the antagonist in the story; because the "Street" represents all of the evil inherent in the bad housing, the bad sanitation, the violence, and the bestiality of a segregated, oppressed, and frustrated people. The depraved superintendent who tries to rape Lutie and who finally proves her undoing, the sinister figures of Junto, the white man who desired Lutie, of Mrs. Hedges, the brothel-keeper, and of Boots Smith, the slimy band-leader, are all parts of the Street and are all in league against the heroic efforts of Lutie to give her son a home and security.

The Street—116th in New York in this case—is symbolical of all the slums of America. Miss Petry has seen the evil effects of such places on the lives of essentially fine characters, and that is the thesis of her work. As a thesis it is sound, but a thesis is one thing, a good novel another. There is almost too much thesis lurking behind the characters in The Street. As a result, some of them become puppets to motivate the plot and not flesh-and-blood human beings. Junto, for instance, the mysterious behind-the-scenes controller of Harlem bands and night spots, is more melodramatic than real. The same holds true for Mrs. Hedges, although she is a fascinating figure.

All the way through the book, the reader keeps wondering why Lutie, who is an intelligent person, doesn't take an intelligent course of action when some emergency arises. This is particularly true at the end when she seeks a lawyer to get her child out of a detention home. As a matter of fact the whole ending seems forced. The author evidently felt that she needed a strong climax and proceeded to obtain one at the expense of reality. A sensational ending it certainly is, but it is not convincing.

In spite of these obvious weaknesses—weaknesses often found in first novels—The Street is a fascinating work. Its sensationalism makes for fast and "easy" reading. Moreover, Miss Petry knows her Street intimately; and her theme, though she has made it Negro, is not essentially racial but human, and therefore has a universal appeal.

Ann Petry, the author, has had a versatile life. She has been a pharmacist, a newspaper woman, a teacher, a writer of children's plays, and an amateur actress. At the present time, she is executive secretary of Negro Women Incorporated, a civic organization interested in local and national legislation. Her thorough knowledge of Harlem was gained through her work as newspaper woman.

Miss Petry's first published work was a short story, "On Saturday the Siren Sounds at Noon," which appeared in the December 1943 *Crisis*. Since that time she has publish several other short stories. In 1945 she received the Houghton Mifflin Literary Fellowship and through its aid finished The Street her first novel.

With her profound knowledge of Negro slum life, her flair for the sensational, and her ability to dramatize social ills, Ann Petry has the makings of a great protest novelist.

In The Street her thesis was not wholly sublimated into art, but with her intelligence and obvious ability she will surely profit from the experience of this first effort. It looks as though the Hard Boiled School has another able scholar.

Source: Arthur P. Davis, "Hard Boiled Fiction," in *The Journal of Negro Education*, Vol. 15, No. 1, Autumn 1946, pp. 648–649.

SOURCES

Baldwin, James. *Notes of a Native Son*. Beacon Press, 1955: 13–23.

Christian, Barbara. "A Checskered Career." *The Woman's Review of Books*. Vol. 9, Nos. 10/11 (July 1974): 18–19.

Davis, Arthur P. "Hard Boiled Fiction." *The Journal of Negro Education*. Vol. 15, No. 4 (Autumn 1946): 648–49.

Gates, Henry Louis, Jr. "In Her Own Write." Forward. *The Schomburg Library of Nineteenth-Century Black Women Writers*. Oxford University Press, 1988.

Greene, Marjorie. "Ann Petry Planned to Write." *Opportunity* 24 (April to June 1946): 78–79.

Hicks, Heather. "Rethinking Realism in Ann Petry's *The Street*." *MELUS*. Vol. 27, No. 4 (Winter 2002): 89–105.

Ivy, James W. "Ann Petry Talks about First Novel." *Crisis* 53 (January 1946): 48–49.

Lattin, Vernon E. "Ann Petry and the American Dream." *Black American Literature Forum*. Vol. 12, No. 2 (Summer 1978): 62–72.

McKay, Nellie. "Ann Petry's *The Street* and *The Narrows*: A Study of the Influence of Class, Race, and Gender on Afro-American Women's Lives." *Women and War*. Ed. Maria Diedrich and Dorothea Fischer-Hornung. Berg, 1990.

Petry, Ann. *The Street*. Houghton Mifflin Company, 1946 and 1974.

Scott, W. "Material Resistance and the Agency of the Body in Ann Petry's *The Street*." *American Literature* 78, No. 1 (2006): 89–116.

Shinn, Thelma J. "Women in the Novels of Ann Petry." *Critique: Studies in Modern Fiction*. 16, No. 1 (1974): 110–120.

FURTHER READING

Evrin, Hazel Arnett. *The Critical Response to Ann Petry*. Praeger, 2005.
    This collection of essays and reviews chronicles the reception history of Petry's fiction and influences on her work.

Holliday, Hilary. *Ann Petry*. Twayne Publishers, 1996.
    This book offers a complete biography of Petry's life.

Locke, Alain and Arnold Rampersad, eds. *The New Negro: Voices of the Harlem Renaissance*. Albert & Charles Boni, Inc., 1925.
    Considered by many as a definitive text of the Harlem Renaissance, this book provides a window into the cultural movement from which Petry's work was generated.

Petry, Elizabeth. *At Home Inside: A Daughter's Tribute to Ann Petry*. University Press of Mississippi, 2009.
    In this book, Ann Petry's daughter lovingly explores the contradictory details of Ann's career and family life.

Tangerine

EDWARD BLOOR
1997

Tangerine, published in 1997, is a best-selling novel for young adults by Edward Bloor. His first published work, *Tangerine* is highly regarded by both critics and readers for its strong characters, interesting setting, and compelling story. The novel was named one of the top ten best books for young adults by the American Library Association and received an Edgar Allan Poe Award nomination for best young adult novel, both in 1998.

Written in diary form, *Tangerine* takes the perspective of Paul Fisher, a legally blind seventh grader who must wear thick glasses to see. Unlike many of the adults around him and his peers, Paul is very perceptive about the problems in his family and in his new home in Tangerine County, Florida. Over the course of the novel, Paul remembers the true story of how he became blind. He also learns to tell the full truth about his family, friends, and the events he witnesses.

Tangerine uses sports to underscore aspects of the story. Paul is an enthusiastic soccer player and becomes a key member of the Tangerine Middle School soccer team. Paul's troubled brother Erik is an extremely talented placekicker for his high school football team. One recurring motif in the novel is Mr. Fisher's obsession with what Paul terms the "Erik Fisher Football Dream," as Paul and Erik's father believes that Erik can become a star in a prestigious college program, if not on a professional level.

Edward Bloor *(Photograph by Pamela Bloor. Reproduced by permission of Edward Bloor.)*

Bloor was inspired to write *Tangerine* after he moved to Florida and began working as a public middle-school and high-school English teacher. Bloor later moved to a neighborhood—one similar to Paul's in the novel—and commuted on the back roads through citrus groves being destroyed for new housing developments. Bloor told Lynda Brill Comerford of *Publishers Weekly* that he considered *Tangerine* a *Florida Gothic*.

AUTHOR BIOGRAPHY

Edward William Bloor was born October 12, 1950, in Trenton, New Jersey, the son of Edward William and Mary (Cowley) Bloor. Educated in Catholic schools, he was an enthusiastic reader and began writing at an early age. As a writer, Bloor wrote copiously from seventh to twelfth grade. At the time, he was influenced by New York City's literary and theatrical scenes. During high school, he wrote plays that were produced at his school and served as the school's literary magazine editor. He was also an enthusiastic athlete, playing soccer, basketball, baseball and football. Bloor went on to play soccer

and to earn an English degree from Fordham University in 1973.

After graduation, Bloor lived in New York, Boston, and England while he tried and failed to become a published author. With his family, he eventually moved to southern Florida. From 1983 to 1986, Bloor worked as an English teacher in both public middle and high schools in Fort Lauderdale. While devising educational materials for his classrooms, he became interested in publishing. Bloor left teaching and became an educational-text editor for Harcourt Brace, a publishing house, in 1986. Through his work, Bloor had to read hundreds of young adult novels and came to realize that he could write in this genre. He began writing, often by dictating into a recorder while commuting to work and while doing such tasks as mowing the lawn.

Through Harcourt, Bloor published his first young adult novel, *Tangerine*, in 1997. It eventually sold nearly a million copies. With the success of the novel, Bloor frequently traveled to book signings and speaking engagements at schools. Bloor continued to both work at Harcourt and write other young adult novels. Bloor also achieved success with his next novel, *Crusader* (1999). Like *Tangerine*, *Story Time* (2004) was nominated for an Edgar Allen Poe Award for best young adult novel. In the years that followed, Bloor wrote the popular novels *London Calling* (2005) and *Taken* (2007). Since then, he's been living, working, and writing in Florida with his schoolteacher wife, Pamela Dixon, and their children, Amanda and Spencer.

PLOT SUMMARY

At the beginning of *Tangerine*, seventh grader Paul Fisher, wearing his thick glasses, is helping his mother Caroline finish closing up the family home in Houston. They are moving to Lake Windsor Downs in Tangerine County, Florida. As he and his mother drive away from their old home, he has vague memories of telling his parents that his elder brother Erik tried to kill him, but his mother dismisses it because of Paul's poor eyesight.

Part 1
FRIDAY, AUGUST 18

As Paul and his mother arrive in Lake Windsor Downs, Paul talks about his father's obsession

MEDIA ADAPTATIONS

- *Tangerine* was recorded as an audio book read by Ramon de Ocampo. It was released by Recorded Books in 2001.
- Edward Bloor maintains a web site at http://www.edwardbloor.net that includes information on *Tangerine* and other novels. It also provides a biography of the author.

with Erik, a star placekicker, landing at a big-time college and perhaps someday going pro.

SATURDAY, AUGUST 19

The next morning, Paul smells fire and alerts his mother. She calls the fire department and is distressed to learn that it is a muck fire that has been burning for years and will continue to burn because it is nearly impossible to put such fires out. Paul's mother is unhappy to know that she must live with the situation.

SATURDAY, AUGUST 19, *LATER*

Paul rides his bike and explores his new surroundings. When he arrives home, he finds his mother talking to Mr. Costello, the head of the development's homeowners' association. Erik and his father arrive home, and Mr. Costello learns that Erik is a high school football star. He goes home to get his son Mike, who is also a highly regarded football player, and they talk about the team.

MONDAY, AUGUST 21

Paul's mother drives him to Lake Windsor Middle School. She is displeased to learn that the seventh and eighth graders, including Paul, have all their classes in portable buildings behind the main school building. She tells Mrs. Gates, the school's principal, that Paul is legally blind without his glasses. Paul thinks he can see clearly and cares only about joining the school's soccer team.

WEDNESDAY, AUGUST 23

Paul, his mother, and his father go to the high school's football tryout camp and watch Erik and the other players demonstrate their skills. After a downpour, Paul introduces himself to Joey Costello, Mike's little brother, and other kids playing with a soccer ball. Paul is not impressed by their abilities.

MONDAY, AUGUST 28

On the first day of school, Paul has a flashback to an early day of kindergarten when his brother made fun of his impaired vision at the bus stop. Erik said that Paul stared at a solar eclipse without protection and damaged his eyes. Although this story gets repeated, Paul does not completely believe it. At school, Paul demonstrates his independence by dismissing his guide for the day.

WEDNESDAY, AUGUST 30

At home, Paul listens to Erik practicing his kicking with the help of a third-string player on the team, Arthur Bauer. Arthur has an SUV and drives Erik around, because Erik does not drive. Paul ponders how Erik will give Arthur enhanced social status.

THURSDAY, AUGUST 31

Paul learns that soccer tryouts will start the next day. To prepare, he goes running with Joey. Joey points out Mr. Donnelly's house, which has been struck repeatedly by lightning. Paul offers a complicated theory about why it happened.

FRIDAY, SEPTEMBER 1

After school, Paul makes the team because no one is turned away. However, only the top fifteen players go to away games. Wearing thick prescription goggles, Paul is nicknamed Mars by teammates. He impresses his teammates with his skills and he is sure he will be the starting goalie.

TUESDAY, SEPTEMBER 5 TO THURSDAY, SEPTEMBER 7

At home, Paul learns from Erik and Arthur that Mike died that afternoon at football practice. He was struck by lightning when he leaned against a goalpost that was hit. When they are outside alone, Erik and Arthur make fun of Mike, how he died, and how his little brother reacted to the situation. Paul is disgusted by them.

At school, there is little attention paid to the death. Paul realizes there are only a few good players on his team and that his brother is key to understanding what he cannot remember how he became blind. The next day, Caroline organizes a meeting at the family home about having football practice during an unsafe time of the day.

Through her efforts, practices are moved to mornings.

FRIDAY, SEPTEMBER 8 TO FRIDAY, SEPTEMBER 8, *LATER*

Paul is upset to learn that he has been kicked off the soccer team because his mother filled out a form that identified him as handicapped. Although Paul's mother assures him that his father can work it out with the coach, Paul's only option is to become the team's manager. Caroline apologizes to Paul for filling out the form and killing his dream. Later that night, the whole family goes to Mike's viewing, where Paul offers support to Joey.

SATURDAY, SEPTEMBER 9

While riding with his mother and Joey to a carnival, Paul learns that Tangerine County used to be the "tangerine capital of the world." At the carnival, Joey points out some kids from Tangerine Middle School that he thinks they need to avoid. Paul admires their skills with a soccer ball. Joey and Paul meet up with other kids from their school, but Paul gets left behind when he gets enthralled by the "Boy Who Never Grew" exhibit in the "Wonders of the World" freak show. As Paul leaves the exhibit, he sees the kids from Tangerine Middle waiting to go inside. Paul does not see Joey again until Caroline comes to pick them up.

MONDAY, SEPTEMBER 11

On a rainy school day, Paul is called into the office with other boys who were at the carnival. They are asked if they vandalized an exhibit in the freak show, they deny it, and Paul accuses the soccer-playing kids from Tangerine Middle School. Walking back to class with the other boys, Paul worries that those kids will learn he told on them. Before they can get back to class, the portable classrooms began sinking because a sinkhole has opened under the field. Paul and Joey help save students trying to escape the portables.

MONDAY, SEPTEMBER 11, *LATER* **TO FRIDAY, SEPTEMBER 15**

While the students and city deal with the collapse of the sinkhole, Paul is proud of his actions. He is out of school for several days while his father, who works for the city as a civil engineer, is promoted to director of civil engineering for the county. It has come to light that his boss, Old Charley Burns, had been taking bribes and allowing development without inspections.

At a later meeting, Paul learns that he can either attend Lake Windsor on a split schedule or transfer to Tangerine for the remainder of the semester. Paul tells his parents that he will go to Tangerine and that there will be no paperwork filled out identifying his blindness so he can play soccer. They agree.

Part 2

MONDAY, SEPTEMBER 18

Paul's mother reluctantly drops him off at Tangerine for his first day. He is assigned an escort for the first day, Theresa Cruz, to show him around. She does not talk much to him, except when Paul asks about the soccer team. Her twin brother Tino is a good player on the team. Paul also discovers that the soccer players who vandalized the carnival are on the team. After school, the team coach, Ms. Bright, allows him on the team but only as a backup. His mother picks Paul up after practice and tells him she removed the form that put him in the handicapped program from his paperwork.

TUESDAY, SEPTEMBER 19

At lunch the next day, Paul meets the tough soccer kids—Victor, Tino, and Hernando—who had been suspended and went to "vandalism jail" for breaking the freak-show exhibit. They admit to their actions, and Paul succeeds in fitting in with them. Later, at soccer practice, Paul is impressed by their talent.

WEDNESDAY, SEPTEMBER 20

When Joey comes over to show Paul his soccer uniform and see Paul's, Erik and Arthur make fun of Mike Costello and Joey's reaction to his death. Joey wants to confront them, but Paul tells him it is not worth it.

FRIDAY, SEPTEMBER 22 TO FRIDAY, SEPTEMBER 22, *LATER*

Tangerine's first soccer game is an away game at a school with both nasty players and mean-spirited fans. During the first half, Paul is amazed by his team's abilities. After Tino starts punching an opposing player for upending him, his coach sends Paul in as a replacement center forward. Paul gets pulled from the game, too, for reacting when he gets mud put in his eyes. The team wins by a score of 2 to 1.

SATURDAY, SEPTEMBER 23

The whole Fisher family attends Erik's first football game. Erik looks like a fool when he kicks at air after not being informed his team would be using a trick play to win the close game. Erik is further humiliated when the local news airs the clip of his dramatic fall into the mud.

TUESDAY, SEPTEMBER 26 TO FRIDAY, SEPTEMBER 29

No one from Paul's family attends his first home soccer game. He is impressed by this school's level of talent as well as the skills of his own team. After Victor is sent to the hospital by Coach Bright for a bleeding wound on his forehead, Paul plays in the second half of the game as Victor's replacement. Paul unexpectedly scores his first goal of the season, and his team wins easily. Victor congratulates him. Later at home, Paul is befuddled when Cara Clifton calls him on the telephone and asks him if he likes Kerri Gardner. He calls his friend Joey, who tells him Kerri was probably listening in on the conversation to find out what he would say about her.

Because Paul's mom calls the local newspaper about the outstanding talent of the girls on his team, Mr. Donnelly from the newspaper shows up at their practice. Shandra runs and hides when she sees the reporter, while the coach questions his motive for covering the story. In the end, only Maya is mentioned in the paper.

MONDAY, OCTOBER 2 TO THURSDAY, OCTOBER 5

Though recent transfer student Joey is reluctant, Paul has him join a group with Henry D., Theresa, and Tino for a class project. Theresa takes charge of the group and tells them they are going to focus on a new type of tangerine her brother Luis has invented, the Golden Dawn. While working on his class project on his father's computer, Paul listens to a meeting of the homeowners' association. Paul learns about a rash of robberies of valuables in the homes that have been tented for the fumigation of insect pests.

On Thursday, Paul is invited to the Cruz house to meet Luis for the project after school and for soccer practice. At the Tomas Cruz Groves/Nursery, Luis shows them around, teaching them about his groves, his nurseries, and how he created the Golden Dawn variety of tangerine. Paul is very impressed and Luis invites him to come again. At home, Paul has another flashback about losing his vision when the family lived in Huntsville, Alabama.

THURSDAY, NOVEMBER 2 TO SATURDAY, NOVEMBER 4

Over the past busy month, Erik has become the star player on his high school team, while Paul has regularly substituted for other players on his winning middle-school soccer team. Acting on Luis's invitation, Paul has his mom drop him off at Cruz Groves on Saturday, November 4. Although Tino is hostile, Luis has Paul help lay hoses around the baby trees and then cut holes in them. After this hard day of work, Tino has new respect for Paul, and Paul tells him that he was the one who told on them that day at the carnival. Tino gives him one kick in the "backside" as punishment.

SUNDAY, NOVEMBER 5

The Fisher family spends the evening at Mr. Donnelly's house. Mr. Donnelly is a booster for the University of Florida, and knows the football coaches there. His guests also have connections to college football. The family hopes to bring Erik's skills to their attention. While Erik is the center of attention, Donnelly also talks to Paul. At home, Paul has another memory about the past and his eyes involving a visit from his grandparents.

TUESDAY, NOVEMBER 7 TO FRIDAY, NOVEMBER 10

In Paul's last home game, he starts at left wing and gets a goal. The game gets called when it starts raining and it goes into the book as a "no game." Friday is the last game of the season and one that determines the championship between Tangerine and Lake Windsor. There is a bigger crowd, which includes Paul's mother. After Victor gets punched in the face by an opposing player, Paul goes into the game in his place. The game is rough, and Shandra gets hurt. Paul replaces her as goalie and lets in one goal. At halftime, Coach Walski tells Coach Bright that Paul is ineligible to play and threatens to turn him in to the referee. Coach Bright counters with the fact that Shandra is Antoine Thomas's sister and that the star football player does not live in Lake Windsor. Walski backs off, and the game continues. The game ends in a tie, and Tangerine is the league champion.

Part 3

MONDAY, NOVEMBER 20

Paul's school-project group comes over to his house to make some decisions about their paper. While they play outside with a soccer ball, Erik and Arthur show up and Erik makes a condescending remark. Tino stands up for himself, and Erik hits him hard. The group leaves, and Paul wonders what he should have done.

TUESDAY, NOVEMBER 21

Still reeling from yesterday's events, Paul accompanies his mother on her errands. Because his mother has a meeting with Erik's school guidance counselor, Paul watches the end of football practice from under the bleachers. He witnesses Luis confronting Erik about Tino, and Arthur hitting Luis's head with a blackjack (a type of small weapon). Antoine Thomas and some other players assist Luis.

THURSDAY, NOVEMBER 23, THANKSGIVING

Writing about yesterday, Paul says that he notices that many kids have been absent from school. Henry D. tells him that it is because of the freezing weather, and that the kids are helping their families save their crops. Paul and Henry D. volunteer at the Cruz's' after school. They work hard to save as many trees as they can using various methods, although Paul is made to stay inside and rest at 2:00 AM Before Luis goes out again, Paul tells him that he witnessed Arthur using the blackjack on his head. In the morning, Paul apologizes to Tino for what happened at his house. Luis also tells him that he, Antoine, and another guy on the football team will get retribution on Erik and Arthur. When Paul's mother picks him up, he is tired and sick so she lets him stay home from Erik's last football game.

FRIDAY, NOVEMBER 24

Paul learns from his dad that the center on the football team seemed to deliberately snap the ball poorly every time Erik had a chance to kick for a point in his last game. Antoine was its star. Paul also makes his dad understand that he never showed any interest in his soccer games this season. A neighbor alerts them to smashed mailboxes in the neighborhood. When Paul goes outside to check them out, he smells the smoke of the muck fire. It triggers the trace of a memory and causes him to faint.

MONDAY, NOVEMBER 27

Paul's mother insists that he stay home from school because of illness. Paul is shocked when Erik comes home unharmed, and later when Kerri calls to ask him to go to a party at Joey's after the football awards banquet on Friday.

TUESDAY, NOVEMBER 28

Going back to school, Paul learns that Luis Cruz was found dead yesterday in one of his groves. Luis died of an aneurysm that doctors believe was caused by a blow to his head. Although others believe Luis was hit by a branch during the freeze, Paul goes home sick and investigates the possibility that the blow from Arthur killed him. Paul concludes that Arthur was at fault.

WEDNESDAY, NOVEMBER 29

Staying home again, Paul gets a call from Theresa, who tells him not to come to Luis's funeral on Thursday because something might happen to him. Paul realizes that they all knew about Luis getting hit by Arthur.

THURSDAY, NOVEMBER 30

Home again, Paul puts on his suit, goes outside by the gray wall, and—in a tribute to Luis—digs until he hits the soil of the tangerine grove.

FRIDAY, DECEMBER 1

Paul remains home during the day, but goes to his brother's football awards that night. During the ceremony, Tino and Victor show up. Tino attacks the unsuspecting Erik, while Victor attacks Arthur. The crowd at the ceremony jumps up and intervenes. Victor escapes, but Tino is put in a headlock by Coach Warner. As the coach tries to take Tino away, Paul jumps on him and Tino is able to make his escape. Paul's father is furious and demands to know who attacked Erik and Arthur, but Paul runs out as well. As he makes his way home, Paul is stopped by Erik and Arthur. Paul shows no fear through Erik and Arthur's attempts to intimidate him. Erik loses his temper before they leave.

When Erik calls Arthur "Castor," Paul remembers what happened to him when he lost his sight. He was about five when Erik and his friend, Vincent Castor, spray-painted a wall. Paul knew they had done it, although he told no one. Erik believed that Paul told on Castor, and punished Paul by holding him down while Castor spray-painted into Paul's eyes. His mother found Paul unconscious and drove him to the hospital.

When Paul arrives home and confronts his parents about what happened. His father says they did not tell him because they did not want him to hate his brother. Paul makes his father cry when he says, "So you figured it would be better if I just hated myself?"

SATURDAY, DECEMBER 2

Joey alerts Paul that Betty Bright is at Mr. Donnelly's house. Paul learns from Shandra that Antoine has decided to tell the truth about his residency because of what happened to Luis and because of the many lies he has had to tell.

Antoine later encourages Paul to speak the truth as well, as he knows Paul witnessed what happened to Luis.

SUNDAY, DECEMBER 3

Mr. Donnelly's story causes a stir. Based on Antoine's sworn statement, all of Lake Windsor's victories and all school records set while he was on the team are nullified. Although the community vilifies Antoine, Paul points out to his father that the truth was right in front of everyone because Antoine was never in Lake Windsor except for school and games.

SUNDAY, DECEMBER 3, *LATER*

At a meeting with local residents who have been robbed, along with the Fisher and Bauer families, Erik and Arthur sport their beat-up faces. Paul's mother informs the people who had been robbed that Erik and Arthur have been committing the crimes. She found the evidence in the family's storage unit, and that she has arranged for items to be returned. The fathers of Erik and Arthur ask those present to accept the return of the items as restitution and that they not press charges. The victims agree reluctantly to the plan.

As the meeting ends, Arthur is arrested for Luis's murder. Arthur's father tells the arresting officer that Arthur is innocent. Paul speaks up and tells the police what he saw Arthur do with the blackjack. Paul also states that Erik told Arthur to do it, and Erik admits to his role in the crime. After the law-enforcement officials leave, Paul's grandparents show up for their scheduled short visit. His grandparents remind his mother and father that they believed Erik needed help when he hurt Paul.

MONDAY, DECEMBER 4

After Paul hands Theresa the final copy of their report, he is expelled for the rest of the school year for "assaulting a teacher or other School Board employee." Paul will complete seventh grade at the local Catholic school. As he leaves Tangerine, the kids congratulate him. On the car ride to the mall, he tells his mother he will be going back to Tangerine Middle School and its soccer team next year.

TUESDAY, DECEMBER 5 TO TUESDAY, DECEMBER 5, *LATER*

The investigation into the murder of Luis continues, and Paul's dad washes his hands of Erik. Tino calls and makes peace with Paul. Tino

also invites Paul to come and help fill the orders for the Golden Dawn tangerine whenever he wants. Later, Paul completes his statement for the police.

WEDNESDAY, DECEMBER 6

Paul has his first day at St. Anthony's. His father drives him to school, pointing out the tree planted in memory of Mike Costello along the way.

CHARACTERS

Adam

Adam is a student at Lake Windsor Middle School. He seems close to Kerri at the carnival.

Tommy Acoso

A native of the Philippines, Tommy is a student at Lake Windsor Middle School and one of the best players on its soccer team.

Ms. Alvarez

Ms. Alvarez is Paul's homeroom teacher at Lake Windsor Middle School.

Arthur Bauer Jr.

A mediocre player on the high school football team, Arthur becomes Erik's flunky. He serves as Erik's holder for kicking, drives him everywhere in his SUV, and becomes his enforcer, as when he hits Luis Cruz on the side of the head with a blackjack. Arthur is also responsible for the actual burglaries in Paul's housing development. At the end of the novel, he is arrested for his crimes.

Arthur Bauer Sr.

The father of Arthur and Paige, he works as a building contractor and a major in the Army National Guard. He tries to keep his son's future intact by getting his robbery victims to agree not to press charges in exchange for the return of the items. His tactic works in the short term, but his son is eventually arrested for his role in the death of Luis Cruz.

Paige Bauer

Paige is Arthur's sister, a sophomore at Lake Windsor Middle School and a cheerleader. Paul thinks she is dating Erik.

Brian Baylor

Brian is a senior on the Lake Windsor High School football team. He plays center and helps sabotage the last game of the season for Erik.

Bud Bridges

Bud Bridges is the principal at Lake Windsor High School. His wife is a teacher at Lake Windsor Middle School.

Mrs. Bridges

Mrs. Bridges is Paul's language-arts teacher at Lake Windsor Middle School. Her husband is the principal at Lake Windsor High School.

Betty Bright

A locally raised track-and-field star who competed internationally, Betty Bright is the soccer coach at Tangerine Middle School. She lets Paul on the team and allows him to play. Coach Bright often acts in support of her players, but does not hesitate to punish them when necessary.

Old Charley Burns

Old Charley Burns is the head of Tangerine County's Civil Engineering Department at the beginning of *Tangerine*. Because he has taken bribes and permitted unchecked, shoddy construction in the area, a sinkhole develops. It takes out the portable classrooms behind the middle school. Burns uses his illegally obtained money to attend as many stock-car races as possible. Soon after Burns's transgressions come to light, he has a heart attack and dies in his lawyer's office.

Vincent Castor

Vincent Castor was Erik's flunky when the family lived in Huntsville, Alabama. It is Vincent who actually sprayed the paint in Paul's eyes when Paul was about five years old. The act made Paul legally blind, but no consequences for Vincent are mentioned. Erik calls Arthur "Castor" late in the book because of the similar role Arthur plays in his life.

Cesar

Cesar is a reserve player on the Tangerine Middle School team.

Cara Clifton

Cara is a student at Lake Windsor Middle School. She is Joey Costello's girlfriend and a close friend of Kerri Gardner.

Mr. Jack Costello

A lawyer and head of the Homeowners' Association, Jack Costello is the father of Mike and Joey Costello. He becomes distraught when his son accidentally dies after being struck by lightning during football practice.

Joey Costello

Joey Costello is Mike Costello's younger brother and is in the same grade as Paul. Like Paul, he enjoys soccer, but Joey is not a great player and eventually quits. Joey becomes very upset when Mike dies but continues to date and attend school. Sometimes a friend of Paul, Joey also briefly attends Tangerine Middle School but responds poorly to Paul's friends there and does not fit in. So, he returns to Lake Windsor Middle School.

Mike Costello

The son of Jack Costello and the older brother of Joey Costello, Mike is a star football player at Lake Windsor High School. He is a lineman, and then becomes the number two quarterback. Football is not Mike's whole life before his death as he has already been accepted into the School of Engineering at Florida State University. In early September, Mike dies during football practice when he is struck by lightning while leaning against a goalpost.

Luis Cruz

Luis Cruz is the older brother of Tino and Theresa Cruz and the son of Tomas Cruz. He walks with a limp because of a childhood work accident with the clippers used to harvest tangerines, but he played goalie for his school soccer teams. Luis's passion is his work, especially his development of a new type of tangerine, the Golden Dawn. Luis appreciates Paul's interest in his work and allows him to help the family business several times. Luis dies of an aneurysm after Arthur hits him in the head with a blackjack on Erik's orders.

Theresa Cruz

Theresa Cruz is a student at Tangerine Middle School. She is the twin sister of Tino Cruz, the sister of Luis Cruz, and the daughter of Tomas Cruz. She is a good student and leads Paul around on his first days at Tangerine. Theresa is friendly with Paul and appreciates his completion of their class project on Luis's Golden Dawn tangerine.

Tino Cruz

Tino Cruz is a student at Tangerine Middle School and a good soccer player on his school's team. He is also the twin brother of Theresa, the brother of Luis, and the son of Tomas Cruz. Although he does not respect Paul much when he comes to Tangerine, he comes to appreciate him after Paul helps save the family's citrus trees during a freeze. Tino does not like to back down from a challenge, and he does not fear the consequences of inflicting retribution. He is suspended several times during the school year for his actions.

Tomas Cruz

Tomas Cruz is the owner of the grove and nursery where his oldest son, Luis, works. He is also the father of Tino and Theresa.

Gino Deluca

A student at Lake Windsor Middle School, he is arguably the best player on their soccer team. Gino serves as the team's captain.

Henry Dilkes

Henry Dilkes, also known as Henry D., is the younger brother of Wayne Dilkes, and he is a student at Tangerine Middle School. He plays soccer and is in the class project group with Paul, Tino, and Theresa. Henry is a good friend to the Cruz twins as well as Paul. With Paul, he works all night to ensure the family's citrus trees survive a freeze.

Wayne Dilkes

The brother of Henry D., Wayne Dilkes is a local volunteer firefighter, spray-truck driver, and exterminator who kills termites and mosquitoes in the Lake Windsor development where Paul resides. Wayne also gives Paul and his brother rides to the Cruz family's grove, sharing his knowledge about the infestations with them along the way.

Bill Donnelly

Bill Donnelly, often called Mr. Donnelly by Paul, lives in his development. His home has been hit by lightning three times, making it impossible to sell and insure it, so he has ten lightning rods along the roof. Mr. Donnelly also is the father of Terry Donnelly and works as a reporter. He writes stories on the amazing girls on Paul's soccer team, on Betty Bright, and on the truth about Antoine Thomas's residency. Mr. Donnelly is also a University of Florida booster and attempts to help Erik and Mr. Fisher by introducing them to other boosters.

Terry Donnelly

The son of Bill Donnelly, he resides with his father in the same development as Paul's family. He plays football at Lake Windsor High School.

Sergeant Edwards

A member of the Tangerine County's Sheriff Department, Sergeant Edwards is in charge of the robbery cases involving Erik and Arthur.

Dolly Elias

Dolly Elias plays fullback and is a good player on the Tangerine Middle School soccer team.

Caroline Fisher

Caroline Fisher is the mother of Paul and Erik, and the wife of Mr. Fisher. While she is more supportive of Paul than her husband, she often so caught up in her own activities and problems that she does not always know what is going on in Paul's life. She does drive him most places, though, and takes charge of dealing with his schools and buying him clothes. Over the course of the novel, she becomes the head of the Architectural Committee of the Homeowners' Association and serves as the block captain for the Neighborhood Watch patrol. If there is a problem, Caroline makes a call or holds a meeting at her home. More than her husband, Mrs. Fisher is at least somewhat aware that Erik's football dreams might not come to fruition early on. She becomes gravely concerned when she discovers the stolen items Erik has been putting in the family storage facility and talks about the situation with the sheriff. Much to her husband's dismay, she has a close relationship with her parents, who visit toward the end of the novel. In *Tangerine*, she acts on her maternal instincts and does her best to support Paul, her husband, and even Erik.

Erik Fisher

Erik Fisher is Paul's high-school-age brother and the reason why Paul is blind. Erik has a mean—if not sadistic—streak, and an ability to manipulate those around him, including Arthur and Paul. He is prone to rages and does not always have control of himself. While Erik only shows a hypocritical side that is positive and polite to most adults, he beats up Tino, has Arthur participate to Luis's murder, and robs local houses with Arthur's help. In the end, Erik's true nature catches up to him, and he loses his football dream to the legal system. It is unclear at the end of the novel what his fate will be.

Mr. Fisher

Paul's father, Mr. Fisher, has come to Florida to work as a civil engineer for Tangerine County's

Civil Engineering Department. After a sinkhole develops at the Lake Windsor Middle School and his former boss Old Charley Burns is revealed to be corrupt, Mr. Fisher becomes the director of the department. More important to the story, Paul's father is the tireless supporter of what Paul terms "the Erik Fisher Football Dream." Essentially ignoring Paul, his needs, and his soccer games, Mr. Fisher focuses on turning Erik's admitted talent for placekicking into a football scholarship at a prestigious school, if not a career in the National Football League. Every action of Mr. Fisher's focuses on that goal until the end of *Tangerine*, when he learns that his dismissal of Paul's needs, including the need to know the truth about why he is legally blind, has deeply affected his young son.

Paul Fisher

The hero, narrator, and primary character in *Tangerine*, Paul Fisher is a seventh grader who has moved to Lake Windsor with his parents and older brother, Erik. Legally blind because his brother and his brother's friend Vincent Castor sprayed paint in his eyes when Paul was only about five years old, Paul wears thick glasses that allow him to see and to play his favorite sport, soccer. As Paul struggles to remember what his brother did to him all those years ago, he encourages others, identifies with the downtrodden, and does his best to help other people, such as the Cruz family and kids at his school. He does not want to be labeled as *handicapped* as he believes he is the only one in his family, and sometimes his local environment, who can truly see. Paul wishes his parents, especially his father, were not so blinded by Erik and his needs, as Paul and his accomplishments are often ignored in favor of Erik's talents on the football field. Over the course of the novel, Paul learns to trust himself and not fear people like Erik. With his newly found confidence, Paul tells the truth about Erik and Arthur when they contribute to Luis Cruz's death. Although this truth makes his family life difficult, it strengthens Paul and helps him continue to grow at the end of the novel.

Kerri Gardner

Kerri Gardner is a student at Lake Windsor Middle School and a friend of Cara Clifton. She first meets Paul when she is assigned to guide him around on his first day, but allows him to go on his own when he asks. Paul has a crush on her and she shows interest in him, but they never get to spend time together.

Mrs. Gates

Mrs. Gates is the principal of Lake Windsor Middle School.

Grandmom and Grandpop

Paul's maternal grandparents, Grandmom and Grandpop, play a limited role in his life but call regularly and express interest in him. His mother is close to them, but his father does not particularly like them or want them around. They visit shortly after the truth about Erik and Arthur comes to light, and they remind Paul's mother and father that they believed Erik needed help when he hurt Paul years ago.

Victor Guzman

Victor Guzman is one of the star players on the Tangerine Middle School team, and its leader. Like Tino Cruz, Victor does not easily back down from a challenge, nor does he fear the consequences of inflicting retribution. He is suspended several times during the school year for his actions. Although Victor initially challenges him, he also comes to appreciate Paul's soccer skills and loyalty as a friend.

Hernando

Hernando is a good player on the Tangerine Middle School team. He is also suspended several times for his actions during the school year.

Mrs. Hoffman

Mrs. Hoffman is Paul's science teacher at Lake Windsor Middle School.

Dr. Grace Johnson

Dr. Johnson is the principal at Tangerine Middle School.

Mano

Mano is a fullback on the Tangerine Middle School soccer team.

Mars

See Paul Fisher

Mr. Murrow

Mr. Murrow is the head of guidance at Lake Windsor Middle School. His wife is a teacher at Tangerine Middle School.

Mrs. Murrow

Mrs. Murrow is Paul's language arts teacher at Tangerine Middle School. She is the wife of

Mr. Murrow, and this fact causes Paul to worry that information about his disability will make its way to Tangerine.

Nita

Nita is the cousin of Maya Pandhi; she is a good player on the Tangerine Middle School soccer team.

Maya Pandhi

Maya is one of the star players for Tangerine Middle School soccer team. She learned to play the sport in England and is featured in Bill Donnelly's article on the star girls on the Tangerine team. Maya is Nita's cousin.

Mrs. Potter

Mrs. Potter is the science teacher at Tangerine Middle School.

Sergeant Rojas

A member of the Tangerine County's Sheriff Department, Sergeant Rojas arrests Arthur for the murder of Luis Cruz. Rojas is in charge of the investigation into the murder.

Antoine Thomas

Antoine Thomas is a senior, the star quarterback of Lake Windsor High School, and the elder brother of Shandra Thomas. By the end of the novel, it is revealed that Antoine has been lying about his residency with the knowledge and help of unnamed others so that he could play football for Lake Windsor. Antoine tells the truth about the matter at the end of the football season, resulting in a nullification of all of Lake Windsor's wins and team records. Antoine proves himself to be a man of honor in another way, as he defends Luis after Arthur hits him, and vows revenge on Erik and Arthur for their actions. Antoine does not like Erik and speaks out against him.

Shandra Thomas

Shandra Thomas is the talented starting goalie on the Tangerine Middle School team. She is the younger sister of Antoine Thomas. Because of that connection and because of Antoine's attendance of Lake Windsor High School, she hides from Bill Donnelly when he comes to write a story about the girls on the Tangerine team.

Tina Turreton

Tina is a student and cheerleader at Lake Windsor High School. She dates Arthur the football player.

Mr. Walski

An eighth-grade teacher at Lake Windsor Middle School, Mr. Walski is also the school's soccer coach. He kicks Paul off the team for insurance reasons when he learns that Paul's file contains the form about his disability. Coach Walski tries to use Paul's alleged ineligibility against the Tangerine Middle School team when they play Lake Windsor at the end of the soccer season.

Mr. Ward

Mr. Ward is Paul's math teacher at Lake Windsor Middle School.

Coach Warner

Coach Warner is the head football coach at Lake Windsor High School. Paul jumps on him at the football awards banquet near the end of the novel to help Tino get free. As a result, Paul is expelled from the school district for the year.

THEMES

Truth versus Lies

One of the primary themes in *Tangerine* is the importance of telling the truth and living the truth as well as the consequences of lies. As star football player Antoine Thomas advises Paul toward the end of the novel, "Don't spend your life hiding under the bleachers, little brother. The truth shall set you free." Paul responds, "Yes! Yes!" Truths and falsehoods are important to nearly every plot in *Tangerine*, even secondary ones. Old Charley Burns, for example, takes bribes and does not find out the truth about the poor quality of most of the construction projects in the area. Because of Burns, a sinkhole develops that engulfs the junior high school portable classrooms. As a result, he must resign.

For Paul, the truth about what happened to make him legally blind is very important. He does not remember until the end of the novel that his older brother Erik held him down and convinced his friend Vincent Castor to force spray paint into five-year-old Paul's eyes. Paul's parents have not told the truth to him about what happened to him and allowed Erik's lie about Paul staring at a solar eclipse to become the accepted truth. Such lies have eaten away at the family's interpersonal relationships and perhaps allowed Paul's parents to rationalize not dealing with Erik's problems. Mr. and

TOPICS FOR FURTHER STUDY

- Using the Internet, research one of the environmental topics touched on in *Tangerine*, such as muck fires, sinkholes, lightning strikes, or weather extremes in Florida. Create a presentation for the class in which you explain the phenomenon in terms of the novel. Include information about how the topic you choose is relevant to your local environment, if applicable.

- After Paul and his friend try to save the Cruzes's trees, they escape the cold by going into a Quonset hut. Research the history of Quonset huts and how they are used today at your library and on the Internet. Write a research paper that includes your findings and how the huts play a role in the novel.

- In a small group, discuss what you think motivates Erik Fisher to act the way he does. Before you meet with the group, have each member find some information on the psychology or sociology of troubled teens

that supports his or her perspective. How do you feel about the "Erik Fisher Football Dream," as Paul calls it, and the breaks often given to sports stars in schools? Present your findings in a short presentation and/or debate for the class.

- At the beginning of *Tangerine*, there is a quotation from a song by the 1960s rock band The Doors called "The Soft Parade." It says, "Successful hills are here to stay. Everything must be this way." In an essay, explain how the song relates to the novel. How do you interpret the quotation, and, perhaps, the song as a whole?

- Watch the film *Bend It Like Beckham* (2002), about a Sikh girl living in England who is obsessed with playing soccer despite her parents' objections. In a paper, compare and contrast the lives and motivations of Jesminder and Paul. How do cultural differences play a role in your interpretation of both the book and the film?

Mrs. Fisher have let the truth become unimportant in their lives—to their own detriment.

Paul gradually remembers more and more about his personal truth as he observes or helps uncover other characters' truths. For example, Paul can see that Erik and Arthur are destructive and only care about their own personal gain, because the truth does not matter to them. Although Paul does not know that they robbed houses in the neighborhood until his mother reveals that painful truth in a meeting at the Fisher home, he knows other truths about them. For example, Paul witnesses how Erik and Arthur make fun of Mike Costello's death and Joey's immediate reaction to it in front of him and Joey yet Erik and Arthur act respectfully in front of Erik and Paul's mother. Erik puts on a similar front whenever adults are around, but reveals his true mean-spirited

nature when alone with his peers or those younger than him.

Antoine is one peer who does not respect Erik because he, like Paul, knows that Erik does not respect or care about the truth. Like Paul, Antoine witnesses Erik order Arthur to use a blackjack on Luis Cruz when he confronts Erik and Arthur about hitting his younger brother, Tino, at the Fisher house. This act eventually causes Luis's death, but not before Antoine and a few other football players vow to help Luis get back at Erik and Arthur. One way Antoine hurts Erik is by telling the truth about his eligibility to play at Lake Windsor to Bill Donnelly. Antoine lives in Tangerine, not Lake Windsor, and plays football at Lake Windsor High School with the full knowledge of the staff. By telling the truth, all of Lake Windsor's wins are nullified, as are the school records set during his playing days. This action makes Erik's short-lived career there also essentially off the books. While the adults lie about not knowing where Antoine lived, Antoine is freed by the truth. So is his sister Shandra, who attends Tangerine Middle School and has to hide from Donnelly when he comes to write about the best girl soccer players at the school.

Life and Death

There are three deaths in *Tangerine*—those of Mike Costello, Luis Cruz, and Old Charley Burns—and each one underscores the importance of life and death to the story. Bloor emphasizes the fragility of life and how close people are to death every day, while also using each death as an example of why the truth is important. Mike Costello dies because he was standing next to a goalpost that was struck by lightning. Because of his death, Caroline Fisher works to get football practices moved to a time when lightning strikes are less common. His death also allows Bloor to show how poorly Erik and Arthur behave. Old Charley Burns's death has a similar purpose. He has a heart attack in his lawyer's office after admitting to taking bribes for years and not investigating construction permits. His actions defrauded the people of Tangerine County and contributed to his death. While Mike's death is a tragic accident and Burns's death a tragic result of his own actions, Luis Cruz's death is the most unnecessary of all. Luis plays a key part in his father's life as well as that of his younger siblings. He helps out with the family business, has developed a new type of tangerine that could put the business on the map, and helps out by driving the twins to and from school. Luis also provides a role model for Paul, who can relate to Luis's passion for tangerines and his open nature. Luis ends up dead because he dared to confront Erik and Arthur over their treatment of Tino at Paul's house. Through his confrontation, Luis ends up showing the depth of Erik and Arthur's disrespect of others. Luis's death is the one that compels Paul to fully confront what happened to him and understand the importance of telling the truth. These deaths each bring the truth about many aspects of the story closer to the light.

Favoritism for Sports Stars

Another idea explored in *Tangerine* is the favoritism shown for people who play sports. Paul repeatedly refers to his father's obsession with Erik as a star football player as the "Erik Fisher Football Dream." Mr. Fisher focuses to the exclusion of other things on getting Erik noticed as an extremely talented placekicker. He believes that Erik can play football for a prestigious university, then perhaps professionally, and does whatever he can to help him reach that goal. Mr. Fisher favors Erik to the extreme because of his talent and ignores Paul and his own solid soccer skills. Mr. Fisher insists on attending every one of Erik's football events but never once attends a game of Paul's and knows nothing about what his younger son does as a member of the soccer team. Mrs. Fisher only attends one game of Paul's, the last one played at Lake Windsor Middle School. She does not place as much importance on Erik's star status and does little more than drive him to and from practices and games. Bloor draws a portrait of the parents as favoring Erik, the arrogant high school sports star, over Paul, the handicapped middle school soccer player. This situation allows Paul to have empathy for others and become more certain that the truth is one of the most important things in life. Such favoritism essentially ends when it is revealed that Erik helped rob neighborhood homes and contributed to the death of Luis. However, the mistakes of the parents only serve to build the character of Paul.

STYLE

Diary-Form Novel

Tangerine is not written as a straight narrative but takes the form of a diary written by Paul Fisher. In place of chapters or other kinds of sections, there are diary entries in which Paul describes the events as he experiences them or understands them. By using such a form, Paul is writing in the first person and everything is filtered through his perspective. Writing in a diary format also allows the character of Paul to express himself in a very personal manner, as a diary is often where people write their innermost thoughts and feelings.

Flashbacks

Scattered throughout *Tangerine* are flashbacks to Paul's past. A *flashback* presents events that occurred before a story began. In Paul's flashbacks, he remembers bits and pieces of the events surrounding the moment when he became legally blind. At the beginning of the novel, Paul reluctantly believes that he was blinded when he looked directly at the sun

Tangerine grove *(Image copyright Inacio Pires, 2009. Used under license from Shutterstock.com)*

during an eclipse. His flashbacks are pieces of his memory. Through them, Paul learns that the story about the eclipse is not true and that Erik and his cohort Vincent Castor forced spray paint into Paul's eyes when he was a small child. The flashbacks help Paul understand the power of the truth.

Setting

The setting is important to fully understanding the themes, characters, and plot of *Tangerine*. The *setting* is the time, place, and culture in which the narrative's action takes place. In *Tangerine*, the setting is Lake Windsor, Florida. As newcomers to the area, Paul and his family encounter unexpected extremes in weather (hot and freezing cold), afternoon thunderstorms with lightning, muck fires, and the citrus industry—both active and buried below ground. The novel takes place in a time contemporary to its publication date—1997—but it is the place and culture of this part of Florida that Bloor uses as a backdrop to the novel's situations and dilemmas. Some aspects of the setting in the novel include the

many residential developments, the racial makeup of the characters, and an emphasis on football culture.

Symbolism

Bloor uses some aspects of the setting of *Tangerine* in a symbolic fashion. In fiction, *symbols* are something that suggests something else without losing their original meaning. In *Tangerine*, Bloor uses symbols that have meaning from their function in the story. For example, the muck fires that continuously blaze and cannot be put out can be seen as a symbol of the long-running fire in the Fisher family over Erik's role in the blinding of Paul and in other transgressions. The sinkhole at the middle school and the termite infestation in parts of Paul's neighborhood also can be interpreted as having symbolic value. The sinkhole symbolizes the greed of such men as Old Charley Burns as well as the emptiness of Lake Windsor, while the termite infestation symbolizes the problematic foundation on which Lake Windsor society is based.

HISTORICAL CONTEXT

Florida

Because of its warm and sunny climate, Florida has seen many cycles of economic growth since it became a state in 1845. It was not until the early twentieth century that Florida became a major tourist center and saw its population greatly increase. After World War II, Florida's population grew because the state became a favorite place for millions of Americans from the North to spend their retirement years. In the late twentieth century, Florida again experienced a booming population and became one of the fastest-growing states in the country.

By 1990, Florida was the fourth-largest state in terms of population, with nearly thirteen million residents, yet only about thirty percent of Florida's residents had been born in that state. Ten years later, Florida was the third-most populated state with nearly sixteen million residents. Aside from retirees, many American newcomers (often from the Northeast and the Midwest) came to take advantage of growing new business enterprises such as the high-tech, banking, and service industries often tied to U.S. Department of Defense contracts and the vast presence of many U.S. military facilities in the state. Florida also saw its population increase because of large-scale migration from countries in the Caribbean and Latin America, especially Cuba and Haiti.

The rapid population growth created issues for Florida in the 1990s. As the average age of the newcomer population lowered in the 1980s and 1990s, there was a greater demand for schools. By the 1990s, schools in Florida had become overcrowded because of the increased number of students. This situation contributed to the use of portable classrooms for whole grades at Lake Windsor Middle School in *Tangerine*. This growing population also put a strain on Florida's natural environment, as resources such as timber and minerals became increasingly exploited. To safeguard the remaining natural environment, the state of Florida created the Department of Environmental Protection in 1993 to implement pollution control laws, better manage water resources, protect coastal and marine resources, and purchase environmentally endangered land tracts.

Citrus Industry

The citrus industry had been part of Florida's history since the late sixteenth century, when citrus trees and shrubs were introduced by the Spanish to the area (as well as to California). By the time Florida became a state in 1845, big groves of wild citrus trees could be found in many forests. The process of domestication soon began, and small groves were planted in the 1830s, although lack of transportation meant that citrus agriculture could not be commercialized until railways reached the interior of the state in the 1870s and 1880s. At that time groves became larger, as crops were able to be shipped and sold out of state. Despite several major freezes in the late nineteenth and early twentieth centuries that destroyed many citrus trees, Florida growers continued to revive the industry, which rapidly expanded throughout the twentieth century. The state became the dominant producer of citrus in the United States by the 1960s. By the early 2000s, Florida produced the vast majority of America's oranges and grapefruits. Florida was also the largest producer of tangerines, which had been introduced to the state in 1876. By 2000, the tangerine industry in Florida brought in $60 million per year. Although Florida's economy has become more diversified over the years, citrus agriculture remained one of the state's leading industries in the 1990s and continued to be into the twenty-first century.

CRITICAL OVERVIEW

Tangerine was widely praised from the time it was published in 1997. Critics and readers alike embraced the book for the way Bloor draws his characters, develops the plot, and depicts life in Florida. Commenting on the audio-book version of the novel, Bette D. Ammon of *Kliatt* called *Tangerine* a "strange and riveting story" and "first-rate." In the *Massachusetts Sunday Telegram*, Nicholas A. Basbanes writes that Bloor "has written a powerful novel that is rich in regional nuance and purpose." Basbanes concludes by labeling the novel "an impressive debut."

Some critics found fault with a few aspects of the novel, although not with the novel as a whole. While Kathleen Squires in *Booklist* believes that the development of Bloor's characters outside of Paul is thin and the story a bit busy, she praises the book overall, calling it a "dark debut novel," and she lauds the "atmospheric portrait of an eerie community." *Publishers Weekly* takes issue

A lightning strike (Image copyright Valdezri, 2009. Used under license from Shutterstock.com)

with the way Bloor leaves some elements unresolved and with his pacing, but praises him, too: "first-novelist Bloor pulls it off, wedding athletic heroics to American gothic with a fluid touch and a flair for dialogue." The review concludes that *Tangerine* is "A sports novel that breaks the mold."

While some reviewers focused on the sports element of the story, other critics praised its environmental aspects. In the *School Library Journal*, Linda K. Ferguson and Joy Sibley write that *Tangerine* "is an excellent example of the conflict between humans and nature." Ferguson and Sibley conclude, "Aside from the conflicts between humans and nature (they just keep coming), the story is filled with humorous yet poignant middle school scenes."

Young readers were also impressed. One young reviewer in the *Hamilton Spectator* comments, "I thought it was really good. It really paints a clear picture in your mind of what's going on. It's a little fuzzy sometimes about what's happening, but it's still good."

CRITICISM

A. Petruso

Petruso has a B.A. in history from the University of Michigan and an M.A. in screenwriting from the University of Texas at Austin. In this essay, she explores how Bloor uses blindness and other vision-related metaphors in the novel.

Throughout Edward Bloor's young adult novel *Tangerine*, the author regularly refers to blindness, eyesight, and vision. These concepts become highly effective metaphors for the situations in which Paul Fisher, his family, and his wide circle of friends and acquaintances find

WHAT DO I READ NEXT?

- *Story Time*, published in 2004, is a young adult novel by Edward Bloor. This humorous ghost story focuses on issues of testing and charter schools through the adventures of young teen protagonists.

- *Who Really Killed Cock Robin?*, published in 1985, is a young adult novel by Jean George, which features some friends who follow the life of a bird and eventually investigate why it dies.

- *Crusader*, published in 1999, is the second young adult novel by Bloor. The novel focuses on fifteen-year-old Roberta Ritter, who lives in south Florida and works at a virtual-reality arcade at a failing mall. She struggles with the lack of positive role models and the racist games played at the arcade while hoping for a career as a journalist.

- *London Calling*, published in 2005, is a young adult novel by Bloor. In the novel, Martin Conway, an eighth-grade misfit attending a prep school in New Jersey, inherits an old radio that allows him to travel back in time to London in the 1940s.

- *Touchdown Pass*, originally published in 1948, is a young adult novel by Clair Bee. This is the first in a long series of sports novels featuring Chip Hilton that Bloor said he read when he was a child and that they influenced his desire to write. Chip is already a football star in high school when he helps discover who committed an act of sabotage.

- *The Absolutely True Diary of a Part-Time Indian*, published in 2007, is a young adult novel by Sherman Alexie. The novel explores issues of identity as a young Native American teenager, Arnold Spirit, transfers from the reservation school to a rich white school. He must deal with issues of identity and fitting in while also confronting problems in his personal life.

- *Go for the Goal: A Champion's Guide to Winning in Soccer and Life*, published in 1999, is a nonfiction book by Mia Hamm and Aaron Heifetz. This book written by Hamm, a soccer champion, and her coauthor includes biographical and instructional information, as well as words to inspire the reader.

themselves. Critics also note Bloor's symbolic use of sight/blindness-related imagery. For example, in a *School Library Journal* review of the audio book version of *Tangerine*, Sarah Flowers comments,

> Paul's eyesight was damaged in a mysterious accident when he was five, and he wears '-bottlel' glasses, but he has clearer vision than the rest of his family—and most of the people in Lake Windsor Downs.

This essay looks at how these metaphors are used in the novel and how they define certain characters therein.

Tangerine's narrator and main character, Paul, is the focal point of many of Bloor's visual metaphors. He is legally blind because of the accident Flowers refers to above and must wear his thick glasses to see, but does not like being labeled "visually impaired." With the glasses or prescription sports goggles, he can see as well as anyone, so he does not need Kerri Gardner as his escort on his first day at Lake Windsor Middle School, and he can play multiple positions on his soccer team. Bloor shows that Paul is more than a kid with what many would consider a handicap, however. Paul can see what such people as his brother, father, and others are really like. Paul's visual problems give him empathy, insight, and an understanding of others that most other characters in the novel lack.

Bloor uses metaphors related to Paul's vision most often when he's talking about Paul's family.

> WHILE LUIS IS NOT BLIND LIKE PAUL, HE HAS A TRUE VISION THAT HAS ALLOWED HIM TO SPEND HIS LIFE CREATING A NEW TYPE OF TANGERINE, THE GOLDEN DAWN, THAT WILL BRING PRESTIGE AND FINANCIAL SUCCESS TO HIS HARDWORKING FAMILY."

Paul has no illusions about his brother, although he cannot remember how he was blinded in the first place and the major role Erik played in the incident until near the end of *Tangerine*. Paul hints at problems with Erik in the prologue, writing in his diary that "I can see everything. I can see things that Mom and Dad can't. Or won't." After his first tour of Lake Windsor Middle School, Paul writes "I can see just fine."

Paul sees that Erik is a phony who shows adults the polite young man he wants them to see. For example, in part one, Erik and his sidekick Arthur solemnly explain to Mrs. Fisher how Mike Costello dies when he is struck by lightning while standing next to a goal post. A few moments later, Paul sees them laughing and making fun of the deceased. Later, when Joey visits Paul at the Fisher house, Erik and Arthur mock Joey to his face about what happened to his brother that tragic day and Joey's immediate reaction to Mike's death.

Over the course of *Tangerine*, Paul points out situation after situation in which Erik shows a respectful public face to adults but treats children and Luis with contempt. By the end of the novel, Paul is aware that Erik made up the story about Paul being blinded by staring directly at a solar eclipse, although that has been the story behind his vision problems for many years. Paul knows he was smarter than that, even when he was five years old, and his recovered memories of the cruel way he lost his sight prove it. He has few illusions about people.

Paul is also conscious of how his vision problem gives him empathy. Unlike Joey—who says racist things about the students at Tangerine Middle School and chooses not to fit in for the few weeks he chooses to go there—Paul comes to love the rough-and-tumble school.

Not only because he becomes a key member of Tangerine's soccer team, but also because many other students see him and accept him for who he is and they allow him to do the same in return. Paul regards the students of Tangerine with empathy by writing early in part two, "At Tangerine Middle, the minorities are the majority. I have no problem with that. I've always felt like a minority myself because of my eyes." Paul even questions Joey when he makes his racist implications about Tangerine Middle School and Theresa Cruz, in particular.

Paul is not the only character for whom Bloor uses sight and vision-related metaphors. Bloor depicts Paul's mother, Caroline, as having some vision about her family life. She is aware of how her husband focuses most of his time and energy on Erik and the "Erik Fisher Football Dream," as Paul calls it. When she first visits Lake Windsor Middle School with Paul early in Part One, she fumes, "Not having a gym, or an auditorium. Two more facts apparently overlooked by your father. And what am I supposed to do?"

Caroline is repeatedly frustrated by her husband's myopic vision where his eldest son is concerned to the detriment of the rest of the family, although she does support Erik's football ambitions. While Paul is fully aware of his father's limited vision, Caroline at least somewhat grasps the concept. In the end, it is Mrs. Fisher, not her husband, who is first forced to face the truth about Erik when she finds the property Erik and Arthur stole in the Fisher family storage unit. She sees the goods, figures out the situation, and calls the authorities.

When writing about the circle of people around Tangerine Middle School, Bloor employs fewer visual metaphors. Like the novel's readers, Paul comes to realize that unlike people who live in Windsor Downs, members of the Cruz family and others who attend or work at Tangerine Middle School choose not to be blind about people. They learn what kind of person Erik is and what kind of person Paul is. They come to appreciate Paul's color-blind friendship, enthusiasm, and honesty. They do not hold Erik, Arthur, and his actions against Paul—except perhaps on the day of Luis's funeral—but see him for himself. As Paul writes in Part Three,

> *The truth about Luis is obvious to all of the people around him. Their lives are not made up bits and pieces of versions of the truth. They don't live that way.*

One character from this part of *Tangerine* that has a distinctive vision is Luis Cruz. Bloor draws a parallel between Luis and Paul in their backgrounds and characterizations. Both male characters have handicaps. Luis walks with a limp because of a work accident involving clippers and his left knee. Luis and Paul also both have played goalie in soccer games while middle school students, and both are passionate about citrus fruit, especially tangerines. Luis once tells Paul, "You know, I walk out here in the mornings sometimes, and I fall on my knees, and I weep, right into the ground. I'm overcome by the beauty of it all." While Luis is not blind like Paul, he has a true vision that has allowed him to spend his life creating a new type of tangerine, the Golden Dawn, that will bring prestige and financial success to his hardworking family. Bloor also demonstrates the effect Luis has on Paul when Paul performs his own funeral ritual for the deceased Luis. After it is done, Paul writes, "It's remarkable. Strange and remarkable. I feel like Luis is a part of me now. I feel like a different person."

Bloor uses visual metaphors involving Luis in other ways. For example, Luis shows his grove and nursery to the kids who work on the school project with Tino and Theresa. He says at one point on the first tour, "If you look out there, you'll see that all of these trees are the same." Bloor links Paul and his visual metaphors with honesty and the truth, and this concept extends to Luis as well. Unlike Paul—who does not confront his family with the truth about Erik because he has repressed it—Luis is not afraid of the truth and confronting Erik and Arthur about hitting Tino at the Fisher house. While Luis ultimately dies of the injuries inflicted by Arthur's blackjack, Luis lets Erik and Arthur see that he will stand up for his younger sibling and that he is not afraid of Erik. This courage and fearless vision later inspires Paul to remember and tell the full truth about what he has seen, both about how Erik harmed him as a small child and about how Erik ordered Arthur to injure Luis.

One way to interpret *Tangerine* is as a celebration of the power of perception. Paul, the person with the physically weakest vision, sees more than most everyone around him. His vision extends to the sky and the minor mystery of the missing koi fish from the pond at Lake Windsor Downs. It is only Paul who looks up and sees ospreys carrying away the fish they hunt to their nests along Route 89. He has to inform the adults, who want to place blame elsewhere the truth about the situation. Similarly, when the truth about Antoine Thomas's residency comes out, Paul perceptively points out to his father how the denial by the adults that they know where Antoine really lives is a case of willful blindness, just as it's a case of willful blindness to deny that Erik and Arthur have been hurting people. Paul exclaims, "it's about your eyesight. Your eyesight, Coach Warner's, and Mr. Bridges's, and everybody else's who's 'shocked' today." Paul, like Luis and others affiliated with Tangerine Middle School, is not afraid of the truth that true vision brings.

Source: A. Petruso, Critical Essay on *Tangerine*, in *Novels for Students*, Gale, Cengage Learning, 2010.

Holly Atkins

In the following interview, Bloor offers background information on himself and Tangerine.

Sink holes, muck fires and deadly lightning strikes—wonders of Florida? Yep. Some would also say they are three good reasons to move to a nice, safe state—like Ohio, maybe.

But not if you're Edward Bloor. When this kind of weird science is the stuff of daily living, you do what comes naturally—write about it.

Young adult author Edward Bloor's novel *Tangerine* bursts with the bittersweetness of our state. Although set in a fictitious town, *Tangerine* will have you nodding along as you read about familiar Florida wonders.

High school football fanatics dreaming of life as Florida Gators. Killing frosts that wipe out a family's citrus grove in a single night. Things that are as much a part of Florida life as palm trees and sandy beaches.

So, join me as I chat with Ed Bloor about Florida, writing and one of my favorite topics—books.

I guess a good place to start would be for you to tell us a little bit about yourself.

Bloor: I was born in Trenton, N.J. I played soccer there from the time I was 8, up into college. I graduated from Fordham University in New York and lived in New York, Boston and England before moving to Florida. (Paul Fisher, the hero of *Tangerine*, and I both look at Florida as outsiders, although I have now been here for over half my life.) I taught middle school language arts in Fort Lauderdale. That's where I met my wife, Pam. She still teaches middle school language arts here in Winter Garden, a small city northwest of Orlando. We have two children—Amanda, 15, and Spencer, 10.

Have you always wanted to be a writer? When did you start writing?

Bloor: Writing has always been a part of my life. Even at a very young age, I wrote plays and stories to amuse my family and friends. I can vividly recall when my seventh–grade teacher challenged me to write and put on a series of silly commercials in front of the whole school. They were a big hit. I was suddenly popular, and I have pursued a career in writing ever since.

Who were your favorite authors growing up?

Bloor: My own reading as a child was consumed by the Chip Hilton sports stories by coach Clair Bee. As I recall, they were all basically the same: Chip and his friends would encounter some obstacle to winning the big game; they would overcome the obstacle, and then they would win the big game. Only the sports changed. Still, I loved them.

Why did you select Florida as the setting for your novel Tangerine?

Bloor: Our part of Florida is in a state of transition between the old citrus economy and the more diverse economy that has replaced it. The destruction of the citrus groves all around me was the inspiration for *Tangerine*, my first young adult novel. That story is about both the people who are moving out and the people who are moving in.

I still have a full–time job, as an editor of reading and language arts textbooks at Harcourt School Publishers. Part of my job here is to read young adult novels. I realized one day that I could write them as well as read them.

Do you have any advice for kids who want to become writers?

The best advice for kids who want to be authors is to write what you know. That's what I did with those silly TV commercials years ago. And that's what I did with *Tangerine*, with its mix of soccer, middle school life and Florida citrus towns.

My second novel, *Crusader*, incorporated some of my other Florida experiences. It is set in Fort Lauderdale, in a high school (I taught high school English very briefly) and revolves around a series of sinister happenings in a mall (I worked in a South Florida mall that is very similar to the one in the book). *Crusader* is aimed at an older teenage audience. It therefore has darker issues, and a little more attitude.

I have been very fortunate with these two novels. I've had the opportunity to travel all over the United States speaking to teachers, librarians and students.

Tangerine has won young reader awards in six states so far. What has struck me during these visits is that people in other states look upon *Tangerine* as a science fiction novel. They cite its deadly lightning strikes, killer mosquitoes, sinkholes, muck fires and so on as wild flights of fancy.

People who live in Florida, of course, realize that these things are the staples of the nightly news. They're what we're used to. They're what we call normal.

Are you working on a new book right now?

My new novel is titled *Story Time*. It is set in an unnamed city. It's a departure from the first two novels in that it is part ghost story and part satire about educational testing. I hope it will be published in the spring of 2003. After that, I am turning my attention to the year 1940 with a novel titled *London Calling*.

I hope to keep writing, and to keep writing in this young adult market for as long as they will have me.

Source: Holly Atkins, "Enjoy This Tangerine, a Slice of Florida," in *St. Petersburg Times*, February 18, 2002, p. 6D.

Lauren Adams

In the review that follows, Adams gives a positive assessment of Tangerine.

Paul Fisher is legally blind and has lived most of his life in the shadow of his football star brother, Erik. But Paul can see; with his prescription goggles he is an excellent soccer player. He can also see things that his parents somehow can't, like what kind of person Erik really is. When the family moves to Tangerine County, Florida, things start to change. Paul's father is still obsessed with the Erik Fisher Football Dream, and his mother with her various committees. But behind the sterile perfection of their housing development lurks a series of bizarre disasters: an underground muck fire burns incessantly with putrid smoke; termites run rampant under the houses; and lightning strikes savagely every afternoon, once killing a boy at football practice. In this eerie atmosphere, random memories start cropping up for Paul, and he senses that knowledge of the mysterious accident that damaged his eyes at age five—an incident his family never discusses but one he knows involves Erik—is almost in his grasp. When Paul's school is sucked into a giant sinkhole during a rainstorm, he transfers to Tangerine Middle School, where the tough kids are in charge. There Paul's decency, sense of humor, and soccer skills win him an unlikely new crew of friends. The nightmarish disasters and Paul's pervasive fear of Erik are balanced in the novel by his genuine love of soccer playing and his joy in the scent and beauty of the Tangerine fields, a joy he shares with tangerine grower Luis. So much happens so quickly that you are pulled right along in the story, and the engaging sport, scenes highlight the personalities of the players as well as the action on the field. Events move even faster after Paul witnesses Erik and his henchman using a blackjack in a vicious assault on Luis, who dies a week later from the blow. All truths finally come pouring out as Paul remembers Erik's horrifying assault on his eyes, and he confronts his parents with all they've been denying. Paul Fisher is an immensely likable character—a bright, funny, straight-talking, stand-up kid—and it's a real pleasure to watch him grow in Tangerine.

Source: Lauren Adams, "*Tangerine*," in *Horn Book Magazine*, Vol. 73, No. 4, July–August 1997, pp. 449–50.

SOURCES

Ammon, Bette D., Review of *Tangerine*, in *Kliatt*, Vol. 36, No. 2, March 2002, p. 53.

Basbanes, Nicholas A., "This spring's offerings seem to run the gamut," in *Sunday Telegram*, April 6, 1997, p. C5.

Bloor, Edward, *Tangerine*, Harcourt Brace & Company, 1997.

Broderick-Price, Brian, "*Tangerine* Offers Action," in *Hamilton Spectator*, September 2, 2000, p. K03.

Comerford, Lynda Brill, "Flying Starts: Children's Authors and Artists Talk About Their Spring '97 Debuts," in *Publishers Weekly*, Vol. 244, No. 26, June 30, 1997, p. 26.

Ferguson, Linda K., and Joy Sibley, "Middle Schoolers Take on the Issues," in *School Library Journal*, June 1999, pp. 34–35.

Flowers, Sarah, Review of *Tangerine*, in *School Library Journal*, March 2002, p. 87.

Review of *Tangerine*, in *Publishers Weekly*, Vol. 244, No. 12, March 24, 1997, p. 84.

Squires, Kathleen, Review of *Tangerine*, in *Booklist*, Vol. 93, No. 18, May 15, 1997, p. 1573.

FURTHER READING

Alexander, Sally Hobart, *Taking Hold: My Journey into Blindness*, Simon & Schuster Children's Publishing, 1994.
This young adult memoir tells the story of a teacher in her twenties who suddenly goes blind and how she deals with the changes in her life.

Friend, Sandra, *Sinkholes*, Pineapple Press, 2002.
This young adult book explains why sinkholes occur and illustrates the text with pictures of sinkholes from around the world.

Laszlo, Pierre, *Citrus: A History*, University of Chicago Press, 2007.
This book provides a history of citrus worldwide, from its roots in Southeast Asia to Africa and Europe, and finally to the Americas in the 1500s. Laszlo also explores how citrus affected various aspects of life, culture, religion, agriculture, and the arts.

Mormino, Gary R., *Land of Sunshine, State of Dreams: A Social History of Modern Florida*, University Press of Florida, 2008.
This social history of Florida chronicles its cycles of development from its days as a Spanish colony to its phenomenal growth at the end of the twentieth century and the beginning of the twenty-first century.

Glossary of Literary Terms

A

Abstract: As an adjective applied to writing or literary works, abstract refers to words or phrases that name things not knowable through the five senses.

Aestheticism: A literary and artistic movement of the nineteenth century. Followers of the movement believed that art should not be mixed with social, political, or moral teaching. The statement "art for art's sake" is a good summary of aestheticism. The movement had its roots in France, but it gained widespread importance in England in the last half of the nineteenth century, where it helped change the Victorian practice of including moral lessons in literature.

Allegory: A narrative technique in which characters representing things or abstract ideas are used to convey a message or teach a lesson. Allegory is typically used to teach moral, ethical, or religious lessons but is sometimes used for satiric or political purposes.

Allusion: A reference to a familiar literary or historical person or event, used to make an idea more easily understood.

Analogy: A comparison of two things made to explain something unfamiliar through its similarities to something familiar, or to prove one point based on the acceptedness of another. Similes and metaphors are types of analogies.

Antagonist: The major character in a narrative or drama who works against the hero or protagonist.

Anthropomorphism: The presentation of animals or objects in human shape or with human characteristics. The term is derived from the Greek word for "human form."

Anti-hero: A central character in a work of literature who lacks traditional heroic qualities such as courage, physical prowess, and fortitude. Anti-heroes typically distrust conventional values and are unable to commit themselves to any ideals. They generally feel helpless in a world over which they have no control. Anti-heroes usually accept, and often celebrate, their positions as social outcasts.

Apprenticeship Novel: See *Bildungsroman*

Archetype: The word archetype is commonly used to describe an original pattern or model from which all other things of the same kind are made. This term was introduced to literary criticism from the psychology of Carl Jung. It expresses Jung's theory that behind every person's "unconscious," or repressed memories of the past, lies the "collective unconscious" of the human race: memories of the countless typical experiences of our ancestors. These memories are said to prompt illogical associations that trigger powerful emotions in the reader. Often, the emotional process is primitive, even primordial. Archetypes are the literary images that grow out of the "collective unconscious." They appear in literature as incidents and plots that repeat basic patterns of life. They may also appear as stereotyped characters.

Avant-garde: French term meaning "vanguard." It is used in literary criticism to describe new writing that rejects traditional approaches to literature in favor of innovations in style or content.

B

Beat Movement: A period featuring a group of American poets and novelists of the 1950s and 1960s—including Jack Kerouac, Allen Ginsberg, Gregory Corso, William S. Burroughs, and Lawrence Ferlinghetti—who rejected established social and literary values. Using such techniques as stream of consciousness writing and jazz-influenced free verse and focusing on unusual or abnormal states of mind—generated by religious ecstasy or the use of drugs—the Beat writers aimed to create works that were unconventional in both form and subject matter.

Bildungsroman: A German word meaning "novel of development." The *bildungsroman* is a study of the maturation of a youthful character, typically brought about through a series of social or sexual encounters that lead to self-awareness. *Bildungsroman* is used interchangeably with *erziehungsroman,* a novel of initiation and education. When a *bildungsroman* is concerned with the development of an artist (as in James Joyce's *A Portrait of the Artist as a Young Man*), it is often termed a *kunstlerroman.*

Black Aesthetic Movement: A period of artistic and literary development among African Americans in the 1960s and early 1970s. This was the first major African-American artistic movement since the Harlem Renaissance and was closely paralleled by the civil rights and black power movements. The black aesthetic writers attempted to produce works of art that would be meaningful to the black masses. Key figures in black aesthetics included one of its founders, poet and playwright Amiri Baraka, formerly known as LeRoi Jones; poet

and essayist Haki R. Madhubuti, formerly Don L. Lee; poet and playwright Sonia Sanchez; and dramatist Ed Bullins.

Black Humor: Writing that places grotesque elements side by side with humorous ones in an attempt to shock the reader, forcing him or her to laugh at the horrifying reality of a disordered world.

Burlesque: Any literary work that uses exaggeration to make its subject appear ridiculous, either by treating a trivial subject with profound seriousness or by treating a dignified subject frivolously. The word "burlesque" may also be used as an adjective, as in "burlesque show," to mean "striptease act."

C

Character: Broadly speaking, a person in a literary work. The actions of characters are what constitute the plot of a story, novel, or poem. There are numerous types of characters, ranging from simple, stereotypical figures to intricate, multifaceted ones. In the techniques of anthropomorphism and personification, animals—and even places or things—can assume aspects of character. "Characterization" is the process by which an author creates vivid, believable characters in a work of art. This may be done in a variety of ways, including (1) direct description of the character by the narrator; (2) the direct presentation of the speech, thoughts, or actions of the character; and (3) the responses of other characters to the character. The term "character" also refers to a form originated by the ancient Greek writer Theophrastus that later became popular in the seventeenth and eighteenth centuries. It is a short essay or sketch of a person who prominently displays a specific attribute or quality, such as miserliness or ambition.

Climax: The turning point in a narrative, the moment when the conflict is at its most intense. Typically, the structure of stories, novels, and plays is one of rising action, in which tension builds to the climax, followed by falling action, in which tension lessens as the story moves to its conclusion.

Colloquialism: A word, phrase, or form of pronunciation that is acceptable in casual conversation but not in formal, written communication. It is considered more acceptable than slang.

Coming of Age Novel: See *Bildungsroman*

Concrete: Concrete is the opposite of abstract, and refers to a thing that actually exists or a description that allows the reader to experience an object or concept with the senses.

Connotation: The impression that a word gives beyond its defined meaning. Connotations may be universally understood or may be significant only to a certain group.

Convention: Any widely accepted literary device, style, or form.

D

Denotation: The definition of a word, apart from the impressions or feelings it creates (connotations) in the reader.

Denouement: A French word meaning "the unknotting." In literary criticism, it denotes the resolution of conflict in fiction or drama. The *denouement* follows the climax and provides an outcome to the primary plot situation as well as an explanation of secondary plot complications. The *denouement* often involves a character's recognition of his or her state of mind or moral condition.

Description: Descriptive writing is intended to allow a reader to picture the scene or setting in which the action of a story takes place. The form this description takes often evokes an intended emotional response— a dark, spooky graveyard will evoke fear, and a peaceful, sunny meadow will evoke calmness.

Dialogue: In its widest sense, dialogue is simply conversation between people in a literary work; in its most restricted sense, it refers specifically to the speech of characters in a drama. As a specific literary genre, a "dialogue" is a composition in which characters debate an issue or idea.

Diction: The selection and arrangement of words in a literary work. Either or both may vary depending on the desired effect. There are four general types of diction: "formal," used in scholarly or lofty writing; "informal," used in relaxed but educated conversation; "colloquial," used in everyday speech; and "slang," containing newly coined words and other terms not accepted in formal usage.

Didactic: A term used to describe works of literature that aim to teach some moral, religious, political, or practical lesson. Although didactic elements are often found in artistically pleasing works, the term "didactic" usually refers to literature in which the message is more important than the form. The term may also be used to criticize a work that the critic finds "overly didactic," that is, heavy-handed in its delivery of a lesson.

Doppelganger: A literary technique by which a character is duplicated (usually in the form of an alter ego, though sometimes as a ghostly counterpart) or divided into two distinct, usually opposite personalities. The use of this character device is widespread in nineteenth- and twentieth-century literature, and indicates a growing awareness among authors that the "self" is really a composite of many "selves."

Double Entendre: A corruption of a French phrase meaning "double meaning." The term is used to indicate a word or phrase that is deliberately ambiguous, especially when one of the meanings is risqué or improper.

Dramatic Irony: Occurs when the audience of a play or the reader of a work of literature knows something that a character in the work itself does not know. The irony is in the contrast between the intended meaning of the statements or actions of a character and the additional information understood by the audience.

Dystopia: An imaginary place in a work of fiction where the characters lead dehumanized, fearful lives.

E

Edwardian: Describes cultural conventions identified with the period of the reign of Edward VII of England (1901-1910). Writers of the Edwardian Age typically displayed a strong reaction against the propriety and conservatism of the Victorian Age. Their work often exhibits distrust of authority in religion, politics, and art and expresses strong doubts about the soundness of conventional values.

Empathy: A sense of shared experience, including emotional and physical feelings, with someone or something other than oneself. Empathy is often used to describe the response of a reader to a literary character.

Enlightenment, The: An eighteenth-century philosophical movement. It began in France but had a wide impact throughout Europe and America. Thinkers of the Enlightenment valued reason and believed that both the individual and society could achieve a state of perfection. Corresponding to this essentially humanist vision was a resistance to religious authority.

Epigram: A saying that makes the speaker's point quickly and concisely. Often used to preface a novel.

Epilogue: A concluding statement or section of a literary work. In dramas, particularly those of the seventeenth and eighteenth centuries, the epilogue is a closing speech, often in verse, delivered by an actor at the end of a play and spoken directly to the audience.

Epiphany: A sudden revelation of truth inspired by a seemingly trivial incident.

Episode: An incident that forms part of a story and is significantly related to it. Episodes may be either self-contained narratives or events that depend on a larger context for their sense and importance.

Epistolary Novel: A novel in the form of letters. The form was particularly popular in the eighteenth century.

Epithet: A word or phrase, often disparaging or abusive, that expresses a character trait of someone or something.

Existentialism: A predominantly twentieth-century philosophy concerned with the nature and perception of human existence. There are two major strains of existentialist thought: atheistic and Christian. Followers of atheistic existentialism believe that the individual is alone in a godless universe and that the basic human condition is one of suffering and loneliness. Nevertheless, because there are no fixed values, individuals can create their own characters—indeed, they can shape themselves—through the exercise of free will. The atheistic strain culminates in and is popularly associated with the works of Jean-Paul Sartre. The Christian existentialists, on the other hand, believe that only in God may people find freedom from life's anguish. The two strains hold certain beliefs in common: that existence cannot be fully understood or described through empirical effort; that anguish is a universal element of life; that individuals must bear responsibility for

their actions; and that there is no common standard of behavior or perception for religious and ethical matters.

Expatriates: See *Expatriatism*

Expatriatism: The practice of leaving one's country to live for an extended period in another country.

Exposition: Writing intended to explain the nature of an idea, thing, or theme. Expository writing is often combined with description, narration, or argument. In dramatic writing, the exposition is the introductory material which presents the characters, setting, and tone of the play.

Expressionism: An indistinct literary term, originally used to describe an early twentieth-century school of German painting. The term applies to almost any mode of unconventional, highly subjective writing that distorts reality in some way.

F

Fable: A prose or verse narrative intended to convey a moral. Animals or inanimate objects with human characteristics often serve as characters in fables.

Falling Action: See *Denouement*

Fantasy: A literary form related to mythology and folklore. Fantasy literature is typically set in non-existent realms and features supernatural beings.

Farce: A type of comedy characterized by broad humor, outlandish incidents, and often vulgar subject matter.

Femme fatale: A French phrase with the literal translation "fatal woman." A *femme fatale* is a sensuous, alluring woman who often leads men into danger or trouble.

Fiction: Any story that is the product of imagination rather than a documentation of fact. characters and events in such narratives may be based in real life but their ultimate form and configuration is a creation of the author.

Figurative Language: A technique in writing in which the author temporarily interrupts the order, construction, or meaning of the writing for a particular effect. This interruption takes the form of one or more figures of speech such as hyperbole, irony, or simile. Figurative language is the opposite of literal language, in which every word is truthful, accurate, and free of exaggeration or embellishment.

Figures of Speech: Writing that differs from customary conventions for construction, meaning, order, or significance for the purpose of a special meaning or effect. There are two major types of figures of speech: rhetorical figures, which do not make changes in the meaning of the words, and tropes, which do.

Fin de siecle: A French term meaning "end of the century." The term is used to denote the last decade of the nineteenth century, a transition period when writers and other artists abandoned old conventions and looked for new techniques and objectives.

First Person: See *Point of View*

Flashback: A device used in literature to present action that occurred before the beginning of the story. Flashbacks are often introduced as the dreams or recollections of one or more characters.

Foil: A character in a work of literature whose physical or psychological qualities contrast strongly with, and therefore highlight, the corresponding qualities of another character.

Folklore: Traditions and myths preserved in a culture or group of people. Typically, these are passed on by word of mouth in various forms—such as legends, songs, and proverbs—or preserved in customs and ceremonies. This term was first used by W. J. Thoms in 1846.

Folktale: A story originating in oral tradition. Folktales fall into a variety of categories, including legends, ghost stories, fairy tales, fables, and anecdotes based on historical figures and events.

Foreshadowing: A device used in literature to create expectation or to set up an explanation of later developments.

Form: The pattern or construction of a work which identifies its genre and distinguishes it from other genres.

G

Genre: A category of literary work. In critical theory, genre may refer to both the content of a given work—tragedy, comedy, pastoral—and to its form, such as poetry, novel, or drama.

Gilded Age: A period in American history during the 1870s characterized by political corruption and materialism. A number of important novels of social and political criticism were written during this time.

Gothicism: In literary criticism, works characterized by a taste for the medieval or morbidly attractive. A gothic novel prominently features elements of horror, the supernatural, gloom, and violence: clanking chains, terror, charnel houses, ghosts, medieval castles, and mysteriously slamming doors. The term "gothic novel" is also applied to novels that lack elements of the traditional Gothic setting but that create a similar atmosphere of terror or dread.

Grotesque: In literary criticism, the subject matter of a work or a style of expression characterized by exaggeration, deformity, freakishness, and disorder. The grotesque often includes an element of comic absurdity.

H

Harlem Renaissance: The Harlem Renaissance of the 1920s is generally considered the first significant movement of black writers and artists in the United States. During this period, new and established black writers published more fiction and poetry than ever before, the first influential black literary journals were established, and black authors and artists received their first widespread recognition and serious critical appraisal. Among the major writers associated with this period are Claude McKay, Jean Toomer, Countee Cullen, Langston Hughes, Arna Bontemps, Nella Larsen, and Zora Neale Hurston.

Hero/Heroine: The principal sympathetic character (male or female) in a literary work. Heroes and heroines typically exhibit admirable traits: idealism, courage, and integrity, for example.

Holocaust Literature: Literature influenced by or written about the Holocaust of World War II. Such literature includes true stories of survival in concentration camps, escape, and life after the war, as well as fictional works and poetry.

Humanism: A philosophy that places faith in the dignity of humankind and rejects the medieval perception of the individual as a weak, fallen creature. "Humanists" typically believe in the perfectibility of human nature and view reason and education as the means to that end.

Hyperbole: In literary criticism, deliberate exaggeration used to achieve an effect.

I

Idiom: A word construction or verbal expression closely associated with a given language.

Image: A concrete representation of an object or sensory experience. Typically, such a representation helps evoke the feelings associated with the object or experience itself. Images are either "literal" or "figurative." Literal images are especially concrete and involve little or no extension of the obvious meaning of the words used to express them. Figurative images do not follow the literal meaning of the words exactly. Images in literature are usually visual, but the term "image" can also refer to the representation of any sensory experience.

Imagery: The array of images in a literary work. Also, figurative language.

In medias res: A Latin term meaning "in the middle of things." It refers to the technique of beginning a story at its midpoint and then using various flashback devices to reveal previous action.

Interior Monologue: A narrative technique in which characters' thoughts are revealed in a way that appears to be uncontrolled by the author. The interior monologue typically aims to reveal the inner self of a character. It portrays emotional experiences as they occur at both a conscious and unconscious level. images are often used to represent sensations or emotions.

Irony: In literary criticism, the effect of language in which the intended meaning is the opposite of what is stated.

J

Jargon: Language that is used or understood only by a select group of people. Jargon may refer to terminology used in a certain profession, such as computer jargon, or it may refer to any nonsensical language that is not understood by most people.

L

Leitmotiv: See *Motif*

Literal Language: An author uses literal language when he or she writes without exaggerating or embellishing the subject matter and without any tools of figurative language.

Lost Generation: A term first used by Gertrude Stein to describe the post-World War I generation of American writers: men and women haunted by a sense of betrayal and emptiness brought about by the destructiveness of the war.

M

Mannerism: Exaggerated, artificial adherence to a literary manner or style. Also, a popular style of the visual arts of late sixteenth-century Europe that was marked by elongation of the human form and by intentional spatial distortion. Literary works that are self-consciously high-toned and artistic are often said to be "mannered."

Metaphor: A figure of speech that expresses an idea through the image of another object. Metaphors suggest the essence of the first object by identifying it with certain qualities of the second object.

Modernism: Modern literary practices. Also, the principles of a literary school that lasted from roughly the beginning of the twentieth century until the end of World War II. Modernism is defined by its rejection of the literary conventions of the nineteenth century and by its opposition to conventional morality, taste, traditions, and economic values.

Mood: The prevailing emotions of a work or of the author in his or her creation of the work. The mood of a work is not always what might be expected based on its subject matter.

Motif: A theme, character type, image, metaphor, or other verbal element that recurs throughout a single work of literature or occurs in a number of different works over a period of time.

Myth: An anonymous tale emerging from the traditional beliefs of a culture or social unit. Myths use supernatural explanations for natural phenomena. They may also explain cosmic issues like creation and death. Collections of myths, known as mythologies, are common to all cultures and nations, but the best-known myths belong to the Norse, Roman, and Greek mythologies.

N

Narration: The telling of a series of events, real or invented. A narration may be either a simple narrative, in which the events are recounted chronologically, or a narrative with a plot, in which the account is given in a style reflecting the author's artistic concept of the story. Narration is sometimes used as a synonym for "storyline."

Narrative: A verse or prose accounting of an event or sequence of events, real or invented. The term is also used as an adjective in the sense "method of narration." For example, in literary criticism, the expression "narrative technique" usually refers to the way the author structures and presents his or her story.

Narrator: The teller of a story. The narrator may be the author or a character in the story through whom the author speaks.

Naturalism: A literary movement of the late nineteenth and early twentieth centuries. The movement's major theorist, French novelist Emile Zola, envisioned a type of fiction that would examine human life with the objectivity of scientific inquiry. The Naturalists typically viewed human beings as either the products of "biological determinism," ruled by hereditary instincts and engaged in an endless struggle for survival, or as the products of "socioeconomic determinism," ruled by social and economic forces beyond their control. In their works, the Naturalists generally ignored the highest levels of society and focused on degradation: poverty, alcoholism, prostitution, insanity, and disease.

Noble Savage: The idea that primitive man is noble and good but becomes evil and corrupted as he becomes civilized. The concept of the noble savage originated in the Renaissance period but is more closely identified with such later writers as Jean-Jacques Rousseau and Aphra Behn.

Novel: A long fictional narrative written in prose, which developed from the novella and other early forms of narrative. A novel is usually organized under a plot or theme with a focus on character development and action.

Novel of Ideas: A novel in which the examination of intellectual issues and concepts takes precedence over characterization or a traditional storyline.

Novel of Manners: A novel that examines the customs and mores of a cultural group.

Novella: An Italian term meaning "story." This term has been especially used to describe fourteenth-century Italian tales, but it also refers to modern short novels.

O

Objective Correlative: An outward set of objects, a situation, or a chain of events corresponding to an inward experience and evoking this experience in the reader. The term frequently appears in modern criticism in discussions of authors' intended effects on the emotional responses of readers.

Objectivity: A quality in writing characterized by the absence of the author's opinion or feeling about the subject matter. Objectivity is an important factor in criticism.

Oedipus Complex: A son's amorous obsession with his mother. The phrase is derived from the story of the ancient Theban hero Oedipus, who unknowingly killed his father and married his mother.

Omniscience: See *Point of View*

Onomatopoeia: The use of words whose sounds express or suggest their meaning. In its simplest sense, onomatopoeia may be represented by words that mimic the sounds they denote such as "hiss" or "meow." At a more subtle level, the pattern and rhythm of sounds and rhymes of a line or poem may be onomatopoeic.

Oxymoron: A phrase combining two contradictory terms. Oxymorons may be intentional or unintentional.

P

Parable: A story intended to teach a moral lesson or answer an ethical question.

Paradox: A statement that appears illogical or contradictory at first, but may actually point to an underlying truth.

Parallelism: A method of comparison of two ideas in which each is developed in the same grammatical structure.

Parody: In literary criticism, this term refers to an imitation of a serious literary work or the signature style of a particular author in a ridiculous manner. A typical parody adopts the style of the original and applies it to an inappropriate subject for humorous effect. Parody is a form of satire and could be considered the literary equivalent of a caricature or cartoon.

Pastoral: A term derived from the Latin word "pastor," meaning shepherd. A pastoral is a literary composition on a rural theme. The conventions of the pastoral were originated by the third-century Greek poet Theocritus, who wrote about the experiences, love affairs, and pastimes of Sicilian shepherds. In a pastoral, characters and language of a courtly nature are often placed in a simple setting. The term pastoral is also used to classify dramas, elegies, and lyrics that exhibit the use of country settings and shepherd characters.

Pen Name: See *Pseudonym*

Persona: A Latin term meaning "mask." *Personae* are the characters in a fictional work of literature. The *persona* generally functions as a mask through which the author tells a story in a voice other than his or her own. A *persona* is usually either a character in a story who acts as a narrator or an "implied author," a voice created by the author to act as the narrator for himself or herself.

Personification: A figure of speech that gives human qualities to abstract ideas, animals, and inanimate objects.

Picaresque Novel: Episodic fiction depicting the adventures of a roguish central character ("picaro" is Spanish for "rogue"). The picaresque hero is commonly a low-born but clever individual who wanders into and out of various affairs of love, danger, and farcical intrigue. These involvements may take place at all social levels and typically present a humorous and wide-ranging satire of a given society.

Plagiarism: Claiming another person's written material as one's own. Plagiarism can take the form of direct, word-for-word copying or the theft of the substance or idea of the work.

Plot: In literary criticism, this term refers to the pattern of events in a narrative or drama. In its simplest sense, the plot guides the author in composing the work and helps the reader follow the work. Typically, plots exhibit causality and unity and have a beginning, a middle, and an end. Sometimes, however, a plot may consist of a series of disconnected events, in which case it is known as an "episodic plot."

Poetic Justice: An outcome in a literary work, not necessarily a poem, in which the good are rewarded and the evil are punished, especially in ways that particularly fit their virtues or crimes.

Poetic License: Distortions of fact and literary convention made by a writer—not always a poet—for the sake of the effect gained. Poetic license is closely related to the concept of "artistic freedom."

Poetics: This term has two closely related meanings. It denotes (1) an aesthetic theory in literary criticism about the essence of poetry or (2) rules prescribing the proper methods, content, style, or diction of poetry. The term poetics may also refer to theories about literature in general, not just poetry.

Point of View: The narrative perspective from which a literary work is presented to the reader. There are four traditional points of view. The "third person omniscient" gives the reader a "godlike" perspective, unrestricted by time or place, from which to see actions and look into the minds of characters. This allows the author to comment openly on characters and events in the work. The "third person" point of view presents the events of the story from outside of any single character's perception, much like the omniscient point of view, but the reader must understand the action as it takes place and without any special insight into characters' minds or motivations. The "first person" or "personal" point of view relates events as they are perceived by a single character. The main character "tells" the story and may offer opinions about the action and characters which differ from those of the author. Much less common than omniscient, third person, and first person is the "second person" point of view, wherein the author tells the story as if it is happening to the reader.

Polemic: A work in which the author takes a stand on a controversial subject, such as abortion or religion. Such works are often extremely argumentative or provocative.

Pornography: Writing intended to provoke feelings of lust in the reader. Such works are often condemned by critics and teachers, but those which can be shown to have literary value are viewed less harshly.

Post-Aesthetic Movement: An artistic response made by African Americans to the black aesthetic movement of the 1960s and early '70s. Writers since that time have adopted a somewhat different tone in their work, with less emphasis placed on the disparity between black and white in the United States. In the words of post-aesthetic authors such as Toni Morrison, John Edgar Wideman, and Kristin Hunter, African Americans are portrayed as looking inward for answers to their own questions, rather than always looking to the outside world.

Postmodernism: Writing from the 1960s forward characterized by experimentation and continuing to apply some of the fundamentals of modernism, which included existentialism and alienation. Postmodernists have gone a step further in the rejection of tradition begun with the modernists by also rejecting traditional forms, preferring the anti-novel over the novel and the anti-hero over the hero.

Primitivism: The belief that primitive peoples were nobler and less flawed than civilized peoples because they had not been subjected to the tainting influence of society.

Prologue: An introductory section of a literary work. It often contains information establishing the situation of the characters or presents information about the setting, time period, or action. In drama, the prologue is spoken by a chorus or by one of the principal characters.

Prose: A literary medium that attempts to mirror the language of everyday speech. It is distinguished from poetry by its use of unmetered, unrhymed language consisting of logically related sentences. Prose is usually grouped into paragraphs that form a cohesive whole such as an essay or a novel.

Prosopopoeia: See *Personification*

Protagonist: The central character of a story who serves as a focus for its themes and incidents and as the principal rationale for its development. The protagonist is sometimes referred to in discussions of modern literature as the hero or anti-hero.

Protest Fiction: Protest fiction has as its primary purpose the protesting of some social injustice, such as racism or discrimination.

Proverb: A brief, sage saying that expresses a truth about life in a striking manner.

Pseudonym: A name assumed by a writer, most often intended to prevent his or her identification as the author of a work. Two or more authors may work together under one pseudonym, or an author may use a different name for each genre he or she publishes in. Some publishing companies maintain "house pseudonyms," under which any number of authors may write installations in a series. Some authors also choose a pseudonym over their real names the way an actor may use a stage name.

Pun: A play on words that have similar sounds but different meanings.

R

Realism: A nineteenth-century European literary movement that sought to portray familiar characters, situations, and settings in a realistic manner. This was done primarily by using an objective narrative point of view and through the buildup of accurate detail. The standard for success of any realistic work depends on how faithfully it transfers common experience into fictional forms. The realistic method may be altered or extended, as in stream of consciousness writing, to record highly subjective experience.

Repartee: Conversation featuring snappy retorts and witticisms.

Resolution: The portion of a story following the climax, in which the conflict is resolved.

Rhetoric: In literary criticism, this term denotes the art of ethical persuasion. In its strictest sense, rhetoric adheres to various principles developed since classical times for arranging facts and ideas in a clear, persuasive, appealing manner. The term is also used to refer to effective prose in general and theories of or methods for composing effective prose.

Rhetorical Question: A question intended to provoke thought, but not an expressed answer, in the reader. It is most commonly used in oratory and other persuasive genres.

Rising Action: The part of a drama where the plot becomes increasingly complicated. Rising action leads up to the climax, or turning point, of a drama.

Roman à clef: A French phrase meaning "novel with a key." It refers to a narrative in which real persons are portrayed under fictitious names.

Romance: A broad term, usually denoting a narrative with exotic, exaggerated, often idealized characters, scenes, and themes.

Romanticism: This term has two widely accepted meanings. In historical criticism, it refers to a European intellectual and artistic movement of the late eighteenth and early nineteenth centuries that sought greater freedom of personal expression than that allowed by the strict rules of literary form and logic of the eighteenth-century neoclassicists. The Romantics preferred emotional and imaginative expression to rational analysis. They considered the individual to be at the center of all experience and so placed him or her atthe center of their art. The Romantics believed that the creative imagination reveals nobler truths—unique feelings and attitudes—than those that could be discovered by logic or by scientific examination. Both the natural world and the state of childhood were important sources for revelations of "eternal truths." "Romanticism" is also used as a general term to refer to a type of sensibility found in all periods of literary history and usually considered to be in opposition to the principles of classicism. In this sense, Romanticism signifies any work or philosophy in which the exotic or dreamlike figure strongly, or that is devoted to individualistic expression, self-analysis, or a pursuit of a higher realm of knowledge than can be discovered by human reason.

Romantics: See *Romanticism*

S

Satire: A work that uses ridicule, humor, and wit to criticize and provoke change in human nature and institutions. There are two major types of satire: "formal" or "direct" satire speaks directly to the reader or to a character in the work; "indirect" satire relies upon the ridiculous behavior of its characters to make its point. Formal satire is

further divided into two manners: the "Horatian," which ridicules gently, and the "Juvenalian," which derides its subjects harshly and bitterly.

Science Fiction: A type of narrative about or based upon real or imagined scientific theories and technology. Science fiction is often peopled with alien creatures and set on other planets or in different dimensions.

Second Person: See *Point of View*

Setting: The time, place, and culture in which the action of a narrative takes place. The elements of setting may include geographic location, characters' physical and mental environments, prevailing cultural attitudes, or the historical time in which the action takes place.

Simile: A comparison, usually using "like" or "as," of two essentially dissimilar things, as in "coffee as cold as ice" or "He sounded like a broken record."

Slang: A type of informal verbal communication that is generally unacceptable for formal writing. Slang words and phrases are often colorful exaggerations used to emphasize the speaker's point; they may also be shortened versions of an often-used word or phrase.

Slave Narrative: Autobiographical accounts of American slave life as told by escaped slaves. These works first appeared during the abolition movement of the 1830s through the 1850s.

Socialist Realism: The Socialist Realism school of literary theory was proposed by Maxim Gorky and established as a dogma by the first Soviet Congress of Writers. It demanded adherence to a communist worldview in works of literature. Its doctrines required an objective viewpoint comprehensible to the working classes and themes of social struggle featuring strong proletarian heroes.

Stereotype: A stereotype was originally the name for a duplication made during the printing process; this led to its modern definition as a person or thing that is (or is assumed to be) the same as all others of its type.

Stream of Consciousness: A narrative technique for rendering the inward experience of a character. This technique is designed to give the impression of an ever-changing series of thoughts, emotions, images, and memories in the spontaneous and seemingly illogical order that they occur in life.

Structure: The form taken by a piece of literature. The structure may be made obvious for ease of understanding, as in nonfiction works, or may obscured for artistic purposes, as in some poetry or seemingly "unstructured" prose.

Sturm und Drang: A German term meaning "storm and stress." It refers to a German literary movement of the 1770s and 1780s that reacted against the order and rationalism of the enlightenment, focusing instead on the intense experience of extraordinary individuals.

Style: A writer's distinctive manner of arranging words to suit his or her ideas and purpose in writing. The unique imprint of the author's personality upon his or her writing, style is the product of an author's way of arranging ideas and his or her use of diction, different sentence structures, rhythm, figures of speech, rhetorical principles, and other elements of composition.

Subjectivity: Writing that expresses the author's personal feelings about his subject, and which may or may not include factual information about the subject.

Subplot: A secondary story in a narrative. A subplot may serve as a motivating or complicating force for the main plot of the work, or it may provide emphasis for, or relief from, the main plot.

Surrealism: A term introduced to criticism by Guillaume Apollinaire and later adopted by Andre Breton. It refers to a French literary and artistic movement founded in the 1920s. The Surrealists sought to express unconscious thoughts and feelings in their works. The best-known technique used for achieving this aim was automatic writing—transcriptions of spontaneous outpourings from the unconscious. The Surrealists proposed to unify the contrary levels of conscious and unconscious, dream and reality, objectivity and subjectivity into a new level of "super-realism."

Suspense: A literary device in which the author maintains the audience's attention through the buildup of events, the outcome of which will soon be revealed.

Symbol: Something that suggests or stands for something else without losing its original identity. In literature, symbols combine their literal meaning with the suggestion of an abstract concept. Literary symbols are of two types: those that carry complex associations of meaning no matter what their contexts, and those that derive their suggestive meaning from their functions in specific literary works.

Symbolism: This term has two widely accepted meanings. In historical criticism, it denotes an early modernist literary movement initiated in France during the nineteenth century that reacted against the prevailing standards of realism. Writers in this movement aimed to evoke, indirectly and symbolically, an order of being beyond the material world of the five senses. Poetic expression of personal emotion figured strongly in the movement, typically by means of a private set of symbols uniquely identifiable with the individual poet. The principal aim of the Symbolists was to express in words the highly complex feelings that grew out of everyday contact with the world. In a broader sense, the term "symbolism" refers to the use of one object to represent another.

T

Tall Tale: A humorous tale told in a straightforward, credible tone but relating absolutely impossible events or feats of the characters. Such tales were commonly told of frontier adventures during the settlement of the west in the United States.

Theme: The main point of a work of literature. The term is used interchangeably with thesis.

Thesis: A thesis is both an essay and the point argued in the essay. Thesis novels and thesis plays share the quality of containing a thesis which is supported through the action of the story.

Third Person: See *Point of View*

Tone: The author's attitude toward his or her audience may be deduced from the tone of the work. A formal tone may create distance or convey politeness, while an informal tone may encourage a friendly, intimate, or intrusive feeling in the reader. The author's attitude toward his or her subject matter may also be deduced from the tone of the words he or she uses in discussing it.

Transcendentalism: An American philosophical and religious movement, based in New England from around 1835 until the Civil War. Transcendentalism was a form of American romanticism that had its roots abroad in the works of Thomas Carlyle, Samuel Coleridge, and Johann Wolfgang von Goethe. The Transcendentalists stressed the importance of intuition and subjective experience in communication with God. They rejected religious dogma and texts in favor of mysticism and scientific naturalism. They pursued truths that lie beyond the "colorless" realms perceived by reason and the senses and were active social reformers in public education, women's rights, and the abolition of slavery.

U

Urban Realism: A branch of realist writing that attempts to accurately reflect the often harsh facts of modern urban existence.

Utopia: A fictional perfect place, such as "paradise" or "heaven."

V

Verisimilitude: Literally, the appearance of truth. In literary criticism, the term refers to aspects of a work of literature that seem true to the reader.

Victorian: Refers broadly to the reign of Queen Victoria of England (1837-1901) and to anything with qualities typical of that era. For example, the qualities of smug narrowmindedness, bourgeois materialism, faith in social progress, and priggish morality are often considered Victorian. This stereotype is contradicted by such dramatic intellectual developments as the theories of Charles Darwin, Karl Marx, and Sigmund Freud (which stirred strong debates in England) and the critical attitudes of serious Victorian writers like Charles Dickens and George Eliot. In literature, the Victorian Period was the great age of the English novel, and the latter part of the era saw the rise of movements such as decadence and symbolism.

W

Weltanschauung: A German term referring to a person's worldview or philosophy.

Weltschmerz: A German term meaning "world pain." It describes a sense of anguish about the nature of existence, usually associated with a melancholy, pessimistic attitude.

Z

Zeitgeist: A German term meaning "spirit of the time." It refers to the moral and intellectual trends of a given era.

Cumulative
Author/Title Index

Cumulative Author/Title Index

Cumulative Nationality/Ethnicity Index

Adams, Richard
    Watership Down: V11
Austen, Jane
    Emma: V21
    Mansfield Park: V29
    Northanger Abbey: V28
    Persuasion: V14
    Pride and Prejudice: V1
    Sense and Sensibility: V18
    Sense and Sensibility (Motion
        picture): V33
Ballard, J. G.
    Empire of the Sun: V8
Blair, Eric Arthur
    Animal Farm: V3
Bowen, Elizabeth Dorothea Cole
    The Death of the Heart: V13
Braithwaite, E. R.
    To Sir, With Love: V30
Brontë, Anne
    The Tenant of Wildfell Hall: V26
Brontë, Charlotte
    Jane Eyre: V4
Brontë, Emily
    Wuthering Heights: V2
Brookner, Anita
    Hotel du Lac: V23
Bunyan, John
    The Pilgrim's Progress: V32
Burgess, Anthony
    A Clockwork Orange: V15
Burney, Fanny
    Evelina: V16
Carroll, Lewis
    *Alice's Adventurers in
        Wonderland:* V7
    Through the Looking-Glass: V27
Christie, Agatha
    The A.B.C. Murders: V30
    Murder on the Orient Express: V33
    Ten Little Indians: V8
Conan Doyle, Arthur, Sir
    The Hound of the Baskervilles: V28
Conrad, Joseph
    Heart of Darkness: V2
    Lord Jim: V16
Defoe, Daniel
    A Journal of the Plague Year: V30
    Moll Flanders: V13
    Robinson Crusoe: V9
Dickens, Charles
    Bleak House: V30
    A Christmas Carol: V10
    David Copperfield: V25
    Great Expectations: V4
    Hard Times: V20
    Nicholas Nickleby: V33
    Oliver Twist: V14
    A Tale of Two Cities: V5
Doyle, Arthur Conan, Sir
    The Hound of the Baskervilles:
        V28

du Maurier, Daphne
    Rebecca: V12
Eliot, George
    Middlemarch: V23
    The Mill on the Floss: V17
    Silas Marner: V20
Fielding, Henry
    Joseph Andrews: V32
    Tom Jones: V18
Foden, Giles
    The Last King of Scotland: V15
Ford, Ford Madox
    The Good Soldier: V28
Forster, E. M.
    A Passage to India: V3
    Howards End: V10
    A Room with a View: V11
Fowles, John
    The French Lieutenant's Woman:
        V21
Golding, William
    Lord of the Flies: V2
Graves, Robert
    I, Claudius: V21
Greene, Graham
    The End of the Affair: V16
    The Power and the Glory: V31
Hardy, Thomas
    Far from the Madding Crowd:
        V19
    Jude the Obscure: V30
    The Mayor of Casterbridge: V15
    The Return of the Native: V11
    Tess of the d'Urbervilles: V3
Huxley, Aldous
    Brave New World: V6
Ishiguro, Kazuo
    The Remains of the Day: V13
James, Henry
    The Ambassadors: V12
    The Portrait of a Lady: V19
    The Turn of the Screw: V16
Kipling, Rudyard
    Kim: V21
Koestler, Arthur
    Darkness at Noon: V19
Lawrence, D. H.
    The Rainbow: V26
    Sons and Lovers: V18
Lessing, Doris
    The Golden Notebook: V27
Lewis, C. S.
    *The Lion, the Witch and the
        Wardrobe:* V24
Llewellyn, Richard
    How Green Was My Valley: V30
Maugham, W. Somerset
    The Razor's Edge: V23
McEwan, Ian
    Atonement: V32
More, Thomas
    Utopia: V29

Orwell, George
    Animal Farm: V3
    1984: V7
Rhys, Jean
    Wide Sargasso Sea: V19
Rushdie, Salman
    The Satanic Verses: V22
Sewell, Anna
    Black Beauty: V22
Shelley, Mary
    Frankenstein: V1
Shute, Nevil
    On the Beach: V9
Spark, Muriel
    The Prime of Miss Jean Brodie:
        V22
Stevenson, Robert Louis
    Dr. Jekyll and Mr. Hyde: V11
    Kidnapped: V33
Swift, Graham
    Waterland: V18
Swift, Jonathan
    Gulliver's Travels: V6
Thackeray, William Makepeace
    Vanity Fair: V13
Tolkien, J. R. R.
    The Hobbit: V8
    The Lord of the Rings: V26
Waugh, Evelyn
    Brideshead Revisited: V13
    Scoop: V17
Wells, H. G.
    The Time Machine: V17
    The War of the Worlds: V20
White, T. H.
    The Once and Future King: V30
Woolf, Virginia
    Mrs. Dalloway: V12
    To the Lighthouse: V8
    The Waves: V28

European American

Hemingway, Ernest
    The Old Man and the Sea: V6
Stowe, Harriet Beecher
    Uncle Tom's Cabin: V6

French

Balzac, Honoré de
    Le Père Goriot: V33
Boulle, Pierre
    The Bridge over the River Kwai:
        V32
Camus, Albert
    The Plague: V16
    The Stranger: V6
Dumas, Alexandre
    The Count of Monte Cristo: V19
    The Three Musketeers: V14
Flaubert, Gustave
    Madame Bovary: V14

Subject/Theme Index

Characterization
  The Adventures of Augie March:
    22, 23
  *Beauty: A Retelling of the Story of
    Beauty and the Beast:* 40
  Intruder in the Dust: 90
  Murder on the Orient Express: 158
  Ordinary People: 230
  Sense and Sensibility: 279, 282
  Tangerine: 330
Christianity
  No Longer at Ease: 201, 211, 216
Civil rights
  The Glory Field: 61
  The Street: 293, 308
  Intruder in the Dust: 76, 80, 82–83
  Ordinary People: 231
Civil War
  The Glory Field: 49, 63, 64
  Intruder in the Dust: 82
Class conflict. *See also* Social class
  Murder on the Orient Express:
    150–151
  Nicholas Nickleby: 174
Classicism
  Sense and Sensibility: 274
Cold War
  The Adventures of Augie March:
    13–14
Colonialism
  No Longer at Ease: 201, 210
Comedy. *See also* Humor
  Nicholas Nickleby: 164
  Sense and Sensibility: 282
Coming of age
  The Adventures of Augie March:
    12
  Kidnapped: 104
  A Lost Lady: 127
  Nicholas Nickleby: 175–176, 178
  Ordinary People: 220
Communism
  The Adventures of Augie March:
    13–14
Conflict
  The Glory Field: 70
  A Lost Lady: 125–127
  No Longer at Ease: 201
  Ordinary People: 222–223
Corruption
  No Longer at Ease: 193, 201–202,
    209–211
Courage
  Kidnapped: 104
Crime
  Intruder in the Dark: 81–82
  Murder on the Orient Express:
    151–152, 157–158
Cultural conflict
  Murder on the Orient Express:
    150–151
  No Longer at Ease: 211

Cultural criticism
  Murder on the Orient Express:
    154–157
Cultural identity
  No Longer at Ease: 209
Culture
  Kidnapped: 104, 105
  Murder on the Orient Express: 150
  No Longer at Ease: 206, 206–207,
    210, 214
  Tangerine: 325

D

Death
  Tangerine: 324
Debt
  Intruder in the Dust: 79–80
Deformity
  Nicholas Nickleby: 185–189
Description (Literature)
  Le Père Goriot: 250, 261
Devil
  Le Père Goriot: 251–252
Discrimination. *See* Prejudice;
  Racism
Dreams
  Ordinary People: 223–224
Drug abuse
  The Glory Field: 48, 61
Dysfunctional families
  Ordinary People: 224, 224–225,
    225
Dysfunctional relationships
  Ordinary People: 225, 229

E

Economics
  Le Père Goriot: 239, 247, 255–258
Education
  No Longer at Ease: 207, 209–210,
    212–213
Empathy
  Tangerine: 328, 329
English history
  Kidnapped: 105–107
Environmentalism
  Tangerine: 327
Epiphanies
  Ordinary People: 226
Escape
  The Street: 298
Ethnic identity
  No Longer at Ease: 209
European culture
  Murder on the Orient Express: 157
  No Longer at Ease: 208, 208–209
Evil
  Le Père Goriot: 251–252
  Nicholas Nickleby: 176
Exile
  Kidnapped: 103–104

Experience
  The Street: 285–286
Exploitation
  Nicholas Nickleby: 174–175

F

Fairy tales
  *Beauty: A Retelling of the Story of
    Beauty and the Beast:* 33–34,
    42–35
Familial love
  The Adventures of Augie March:
    11
  Le Père Goriot: 248, 257
  Ordinary People: 237
Family
  The Glory Field: 47, 63, 66
  *Beauty: A Retelling of the Story of
    Beauty and the Beast:* 28, 32,
    39–40
  Nicholas Nickleby: 181
  Ordinary People: 224–225
Family relationships
  The Glory Field: 59–60
  Le Père Goriot: 257
  Ordinary People: 221–223, 224,
    224–225
Fantasy fiction
  *Beauty: A Retelling of the Story
    of Beauty and the Beast:* 34, 35,
    39, 41
Fate
  The Adventures of Augie March:
    18
  *Beauty: A Retelling of the Story of
    Beauty and the Beast:* 24, 33
Father-child relationships
  Le Père Goriot: 245, 255–257
  Ordinary People: 225, 226, 228,
    229, 229–230
  Tangerine: 317, 321, 324, 329
Fear
  Ordinary People: 233
Female identity
  *Beauty: A Retelling of the Story of
    Beauty and the Beast:* 33, 39–41,
    41–42
Female-male relations
  *Beauty: A Retelling of the Story of
    Beauty and the Beast:* 40, 42
  Ordinary People: 225, 226, 228,
    232, 276
Feminism
  *Beauty: A Retelling of the Story of
    Beauty and the Beast:* 34–35
  Ordinary People: 231
Fidelity. *See* Adultery
Flashbacks
  Ordinary People: 222, 223, 225,
    230–231
  Tangerine: 324–325

Subject/Theme Index (side)